THE LITERATURE OF POLITICAL ECONOMY

Samuel Hollander is widely recognized as one of the most important and controversial historians of economic thought. This second volume collects together essays extending beyond classical economics, the subject with which he is most associated.

The collection includes:

- An autobiographical introduction
- Studies in Scholastic, Smithian and Marshallian literature
- Papers on the Corn-Law pamphlets of 1815, the post-Ricardian dissension, and the 'marginal revolution'
- Essays on T.R. Malthus, including four bibliographical studies
- Reviews of a broad range of important books published in the last thirty years.

Samuel Hollander is University Professor of Economics at the University of Toronto and Fellow of the Royal Society of Canada.

THE LITERATURE OF POLITICAL ECONOMY

Collected Essays II

Samuel Hollander

Routledge
Taylor & Francis Group

LONDON AND NEW YORK

First published 1995
by Routledge
2 Park Square, Milton Park, Abingdon, Oxfordshire OX14 4RN

Second edition 1998
Simultaneously published in the USA and Canada
by Routledge
711 Third Avenue, New York, NY 10017

First issued in paperback 2015

Routledge is an imprint of the Taylor and Francis Group, an informa business

British Library Cataloguing in Publication Data
A catalogue record for this book is available from the British Library

Library of Congress Cataloguing in Publication Data
Hollander, Samuel.
The literature of political economy/Samuel Hollander.
Includes bibliographical references and index.
1. Economics. 2. Economics – Bibliography. I. Title
HB71.H69 1997
97–11430
016.33–dc21
CIP

ISBN 13: 978-0-415-75642-6 (pbk)
ISBN 13: 978-0-415-11429-5 (hbk)

For Isaac, Ilana, Amber and Jasmine with my love

and in memory of two good friends,
Martin Bronfenbrenner and Giovanni Caravale

CONTENTS

CONTENTS

Part IV. NINETEENTH-CENTURY LITERATURE

Part V. MALTHUS

Part VI. SHORT REVIEWS

CONTENTS

NOTES ON CHAPTERS

12 The Corn-Law Pamphlet Literature of 1815: Malthus, West, Ricardo and Torrens. A shorter version of this chapter is published in German in the series Klassiker der Nationalökonomie as 'Die "Corn-Law-Pamphlete" von 1815', *Vademecum zu den klassikern der Differentialrenten Theorie*, Düsseldorf: Verlag Wirtschaft und Finanzen GMBH, 1996, 85–131.

13 On *The Works of Thomas Robert Malthus*, *Journal of Economic History*, 48, December 1988, 987–9.

14 New Editions of Malthus, *Utilitas*, 3, November 1991, 303–10.

15 On Malthus's Physiocratic References, *History of Political Economy*, 24, Summer 1992, 369–80.

16 Malthus's Abandonment of Agricultural Protectionism: A Discovery in the History of Economic Thought, *The American Economic Review*, 82, 3, June 1992, 650–9.

17 More on Malthus and Agricultural Protection, *History of Political Economy*, 27, 3, 1995, 531–7.

18 This chapter is a revised (shorter) version of the article 'Malthus as Physiocrat: Surplus versus Scarcity' published in *Economie et Société*, Série Oeconomia, Histoire de la Pensée Economique, P.E. no. 22–23, 1995, 79–116.

19 Introduction to facsimile reprints of T. R. Malthus, *An Essay on Population*, The Six Editions, London: Routledge/Thoemmes Press, 1996, vol. I, v–lx.

20 On the Authorship of 'Spence on Commerce' in *The Edinburgh Review*, January 1808, *Victorian Periodicals Review*, 29, Winter 1996, 315–29.

PREFACE

The memoir with which this collection opens has appeared elsewhere in print but I have added an addendum bringing the story up to date. Chapters 2 and 3 also belong in the Biographical part; it will be evident why from the memoir. I reproduce in Parts II and III various early essays which I think still have some merit, by and large, and to which I would ideally like to return. I have allowed into Part V very few of those of my recent contributions on Malthus which have been absorbed into my *Economics of Thomas Robert Malthus* (1997 Toronto: University of Toronto Press). Thus essay 16 and its companion and also 18 are included, because they are my particular favourites in their original (brief) form. The four bibliographical essays (13, 14, 15, 20) do not appear in *ETRM*, and 19 contains a summary statement of parts of that work. Essays concerning J. S. Mill, Marx and Sraffa are excluded from this collection. Ricardo already has a home of his own in my first collection.

I have added a final Part of short reviews, with the hope that they will be found fair and judicious, satisfying the minimum obligation of a reviewer, which is to inform the reader of the contents and object of the book in question (an obligation that I have learned to my cost is far from universally recognized). One's position does, fortunately, change over time. I would now tone down the strong statement regarding James Mill on p. 365. I have long since abandoned the position expressed on p. 373-4 entailing J. S. Mill's economics as inherently contradictory and with it the various implications for the status of his innovations; I would not now speak of 'the debilitating effects of classical orthodoxy' (p. 368); and I no longer question (as on p. 377) the validity of the notion of a 'classical' tradition especially with respect to method. Finally, I find myself accepting in 1976 the then-standard emphasis on Ricardian comparative-statics methodology and the related constant-wage interpretation of Ricardian growth theory (pp. 30, 378-80).

I am saddened to learn of the death of two friends, Martin Bronfenbrenner and Giovanni Caravale. I am overwhelmed that Martin, in a review of my first volume of essays for *History of Political Economy*, (Spring 1997), should have found the strength in his last days to convey his appreciation of some of my contributions.

Samuel Hollander
Toronto, Ontario

ACKNOWLEDGEMENTS

Acknowledgement is due to the following sources for permission to reproduce the chapters in this volume. The History of Economics Society for chapter 1 and section 21.14; Duke University Press for chapters 2, 15, 17; the Canadian Economics Association for chapters 3, 4 and sections 21.2, 21.3, 21.7, 21.8; Helbing & Lichtenhahn Verlag AG for chapter 5; the *Southern Economic Association* for chapter 6; the Royal Society of Canada for chapter 7; the Journal of Law and Economics for chapter 8; Oxford University Press for chapters 9 and 14; Academic Press Ltd for chapter 10; the JAI Press for chapter 11; Cambridge University Press for chapter 13; the Bentham Project for section 21.1; the American Economic Association for chapter 16 and sections 21.4, 21.9; the Victorian Periodicals Review for chapter 20; The Times Supplements Ltd for 21.5; Indiana University Press for 21.10; Blackwell Publishers for 21.11 and the North American Conference on British Studies for 21.12.

I am most happy to express appreciation for the generous assistance provided by Gerald Schwartz of the Onex Corporation, Toronto; by the Social Sciences and Humanities Research Council of Canada; and by the Acting Dean of Arts and Science, the Vice-President of Research and International Relations, and the Humanities and Social Sciences Committee at the University of Toronto. In regard to research funding, as well as moral support, I am greatly obliged to the initiatives taken by my friend Ian Mirlin.

Part I

BIOGRAPHICAL PERSPECTIVES

1

'IT'S AN ILL WIND ...'

A memoir*

My candle burns at both ends;
It will not last the night;
But ah, my foes, and oh, my friends –
It gives a lovely light!

(Edna St Vincent Millay)

I can conceive of few academics presumptuous or foolhardy enough to write an 'intellectual autobiography' unless invited to do so.[1] It is no easy assignment. One seeks to protect a core of privacy; there is a residual subjectivity regarding events and persons that cannot be eliminated; one is obliged to tone things down for practical reasons. Even if one can hope to tell the 'truth' it will not be the whole truth – certainly not in a mere twenty pages. It must also be said that any linkages that might be suggested between character or experience and professional contribution (and an intellectual autobiography of course seeks out such linkages) can never progress beyond the stage of hypothesis; neither necessary nor sufficient causation is at issue. Yet I myself have learned something from this exercise; perhaps my readers will too.

The present account does not address the so-called New View of Ricardo which has received so much attention over the past twenty years. I have dealt with that matter in a companion piece (Hollander 1995: 1–15). My concern here is with rather more intimate matters. And I shall start near the beginning with the emergence of a theme whose persistence comes as rather a surprise even to me.

EARLY DAYS

My first conscious religious experience occurred sometime before age five when I was warned: 'Get off that horse, or your father will kill you.' It was a milk-delivery van in Letchworth, Hertfordshire, in the English Home Counties where my family had been evacuated during the London Blitz.

---

* This paper is republished with a few minor amendments.

And it was the Sabbath, on which day horse riding – and very much else – is forbidden by Jewish religious law.[2] Thus at a tender age I was inducted into a complex world of social control. The dietary laws are particularly potent as will become clear.[3] Those who accept the 'yoke' full-heartedly enjoy a profoundly meaningful and comforting existence. But many 'orthodox' treat the regulations somewhat selectively. My own childhood was a training in ambivalence, as I shall explain.

My father had left Austrian Galicia with his parents and siblings just before 1914 – the males to Holland and the females to Vienna. In 1918 the family joined up in Scheveningen and unsuccessfully tried the diamond business. My father emigrated in 1925 to Britain where he set up a successful clothing factory. He himself had no formal education, but was astute in business and also possessed great intellectual ability, as indicated by his Talmudic competence, attained informally and with extraordinary application at least from his arrival in Letchworth in 1940 until the end of his life in 1991. He was the sole support of his parents and several of his brothers and sisters who in the mid-1930s had emigrated to Palestine. (The one sister who remained behind was murdered in the Nazi clearing of the Jewish hospital in Apeldoorn.) He attached himself closely to religious teachers, relying on their advice in many personal matters; and after our return to London in 1951 he took an active role in the synagogue of a Chassidic rabbi in his father's tradition, a scholar of considerable distinction with whom I also studied and whose school my son attended many years later. It is not surprising, given his own background and experience, that my father was far from appreciative of the cultural, even the utilitarian, function of secular studies. Certainly the 'university' was suspect in the orthodox community at that time.

My mother in major respects stood at the other pole. She was born in London within sound of Bow bells of immigrants from Galicia, the youngest of eleven children, all except for her born in Cracow. She was educated, of all places, in a German Lutheran school located in east London. She became an accomplished pianist who in the mid-twenties was offered a position by the BBC though forbidden by her father to accept it: 'Jewish daughters do not play piano for the BBC.' Yet, strange to relate, her father permitted her to eat milk dishes after meat 'as soon as she felt hungry', rather than wait the statutory six (or three or one) hours; here is a pattern I cannot quite appreciate. She was a voracious reader in German and English secular literature with an extraordinary memory. It was in her late eighties that she recommended to me *The Well of Loneliness* by Radclyffe Hall (1928), a Lesbian first, once proscribed in Britain. And she had the sharpest wit and sense of humour. I have been told that at the time of her marriage in 1931 she was more 'orthodox' in practice than my father; if this is so then the roles were soon to be reversed. For it was he not she who objected to Sabbath horse riding. Indeed, she was ready to bend the rules. An illustration: the British

Rabbinate had issued a ruling that turbot – then thought to be a question-able fish for reasons I need not enter into here – was permitted in wartime. My mother made a simple extension. She would take my sister and myself into the local café for very doubtful cakes on the grounds that 'there was a war on', cautioning us to say nothing. I did not at the time appreciate how my father failed to realize that a state of hostilities existed with Germany – everyone was talking about it – but was clever enough to obey instructions.

The adult household was completed by an aunt, my mother's sister, blind from her teenage years. Her kindly presence counteracted a certain pervasive tension. Yet I cannot afford to be too critical, for the ambivalence and clash of temperaments that I experienced in my parents' home was later repeated in my own.

I return to the opening episode. It would be painting a misleading picture to leave an impression that the Sabbath was a grey day. It was, for one thing, a day of rest from studying – apart from the dreaded test of the week's scholarly accomplishments; and there were no injunctions against children's games. (There was at Letchworth a splendid quarry-like indenta-tion known as the Roman Camp that served as our Sabbath sporting arena.) And paradoxical as it may appear, synagogue decorum is more relaxed the more orthodox the establishment, possibly reflecting a familiarity with and affection for the Deity. The restrictions thus went hand in hand with a surprising degree of freedom; perhaps too much. I also wish to avoid giving an impression that our community was in any way 'homogeneous'. To the contrary, it was made up largely of refugees from all quarters of Europe, each with his own particular traditions, generating clashes of practice and char-acter. Nonetheless, there was sufficient common ground to allow for the maintenance of a vibrant communal life turning about the tiny synagogue.[4]

One obvious consequence of the orthodox practices is to create obstacles to 'fraternization' with the locals. I do not, for example, recall ever visiting the homes of my non-Jewish schoolfriends, primary or secondary. This barrier has existed to some extent until the present day. In any event, there was scarcely time for socializing. As I explain elsewhere in this document, it is common practice in the orthodox community to put a high premium on competence in Talmudic reasoning. My own training began at age seven in two-hour evening sessions held in Yiddish, though I distinctly recall real-izing at the time that it was a premature exercise since I still had difficulty with the prayer book and was not yet comfortable with Yiddish.

I have at hand a family tree relating to my mother's maternal ancestry which conveys an indication of a very extensive rabbinical 'gene pool', and shows some late medieval links with Karl Marx, which (when I have alluded to them in the abstract) seem, I cannot imagine why, to upset some of my Sraffian friends. Specifically, Marx and I share common ancestors in Rabbi Jehiel Luria II (d. 1470), head of the ecclesiastical court in Brest-Litovsk, Poland; and in R. Israel Isserlein of Cracow (d. 1558) and his wife Dinah

Malka (1485–1553). (Students think of Marx as a disembodied spirit, and my chart – which I would happily send to anyone interested in genealogy – should disabuse them.) I might add that my maternal grandmother's line flows from the great legal codifier R. Moses Isserles of Cracow (circa 1520–72) – a son of R. Isserlein – and his *first* wife; and the nineteenth-century composer Felix Mendelssohn-Bartholdy can be traced back to R. Isserles and his *second* wife. I mention this connection since Felix's grandfather, Moses Mendelssohn of Dessau (1729–86), figures large in my pantheon of heroes. Notwithstanding a hostile orthodox reaction on doctrinal grounds, Moses insisted always on the importance of the ceremonial law in practice, that is, on conformity in action. He personifies the encounter between rabbinic Judaism and the so-called 'Enlightenment'.[5] Since I am still trapped in that time warp, Moses' dilemmas constitute the real thing for me.

EDUCATION CIRCA 1941–59

My primary secular education (1941–8) was at a small private school in Letchworth run by two liberated and progressive ladies. (I use the term 'lady' deliberately; to me it is not a four-letter word.) Those were splendid times, rather easy-going with much attention given to dramatics (Shakespeare in particular), music and exercise with emphasis on country dancing. I worshipped my teachers – a general trait that only ended when I became a teacher myself. There was no interfaith tension whatsoever; Jewish pupils simply left the room when 'All things bright and beautiful' was sung each morning. School was an oasis – from domestic tensions and also from tension on the street, where it was sometimes dangerous for Jewish children to walk alone because of stone-throwing louts (for Letchworth is in a chalky area with many stones at hand) shouting: 'Go back to Palestine!' Ironically, the Royal Navy was at this time placing severe obstacles in the way of this particular solution. I might add too that some synagogue members (mainly the Hungarians) were opponents of Zionism on religious grounds and had no wish to go to godless Palestine.

I am better able to interpret my experiences after discussions with an undergraduate student of Indian extraction whose family had emigrated from East Africa and settled in a small English town. His account duplicates my own. It is also certain that were, for example, some non-Chassidic group to settle in Jerusalem's Mea Shearim quarter they would not be made welcome. Individuals are one thing, groups another; especially if the newcomers are highly visible and successful into the bargain. I stray into a most difficult area, and will say no more except that I think of Britain with deep affection. In a sense, I never left the country in 1959 since, apart from my professional activities, much of my leisure reading revolves about British rather than North American themes. My perspective is perhaps filtered through lenses tinted by those two ladies mentioned above. But there is much more to it than that. Children were affected in the manner described above; adults might scarcely have been aware of any hostility. In any event, the *rule of law* prevailed.

The transition at age eleven to the local grammar school proved less satisfactory, for the bully boys (including a few of the staff) were more in evidence. But the standard of instruction was, on the whole, surprisingly good for so small a town. Physics proved a disaster; this subject was taught late on Friday afternoons and Jewish students were obliged to leave early in the winter months, generating an unholy muddle in my mind regarding the physical sciences. History, fortunately, was not taught on Friday, or I might not be writing this particular record.

By this time (1948–9) most Jewish families had returned to London. Consequently I lost the company of several cousins with whom I was (and to this day remain) very close. So my social life was now extremely limited – almost non-existent in fact, having in mind the obstacles in the way of inter-faith contact. A premature seriousness was thus imposed on me by events. My ambition to spend the future as a bus driver (I was quite normal in that regard) was now replaced by more bookish interests. I certainly recall being impressed by the gravity of the atmosphere upon the announcement of the 1949 devaluation; and was exercised by the observation that dried bananas, available in wartime, were no longer to be had for love or money, whereas the reverse held true of racing cycles.

Our own return to London was delayed until 1951, when I attended what was then Hendon County School. There the standard of teaching extended from the very poor – in one case amounting to the copying of remarkably written copper-plate notes from the board (remarkable because the teacher was often drunk) with not a word of explanation or discussion – to the outstanding, especially (as far as I was concerned) in literature and history. I much appreciate the instruction I received from those dedicated teachers, brief as it was. For my formal secondary schooling ended in 1953 at age sixteen, as I shall now explain.

It is customary for orthodox Jewish families to send their sons away for Talmudical training, though not necessarily to the end of entering the rabbinate. I did not resist this practice for myself, but did take Alfred Marshall with me (having learned of Marshall from an advisor at school since it was expected that I would return to enter the sixth form) to Gateshead-on-Tyne, where is located the most prominent Talmudical academy in Europe. I do not know what Gateshead looks like today; but it was certainly not very inviting in 1953. I would not be surprised if the location in a coal-mining area was chosen for that very reason, to minimize 'distractions'. Of course there were distractions. I was tested with one such on the train down in the shape of a nurse from the Royal Newcastle Infirmary; it was not a difficult test to pass considering the large number of academy students on that particular train.

7

The regime was strict, with relentless pressure to study; but self-imposed discipline pushed me to work sixteen hours a day six days a week – the main term lasting from October to April with no break – and this far surpassed anything imposed upon me. Because it was known that I had the capacity and willingness to work, I was allowed considerable freedom to follow a routine of my own making, a flexibility on the part of the staff which made the entire episode tolerable. Thus, for example, I had permission to swim daily – and this in place of public prayers – provided of course there were no females in the pool (at the unearthly hour I chose to exercise there were no males either). I also read a daily newspaper; and I wore 'unorthodox' clothing. For a short period I even had a picture of Joseph Stalin on the wall. (This last was too much for my roommate, so Stalin came down.) I might add here that my admiration for this monster went back much further. In fact, as a young boy – the precise date escapes me – I made my way to the Soviet Embassy in London to make enquiries regarding visitor regulations and vividly recall the stolid faces of the embassy staff staring at me through the windows on my retreat to the gates. I put this infatuation down *inter alia* to unhappiness with my own domestic situation (the 'push' factor) coupled with admiration for the Soviet Union in its defeat of Nazi Germany (the 'pull' factor). I did not fully shake off this regrettable attitude until 1968, though at no time was I ever inclined to attach myself to a political party. It was all in the realm of theory.

Despite all this, I fitted in surprisingly well. The average level of intelligence at Gateshead was extraordinarily high. But the training was narrow. There was an absence of any historical dimension, for time is filtered out in traditional method (about which more presently); and Bible study and religious law – ethics somewhat less so – were secondary to Talmudic logic with a premium on the devising of innovatory logical glosses. None of this, of course, came as a surprise; I had been brought up on it.

There were certainly those who went beyond the bounds of all reason in their hostility to the twentieth century – I recall one such exclaiming: 'Einstein! Let his name and memory be erased'; and those whose practice was quite medieval – one roommate wore gloves at night and dipped his right arm up to his elbow in icy water upon awakening (happily after removing his gloves). But such types were a source of entertainment and I regretted there were not more of them to brighten my life. Certainly the rabbis were not of this sort, and for them I had enormous respect.

My decision to leave Gateshead earlier than I now think was desirable – having in mind the objective of the training, which is to feel at home with any Talmudic text – reflected a concern to assure myself a university place, for there was some doubt as to how long and to what extent my father would be prepared to finance my secular studies. Thus it was that late in 1954 I returned to London to attend (in succession) Hendon Technical College and Kilburn Polytechnic where I satisfied in short order, and with some distinction, the then 'Advanced Level' requirements for university entrance. The transition was an easy one: I was self-motivated and hugely industrious; and delighted with the range of young men and women and the mature students from varied parts of the world who were seeking educational advancement outside the regular school system. I was, I think, ready for university.

My only regret, in recalling this period, is the waste of some nine months between the completion of the entrance exams and the commencement of my first academic year at the London School of Economics in October 1956. (My late friend, the economic historian Karl Helleiner, liked to call me a Puritan, and of course he was right.) Those months might have been spent to good purpose back in Gateshead or some equivalent establishment. In fact, I spent them in my father's factory endlessly sticking labels on parcels. For all that, there was some benefit. I was in the unskilled work force engaged in repetitive specialized acts so that Adam Smith's pin factory was to have meaning. And I made new friends among my co-workers; I was certainly made to feel comfortable on my necessarily surreptitious visits to their homes.

It was also during this pre-university hiatus that I first read Robbins' *Nature and Significance of Economic Science*, though I do not recall who introduced me to it; I may have found it by accident at the library. The idea that I might actually be privileged to see its author, even if at a distance, boggled the mind. That I gave private lessons in economic history, and bought a cat which we called 'Ricardo' for a girlfriend, suggests to me that by this time I had decided on the direction I intended to follow.

I turn then to the LSE, whose one hundredth anniversary is currently being celebrated. It comes as a surprise to my students to learn that there were no examinations – none for which we received 'credits' – until the end of the second year of the B.Sc.Econ. degree. This could be and often was an invitation to disaster; but it was helpful in my own case since I worked so well under my own steam. I lived in the library and am surprised that my lungs held out, considering the yellow fog that infiltrated the place.

One word describes my attitude to the material in the 'Economics: Analytical and Descriptive' course – general economic theory and economic history but especially the classics – 'romantic'; I was in love with the great economists of the eighteenth and nineteenth centuries. History of economics had a high profile in the course and my burning interest in it was encouraged by adult debate with my teachers, especially Bernard Corry and Kurt Klappholz, in addition to Lionel Robbins, and also with fellow students, preeminently David Laidler who arrived at the same time as I did. Don Patinkin's *Money, Interest and Prices*, then just published, also exerted an impact. I became convinced at this time that received opinion on Adam Smith's 'paradox of value' was faulty, and held my own when Marian Bowley of University College lectured to students and faculty on the issue.

In economic theory, we received excellent instruction from Kelvin

Lancaster (my personal advisor), Roger Opie, S. A. Ozga, Ezra Mishan and G. C. Archibald. In applied economics we had Frank Paish, Henry Phelps-Brown and Jack Wiseman (I can still hear his Yorkshire-accented: 'What are the implications for policy?' reiterated at every opportunity). Karl Popper was all the rage. We were fortunate to hear lectures in political theory by Elie Kedourie and the great Michael Oakeshott – who incidentally at around this time was arrested on a Brighton beach for bathing in the nude. (Today on some Brighton beaches it is more likely that he would be arrested for bathing in a costume.) It was J. Potter in Economic History who inculcated what I already realized – that Talmudic method is not always appropriate and might be positively misleading. (I had somehow managed to prove convincingly that strike activity is greatest during depressions.)

My years at LSE would have been happy ones indeed were it not for the pressures emanating from the absolute necessity, as I then saw it, to obtain a First-class degree. For I could envisage no alternative to an academic career and a First was effectively a *sine qua non*. The tension was hideously aggravated by the strong opposition of my parents to my marriage, for I had found time during a visit to Paris in the summer of 1957 – the end of my first year – to become engaged to the sister of an acquaintance met at Gateshead. Their opposition turned partly on the prejudice (at that time) of Ashkenazic towards Sephardic Jews (doubtless reciprocated). This, in my naiveté, came as a shock since my fiancée descended from orthodox Egyptian and Turkish families each of considerable pedigree (one Italian, the other Spanish) and I had been certain of my parents' approval. They also suspected that I would be incapable of 'making a living', an attitude of mind I inherited from them that may have depressed my salary over the years. Since my fiancée insisted on obtaining my parents' blessing for the union, I was caught in a severe bind; but my determination was unaffected, and my parents ultimately relented though subject to my obtaining a First. Thus it was that very much indeed depended on where my name would appear on the boards outside Senate House, University of London, where examination results are posted.

In the event I got my First (along with Laidler) – though I remained subject to severe insomnia for years afterwards. Rapid wedding arrangements – we were married in Paris by my teacher, my father's Chassidic rabbi – were followed by a trans-Atlantic honeymoon on the Queen Mary on my way to graduate school. At this time my wife spoke no English (I sometimes suspect she may have misunderstood my proposal of marriage). The transition for her especially was not to be an easy one.

Before proceeding to the next stage, I must state that Lionel Robbins has been, to my mind, the greatest single influence on my career, as he has been for so many other academics. When he passed away in 1984 I felt that a fixed star in my firmament had disappeared. I still feel the loss. I attended in my third year his inspiring lectures in the history of thought and also his seminar late on Friday afternoons. (This scheduling is of some significance for it obliged me to walk home in the winter months – several miles – and provided me with an unsurpassed opportunity to seep up some London atmosphere.) He was instrumental in my choosing Princeton as graduate school – he was a close friend of Professors William Baumol and Jacob Viner – and in my appointment at the University of Toronto. He gave me moral support and very substantial advice with respect to my researches on Smith, David Ricardo and J. S. Mill. And he taught me (or tried to teach me) how best to respond to critics: 'Congratulations on letter appearing in TLS,' he telegraphed with respect to a reply to an unfriendly review of my *Ricardo* – the letter constituting a revised version, following his suggestions, of an original he warned me not to send: 'a display of pity yes, anger never'. He and Iris welcomed me at their home whenever I was in London. His typical kindness is manifest in his personally delivering over several weeks in 1974 a flow of books from his own library – including an 1803 edition of the *Essay on Population* – when I was restricted to my house in London with a broken leg. Lionel, much later, asked to meet my father, and visited him in the empty shell of his London home shortly before he emigrated to Canada in 1980. It was a most successful encounter. The two elderly gentlemen taking tea together on a packing case make a picture that I shall always treasure.

GRADUATE SCHOOL, 1959–63

As already explained, to be assured of an academic career in Britain in the late 1950s required not a doctorate but a First-class Bachelor's degree. But it was not to be presumed; so I took out some insurance by applying to two US graduate schools, Stanford and Princeton, after speaking with Maurice (now Lord) Peston who had recently returned from Princeton. Both schools accepted me and I was obliged to choose between them before the B.Sc.Econ. results were posted. I got my First and along with it the Gonner Prize (which included volume 2 of Sraffa's *Ricardo*) and a University Postgraduate Scholarship. But I was advised to take advantage of a Fulbright Travel Award and follow up the Princeton opportunity for some formal training. I took the advice, though with no real idea of what this would entail. Certainly it was not then our intention to spend four years away from Europe.

One of my reasons for selecting Princeton over Stanford was the presence there of Jacob Viner, whose retirement had been delayed. His course was, as one would expect, first rate, and I still find his notes valuable. But it was necessary not to allow oneself to be intimidated by him. His first question on meeting me was: 'Who was Hardy Canute?' And he strongly asserted (quite inexplicably) that there are no biological analogies in Alfred Marshall's work. He was also intolerant when it came to Marx, whose writings on value he likened to the ink splatterings made by a monkey. But I am privileged to have studied with the author of *Studies in the Theory of International Trade*, which is surely one of the finest works in doctrinal history ever written.

At the time of my arrival in Princeton there were no formal courses in mathematical economics. I made arrangements with Harold Kuhn, who helped me with Robert Dorfman, Paul Samuelson and Robert Solow; and I used James Henderson's and Richard Quandt's text assiduously. (Quandt was my personal advisor and I am indebted to him for his encouragement.) But it was clear to all, and especially to myself as I had suspected since age five – a school report dated July 1942 mentions that 'Samuel became over-anxious regarding number-work' but errs by adding that 'now he derives much pleasure from this subject' – that I was not cut out to be a mathematical economist.

The choice of dissertation was particularly difficult. I had not intended to proceed to a doctorate at Princeton. The issue did not arise until after the comprehensive examinations, when I indicated to William Baumol, who had kept a kindly eye on me since my arrival, that my wife and I (by then we also had a daughter) planned to return to Britain. He dissuaded me, and I found myself faced with the choice of proceeding either to research in the history of economic thought with little formal supervision – Viner had by then retired – and also no clearly defined project, only a vague wish to write on the British classics, or to some alternative. Fritz Machlup, who had come from Johns Hopkins to succeed Viner, provided the solution. He was then organizing an army of graduate students in a project financed by the Ford Foundation on the economics of innovation. For him a dissertation was one further hurdle to overcome on the way to the doctorate in no more than two years, certainly not one's *magnum opus*. I followed his advice to undertake one of the forty-odd studies he had listed; and not being really interested in any of them I selected the first: Investment and Innovation. It proved to be an inspired choice.

At the very outset of my investigation an extraordinary offer by the DuPont Company gave me access to some thirty years of detailed cost and investment data relating to rayon manufacture at several of their North American plants, and also to the scientists and officers who had been engaged in decision-making over that period. I do not recall by what persuasive arguments I convinced DuPont to yield up materials of this richness to an outsider. I was also able to obtain supplementary information from suppliers of materials and equipment. Many days were devoted in the New York Public Library to the *Rayon Textile Monthly* and *Chemical Industries* and such like; and I made frequent trips to Wilmington, Delaware (DuPont's head office) and to the homes of active and retired informants, several of whom showed great kindness to my small family. The wealth of data and information and the acquired knowledge of the production process allowed me to measure the impact of innovation – distinguishing between 'major' and 'minor' categories – on productivity improvement, to evaluate the degree of capital embodiment required and the extent of patent protection, and to treat related issues in the economics of innovation. The thesis was published with only minor revisions by the MIT Press (Hollander 1965) and to this day is regularly referred to in the widest range of journals.

At the time it pleased me to know that both Adam Smith and Alfred Marshall would have approved of the exercise. And with this single venture into Industrial Organization I obtained my licence to devote the rest of my life to the history of economics. The exercise was of permanent value in other respects too. I had dirtied my hands with *real* economics; and I was made suspicious of the one-sided Popperian perception of scientific activity with its neglect of the inductive dimension.[6]

TORONTO, 1963–95

My initial appointment at Toronto resulted from a series of unlikely misunderstandings. It was a rule at Princeton that graduate students who had a paper accepted for publication would be excused from one of their PhD field examinations; the rule was designed to introduce us to the real world of academia and has since, I understand, been abandoned. It so happened that I had brought with me an undergraduate paper on Marshall's Representative Firm. Baumol helped me rework it – an incomparable training – and in 1960 it was accepted by the then *Canadian Journal of Economics and Political Science* [chapter 4 in this collection]. Shortly thereafter Harry Johnson, speaking to the student body, suggested that if we should have any difficulty publishing in a journal we might try the *CJEPS*. At the December 1962 slave market held in New York I had a chance encounter with him in the elevator, and plucked up courage to ask him whether he had meant what he had told us, since I was *parti pris*. He was kind enough to assure me that he had not, and that he had made an inappropriate joke. In any event, he took down details of my work and interests in his famous black book – by this time I had published my second article ('On Malthus and Keynes') in the *Economic Journal*. This he followed up with a letter informing me of an editorial opening at the University of Toronto Press J. S. Mill project, then at the start of what was to be a thirty-year odyssey. The Press replied that there was no opening, and suggested that Johnson might in fact have intended the Political Economy Department at the University. On enquiry, the department chairman, the economic historian Tom Easterbrook, wrote to say that there would indeed be an opening in the history of thought, considering Professor Vincent Bladen's imminent retirement. Thanking me for reminding him of the department's requirements, Easterbrook invited me for an interview with Bladen.

There were thus no advertisements, phoney or otherwise; no unbecoming bedroom encounters with departmental representatives; not even a workshop to address. Bladen liked me and I liked him and that was that. There were, of course, letters of recommendation but in one respect these worked to my disadvantage. As I later discovered, they were so flattering that Easterbrook sniffed out an element of economic rent in the salary he had been prepared to offer: 'Why, with such letters, would SH wish to come to Toronto?' – a very Canadian reaction; 'we can reduce our offer'. I am sorry I never had the opportunity to let him know that I had had the better of him; for I could have been hired for considerably less. It was a quantum leap from my $2,000 student grant to a salary of $7,500.

I had had also at this time, thanks to Lord Robbins, an offer from the University of Hull back home; I visited Franklin and Marshall College in the beautiful Pennsylvania Dutch countryside; and I gave a test lecture on J. S. Mill at Austin, Texas, where there was an opening in the history of thought. But the Toronto prospect was the most promising, and I did not explore these or any other possibilities further. And I have now been at Toronto for thirty-two years.

The present Department of Economics was created in 1982 when it was carved out of the Department of Political Economy. Political Economy at its inception in 1888 comprised economics, political science, law (until 1930), and history (until it gradually emerged as an independent subject over the years 1895–1910); and to it were added commerce and finance (in 1909) and sociology in 1932 (until 1963). The breakup of the department – more a faculty – was largely instigated by economists, notwithstanding the considerable decentralization that had evolved among the three remaining disciplines, on the grounds that it was professionally unwise to be distinguished by an appellation which was easily misunderstood, thereby dissuading potential faculty and students. It was sensible to set up a department of economics on a par with other North American departments, allowing it to acquire (or was it to maintain?) its natural and rightful place in the sun as the 'Harvard of the North'.[7]

Those who wished to retain the political economy umbrella did so for a variety of reasons. My own opposition to the disestablishment reflected a concern that the diversity and tolerance that had characterized political economy would be undermined by the break. These features had worked greatly in my favour since my arrival, allowing me to teach and do research in the history of economics without let or hindrance and without having to pretend that I was engaged in some other more useful activity. (I have recently encountered a 'computable dynamic model' of some eighteenth-century propositions in theory – rational reconstruction with a vengeance – that yields nothing beyond the results stated so clearly in the original prose.) I might mention at this point that my initial plan – once the DuPont study was at the publishers in 1964 – had been a volume on classical economics. This I did not achieve until 1987, for it became clear very soon that each of the great economists would require a book (if not two) of his own.

14

I had been engaged by Bladen to continue a tradition according a central position, on intellectual principle, to the history of economic thought in undergraduate training. W. J. Ashley was first Professor of Political Economy (1888–92) and was instrumental in assuring the appointment of James Mavor, with a similar historical bias, who held the professorship, as Professor of Political Economy and Constitutional History, until 1923; Harold Innis joined the department in 1921 and was Head from 1937 until his death in 1952; C. R. Fay held a chair in economic history from 1921 until 1930 when he returned to Cambridge; Bladen arrived in 1922 and taught a compulsory honours course in the literature of political economy for several decades. (It is indicative of the character of the department that the economics of socialism and Karl Marx figured quite prominently in the curriculum of the 1920s and 1930s.) It was with the hope of continuing this tradition on his imminent retirement that Bladen recommended my appointment. But to my good fortune, he never really retired. He had much to offer on Smith – my *Smith* is dedicated to him – and Mill; and for several years we shared, to mutual advantage, teaching responsibilities in our subject.

I have had occasion to describe in print the expansion of economic thought at Toronto by the early 1970s (Hollander 1975 [chapter 2]). Things were certainly looking up then. The presence in the department of Brough Macpherson, author of *Possessive Individualism*, and in English of Jack Robson and his team of Mill researchers, provided further attractions. At this time too William Jaffé, after retirement from Northwestern University and a series of visiting professorships, took up an appointment at York University which he held for the last decade of his life, from 1970 to 1980. I took full advantage of his linguistic, editorial, scholarly and theoretical skills.[8] When I think of his struggle for recognition of our field – that he was obliged to continue with annual appointments until age eighty-two is itself suggestive – I count my blessings.

My worst fears were not in fact realized with the above-mentioned split. The new department of economics lived up to a commitment to respect the traditional strengths. A third-year undergraduate course in the history of thought is still compulsory for economic specialists. And graduate history of thought has flourished, and this despite subtle pressures on students to work in more 'relevant' fields. Indeed, economic development and history of thought have an enviable record as far as concerns the generation and place-ment of doctoral students. Also indicative is a 'breadth' requirement for all economists in the PhD programme that can be satisfied by a year's course in economic history or the history of economic thought.

This last sentence should now be written in the past tense. It came as a complete surprise to me in February this year to find a proposal in my mail box from the graduate coordinator recommending the elimination of the economic history/history of thought requirement as part of a package designed to correct a perceived failure of the graduate programme –

precisely the complaint that had led to the creation of the department in the first place: 'Our graduate programme can and should be better. We have difficulty attracting the best domestic students and, at the other end, have some difficulty placing students. Our students currently take a full-year course in economic history or history of thought in either the second or third year of the programme. In my view, the opportunity cost imposed by the current requirement at Toronto is too high . . . so that requirement should now be eliminated.'

As I see it, the proposal was more than the product of a single individual's prejudices; it reflected a perspective on training in economics shared by the leadership and possibly by a majority of the faculty – of this I cannot be sure since no vote was ever taken – coupled with the wish to imitate programmes elsewhere. In any event, the department imposed the change without feeling it necessary to provide any reasoned substantiation of the assertion that the 'opportunity cost' of the requirement was 'too high' – to face up to Sir John Hicks's position that 'economics is more like art or philosophy than science, in the use that it can make of its own history' (Hicks 1983: 4) or to Friedrich A. von Hayek's view of the social sciences as subject to an '*essential* complexity from which the natural sciences are free' (von Hayek 1989 [1974]); nor did it see fit to offer any explanation of the academic success of those who had had the courage to write their dissertation in our field. To be more accurate, there was one substantive response: 'Do you think,' a colleague asked of me, 'that it is our function to produce educated doctoral students? Our function is to produce welders.' I am grateful to him for coining so graphic a description of what is going on in the profession – notwithstanding the periodic laments by presidents of the American Economic Association – of which the recent events in Toronto are a mere reflection.[9]

The abandonment of any pretence to keep to the understanding of 1982 is clear. Its delay by some thirteen years can perhaps be partly explained by the high visibility of the history of thought, as manifested in my election to the Royal Society of Canada in 1976 and my appointment to a University Professorship in 1984 – largely an honorific title at Toronto (bar some excellent cucumber sandwiches once a year) but more tangible in other major North American institutions – and more generally by the recognition by Canadian academics of the traditional strengths of the department, as reflected, for example, in a recent External Evaluation. But perhaps the *dictat* was inevitable once the old guard had retired or approached retirement.

In opposing the change, I did not stand quite alone. Gerry Helleiner – Karl's son – and Sue Horton, both development specialists, protested vehemently. In my opinion, the welding syndrome certainly threatens the viability of economic development as a subject treated with due allowance for history and institutional arrangement; and economic development thus treated has been quantitatively the single most important subject in the department over the past two decades in terms of doctorates. In sharp contrast was a deafening silence from the economic historians. Notwithstanding the relatively large numbers of faculty in that subject, it had attracted not a single doctoral student for a decade and no graduate student had chosen to satisfy the PhD requirement by way of the economic history option. There was nothing for them to lose by acceptance of the proposal.

In and of itself the new regime is not necessarily an immediate threat to the history of economic thought at Toronto; MA and PhD students may still take the course if they wish, and students may still choose to write a dissertation in the field. But the message directed to incoming students is clear. (It was, interestingly, from among the students that much opposition to the change emanated.) And most revealing of the effort to replicate the 'top' American schools (perhaps more immediately the 'top' Canadian schools) is the exclusion of economic thought from long-run staffing plans for the department. Students who might wish to work in the history of thought will in the near future be obliged now to do an empirical study of DuPont plants – if they can obtain the data.

Only a short while ago I wrote in response to a proposal that the history of economics be transferred to the history of science programme that, though I welcomed serious contact with historians of science,

> we would be failing to meet our educational responsibilities were a strengthening of those ties to reflect a deliberate 'break-away' from economics rather than a deliberate attempt to have the best of both worlds. I am not yet ready to see economists as unredeemable Philistines. Should this prove too optimistic, the case may have to be carried over the heads of the individual departments to the university and even beyond. In the meantime our duty is to encourage students of economics, graduate and undergraduate, to take the history of their subject seriously. They cannot do so if no one is there to provide them with the opportunity and set an example.
>
> (Hollander 1992: 214)

All of this has been superannuated by events. The Graduate School showed no interest in the changes and did not insist on a reasoned justification. (The university is in fact in the process of relinquishing much of the authority hitherto exercised by the Graduate School to the departments.) My argument had taken for granted the rule of reason. I had forgotten my Kant: '*der Besitz der Gewalt das freie Urteil der Vernunft unvermeidlich verdirbt*' (the possession of power ruins the free use of reason).

I stand by my conviction that major benefits accrue to both undergraduate and graduate students in economics who have some familiarity with the great literature of their subject. Apart from a better comprehension of economics *qua* analysis there is scarcely a single current policy issue that did

17

not receive attention from brilliant minds in the past. Economists cannot afford to neglect this vast mine of intelligent discussion. That our subject has attracted some of the brightest students at Toronto and that they have set up their own spheres of influence, satisfies me that it has not all been a waste of time. As for my own written output, it will be little affected, for my intellectual contacts have always been almost entirely extra-departmental.

But it's an ill wind. Sad as it may be, the refusal of my department to build on its traditional strengths has had the positive effect of making me begin to consider available options, including that of early retirement from Toronto – though not retirement from scholarship, for I still hope to complete my plan of proceeding to a study of the economics of my distant relative Karl Marx, by all indications a task of several years. That I should leave Toronto vertically rather than be carried out feet first is not an unpleasing prospect.

TRAVEL

To return to happier days. It has been my good fortune to have been able to take leaves of absence approximately every five years on average; and to have travelled frequently as guest lecturer. Each location has attached to it in my mind some long-term research project. I connect Florence and London with *Ricardo*; Jerusalem with *Mill*; Jerusalem again, Melbourne (La Trobe University) and Auckland with *Malthus*. These expeditions have proven rewarding, both personally and professionally. For one thing, my daughter and son benefited hugely from their experiences in Italy, Britain and Israel. (Both have settled in Israel.) As for myself, the leave taken in Britain in 1974 provided the opportunity to work with Sir John Hicks and seduce him from the fix-wage interpretation of Ricardo – a high point of my career. But of all my expeditions those to New Zealand in 1985 and 1988 have pleased me most, thanks to Tony Endres and his colleagues at Auckland. The University's Department of Economics has been a true pleasure to work in.

Without my wife at my side these ventures would have been all but impossible, considering the above-mentioned restrictions, which become particularly onerous when foreign travel is involved. On the whole we have experienced great goodwill on the part of our hosts, who have attempted to find practical ways to overcome the difficulties – nicely thwarting one of their purposes!

Occasionally there have been less understanding encounters. My neighbour at one conference dinner in 1982, a woman of considerable academic stature, asked me if I thought the Deity cared whether I ate a steak such as she had on her plate. I could only reply that 'God alone knows'. It scarcely seemed worthwhile to explain that adherence to ancient practice does not necessarily imply backwardness; or that, from my perspective, God did not come (immediately) into the picture. (The cost of that particular dinner was shared equally among all participants, for I could not possibly protest on my own behalf; my hard-boiled egg cost me more than the equivalent of $30.) I recall also the embarrassed chairman who had to kick his colleague under the table when the latter began to mock some orthodox Jewish academic for surviving on bananas when he travelled, unaware that one such survivor was seated opposite him. And there was a perverse interpretation, offered by an otherwise very sensible observer, of my refusal to drink the wine that was being served at some dinner as an indication that I was 'on the wagon', a charge repeated to graduate students at an American institution and thence relayed to me, for the academic world is small and gossipy. The rabbinical ordinance dictating my refusal at that time does not, however, extend to all spirits – my illustrious ancestor R. Moses Isserles has some quite 'liberal' things to say on the matter of wine itself – and the individual in question must have believed that I had failed in my effort to 'dry out' when he observed me imbibing on some other occasion. All of this is small beer; but it does add variety.

SOME CONCLUSIONS

At the most general level it seems to me that my practices have saved me from myself. The Sabbath day has protected me from some of the effects of my workaholism, by providing at regular intervals that minimum of tranquillity required for the maintenance of sanity; that my insomnia afflicted me on all nights except Friday is revealing. (And I don't much care for horse riding anyway.) Unfortunately, that workaholism itself can perhaps be traced to the same source. Apart from the danger of wasting time, which was always a standard refrain, there is the drive to prove oneself in a 'hostile' environment – a much recorded sociological phenomenon – the hostility, however, emanating in my case from within as much as from without the community.

As for specifics, I have already mentioned that traditional Talmudic scholarship is ahistorical; history can be dangerous, for it threatens the notion of a seamless whole whereby the forefathers, some three and a half to four millennia ago, are perceived to have obeyed the Law before it was handed down at Sinai.[10] And, of course, there is the Creationism that is taken for granted.[11] If then I have devoted myself to history it must be in spite of, not because of, my training unless by way of reaction. I do, however, admit to finding the notion that time moves in all directions touching and have recently learned much in this regard from the writings of my paternal grandfather, an adept Bible critic who practised a sort of 'bounded deconstruction' whereby anything goes in biblical exegesis provided the outcome satisfies the orthodox codes of law and morality (I. M. Hollander 1956–7). But only on the day of rest, in small doses and after a glass of whisky, do I permit myself the luxury.

19

My hostility towards 'deconstruction'[12] and my inclination towards 'positivism' requires elaboration. I am old-fashioned enough to seek to isolate what someone patently sane intended by his utterances; and believe the position to the contrary, embodied in the dismissal of authorial intent, to constitute a threat to the very concept of a university.[13] I suspect that my stance has been reinforced by the training in textual interpretation I received almost since birth, though not my grandfather's variety, which is too modern for my liking. That same training has led me, I believe, to avoid premature recourse to charges of inconsistency. And it might also have generated a bias towards emphasizing continuities in intellectual development, though (I hasten to add) not to the extent of perceiving them where they do not exist. I must justify this latter qualification. At one time I subscribed pretty much to Piero Sraffa's reading of Ricardo (Hollander 1973: 14, 186); and also perceived J. S. Mill as riddled with inconsistency in maintaining features of both 'Ricardianism' and 'neoclassicism' (Hollander 1976). My continuity position developed with the evidence; it was not ready made.

That I am greatly attracted to the utilitarianism that runs through the British classical school might seem paradoxical, since that perspective was, of course, designed as a counter to natural law and other varieties of 'absolutism'. Yet rabbinical Judaism has a pervasive utilitarian component, as illustrated by legal devices to allow interest payment and receipt, and – my favourite – by a nice 'Malthusian' injunction against sex in marriage during periods of famine, notwithstanding the general rule to be fruitful and multiply. One problem has been to allow innovations without threat to authority and social control; the solution is to represent them not as responses to specific contemporary problems, but as the drawing out of implications to be found in the scriptures.[14]

It has been said often enough that my work is 'controversial'. This is so, and perhaps appropriately, for controversy (in the best sense of that word) is the essence of the exegetical procedures in which I have been trained. Moreover, life at the interface of my 'two worlds' may well tend to encourage a certain independence of mind. I stand by the optimistic title of this memoir.

AN ADDENDUM

I told Mr Johnson that I put down all sorts of little incidents in it [the journal]. 'Sir,' said he, 'there is nothing too little for so little a creature as man. It is by studying little things that we attain the great knowledge of having as little misery and as much happiness as possible.'

(Boswell 1950: 305)

My first effort at autobiography has generated friendly and positive responses for which I am grateful. I take this occasion to add a point or two by way of clarification.[15]

I wish to emphasize first, that my comments on the absence of history from my course of Talmudic training (above, p. 8) refer specifically to the particular curriculum characterizing the traditional academies. I was not commenting upon the role of history in Talmudic literature in any other sense. Second, it is also essential to specify that the general approach at Gateshead reflected the logical and shrewd style characteristic of the old Lithuanian academies, rather than the scholastic and sophistic style of the Polish Talmudists. Third, some readers did not quite appreciate the significance of my allusion to turbot as a 'questionable fish' (above, p. 5). I do not blame them.[16] To give some flavour of how serious the issue is in the orthodox world – and to correct a minor error – I quote from an account of decisions taken by the London ecclesiastical court (Beth Din) in 1822 and 1954:

> Shortly before the High Holy-Days of 1822 the Beth Din received a communication from Newcastle-upon-Tyne asking if the fish 'called Turbot' could be eaten by Jews. The Chief Rabbi answered in the affirmative and stated that permission to eat the particular sea-water fish had been authorised in two responses – one issued by his own father while rabbi in London, and the other by his father's illustrious brother, Rabbi Saul of Amsterdam. Hirschell stated that they had both based their decisions on documents in the Beth Din of Venice. This ruling of 1822, issued by the Ab Beth Din of London, was accepted by British Jewry for the following 132 years. However, an event took place in London during 1954 which made it apparent that the then members of the London Beth Din were unaware of Hirschell's ruling. At a festive dinner at a London hotel the fish course was turbot and one of the distinguished guests accused the caterer of serving *trefa* (non-kosher) fish. A piscatorial furore ensued, and for the following few weeks countless so-called experts gave their views for or against the *kashrut* of the fish. The climax came on November 2, 1954, when the Beth Din issued a ruling that turbot was not to be included in the list of kosher foods. The ruling was unique in that the then Chief Rabbi and his *dayanim* overruled the decisions of two former heads of their own Beth Din!
>
> (Simons 1980: 68)[17]

In the memoir I illustrated the complexities of the dietary rules by this particular instance, because it is one that I recall vividly from my childhood. But the example casts light on an entire life-style and the broader picture should be kept in mind. Thus the fact that turbot was not generally acceptable in my parents' home confirms a stricter degree of observance than that enjoined by the London court at the period in question, and reflects the great stringency of the European immigrant communities. And the relaxation during the war years was not (it appears from Simons) on the part of the London court as I thought – since until 1954 that court was permissive in its ruling – but rather on that of the stricter independent orthodox communities.

I turn to a related matter. The clash between the Enlightenment philosophy and rabbinic Judaism on which I put considerable stress (above, p. 6) may be nicely illustrated by an extraordinary apology to readers from the Editorial Board of *The Jewish Observer*, an orthodox American journal, for having published a piece on Moses Mendelssohn, albeit one that had identified his 'fatal flaws': 'We see that we were indeed in error in publishing an article on Mendelssohn. For this we apologize to our readers. All the more are we pained by the indication from the responses that the article was interpreted as a watering down of the traditional opposition to Mendelssohn' (*The Jewish Observer* 1987). This response will (like the turbot case) help convey some of the background which I sought, perhaps too briefly, to reconstruct.

To summarize: I accept for myself the regulations of my religion but with a strong preference for lenient rulings; for me a good rabbi has always been one who can say 'yes'. I reject the intolerance that sometimes attaches to (or rather seems endemic in) organized 'conservative' religion, and strenuously oppose any sort of theocratic organization – Mendelssohn's position of course. I have been asked by readers of the memoir how I can reconcile these two orientations. I can only answer in the words of the late Benny Hill: 'With considerable difficulty.' For all that, I have not yet fallen off the tightrope and, God willing, can stay up into the foreseeable future.

This leads me to a matter which I deliberately avoided in the memoir, but which I now think has to be brought into the open notwithstanding the risk that a charge of paranoia will be brought against me. I allude to the irrational (and, it pains me to say it, even malevolent) nature of a few of the reactions to my researches on Ricardo and the classics.[18]

A little background from another field (epidemiology) will set the stage. Peter Duesberg, a professor of molecular cell biology at Berkeley, takes the minority view that AIDS is drug-induced, not virus-induced (Horton 1996). What does the scientific establishment do to a scientist whose work is out of step with majority opinion? Cut off his funding. And peer pressure reflecting scientific consensus can be crippling so that 'few scientists are any longer willing to question, even privately, the consensus view in any field' (Duesberg, in Horton 1996: 20). Duesberg was badly hit by the establishment.[19] I myself have never suffered serious consequences for my position on the classics. Imagine then my astonishment to read a referee's report relating to a recent request for research funding from Ottawa. The referee seems to have read my memoir: 'Now of course, both Hollander and his critics have the right to be heard. But his request for funds to support a further series of articles defending his view of classical economics seems to me quite unreasonable. It reflects his tendency towards research overkill, behind which is a Talmudic mind (he is Jewish, and he did spend a year as a trainee for the rabbinate) and a fierce conviction that by sheer effort and willpower he can ensure that his view will prevail.' He then proceeds with the original argument that since I would do the research anyway, why waste the state's precious funds: 'his very large research output and writings in response to critics seems to demonstrate that he is perfectly capable of defending, reiterating, and elaborating his views without further outside research assistance'. There was all the more reason to put the Research Council's investment 'to better use', since '[s]ome time between his *Ricardo* (1979) and his *Mill* (1985), most of the leading English-speaking specialists on classical economics' – he cites six by name – 'expressed their disagreement with Hollander's aim of proving his claim "that the Ricardo–Mill theory . . . is directly in line with modern doctrine" '.

One must not lose perspective. Duesberg's position, if correct, has societal implications of enormous importance; the interpretation of Ricardo is inconsequential in comparison. And fortunately I received my funding, the grants committee dissociating itself from the hostile report, and placing me high in its ranking. (The Canadian government is serious and sent my modest proposal to *five* referees, who covered the entire spectrum of opinion.) I raise the issue only to show how an effort was made to deny funding for my work on the grounds that I must be wrong since an (alleged) majority of English-language critics says I am; and how incensed the referee must be to make no attempt to disguise his regrettable biases and to fall back on the perverse case that a productive scholar is to be penalized for his productivity.

Though the referee had apparently read my memoir, he got it wrong in one respect: I was never a trainee for the rabbinate as I made it clear (above, p. 7, 8). But my training did instil in me a respect for the texts, particularly an appreciation of the necessity to read *in context*. It is disrespect for the texts that is the source of the myth-making that bedevils the history of economics. A sad instance close to home is provided by what masquerades as a 'review' of my first collection of essays. In the introduction to that collection I quote a list of ten assertions regarding Ricardo which had been *attributed to me* by a hostile critic and observe: 'I actually go a long way with Professor [Mark] Blaug. *Many of the assertions are false* (especially those containing "never" or its equivalent). *But these I do not recognize as my own*, claiming for myself and attributing to Ricardo a modicum of subtlety and sophistication' (Hollander 1995: 2; emphasis added). Now in his response, the intemperate critic rips my three-sentence statement apart, suppresses the second and third sentences, and leaves me exposed to ridicule: 'Professor Hollander sets out my list of ten of his iconoclastic assertions about Ricardo, every one of which I claim are false, and calmly concludes: "I actually go a long way with Professor Blaug" (p. 2). He can say this because his method ensures that even his own interpretative conclusions exhibit the dictum that "anything goes"'. (Blaug 1996: 23). Such a spectacle on the part of an established scholar is enough to make one weep. As for a lament at the close of the tirade that 'reading Hollander is always irritating and sometimes dangerous to one's mental health' and akin to 'wallowing in mud' (24), perhaps I can make amends. I would be happy to provide details of a promotional notice appearing in Canada's national daily under 'Country Inns and Outings': ' "Dirty Weekend" takes on a whole new meaning. . . . Relax your aching muscles in our new Total Immersion Hot Moor Mud Baths. Clip this ad and receive two Mud Baths *for the price of one*.' A dip in our Hot Moor Mud Baths might help repair the damage to my critic's mental health for which he holds me responsible.

With respect to another recent episode, I readily plead *mea culpa*; the excitement of research led me to a gross error that has now been corrected (Hollander 1996). I allude to my report at the January 1995 meeting of the AEA in Washington of the possible emergence in the Sraffa archives of Ricardo's famous 'Lost Papers on the Profits of Capital'. Given my certitude that the hand was Ricardo's, I was faced with two possibilities. That Sraffa, who must have known of this paper, chose to suppress it. That Sraffa must have mistaken Ricardo's hand for Bentham's, for which reason he did not publish the piece in the *Works and Correspondence*. (The document is described by Sraffa as a 'paper probably in Bentham's hand-writing on the effects on profits of cultivating successive qualities of land', and also as 'Bentham on Rent'.) The first of these possibilities, I dismissed immediately. (I now believe the document to be in James Mill's hand, and possibly the Bentham item reported by Sraffa, Mill acting as Bentham's amanuensis.)

Why do I raise this particular issue? It is because the original attribution to Ricardo engendered a charge against me of dishonesty, indeed of *lèse-majesté*, by an outraged defender of the faith. His widely circulated censure uses at the masthead the Chinese proverb: 'The Truth cannot be erased. *Neither can Falsehood*' (italicized in the original), and it reflects his high dudgeon at an imaginary implication:

> Hollander suggests that Sraffa might have not recognized the manuscript to be in Ricardo's hand, and assumed it to be by (probably) Bentham. This however must appear so incredible to any reader in his right mind that another explanation naturally suggests itself: Sraffa must have suppressed the paper. And the fact that it was not found among Ricardo's papers in Cambridge University Library, where it actually belongs, but among Sraffa's papers, might make this explanation appear (superficially) plausible; moreover apart from considerations relating to Sraffa's integrity and scholarship . . . one would deem him an idiot if he suppressed a manuscript of Ricardo and then left it in his own collection of autographs.

It did not cross my critic's mind that honest mistakes are possible and that at no time did I question Sraffa's editorial integrity. The interested reader might refer to de Vivo 1996 to find the complaint – though by then wholly irrelevant – alluded to in print.

It is evident from these episodes that the history of economics is highly charged with emotion – or should I say with 'religious' fervour? And with the fervour comes a danger of intellectual fascism against which one must be ever alert, for liberty requires eternal vigilance, as we were taught by the Lord Mayor of Dublin in 1790. Nevertheless, my own experience makes me hopeful – it *is* possible to swim against the tide – for we are blessed with a variety of research centres and outlets for publication. I am not sure though that my inveterate habit of responding to critics has been to good purpose. James Boswell would have doubted it: '[I]t would be an endless task for an author to point out upon every occasion the precise object he has in view. Contenting himself with the approbation of readers of discernment and taste, he ought not to complain that some are found who cannot or will not understand him' (Boswell 1961 [1773]: 223n). But though I was, I now admit, childishly naive in taking it for granted that rational debate is always welcome, I very much doubt that I will ever wholly abandon belief in the dictum: *de la discussion jaillit la lumière* (though I shall be more discriminating in future). I have my Talmudic training to blame for that. And fortunately we do have a model to emulate: 'And now my dear Malthus I have done. Like other disputants after such discussion we each retain our opinions. These discussions however never influence our friendship; I should not like you more than I do if you agreed in opinion with me' (Ricardo to Malthus, 31 August 1823; Ricardo 1951–73, IX: 382). That too, though Ricardo might not have realized it, is the Talmudic mode.

NOTES

1 One must admit to being flattered by such an invitation. Here I am reminded of a report from a colleague a while ago that one of my students had referred to me either as a 'great' or as a 'good' man, he could not recall which. My response at that time was that into which category one would best like to fall depends on one's age, so that I still preferred the first. It has now become (almost) a matter of indifference.

2 The formal rationale offered is lest one might break off a branch from a tree, an act proscribed by Torah Law (the Law as derived by the rabbis from the biblical texts on the basis of complex hermeneutical rules). But this it seems to me is a fiction, designed to link all rabbinical interventions to the Pentateuch; the essential logic is to prevent behaviour that would damage the spirit or character of the Sabbath. This example can serve as template: swimming, for example, is forbidden for analogous reasons.

3 Strictly speaking, the restrictions apply only after confirmation (at the age of thirteen for boys) but it was apparently perceived to be never too young to learn.

4 There were other quorums. One was organized by the Sassoon family of Bombay. But this was to us another world.

5 See Altmann 1973. Another scholar, of the following century, who is sympathetic to me in this regard, is Heinrich Graetz (1974 [1891]).

6 I am interested to find a recent confirmation of this suspicion in Papineau 1995.

7 For a history of the department, see Drummond 1983.

8 For a memorial evaluation, see Hollander 1981 [chapter 3 in this volume].

9 The notion of a single-term requirement – a Canadian term is considerably shorter than a US semester – was rather casually floated. But in my opinion serious treatment of our subject would be impossible in anything much less than a Canadian academic year.

10 On the matter of *time* in this context see the brief but instructive comments by Ephraim Kleiman (1994) and Ismar Schorsch (1994).

11 At the Gateshead academy the nineteenth-century 'watchmaker' argument was used to support the notion of creation (just short of 6,000 years ago). Fortunately, neither this nor other features of the belief system took centre stage.

12 The best account known to me is by Jonathan Lynn (1994, chapter 19).

13 The worst may be over in this age of financial constraint, but only to be replaced by a new threat from a perspective on knowledge not in terms of *education* but as *means* – we are back to the 'welding syndrome'.

14 Two examples of interventions which tighten rather than loosen the reins will be found in note 2.

15 I should also add a note on my Toronto career which so much preoccupied me in the memoir. In the summer of 1996 faculty members in my age group were offered the proverbial golden handshake on agreeing to early retirement. I signed a futures contract to leave at the end of the 1997–8 academic year. And I acted wisely and with prescience; for my graduate course, which had flourished for years generating a number of wonderful doctoral candidates, no longer has students thus undermining my *raison d'être* at this institution.

16 The issue turns on the biblical injunction: 'These you may eat of all that are in the waters: all that have fins and scales may you eat. And whatsoever has not fins and scales you may not eat; it is unclean for you' (Deuteronomy XIV. 9–10; also Leviticus XI. 9–10, 12). Questions arise because of the uncharacteristic scales of the European turbot (*Scophthalmus maximus* or *Psetta maximus*). Other varieties of turbot are permitted by all branches of orthodoxy.

17 I thank Professor Judah Sanders of Concordia University (a Letchworth cousin) for bringing this episode to my attention.

18 The following comments draw upon an address – an after-dinner address – which I gave to the conference on Time and Economics held at Glendon College (Toronto) in June 1996.

19 The dire consequences for those who do not toe the party line may also be illustrated from literary theory (Anon. 1995: 30–3).

REFERENCES

Altmann, Alexander (1973) *Moses Mendelssohn. A Biographical Sketch*, London: Routledge and Kegan Paul.

Anon. (1995) 'An Open Letter', *PN Review*, 21, 5 (May–June): 30–3.

Blaug, Mark (1996) 'Taking Hollander Seriously: *Ricardo–The New View*', *History of Economic Thought Newsletter*, 56 (Summer): 22–4.

Boswell, James (1950) *London Journal 1762–1763*, ed. F. A. Pottle, New York: McGraw-Hill.

—— (1961) *Journal of a Tour of the Hebrides with Samuel Johnson, LLD* [1773], ed. F. A. Pottle and C. H. Bennett, New York: McGraw-Hill.

Drummond, Ian (1983) *Political Economy at the University of Toronto: A History of the Department, 1888–1982*, Toronto: University of Toronto Faculty of Arts and Science.

Graetz, Heinrich (1974) [1891] *History of the Jews*, Philadelphia: Jewish Publication Society of America.

von Hayek, F. A. (1989) [1974] 'The Pretence of Knowledge: Nobel Memorial Lecture', *American Economic Review*, 79: 3–7.

Hicks, J. R (1983) 'Revolutions in Economics', in *Collected Essays on Economic Theory: III Classics and Moderns*, Cambridge: Harvard University Press, 3–16.

Hollander, Isaac M. (1956–7) [5717] *Sefer Rekué Pachim*, London.

Hollander, Samuel (1965) *The Sources of Increased Efficiency: A Study of DuPont Rayon Plants*, Cambridge, Mass.: MIT Press.

—— (1973) *The Economics of Adam Smith*, Studies in Classical Political Economy, Vol. I, Toronto and Buffalo: University of Toronto Press.

—— (1975) 'On the Teaching of the History of Economic Thought', *History of Political Economy*, 7 (Spring): 115–21.

—— (1976) 'Ricardianism, J. S. Mill and the Neoclassical Challenge', in J. M. Robson and M. Laine (eds) *James and J. S. Mill: Papers of the Centenary Conference*, Toronto: University of Toronto Press, 67–85.

—— (1981) 'In Memoriam: William Jaffé, 1898–1980', *Canadian Journal of Economics*, 14 (February): 106–9.

—— (1992) Symposium on 'History of Economics as History of Science', *History of Political Economy*, 24 (Spring): 212–14.

—— (1995) *Ricardo–the New View. Collected Essays I*, London and New York: Routledge.

—— (1996) 'Notes on a Possible Bentham Manuscript: A Mystery Unresolved', *Cambridge Journal of Economics*, 20 (September): 623–35.

Horton, Richard (1996) 'Truth and Heresy about AIDS', *The New York Review of Books*, 18 (May 23): 14–20.

The Jewish Observer (1987) 'An Editorial Statement on ' "The Enigma of Moses Mendelssohn",' 19 (January): 13.

Kleiman, Ephraim (1994) Review of *Economic Analysis in Talmudic Literature* by Roman A. Ohrenstein and Barry Gordon, *Journal of the History of Economic Thought*, 16 (Spring): 161–3.

Lynn, Jonathan (1994) *Mayday*, London: Penguin Books.

Papineau, David (1995) 'Open Society, Closed Thinker', *Times Literary Supplement*, No. 4812, 23 June, 4–5.

Ricardo, David (1951–73) *The Works and Correspondence, IX: Letters July 1821–1823*, (ed.) P. Sraffa, Cambridge: Cambridge University Press.

Schorsch, Ismar (1994) *From Text to Context: The Turn to History in Modern Judaism*, Hanover, New Hampshire: University Press of New England.

Simons, Hyman A. (1980) *Forty Years a Chief Rabbi: The Life and Times of Solomon Hirschell*, London: Robson Books.

de Vivo, Giancarlo (1996) 'Piero Sraffa and the Mill–Ricardo Papers: A Comment', *Cambridge Journal of Economics*, 20 (September): 637–9.

2

ON THE TEACHING OF THE
HISTORY OF ECONOMIC THOUGHT
Attack the best defence*

I.

At the University of Toronto the History of Economic Thought has always played, and continues to play, a significant part in the undergraduate programme and in recent years has expanded also at the graduate level. Eighty-five students (graduate and undergraduate) took the subject in 1972–3, which is approximately twice the number in the late 1960s.

The principal pedagogic value of the subject is, I believe, the cultivation of the critical faculties, and above all the development of the wherewithal to place current procedures in a balanced perspective. This desideratum calls for a particular emphasis upon *issues* and *controversies*.

In the first place, the course should concentrate upon the kinds of problems which have attracted the attention of the great economists and the extent to which these problems have been solved or await solution; by this procedure a more or less objective evaluation of current preoccupations and procedures may be approached. Examples of the kind of issues which might be raised are these:

- the Ricardian preoccupation with the effects of wage changes upon profits and the price level, which question became increasingly significant with the growth of trade unions in the 1860s and is reflected in Mill's work (and that of Marx);
- the desirability of economic growth as analysed by Smith, with particular reference to the beneficial effects of expansion for the working masses;
- the stationary state as envisaged by Smith and Mill;
- the extent of justifiable protection and planning in the case of developing countries, entering the race late, as discussed by Tucker and Smith;
- the uses of economic knowledge (e.g. economics envisaged by Smith and Mill as a weapon for social improvement);
- the justice of the distributive shares; here the discussions in the scholastic literature of just wages and just prices are particularly significant;

* This paper constitutes the greater part of my contribution to a symposium held at Bristol, 1973, on teaching the history of economic thought.

28

- the scope of government intervention; and the ends of economic activity;
- the nature of profit and the alternative conceptions of 'surplus';
- the increasing returns issue;

and so on. Many of these issues are *normative* and this alone is an important lesson to get across. The work of Ricardo – the economist's economist – and not only that of Smith, Mill, Marx, and Marshall, is imbued with concern with normative matters. Not only are many of these questions still very much open issues; they are not even raised by students who are not faced by them in the thought course.

It is not out of place, in this context, to bring to the attention of the student that the concern of the great economists with 'fundamental' social issues did not disguise an inability to deal with more mundane matters of applied economics. In this regard Professor Stigler's 'alternative view' of the Classicals is quite crucial to a correct perspective.

Apart from the question of the problems considered important by our great forebears, attention must be paid to the way in which the problems were handled. The recent criticisms by Professor Phelps Brown – and related arguments by Professor Leontief – that much of modern academic economics is impaired by the adoption of assumptions 'plucked from the air' indicates that the great debates of the 1930s and 1950s, engendered in particular by Lord Robbins and Professor Friedman, remain very much open. To my mind, these can be approached in a mature manner only with the help of some acquaintance with a variety of alternative practices. The same is true of Professor Kaldor's recent strictures concerning equilibrium economics; and of criticism relating to the so-called 'Ricardian vice' involving a too-rapid transfer from theory to prescription. The student familiar with a broad literature is in a far better position to evaluate their validity.

As examples of interesting methodological subjects I would note these:

- the nature of the economic man (rational maximizing assumption) in pre-Smithian (including mercantilist), Smithian, and Classical literature;
- the role of factual information, e.g. in mercantilism; in Petty; in Cantillon; in Physiocracy; in the *Wealth of Nations*; in Malthus' *Essay*; in the Corn Law literature; in Ricardo (e.g. his emphasis on labour, his arithmetical illustrations, etc.);
- the rationale for the choice of particular behavioural assumptions such as the interest–savings nexus in eighteenth-century literature and in the work of Ricardo and Marx, and Senior and Mill;
- the basis for the choice by Ricardo of extreme values for a variety of elasticities;
- Mill's methodological distinction between categories of economic 'laws' as framework for an appreciation of institutional assumptions in economics;
- the nature of the distinction between productive and unproductive labour and its validity in light of alternative institutional frameworks.

The methodological issues come to a head in the great debates or controversies, either 'formal' or 'informal'. Here I have in mind, for example:

- the issues discussed in Letwin's *Origins of Scientific Economics*;
- the features distinguishing the Smithian, Ricardian, and Neoclassical paradigms;
- Bailey's condemnation of the extreme simplification characteristic of Ricardian method and his plea for greater generality; his charges that Ricardo failed to understand the nature of the analytical operations he was undertaking, refused to re-examine first principles despite 'the strangeness of the results at which he arrived' (committing consequently 'oversights in his premisses and assumptions for which no subsequent severity of logic could compensate'), and was careless in the use of terms;
- the strictures directed against Ricardo by Torrens relating to the former's 'hasty and premature generalizations, bestowing universality upon one leading particular, and attributing to the exclusive agency of a single cause, effects resulting from the combined operation of many' – and (I must add) Torrens's candid retractions;
- Ricardo's objections to the so-called French tradition (also that of Malthus) of regarding commodities and factor services as subject to the same pricing rules;
- the great Malthus–Ricardo debates;
- Mill's objections to Jevons's rendition of consumption theory in mathematical terms;
- Marx's criticism of the post-Ricardian English 'dissenters';
- the reversion to the Smithian tradition of political economy by McCulloch and J. S. Mill and their plea for a full integration of economic theory and its application, and their criticisms of Senior's formal limitation of the sphere of the science (incidentally, it is not clear that the stereotype version of Ricardo's procedures – his 'premature generalizations and pure abstractions' – is justified);
- Steuart's early appeal for a *balanced* use of the inductive and deductive methods whereby induction from statistical data was to establish the hypotheses and deduction to derive logical principles; and his concern with the potential misuse of deductive method in applications to practical issues – 'the habit of running into what the French call systèmes' which represent 'a chain of contingent consequences, drawn from a few fundamental maxims, adopted, perhaps, rashly' and applied 'far beyond the limits of the ideas present to his understanding, when he made his definition'; his plea for a recognition of the complexity of verification is an extraordinary statement;
- the historicist objections to Classical and Austrian theorizing;
- Austrian, Lausanne, Cambridge procedures.

Thus far I have envisaged the intellectual value of the history of economic thought to lie in its ability to sharpen the student's critical faculties and sense of perspective. I also believe that familiarity with the early literature may well be an important potential source for novel hypotheses. A most striking instance is provided by Sir John Hicks's development of the materials in Ricardo's chapter 31 in an attempt to understand the experience of the labouring class during the early nineteenth century, particularly the delay in any significant rise in living standards. And as for protection against routine journalistic panaceas, there is no better antidote than a close study of the mercantilist and physiocratic literature.

If I have emphasized the utilitarian function of the subject, it is because I have grown accustomed to the need, every so often, to convince my colleagues of the significance of the course in the programme and find that this sort of case is appreciated. But apart from the 'practical' usefulness of the subject, I would emphasize Jacob Viner's 'modest proposal' twenty-three years ago for 'Some Stress on Scholarship in Graduate Training'. I require of my students, despite their occasional objections, the strictest adherence to the traditional conventions. The requirements of objectivity and judiciousness too have a 'utilitarian' dimension as anyone must realize who relies on Keynes himself to evaluate Keynes's relationship with his predecessors.

I have thus far said nothing of the broad issues relating to the sociology of knowledge, particularly the conceptions of scientific development in terms of cumulative improvements on the one hand and revolutionary changes on the other. This matter cannot be neglected and in a sense constitutes the 'ultimate' objective. Obviously Kuhn's work and the journal literature regarding its applicability to economics require close attention. Here the direct contributions both of Smith and of Mill are highly relevant; and it is surprising that our branch of the profession has only now become so enamoured of these matters. Yet I find these issues overwhelming in their complexity and feel that much more spadework is required before anything really worthwhile can be said. I trust that we will keep our feet firmly planted on the ground when engaging our renewed concern with these important matters.

II.

I do not believe there is any single 'correct' approach to the subject and encourage students to follow their own predilections in essays and examinations. . . . My courses have a predominantly analytical content but one which emphasizes a number of necessary preconditions for such an approach, and which explicitly allows for an environmental or relativist dimension. It is my objective to draw a picture of various *systems* of analysis, with emphasis upon the internal cohesion of each system rather than to describe a sequence of issues seriatim from system to system.

It is my usual practice to introduce, at the outset of the course, the general problem whether the development of economic analysis has been largely a matter of purely intellectual progression, or whether, and in what cases how, it has been influenced by external forces, both economic and extra-economic. Students are encouraged to think about this issue during the course of their reading. Within this introductory context, I present the Marxian position that much of nineteenth-century economics was really the ideology of the industrial and commercial bourgeoisie and illustrate by a few instances such as Senior's abstinence conception and the development of marginalism. The legitimacy of the Marxian claim regarding 'progress' only up to and including Smith and Ricardo (and subsequently in Marx) is then raised, with particular reference to the standard of reference chosen by which such judgements are made. Schumpeter's alternative position is then described, with illustrations, and some problems are raised relating particularly to the procedures whereby ideology is, in his view, squeezed out and objective standards for judging contributions achieved. This provides the cue, by way of contrast, for some discussion of Kuhn's work relating to the incommensurability of alternative paradigms, and also for the broad question of historical 'relativism'.

It is my object in all this, in the first place, to familiarize the student with the alternative approaches in the secondary literature for his or her guidance, and secondly to suggest the dangers of starting with any preconceived notions. I strongly believe that we are in no position to state general theories of intellectual development either of an environmental or any other kind; what is required is evidence accumulated by a case study approach. The distinction between 'absolutism' and 'relativism', while useful conceptually, is probably misleading in practice. Both approaches may be relevant, depending on the precise individual or problem under discussion, and neither can be ruled out *a priori* without great risk.

An illustration of the issue is in order from the Smithian case. It is never difficult to find very childish examples of relativism. Yet in the case of Smith an understanding of the eighteenth-century industrial structure and his vision thereof are absolutely essential prerequisites for an appreciation of the implicit assumptions of his basic growth model and an evaluation of the objectives of his theorizing. Once the relevant domain has been defined, the analytical issues relating to the internal coherence of his analysis – envisaged as a whole – can then be raised.

In other cases the environmental influence may be less significant. But even when attention is focused upon the purely analytical content of a body of thought, it is essential to bear in mind a variety of complicating matters:

1 The legitimacy of utilizing the categories of modern theory in interpretation of a particular body of literature itself requires justification in each instance.

2 Even when we are assured of a common basic theory, the present state of the science cannot be used for 'evaluation' or 'ranking', but may be used only to provide a helpful catalogue of questions.

3 For 'evaluation', contemporary standards are the relevant ones.

The need to allow both for analytical (absolutist) and historical (relativist) approaches can perhaps also be supported by reference to Schumpeter's position. Although Schumpeter's 'main purpose' in the *History of Economic Analysis* was 'to describe what may be called the process of Filiation of Scientific Ideas – the process by which men's efforts to understand economic phenomena produce, improve, and pull down analytical structures in an unending sequence', he nonetheless allowed for the influence of external events, recognizing a variety of obstacles in the way of the progressive development of economic analysis: 'Scientific analysis is not simply a logically consistent process that starts with some primitive notions and then adds to the stock in a straight-line fashion. It is not simply progressive discovery of an objective reality – as is, for example, discovery in the basin of the Congo. Rather it is an incessant struggle with creations of our own and our predecessors' minds and it "progresses", if at all, in a criss-cross fashion, not as logic, but as the impact of new ideas or observations or needs, and also as the bents and temperaments of new men dictate.' These impediments derive essentially from two related facts. First, the subject matter of economics is a 'unique process in historic time' to the extent that the source of the materials used is derived from specific historical experiences. Since it is impossible for an economist to use more material than is actually available, theoretical results which are achieved at any time may not be justified in the light of further experience. Moreover the institutional frameworks which are subsumed under theoretical models have application to specific historical conditions. It follows that the scope and validity of 'economic laws' work out differently in different institutional circumstances. (These conditions provide the rationale for the role accorded by Schumpeter to economic history of *primus inter pares* amongst the fundamental fields of economic analysis – namely, economic history, statistics, economic theory, and economic sociology.)

Historical relativity intrudes also by a second route. The economist himself 'is the product of a given social environment – and of his particular location in this environment – that condition him to see certain things rather than others, and to see them in a certain light. And even this is not all: environmental factors may even endow the observer with a subconscious craving to see things in a certain light!'

III.

Professor William Jaffé has observed that 'the study of the subject has come to a paradoxical pass; while research is advancing apace, the teaching of the subject has been in rapid decline. . . . Graduate instruction in the discipline has all but disappeared in the major universities; and undergraduate instruction has been demoted to the point where the courses in the history of economics are largely entrusted to professors who, though they may have a dilettantish interest in the subject, are without any specialist training for its development. . . . In the more prestigious centres of learning, promising graduate students evincing a desire to write a thesis in the field are discouraged from doing so; indirectly by the absence of a professor to guide them and directly by the counsels of their advisers that the subject is without any future and is beneath a good student's talents.' This is probably a fair statement of the pattern over time and the current state of affairs in North America as a whole.

I can see evidence of a revival of interest in the subject but trust that this does not reflect the winter of our discontent, only to pass with the coming of springtime. I do not believe the subject is a luxury. The subject will only be taken seriously if a positive case is made for it as a *necessary* part of training — on a par, for example, with mathematical economics.

3

IN MEMORIAM
William Jaffé, 1898–1980

William Jaffé, the leading authority on the history of general-equilibrium theory, died in Toronto on 17 August 1980 aged eighty-two years. His constant fear that his researches (begun over half a century ago) would remain unfinished has come to pass. He died in harness, engaged on the 'Life and Writings of Léon Walras, 1834–1910'. We must be thankful that his papers are in the expert hands of Professor D. A. Walker of the Indiana University of Pennsylvania, as he wished, so that the finished portions of the 'Life' will not be lost to us. We have also the series of seminal articles, many of them written in very recent years – the latest item from his pen appeared in the June 1980 issue of the *Journal of Economic Literature* and yet another is in press – dealing with the origins of Walras's system; the relation of Walras's theoretical contributions to those of his predecessors and contemporaries; and the critical evaluations and emendations of Walras's theories of general equilibrium, capital, and money in the twentieth-century literature (including the recent interpretation by Michio Morishima). It is hoped that these articles will appear, under Donald Walker's direction, as Jaffé planned, in a volume of collected essays [1983].

Professor Jaffé was born on 16 June 1898 in New York City of Jewish immigrant parents from Russia. He received his BA (English and Classics) at the City College in 1917 and his MA (history) at Columbia the following year. His doctoral dissertation, 'Les théories économiques et sociales de Thorstein Veblen', written for the Université de Paris (Faculté de Droit) was published in 1924. From 1928 until the mid-1960s he taught at Northwestern University. Thereafter, he held a series of visiting professorships (at the Université d'Algers, Harvard, and UBC) until his appointment as Professor of Economics at York University, where he taught for the last decade of his life. Jaffé was a Foreign Member of the Royal Netherlands Academy of Science and Letters, a Corresponding Fellow of the British Academy, Chevalier de la Légion d'Honneur, and Fellow of the Royal Society of Canada.

The major works upon which Professor Jaffé's fame rests are his edition of

Walras's *Elements of Pure Economics* in beautiful translation (1954), and the massive *Correspondence of Léon Walras and Related Papers* (1965).

The former, published under the joint auspices of the American Economic Association and the Royal Economic Society, provides a formidable *apparatus criticus* and commentary, which renders the original formal statement of the theory of general equilibrium intelligible to the English-speaking world of theoretical economists and provides, at the same time, an invaluable instrument of research for scholars interested in the history of nineteenth-century economic analysis. That Jaffé's translation was the first to be made *in any language* of what surely is, directly or indirectly, one of the most influential books of the modern era is an index of the enormity of the task involved, reflecting not only the difficulty of the subject matter itself but the complex formulation, primitive mathematics, and crabbed prose of the original.

The same formidable battery of linguistic, editorial, scholarly and theoretical skills was brought to bear in the preparation of the *Correspondence*, published under the auspices of the Royal Netherlands Academy of Science and Letters. The stated purpose of this compilation was to show Walras 'as a working economist', to reveal 'the man himself in the exercise of his profession'. This marvellous edition succeeds eminently in the task and places at the disposal of historians of neo-classical economics a powerful research tool. While a selection from the extant materials was necessary, the precise formulation of the principles of selection as well as internal evidence (including evidence derived from a series of hitherto unpublished papers given in full text or summary to supplement the letters) make it clear that the content of Walras's extant literary remains has been exhausted, something which unfortunately cannot always be said of such ventures. The location, arrangement, and deciphering of Walras's letters constitute perhaps the most complex editorial task ever attempted in the history of economics. A quantitative index of what this work entailed is provided by the number of letters incorporated – some 1,900 written from and to Walras in four languages between 1857 and 1910. But even these data are scant witness to the veritable editorial odyssey upon which Jaffé embarked alone in 1930 – and within an environment of general unconcern with the history of their subject by economists.

An essential principle governed Professor Jaffé's historiographical procedures; since the construction of hypotheses is a creative act amenable to investigation only by use of *psychological* – as distinct from *logical* – categories (a position also adopted by Karl Popper and Milton Friedman) it follows that an integration of analysis and biography, and thus a place for genuine history, is essential if we are to understand the origins and the impact of the contributions made by the great innovators, rather than restrict ourselves to the internal consistency or empirical relevance of a novel analytical theory. The principle yielded significant results, a few of which are as follows. There are suggestive hypotheses regarding the belated introduction of mathematics in economics. There is the fascinating story of the gestation of the *Elements* which casts light, with regard to economics, on many of the sociological issues isolated by Robert Merton – priorities in scientific discovery, behaviour patterns of scientists, multiple discoveries, ethnocentrism in science, and so forth. We can no longer identify Walras, Jevons, and Menger as independent discoverers of the marginal utility theory without reference to the distinctive objectives and design of their individual contributions. (In Walras's case, Jaffé insisted, the primary objective was not the theory of consumption at all but the theory of exchange, or catallactics.) The old saw that marginal utility was invented to refute the labour theory for *apologetic* reasons should never again be encountered; it was, Jaffé showed, *la question sociale* – the poverty of the labouring masses – which governed the scientific work of Walras and his father.

Here, it seems to me, will be found Jaffé's major contribution, for what he showed by his investigation of the biographical dimension – Walras's personal experience (including his education, both formal and informal), the attitudes of his social class, the traditions of the economic literature and the intellectual climate of the day – is the 'ideological' and 'metaphysical' substratum underlying Walras's work *including the analytical contributions*, or what he termed 'the normative bias' of Walras's economics. It is heartbreaking that the debate with Morishima in the *JEL* touching upon Walras's 'ultimate aim' in the *Elements* – with its implications for the intended scope of that work (its status as 'realistic utopia' as Jaffé believed, or as representation of 'how the capitalist system works' as Morishima believes), and more specifically its implications for the precise nature of the entrepreneur, *tâtonnement*, money, capital formation, and economic progress – should have been cut short. It is particularly sad since in this debate are also to be found the ingredients which will allow a clearer appreciation of the relationships between the classical and the Walrasian approaches to production and growth.

Jaffé's comments on the occasion of his induction at the Royal Society of Canada in May 1979, when he protested the present-day separation of the humanities from the sciences, touched upon the matter of his historiographical method:

> One of the dominant purposes of my writing and teaching has been to study this ill-conceived progressively widening gap. And if I have given so much attention to Léon Walras, a titan among the nineteenth-century founders of modern mathematical economics, it is because I found in him a kindred spirit. . . . Once one penetrates beneath the surface of his papers bristling with sets of simultaneous equations, one perceives that these pages were designed as a systematic expression of a social ideal—perhaps not wholly your ideal or mine, but a social ideal nevertheless. And the ideal was that of justice embracing

the traditional concepts of commutative and distributive justice that have come down to us from classical antiquity and the middle ages in the literature of the humanities.

To penetrate beneath the surface of the formal models, however, is no simple task; it requires the skills of an historian as well as those of an economist and a keen appreciation of the general issues which preoccupy historians, philosophers, and sociologists of science – a rare combination. Jaffé's masterly command of these skills and his wide intellectual interests go a long way to explain the fruitfulness and quality of his contributions to the history of economics.

No one stood higher in the esteem of his colleagues than did Bill Jaffé. It is a consolation that in April 1980 the History of Economics Society acknowledged their respect by nominating him first Distinguished Fellow of the organization. This gesture without doubt brightened his last days.

REFERENCES

Jaffé, William (ed.) (1965) *Correspondence of Léon Walras and Related Papers*, Amsterdam: North Holland.

—— (1980) 'Walras's Economics As Others See It', *Journal of Economic Literature*, 18 (June): 528–49.

—— (1983) *William Jaffé's Essays on Walras*, ed. D. A. Walker, Cambridge: Cambridge University Press.

Morishima, Michio (1977) *Walras's Economics: A Pure Theory of Capital and Money*, Cambridge: Cambridge University Press.

Walras, Léon (1954) *Elements of Pure Economics*, 4th definitive edn (1926), translated by William Jaffé, London: George Allen and Unwin.

Part II

THREE EARLY PAPERS

4

THE REPRESENTATIVE FIRM AND IMPERFECT COMPETITION*

In a recent paper, J. N. Wolfe (1954) has interpreted P. Sraffa (1926) as having exposed a logical inconsistency in Marshall's *Principles of Economics* (8th edn, 1920). According to Wolfe, Sraffa interpreted Marshall as being concerned with perfect competition and yet as allowing his representative firm to possess unexhausted internal economies; he therefore believed that Marshall was inconsistent, for the two phenomena are incompatible. Wolfe himself interprets the Marshallian representative firm as an oligopoly model.

This essay discusses the following points. First, it will be shown that Marshall's model when discussing increasing returns and the representative firm involved neither perfect competition nor oligopoly but imperfect competition. Second, I shall argue that the representative firm was largely designed to describe the problems which exist when product differentiation is recognized but when the industry is retained as a meaningful concept. That is, Marshall faces the same difficulties as those faced by J. Robinson and E. Chamberlin, but his solution involves a different approach. This is not to suggest that there was no need for the Robinson and Chamberlin volumes; indeed their appearance, together with Sraffa's article, reflected the unsatisfactory state in which Marshall left his analysis on this topic. Third, it follows from our interpretation that for Marshall the representative firm was a structure of the mind, a tool of analysis, and not a real firm. To clarify his views, I reproduce certain passages from which it is clear that he is not guilty of logical inconsistency either in the case of actual firms, or in the case of the representative firm.

I.

I turn now to the first objective. Several recent papers[1] have disagreed on the market structure which Marshall subsumed under his discussion of the representative firm. There seems little doubt that a perfectly competitive model is used to a large extent, as, for example, early in Book V;

---

* The author is indebted to Professor W. J. Baumol for criticism and advice.

nevertheless in his discussion of industries with increasing returns, where the representative firm figures so predominantly, Marshall was definitely concerned with imperfect competition, that is with product differentiation or with any form of consumer preference for the product of one firm over that of another. Marshall introduces Book V, chapter XII as an examination of 'some difficulties connected with the relations of demand and supply as regards commodities the production of which tends to increasing return' (1920: 455). He next points out that the 'tendency to a fall in the price of a commodity as a result of a gradual development of the industry by which it is made is quite a different thing from the tendency to the rapid introduction of new economies by an individual firm that is increasing its business' (457).

The first of the two specific differences given is that during a general growth of an industry, an actual firm undergoes a life cycle: it grows and declines 'like the leaves on a tree'. 'Thus the rise and fall of individual firms may be frequent, while a great industry is going through one long oscillation, or even moving steadily forward' (457). 'We must take account of the fact that very few firms have a long-continued life of active progress' (459). The second difference is that: 'When we are considering an individual producer, we must couple his supply curve – *not with the general demand curve* for his commodity in the wide market, but – *with the particular demand curve of his own special market*' (458; emphasis added). 'The relations between the individual producer *and his special market* differ . . . from those between the whole body of producers and the general market' (459; emphasis added).

Thus far it is clear that the model is either one of imperfect competition or oligopoly. But the discussion relates to the case where the firm's 'production is but small relatively to the broad market for which in a more general sense it may be said to produce' (458), a remark which excludes oligopoly, and there seems little doubt, therefore, that Marshall is discussing a case of imperfect competition.

II.

We next turn to the main consideration of this paper, namely, the purpose for which the representative firm was, at least to some extent, designed. It is clear that product differentiation is recognized; how else is the 'particular demand curve' to make sense? At the same time, however, Marshall continues to refer to the industry; he still finds it a meaningful concept. We will now show that it is just at this stage that the representative firm is used:

Thus the history of the individual firm cannot be made into the history of an industry. And yet . . . the aggregate production for a general market is the outcome of the motives which induce individual producers to expand or contract their production. *It is just here that our device of a representative firm comes to our aid.* We imagine to ourselves at any time a firm that has its fair share of those internal and external economies which appertain to the aggregate scale of production in the industry to which it belongs.

(Marshall 1920: 459–60; emphasis added)

Marshall expresses at this stage the desire to reconcile the industry with those firms constituting it despite the product differentiation which exists, and despite the dynamic changes which individual firms undergo.

J. Robinson (1933) has drawn up industry demand and supply curves even in differentiated industries. However, recognizing the difficulties involved she postulates identical demand and cost curves both before and after changes in demand. E. Chamberlin (1950) avoids drawing industry curves but, as R. Triffin (1940) has pointed out, his assumptions imply that firms are identical. Triffin himself, following Sraffa's lead, denies the meaningfulness of the industry in such circumstances.

Marshall approaches the problem neither by abandoning the industry nor by making the assumptions of uniformity which suck all interest from a discussion of differentiated products. Marshall uses the representative firm.

A passage from Robinson is of interest here:

It might be possible . . . to draw an industry's supply curve without assuming each firm to be of equilibrium size. The attempt to do so introduces many formidable difficulties . . . and they have received more attention from economists than the difficulties connected with the imperfection of markets. Various devices have been suggested to overcome them, of which the most familiar is Marshall's Representative Firm. Since these devices are not designed to deal with the fundamental difficulty involved in the notion of a supply curve under imperfect competition, they must be taken to represent an attempt to deal with an imaginary world in which the market is perfect, but in which firms take time to reach their equilibrium size.

(Robinson 1933: 91)

The main argument of this paper is that one of the most significant uses to which Marshall put the concept was in fact 'to deal with the fundamental difficulty involved in the notion of a supply curve under imperfect competition'. The concept was, it is true, also used to study disequilibria or the 'dynamic' changes of actual firms, as Robinson suggests, but this holds for imperfect as well as perfect competition. We turn now to discuss the details of the analysis.

Our attention will be centred predominantly on the discussion of 'incidents of the tendency to increasing return' (Marshall 1920, V, ch. 12). As a preliminary we will establish two relevant factors. First, in very general terms, Marshall hoped with the use of his representative firm to analyse the normal cost of production of a commodity under a restrictive condition: 'We shall have to analyse carefully the normal cost of producing a commodity relatively to a given aggregate volume of production; and for this purpose we shall have to study *the expenses of a representative producer* for that aggregate volume' (Marshall 1920: 317). The restrictive condition is the fact that costs of production of the representative firm are examined 'relatively to a given aggregate volume of production'.

Second, it is clear that the representative firm is needed largely to explain long-run industry phenomena; specifically, it is representative with regard to the extent to which economies of large-scale production have extended generally in the industry. 'Thus a representative firm is in a sense an average firm . . . at which we have to look to see how far the economies, *internal and external*, of production on a large scale have extended generally in the industry' (318).

These two factors are consistent with the interpretation of the representative firm given by R. Frisch. The representative firm, Frisch argues, is a construct of the mind, giving a miniature representation of the supply side of the market. It describes the reaction of total industry supply in the process of long-run adaptation to changes in total demand. Its volume of production varies proportionally with the aggregate volume of production in the industry and its unit costs represent average unit costs. Frisch stresses two points. First, in the stationary state, when an industry is in equilibrium, actual firms, according to Marshall, still undergo a process of development and decline. However, the total production for the market is by definition constant and therefore so must be the output of the representative firm. In this respect the construct does not follow the same laws as actual firms. Second, when we say for example that the representative firm is earning, at any time, 'more than normal profits', we are simply saying *in shorthand* that a majority of firms in the industry are earning super-normal profits. This is the cause of an increase in output by the industry, for the growth of firms is speeded up (or their decline is decelerated). Normal profit for the representative firm *means* that the industry is neither growing nor declining since the growth of some actual firms is exactly balanced by the decline of others. On the basis of these characteristics, Frisch draws up the long-run cost curve of the representative firm for perfect competition.

Let us adapt this interpretation to the case of imperfect competition which, as we have tried to show, is Marshall's main concern. In Figure 1, OA_1 represents a given level of industry output.[2] Following our definitions, to any given total output there corresponds a given magnitude of production by the representative firm. This can be shown by OB_1 if the axis is suitably reinterpreted. At output OB_1 the unit production costs of the representative firm are B_1N. These unit costs are the average unit costs of production in the industry, determined by the extent to which 'economies internal and external of production on a large scale have extended generally in the industry'. The average price is B_1M so that the representative firm is earning super-normal profits. The industry will therefore expand to OA_2, where normal profits are earned by the representative firm. The expansion involves increased growth by some actual firms and a decreased rate of decline by others. The model applies to the long run.

This approach differs from that of Frisch in that it allows specifically for product differentiation. The price referred to is an *average* price and not a common market price. A large number of actual prices may in fact exist since actual firms produce differentiated commodities. Some arbitrary rule must be assumed to allow one to talk of OX units of a differentiated product.

No assumptions have been introduced to make identical either the cost curves of actual firms or their respective demand (sales) curves. Each actual firm may retain its individuality, unlike the firms postulated by Robinson and Chamberlin.

It should be pointed out that the function of the representative firm is basically to *describe* the link between the industry and individual differentiated firms in circumstances where the imperfections are not assumed away

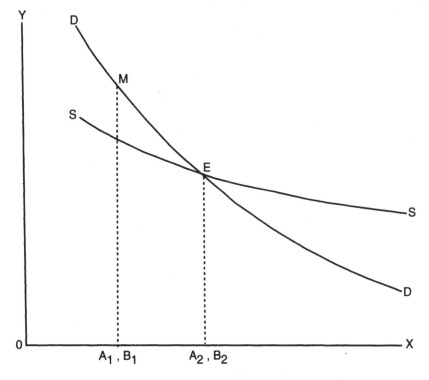

Figure 1
Y axis: Average price of the differentiated product
X axis: Output of industry and of representative firm
SS curve: Long period unit cost curve of the representative firm

(and where 'dynamic' changes are occurring). It certainly does not solve the problems presented by such a model.

III.

The final aim of this paper is to counter the notion that Marshall is guilty of the logical inconsistency referred to in the introduction. Our interpretation has taken the representative firm to be a construct of the mind rather than a real firm.

One or more actual firms may at some moment be characterized by one of the features of the theoretical (representative) firm; they too may have a 'fair share' of economies. This does not mean that the actual firms become representative firms because the representative firm possesses several other peculiar features which no existing firm can possess,[3] as has already been shown.

Our diagram, unlike Frisch's, portrays a continuously declining long-run unit cost curve, that is, the representative firm possesses 'unexhausted economies of scale'. The diagram corresponds to the discussion in Marshall (1920, V, ch. 12) of increasing return industries since the firm is a miniature representation of the supply side of the market.

The present argument in no way bears out J. N. Wolfe's interpretation of Sraffa to the effect that Marshall had fallen into a logical inconsistency. The unexhausted economies under discussion are those of the *representative* firm, and nothing we have said so far reflects on Marshall's position on scale economies and *real* firms. The same applies to those sections of the *Principles* where perfect competition is under discussion.

It may be of interest to point out some significant passages where Marshall rules out any tendency to complete monopolization of an industry by a single real-life firm. He points out that in those cases where for technological reasons expansion of output leads to lower average cost, the problems of marketing prevent expansion of an unlimited nature:

> If then [a producer] can double his production, and sell anything like his old rate, he will have more than doubled his profits. . . . [4]It seems at first that no point is marked out at which he needs stop . . . he might then gather into his hands the whole volume of production in his branch of trade for his district. And if his goods were not very difficult of transport nor of marketing, he might extend this district very wide, and attain something like a limited monopoly; that is, of a monopoly limited by the consideration that a very high price would bring rival producers into the field. . . .
>
> But the continued very rapid growth of his firm requires the presence of two conditions which are seldom combined in the same industry. There are many trades in which an individual producer could

secure much increased 'internal' economies by a great increase of his output; and there are many in which he could market that output easily; yet there are few in which he could do both and this is not accidental, but almost a necessary result. For in most of those trades in which the economies of production on a large scale are of first rate importance, marketing is difficult.

(Marshall 1920: 285–6)

Perfect competition is almost by definition a structure where marketing is not difficult; but it is in just these perfectly competitive industries where economies of scale are not of first-rate importance.

Consider, too, Marshall's well-known criticism of Cournot and others who 'had before them what is in effect the supply schedule of an individual firm; representing that an increase in its output gives it command over so great internal economies as much to diminish its expenses of production, ... without noticing that their premises lead inevitably to the conclusion that, whatever firm first gets a good start, will obtain a monopoly of the whole business of its trade in its district' (459). This procedure is categorically rejected from the *Principles*.

Finally, add to the above Marshall's 'life cycles' which characterize actual firms (and which imply the ultimate decline of firms), and it is clear that there are no grounds for the criticism that Marshall was logically inconsistent. This is true, as we have shown, both with regard to his treatment of the representative firm and his treatment of actual firms.

NOTES

1 Wolfe, 'The Representative Firm', 1954; R. Frisch, 'Alfred Marshall's Theory of Value', 1950; D. Hague, 'Alfred Marshall and the Representative Firm', 1958.
2 The figure is drawn upon the assumption of stability in the Marshallian sense with the D curve cutting the S curve from above. The unstable case is not discussed here.
3 Much of the controversy over the representative firm is apparently due to the use of the term 'firm'.
4 The discussion is one where a 'large business can command very important advantages which are beyond the reach of a small business'.

REFERENCES

Chamberlin, E. (1950) *Theory of Monopolistic Competition*, 6th edn, Cambridge, Mass.: Harvard University Press.
Frisch, R. (1950) 'Alfred Marshall's Theory of Value', *Quarterly Journal of Economics*, 64 (November): 495–524.
Hague, D. (1958) 'Alfred Marshall and the Representative Firm', *Economic Journal*, 68 (December): 673–90.
Marshall, Alfred (1920) *Principles of Economics*, 8th edn, London: Macmillan.
Robinson, J. (1933) *Economics of Imperfect Competition*, London: Macmillan.

Sraffa, P. (1926) 'Laws of Returns Under Competitive Conditions', *Economic Journal*, 36 (December): 535–50.

Triffin, R. (1940) *Monopolistic Competition & General Equilibrium*, Cambridge, Mass.: Harvard University Press.

Wolfe, J. N. (1954) 'The Representative Firm', *Economic Journal*, 64 (June): 337–49.

5

ON THE INTERPRETATION OF THE JUST PRICE*

Carius vendere quam valeat – here indeed is a very fine hare which, with no obvious asthmatic symptoms, is still gallantly breasting the uplands, pursued from afar by a great company of short-winded metaphysicians and economists.

Sir Alexander Gray

At one time it was regarded almost as a truism that by the 'just price' the schoolmen, including St Thomas Aquinas, were referring to a 'normal' price dependent upon costs of production, rather than a fluctuating price dependent upon the chances of the market. Production costs, it was believed, were determined by a deserved standard of living on behalf of the producers, and would not of course include interest (Ashley 1896: 500).[1] Recently, the debate has been re-opened and the circle has made a complete turn. The idea that the just price was directly related to costs is now denied by some authors. It is argued that the just price was the going market price, and particular emphasis was placed on demand and utility (Noonan 1957: 84–6). Others agree that the price determined in a competitive market was considered by the main stream of scholastic thought to be the just price; however, passages exist where it would seem that cost ratios play an important role. It is therefore argued that 'beyond doubt . . . he [Aquinas] considered the market price as just' but the market price would 'tend to coincide with cost or to oscillate around this point like the swing of a pendulum' (de Roover 1958: 422).

These interpretations all appear to be based on the implied assumption that there is to be found in Aquinas a single version of the just price. In some cases it is further implied that one can expect to find consistent economic analysis reflected in his discussion of the issue. But it should always be remembered that the early writers were not primarily concerned with economic processes. To ignore this fact, given the natural desire to find predecessors, can lead to serious distortion.

* I am indebted to Professors K. F. Helleiner, A. Kruger, C. B. Macpherson, and A. Rotstein for very helpful comments. This paper was read at the meetings of the Canadian Political Science Association in Vancouver, June 1965.

In this note we shall argue that there is strong evidence to support the claim that the just price was in fact related to costs within the medieval context of social status. On the other hand it is also clear that Aquinas did at times define the just price as the market price. *Both versions are to be found depending upon the problem under investigation,* and statements made within one context need not be applicable to the other. Attempts to discern a single version of the just price even in the work of a single author may be misleading. We shall also argue that there is little evidence to show that Aquinas related analytically the market price to production costs in the classical or neo-classical fashion.

As a preliminary it will be necessary to clarify the position on justice in exchange adopted by Aristotle and the comments thereon by Aquinas (Section I). We shall then turn to the discussion of the issue in Aquinas's independent writings (Section II). Finally, we shall consider the proposition that it is possible to interpret Aquinas in terms of a neo-classical theory of price determination (Section III).

I.

The Aristotelian comments in the *Nicomachean Ethics*[2] on just rates of exchange between craftsmen is the traditional starting-point for the analysis of the scholastic doctrine on just price. The context is the definition and analysis of commutative justice: 'Therefore, that which is just is an equal, a mean between more and less in such a way that gain is taken as more, and loss as less' (Aristotle 1964: Book V, Lecture VI, 1131 b 25, 409). The principle is applied to the exchange of products by specialist craftsmen: 'This is true also in other arts, for they would be destroyed if the craftsman doing the quality and quantity of work which he should is not supported accordingly' (V, VII, 1132 a 25, 414).

Aristotle then elaborates in passages which are of sufficient importance to our subject to be quoted in detail.

A conjunction by means of a diagonal shows how to make that compensation which is according to proportionality. Let *A* be a builder, *B* a shoemaker, *G* a house, and *D* a sandal. It is necessary that a builder should take from the shoemaker his product and in return give what he himself makes. If first an equality according to proportionality be found and then reciprocation be made, it will be as we have said. But if not, there will not be an equality – and the state would not continue to exist – because nothing hinders the work of one craftsman from being of more value than the work of another. Therefore, these things must be equated.

This is to be observed also in the other arts, for they would be destroyed if a workman did not receive according to the quantity and quality of what he produced. Between two doctors an exchange does not take place but between a doctor and a farmer who are altogether different and unequal. These then must be equated. [V, VIII, 1132 b 21, 418–19]

Therefore all things capable of exchange ought to be compared in some way. For this purpose money was invented and became a kind of medium measuring everything including excess and deficit.

A certain number of sandals are equal in value to a house or to a quantity of food. Therefore, as many sandals must be exchanged for a house or a quantity of food in proportion as the builder contributes more than the shoemaker (or the farmer). If this is not observed, there will be neither exchange nor sharing. But this reciprocation will not be possible unless things are equated.

Therefore, it is reasonable to measure all things by one norm. . . . This norm in reality is demand which connects all things. If men were not in need there would be no exchange, or if they did not have a similar demand, exchange would not be the same. Money originated by agreement on account of necessary exchange. . . .

When things have been equated there will be reciprocation, so that as the farmer is to the shoemaker, the amount of the shoemaker's work is to the amount of the farmer's work. When things are to be exchanged they ought to be represented in a figure showing proportionality. If this is not done one extreme will have both excesses, but when all have what is theirs they will be equal, and will do business with one another because this equality can be brought about for them. . . .

. . . if there is no such reciprocation, there will not be any sharing of goods. [V, IX, 1133 a 18, 423–4]

(Aristotle 1964)

Conflicting versions of Aristotle's just price doctrine are to be found in the literature. Traditionally, the above passages have been taken as evidence that Aristotle maintained a cost theory of the just price. This view has been challenged: J. T. Noonan, for example, argues that Aristotle's example of commutative justice – 'the builder's work in building the house equalling the shoemaker's work in making the shoes' – is 'not pressed, and it seems clear that Aristotle intended it only as an illustration, not an absolute affirmation that equality in exchange demanded an equality of labor being matched; a little after this passage, he explicitly says that value is determined by need' (Noonan 1957: 86). Similarly, J. J. Spengler concludes that 'Aristotle, with his emphasis upon demand and his neglect of costs, was a forerunner of the Austrian rather than the English classical school' (Spengler 1955: 388). It has also been argued that Aristotle assumed the *coincidence* of both criteria in the sense that 'that which is the more costly to supply (in terms of labor expended and skill exerted) will be that which is the more eagerly desired' (Gordon 1964).

Whether or not Aquinas adopted Aristotle's position in his *Commentary* is also a matter for debate. According to Noonan (1957: 86) 'a repetition of Aristotle in a commentary on him cannot be taken as an expression of the commentator's view'.

It appears likely, however, that Aristotle did present a doctrine of just price based upon costs. Moreover, it is probable that Aquinas ascribed to this doctrine. For it is not quite true to say that he merely repeated Aristotle *verbatim*, as Noonan argues; at certain critical junctures he clarified serious ambiguities.

Several phrases included in the passages quoted earlier leave some room for uncertainty: 'nothing hinders the work of one craftsman from being of more value than the work of another';[3] 'as many sandals must be exchanged for a house . . . in proportion as the builder contributes more than the shoe-maker'; the arts 'would be destroyed if a workman did not receive according to the quantity and quality of what he produced'.[4] But according to the *Commentary* by Aquinas the 'superiority' of one craftsman over another – the proportion by which the one 'contributes' more than the other – refers to the *relative costs incurred in production*:

> The arts would be destroyed if the craftsman, who works at some handicraft, would not be supported, i.e., would not receive for his workmanship, according to the quantity and quality of what he produced. [Book V, Lecture VII, 416]
>
> . . . proportionality must be employed in order to bring about an equality of things because the work of one craftsman is of more value than the work of another, e.g., the building of a house than the production of a penknife. . . . [V, VIII, 420]
>
> . . . first an equality according to proportionality is found so that on one side a certain number of sandals be fixed as equal to one house (for a builder incurs more expense in building one house than a shoe-maker in making one sandal: *nam plures expensas facit aedificator in una domo, quam coriarius in uno calceamento*). . . . [V, VIII, 421]
>
> In order then to have just exchange, as many sandals must be exchanged for one house . . . as the builder . . . exceeds the shoemaker in his labor and costs [*in labore et in expensis*]. If this is not observed, there will be no exchange of things and men will not share their goods with one another. [V, IX, 426]
>
> This is done in such a manner that as the farmer . . . excels the shoe-maker . . . in the same proportion the work of the shoemaker exceeds in number the work of the farmer, so that many sandals are exchanged for one bushel of wheat. . . . If this was not done . . . if a farmer gave a bushel of wheat for a sandal, he would have a surplus of labour in his

product and would have an excess of loss because he would be giving more than he would receive. But when all have what is theirs, they are in this way equal and do business with one another because the equality previously mentioned is possible for them. [V, IX, 426–7]

(Aquinas 1964)[5]

Aquinas interprets Aristotle's doctrine as one based on cost ratios and does not simply repeat him word for word. This would suggest that he was in agreement with the view that the just price must reflect relative costs. Moreover, in the questions on 'economic' matters in *Summa Theologica*, to be discussed presently, references to the Philosopher's *Ethics* are so frequent as to imply strongly such accord.

What role was played by 'demand' or 'need' in Aristotle's scheme? Immediately after the apparent definition of justice in terms of costs, Aristotle, as we have seen, writes 'it is reasonable to measure all things by one norm. . . . This norm in reality is demand which connects all things. If men were not in need there would be no exchange, or if they did not have a similar demand, exchange would not be the same. Money originated by agreement on account of necessary exchange.' These remarks are continued in the following passages:

That human demand connects everything as by a kind of measure is evident because when men are so mutually situated that both or at least one is not in need, they do not exchange their goods. But they engage in exchange when one needs what the other has, e.g., wine, and they give grain for it. An equation then must be made between these goods.

For future exchanges money is, as it were, a guarantee that a man, who has no present need, will be helped when he is in want later on. However, currency suffers like other things, for it is not always of the same value; although it tends to be more stable than other things.

Everything then must be evaluated in money, for in this way exchange will always take place and consequently association among men. Money equates goods making them commensurate after the manner of a measure. . . .

It is impossible that things so greatly different be made commensurate according to reality, but they agree sufficiently by comparison with the needs of man, and so there must be one measure determined by man. And this is called money, which makes all things commensurate inasmuch as they are measured in money.

Let A represent a house and B five minae. Let G represent a bed worth one mina. The bed then will be one fifth the value of the house. . . . Likewise it is obvious that barter took place before money existed. But it makes no difference whether five beds or the value of five beds are given.

(Aristotle 1964: V, IX, 1133 a 18, 424–5)

It is apparent that Aristotle in the chapter on money was increasing the complexity of his 'model'. It will be noted, however, that these statements occur immediately after the establishment of the rule that the just price is determined by relative costs. Furthermore, the existence of money does not alter the 'real' situation: 'Likewise it is obvious that barter took place before money existed. But it makes no difference whether five beds or the value of five beds are given.' With these considerations in mind let us turn once more for clarification by Aquinas. 'He says first, in order that the products of the different workmen be equated and thus become possible to exchange, it is necessary that all things capable of exchange should be comparable in some way with one another so that it can be known which of them has greater value and which less. It was for this purpose that money or currency was invented, to measure the price of such things' (1964: V, IX, 425–6).

It is clear that no additional rules were introduced at this point to explain the determination of exchange ratios, for Aquinas then refers back to the original rule; the just price still depends upon relative costs: 'In order then to have just exchange, as many sandals must be exchanged for one house . . . as the builder . . . exceeds the shoemaker in his labor and costs. . . . But what has been said, that a number of sandals are exchanged for one house, is not possible unless the sandals are equated with the house in some way' (1964: V, IX, 426). This 'commensuration' is made by means of money. Money, however, is merely a 'convention'. Behind the creation of money lies the phenomenon of human need: 'He states that for this reason it is possible to equate things because all things can be measured by some one standard. . . . But this one standard which truly measures all things is demand. This includes all commutable things inasmuch as everything has a reference to human need. Articles are not valued according to the dignity of their nature, otherwise a mouse . . . should be of greater value than a pearl. . . . But they are priced according as man stands in need of them for his own use' (1964: V, IX, 426). Considered in isolation this latter statement might suggest that (in Aquinas's view) Aristotle had stated a law of just exchange squarely based upon relative utility. Taken in the general context, however, it seems clear that this conclusion would be incorrect. For Aquinas continues: 'An indication of this is that if men were not in need there would be no exchange, or if they did not have a similar need, i.e., of these things, exchange would not be the same because men would not exchange what they have for things they did not need.'

What Aristotle seems to be indicating, and what Aquinas makes more explicit, is not that the just exchange ratios will be *determined* by the relative strength of 'needs', but that in the broadest sense *human* needs underlie the system of specialization and exchange, and the convention 'money'. But the classical economists too were in full agreement with such propositions. Demand is clearly recognized as the binding force of society for specialization depends upon mutual demands. Moreover, the classics state explicitly that utility is 'absolutely essential' to exchange value. But they do not conclude that exchange value will, therefore, be determined thereby.

While relative costs appear to govern the just price Aristotle does not explain how the costs are determined. But it is probable that the position of the producer in the 'social hierarchy' would be relied upon to determine the weight attached to his 'effort'. Certainly the ranking of different occupations plays an important part in the work of Aristotle. If this is the case, then the absence of an *explanation* of cost determination is not a critical omission for relative costs would be largely *data*.

We have referred to the view that Aristotle assumed the *coincidence* of both relative cost and relative utility. In this interpretation by B. J. Gordon both cost and utility receive equal weight as determinants of Aristotle's exchange rate. Textual evidence is brought to suggest that the higher the cost of obtaining a good the greater the want-satisfying power thereof (Gordon 1964: 124).[6] While it is probably correct to say that Aristotle did not envisage a potential divergence between relative costs and relative utility, it is important to bear in mind that in fact Aristotle did not emphasize relative utility. This would perhaps be of little relevance if his account of the 'determination' of the just price was analytical. But, as we shall try to show presently, Aristotle did not give an analytical explanation of the determination of price. His doctrine was an ethical 'prescription'. As far as the *influence* of such a doctrine is concerned the emphasis given to costs of production would appear to be of great consequence, for later authors may not adopt the strict relationship between the two 'variables'.

II.

We have noted above the viewpoint that the comments on the *Nicomachean Ethics* should not be taken as an expression of Aquinas's opinion. Noonan points out that in Aquinas's own work we cannot find views similar to those expressed in his *Commentary*. In the case of Aquinas and other scholastic authors 'the just price is seen to be the price where demand and supply meet: in short, the market price' (Noonan 1957: 85). For the most part the scholastics assumed

> that any man engaged in an honest trade may and will charge enough to support himself and his family. But they do not believe that the just price on the seller's part will be determined by the cost of his labor alone. St Thomas teaches explicitly that value may increase by a change in place or time alone without labor or risk by a good's owner; and the other writers . . . who teach that value changes with changes in demand or supply, show no disposition to assert that changes must reflect the cost of labor. Labor will influence cost and so the supply; but no scholastic teaches that it is the sole determinant of value.
>
> (Noonan 1957: 87)

On the other hand, in the previous section we argued that Aquinas in fact does appear to agree with the Aristotelian doctrine of justice in exchange and explicitly refers to cost ratios as the determinant of just prices. Older scholarship, moreover, placed great emphasis on production costs: 'Knies and others have remarked that what the doctrine of just price aimed at may be described as a *normal* price, in accordance with *cost of production*, instead of a fluctuating price dependent upon the changes of the market. This is an accurate description, if it be understood that cost of production was to be determined by a fixed standard of living on the part of the producers, and was not to include any element of *interest*' (Ashley 1896:#500). In principle, according to this view of the matter, it would be possible for each individual producer to determine for himself the just price of his product 'by reckoning what he needed to support his rank'. This was explicitly argued by Langenstein but was probably 'assumed as a matter of course by Aquinas and other writers'.

We turn now to examine these interpretations. We shall argue that the assumption of a single criterion of justice is false. A different rule was adopted in different circumstances.

There is little doubt that at times St Thomas referred in his discussion of just exchange to the market price. This is obviously the case in his *Summa Theologica*. Responding to the question 'Whether a seller is bound to declare a defect in a thing sold?', St Thomas raises a possible analogy suggesting that the seller need not do so, and finally denies its relevance:

> if a man is bound to declare a defect in a thing sold, this is only in order that the price may be lowered. But sometimes the price may be lowered even apart from any defect in the thing sold, for some other reason; for example, if a seller, bringing wheat to a place where grain is dear, knows that many are following with more wheat, knowledge of which on the part of the buyers would cause them to pay less. This, however, the seller does not have to tell, apparently. Hence for analogous reasons, he does not have to declare defects in the thing sold. . . .
>
> In reply . . . it is to be said that a defect in a thing makes its present value less than it seems; but in this case the thing is expected to fall in value in the future through the arrival of merchants, which is not expected by the buyers; hence a seller who sells at the prevailing price does not seem to act contrary to justice, in not telling what is going to happen. If, however, he did tell, or lowered his price, he would act more virtuously; though he does not seem to be bound by the requirements of justice to do this.
>
> (Aquinas, Question LXXVII, Article III, in Monroe 1951: 60–2)

Clearly to sell at the prevailing price is to act 'justly'. The just price in this context is simply the market price.

Similarly in answer to the question 'Whether in trading it is lawful to sell a thing for more than was paid for it?', Aquinas argues at one point that 'it can be done lawfully . . . because the price has changed with a change of place or time' (LXXVII, IV, in Monroe 1951: 64). Elsewhere he is equally explicit: 'For if the merchants of Tuscany, bringing cloth from the Fair of Lagny, to wait for it [payment?] until Easter, sell the cloth for more than it is worth in the general market, there is no doubt that this is usury.'[7]

What must not be forgotten, however, is that all these references apply *specifically to the merchant or trader*. The problems of conscience, with which Aquinas had to deal, apparently arose within the particular context of *trading* rather than within that of *production*. There is no *a priori* reason to generalize from the former to the latter problem.

The just price is frequently defined as that price which reflects 'the community's estimate' of the product. The market price may be considered 'lawful' simply because it is the most suitable indicator of the entire set of objective and subjective elements which forms the community estimate. But there is a less positive view that seems to be closer to the truth. Clearly, at least part of the reason for the adoption of the market price as the criterion lay in the desire to avoid monopolistic and monopsonistic exploitation. If this end could be achieved by means of the market then all well and good. But in some circumstances there may have existed equally satisfactory, if not preferable, criteria. To say that the essence of the matter is the avoidance of exploitation by *individual* sellers and buyers need not lead to the conclusion that exchange at competitive market prices is the only solution. There may be others. Thus, for example, it was generally accepted that the 'common estimate' may be determined by the civil authority.

Now the ideal, and perhaps typical, economic organization with which Aquinas was familiar has been described as one of 'non-competing groups', where complementary functions were carried on largely by guilds 'each of which was an organ for fulfilling some requisite of community life'. 'Because social relations are governed by justice . . . exchange must take place according to the community's estimate of the social utility of the two products, because the producer who expects sustenance from society in return for his labour, by performing his function in the social organism, has earned his right to a just return. The factors that will normally determine the community estimate of social utility are labour, cost of materials, risk, and carriage charges' (Dempsey 1958: 426). Competition was 'far from Aquinas's mind': 'In the temporal commonwealth, peace departs because the individual citizens seek only their own good. . . . Rather through diversity of function and status is the peace of temporal commonwealths promoted inasmuch as thereby there are many who participate in public affairs' (Aquinas, cited 423). But the discussions of justice in exchange which turn to the market do not seem to be applicable to such a system. And in his independent work Aquinas does not treat the problem of justice within the stratified society based upon status and rank. It may be suggested that this was simply because the rules of justice were here self-evident. They had been laid down by Aristotle and were perfectly acceptable. The serious problems which had to be dealt with were those arising outside the 'traditional' sector.

In the trading market, and particularly the international fairs, the stratified social relationships had presumably far less meaning, and the Aristotelian principles would have been impractical to apply and, therefore, largely irrelevant. This may have also been true where production was discontinuous, or where there occurred commonly violent changes in output. In these instances the only solution would be to rely on the market price, if such a price existed. But this statement must be qualified, for the hesitancy with which Aquinas permits the adoption of this standard strongly implies that it was acceptable *faute de mieux*.

Consider the reply to the question already referred to: 'Whether in trading it is lawful to sell a thing for more than was paid for it?'

> Gain, however, which is the end of trading, though it does not logically involve anything honorable or necessary, does not logically involve anything sinful or contrary to virtue; hence there is no reason why gain may not be directed to some necessary or even honorable end; and so trading will be rendered lawful; as when a man uses moderate gains acquired in trade for the support of his household, or even to help the needy; or even when a man devotes himself to trade for the public welfare, lest there be a lack of things necessary for the life of the country; and seeks gain, not as an end, but as a reward for his efforts.
>
> In reply to the first argument, then, it is to be said that the words of Chrysostom [that gain is sinful] are to be understood as applying to trade insofar as gain is its ultimate end; and this seems to be the case chiefly when a man sells a thing at a higher price without making any change in it: for if he charges a higher price for a thing that has been improved, he seems to receive a reward for his efforts; though the gain itself may also be sought, not as an ultimate end, but for some other necessary or honorable end, as explained above.
>
> In reply to the second argument, it is to be said that not everyone who sells for more than he paid is a trader, but only the one who buys for the express purpose of selling dearer. Now if he buys a thing, not for the purpose of selling it, but with the intention of keeping it, and later wishes to sell it, for some reason, it is not trading, though he sells at a higher price. For this can be done lawfully, either because he has improved the thing in some way, or because the price has changed with a change of place or time, or because of the risk he takes in transporting the thing from one place to another, or even in having it transported for him.
>
> (Aquinas, Question LXXVII, Article IV, in Monroe 1951: 63–4)

Clearly, should it happen that the selling price exceeds the purchase price of the commodity, a trader is in danger of sinful behaviour by relying on the market. He must be able to justify the excess which, incidentally, should be 'moderate'. Moreover, either the use to which this moderate gain is put must be suitable, or it must be possible to view the 'gain' as a 'reward for his efforts'. Specifically, a return to labour, a return to risk-taking, and transportation costs are enumerated. The case where one is justified in earning the excess simply 'because the price of a thing has changed with the change of place or time' occurs in a particular context; namely where the individual had not originally purchased the commodity with the intention to resell it, that is, where the individual is not strictly a trader at all. Such qualifications suggest that Aquinas accepted the market price as just most hesitantly, and would not have recommended its adoption as a general rule.[8]

The case may be concluded as follows: there are to be found in Aquinas several distinct versions of justice in exchange. One was based on an exchange determined by the hierarchies of producers. This version would appear to be relevant in a social system where rank is well determined. Another criterion was the prevailing market price and this would apply with qualification, in circumstances where status and rank were not clearly defined, and where market determination of price was the rule.[9] In the following section we will have occasion to consider in greater detail the conditions which should be satisfied for the market price to constitute a just price.

III.

We turn finally to consider one further interpretation of the just price. An attempt has been made to reconcile the apparently divergent propositions to be found in the writings of Aquinas. Professor de Roover recognizes both the references to cost ratios in the *Commentary* and the references to market prices elsewhere and combines them into a consistent whole by suggesting that according to Aquinas the 'arts and crafts would be doomed to destruction if the producer did not recover his outlays in the sale of his product. In other words, the market price could not fall permanently below cost', but would tend 'to coincide with cost or to oscillate around this point like the swing of a pendulum' (de Roover 1958:422). Elsewhere de Roover makes his point in even stronger terms: 'A vrai dire, c'est une théorie surprenante par sa modernité, et qui s'accorde entièrement avec les enseignements de l'économie politique suivant laquelle le prix courant tend à osciller autour du coût de production comme le balancier d'une pendule, bien entendu sous un régime de libre concurrence' (de Roover 1962: 154).[10]

This view would appear to be unjustified. The only reason for offering the interpretation is apparently that there would otherwise be a 'contradiction' between Aquinas's argument that the just price is the market price and his comments on Aristotle's cost ratios. However, there is no reason to expect that it is necessary to avoid 'contradictions'. Aquinas was not an analyst of economic phenomena, and we cannot ascribe to him a full-fledged Marshallian theory of price determination involving a recognition of the relationship between supply curves of various 'runs'.

In support of this view let us turn back to Aristotle's treatment of justice in exchange and the comments thereon by Aquinas. It is tempting to see in the statement that without justice 'the arts would be destroyed' an argument to the effect that unless outlays are recovered the producer would be doomed to destruction, so that the market price could not fall permanently below costs. However, while it is certainly true that price cannot fall permanently below cost it is not by means of a classical or neo-classical mechanism that this fact is assured. It does not seem to be the case, in other words, that the price would tend to oscillate around costs 'like the swing of a pendulum'. Aristotle and Aquinas were treating a problem which did not concern the classical or later writers. They seem to be referring to the possibility that unless the exchange rate reflected relative costs of production the social structure, in particular the system of specialization, would collapse: 'as many sandals must be exchanged for one house . . . as the builder . . . exceeds the shoemaker in his labour and costs. If this is not observed, there will be no exchange of things and men will not share their goods with one another.' On the other hand, if the rules of justice are followed there will be mutual inter-change between the specialist craftsmen: 'But when all have what is theirs, they are in this way equal and do business with one another because the quality previously mentioned is possible for them' (quoted above, p. 52–3).

It is essential to recognize that neither Aristotle nor Aquinas in his *Commentary* explain how the exchange ratios will come to reflect costs of production. The topic under discussion was exchange between individual craftsmen, who were not to engage in any form of bargaining; the just rate was well defined *prior* to the act of exchange. One cannot find an argument to the effect that resources will move from one occupation to another in response to relative profitability. There is no indication of the manner in which an unprofitable trade will decline and a profitable trade expand. In short, there is no mechanism whereby current prices are related to produc-tion costs. Yet such a mechanism is essential if one wishes to explain a tendency to long-run equilibrium. It is evident that social opprobrium or the 'self-interest' and above all the 'conscience' of the craftsmen must have been relied upon. There is no economic mechanism to explain the cost 'determination' of price.

When we consider the discussion by St Thomas in *Summa Theologica*, and elsewhere, the conclusion must still be that he failed to relate the market price and production costs. Although it is clear that the mechanics of market price determination were understood, no consideration was given to the consequences of a failure to cover long-run costs. The extent to which the relationship between market price and costs was dealt with may be illustrated by the response made to an argument that traders should be permitted to charge for usurious payments they had undertaken. These individuals 'wish to recover that usury by selling the cloth at more than its worth':

> Nor are they excused by the fact that they wish to indemnify themselves, for no one should indemnify himself by committing mortal sin. And although they can in selling the cloth lawfully recover other expenses lawfully contracted, for example, the cost of transporting the cloth, still they cannot recover the usury they paid, for this was an unjust payment; especially since by paying usury they sinned as giving the usurers an occasion for sinning, since the necessity which is urged – namely that they may live more respectably and do a bigger trade – is not such a necessity as suffices to excuse the aforesaid sin. This is clear by comparison; for a man could not in selling cloth recover expenses which he might have incurred carelessly and imprudently.[11]
>
> (Aquinas, quoted in O'Rahilly 1928:165)

We have seen earlier that to justify the 'gain' of a trader Aquinas insisted that a return to effort of some kind must be reflected, although there are acceptable claims to the excess of purchase price over sales price based upon the *use* to which the excess is put. Now in the above passage Aquinas is considering the problem of 'loss'. If the going market price should fail to cover costs, the trader may legitimately charge a price higher than that ruling in the market, should an opportunity present itself, providing that his costs are legitimate claims. If the costs represent interest payments, or if they are 'abnormally' high because of his carelessness and imprudence, he must charge the going market price, and suffer the loss.

We can discern in this discussion a sense in which Aquinas may be said to be groping towards the idea of normal long-run competitive price. In the first place, it will be noted that the nature of 'costs' in the treatment of problems relating to trading is more sophisticated than is that to be found in the *Commentary* for Aquinas no longer restricted himself to the simple labour costs of specialist craftsmen. Second, whereas a market price which permitted 'gain' was satisfactory if the seller's costs were reflected thereby, a market price which failed to cover legitimate and 'normal' expenses was not obligatory. But this result, reflecting both an absence of pure profit and of loss, will be attained in the long run by the neo-classical competitive process. Our point, however, is that Aquinas did not reach his conclusions by means of analytical reasoning. He did not explain how the market price would come to reflect normal costs of production. In brief, he did not trace through the consequences of a failure to cover supply price; this problem did not concern him. St Thomas was prescribing certain 'just' courses of action which suggest that he envisaged the market price as satisfactory provided that it did not permit pure profit on the one hand, and did not lead to losses on the other. This conclusion must of course be qualified, for a pure profit would in some cases be permissible if it were utilized in a satisfactory manner, and the seller must suffer losses due to his own carelessness. Thus cases can be found where the market price may be charged although the consequence would be profit, or must be charged despite the losses which would ensue.

IV.

It has been argued that 'preoccupation with the ethics of pricing . . . is precisely one of the strongest motives a man can possibly have for analysing actual market mechanisms' (Schumpeter 1954: 60). It is true that the ethics of pricing *may* lead to analysis of economic phenomena, but the question is whether St Thomas can be said to have taken the step from ethics to analysis.

It is probable that Aquinas by his own experience and observation would not have been led to recognize the influence of the current price on supply, and thereby the mechanism of adaptation of supply to demand which assures the long-run cost determination of price. Resource mobility would have been low even in the long run and any relationship between market price, the relative profitability of operations, and production costs would probably have been clouded.[12]

It is clear that Aquinas was concerned with giving advice to individuals concerned with the morality of their actions. Certain charges can morally be made. By implication it may be argued that this is also a recognition that these functions (of labour, risk-taking, and transportation) have a *supply* price which, if not covered, would lead to the withdrawal of factors from the particular occupation. But this is no more than an implication; the full recognition was at no point made. What is implicit in a man's writings and what the man himself recognized in them are two distinct questions. The step from ethics to analysis was a task for the future.

NOTES

1 The idea of a just price related to social hierarchy and a corresponding standard of living related to status can be traced back to the interpretations of the German Historical School, in particular to Sombart and Roscher. See de Roover 1958: 418–34; Ashley 1893, Part 2: 391 ff.

2 Volume 1 in the Library of Living Catholic Thought series (Chicago: Henry Regnery Company, 1964), contains St Thomas Aquinas's *Commentary on the Nicomachean Ethics* and also the relevant passages from Aristotle. The new translations of Aquinas and Aristotle are by C. I. Litzinger. Page references are to this translation.

3 The phrase has been translated by W. D. Ross as: 'for there is nothing to prevent the work of one from being better than that of the others'. Cf. Spengler 1955: 384.

4 Alternatively rendered as 'they would be destroyed, if the effect upon the patient were not, in kind, quantity and quality, the same as the effort of the agent' in the translation by J. E. Welldon in Monroe 1951: 27–8.

5 I have given the Latin original of the key phrases found in *In Decem Libros Ethicorum Aristotelis ad Nicomachum* (Pirotta and Gillet, eds, 1934:326).

6 Examples of this relationship quoted by Gordon are the following statements: 'Thus gold is a better thing than iron; though less useful: it is harder to get, and therefore better worth the getting'; 'we appreciate better the possession of things that cannot be easily acquired'; 'all men love more what they have won by labour . . .', from the *Rhetoric*, *Topica*, and the *Ethics* respectively. In his paper, Gordon also emphasizes the ranking of skills which is to be found in Aristotle; this ranking is 'non-economic' and based on criteria such as the extent to which 'the body must be deteriorated', and the element of chance involved (Gordon 1964: 126).

One possible approach to the relationship between cost and utility may be added here. Aristotle may not have been concerned, when he referred to 'demand' and 'need' in our texts, with the *individuals* concerned. But the ranking of each occupation (and consequently production costs) may partly be dependent upon the *social* demand for, or rather the importance attached by *society as a whole* to, the relevant products. In this case too, *both* costs and 'utility' play a role although once again it is the former which receive the emphasis, the latter being of indirect relevance.

7 From a letter translated and analysed by Alfred O'Rahilly (1928: 165).

8 Indeed, it has been argued that the very notion of commutative justice is superseded and contradicted by that of market price. This view is implicit in Hobbes. Cf. Macpherson 1962: 63.

9 We have also noted that the prices set by civil authority were acceptable. Moreover, there was considerable flexibility. For example, a seller of a thing who is 'injured if he is deprived of it' may allow for this (Aquinas, LXXVII, I, in Monroe 1951: 55). But the discussion here pertains not to the case of specialist craftsmen or to traders, but rather to an 'occasional' exchange of objects.

10 A somewhat similar view is taken by Joseph A. Schumpeter. According to Schumpeter, Aquinas's just price was, as it was for Aristotle, 'simply normal competitive price' (1954:93). Some passages suggest 'that, by implication, at least, he did relate just price to cost'. But it was Duns Scotus who must be credited with 'having discovered the condition of competitive equilibrium which came to be known in the nineteenth century as the Law of Cost. This is not imputing too much: for if we identify the just price of a good with its competitive common value, as Duns Scotus certainly did, and if we further equate that just price to the cost of the good (taking account of risk, as he did not fail to observe), then we have ipso facto, at least by implication, stated the law of cost not only as a normative but also as an analytic proposition'.

11 It is evident from the context that the term 'its worth' refers to the going market price (see above, p. 57). Considered in isolation, the statement that 'a man could not in selling cloth recover expenses which he might have incurred carelessly and imprudently', might be interpreted as a highly sophisticated recognition of the fact that the competitive market price will, in the long run, cover normal costs so that the individual seller – selling at the going price – would be *unable* to cover his abnormally high costs. However, Aquinas seems rather to have in mind the individual who has an opportunity to charge a price in excess of the current market price in a particular transaction. He was

morally prohibited from so doing if his costs were carelessly incurred, but might do so if his costs were legitimate and normal claims. Furthermore, even if the former interpretation were in fact correct, there is still to be found no economic mechanism by which the result is assured.

12 See for example the discussion of supply elasticity in agriculture, in Postan and Rich 1952: 166–7, 211.

REFERENCES

Aquinas, St Thomas (1951) *Summa Theologica*, in *Early Economic Thought: Selections from Economic Literature Prior to Adam smith*, A. E. Monroe (ed.), Cambridge: Harvard University press.
—— (1964) *Commentary on the Nicomachean Ethics*, translated by C. I. Litzinger, Vol. 1, Library of Living Catholic Thought series, Chicago: Henry Regnery Company.
Aristotle (1964) *Nicomachean Ethics*, translated by C. I. Litzinger, Vol. 1, Library of Living Catholic Thought series, Chicago: Henry Regnery Company.
Ashley, W. J. (1893) *English Economic History*, 2nd edn, New York: G. P. Putnam's Sons; London: Longmans and Co.
—— (1896) 'Justum Pretium', *Dictionary of Political Economy*, R.H.I. Palgrave (ed.), 1st edn, Vol. 2, London: Macmillan.
Dempsey, Bernard W. (1958) *The Functional Economy*, Englewood Cliffs: Prentice-Hall.
Gordon, Barry J. (1964) 'Aristotle and the Development of Value Theory', *Quarterly Journal of Economics*, 78 (February): 115–28.
Macpherson, C. B. (1962) *The Political Theory of Possessive Individualism: Hobbes to Locke*, Oxford: Clarendon Press.
Monroe, Arthur E. (1951) *Early Economic Thought*, Cambridge, Mass.: Harvard University Press.
Noonan, Jr, John T. (1957) *The Scholastic Analysis of Usury*, Cambridge, Mass.: Harvard University Press.
O'Rahilly, Alfred (1928) 'Notes on St Thomas; III – St Thomas on Credit', *Irish Ecclesiastical Record*, 31 (February).
Pirotta, A. M. and M. S. Gillet (eds) (1934) *In Decem Libros Ethicorum Aristotelis ad Nicomachum*, Turin: Marietti.
Postan, M. and E. E. Rich (eds) (1952), *Trade and Industry in the Middle Ages*, Vol. II of *The Cambridge Economic History of Europe*, Cambridge: Cambridge University Press.
de Roover, Raymond (1958) 'The Concept of the Just Price: Theory and Economic Policy', *The Journal of Economic History*, 18 (December): 418–34.
—— (1962) 'La Doctrine Scolastic en Matière de Monopole et Son Application à la Politique Economique des Communes Italiennes' in *Studi in Onore di Amintore Fanfani*, Milan: Dott. A. Giuffrè.
Schumpeter, Joseph A. (1954) *History of Economic Analysis*, New York: Oxford University Press.
Spengler, Joseph J. (1955) 'Aristotle on Economic Imputation and Related Matters', *Southern Economic Journal*, 21 (April): 371–89.

6

THE ROLE OF THE STATE IN
VOCATIONAL TRAINING
The classical economists' view*

The general consensus of opinion in the recent literature is that the British classical economists were substantially in favour of considerable government intervention in education.[1] Yet there is one aspect of the problem, of much relevance today, which has received little attention. This is the issue of vocational training. Did the classical economists extend their argument in favour of intervention to vocational training, or were they willing to leave this branch of education to the free market?[2]

In this essay we discuss this issue specifically. The first impression, we shall see, is in fact one of hostility to government intervention even by those who were aware of serious impediments to labour mobility which prevent the private market from generating 'adequate' supplies of skilled labour. On the other hand, it is possible to delineate the circumstances wherein at least some of the economists would have supported intervention. It will become clear that the classical case in favour of public support for *elementary* education has implications for the present issue which cannot be neglected. For amongst the benefits envisaged from extended elementary education are precisely those which would today – when a 'literate' working population is taken for granted – more commonly be attributed to vocational training. Moreover, as in the case of many other policy issues some attention must be paid to the Malthusian population reaction for a full understanding of the classical position. Our conclusion is that the absence of an *explicit* call for public aid to vocational training cannot be said to reflect a rejection 'in principle' of such intervention.

We examine first the assumptions regarding the degree of labour mobility which are to be found in the classical literature on the wage structure. We then consider the principal arguments of the economists in support of government intervention in the provision of elementary education. Finally, we attempt to explain the absence of an explicit case for public

* I would like to thank my colleagues V. W. Bladen, R. S. Blair and K. F. Helleiner, and Kurt Klappholz of the London School of Economics for helpful suggestions.

support of vocational training even on the part of those who particularly emphasized the existence of permanent monopoly earnings in skilled trades.

I.

Adam Smith recognized institutional impediments to the process by which wages in different occupations were kept in line, particularly contemporary apprenticeship and corporation laws. But apart from these artificial constraints he was confident that the market process would generate adequate supplies of skilled labour. All this is well known. But it might be worthwhile to illustrate the extent to which Smith, and later classical writers, tended to play down the restraints imposed on mobility by the difficulty of acquiring the necessary skills. For example, in a discussion of the consequences of abolishing trade barriers, Smith denied that long-term unemployment would result, on the grounds that workers may easily transfer from one trade to another: 'Though a great number of people should, by thus restoring the freedom of trade, be thrown all at once out of their ordinary employment and common method of subsistence, it would by no means follow that they would thereby be deprived either of employment or subsistence. . . . To the greater part of manufactures . . . there are other collateral manufactures of so similar a nature, that a worker can easily transfer his industry from one of them to another' (Smith 1937 [1776]: 436–7). It was in fact precisely upon these grounds that Smith condemned contemporary practices relating to apprenticeship: 'Long apprenticeships are altogether unnecessary. The arts, which are much superior to common trades, such as those of making clocks and watches, contain no such mystery as to require a long course of instruction. . . . How to apply the instruments and how to construct the machines, cannot well require more than the lessons of a few weeks, perhaps those of a few days might be sufficient. In the common mechanical trades, those of a few days might certainly be sufficient' (1937 [1776]: 123).

In fact, according to Smith the degree of skill required in manufacturing was less than that in agriculture where the system of apprenticeship was not applied: 'There is scarce any common mechanic trade . . . of which all the operations may not be as completely and distinctly explained in a pamphlet of a very few pages. . . . Not only the art of the farmer, the general direction of the operations of husbandry, but many inferior branches of country labour, require much more skill and experience than the greater part of mechanic trades. The man who works upon brass and iron, works with instruments and upon materials of which the temper is always the same, or very nearly the same' (1937 [1776]: 126–7).[3]

Optimism regarding the ease of acquiring skills was apparently quite widespread. Thus Jeremy Bentham, when discussing the kinds of work appropriate for handicapped 'industry-house' inmates, says that extensions in specialization tended to reduce the need for skilled labour: 'The stock of *every-man's-work* operations being increased more and more by the division of labour . . . the stock of work adapted to these confined-ability hands will receive a proportionate increase' (Bentham 1962, VIII: 389).[4]

Similarly, J. R. McCulloch repeated Smith's theme that the acquisition of new skills posed no serious problem, and applied it both to the issue of free trade and to that of the technological displacement of labour: 'most industrial undertakings have so many things in common, that individuals familiar with one have seldom much difficulty in accommodating themselves to others' (1965 [1864]: 101).[5]

The Report of the Hand-Loom Weavers Commission supported proposals that the state establish institutions of 'design' with the aim of 'increasing the number of good designers actually engaged in the business of manufacturing' (Parliamentary Papers 1841, X: 81).[6] But the basic objective was to increase the competitiveness of English cloth exports in the light of similar measures adopted by the French government. This appears to be the only case in the report for government support of training in skills. Certainly if acquiring skills was considered problematical, the issue would have been raised in a study such as that of the hand-loom weavers' plight.

It is also notable that the Poor-Law Report of 1834 had nothing to say about the problem involved in the acquisition of skills. Its main concern in the matter of training was with the 'religious and moral education of the labouring classes' (Parliamentary Papers 1834, XXVII: 205).

Although Smith emphasized the ease with which skills may be acquired by the working class, he was, at the same time, acutely aware of the fact that workers could not afford a costly education: 'the common people . . . have little time to spare for education. Their parents can scarce afford to maintain them even in infancy. As soon as they are able to work, they must apply to some trade by which they can earn their subsistence' (1937 [1776]: 737). Smith did not evidently fear that the exclusion of workers from occupations requiring a heavy preliminary 'investment' in education in any way prevented the process of net equalization of returns. He apparently presumed that a sufficient number of relatively wealthy individuals were available to assure that, in the long run, excessive returns in such occupations would be eliminated.

The Smithian analysis was severely criticized by J. S. Mill. Although Smith had recognized that monetary returns in any occupation must in equilibrium suffice to indemnify education costs, he had failed to consider the possibility that returns might persist which exceed the amount required, apart from instances of excessive returns due to institutional constraints on entry into skilled trades. In fact, Mill argued, both *financial and social obstacles* prevented the attainment of skills by sufficiently large numbers to assure the eradication of monopoly returns in skilled trades even in the absence of institutional constraints (Mill 1965 [1848–71]: 386–7). In the *Wealth of Nations* the analysis of the wage structure referred essentially to the earnings of the 'working class'; professional men were a non-competing group. The recognition by Mill that *within* the working class there were non-competing groups was the essence of the change.

But Mill's objections went further. According to Smith it was to be expected that the least pleasant occupations would, *ceteris paribus*, be the highest paid. It was pointed out by Mill that at best – that is apart from the presence of impediments to mobility which hamper the process of net equalization – the result envisaged presumes that the aggregate labour market is in equilibrium. Should unemployment exist in the labour force as a whole, it is likely that the least agreeable (and unskilled) trades would be the worst paid since the excess supply would tend to be relatively greater in such trades:

> If the labourers in the aggregate, instead of exceeding, fell short of the amount of employment, work which was generally disliked would not be undertaken, except for more than ordinary wages. But when the supply of labour so far exceeds the demand that to find employment at all is an uncertainty, and to be offered it on any terms a favour, the case is totally the reverse. Desirable labourers, those whom every one is anxious to have, can still exercise a choice. The undesirable must take what they can get. The more revolting the occupation, the more certain it is to receive the minimum of remuneration, because it devolves on the most helpless and degraded, on those who from squalid poverty, or from want of skill and education, are rejected from all other employments. Partly from this cause, and partly from the natural and artificial monopolies . . . the inequalities of wages are generally in an opposite direction to the equitable principle of compensation erroneously represented by Adam Smith as the general law of the remuneration of labour.
>
> (Mill 1965 [1848–71]: 383)

It is a striking phenomenon to find in the work of a leading classical economist an objection to the Smithian principles of relative wage-rate determination based on the presumption that typically unemployment existed in the labour market as a whole. Excessive or monopoly returns were thus regarded by Mill to be the *rule*, and to result both from relatively great excess labour supply in unskilled trades, and the various impediments to mobility referred to earlier.

II.

We turn now to consider the classical arguments in support of government intervention in education. Our particular concern is the apparent contrast in this respect between elementary and vocational training.

It has been made quite clear in the recent secondary literature that the classics based a case for government intervention on the grounds of a divergence between social and private returns. Insofar as *vocational* training is concerned, however, Smith considered that private and social returns coincide so that the market can be relied upon to generate adequate investment. Consider for example Smith's references to an earlier discussion by David Hume to this effect:

> 'Most of the arts and professions in a state', says by far the most illustrious philosopher and historian of the present age, 'are of such a nature, that while they promote the interests of the society, they are also useful and agreeable to some individuals; and in that case, the constant rule of the magistrate, except, perhaps, on the first introduction of any art, is, to leave the profession to itself, and trust its encouragement to the individuals who reap the benefit of it. The artizans, finding their profits to rise by the favour of their customers, increase, as much as possible, their skill and industry; and as matters are not disturbed by any injudicious tampering, the commodity is always sure to be at all times, nearly proportional to the demand'.
>
> (Smith 1937 [1776]: 742)

A clearer statement to the effect that normally social and private returns may be presumed to coincide cannot be imagined. Yet the allowance that government aid might be called for 'on the first introduction of any art' should be noted carefully for it is possible that Hume and Smith would have adopted a different attitude in an economy undergoing rapid changes in products and processes.

Some reference may be made at this juncture to Smith's recommendation that a modernized curriculum was desirable. Elementary education should be extended to 'geometry and mechanics': 'If in those little schools . . . they were instructed in the elementary parts of geometry and mechanics, the literary education of this rank of people would perhaps be as complete as it can be. There is scarce a common trade which does not afford some opportunities of applying to it the principles of geometry and mechanics, and which would not therefore gradually exercise and improve the common people in those principles, the necessary introduction to the most sublime as well as the most useful sciences' (1937 [1776]: 737–8).[7] To some extent it may appear that vocational training is implied in the above recommendation and indeed that Smith was implicitly recognizing the impediments to mobility created by limited educational opportunities. But on balance it would appear that the emphasis is upon elementary education rather than on the training of specific skills, although it is significant that a relatively ambitious programme was recommended in order to raise the productivity of the working force.

James Mill, too, apparently believed that in the case of vocational skills intervention was uncalled for. As he wrote in his celebrated article for the *Encyclopaedia Britannica* (1818) on 'Education': 'Whether these

69

apprenticeships, as they have hitherto been managed, have been good instruments of education, is a question of importance, about which there is now, among enlightened men, hardly any diversity of opinion. When the legislature undertakes to do for every man, what every man had abundant motives to do for himself, and better means than the legislature; the legislature takes a very unnecessary, and commonly a not very innocent trouble' (James Mill, in Cavenagh 1931: 66).[8]

A case for government support of *basic research* on the grounds of a divergence between social and private returns may be found in the work of J. S. Mill, but the argument is not applied generally to vocational education:

> The cultivation of speculative knowledge, though one of the most useful of all employments, is a service rendered to a community collectively, not individually, and one consequently for which it is, *prima facie*, reasonable that the community collectively should pay: since it gives no claim on any individual for a pecuniary remuneration; and unless a provision is made for such services from some public fund, there is not only no encouragement to them, but there is as much discouragement as is implied in the impossibility of gaining a living by such pursuits. . . . It is highly desirable, therefore, that there should be a mode of insuring to the public the services of scientific discoverers, and perhaps of some other classes of savants, by affording them the means of support consistently with devoting a sufficient portion of time to their peculiar pursuits.
>
> (Mill 1965 [1848–71]: 968–9)[9]

Mill was in favour of the use of endowments, under state control, to finance the further education of the 'élite' amongst the workers who had demonstrated superior ability at the elementary level. But his concern was with *general* secondary and even university education, not vocational training. The argument was based partly upon the desire for greater equality of opportunity, although it is also quite clear that the purely economic advantages of the policy to society as a whole were recognized:

> The State does not owe gratuitous education to those who can pay for it. The State owes no more than elementary education to the entire body of those who cannot pay for it. But the superior education which it does not owe to the whole of the poorer population, it owes to the *élite* of them – to those who have earned the preference by labour, and have shown by the results that they have the capacities worth securing for the higher departments of intellectual work, never supplied in due proportion to the demand. . . . The gain to society, by making available for its most difficult work, not those alone who can afford to qualify themselves, but all those who would qualify themselves if they could afford it, would be but part of the benefit. I believe there is no

single thing which would go so far to heal class differences, and diminish the just dissatisfaction which the best of the poorer classes of the nation feel with their position in it.

(Mill 1967 [1869]: 627–8)[10]

An argument for state intervention may arise where consumer knowledge is limited because of the nature of the product in question. Such a case was developed by Mill to support a claim for government intervention in education:

> [The consumer] is generally the best judge . . . of the material objects produced for his use. . . . But there are other things, of the worth of which the demand of the market is by no means a test; things of which the utility does not consist in ministering to inclinations, nor in serving the daily uses of life, and the want of which is least felt where the need is greatest. This is particularly true of those things which are chiefly useful as tending to raise the character of human beings. The uncultivated cannot be the competent judges of cultivation. . . . It will continually happen, on the voluntary system, that the end not being desired, the means will not be provided at all, or that, the persons requiring improvement having an imperfect or altogether erroneous conception of what they want, the supply called forth by the demand of the market will be anything but what is really required. . . . Education, therefore, is one of those things which it is admissible in principle that a government should provide for the people.
>
> (Mill 1965 [1848–71]: 947–8)

It is not easy to judge the range of cases to which Mill intended such an argument to apply. Presumably in principle it might be extended, where circumstances require it, to justify considerable state intervention in all branches of education. But the references to 'things which are chiefly useful as tending to raise the character of human beings' and the view that 'the uncultivated cannot be the competent judges of cultivation' would suggest that the argument was intended by Mill to apply to general rather than to vocational training.[11]

III.

From what has been said in the previous section it would appear that the classical economists favoured public aid to elementary schooling but not to vocational training. But it is essential to make it clear that in arguing their case, the classicists paid attention not only to beneficial 'social' effects of a general kind resulting from literacy, but also to specifically economic advantages.[12] In fact, to the extent that many workers were initially receiving no education, or very little education, or education of very low quality, the introduction of adequate elementary training would tend to increase mobility. Indeed, starting from an illiterate base it is difficult to distinguish elementary from vocational training since, frequently, the former is a necessary prerequisite of the latter.

The economic advantages are implied in the elementary-school curriculum recommended by Adam Smith which included, as we have seen earlier, 'the principles of geometry and mechanics . . . the necessary introduction to the most sublime as well as the most useful sciences'. It will also be recalled that amongst the stultifying effects of specialization Smith included the danger that the industrial worker would find it ultimately impossible to operate 'in any other employment than that to which he has been bred' (1937 [1776]: 735). We conclude that Smith's optimism regarding the high degree of mobility – upon which was based his confidence in the operation of the free market in the provision of skills – was contingent upon a necessary minimum degree of elementary training.

A number of further examples in the classical literature of the purely economic effects of elementary education will now be given. Senior included amongst the specifically economic advantages of elementary education a resultant increase in labour skills: 'No country is so poor as to be unable to bear the expense of good elementary schools. Strictly speaking it is not an expense. The money so employed is much more than repaid by the superiority in diligence, in skill, in economy, in health – in short, in all the qualities which fit men to produce and to preserve wealth, of an educated over an uneducated community' (from Lecture Notes 1847–8, Senior 1928, II: 328–9).[13]

Furthermore, it was an argument of the Hand-Loom Weavers Commission that mobility would be enhanced *indirectly* by the encouragement given students in elementary courses to avoid or leave declining industries, or at least to desist from automatically putting their own children into their trades regardless of long-term prospects. It was hoped that 'the exercise of the activity, intelligence, self-denial, and prudence to which we have alluded, might proportion their number to their employments as to secure good average wages' (Parliamentary Papers 1841, X: 120).[14]

McCulloch included 'the dexterity, skill and intelligence' of the working class in his definition of national capital and carried on to support the educational movements of his time: 'An ignorant and uneducated people, though possessed of all the materials and powers necessary for the production of wealth, are uniformly sunk in poverty and barbarism: and until their mental powers begin to expand, and they learn to exercise the empire of mind over matter, the avenues to improvement are shut against them, and they have neither the power nor the wish to emerge from their degraded condition' (McCulloch 1965 [1864]: 67).[15]

J. S. Mill was particularly careful to specify increased labour mobility amongst the social advantages of elementary training. Thus in a discussion of the benefits he included an improvement in the ability of a worker to undertake tasks which extended beyond the routine:

A thing not yet so well understood and recognised, is the economical value of the general diffusion of intelligence among the people. The number of persons fitted to direct and superintend any industrial enterprise, or even to execute any process which cannot be reduced almost to an affair of memory and routine, is always far short of the demand; as is evident from the enormous difference between the salaries paid to such persons, and the wages of ordinary labour. The deficiency of practical good sense, which renders the majority of the labouring class such bad calculators . . . must disqualify them for any but a low grade of intelligent labour, and render their industry far less productive than with equal energy it otherwise might be. The importance, even in this limited aspect, of popular education, is well worthy of the attention of politicians especially in England.

(Mill 1965 [1848–71]: 107–8)[16]

Mill recognized the social changes underway in Britain which were breaking down traditional impediments to mobility: 'The changes, however, now so rapidly taking place in usages and ideas, are undermining all these distinctions [between social groups]; the habits or disabilities which chained people to their hereditary condition are fast wearing away, and every class is exposed to increased and increasing competition from at least the class immediately below it' (1965 [1848–71]: 388). These social changes included the ever-growing numbers of the working class who were receiving basic elementary education: 'Since reading and writing have been brought within the reach of a multitude, the monopoly price of the lower grade of educated employments has greatly fallen, the competition for them having increased in an almost incredible degree' (386–7). Yet the full effects on mobility of universal elementary education at an adequate standard still remained to be seen: 'The small degree of education required [of a clerk] being not even yet so generally diffused as to call forth the natural number of competitors' (387).[17]

Thus, Mill's pessimism regarding the degree of labour mobility tended to diminish with the extension of the elementary-school programmes. And the confidence of Smith and others in the ability of labourers to acquire technical training was partly based upon the assumption that a satisfactory system of elementary education was available.

IV.

It is not particularly surprising to find Smith opposed to government aid to vocational training, for, as we have seen, he adopted the view that in the absence of artificial restrictions and, it should be added, with the extension of elementary education, monopoly returns would be competed away. Accordingly, the consequence of government intervention would be to drive the returns to skilled trades below the competitive level and thereby

73

generate 'inadequate' wage differentials. Smith's argument was made with particular reference to the professions but there is no reason to believe that he intended it to be in any way limited to particular occupations:

> It has been considered as of so much importance that a proper number of young people should be educated for certain professions, that, sometimes the public, and sometimes the piety of private founders have established many pensions, scholarships, exhibitions, bursaries, &c. for this purpose, which draw more people into those trades than could otherwise pretend to follow them. . . . The long, tedious, and expensive education, therefore, of those who are [educated altogether at their own expense], will not always procure them a suitable reward . . . and in this manner the competition of the poor takes away the reward of the rich.
>
> (Smith 1937 [1776]: 129–30)

These remarks may be applied to all those writers who shared Smith's optimism regarding the ease of training, and who attributed immobility of labour largely to 'artificial' constraints (including those due to unionization), rather than to financial (and social) obstacles which hinder a worker from acquiring skills and which thus permit permanent monopoly earnings in skilled trades.

More surprising is the attitude of J. S. Mill, who laid such great emphasis upon the existence of non-competing groups within the labouring class and who clearly explained that *in the past* monopoly returns had been reduced by government intervention: 'While it is true, as a general rule, that the earnings of skilled labour, and especially of any labour which requires school education, are at a monopoly rate, from the impossibility, to the mass of the people, of obtaining that education; it is also true that the policy of nations, or the bounty of individuals, formerly did much to counteract the effect of this limitation of competition, by offering eleemosynary instruction to a much larger class of persons than could have obtained the same advantages by paying their price' (Mill 1965 [1848–71]: 388–9). But at no point did he present a general case in favour of government support of vocational training on the grounds that monopoly returns would thereby be reduced.[18]

To some extent Mill's attitude may be explained along the lines suggested above, namely by his belief that the achievement of an adequate *elementary* programme might suffice to correct restrictions upon mobility. But there is a further reason for Mill's attitude. Mill took a much more serious view of the 'population problem' than did other classical economists after the mid-1830s, and he feared that too rapid a dissolution of the impediments to upward mobility would simply lead to increased population and a lower average wage rate. This argument is stated clearly in the following passage:

> The general relaxation of conventional barriers, and the increased facilities of education which already are, and will be in a much greater

degree, brought within the reach of all, tend to produce, among many excellent effects, one which is the reverse; they tend to bring down the wages of skilled labour. The inequality of remuneration between the skilled and the unskilled is, without doubt, very much greater than is justifiable; but it is desirable that this should be corrected by raising the unskilled, not by lowering the skilled. If, however, the other changes taking place in society are not accompanied by a strengthening of the checks to population on the part of labourers generally, there will be a tendency to bring the lower grades of skilled labourers under the influence of a rate of increase regulated by a lower standard of living than their own, and thus to deteriorate their condition without raising that of the general mass; the stimulus given to the multiplication of the lowest class being sufficient to fill up without difficulty the additional space gained by them from those immediately above.

(Mill 1965 [1848–71]: 388)

Mill was, therefore, apparently willing to tolerate the excessive wage differentials between skilled and unskilled occupations at least until the population issue had been resolved.

The significance of the Malthusian population reaction in accounting for Mill's position on key policy issues, including that of vocational training, cannot be exaggerated. Precisely the same argument was repeated by Mill in his justification of the restrictive practices of unions in skilled trades. For he refused to condemn unions out of hand, despite his acceptance of evidence that movement out of depressed trades was severely impeded by union activity: 'Notwithstanding, however, the cruel manner in which the exclusive principle of these combinations operates in a case of this peculiar nature, the question, whether they are on the whole more useful or mischievous, requires to be decided on an enlarged consideration of consequences, among which such a fact as this is not one of the most important items' (1965 [1848–71]: 397). (The reference is to the evidence of the Hand-Loom Weavers Commission.) The problem of inadequate restraint over the rate of growth of population was of overwhelming importance. And generally, Mill was willing to tolerate unions which succeeded in raising wages over the competitive level despite the nefarious effects on the non-unionized sector, until population restraint came to be exercised:

if the present state of the general habits of the people were to remain for ever unimproved, these partial combinations, in so far as they do succeed in keeping up the wages of any trade by limiting its numbers, might be looked upon as simply entrenching around a particular spot against the inroads of over-population, and making the wages of the class depend upon their own rate of increase, instead of depending on that of a more reckless and improvident class than themselves. What at first sight seems the injustice of excluding the more numerous body

75

from sharing the gains of a comparatively few, disappears when we consider that by being admitted they would not be made better off, for more than a short time; the only permanent effect which their admission would produce, would be to lower the others to their own level.

(Mill 1965 [1848–71]: 397–8)[19]

V.

We conclude from the preceding discussion that the absence in the classical literature of an explicit case favouring public support of vocational training need not be interpreted as a reflection of hostility in principle to such intervention. In the first place, when a classical author formally condemned state intervention in the matter of technical education it was frequently in the context of an attack upon the apprenticeship laws. But a call for the abolition of such contemporary forms of interference does not necessarily imply a condemnation of all forms. In fact, it seems clear that the economists had not yet fully made up their minds as to the best alternative to the traditional methods whereby labourers acquired technical training.

In the second place, the widespread confidence in the ability of labourers to acquire skills without undue difficulty was based, in part at least, upon the assumption that a satisfactory standard of elementary training was available. But this prerequisite had, even by 1871, at the time of J. S. Mill's final edition of the *Principles*, not yet been satisfied, so that the basis for optimism was never fully tested during the classical period. There is every reason to believe that the classical economists would have altered their position in the event that good elementary education failed to produce the expected results. The recognition by several economists of a divergence between private and social returns in the case of basic scientific research might in principle be extended to a wide variety of cases.

But the classical writers did not expect that even the best elementary education would make government intervention unnecessary in all circumstances. We have, for example, noted the admission, albeit casual, by Hume and Smith that in the case of *new* trades the coincidence of private and social returns to investment in vocational training might be disturbed, and accordingly government intervention justified. It is also clear that J. S. Mill's opposition to government intervention in the matter of technical skills significantly weakened as the pressure of population eased.

REPLY TO E. G. WEST (1969)[20]

My remarks on Professor West's position (*Southern Economic Journal*, April 1968; 522n [above, note 17]) were based upon his 'Private versus Public Education: A Classical Economic Dispute', *Journal of Political Economy*, October 1964. I found no convincing evidence in that article to counter the view that the Royal Commission of 1861 underrated the deficiencies of the educational system. But my intention was not, in fact, to state my own view – one way or the other – regarding the validity of the findings of 1861. What troubled me was the implication of the article that Mill and Senior were too prejudiced to examine the evidence objectively, having long before made up their minds. As I pointed out, McCulloch, for example, was equally critical of the private system, and expressed himself strongly to this effect as late as in 1864. Moreover, Lowe, who – according to the *JPE* article itself – cannot be charged with mistrust of parental choice or with Benthamite predilections in educational matters, had absolutely no confidence in the Commission's statistical findings. I can only repeat Lowe's statement: 'It would be paying too great a compliment to those figures to base any calculation on them.' The Commission evidently failed – whether or not for good reason – to convince economists and educationalists of widely differing philosophies.

NOTES

1 Cf. West 1967: 'The classical economists, as is commonly known, were in favour of appreciable government intervention in English education' (378).

2 At one point in his recent paper W. L. Miller touches briefly upon the issue of vocational training in a discussion of J. S. Mill: 'he did not expect much good to come from application of the market principle to education except perhaps in vocational training'. See Miller 1966, 304.

3 Smith recognized *geographical* immobility apparently unrelated to the laws of the land. In commenting on an observed permanent difference between real wages paid to town and to country labourers he remarked: 'After all that has been said of the levity and inconstancy of human nature, it appears evidently from experience that a man is of all sorts of luggage the most difficult to be transported' (Smith 1937 [1776]: 75).

   In his highly optimistic treatment of *occupational* mobility Smith apparently believed that this observation was irrelevant. (This problem is mentioned by Francis A. Walker, 1876: 193.) The equalization process whereby money-wage differentials compensate for subjective evaluations of work and other non-monetary characteristics attached to each occupation requires of course the assumption of 'mobility', or rather *enough* mobility to meet the conditions of net equalization without creating chaos. Some degree of inertia and of attachment to locality relating to the risk and cost of moving must exist. Yet Smith's references to geographical immobility imply a degree of inertia in *excess* of this required amount.

   Insofar as Smith was writing a 'tract for the times' his position may be understood as calling for the removal of the *grossest* institutional impediments to mobility first. Remaining obstacles would be of relatively smaller significance and could be dealt with afterwards.

4 From *Outline of a Work Entitled Pauper Management Improved* (1797). It is also to be noted that in his exhaustive classification of types of unemployed Bentham did not consider the class of workers displaced by changing techniques as being in any danger of permanent unemployment. See *Situation and Relief of the Poor* (1797) in Bentham 1962, VIII: 361 ff. This may, however, be because of

the training which would be acquired whilst in the industry house. For a fuller discussion see note 11 below.

5 One difference which may be important between Smith and McCulloch is that whereas the latter apparently presumes some initial skill in discussing the ease of transferring to other occupations, Smith plays down the problems involved even in the first acquisition of a skill.

6 Unionization was stressed as a cause contributing to the long-run depressed state of hand-loom workers. Displaced workers were unable to transfer to other industries because of the exclusive behaviour of unions elsewhere (Parliamentary Papers 1841: 38).

   In 1837 the Board of Trade had actually established a school of design 'but little interest was taken in providing theoretical instruction in subjects connected with industry and manufactures' (Woodward 1946: 480–1).

7 The government would establish parish schools. But the teacher would be paid only in part from public funds. Fees would be charged to assure against the 'dereliction of his duty'.

8 'Education' (probably written in 1818), in Supplement to Encyclopaedia Britannica, 5th edn, edited by Macvey Napier; reprinted in F. A. Cavenagh (ed.) 1931. Yet Mill concludes the discussion on a note of uncertainty: 'Into the details, however, of the best mode of teaching, to the working people, the arts by which the different commodities useful or agreeable to man are provided, we cannot possibly enter.' His opposition to intervention may, in fact, represent the specific hostility to the contemporary apprenticeship laws.

   James Mill, Bentham, Ricardo and other classical economists, it is well known, were much in favour of the various 'mechanics' institutions' that were being established during the early nineteenth century. See for example Adamson 1925: 27 ff.; and Woodward 1946: 474 ff.

9 Mill was by no means unique in his call for state subsidization of basic scientific research. For example, J. B. Say made a similar plea:

Thus, none but elementary and abstract science, – the highest and the lowest branches of knowledge, are so much less favoured in the natural course of things, and so little stimulated by the competition of demand, as to require the aid of that authority, which is created purposely to watch over the public interests. . . .
   I would not be understood to find fault with public establishments for purposes of education, in other branches than those I have been describing. . . . But care must be taken, that encouragement of one branch shall not operate to discourage another. This is the general mischief of premiums awarded by the public.

(J. B. Say 1964 [1880]: 437)

   An equally strong argument is also to be found in Charles Babbage 1963 [1835]: 380.

10 Mill here supports the view of the Schools Enquiry Commission of 1867–8. Post-elementary schooling of 'deserving' working-class students would be supported by scholarships financed out of private endowments, but administered under state control (Mill (1967) [1869]: 626–7). The references to post-elementary schooling are to secondary and university schools, and not to vocational training. It should be borne in mind that Mill very strongly believed that universities were not to provide professional training. (See, for example, his Inaugural Address at St. Andrews, Mill 1984 [1867], XXI: 218.)
   Mill adds that endowments might similarly be used to subsidize university

professors in subjects otherwise neglected, such as comparative philology, history and 'the highest branches of almost all sciences, even physical' (1967 [1869]: 628).

11   The position of Bentham with respect to intervention in technical training is of particular interest since he is regarded as an interventionist *par excellence* in matters of education. (Cf. Hutchison 1956: 'There should be', in Bentham's view, 'government activity in everything connected with the propagation of knowledge – universities, schools, agricultural and scientific research and the collection of statistics.')

It is true that he was strongly in favour of general education at public expense. Attention was devoted particularly to the broad social benefits of extended elementary education. See for example *Principles of Penal Law*: 'But in regarding education as an indirect mode of preventing offences, it requires an essential reform. The most neglected class must become the principal object of care. The less parents are able to discharge this duty, the more necessary is it for government to fulfil it' (Bentham 1962, I:570). But his view on intervention in the provision of skills is not so clear.

Bentham was in fact strongly opposed to the clause in Pitt's proposed bill on the poor laws (introduced in 1796) which would have allowed for the payment by the government of the apprenticeship fees of some of the poor. See *Observations on the Poor Bill* (1797) in Bentham 1962, VIII: 452 ff. The reasoning, however, is difficult to appreciate. Such intervention, Bentham argued, would *not* reduce monopoly earnings in skilled trades since labourers hitherto protected would merely be displaced; there would be no net addition to the supply of skilled labour.

This argument is all the more extraordinary since he was in favour of the formal training of (non-adult) paupers in vocational skills within the context of his plan for a National Charity Company (*Pauper Management Improved*, Bentham 1962, VIII: 369 ff.). One of the objectives of such training was precisely to permit pauper children to rise in the social scale upon entry into the labour market. In fact the Company would even be given 'powers for apprehending non-adults of diverse descriptions, being without prospect of honest education, and causing them to be bound to the company in quality of apprentices' (370). More generally, amongst the advantages of providing apprenticeship in the industry houses under Company control would be 'to the child instruction, intellectual, moral, and religious; inbred habits of systematical frugality – certain security from vice and criminality – certainty of employment during the apprenticeship, and even afterwards – chance of promotion to rank and affluence' (385).

Adults, too, would be given help both formally and informally in the acquisition of technical skills. Thus, for example, even self-maintaining poor might be permitted to attend the formal lessons given to internee apprentices and others as auditors. Techniques learned in the industry houses by habitual practice might be communicated to outsiders 'by courses of instruction'. And special courses to outsiders might be given, possibly for 'a small fee' in the case of the 'superior classes but free for others'. In fact Bentham implies that such instruction might be able to replace the contemporary apprenticeship system in some trades:

A system of instruction being thus provided, and rendered universally accessible, the having partaken of the benefit of it might be rendered a condition necessary to the faculty of practicing anywhere in the character of a *farrier*. This might be accomplished, in the instance of this occupation, without private hardship, or public expense; which, in regard to occupations in general, has been so vainly aimed at, and at the expense of such an enormous mass of hardship, by the *statute of apprenticeships.*

(Bentham 1962, VIII: 427–8)

In these proposals there is no repetition of the objection to Pitt's clause in favour of government subsidization of apprentice fees, namely that there would result no net increase in the supply of skilled labour. Although we cannot explain the latter argument, several reasons can be suggested for the opposition to government subsidies despite his support of such activity by the National Charity Company. In the first place he was extremely hostile to the contemporary apprentice laws 'against which many have protested, and for which nobody has ever pretended to find a use' (401); government subsidies would merely shore up the system.

Second, at least at this stage of his thinking, he had no confidence in direct government intervention either in the labour or in other markets. For example, he wrote that it is only in the provision of information services regarding market opportunities 'that government can occupy itself, to any good effect, either in raising, sinking, or steadying prices: operating not by the *creation* of inducements, but by bringing into *notice* inducements which spring of themselves from other sources' (400n). By contrast, the National Charity Company was to be a private joint-stock company after the manner of the Bank of England or the East-India Company (although there would also be some initial reliance for finance upon local poor rates), and great things were expected from this profit-seeking enterprise, which would, incidentally, be under government inspection (369). But the fact is, as Bentham himself admitted, that the full implications of the proposal with regard to the training of the young had not been thought through. These aspects of his proposal would depend upon a broader investigation of the problem of pauper education which had yet to be made: 'An inquiry concerning the best method of providing for the non-adult classes of the pauper population coming under the management of the proposed Company . . . requires for its answer a complete plan of education, adapted to this numerous division of the community' (395).

12 It has been suggested that McCulloch was exceptional among the classical economists in relating education to economic growth. Cf. West 1965: 119. This evaluation appears to be much exaggerated as we shall see.

It has also become common in evaluating the classical theory of economic policy to talk of state intervention in elementary education as representing part of the construction of a 'framework' within which freedom of enterprise was to operate. Cf. Samuels 1966: 14 ff. This formulation may be misleading insofar as even intervention at the elementary level has widespread implications for labour productivity and mobility and hence for resource allocation in general.

13 It may be added that Senior also referred to the effect of elementary education upon 'security' and consequently upon wealth (reproduced from Lectures 1848–9, Senior 1928, I: 193 ff.).

14 The argument was, however, severely qualified. In unskilled trades there was little hope that the labour supply could be permanently reduced, since even women and children were able to enter at will from outside. The only solution in this class was to 'raise the condition of the whole body of labourers' (*loc. cit.*), referring perhaps to an easing of the pressure of excess population. It was in *skilled* trades, into which the unemployed cannot flood from outside, that elementary education was likely to be successful in reducing the labour supply.

15 A particularly important consequence was noted by James Mill who recognized

the increase in productivity which would result from entry into the labour market at a later age: 'With a view to the productive powers of their very labour, it is desirable that the animal frame should not be devoted to it before a certain age, before it has approached the point of maturity' (James Mill, in Cavenagh 1931: 62).

16 An equally full discussion of the purely economic effects of elementary schooling – including those on productivity and mobility – will be found in Fawcett 1871: 137 ff.

17 Misgivings regarding the extent of provision by the private school sector – even though aided in some cases by state grants – were expressed even more strongly in Mill's chapter 'Of the Grounds and Limits of the *Laisser-Faire* or Non-Interference Principle': 'The education provided in this country on the voluntary principle has of late been much discussed, that it is needless in this place to criticise it minutely, and I shall merely express my conviction, that even in quantity it is, and is likely to remain, altogether insufficient, while in quality, though with some slight tendency to improvement, it is never good except by some rare accident, and generally so bad as to be little more than nominal' (Mill 1965 [1848–71]: 949–50).

In the editions of 1848, 1849 and 1852, Mill accordingly called upon the government 'to supply the defect, by providing elementary schools'; in later editions the government was to 'supply the defect, by giving pecuniary support to elementary schools'. The object in both formulations was to make such schools 'accessible to all the children of the poor, either freely, or for a payment too inconsiderable to be felt'.

It has been argued in a recent paper that this depressing evaluation of the private system by J. S. Mill (which was made also by Senior) was – at least by the early 1860s – quite unjustified. The Royal Commission on Popular Education which reported in 1861 presented data showing that almost the entire population of children of elementary-school age was in fact provided for. This same paper implies too that the evaluation of poor quality in the private schools by Mill and Senior was unjustified. Cf. West 1964. West attributes the (unjustified) hostility to the private system of both Mill and Senior to their mistrust of parental freedom of choice in the matter of education, and their flirtation with some of the Benthamite preferences regarding educational methods.

Professor West's argument is not convincing. It is frequently argued in social histories that the Royal Commission grossly underrated the deficiencies of the educational system. The true state of affairs came to light only after the passage of the Forster Act in 1871. See, for example, Adams 1882, 179 ff.; Adamson 1919, 303 ff.; and Woodward 1946: 462. West brings no substantial evidence to counter these evaluations. Indeed Robert Lowe – who receives such an excellent press in West's paper – made it quite clear in a parliamentary debate that he did not take the data offered by the Royal Commission seriously: 'It would be paying too great a compliment to those figures to base any calculation on them' (quoted in Adams 1882: 182).

Furthermore, whatever might have been the Benthamite predilections of Senior and J. S. Mill, we also have the very strong criticism by McCulloch of the system, as late as in 1864, three years after the Royal Commission had presented its evidence:

It is now, indeed, very generally acknowledged, that the providing of elementary instruction, for all classes of its subjects is one of the most pressing duties of government; and during the last half-century, and especially since the termination of the late French war, some of the principal Continental states have taken every means in their power to ensure the efficient discharge of this important duty. But except in Scotland, no plan of national education has been organized in any part of the United Kingdom. And though much has been done to supply this deficiency by benevolent individuals and societies, and more recently by government, a great deal remains to be accomplished, both as respects the diffusion of instruction, and the improvement of its quality.

(McCulloch 1965 [1864]: 396)

Thus 'statutory provision' was required for the education of the public. Moreover 'the public are entitled to superintend its own schools, to decide upon the qualification of the masters, and the species of instruction to be afforded to the pupils. But, in the case of private schools, these important matters are left to the discretion of irresponsible individuals; and the masters and the instruction may be alike deficient' (399). McCulloch did not call for the *immediate* establishment of a system of state schools because of the numerous administrative and religious difficulties which were in the way, but he did recommend an extension of the system of parliamentary grants supplemented by government inspection of all schools (401).

18 Immediately after stating the beneficial consequence of government intervention *in the past* in reducing monopoly returns in skilled trades, Mill gives the extract from Smith, referred to in the previous paragraph, to the effect that in certain professions an inadequate return had been generated. Of itself the use of this extract by Mill cannot be regarded as 'proof' that he was prepared to accept Smith's argument. It may merely be the case that he found Smith's exposition of the general principle that returns would tend to decline with government intervention very clear. Nonetheless, the fact remains that Mill did not go on to argue that governments should aid in the acquisition of skills.

19 In the fifth edition of 1862 and thereafter. Subtle changes of emphasis are to be noted between editions. In the first and second editions (1848 and 1849) Mill stated categorically: 'I find it impossible to wish, in the present state of the general habits of the people, that no such combinations existed' (397n). In the third and fourth editions (1852 and 1857) Mill was less certain that unions are to be justified:

The time, however, is past when the friends of human improvement can look with complacency on the attempts of small sections of the community, whether belonging to the labouring or any other class, to organize a separate class interest in antagonism to the general body of labourers, and to protect that interest by shutting out, even if only by a moral compulsion, all competitors from their more highly paid department. The mass of the people are no longer to be thrown out of the account, as too hopelessly brutal to be capable of benefiting themselves by any opening made for them, and sure only, if admitted into competition, to lower others to their own level.

(Mill 1965 [1848–71]: 397n)

A similar change in emphasis appears towards the close of the book. In 1848 and 1849 Mill stated: 'Combinations to keep up wages are therefore not only permissible, but useful, whenever really calculated to have that effect' (931n), namely of protecting a group against population pressure exerted by the masses who are excluded. Thereafter, there seems to be greater doubt: 'If, therefore, no improvement were to be hoped for in the general circumstances of the working classes, the success of a portion of them, however small, in keeping their wages by combination above the market rate, would be wholly a matter of satisfaction. But when the elevation of the character and condition of the entire body has at last become a thing not beyond the reach of rational effort, it is time that the better paid classes of skilled artisans should seek their own advantage in common with, and not by the exclusion of, their fellow-labourers' (Mill 1965 [1848–71]: 931). The changes in emphasis reflect greater optimism regarding the progress of population restraint.

20 'Classical Economic Views of the Role of the State in Victorian Education: Comment', *The Southern Economic Journal*, 35, 4, April 1969.

REFERENCES

Adams, Francis (1882) *History of the Elementary School Contest in England*, London: Chapman and Hall.

Adamson, J. W. (1919) *A Short History of Education*, Cambridge: Cambridge University Press.

—— (1925) *An Outline of English Education, 1760–1902*, Cambridge: Cambridge University Press.

Babbage, Charles (1963) [1835] *On the Economy of Machinery and Manufactures*, London, 1835; New York, 1963: Augustus M. Kelley.

Bentham, Jeremy (1962) *The Works of Jeremy Bentham*, ed. John Bowring, 1838–43, New York: Russell and Russell.

Cavenagh, F. A. (ed.) (1931) *James and John Stuart Mill on Education*, Cambridge: Cambridge University Press.

Fawcett, Henry (1871) *Pauperism: Its Causes and Remedies*, London: Macmillan.

Hutchison, T. W. (1956) 'Bentham as an Economist', *Economic Journal*, 66 (June): 288–306.

McCulloch, J. R. (1965) [1864] *Principles of Political Economy*, 5th edn [1865], New York: Augustus M. Kelley.

Mill, James (1818) 'Education' in Supplement to *Encyclopaedia Britannica*, 5th edn, Macvey Napier (ed.); reprinted in Cavenagh 1931.

Mill, J. S. (1965) [1848–71] *Principles of Political Economy, Collected Works*, II, III, Toronto: University of Toronto Press.

—— (1967) [1869] 'Endowments', *Fortnightly Review*, n.s. V, April 1869: 377–90; in *Essays on Economics and Society, Collected Works*, V, Toronto, 613–29.

—— (1984) [1867] 'Inaugural Address Delivered to the University of St Andrews', in *Essays on Equality, Law, and Education, Collected Works*, XXI, Toronto, 215–57.

Miller, William L. (1966) 'The Economics of Education in English Classical Economics', *Southern Economic Journal*, 32 (January): 294–309.

Parliamentary Papers (1834) 'Report of the Royal Commission of Inquiry into the Administration and Practical Operation of the Poor Laws', XXVII–XXXIX.

—— (1841) 'Report of the Royal Commission on the Hand-Loom Weavers', X.

Samuels, Warren J. (1966) *The Classical Theory of Economic Policy*, Cleveland, Ohio: World Publishing Co.

Say, J. B. (1964) [1880] *Treatise on Political Economy*, Philadelphia, 1880; New York, 1964: Augustus M. Kelley.

Senior, N. W. (1928) *Industrial Efficiency and Social Economy*, ed. S. Leon Levy, New York: Henry Holt.

Smith, Adam (1937) [1776] *The Wealth of Nations*, New York: Modern Library.

Walker, Francis A. (1876) *The Wages Question*, New York: Henry Holt.

West, E. G. (1964) 'Private versus Public Education: A Classical Economic Dispute', *Journal of Political Economy*, 30 (October): 464–75.

—— (1965) *Education and the State: A Study in Political Economy*, London: The Institute of Economic Affairs.

—— (1967) 'Tom Paine's Voucher Scheme for Public Education', *Southern Economic Journal*, 33 (January): 378–82.

—— (1969) 'Classical Economic Views of the Role of the State in Victorian Education: Comment', *The Southern Economic Journal*, 35,4 (April).

Woodward, E. L. (1946) *The Age of Reform, 1816–1870*, Oxford: Clarendon Press.

Part III

ADAM SMITH

THE HISTORICAL DIMENSION OF THE *WEALTH OF NATIONS**

I. ECONOMIC THEORY AND HISTORY

Since the publication of the *Principles of Political Economy* in 1817 it has been common to read of a sharp breakaway by Ricardo from Smithian methodology. An early statement of the contrast discerned is by Simonde de Sismondi who compared Smith's view of political economy as *'une science d'expérience'* with Ricardo's speculations (1951 [1827], I: 69–70). Statements to much the same effect appear in two important new works on classical economics – Sowell 1974: 113–14 and O'Brien 1975: 67.[1]

The presumed contrast between Smithian and Ricardian procedures is frequently related to Smith's place within the Scottish Historical School – that group of historians which includes Adam Ferguson, William Robertson, and John Millar – whose members, it is said, 'were concerned to base their social and economic generalizations on firm historical facts, and were opposed to abstract speculation and conjecture' (O'Brien 1975: 66–7).[2] More generally, it has been observed that 'the idea of the progress of society can be described as the historical frame of reference of the *Wealth of Nations*' (Forbes 1954: 648).[3] There is no comparable dimension in Ricardo's *Principles*.

On our reading of the primary literature, the sharp contrast between a Smithian empirico-historical approach and a Ricardian hypothetico-deductive approach is invalid. Ricardo's procedures were derived from a pattern formulated by Smith.

Smith's main object in the *Wealth of Nations* was the formulation of a reform programme on the basis of an analytical model of the operation of a capitalist exchange economy. More specifically, he wished to demonstrate the adverse effects upon development of distortions in resource allocation due to a variety of contemporary policies and institutions which remained in force

---

* A longer version of this paper, entitled 'The Wealth of Nations: Foundation of Classical (Ricardian) Economics', was read at the meetings of the Royal Society of Canada, Quebec City, 8 June 1976. An earlier version was prepared for the Harry Girvetz Memorial Lecture Series on Adam Smith, the University of California (Santa Barbara), 29 January 1976.

without the justification they might once have had. At the same time he isolated contemporary institutions which had a favourable effect on growth. The understanding of the origins of such institutions could only be appreciated in terms of an historical account, and here we discern a fundamental function of the historical dimension of the *Wealth of Nations*. Smith engaged not merely in description of the historical record, as he understood it – particularly the transition from an agricultural system (entailing a *service* nexus) to a mixed system (entailing a *money* nexus) – but also in interpretation. Both the theme and the principles involved in its interpretation, namely a materialist conception of history and a general notion of the temporal priority of agriculture over commerce during the course of 'normal' development, were characteristic of the Scottish historical literature. But two points require emphasis: The historical analysis is best viewed as a digression, for the recommendations for the reform of actual institutions and policies – the statement of which constitutes the prime objective of the *Wealth of Nations* – are based upon a rather precise analytical model of the 'progress of society' applicable to a competitive capitalist exchange economy. The model of development utilized in this context is a classic example of hypothetico-deductive theorizing and cries out for mathematical formulation. (A second prime example of such method in the *Wealth of Nations* is the theory of value and distribution, which is in some respects even more important from the point of view of its influence on nineteenth-century thought.) At the same time it must be emphasized that, in any event, there is no *clash* between the stadial sequence discerned by the Scottish Historical School – aspects of which are to be found in the *Wealth of Nations* – and that which is entailed in the Smithian analytical model, although the latter is designed for the analysis of economic process in the final 'stage' and stands on its own feet independently of the Scottish procedures.[4]

Inquiry into the origins of contemporary institutional arrangements was one major function of the historical investigation in the *Wealth of Nations*. A second function concerns the behavioural axiom. The theoretical models of the *Wealth of Nations* were based squarely on the behavioural assumptions characterizing 'economic man', for the proposition that self-interest is the governing motive throughout time and space as far as concerns man in his economic affairs is Smith's fundamental *axiom*. But the scope for the various constituent elements incorporated within 'self-interested' motivation varies considerably according to the institutional framework, and for this proposition Smith sought evidence from the record. Smith went to great lengths to build up, from both contemporary and historical evidence, the self-interested patterns of behaviour for which there is scope in a capitalist exchange society. The essence of his position turns upon an environmental approach to behaviour and this too is characteristic of the Scottish historians. The effort to provide a sound empirical basis for at least certain aspects of the premise can be easily documented.

In what follows we develop in some detail the nature of the historical dimension of the *Wealth of Nations*. Particular attention will be paid to the perspectives characteristic of the Scottish Historical School. The basis for Smith's premise of self-interest is discussed by the present author elsewhere, (see essay 8).

II. THE HISTORICAL DIMENSION

Two of the fundamental propositions which have been discerned in the literature as common to the Scottish Historical School are that the 'mode of subsistence' existing at any time determines the legal and institutional framework; and that there exists a causal connection between property relationships and the nature and degree of government authority. These propositions combined with a standard position regarding the 'uniformity of the human constitution' – in which 'self-love' coupled with an environmental approach to behaviour plays a large role – were applied in an investigation of historical progress. The focus of the investigation was the nature of social progress, envisaged as a process of development of the productive forces through four main stages – an initial primitive stage of hunting, succeeded by stages of pasturage, agriculture, and commerce (the exchange economy) – generating a process of constant change in civil society.[5]

There is much new evidence regarding the extent of Smith's contribution to the historico-sociological tradition.[6] Nevertheless, although it is true that characteristics of the 'Scottish' approach may be detected in the *Wealth of Nations*, and in some specific contexts are even the focus of attention, the work as a whole is not governed by the tradition.[7]

In the first place, the transfer from a simple or 'rude' to a complex or 'civilized' economy involving private property in land and the accumulation of stock is at key junctures glossed over. This approach does not suggest a keen interest in the early stages of the Scottish developmental sequence. For example, it is sometimes implied that the advantages of specialization, and the necessary capital accumulation to support division of labour, were potentially available in the simple economy: 'Had this [simple] state continued, the wages of labour would have augmented with all those improvements in its productive powers, to which the division of labour gives occasion' (Smith 1937 [1776]: 64). At the same time Smith asserts that 'this original state of things, in which the labourer enjoyed the whole produce of his own labour . . . was at an end . . . long before the most considerable improvements were made in the productive powers of labour, and it would be to no purpose to trace further what might have been its effects upon the recompense or wages of labour' (65).[8] The early stage is rapidly passed over, and the nature of the transition is not examined carefully. Apart from the discussion in Book V, the notion of a hunting 'stage' is used largely as a *fiction* for analytical purposes rather than for its own sake as part of a treatment of historical development, and the key historical facts relating to the institution of wage labour dependent upon the capitalist employer – as distinct from self-employed or independent labour – are not brought conspicuously to the reader's attention. Thus the fundamental fact, noted by Smith in Book I, that 'in every part of Europe, twenty workmen serve under a master for one that is independent' (66), is not accounted for, except perhaps by implication and this despite a rather harsh evaluation of the system (reminiscent of Josiah Tucker).[9] It would appear in fact that Smith's preoccupation was with the operation of an existing capitalist exchange economy – with the fourth stage, so to speak, of the stadial sequence or, more accurately, a late period (or even the 'final' period) of the fourth stage.[10]

Our conclusion is reinforced by reference to Book III itself, which is preoccupied with the transfer from an agricultural to an exchange economy, entailing the transition from a service nexus ('dependency'), wherein the authority of the dominant class derives from ownership of the means of subsistence, to a cash nexus ('independency'), a theme truly characteristic of the Historical School.

The temporal priority of agriculture, a theme consistent with the position of the Scottish historians, is justified briefly:

> As subsistence is, in the nature of things, prior to conveniency and luxury, so the industry which procures the former, must necessarily be prior to that which ministers to the latter. The cultivation and improvement of the country, therefore, which affords subsistence, must, necessarily, be prior to the increase of the town, which furnishes only the means of conveniency and luxury. It is the surplus produce of the country only, or what is over and above the maintenance of the cultivators, that constitutes the subsistence of the town, which can therefore increase only with the increase of this surplus produce. . . . If human institutions had never thwarted those natural inclinations, the towns could no-where have increased beyond what the improvement and cultivation of the territory in which they were situated could support; till such time, at least, as the whole of that territory was completely cultivated and improved.
>
> According to the natural course of things, therefore, the greater part of the capital of every growing society is, first, directed to agriculture, afterwards to manufactures, and last of all to foreign commerce. This order of things is so very natural, that in every society that had any territory, it has always, I believe, been in some degree observed. Some of their lands must have been cultivated before any considerable towns could be established, and some sort of coarse industry of the manufacturing kind must have been carried on in those towns, before they could well think of employing themselves in foreign commerce.
>
> (Smith 1937 [1776]: 357, 360)

But what must also be noted of the above extracts is the insufficient ground-work they provide for the 'natural course of things'.[11] Smith does not spend much time laying out the basis for the normal stadial sequence, and we cannot be sure that he had in mind in the present context a well-founded theory of the progress of society.[12] In any event in Book III he was largely concerned with the actual historical record which entailed a distorted pattern of development and sought hypotheses to explain the record as he read it, as we shall now see.

The breakdown of feudalism entailing a master–slave relation, a primary issue in Book III, and the growth of a *métayer* system is accounted for largely in terms of the self-interested behaviour of landlords faced by altered objective conditions (rendering them increasingly unwilling to accept the inefficient slave system) coupled with pressure from the sovereign. The inefficiency of slave labour (compared with that of a *métayer* system) is in turn accounted for in terms of the effect of property ownership and income upon effort (356–7). A second fundamentally important historical phase is the transition from a *métayer* organization to one of tenant farming. While the share-cropper was induced to cultivate well with the stock provided by the landlord – in sharp contrast with the slave – it was not in his interest to save and invest his *own* capital since the landlord shared the produce (368).[13]

The change in objective circumstances with which landlords were faced, according to Smith's account, involved the growth of manufacturing and commerce in the towns where the system of 'villeinage and slavery' was initially abolished in consequence of the self-interested action of the sovereign who sought allies against the lords (377). Much is then made of the relatively rapid development of the towns in consequence of the effects of 'order and good government' upon effort (379).

The effect of the growth of manufactures and foreign commerce to which we have alluded was the creation of a market for agricultural produce in exchange for luxury goods. Landlords were now motivated to increase their rents by way of altered tenure systems even if it meant the surrender of some of their personal power: 'What all the violence of the feudal institutions could never have effected, the silent and insensible operation of foreign commerce and manufactures gradually brought about' (388). An institutional framework came into being wherein the great proprietors were 'insignificant', and 'a regular government was established in the country as well as in the city, nobody having sufficient power to disturb its operations in the one, any more than in the other' (390).[14]

Now the priority of the agricultural stage and the substitution of a cash for a service nexus – in effect the transition from the agricultural stage – is discussed by various members of the Scottish Historical School, such as John Millar, and also by Sir James Steuart. (Cf. Skinner 1965: 10f.) Nevertheless, the undermining of the authority of the great landlords by foreign commerce and manufactures is an insight attributed explicitly by Smith to

Hume alone.[15] Moreover, and this is the point that we wish to emphasize in particular, Smith's concern in the *Wealth of Nations* is with the distorted pattern of events which had occurred, that is to say the dependency of agricultural development upon the prior expansion of manufacturing and commerce, rather than the 'normal' relationship: 'It is thus that through the greater part of Europe the commerce and manufacture of cities, instead of being the effect, have been the cause and occasion of the improvement and cultivation of the country' (Smith 1937 [1776]: 392).[16] At least for Smith the progress of society was certainly not an inevitable one as is implied by some accounts of the Scottish tradition.[17] It will also be observed that much is made of the 'fortuitous' role played by individuals, particularly the 'sovereigns', in contributing to the distortion of the natural stadial order; there is, in brief, no simple one-way relation from the mode of subsistence to institutions and governmental forms.[18]

Furthermore, there is a very good deal of 'reading back' into the historical record patterns of behaviour envisaged in contemporary society thus belying to some extent accounts of the Historical School which emphasize a preoccupation with the 'real facts of history'. Despite the overwhelming significance of the breakdown of feudalism, Smith himself conceded that 'the time and manner . . . in which so important a revolution was brought about, is one of the most obscure points in modern history' (367).[19]

It is appropriate to refer at this point to Dugald Stewart's celebrated description of 'theoretical or conjectural history' (which is identified also with Hume's 'natural history' and the French 'histoire raisonnée'): 'When we cannot trace the process by which an event *has been* produced, it is often of importance to be able to shew how it *may have been* produced by natural causes. . . . [The] mind is not only to a certain degree satisfied, but a check is given to that indolent philosophy, which refers to a miracle, whatever appearances, both in the natural and moral worlds, it is unable to explain' (Stewart 1966 [1793]: 33–4).[20] Stewart's account may well be relevant as a description of Smith's procedures in Book III of the *Wealth of Nations*.[21]

Quite apart from the validity of the term 'conjectural' history as a description of Smith's Book III, the relative disinterest therein with the earlier stages of the Scottish stadial sequence and the preoccupation with the distorted pattern of development of the later stages imply that the incorporation of the materials into the *Wealth of Nations* was designed with an eye upon something other than the account of major historical transitions in terms of the standard stadial model. His objective is, in fact, clarified in an introductory note to the third and fourth books:

> In all the great countries of Europe, however, much good land still remains uncultivated, and the greater part of what is cultivated, is far from being improved to the degree of which it is capable. Agriculture, therefore, is almost every-where capable of absorbing a much greater

capital than has ever yet been employed in it. What circumstances in the policy of Europe have given the trades which are carried on in towns so great an advantage over that which is carried on in the country, that private persons frequently find it more for their advantage to employ their capitals in the most distant carrying trades of Asia and America, than in the improvement and cultivation of the most fertile fields in their own neighbourhood, I shall endeavour to explain at full length in the two following books.

(Smith 1937 [1776]: 355)

Smith thus chose to incorporate the historical materials of Book III – older than most of the *Wealth of Nations* – into his general study in order to throw light upon contemporary institutions. History had left its mark on the modern states of Europe: 'The manners and customs which the nature of their original government introduced, and which remained after that government was greatly altered, necessarily forced them into [an] unnatural and retrograde order' (360).

Smith had particularly harsh words for the law of primogeniture and the system of entails – archaic remnants of the feudal period – which encouraged the maintenance of great estates, the proprietors of which were notoriously poor improvers (361f.). The impediments constraining the creation of small estates had also reduced the supply of land offered for sale so that the price of land was extremely high – 'a monopoly price' (392–3).[22] In England itself the distortions were less severe. The security of long leases characteristic of the English system of tenant farming (the origins of which were explained at length as we have seen) and the independence and respect enjoyed by the class of farmers had profoundly influenced the national growth rate compared at least to that of Continental Europe: 'the laws and customs so favourable to yeomanry have perhaps contributed more to the present grandeur of England, than all their boasted regulations of commerce taken together' (369). But even in the English case, and certainly in the Scottish, there was much to be done to clear away the institutional debris. For example, while 'the common law of England . . . is said to abhor perpetuities, and they are accordingly more restricted there than in any other European monarchy . . . even England is not altogether without them. In Scotland, more than one-fifth, perhaps more than one-third part of the whole lands of the country, are at present supposed to be under strict entail' (363).[23] Thus, while British agriculture had 'no doubt' advanced since the reign of Elizabeth,[24] it had followed 'slowly, and at a distance, the more rapid progress of commerce and manufactures', and the cultivation of 'the far greater part' of the country remained 'much inferior to what it might be' (393). Yet agricultural progress might have been much slower: 'What would it have been, had the law given no direct encouragement to agriculture besides what arises indirectly from the progress of commerce, and had left the yeomanry in the same condition as in most other countries of Europe?' (394).

There is, we conclude, an historical dimension to the *Wealth of Nations* characteristic in some respects, although by no means all, of the Scottish Historical School. The historical work is interesting in its own right but – as far as concerns Smith's objectives in the *Wealth of Nations* – mainly because it strengthens the understanding of the contemporary exchange economy. This observation applies to the institutional arrangements which Smith fought to have disbanded and to those institutions which were favourable to growth, the roots of both of which were to be found in past ages. (It also applies, it may be shown, to the analysis of the relationship between the constant behavioural motive of 'self-interest' and the institutional and legal framework within which the 'economic man' operates.)

Yet once the basic framework relevant for a capitalist exchange system had been constructed, the historical scaffolding was no longer formally essential, and could be removed. We refer now to Smith's use of an analytical model of investment priorities over time in making his case for the abandonment of various institutional arrangements. This conclusion is further reinforced by the Smithian analysis of the theory of value-and-distribution as applied to contemporary policy issues. Here the historical dimension fades away completely. Nor is this surprising, for the Scottish historical writers had little to offer on the mechanisms at work within an already well-developed capitalist exchange economy.

III. THE FOUNDATION OF SMITH'S REFORM PROGRAMME

The model of investment priorities turns upon the fundamental proposition regarding profit-maximizing behaviour on the part of the capitalist ('the consideration of his own private profit') which Smith actually states, too hastily on his own grounds, to be 'the sole motive which determines the owner of any capital to employ it either in agriculture, in manufactures, or in some particular branch of the wholesale or retail trade' (Smith 1937 [1776]: 355).[25] It is precisely in this context that we find the most celebrated statements of the operation of economic man (and the consistency of private and public interests).[26] It is on the basis of this behavioural assumption regarding profit-maximizing motivation, taking for granted a capitalistic form of environment, combined with assumptions relating to the changes over time in the productive factor base (relating particularly to the land-labour and the capital-labour ratios), that Smith constructed his rather sophisticated theory of the secular pattern of development.[27] Smith's primary concern was, we believe, the economic development of contemporary Britain (defined in terms of real national income per capita), and his objective, it would appear, was to demonstrate that reliance upon the operation of the competitive mechanism of resource allocation, within a suitable institutional framework, would assure the maximization at any time of the national income generated by the community's resources. Society could thereby most effectively provide the means for a rapid rate of capital accumulation, and thus satisfactory living standards for the common people, and allow for the financing of government services. The argument proceeds in terms of a model of economic process, that is to say a mutually interdependent *system* of cause and effect relationships, appropriate for a capitalistic form of organization.[28] The analysis extends far beyond a demonstration of the non-chaotic nature of the competitive price mechanism in a static context for it encompasses the effects of differential factor proportions upon the pattern of activity and applies the principle to the issue of investment priorities *over time*. Smith's 'system' can thus be construed as a model of capitalistic economic process in a developmental context designed to elucidate the inter-relations between apparently disparate variables upon the basis of a small number of fundamental principles.

But the model was not devised for its own sake – although doubtless it satisfied an aesthetic taste – the *esprit de rationalité* of which so much is made in the 'Essay on Astronomy'. The model was used to interpret the observed differentials between the growth rates and patterns of resource allocation of the North American colonies and those of various European countries.[29] It also served for 'prediction' of the probable future course of American development under alternative Imperial regulations. The main function of the entire construct, however, was to provide an ideal pattern against which actual European and British progress could be measured, and thus to discern the steps required to correct divergencies from the norm. It is the analysis of investment patterns in an established exchange system characterized by capitalistic institutions which provides the model of the 'progress of society' used as the basis of the 'very violent attack . . . upon the whole commercial system of Great Britain', as Smith himself describes the *Wealth of Nations* (Scott 1965 [1937]: 283).[30]

We certainly do not intend to suggest that Smith contributed nothing in the *Wealth of Nations* to the 'materialist conception of history' characteristic of the Scottish School. His account of the breakdown of feudalism and the development of a 'commercial' system – the materials of Book III – rules out any such extreme position. Moreover, Book V is in part devoted to what Smith referred to as the general principles of law and government, and the revolutions they had undergone in different periods of society. Our proposition relates to the conceptual framework accounting for secular development patterns used as the basis for recommendations regarding policy reform, Smith's predominant concern. This is provided not by a structure such as the 'four stages' theory but by the model we have outlined above, which takes for granted capitalistic institutions and a fully developed exchange system, and proceeds to outline 'the natural progress of opulence' within such a framework.[31]

NOTES

1 For a detailed account of Smithian procedure along precisely these lines see Bittermann 1940, esp. 500–2. Bittermann maintains that 'Adam Smith's methodology was essentially empirical, deriving its inspiration from Newton and Hume, in contrast to the rationalistic method of the natural-law school of thought' (497). Also Sowell 1974:113–14.

2 See also Macfie 1967: 29–30. Here very great weight indeed is placed upon the philosophic, historical, and sociological dimensions of Smithian economics – a 'synthetic', in contrast to the modern or 'analytical', approach. Those writing in the Scottish tradition 'are not concerned with logical processes or sequences, or the framing of abstract hypotheses and their analysis to their utmost limits. They wish to build a truly balanced picture of social life as they found it and the force which controlled it', and Smith, in fact, devoted only a fraction of his *Wealth of Nations* to economic analysis as such (29–30). See also: 'The whole Scots sequence cleaves to actual events, to historical and institutional relations growing between them, and to individual experiences that support and develop the argument. But such individual factors do not lend themselves to mathematical or purely deductive logical treatment . . . the Scottish philosophical and the mathematical methods do not blend' (Macfie 1967: 23).

3 'The idea of the progress of society can be described as the historical frame of reference of the *Wealth of Nations* – a fact that seems to have been ignored in the long debate as to how far Smith's method is really deductive or empirical. This is especially clear not only in Book III (the natural progress of opulence), which as W. R. Scott has shown, is the oldest part of the *Wealth of Nations*, traceable back to the Edinburgh lectures, but also in Book V (revenue), in which Smith shows how the expense of defence, justice, public works and institutions, education etc. varies in the different stages of society' (Forbes 1954: 648).

4 There is no clash between Smithian economic method as here conceived and Smith's approach to the notion of the progress of society incorporated within the stadial conception in so far as the latter constitutes an effort to apply to history Newtonian methodology whereby we 'lay down certain principles, primary or proved, in the beginning, from whence we account for the several phenomena, connecting all together by the same chain'. Cf. Skinner 1975: 169. (Cf. also Coats 1975: 224–5.)

5 In this summary paragraph we rely largely upon the splendid accounts given by R. L. Meek and A. S. Skinner. Cf. Meek 1967: 34–50, 1971: 9–27; Skinner 1965: 1–22. See also Skinner 1975: 154f.

6 Meek's discussion of the 'Four Stages' theory draws upon a newly discovered set of student's notes taken of Smith's early Glasgow lectures (and emphasizes intellectual developments proceeding in France similar in many respects to those in Scotland). (Smith's early preoccupation with the progress of society is discussed by Cannan in his account of the lecture notes available to him. Cf. his Introduction to the *Wealth of Nations*, xxxii f.) The 'stages' theory, as here described, envisaged development 'as proceeding through four normally consecutive stages, each based on a particular mode of "subsistence" – viz., hunting, pasturage, agriculture, and commerce. To each stage there corresponded different ideas and institutions relating to property; to each there corresponded different ideas and institutions relating to government; and in relation to each, general statements could be made about the state of manners and morals, the social surplus, the legal system, the division of labour, etc.' (Meek 1971: 10).

Meek's account of the early lectures tends to confirm the weight given to the materialist conception of history in Dugald Stewart's memoir. For Stewart refers to a report of Smith's Glasgow lectures which emphasized his endeavour – following Montesquieu – 'to trace the gradual progress of jurisprudence, both public and private, from the rudest to the most refined ages, and to point out the effects of those arts which contribute to subsistence, and to the accumulation of property, in producing correspondent improvements or alterations in law and government. This important branch of his labours he also intended to give to the public; but this intention, which is mentioned in the conclusion of *The Theory of Moral Sentiments*, he did not live to fulfil' (Stewart 1966 [1793]: 12).

But the report of the lectures recorded by Stewart refers also to the *Wealth of Nations*: 'In the last part of his lectures, he examined those political regulations which are founded, not upon the principle of *justice*, but that of *expediency*, and which are calculated to increase the riches, the power, and the prosperity of a State. Under this view, he considered the political institutions relating to commerce, to finances, to ecclesiastical and military establishments. What he delivered on these subjects contained the substance of the work he afterwards published under the title of *An Inquiry into the Nature and Causes of the Wealth of Nations*.' In his Advertisement to the sixth (1790) edition of *The Theory of Moral Sentiments*, Smith himself refers to his promise in the first edition (1759) to make a study 'of the general principles of law and government, and the different revolutions they had undergone in the different ages and periods of society'. This task he had undertaken, he writes, in the *Wealth of Nations* as far as concerned policy, revenue and arms (but he had not achieved his objective in the matter of jurisprudence). See Rae 1965 [1895]: 426.

7 The point which we now emphasize is that the observations regarding the *Wealth of Nations* by Stewart, and Smith himself, discussed in the previous note, describe particular sections of Books III and V. (It is in Book V where the significant references to the first two 'stages' – those of hunting and pasturage and their determining influence on governmental forms – will be found. For a detailed textual account of the stages of hunting and pasturage as developed in Book V, see Skinner 1975: 156–8.) But the governing theme of the developmental process, in the book as a whole, runs along *different* lines.

8 Smith was by no means consistent regarding the proposition that it is only in the modern economy that the division of labour is applied thus necessitating capital advances (1937 [1776]: 259).

9 'Nothing can be more absurd, however, than to imagine that men in general should work less when they work for themselves, than when they work for other people. A poor independent workman will generally be more industrious than even a journeyman who works by the piece. The one enjoys the whole produce of his own industry the other shares it with his master. The one, in his separate independent state, is less liable to the temptations of bad company, which in large manufactories so frequently ruin the morals of the other' (Smith 1937 [1776]: 83–4).
It may also be noted that Smith had very little to say on the distinction between the *merchant* and the *capitalist employer of wage labour*.
There are, however, references in *Wealth of Nations*, Book III, chapter IV, to the 'dependency' of landless individuals upon the authority of a land-owning class controlling the means of subsistence, a topic to which we turn below. Thus the landowner is 'surrounded with a multitude of retainers and dependants, who having no other equivalent to give in return for their

subsistence . . . must obey him for the same reason that soldiers must obey the prince who pays them' (385). And a contrast is drawn between this form of dependency and the 'independency' of labourers in an exchange system. In this system although the wealthy consumer 'contributes to . . . the maintenance of them all, they are all more or less independent of him, because generally they can all be maintained without him' (389). See also the reference to 'our present sense of the word Freedom' (375).

10 Smith's general preoccupation with the analysis of the *capitalist* economy is emphasized in the accounts by Skinner (in his Introduction to the *Wealth of Nations*) 1970: 12, 42–3, 75–6; 1974: 6, 20; and 1975: 168. See also Meek 1965: 6–7; and 1976: 220.

A recent account of 'The Development of Adam Smith's Ideas on the Division of Labour' by Meek and Skinner (1973) provides further evidence to the same effect. For it would appear that Smith 'purged' the discussion of division of labour in Book I of the *Wealth of Nations* of various 'sociological' illustrations which appear in earlier formulations (1108n). In one *omitted* passage, indeed, 'Smith *explicitly* established a connection between mode of subsistence, size of community, and division of labour, illustrating the point in terms of three distinct economic types (hunting, pasturage, and agriculture)' (1109). The authors do not consider Smith's decision to omit the passage to be an improvement; be that as it may, the decision suggests that the themes were of secondary importance as far as concerns the *Wealth of Nations*.

11 Some complications inherent in the notion of agricultural priority are briefly alluded to in the following extract: 'The town, indeed, may not always derive its whole subsistence from the country in its neighbourhood, or even from the territory to which it belongs, but from very distant countries; and this, though it forms no exception from the general rule, has occasioned considerable variations in the progress of opulence in different ages and nations. . . . That order of things which necessity imposes in general, though not in every particular country, is, in every particular country, promoted by the natural inclinations of man' (Smith 1937 [1776]: 357).

12 In addition to the casual observations in the extracts given in our text, Smith refers to the relatively low risk supposedly attaching to agricultural investment – an observation which seems more appropriate for an advanced economy than for an economy such as that presumably characteristic of the early period with which he (formally) seems to have been dealing: 'Upon equal or near equal profits, most men will chuse to employ their capitals rather in the improvement and cultivation of land, than either in manufactures or in foreign trade. The man who employs his capital in land, has it more under his view and command, and his fortune is much less liable to accidents, than that of the trader' (357–8). Relevant also is the assertion that 'as to cultivate the ground was the original destination of man, so in every stage of his existence he seems to retain a predilection for this primitive employment', because of the non-monetary advantages of country life – the beauty of the countryside, the tranquility of mind promoted, the independency – doubtless introspective considerations which reflect also the good press for agriculture at the time. (The extracts appear to neglect the 'normal' stadial sequence which gives priority to the hunting and pasturage stages.)

13 Reference to capitalist farmers is here apparent, but nothing is said of the employment of wage labour.

14 In this context of 'economic determinism' we find a basic summary of the role of self-interest and the unintended consequences of self-interested behaviour

(Smith 1937 [1776]: 391–2). For a veritable catalogue of instances of what is called 'the law of the heterogeneity of ends' – the *unintended* consequences of behaviour – both in the *Wealth of Nations* and in other writers of the day, see Forbes 1954: 653–8.

15 Smith 1937 [1776]: 385: 'Mr. Hume is the only writer who, so far as I know, has hitherto taken note of it.' Skinner has observed that since Steuart, Ferguson, Millar, and Kames had all written to the same effect by 1776, Smith's citation of Hume alone 'provides further evidence as to the age of this section (Book III) of the work' (Skinner 1975: 165n).

It should, however, be noted that Smith left a role for the feudal law in the decline of the authority of the great landlords, for he envisaged it as attempting 'to moderate the authority of the great allodial lords'. But it was *insufficiently effective* (Smith 1937 [1776]: 388).

16 Cf. also:

But though this natural order of things must have taken place in some degree in every such society [that has any territory], it has, in all the modern states of Europe been, in many respects entirely inverted. The foreign commerce of some of their cities has introduced all their finer manufactures, or such as were fit for distant sale; and manufactures and foreign commerce together, have given birth to the principal improvements of agriculture. The manners and customs which the nature of their original government has introduced and which remained after that government was greatly altered, necessarily forced them into this unnatural and retrograde order.

(Smith 1937 [1776]: 360)

An observation by Dugald Stewart is also relevant: 'What the circumstances are, which, in modern Europe, have contributed to disturb this order of nature, and, in particular, to encourage the industry of towns, at the expense of that of the country, Mr Smith has investigated with great ingenuity, and in such a manner, as to throw much new light on the history of that state of society which prevails in this quarter of the globe' (Stewart 1966 [1793]: 60–1).

17 Skinner refers to the emphasis given by the Scottish historians 'to the historically inevitable development of productive forces' (1965: 7). In his introduction to the *Wealth of Nations* (1970), this notion is apparently attributed to Smith himself (40). But see Skinner 1975: 175, where reference is made to 'Smith's use of the economic stages' as 'general categories in terms of which the experience of different peoples can be interpreted rather than as templates to which that experience must be made to conform'. Cf. also Coats: 'Book III . . . is specifically designed to show how . . . the "natural" course of events has repeatedly been perverted or checked by human interference' (Coats 1975: 223; see also 232).

18 See Skinner 1975: 161, 162, 164, and 168 for a variety of references to *political* as distinct from *economic* determinants of institutional arrangements of various kinds which seem to belie the great emphasis placed elsewhere in his paper upon 'the almost Marxian reliance which is placed [by Smith] on economic forces' (155).

19 But see the discussion of various privileges granted to townspeople by the sovereign where we see Smith attempting to avoid purely 'conjectural' statements as far as possible: 'Whether such privileges had before been usually granted along with the freedom of trade, to particular burghers, as individuals, I know not, I reckon it not improbable that they were, though I cannot

produce any direct evidence of it. But however this may have been, the principal attributes of villanage and slavery being thus taken away from them, they
now, at least, became really free in our present sense of the word Freedom'
(375).

20 Cf. also the remarkable assertion: 'In most cases, it is of more importance to
ascertain the progress that is most simple, than the progress that is most agreeable to fact; for, paradoxical as the proposition may appear, it is certainly true,
that the real progress is not always the most natural. It may have been determined by particular accidents, which are not likely again to occur, and which
cannot be considered as forming any part of that general provision which
nature has made for the improvement of the race' (37).

21 Stewart, in point of fact, included Smith's discussions of Book III as falling
within the category of 'conjectural' history (1966 [1793]: 36). Some questions
have, however, been raised regarding the justice of Stewart's designation of the
method of the Scottish historians in the light of their formal adherence to the
principle of empirical evidence. Thus Meek objects that the Scottish school
'tried consciously to base itself on the study of concrete historical facts, in
opposition to the abstract speculation and conjecture (particularly with regard
to the so-called "state of nature") which had so often been employed in the
past' (Meek 1967: 38).

Meek also suggests (1976: 237–8) that Stewart did *not* have 'mainly in
mind' the four stages theory in his description of conjectural history but rather
what Meek refers to as 'Smith's theory of "the natural progress of opulence" –
the theory that capital is "naturally" directed first to agriculture, then to
manufacture, and finally to commerce. And as applied to *this* theory, what
Stewart says is perfectly true'. This suggestion is not totally convincing. There
is admittedly some ambiguity attaching to certain passages in Book III,
chapter I (cf. note 12, above), but the Book as a whole entails themes falling
within the range of the Scottish historical tradition, and, as remarked in our
text, there is evidence of a reading back of contemporary behaviour patterns
into the record.

22 If landed property were divided equally between the children of the owner,
then upon his death, much of the estate would be put on the market, and the
artificial scarcity in Europe somewhat reduced. The problem did not exist in
North America where 'uncultivated land' was available 'almost for nothing,
or at a price below the value of the natural produce; a thing impossible in
Europe, or, indeed, in any country where all lands have long been private
property'.

23 A further contemporary distortion was the monopoly granted to British
merchants in the colony trade. The effect, in the first instance, was an increase
in the rate of profit on *mercantile trade* which rendered investment in domestic
land improvement relatively unattractive. Moreover, the increase in the *average*
profit rate tended to keep up the interest rate to the detriment of landowners
by lowering the price of land relative to the rent yielded: 'The price of land in
proportion to the rent which it affords, the number of years purchase which is
commonly paid for it, necessarily falls as the rate of interest rises' (Smith 1937
[1776]: 577).

24 When the legislature began to be 'peculiarly attentive to the interests of
commerce and manufactures'.

25 See above, note 12, for the discussion of risk differentials which appears more
appropriate for the capitalist exchange economy than for the historical context
within which it appears.

26 Cf.:

> Every individual is continually exerting himself to find out the most advantageous employment of whatever capital he can command. It is his own advantage, indeed, and not that of the society which he has in view. But the study of his own advantage naturally, or rather necessarily leads him to prefer that employment which is most advantageous to society. . . . He generally, indeed, neither intends to promote the public interest, nor knows how much he is promoting it. By preferring the support of domestic to that of foreign industry, he intends only his own security; and by directing that industry in such a manner as its produce may be of the greatest value, he intends only his own gain, and he is in this, as in many other cases, led by an invisible hand to promote an end which was no part of his intention.
> (Smith 1937 [1776]: 421–3)

27 See my *Economics of Adam Smith* (Hollander 1973), chapter 10, for details of the model including the role of international trade theory therein.

28 While the theory of temporal investment priorities has not perhaps been sufficiently appreciated in the secondary literature, there is a good deal of emphasis upon the 'system-building' aspect of Smith's work in general terms. See, in particular, Letwin 1964: 227–8; J. H. Hollander 1966 [1928]: 19: 'But if the *Wealth of Nations* showed little trace of scientific self-consciousness, it was distinguished in a very high degree by the second and more notable characteristic of an epoch-making work – a body of principles setting forth the uniformities and sequences that obtain in the subject matter assembled. As against the detached solutions of monograph writers or the unfulfilled engagements of more ambitious projectors, Adam Smith visualized the broad extent of economic purpose and result and ventured interpretations of that which he saw or pictured.'

Jacob Viner has similarly observed that Smith's major contribution is his 'detailed and elaborate application to the wilderness of economic phenomena of the unifying concept of a co-ordinated and mutually interdependent system of cause and effect relationships which philosophers and theologians had already applied to the world in general. Smith's doctrine that economic phenomena were manifestations of an underlying order in nature, governed by natural forces, gave to English economics for the first time a definite trend toward logically consistent synthesis of economic relationships, toward "system-building" ' (Viner 1966 [1928]: 116–17).

The criticism by J. A. Schumpeter (1954: 184–5) to the effect that Smith's 'mental structure was up to mastering the unwieldy material that flowed from many sources and to subjecting it, with a strong hand, to a rule of a small number of coherent principles' would doubtless have been read as high praise indeed by Smith himself. For this is precisely a function of the scientist which he regarded to be quite essential as is clear, for example, from the following reference in the *Edinburgh Review* of 1755: 'It seems to be the peculiar talent of the French nation, to arrange every subject in that natural and simple order, which carries the attention, without any effort, along with it. The English seem to have employed themselves entirely in inventing, and to have disdained the more inglorious but not less useful labour of arranging and methodizing their discoveries, and of expressing them in the most simple and natural manner. There is not only no tolerable system of natural philosophy in the English language, but there is not even any tolerable system of any part of it' (Smith 1967: 18–19).

29 Similarly, that part of the model relating to secular changes within the agricultural sector itself is used to interpret contemporary and historical patterns of land use.

30 Dugald Stewart observed: 'To direct the policy of nations with respect to one most important class of its laws, those which form its system of Political Economy, is the great aim of Mr Smith's *Inquiry*. His object was "to ascertain the general principles of justice and of expediency, which ought to guide the institutions of legislators on these important articles" ' (Stewart 1966 [1793]: 56–7).

31 In his discussion of 'Adam Smith and the Mercantile System' (1975) Professor Coats sets out to reconsider Smith's 'account of the mercantile system in relation to his theory of history and politics and his view of long-run socio-economic development' (218). The attack on mercantilism should not be viewed, runs the argument, 'simply and solely as an analysis of impediments to the smooth functioning of the competitive market economy' but rather as 'an integral part of a larger system of moral, socio-philosophical, historical and political ideas' (221). Yet Charles Wilson is quoted approvingly to the effect that 'the arguments of *The Wealth of Nations* were the product of logic working upon material drawn from the observation of three relatively mature mercantile economies: those of England, France and Holland. They did not have the same appeal to those who were still concerned with the earlier stages of the transition from agrarian to mercantile economy' (235). And Coats concludes: Smith's 'protest was directed against a body of restrictive regulations which had long outgrown their usefulness in Britain; and it was backed by a powerful corpus of analysis, much of which has survived to this day' (236).

REFERENCES

Bittermann, Henry J. (1940) 'Adam Smith's Empiricism and the Law of Nature, I', *Journal of Political Economy*, 48 (August): 487–520.

Coats, A. W. (1975) 'Adam Smith and the Mercantile System', in A. S. Skinner and T. Wilson (eds), *Essays on Adam Smith*, Oxford: Clarendon Press, 218–36.

Forbes, Duncan (1954) ' "Scientific" Whiggism: Adam Smith and John Millar', *The Cambridge Journal*, 7 (August): 643–70.

Hollander, J. H. (1966) [1928] 'The Dawn of a Science', in J. M. Clark *et al.*, *Adam Smith, 1776–1926*, New York: Augustus M. Kelley, 1–21.

Hollander, Samuel (1973) *The Economics of Adam Smith, Studies in Classical Political Economy, Vol. I*, Toronto and Buffalo: University of Toronto Press.

Letwin, William (1964) *The Origins of Scientific Economics*, London: Methuen.

Macfie, A. L. (1967) *The Individual in Society*, London: George Allen and Unwin.

Meek, R. L. (1965) *The Rise and Fall of the Concept of the Economic Machine*, Leicester: University of Leicester Press.

—— (1967) 'The Scottish Contribution to Marxist Sociology', in *Economics and Ideology and Other Essays*, London: Chapman and Hall, 34–50.

—— (1971) 'Smith, Turgot, and the 'Four Stages' Theory', *History of Political Economy*, 3 (Spring): 9–27.

—— (1976) *Social Science and the Ignoble Savage*, Cambridge: Cambridge University Press.

Meek, R. L. and Skinner, A. S. (1973) 'The Development of Adam Smith's Ideas on the Division of Labour', *Economic Journal*, 83 (December): 1094–116.

O'Brien, D. P. (1975) *The Classical Economists*, Oxford: Clarendon Press.

Rae, John (1965) [1895] *Life of Adam Smith*, New York: Augustus M. Kelley.

Schumpeter, J. A. (1954) *History of Economic Analysis*, New York: Oxford University Press.

Scott, W. R. (1965) [1937] *Adam Smith as Student and Professor*, New York: Augustus M. Kelley.

de Sismondi, Simonde (1951) *Nouveaux Principes d'Economie Politique*, ed. G. Sotiroff, 2nd edn, 1827, Geneva: Edition Jeheber.

Skinner, Andrew S. (1965) 'Economics and History – the Scottish Enlightenment', *Scottish Journal of Political Economy*, 12 (February): 1–22.

—— (1970) 'Introduction' to the *Wealth of Nations*, Harmondsworth: Penguin Classics.

—— (1974) *Adam Smith and the Role of the State*, Glasgow: University of Glasgow Press.

—— (1975) 'Adam Smith: An Economic Interpretation of History', in A. S. Skinner and T. Wilson (eds) *Essays on Adam Smith*, Oxford: Clarendon Press, 154–78.

Smith, Adam (1937) [1776] *An Inquiry into the nature and causes of the Wealth of Nations*, New York: Modern Library.

—— (1967) *The Early Writings of Adam Smith*, ed. J. R. Lindgren, New York: Augustus M. Kelley.

—— (1976) *The Theory of Moral Sentiments*, ed. D. D. Raphael and A. L. Macfie, Oxford: Clarendon Press.

Sowell, Thomas (1974) *Classical Economics Reconsidered*, Princeton: Princeton University Press.

Stewart, Dugald (1966) [1793] *Biographical Memoir of Adam Smith*, ed. Sir W. Hamilton, Edinburgh, 1858; 1966, New York: Augustus M. Kelley.

Viner, Jacob (1966) [1928] 'Adam Smith and Laissez Faire', in J. M. Clark *et al.*, *Adam Smith, 1776–1926*, New York: Augustus M. Kelley, 116–55.

8

ADAM SMITH AND THE SELF-INTEREST AXIOM

I. INTRODUCTION

John Rae, in 1834, objected to *The Wealth of Nations* on the grounds that it constituted a totally unscientific work. Smithian procedure, as he saw it, was non-experimental *for Smith failed to justify empirically his axioms* (and this despite Bacon's earlier warning against the propensity to generalize from a few familiar notions, and indictment of such procedures as evidence of a disinterest in attaining 'a knowledge of nature') (Rae 1834: 334–5). Marshall took a more positive attitude towards Smithian procedure but it appears from the celebrated Appendix to the *Principles* on the history of economics that he greatly played down the 'inductive' dimension (1961 [1920]: 759n). According to Marshall's evaluation, history provided Smith with 'illustrations' and thus made his exposition more palatable, but close induction from the evidence played little part in his procedure. In particular, the basic behavioural assumptions are said to be purely *axiomatic* or, at the most, only supported by very casual observation.[1] Much the same view seems to have been taken by J. E. Cairnes who observed that 'when [Smith] has recourse to history, it is always in illustration or confirmation; he never makes it the basis of his doctrines. He first lays the foundation deep in the principles of human nature and the physical facts of the external world; the subsequent reference to historical events is merely in illustration of the mode in which the laws thus established operate' (1888: 114–15).[2] And Bagehot's assertion that Smith maintained *as a fact* that 'there was a Scotchman inside every man' on a feeble basis of evidence is well known (1911: 125–6).

In this essay we shall attempt to demonstrate that in fact Smith went to great lengths to build up, from both contemporary and historical evidence, the self-interested patterns of behaviour for which there is scope in a capitalist exchange society. The essence of his position turns upon an environmental approach to behaviour (characteristic of the Scottish historians as a whole). In brief, self-interest as the governing motive throughout time and space as far as concerns man in his economic affairs is indeed

Smith's fundamental axiom, but the scope for the various constituent elements incorporated within 'self-interested' motivation varies considerably according to the institutional framework, and for *this* proposition Smith sought evidence from the record. To set the stage, a word is in order regarding Smith's formal discussion of scientific systems.

II. ASPECTS OF SCIENTIFIC METHOD

In Smith's posthumously published *Essay on the History of Astronomy* much attention is paid to the derivation of the axioms or premises of 'systems', and also to the question of 'verification'. As far as concerns the gravitational premise of Newton's *Principia* Smith emphasized an aesthetic dimension, namely the *familiarity* of the principle involved: 'The superior genius and sagacity of Sir Isaac Newton . . . made the most happy, and, we may now say, the greatest and most admirable improvement that was ever made in philosophy, when he discovered, that he could join together the movements of the Planets by so familiar a principle of connection, which completely removed all the difficulties the imagination had hitherto felt in attending to them' (Smith 1967 [1795]: 100).[3] The general acceptability of a system hinged critically upon this quality which should not therefore be played down: 'We observe in general,' wrote Smith, 'that no system, how well soever in other respects supported, has ever been able to gain any general credit on the world, whose connecting principles were not such as were familiar to all mankind' (46).

But the general acceptability of the basic axiom is one matter,[4] and the discovery thereof quite another. At a general level Smith compares the process of discovery with one attending a play who imagines the back-stage machinery which might account for the visible movements on the stage, or to one who observing a card game seeks to work out from his observations the rules of play (41, 43). As far as concerns Newton's discovery Smith refers to an initial dissatisfaction with the ability of Descartian principles to account for Kepler's laws of planetary motion (99–100). The gravitational principle itself was derived by a process of logical deduction from the evidence (100).

Thus far the whole structure still remained at the hypothetical stage. But, Smith continues, 'having thus shown, that gravity might be the connecting principle which joined together the movements of the Planets, [Newton] endeavoured next to prove that it really was so' (100–1).[5] And here Smith introduces the matters of explanation and testing by prediction:

His principles, it must be acknowledged, have a degree of firmness and solidity that we should in vain look for in any other system. The most sceptical cannot avoid feeling this. They not only connect together most perfectly all the phaenomena of the Heavens, which had been observed before his time; but those also which the persevering industry and more perfect instruments of later Astronomers have made known to us have been either easily and immediately explained by the application of his principles, or have been explained in consequence of more laborious and accurate calculations from these principles, than had been instituted before.

(Smith 1967 [1795]: 108)[6]

Some examples may be briefly given: 'from mechanical principles [Newton] concluded, that, as the parts of the Earth must be more agitated by her diurnal revolution at the Equator, than at the Poles, they must necessarily be somewhat elevated at the first, and flattened at the second' – a 'prediction' confirmed by subsequent observation (103). On the basis of Newton's principles, Smith observed further, 'His followers have . . . ventured even to predict the returns of several [planets], particularly of one which is to make its appearance in 1758. We must wait for that time before we can determine, whether his philosophy corresponds as happily to this part of the system as to all the others' (106).[7]

There is every reason to believe that Smith retained his original position regarding scientific method throughout his later career.[8] In the *Wealth of Nations* we find the 'origins' of scientific investigation outlined, although briefly, along the same lines as in the 'history of astronomy'.[9] The nature of 'systems' is again raised in an excursion into 'conjectural history' regarding the development of ethics or moral philosophy. The following brief passage describes the early transition from *theory* to *science*:

> They might continue in this manner for a long time merely to multiply the number of those maxims of prudence and morality, without even attempting to arrange them in any very distinct or methodical order, much less to connect them together by one or more general principles, from which they were all deducible, like effects from their natural causes. The beauty of a systematical arrangement of different observations connected by a few common principles, was first seen in the rude essays of those ancient times towards a system of natural philosophy. Something of the same kind was afterwards attempted in morals. The maxims of common life were arranged in some methodical order, and connected together by a few common principles, in the same manner as they had attempted to arrange and connect the phenomena of nature. The science which pretends to investigate and explain those connecting principles, is what is properly called moral philosophy.
>
> (Smith 1937 [1776]: 724)[10]

And in the *Theory of Moral Sentiments* Smith once more uses the analogy between a system and a 'machine' and applies it to the case of social studies: 'Human society, when we contemplate it in a certain abstract and philosophical light, appears like a great, an immense machine, whose regular and harmonious movements produce a thousand agreeable effects' (Smith 1853 [1759–90]: 463–4).[11] We shall consider in what follows how Smith's own work in the *Wealth of Nations* compares with the foregoing conception of scientific method, with particular reference to the fundamental premise of self-interest.

III. SELF-INTEREST– A 'FAMILIAR' PREMISE

We have encountered in our discussion of Smith's approach towards Newtonian method an emphasis upon the requirement of 'familiarity' with the premises of a scientific system. There can be no doubt that the basic behavioural motivation of the *Wealth of Nations* – that of 'self-interest' – satisfied this condition. The recognition of the desire for 'profit' as a controlling motive in economic behaviour has an ancient history and both the mercantilist and philosophic literatures, including the Scottish historical literature, are replete with the assumption.[12] And Smith, as is clear from the *Theory of Moral Sentiments* had from an early stage adopted the assumption as a central element in his conception of motivation. There is no break between his two major works on this matter[13] and it will be helpful to have before us some aspects of the earlier statement.

The motive of 'self-love' is synonymous with that of 'prudence' and the virtue of prudence is defined in the following terms:

> The qualities most useful to ourselves are, first of all, superior reason and understanding, by which we are capable of discerning the remote consequences of all our actions, and of foreseeing the advantage or detriment which is likely to result from them; and, secondly, self-command, by which we are enabled to abstain from present pleasure or to endure present pain, in order to obtain a greater pleasure or to avoid a greater pain in some future time. In the union of those two qualities consists the virtue of prudence, of all the virtues that which is most useful to the individual.
>
> (Smith 1853 [1759–90]: 271–2)

The 'man of prudence' receives an excellent press, for the 'impartial spectator' approves of prudent behaviour.[14] Smith goes out of his way to reject those systems of thought which identify virtue with 'benevolence'. Thus Francis Hutcheson's *Inquiry Concerning Virtue* is criticized for failing to appreciate that 'regard to our own private happiness and interest . . . appear upon many occasions very laudable principles of action' (Smith 1853 [1759–90]: 445);[15] while conversely, 'carelessness and want of economy are universally disapproved of, not, however, as proceeding from a want of benevolence, but from a want of the proper attention to the objects of self-interest' (446).

Self-interested behaviour, Smith observes, is inherent 'in the very nature of our being'; there is therefore no reason for surprise at the common estimate which finds a central place for it in virtuous behaviour:

Though the standard by which casuists frequently determine what is right or wrong in human conduct be its tendency to the welfare or disorder of society, it does not follow that a regard to the welfare of society should be the sole virtuous motive of action, but only that, in any competition, it ought to cast the balance against all other motives.

Benevolence may, perhaps, be the sole principle of action in the Deity, and there are several not improbable arguments which tend to persuade us that it is so. It is not easy to conceive what other motive an independent and all-perfect Being, who stands in need of nothing external, and whose happiness is complete in himself, can act from. But whatever may be the case with the Deity, so imperfect a creature as man, the support of whose existence requires so many things external to him, must often act from many other motives. The condition of human nature were peculiarly hard if those affections which, by the very nature of our being, ought frequently to influence our conduct, could, upon no occasion, appear virtuous, or deserve esteem and commendation from any body.

(Smith 1853 [1759–90]: 446–7)

Now it cannot be positively ruled out that Smith introduced the 'economic man' into the *Wealth of Nations* as a deliberate abstraction for analytical purposes as did J. S. Mill (1967 [1836]: 326). But a much more likely interpretation is that which attributes to Smith concern with the 'entire man' *in the anonymous market place* where there is little scope for social sentiments.[16] In his inquiry regarding the economic order Smith adopts this motive force as the overwhelmingly most significant at work and there is little to suggest that he was devising a deliberate abstraction. It is a picture of *actual* behaviour that he believes he is portraying:

But man has almost constant occasion for the help of his brethren, and it is in vain for him to expect it from their benevolence only. He will be more likely to prevail if he can interest their self-love in his favour, and shew them that it is for their own advantage to do for him what he requires of them. Whoever offers to another a bargain of any kind, proposes to do this. Give me that which I want, and you shall have this which you want, is the meaning of every such offer; and it is in this manner that we obtain from one another the far greater part of those good offices which we stand in need of. It is not from the benevolence of the butcher, the brewer, or the baker, that we expect our dinner, but from their regard to their own interest. We address ourselves, not to their humanity but to their self-love, and never talk to them of our own necessities but of their advantages.

(Smith 1937 [1776]: 14)

Smith describes the division of labour at the very outset of the work as 'the necessary, though very slow and gradual, consequence of a certain propensity in human nature . . . the propensity to truck, barter, and exchange one thing for another'. It is not, he insisted, 'originally the effect of any human wisdom, which forsees and intends that general opulence to which it gives occasion'. Of this propensity he observes further that whether it 'be one of those original principles in human nature, of which no further account can be given; or whether, as seems more probable, it be the necessary consequence of the faculties of reason and speech, it belongs not to our present subject to enquire' (13). Nevertheless, despite this disclaimer Smith did contemplate further the origin of the propensity and this he found to lie partly at least in the perception on the part of each individual that by means of exchange his well-being is increased. This perception is attributed to the 'hunters and shepherds' of the very simplest form of human society: 'In a tribe of hunters or shepherds a particular person makes bows and arrows, for example, with more readiness and dexterity than any other. He frequently exchanges them for cattle or for venison with his companions; and he finds at last that he can in this manner get more cattle and venison, than if he himself went to the field to catch them. *From a regard to his own interest, therefore, the making of bows and arrows grows to be his chief business*' (15; emphasis added).[17] That individuals, even in primitive society, are motivated by self-interest in the narrow sense of wealth accumulation is taken for granted without question – and without evidence obviously on the grounds that the attribute is an immutable fact of nature.

IV. AN ENVIRONMENTAL APPROACH TO SELF-INTEREST

Smith's theoretical model was constructed on the basis of self-interested motivation, and the actual record was interpreted in such terms as we have seen. But it is quite clear that while 'self-interested' man of actual history is identified with the 'self-interested' man of the *theoretical* models of development and value-and-distribution – for Smith did not think in terms of a *fictitious* individual – the two categories should be distinguished in terms of the opportunities open to them. The economic man in history is an individual whose behaviour reflects self-love in *all* its possible manifestations; nothing is excluded (in trading relations) except actions designed to promote the well-being of others.[18] But while we are provided with a vantage point from which we may view and interpret actual behaviour, the maximand is very broad indeed. By contrast, the opportunities open for many of the manifestations of self-love are far fewer in the context of Smith's theoretical models. We touch now upon the constraints imposed by the environmental characteristics of capitalistic society. Smith went a considerable way towards defining the interrelationship between the environment and self-interested behaviour.[19] We shall give some illustrations in what follows.

The historical treatment of land-tenure arrangements yields some fundamental insights into the constraints imposed on various categories of self-interested behaviour by legal and institutional forms. According to Smith's account of feudalism, slavery had entailed the use of inefficient methods.[20] Smith concluded that *where the law permitted the institution*, masters were sometimes prepared to surrender profitability to the psychic pleasures derived from domineering, subject always to limits to how far the trade-off would be carried: 'The pride of man makes him love to domineer, and nothing mortifies him so much as to be obliged to condescend to persuade his inferiors. Wherever the law allows it, and the nature of the work can afford it, therefore, he will generally prefer the service of slaves to that of freemen' (Smith 1937 [1776]: 365). It should also be noted that the ability to finance 'pride' out of profits, was, Smith believed, partly at least due to the existence of monopoly and (by implication) could be thwarted by a competitive environment (157–8).

J. S. Mill laid down in describing his (fictitious) economic man 'the entire abstraction of every other human passion or motive' except for the 'desire of wealth', and two *antagonistic* principles – the 'aversion to labour', and the 'desire of the present enjoyment of costly indulgences'.[21] Now the first two 'motives' appear also in Smith's conception of the (whole) man in commercial activity. But the third does not. Indeed the reverse assumption is made the basis of an assertion, the significance of which it is difficult to exaggerate. It is a *savings propensity*, rather than the desire for the present consumption of 'costly indulgences' ('prodigality' or 'vanity' to use Smith's terms), which is given pride of place:

> With regard to profusion, the principle which prompts to expence, is the passion for present enjoyment; which, though sometimes violent and very difficult to be restrained, is in general only momentary and occasional. But the principle which prompts to save, is the desire of bettering our condition, a desire which, though generally calm and dispassionate, comes with us from the womb, and never leaves us till we go into the grave. In the whole interval which separates those two moments, there is scarce perhaps a single instant in which any man is so perfectly and completely satisfied with his situation, as to be without any wish of alteration or improvement of any kind. An augmentation of fortune is the means by which the greater part of men propose and wish to better their condition. It is the means the most vulgar and the most obvious; and the most likely way of augmenting their fortune, is to save and accumulate some part of what they acquire, either regularly and annually, or upon some extraordinary occasions. Though the principle of expence, therefore, prevails in

almost all men upon some occasions, and in some men upon almost all occasions, yet in the greater part of men, taking the whole course of their life at an average, the principle of frugality seems not only to predominate, but to predominate very greatly.

(Smith 1937 [1776]: 324–5)

The principle served as rationale for an identification of the rent of land and the interest on capital as far as concerns their respective supply prices. In effect, the notion of 'abstinence' as a pain cost is rejected by Smith (Hollander 1973, 167n).

Now the powerful propensity to save – 'the universal, continual, and uninterrupted effort to better their own condition' – is much strengthened by an appropriate legal framework: 'It is this effort, protected by law and allowed by liberty to exert itself in the manner that is most advantageous, which has maintained the progress of England towards opulence and improvement in almost all former times, and which, it is to be hoped, will do so in all future times' (Smith 1937 [1776]: 329).

An exception to the general rule regarding the propensity to save (and invest) emerges in the discussion of the behaviour characteristic of recipients of great fortunes – their desire for luxury consumption pushed to extreme (their 'vanity'). The point is made most clearly in a discussion of land improvement:

To improve land with profit, like all other commercial projects, requires an exact attention to small savings and small gains, of which a man born to a great fortune, even though naturally frugal, is very seldom capable. The situation of such a person naturally disposes him to attend rather to ornament which pleases his fancy, than to profit for which he has so little occasion. The elegance of his dress, of his equipage, of his house, and household furniture, are objects which from his infancy he has been accustomed to have some anxiety about. The turn of mind which this habit naturally forms, follows him when he comes to think of the improvement of land. He embellishes perhaps four or five hundred acres in the neighbourhood of his house, at ten times the expence which the land is worth after all his improvements; and finds that if he was to improve his whole estate in the same manner, and he has little taste for any other, he would be a bankrupt before he had finished the tenth part of it.

(Smith 1937 [1776]: 364)[22]

It is the small proprietor who is 'generally of all improvers the most industrious, the most intelligent, and the most successful' (392).[23] In 'commercial' societies, however, the propensity towards 'vanity' is likely to prove to be its own worst enemy:

In countries where a rich man can spend his revenue in no other way than by maintaining as many people as it can maintain, he is not apt to run out, and his benevolence it seems is seldom so violent as to attempt to maintain more than he can afford. But where he can spend the greatest revenue upon his own person, he frequently has no bounds to his expence, because he frequently has no bounds to his vanity, or to his affection for his own person. In commercial countries, therefore, riches, in spite of the most violent regulations of law to prevent their dissipation, very seldom remain long in the same family.

(Smith 1937 [1776]: 391)[24]

Accordingly, while there is scope for 'vanity' in commercial society, the great fortunes which are required to give it effect are likely to be threatened.

The environment is of fundamental import for the supply of effort. Let us recall the positive effects on effort of a framework of 'order and good government' and the legal protection of property (379, 365n respectively). But the magnitude of the wages paid are also of significance. In the *Lectures*, Smith relates crime and disorder to the 'corruption' of men by 'dependency', and this in turn to the lower earnings of labourers in menial service compared to those in commerce and manufactures: 'The establishment of commerce and manufactures, which brings about this independency, is the best police for preventing crimes. The common people have better wages in this way than in any other, and in consequence of this a general probity of manners takes place through the whole country. Nobody will be so mad as to expose himself upon the highway, when he can make better bread in an honest and industrious manner' (Smith 1896 [1763]: 155–6).[25] It is here very strongly implied that an increase in wages calls forth an increased supply of effort. This conception reappears in the *Wealth of Nations* where reference is made to the allocation of income between the productive and unproductive sectors:

The proportion between those different funds necessarily determines in every country the general character of the inhabitants as to industry or idleness. We are more industrious than our forefathers; because in the present times the funds destined for the maintenance of industry, are much greater in proportion to those which are likely to be employed in the maintenance of idleness, than they were two or three centuries ago. Our ancestors were idle for want of a sufficient encouragement to industry. It is better, says the proverb, to play for nothing, than to work for nothing.

(Smith 1937 [1776]: 319)[26]

The differential (self-interested) behaviour pattern of the two 'classes' of labourers is most conspicuous in the *Wealth of Nations*. In the context of the effect on consumption patterns of excise taxes imposed on luxury goods, Smith distinguishes between, on the one hand, 'the sober and industrious poor' – the productive workers – upon whom the taxes 'act as sumptuary laws, and dispose them either to moderate, or to refrain altogether from the use of superfluities which they can no longer easily afford'; and on the other, the 'dissolute and disorderly' – the menials – who 'might continue to indulge themselves in the use of such commodities after this rise of price in the same manner as before' (823). If we consider Smith's position as a whole it would appear that the generally low earnings of service labour generate 'irresponsible' behaviour which extends to consumption patterns.

In general terms it may be said that Smith recognized the possibility of dealing fruitfully with population in terms of conventional economic theory. This is clear from the account given of the very rapid growth rate of population in North America compared with that of Europe which Smith (partly) explained in terms of the high earnings which rendered 'the value of children . . . the greatest of all encouragements to marriage' (71). 'Labour is there so well rewarded that a numerous family of children, instead of being a burthen is a source of opulence and prosperity to the parents' (70). But the death rate – particularly the infantile death rate – is also relevant and thus the physical quality of the human stock. From this perspective much depended upon the consumption pattern – its allocation to wholesome foods, for example. The imposition of excise taxes, which *reduces* the real wage, might stimulate population growth to the extent that it encourages substitution against 'superfluities' (823–4). But such 'economising behaviour' is limited to the productive sector alone. Indeed the entire population reaction is largely applied to this sector.

Clearly environmental factors determine the range of relevant self-interested behaviour patterns. The self-interested man of Smithian economic theory, applicable largely to a capitalist exchange economy and assuming 'order and good government', is thus a rather carefully specified individual, who has limited opportunities for indulging his various tastes such as that for 'pride' – while 'vain' behaviour would be ultimately self-defeating – and who has a rather elastic (positively sloped) supply curve of effort.[27] But whence the *evidence?*

To some extent – and at a broad conceptual level – Smith's position was simply dictated by a variety of axiomatic presumptions including the initial axiom according to which benevolence is ruled out in trading relations. Thus, for example, if we assume with Smith that slave labour is inefficient labour (because of a lack of motivation towards effort), and also rule out benevolence, we arrive very easily at his celebrated interpretation of the decision of some slave holders to free their slaves: 'The planting of sugar and tobacco can afford the expence of slave cultivation. The raising of corn, it seems, in the present times, cannot. In the English colonies, of which the principal produce is corn, the far greater part of the work is done by freemen. The late resolution of the Quakers in Pennsylvania to set at liberty all their negro slaves, may satisfy us that their number cannot be very great.

Had they made any considerable part of their property, such a resolution could never have been agreed to' (Smith 1937 [1776]: 365–6).[28] Similarly, the same axioms and presumptions dictated the Smithian interpretation of the disintegration of feudalism.

But a considerable part of the picture describing self-interested man is drawn from observation. Here it is essential to emphasize the fact that the contemporary world provided so broad a spectrum of institutions and stages of development that a comparative study of behaviour was potentially most fruitful.[29] Smith worked wonders with the materials available. When combined with the notion of the 'uniformity of the human constitution' even over very long stretches of time, we are enabled to observe in this manner *historical* man.[30] We will give some illustrations of Smithian procedure.

It is clear that the geographical range from which Smith drew his observations was sufficient to convince him that 'national character' had little to do with behaviour patterns. The point appears particularly clearly in the Glasgow lectures of 1763:

> It remains now that we consider the last division of police, and show the influence of commerce on the manners of a people. Whenever commerce is introduced into any country probity and punctuality always accompany it. These virtues in a rude and barbarous country are almost unknown. Of all the nations in Europe, the Dutch, the most commercial, are the most faithful to their word. The English are more so than the Scotch, but much inferior to the Dutch, and in the remote parts of this country they [are] far less so than in the commercial parts of it. This is not at all to be imputed to national character, as some pretend; there is no natural reason why an Englishman or a Scotchman should not be as punctual in performing agreements as a Dutchman. It is far more reducible to self-interest, that general principle which regulates the actions of every man, and which leads men to act in a certain manner from views of advantage, and is as deeply implanted in an Englishman as a Dutchman.
>
> (Smith 1896 [1763]: 253)[31]

The attitude to work in a 'capitalist' – as distinct from a 'service' – environment is carefully illustrated from contemporary observation of the effect of high wages on behaviour. It is probable that Smith's assertions regarding the inefficiency of *slave* labour were partially drawn from such sources: 'In mercantile and manufacturing towns, where the inferior ranks of people are chiefly maintained by the employment of capital, they are in general industrious, sober, and thriving; as in many English, and in most Dutch towns. In those towns which are principally supported by the constant or occasional residence of a court, and in which the inferior ranks of people are chiefly maintained by the spending of revenue, they are in general idle, dissolute, and poor; as at Rome, Versailles, Compiegne, and Fontainbleau' (Smith 1937 [1776]: 319).[32]

Smith's conception of the proclivities of the great landed rentiers of which so much is made in the historical investigation is in large part drawn from observation of the contemporary world: 'There still remain in both parts of the united kingdom some great estates which have continued without interruption in the hands of the same family since the times of feudal anarchy. Compare the present condition of those estates with the possessions of the small proprietors in their neighbourhood, and you will require no other argument to convince you how unfavourable such extensive property is to improvement' (364). The habits of the merchant are similarly illustrated: 'Whoever has had the fortune to live in a mercantile town situated in an unimproved country, must have frequently observed how much more spirited the operations of merchants were in this way, than those of mere country gentlemen. The habits, besides, of order, economy and attention, to which mercantile business naturally forms a merchant, render him much fitter to execute, with profit and success, any project of improvement' (385).

We turn next to the assertions made regarding the savings propensity. Smith's position had much in common with that of other eighteenth-century writers who frequently took for granted that the total available supply of investible funds was determined by sociological and institutional factors rather than the rate of interest. But he relies also upon his reading of the historical and contemporary record:

> This frugality and good conduct, however, is upon most occasions, it appears from experience, sufficient to compensate, not only the private prodigality and misconduct of individuals, but the public extravagance of government. The uniform, constant, and uninterrupted effort of every man to better his condition, the principle from which public and national, as well as private opulence is originally derived, is frequently powerful enough to maintain the natural progress of things toward improvement, in spite both of the extravagance of government, and of the greatest errors of administration. Like the unknown principle of animal life, it frequently restores health and vigour to the constitution, in spite, not only of the disease, but of the absurd prescriptions of the doctor.
>
> (Smith 1937 [1776]: 326)

The evidence to which Smith refers relates to the (supposedly) rising capital stocks 'of almost all nations, in all tolerably quiet and peaceable times, even of those who have not enjoyed the most prudent and parsimonious governments' (327). The great care needed in drawing accurate inductions from the evidence is here alluded to.[33]

The same kind of approach is followed in support of the contention that 'imprudent' behaviour is the exception rather than the rule. Here direct reference is made to contemporary experience.[34]

Finally, we may illustrate Smith's 'inductive' procedures from the celebrated chapter on the wage structure, according to which 'every man's interest would prompt him to seek the advantageous, and to shun the disadvantageous employment' (99). While much work had already been accomplished on this issue (especially by Cantillon, Mandeville and Hume) Smith's own observations apparently enabled him to fill in further details of the general picture of self-interested behaviour. He himself refers to the five 'circumstances' which 'so far as I have been able to observe, make up for a small pecuniary gain in some employments, and counter-balance a great one in others'.[35]

V. CONCLUSION

It will be clear from our account that Smith went to great lengths to avoid establishing an economic 'system' upon purely 'hypothetical' axioms. He used the historical and contemporary records in a masterly fashion to define the manifestation of the 'familiar' behaviour axiom of self-interest – which excludes benevolence in the commercial sphere – in a capitalist exchange system.[36] In this regard he proceeded consistently with his evaluation of Newton's approach in the natural sciences (and it may be added in conformity with the recommendations of Hume and the Scottish historical writers).

Smith's admiration for Newtonian method carries over also to the *deductive* aspects of model building. His 'system' relating to the competitive mechanism of investment priorities over time and the theory of value-and-distribution, are outstanding examples of deductive theorizing of the type subsequently carried further by Ricardo. But when we turn to the *uses of theory* we must emphasize a significant divergence from 'Newtonian' procedure. To presume that we can fully appreciate Smith's method in economics by reference to his observations regarding ideal procedure in the early *Essay on Astronomy* is not justifiable. We refer to the fact that he had little confidence in testing procedures for the verification of the deductions drawn from economic models, in contrast to models in the natural sciences. In the last resort, the results derived would *inevitably* be 'conjectural inference'.

NOTES

1 The fundamentally significant contribution made by Smith, in Marshall's view, was to abstract theory: 'he was the first to make a careful and scientific inquiry into the manner in which value measures human motive, on the one side measuring the desire of purchasers to obtain wealth, and on the other the efforts and sacrifices (or "Real Cost of Production") undergone by its producers ... the advance made by him was so great that he really opened out this new point of view, and by so doing made an epoch' (Marshall 1961 [1920]: 758–9).

2 See also where Cairnes refers to the *intuitive* – as distinct from the *inductive* – foundation for the premises of political economy (1888: 88).

3 Similarly: 'The gravity of matter is, of all its qualities, after its inertness, that which is most familiar to us' (Smith 1967 [1795]: 107); the Newtonian system was 'the greatest discovery that ever was made by man, the discovery of an immense chain of the most important and sublime truths, all closely connected

together, by one capital fact, of the reality of which we have daily experience' (108). In his lectures on rhetoric Smith also alluded to the 'pleasure' which we see in 'the phenomena which we reckoned the most unaccountable, all deduced from some principle (commonly a well-known one) and all united in one chain, far superior to what we feel from the unconnected method, where everything is accounted for by itself, without any reference to the others' (Smith 1963 [1762–3]: 140).

4 In fact, Smith observes, there were simpler and even more 'familiar' premises such as that of Descartes which did not serve as well as that of gravity (1967 [1795]: 100).

5 A word is in order regarding the Newtonian dictum *'Hypotheses non fango'* ('I do not frame hypotheses'). His objection was to the 'rationalistic' method of deducing effects from *assumed a priori causes* for which there was no empirical support, as distinct from his own practice of deriving the gravitational principle by a mathematical demonstration of its effects. Moreover, the 'cause' of the properties of gravity was not necessarily essential to the exercise. (In the account given in the lectures on rhetoric Smith referred to the initial principles of a system as 'primary or proved'. It is possible that Smith had this matter in mind, himself adopting the Newtonian position.) On this general issue see Bitterman 1940; Baker 1975: 85n; and Hanson 1970.

Mention should also be made of David Hume's insistence upon the uselessness in social science, as in natural science, of abstract speculation and conjecture: 'Men are now cured of their passion for hypotheses and systems in natural philosophy, and will harken to no arguments but those which are derived from experience. It is full time they should attempt a like reformation in all moral disquisitions' (Hume 1898b [1751]: 174). See also Hume 1882 [1739–40]: 308. For a general discussion of Hume's methodology and procedures, see Rotwein 1955.

6 The 'principle' refers to 'the universality of gravity, and that it decreases as the squares of the distance increase' (Smith 1967 [1795]: 107).

7 On this the editors, Black and Hutton, remarked: 'It must be observed, that the whole of this Essay was written previous to the date here mentioned; and that the return of the comet happened agreeably to the prediction.'

A recent paper dealing with the Smithian approach to the natural sciences asserts that 'Smith judges a hypothesis by its ability to gain some sort of consensus' without providing 'any definite set of rules or logic by which to weigh an hypothesis' (Myers 1975: 284). This observation neglects Smith's very extensive discussion of the predictive accuracy of a model.

8 See on this matter Thomson 1965: 229–33.

9 The great phenomena of nature, the revolutions of the heavenly bodies, eclipses, comets; thunder, lightning, and other extraordinary meteors; the generation, the life, growth and dissolution of plants and animals; are objects which, as they necessarily excite the wonder, so they naturally call forth the curiosity, of mankind to enquire into their causes. Superstition first attempted to satisfy this curiosity, by referring all those wonderful appearances to the immediate agency of the gods. Philosophy afterwards endeavoured to account for them, from more familiar causes, or from such as mankind were better acquainted with, than the agency of the gods.

(Smith 1937 [1776]: 723–4)

10 Smith had harsh words for the irresponsibility of the early system builders, but saw the rise of logic as a corrective.

11 See the reference to 'the wheels of the political machine', Smith 1853 [1759–90]: 265.

12 On the mercantilist literature see Hollander 1973: 34n; and Viner 1960: 57.

For a view of self-interest in the work of Thomas Hobbes which emphasizes the wealth-seeking proclivity see Macpherson 1962: 9–159. It is particularly important to bear in mind that 'power', as defined by Hobbes, is sought after to assure the present means to a future flow of utilities. It is Macpherson's judgement that Hobbes drew from observation of his own society even when dealing with man in the state of nature.

The philosophic literature is discussed in a study of a variety of other writers in Myers 1972. See also the use of the assumption of self-love amongst writers of the Scottish Historical School in Skinner 1965: 5–6.

13 But for a recent argument to the contrary see Mini 1974: 78–9.

14 See Smith 1853 [1759–90]: 314:

In the steadiness of his industry and frugality, in his steadily sacrificing the ease and enjoyment of the present moment for the probable expectation of the still greater ease and enjoyment of a more distant but more lasting period of time, the prudent man is always both supported and rewarded by the entire approbation of the impartial spectator, and of the representative of the impartial spectator, the man within the breast. The impartial spectator does not feel himself worn out by the present labour of those whose conduct he surveys; nor does he feel himself solicited by the importunate calls of their present appetites. To him their present, and what is likely to be their future situation, are very nearly the same: he sees them nearly at the same distance, and is affected by them very nearly in the same manner: he knows, however, that to the persons principally concerned they are very far from being the same, and that they naturally effect *them* in a very different manner. He cannot, therefore, but approve, and even applaud, that proper exertion of self-command which enables them to act as if their present and their future situation affected them nearly in the same manner in which they affect him.

15 The passage continues: 'The habits of economy, industry, discretion, attention and application of thought, are generally supposed to be cultivated from self-interested motives, and at the same time are apprehended to be very praiseworthy qualities, which deserve the esteem and approbation of every body.' See also Smith 1853 [1759–90]: 385, 452.

16 See Jacob Viner:

In commercial activity the economic end fails to act in isolation only to the extent to which one party to an economic transaction concerns himself with the motives or welfare of the other. With the growing degree of impersonality this moral factor becomes negligible; and the economic transaction becomes non-moral in the sense that each party excludes the other from his moral situation. The parties may not know each other, may deal only through an intermediary, human or mechanical, and except for the plane of competition as dictated by the various relevant forms of social control neither is influenced by anything but his immediate economic end.

(Viner 1962: 114)

It is precisely this kind of conception which carries us a long way towards appreciating the intended scope of the *Wealth of Nations* compared to that of the *Theory of Moral Sentiments*.

The point is restated thus by Viner:

In his economic analysis Smith operates from the categorical premise that the economic relations between men are in effect fundamentally impersonal, anonymous, infinitely 'distant', so that the sentiments, with the one exception of 'justice', remain dormant, are not aroused into action. It would not be difficult to follow Smith in this respect when he is considering, for example, commercial transactions carried out by professional merchants of whom one, say, is resident in England and the other in Turkey, and the only communication between them is through equally anonymous intermediaries, or by mail. Smith, however, in his general treatment of the market, although often not when he is dealing with particular cases, writes as if he accepts as realistic the same psychological assumptions when he is considering the relationships of master and servant, landlord and tenant-farmer, employer and employee, as when he is discussing foreign trade.

(Viner 1972: 82)

For an alternative view, see Anspach 1972: 195–6.

17 It would thus appear that the exchanges which occur even in a society where there is very little specialization is a reflection of the 'propensity to truck', but it is reason – observation of the advantageous effects of this practice – that sets in motion a *full-fledged trend* towards specialization.

Professor Viner has observed that 'the important thing for the interpreter of Smith is to note how low down in this scale [of psychological traits] reason enters into the picture as a factor influencing social behaviour'. In the 'sub-rational area' including the apparatus of 'sentiments' Smith, Viner continues, 'perhaps even includes the psychological drives which lead man to engage in trade', as in his reference to the propensity to truck (Viner 1972: 78–9). Nevertheless, Viner concludes: 'That the propensity in its further development in man, its evolution into division of labour, operates with the aid of reason and calculation, Smith does not for a moment question' (80).

18 Smith firmly rejected the view that *all* human motivation can be reduced to self-love: 'That whole account of human nature, however, which deduces all sentiments and affections from self-love, which has made so much noise in the world, but which, so far as I know, has never yet been fully and distinctly explained, seems to me to have arisen from some confused misapprehension of the system of sympathy' (1853 [1759–90]: 466). Smith here specifically refers to Hobbes (463). On Hobbes's position see Macpherson 1962: 32.

19 It is sometimes argued that the *Wealth of Nations* reveals a largely one-way relation between the individual and the social order, namely one starting from the individual and interpreting institutions and social phenomena as the results of his instincts or characteristics. It is only in the *Theory of Moral Sentiments* that Smith shows any realization of the reverse sequence according to which 'the concrete social environment must also be taken into consideration in explaining the nature of the individual man' (Morrow 1928: 172). But see Viner 1972: 84. It will become clear from our investigation that while the 'nature of man' in the *Wealth of Nations* is assumed to be immutable throughout time and space, the environment plays a vital role in providing scope for various aspects of behaviour.

For a splendid account of many of the *detailed* institutional arrangements which Smith proposes for the best assurance of a coincidence between the private and the general interest, see Rosenberg 1960. Our concern here is less with the recommended programme of institutional reform, and rather more with the manner in which the transition to capitalism reduced some of the opportunities for the less desirable manifestations of self-interest and also with the source of Smith's position in observation of the historical and contemporary record.

20 The inefficiency of slave labour (compared with that of a *métayer* system) is accounted for in terms of the effect of property ownership and income by result upon effort:

Such [*métayer*] tenants, being freemen, are capable of acquiring property, and having a certain proportion of the produce of the land, they have a plain interest that the whole produce should be as great as possible, in order that their own proportion may be so. A slave, on the contrary, who can acquire nothing but his maintenance, consults his own ease by making the land produce as little as possible over and above that maintenance. It is probable that it was partly upon account of this advantage, and partly upon account of the encroachments which the sovereign, always jealous of the great lords, gradually encouraged their villains to make upon their authority, and which seem at last to have been such as rendered this species of servitude altogether inconvenient, that tenure in villanage gradually wore out through the greater part of Europe.

(Smith 1937 [1776]: 366–7)

See also: 'The experience of all ages and nations, I believe, demonstrates that the work done by slaves, though it appears to cost only their maintenance, is in the end the dearest of any. A person who can acquire no property, can have no other interest but to eat as much and to labour as little as possible. Whatever work he does beyond what is sufficient to purchase his own maintenance, can be squeezed out of him by violence only, and not by any interest of his own' (365).

21 He continues: These political economy takes, 'to a certain extent, into its calculations, because these do not merely, like other desires, occasionally conflict with the pursuit of wealth, but accompany it always as a drag, or impediment, and are therefore inseparably mixed up in the consideration of it' (Mill 1967 [1836]: 321–2).

22 The same observations regarding the effects of very large incomes are applied to the business class: 'The high rate of profit seems every where to destroy that parsimony which in other circumstances is natural to the character of the merchant. When profits are high, that sober virtue seems to be superfluous, and expensive luxury to suit better the affluence of his situation' (Smith 1937 [1776]: 578).

23 See also:

the wealth acquired by the inhabitants of cities was frequently employed in purchasing such lands as were to be sold, of which a great part would frequently be uncultivated. Merchants are commonly ambitious of becoming country gentlemen, and when they do, they are generally the best of all improvers. A merchant is accustomed to employ his money chiefly in profitable projects; whereas a mere country gentleman is accustomed to employ it chiefly in expence. The one often sees his money go from him and return to him again with a profit: the other when once he parts with it, seldom expects to see any more of it. Those different habits naturally affect their temper and disposition in every sort of business. A merchant is commonly a bold; a country gentleman, a timid undertaker. The one is not afraid to lay out at once a large capital upon the improvement of his land, when he has a probable prospect of raising the value of it in proportion to the expence. The other, if he has any capital, which is not always the case, seldom ventures to employ it in this manner. If he improves at all, it is commonly not with a capital, but with what he can save out of his annual revenue.

(Smith 1937 [1776]: 384–5)

24 The constrained role of 'benevolence' even in the 'non-commercial' context will be remarked.

25 Reference is also made to the *steadier* wages paid in the commercial sector.

26 Elsewhere Smith asserts even more strongly that 'the liberal reward of labour . . . increases the industry of the common people. . . . Some workmen, indeed, when they can earn in four days what will maintain them through the week, will be idle the other three. This however, is by no means the case with the greater part. Workmen, on the contrary, when they are liberally paid by the piece, are very apt to over-work themselves, and to ruin their health and constitution in a few years' (Smith 1937 [1776]: 81–2). See also: 'An apprentice is likely to be idle, and almost always is so, because he has no immediate interest to be otherwise. In the inferior employments, the sweets of labour consist altogether in the recompence of labour' (122).

27 We recall, however, that Smith was also engaged in a specification of detailed institutional recommendations designed to improve the coincidence of self-interested behaviour and the social interest. There were also aspects of contemporary capitalistic society, such as the joint-stock company, and various negative consequences of division of labour, which should be corrected. On some of these aspects, see Rosenberg 1960.

28 For a brief discussion of the *factual* basis for Smith's position, see Viner 1972: 83–4.

On our reading of this troublesome passage Smith's reference to the small numbers of slaves in corn production reflects the extremely low profitability of slavery in that crop compared to a free-labour system. But sometimes masters were prepared to sacrifice *some* profits for satisfaction of their love of domineering – as in sugar and tobacco production.

29 The contrast between the Highland and Lowland economies is particularly important; see Meek 1967: 47.

30 That mankind is much alike throughout time and space, is an assumption conspicuous in the context of 'real value', as labour commanded. It is a presumption very carefully stated by Hume:

It is universally acknowledged, that there is a great uniformity among the actions of men, in all nations and ages, and that human nature remains still the same, in its principles and operations. . . . Would you know the sentiments, inclinations, and course of life of the Greeks and Romans? Study well the temper and actions of the French and English: You cannot be much mistaken in transferring to the former *most* of the observations, which you have made with regard to the latter. Mankind are so much the same, in all times and places, that history informs us of nothing new or strange in this particular.

(Hume 1898a [1748]: 68)

But we have seen that Smith went to some lengths to show how the constant principle of self-interested behaviour manifested itself in *different* circumstances; he might therefore have found Hume's further assertions regarding history unsatisfactory. We have in mind the position that, 'its chief use is only to discover the constant and universal principles of human nature by showing men in all varieties of circumstances and situations, and furnishing us with materials from which we may form our observations and become acquainted

121

with the regular springs of human action and behaviour'. (See on this matter Skinner 1965: 5.)

The practice of 'reading back' into other ages and into theoretical social structures the behavioural patterns observed in contemporary society is also common to Hobbes. See on this issue Macpherson 1962: 17n.

31 Much is made of the effect of 'frequency of dealings' in commercial society upon behaviour: 'A dealer is afraid of losing his character, and is scrupulous in observing every engagement. . . . Wherever dealings are frequent, a man does not expect to gain so much by any one contract, as by probity and punctuality, in the whole, and a prudent dealer, who is sensible of his real interest, would rather choose to lose what he has a right to, than give any ground for suspicion' (Smith 1896 [1763]: 253–5).

32 A change may here be discerned from the approach adopted in Smith's *Lectures* where he cites approvingly an (anonymous) mercantilist pamphlet purporting to show 'by arguments drawn from experience that nothing but necessity will enforce labour' (1896 [1763]: 257n). The asserted facts are related by Smith to a lack of education and also a premature failure of parental authority in consequence of early entry into the labour market in 'commercial' society.

33 When we compare, therefore, the state of a nation at two different periods, and find, that the annual produce of its land and labour is evidently greater at the latter than at the former, that its lands are better cultivated, its manufactures more numerous and more flourishing, and its trade more extensive, we may be assured that its capital must have increased during the interval between those two periods, and that more must have been added to it by the good conduct of some, than had been taken from it either by the private misconduct of others, or by the public extravagance of government. But we shall find this to have been the case of almost all nations, in all tolerably quiet and peaceable times, even of those who have not enjoyed the most prudent and parsimonious governments. To form a right judgment of it, indeed, we must compare the state of the country at periods somewhat distant from one another. The progress is frequently so gradual, that, at near periods, the improvement is not only not sensible, but from the declension either of certain branches of industry, or of certain districts of the country, things which sometimes happen though the country in general be in great prosperity, there frequently arises a suspicion, that the riches and industry of the whole are decaying.

(Smith 1937 [1776]: 326–7)

34 With regard to misconduct, the number of prudent and successful undertakings is every-where much greater than that of injudicious and unsuccessful ones. After all our complaints of the frequency of bankruptcies, the unhappy men who fall into this misfortune make but a very small part of the whole number engaged in trade, and all other sorts of business; not much more perhaps than one in a thousand. Bankruptcy is perhaps the greatest and most humiliating calamity which can befall an innocent man. The greater part of men, therefore, are sufficiently careful to avoid it. Some, indeed, do not avoid it; as some do not avoid the gallows.

(Smith 1937 [1776]: 325)

35 Smith had in mind: 'first, the agreeableness or disagreeableness of the employments themselves; secondly, the easiness and cheapness, or the difficulty and expence of learning them; thirdly, the constancy or inconstancy of employment in them; fourthly, the small or great trust which must be reposed in those who

exercise them; and fifthly, the probability or improbability of success in them' (1937 [1776]: 100).

To illustrate Smith's actual procedures in this context: in analysing an observed differential in favour of masons and bricklayers compared to common labour, Smith precludes the possibility that educational costs play any large part since 'no species of skilled labour . . . seems more easy to learn than that of masons and bricklayers'; accordingly he concludes – having evidently ruled out any other candidates as conceivably relevant – that 'the high wages of those workmen . . . are not so much the recompence of their skill, as the compensation for the inconstancy of their employment' (103).

In the analysis of the apparently high earnings of colliers relative to common labour Smith concluded that the differential represented a not excessive return for 'the hardship, disagreeableness, and dirtiness' (104) on the grounds that considerable mobility existed in this section of the labour market, so that the pattern could not convincingly be interpreted as nothing more than a temporary phenomenon. However, Smith also refers to a structure which 'ought' to emerge (102, 104), implying thereby an initially formulated hypothetical pattern. In this case Smith may have been attempting to 'test' the theory from the evidence.

The quality of the induction in the chapter is a matter which we do not here take up. (See the discussion in Hollander 1973: 130n.) It may, however, be noted that Smith's treatment of the second example given above is unsatisfactory. In the *Lectures*, Smith observed that the relatively high return to Scottish colliers could be partly accounted for by their objection to *bondage*; they escaped to Newcastle where 'though they have less wages . . . they have liberty' (1896 [1763]: 100). There is no mention of this in the *Wealth of Nations*.

36 It should, however, be emphasized that there still remained scope even in capitalist society for various self-interested motives apart from the desire for income and the aversion to effort. Thus, for example, 'honour' still plays a part (Smith 1937 [1776–90]: 100). And a place is given to 'pride' in a discussion of impediments to capital flows into the agriculture sector – an 'inferior station' (371).

REFERENCES

Anspach, Ralph (1972) 'The Implications of the *Theory of Moral Sentiments* for Adam Smith's Economic Thought', *History of Political Economy*, 4, 1: 176–206.
Bagehot, Walter (1911) *Economic Studies*, Richard Holt Hutton (ed.), London: Longmans, Green and Co.
Baker, Keith Michael (1975) *Condorcet: From Natural Philosophy to Social Mathematics*, Chicago: University of Chicago Press.
Bittermann, Henry J. (1940) 'Adam Smith's Empiricism and the Law of Nature, I', *Journal of Political Economy*, 48, 3 (August): 487–520.
Cairnes, J. E. (1888) *The Character and Logical Method of Political Economy*, 2nd edn, London: Macmillan.
Hanson, N. R. (1970) 'Hypotheses Fingo', in Robert E. Butts and John W. Davis (eds) *The Methodological Heritage of Newton*, Toronto: University of Toronto Press, 14–33.
Hollander, Samuel (1973) *The Economics of Adam Smith*, Toronto: University of Toronto Press.
—— (1976) 'The Historical Dimension of the *Wealth of Nations*', *Transactions of the Royal Society of Canada*, 14, 277–92.

Hume, David (1882) [1739–40] *A Treatise of Human Nature*, T. H. Green and T. H. Grose (eds), London: Longmans, Green and Co.

—— (1898a) [1748] 'An Enquiry Concerning Human Understanding', *Essays: Moral, Political and Literary*, Vol. 2, T. H. Green and T. H. Grose (eds), London: Longmans, Green and Co., 1–135.

—— (1898b) [1751] 'An Enquiry Concerning the Principles of Morals', *Essays: Moral, Political and Literary*, Vol. 2, T. H. Green and T. H. Grose (eds), London: Longmans, Green and Co., 157–287.

Macpherson, C. B. (1962) *The Political Theory of Possessive Individualism: Hobbes to Locke*, Oxford: Clarendon Press.

Marshall, Alfred (1961) [1920] *Principles of Economics*, Vol. 1, 9th Variorum edn, C. W. Guillehaud (ed.), Cambridge: Cambridge University Press.

Meek, Ronald L. (1967) *Economics and Ideology, and Other Essays*, London: Chapman and Hall.

Mill, J. S. (1967) [1836] 'On the Definition of Political Economy' in *Collected Works of John Stuart Mill*, Vol. 4, Toronto: University of Toronto Press, 309–39.

Mini, Piero V. (1974) *Philosophy and Economics*, Gainesville: University Presses of Florida.

Morrow, Glenn R. (1928) 'Adam Smith: Moralist and Philosopher', in J. M. Clarke *et al.*, *Adam Smith, 1776–1926*, Chicago: University of Chicago Press, 156–79.

Myers, M. L. (1972) 'Philosophical Anticipations of Laissez-Faire', *History of Political Economy*, 4, 1: 163–75.

—— (1975) 'Adam Smith as Critic of Ideas', *Journal of the History of Ideas*, 36, 2 (April–June): 281–96.

Rae, John (1834) *Statement of Some New Principles on the Subject of Political Economy*, Boston: Hilliard Gray and Co.

Rosenberg, Nathan (1960) 'Some Institutional Aspects of *The Wealth of Nations*', *Journal of Political Economy*, 68, 4 (December): 557–70.

Rotwein, E. (1955) Introduction to *David Hume: Writings on Economics*, London: Nelson, ix–cxi.

Skinner, A. (1965) 'Economics and History – The Scottish Enlightenment', *Scottish Journal of Political Economy*, 12, 1: 1–22.

Smith, Adam (1853) [1759–90] *The Theory of Moral Sentiments*, London: Henry G. Bohn.

—— (1896) [1763] *Lectures on Justice, Police, Revenue and Arms*, Edwin Cannan (ed.), Oxford: Clarendon Press.

—— (1937) [1776] *An Inquiry into the Nature and Causes of the Wealth of Nations*, Edwin Cannan (ed.), New York: Modern Library.

—— (1963) [1762–3] *Lectures on Rhetoric and Belles Lettres*, John M. Lothian (ed.), London: Thomas Nelson and Sons.

—— (1967) [1795] *Essays on Philosophical Subjects*, in J. Ralph Lindgren (ed.), *The Early Writings of Adam Smith*, New York: Augustus M. Kelley, 29–223.

Thomson, Herbert F. (1965) 'Adam Smith's Philosophy of Science', *Quarterly Journal of Economics*, 79, 2 (May): 212–33.

Viner, Jacob (1960) 'On the Intellectual History of Laissez Faire', *The Journal of Law and Economics*, 3 (October): 45–69.

—— (1962) 'Some Problems of Logical Method in Political Economy', in Earl J. Hamilton *et al.* (eds), *Landmarks in Political Economy*, Chicago: University of Chicago Press, 101–24.

—— (1972) *The Role of Providence in the Social Order: An Essay in Intellectual History*, Philadelphia: American Philosophical Society.

Part IV

NINETEENTH-CENTURY LITERATURE

9

THE POST-RICARDIAN DISSENSION
A case-study in economics and ideology*

That the roots of early British socialism can be traced to Ricardo is an important theme in Marxian historiography. The writings of Piercy Ravenstone and Thomas Hodgskin – among other opponents of 'bourgeois' political economy – were said by Marx to 'derive from the Ricardian form' and Marx discussed 'the opposition evoked by the Ricardian theory' (Marx 1971: 238, 258). The derivation in question was a complex one, entailing adoption and development of Ricardian value theory rid, however, of any allowances for the independent productivity of capital. The champions of the proletariat 'seize[d] on this contradiction, for which they found the theoretical ground already prepared. Labour is the sole source of exchange value and the only active creator of use-value. This is what you say. On the other hand, you say that *capital* is everything, and the worker is nothing or a mere production cost of capital. You have refuted yourselves. Capital is *nothing* but defrauding of the worker. *Labour* is *everything*. This, in fact, is the ultimate meaning of all the writings which defend the interests of the proletariat from the Ricardian stand-point basing themselves on his assumptions' (260). As one example, Thomas Hodgskin's insistence upon the non-productivity of capital was the 'inevitable consequence of Ricardo's presentation' (266).[1] What was involved, according to Marx, is a kind of *inversion* of the Ricardian analysis.[2]

There is a second closely related feature of Marx's reading of the record. It is that the 'bourgeois' reaction against Ricardo – the so-called 'dissenting' literature of the 1830s and 1840s – must be understood as a reaction to the use made of Ricardian doctrine by the labour writers. What is referred to as 'vulgar' political economy 'only becomes widespread', Marx wrote,

> when political economy itself has, as a result of its analysis, under-mined and impaired its own premises and consequently the opposition to political economy has come into being in more or less economic, utopian, critical and revolutionary forms. . . . *Ricardo* and the further advance of political economy caused by him provide new nourishment

* I am much indebted to Professor R. D. C. Black for helpful comments.

for the vulgar economist . . . : the more economic theory is perfected, that is, the deeper it penetrates its subject-matter and the more it develops as a contradictory system, the more is it confronted by its own, increasingly independent, vulgar element, enriched with material which it dresses up in its own way until finally it finds its most apt expression in academically syncretic and unprincipled eclectic compilations.

(Marx 1971: 501)

Furthermore, 'vulgar political economy deliberately becomes increasingly *apologetic* and makes strenuous attempts to talk out of existence the ideas which contain the contradictions' – contradictions, which were 'in the process of being worked out in socialism and the struggles of the time' (501). It is precisely this reading of the record that re-appears in the famous Afterword to the second German edition of *Capital* (1873) where Ricardo is portrayed as the 'last great representative of political economy', and the year 1830 as the watershed between 'scientific' and 'apologetic' economics: 'In France and in England the bourgeoisie had conquered political power. Thenceforth, the class-struggle, practically as well as theoretically, took on more and more outspoken and threatening forms. It sounded the knell of scientific bourgeois economy. It was thenceforth no longer a question, whether this theorem or that was true, but whether it was useful to capital or harmful, expedient or inexpedient, politically dangerous or not. In place of disinterested inquiries, there were hired prize-fighters; in place of genuine scientific research, the bad conscience and evil intent of apologetic' (Marx 1965 [1873]: 15).[3]

Marx's reading of the motivation behind the dissenting literature was accepted by Professor Meek in his well-known analysis of 'the decline of Ricardian economics in England'.[4] To explain 'the strength, vigour and virtual universality of the early reaction against Ricardo' resort had to be made 'above all . . . to the fact that a number of elements in his system seemed to set limits to the prospects of uninterrupted and harmonious progress under capitalism. In particular, the work of the Ricardian socialists revealed certain disharmonies and pessimistic implications of Ricardo's system so forcibly that the economists of the day could hardly avoid being influenced by them in the course of their evaluation of Ricardo.' Similarly, 'the majority of economists were very much aware of the dangerous use to which a number of radical writers were putting certain Ricardian concepts'. As far as concerns the theoretical core of Ricardianism the 'concepts of value as embodied labour and profit as a kind of surplus value, which had proved so useful to the radicals, were among the first to be amended or rejected: value began to be conceived in terms of utility or cost of production, or sometimes (as with [Samuel] Bailey) as little more than a mere relation, and profit came to be explained not as the result of something which the labourer did but as the result of and reward for something which either the capitalist or his capital did' (Meek 1967: 68–9, 70, 72).[5]

I propose to treat the Marxian interpretation of the dissent in theory as an hypothesis to be evaluated against the evidence.[6] Because of the complexity of the issues involved it will be helpful to summarize my conclusions at the outset.

It was Marx's position, we have seen, that the socialist writers of the 1820s drew upon Ricardo's value theory to reach their conclusions regarding labour's right to the whole produce but rejected those elements of the Ricardian structure which allowed a positive role to capital. Now the record suggests that the first part of the argument – at least as far as concerns the works of Piercy Ravenstone, William Thompson and Thomas Hodgskin, the best known of the labour writers of the decade in question – cannot be substantiated at all. No use whatsoever was made of Ricardo's labour theory.[7] Hodgskin (unlike the others) did, however, make use of other aspects of the doctrine – the inverse profit–wage relation, the subsistence wage and the differential rent conception. But his usage, I shall show, was an ironical one; he himself was unconvinced by their merit. There is more to the second strand to Marx's case – the socialist critique of the positive role attributed to capital by Ricardo. Yet Marx understates the strength of the 'socialist' objections. The fact is that it is difficult to imagine a stronger critic of Ricardianism than Hodgskin. He condemned it as an apologia for the institutional *status quo* – a defence of the capitalist as well as the land-lord; he read it as providing a justification for the contemporary distribution of income; on his reading it failed to bring to light class conflict; and he rejected its pessimistic underpinnings even as characteristic of contemporary society. Hodgskin's opposition is quite evident despite the formal use that he made on occasion of aspects of Ricardian theory.

The vehement anti-Ricardianism of the labour writers – particularly Hodgskin – makes it very difficult to believe that the dissenters could have reacted against a dangerous *use* of the orthodox doctrine for socialistic ends. We must, of course, not rely entirely upon circumstantial evidence, particu-larly in the light of passages which, taken in isolation, indicate a reliance on certain Ricardian conceptions (though positively not Ricardian value theory). It is always possible that the dissenters failed to recognize the hostility towards Ricardian doctrine on the part of the labour writers. I can, however, find no evidence that any link such as that specified by the Marxist historians was defined.[8] For example, the fallacious position that labour is responsible for all wealth was attributed by Samuel Read to Ricardo, Smith and Hodgskin. But while Smith was treated less harshly than either Hodgskin or Ricardo, no relationship whatsoever is drawn between the latter two, who are treated apart. G. Poulett Scrope included Malthus in his list of culprits as well as Smith, Ricardo and Hodgskin. Richard Whately directed his critical attention at McCulloch and James Mill for their reduction of capital to accumulated labour and their opinion that 'time is a mere word', but neither he nor Scrope linked the socialists with Ricardian theory. And Mountifort Longfield, who may have alluded to Hodgskin, does not suggest any such connection. To the extent that these dissenters believed that Ricardo's analysis of value, particularly as interpreted by McCulloch and James Mill, justified the notion of interest as an 'exploitation' income, their objections did not follow from any dangerous use which they believed the socialists were making of Ricardian theory. The notion of class hostility, supposedly engendered by Ricardo's theory, providing a handle for the anarchists was, however, a central complaint of one of the most faithful of Ricardo's followers – Thomas De Quincey. It becomes even more difficult to argue that the theoretical opposition to Ricardo of the 1830s can be somehow related to the dangerous use which the socialists were making of Ricardian economics.

I come now to a feature of the record that, at first sight, may seem an extraordinary paradox. Scrope – the first of the abstinence writers – was fundamentally opposed to Ricardianism because that doctrine, he believed, lent itself to social apologetics and this, in part, because of its neglect of the implications for social welfare of unequal distribution. Scrope was a *reformer* who saw in orthodox doctrine a rock against which proposals for social improvement must inevitably be destroyed.[9] The parallels between Scrope and, for example, William Thompson regarding their attitudes to Ricardo are quite remarkable. To this extent Marx's interpretation seems to be the exact reverse of the actual course of events.

My reading also has clear implications for an interpretation of the bourgeois dissent subtly different from that which turned on the use made of Ricardo's theory by the labour writers. It is the argument, sometimes offered as an alternative and sometimes as an additional consideration, that the bourgeois economists found the Ricardian doctrine unable to serve as a *convincing reply* – an apologetic reply – to the labour writers. As Meek formulated the proposition: Scrope, Read and Longfield 'tended towards the idea that if a doctrine "inculcated pernicious principles", if it denied that wealth under free competition was consigned to its "proper" owners, or if it could be so interpreted as to impugn the motives or capacity of the Almighty, then that doctrine must necessarily be false' (Meek 1967: 71). (For further details of this argument as it is applied to Scrope, see below, p. 147.)[10]

Now in considering this matter we must ask to what end did the dissenters seek to reply to the labour writers. It was positively not to the end of justifying contemporary capitalism as is implied by the hypothesis. Provided this fundamental correction of the record is recognized it may be allowed that several major dissenters expressed their dissatisfaction with specific aspects of Ricardianism, particularly its supposed implications regarding class conflict and its supposed 'pessimism'.[11]

We have not, however, reached the end of this tortuous journey.

Allowance must also be made for the fact that Longfield cannot be classified as a thorough-going opponent of Ricardo. He retained enough of the Ricardian framework for it to be more accurate to say that he actually *used* the orthodox doctrine in making his reply to the radicals, and this he did partly by interpreting it in a manner which avoided the criticism that it portrayed a picture of class warfare, and partly by his analytical innovations.

I. THOMAS HODGSKIN AS CRITIC OF RICARDIANISM

Limited space obliges me to devote my attention in this section to Thomas Hodgskin, although it can be shown that the hostility towards the Ricardians is apparent also in the works of Ravenstone and Thompson. But, in any event, for my main purpose in this essay – the motivation for the bourgeois dissension – Hodgskin must be the primary concern because his works were particularly well known to the bourgeois dissenters.

Hodgskin's hostility towards Ricardo and the Ricardians is apparent both in his correspondence and in his pamphlets. For our purposes, Hodgskin's correspondence cannot be given the same weighting as the pamphlets of 1825 and 1827. A brief account of his position as it appears in his early letters will, however, set the stage. It is also clear from his reviews for the *Economist* of the 1840s and 1850s that his criticisms of Ricardo remained largely unchanged with the passage of time.[12]

A general statement of position with special reference to Hodgskin's objections to Ricardo will be found in a letter to Francis Place of May 1820 discussing a plan of work submitted to Place a short while earlier (cited in Halévy 1956: 66f). Here he refers frankly to his own 'prejudiced' objections to Ricardo before turning to technical matters. It is the pessimism engendered by Ricardian conceptions and their justification of the *status quo* to which he objected: 'I have . . . no hesitation in saying that I dislike Ricardo's opinions because they go to justify the present political situation of society, and to set bounds to our hopes of future improvement' (67).[13]

First, on Ricardianism as a defence of the existing social structure Hodgskin made the following observation:

> They have the first effect by justifying our great Land-Leviathans in their enormous exactions. *Wealth* is but another name for political power, and with an aristocracy of Land-lords such as at present exists anything like democracy is impossible. We are all subjects of Nature, and we can only be either happy or great by obeying her laws. And if Rent, such as it at present exists, be according to Mr Ricardo the natural result of the progress of Society, then every attempt to rid us of the control of a wealthy aristocracy must be ultimately unsuccessful and in its progress mischievous. I am a *democrat*. Mr Ricardo's doctrines are the strongest support I know, as far as reasoning goes, to aristocracy,

and therefore I dislike them. This is the source of one of my prejudices against them which I thus honestly and openly confess.

(Hodgskin, cited in Halévy 1956: 67)[14]

Hodgskin had some particularly strong words for Ricardo's Preface: 'The two first sentences of the book are radically false. The circumstances there ascribed will undoubtedly have a wonderful influence on the whole quantity of produce, but the manner in which it is distributed will depend entirely and exclusively on political regulations. No circumstances of *soil*, *capital* nor ingenuity will ever make the distribution of wealth the same in the United States of America in which slavery is unknown [*sic*] and in our Empire of India' (78).[15]

Second, regarding the 'pessimism' engendered by Ricardo, Hodgskin wrote in the following strong terms:

> Mr R's opinions set bounds to our hopes for the future progress of mankind in a more definite manner even than the opinions of Mr Malthus. It is, namely, Mr Ricardo's opinion that the rate of all profit is ultimately determined by the rate of profit gained by capital employed on land, that this is constantly diminishing by a necessity for having recourse to poorer soils, and that there is a point, limited by the natural interest of capital and from which most European societies are not far removed, at which improvement must stop. I have always supposed from the progress men have hitherto made that it is impossible for us to limit their future progress. Mr R's doctrines do this exactly and they do it on natural grounds, and because they are thus opposed to this other prejudice of mine, I dislike them very much.

(Hodgskin, cited in Halévy 1956: 67–8)

Hodgskin did not in fact deny that there existed *at any time* a differential rent between good and poor soils, or indeed 'that the necessity of having recourse to these worse soils has increased rent in modern times', especially during the preceding fifty years. His objections – which drew in part upon Smith – were to the implied notion of the *origin* of rent in Ricardo's account; to Ricardo's exaggerated emphasis on a single and relatively unimportant aspect of the rent phenomenon; and, it would appear, to the conception of no-rent land at the margin of cultivation. Moreover, the notion of the 'original and indestructible powers' of the soil is rejected as meaningless 'independent of human labour'; and even that of 'poor' and 'good' soil is questioned on the grounds that 'what are now called the very worst soils may, by some improvements or alterations in the mode of agriculture, be made as productive as what are now called the best' (68–9).[16]

Hodgskin drew upon Hume, Robertson, Millar, Kames and Smith to support the position that a slave system originally existed throughout Europe; in such origins he envisaged the basis for contemporary rent and wage payments, both of which could only be appreciated in historical terms.[17] His entire intellectual perspective rendered Ricardian procedures alien. And although he observed that Ricardo 'found labour rewarded in our society as if the labourer were a slave', he characteristically objected to the supposed implicit presumption that this constituted 'his natural condition' rather than (using Halévy's term) 'a servile custom perpetuated by the laws of men' (Halévy 1956: 72–3, 64). What concerned him was the belief that political economy confused *artificial* institutions with a *natural* social order and tended in consequence to justify the contemporary distributive arrangements.

I turn next to Hodgskin's position on value. Here too he was critical of Ricardo and adopted a position closer to that of Adam Smith. His main point is that rent and profits *enhance prices to the labourer* in his capacity as consumer:

> If Mr R's account of the origin of rent be true and it never amounts to more than the difference between the produce of good and bad land, then Rent can never enhance Price.... If the origin which I have ascribed to Rent be correct, it enhances the price of every thing....
>
> Mr R. has involved this part of the subject in considerable confusion by *supposing* the buyers or the community who pay prices are different from the three great classes, to wit landlords, capitalists and labourers, among whom he divides the produce of the earth.... Now Rent is a part of the produce of labour, taken by a person who does not labour, and, of course, if the labourer wishes to obtain for his own use a quantity of produce equal to the quantity obtained which he has shared with the *lord*, he must double, treble and in the present day must multiply his labour manyfold to obtain it. Rent, therefore, enhances price, by the whole of amount of Rent. Profit, being in like manner a diminution to the labourer of the value of his produce, enhances the price of everything into which it enters to the labourer. It is in this sense in which A. Smith says rent and profit enhance price, and considers the whole produce to be divided into these and wages or among the three classes mentioned. No truth in the whole course of reason was ever more self-evident. It is abundantly clear that rent and profit cannot enhance the quantity of labour necessary to obtain any commodity from nature, but they enhance its price to the labourer by their whole sum.
>
> (Hodgskin, cited in Halévy 1956: 72f)

On these grounds Hodgskin complained of the 'want of an accurate distinction between *natural price* and *exchangeable value*' on Ricardo's part: 'Natural price is measured by the quantity of labour necessary to produce any commodity: its exchangeable value, or what another will give or is obliged to give for this commodity when produced, may or may not be equal to the quantity of labour employed in its production. Mr Ricardo has, I think, made a mistake by supposing these two things to be equal. They are not, or the wages of labour would always be equal to the produce of labour' (74–5). Hodgskin thus objected to Ricardo's measure of cost price in terms of labour embodied on the grounds that it *failed to express the exploitative nature of the returns to land and capital* – that they constitute 'a diminution to the labourer of the value of this product'.[18] In this respect, he believed, Smith had succeeded by adopting what today is referred to as an 'adding-up-components theory' of price.

In an earlier letter to Place of September 1818 Hodgskin, who had just read McCulloch's famous *Edinburgh Review* article on Ricardo's *Principles*, but not the *Principles* itself, took Ricardo to task to similar effect: 'I see no natural cause either why *capital* which is merely the saving of labour and which of itself produces nothing should be considered as affecting real price – if that is always to be considered as accurately measured by the quantity of labour. . . . Its profits are merely a portion of the produce of labour which the capitalist, without any other rights than what laws give him, takes to himself' (40). This was his first reaction – before he had read the *Principles* itself. At most it can formally be said with Halévy that 'he had seen what he could take from Ricardo's theories and on what points he would be at variance with him'. But all he took from McCulloch's *compte rendu* was the labour measure of 'real value'; his general reaction was clearly a negative one from the outset. After reading the original text his hostility hardened, as we have seen, into a specific charge *that Ricardo's formulation – unlike Smith's – failed to bring to the fore the exploitative nature of profits*. On one point alone did he express approval, namely on Ricardo's 'explanation of the manner in which fixed-capital tends to lower the prices of all commodities into which it enters'; this he held to be 'the best and only good part of his book'. His general reaction to Ricardian theoretical procedures was as hostile as that of any 'dissenter': 'I think I never saw a book more destitute of facts than Mr R's, which, at the same time, has had so much weight. To me it appears to rest entirely on arbitrary definitions and strange assumptions. . . . I may have read this book prejudiced against it. I believe I have; but, after making every allowance for my prejudices, it does appear to be built on no sort of facts, to contradict many and to have little more merit than a "bewildering subtlety" ' (77–8; emphasis added).

The main 'positive' aspect of *Labour Defended Against the Claims of Capital* turns upon a rejection of the conception of 'advance' economics; the adoption of time-consuming processes did *not* require the actual provision of stocks of accumulated capital goods. The emphasis is placed upon synchronized activity, and the entire notion of an annual production period abandoned: 'It is this *assurance*, this *knowledge*, this *confidence* of obtaining subsistence and reward, which enables and induces men to undertake long and complicated operations, and the question is, do men derive this assurance from a stock of goods already provided (saved from the produce of previous labour) and ready to pay them, or from any other source?' (Hodgskin 1825: 37).[19] The answer is in the negative: 'Those who undertake [processes extending beyond a year] must rely ... not on any commodities already created, but that other men will labour and produce what they are to subsist on till their own products are completed. Thus should the labourer admit that some accumulation of circulating capital is necessary for operations terminated within the year – and I have shown how very limited that admission ought to be, if made at all – it is plain that in all operations which extend beyond a year the labourer does not, and he cannot, rely on *accumulated* capital' (47). In brief: 'If we duly consider the number and importance of those wealth-producing operations which are not completed within the year, and the numberless products of daily labour, necessary to subsistence, which are consumed as soon as produced, we shall, I think, be sensible that the success and productive power of every different species of labour is at all times more dependent on the coexisting productive labour of other men than on any accumulation of circulating capital' (Hodgskin 1825: 50–1).[20]

Hodgskin conceded that labour productivity was greatly enhanced by the use of *fixed* capital, but fixed capital was itself the product of labour – a fact which, he insisted, did not justify the payment of profit to its owner – and was useless apart from current operating labour: 'It is plainly not the previous creation of these things which entitles them to profit. . . . Fixed capital does not derive its utility from previous, but present labour; and does not bring its owner a profit because it has been stored-up, but because it is a means of obtaining a command over labour' (55).

In his account of the prerequisites for the creation and utilization of fixed capital no emphasis at all was placed upon savings. What was called for is 'knowledge and ingenuity for inventing machines' – and Hodgskin complained of the failure to give inventors their due reward, which would include payment covering 'the manual skill and dexterity for carrying these inventions into execution', and 'the skill and labour to use these instruments after they are made' (63–4).

One further point is the observation that profit is paid to the owners of *both* circulating and fixed capital while the functions of the two categories differ significantly. From this fact Hodgskin deduced 'that the share claimed by the capitalist for the use of fixed capital is not derived from the instruments increasing the efficiency of labour, or from the utility of these instruments; and profit is derived in both cases from the power which the capitalist has over the labourer who consumes the circulating, and who uses the fixed, capital' (70).

Hodgskin's rejection of 'advance' economics and his championship of the notion of 'synchronised' activity – a position which shows a deep appreciation of the distinction between *stock* and *flow* – provides the background to his attack upon Ricardian economics as an apologetic doctrine: 'I shall content myself . . . with examining the claims of the capitalists, *as supported by the theories of political economy*' (27; emphasis added). The economists with whom Hodgskin specifically took issue were McCulloch and James Mill who were both regarded as providing a defence and justification of the contemporary social system: 'Several good and great men, whom we must all respect and esteem, seeing that capital did obtain all the large share I have mentioned, and being more willing, apparently, to defend and to explain the present order of society than to ascertain whether it could be improved, have endeavoured to point out the method in which capital aids production' (32). McCulloch and Mill he regarded as 'by far the most efficient and eloquent supporters of the doctrine *I do not assent to*' (33; emphasis added).[21] Similarly, he complained that economists spoke of capitalists as the 'benefactors' of the labourer rather than the 'appropriators' of his produce: 'such are the doctrines of political economy; and capitalists may well be pleased with a science which both justifies their claims and holds them up to our admiration, as the great means of civilising and improving the world' (72-3). *It is difficult to exaggerate the significance of Hodgskin's charge that the Ricardians provided an apologetic doctrine justifying the extractions of the capitalist.*[22]

That profit (interest) is necessary as 'motives for accumulation and improvement' was 'a false view', arising 'from attributing to capital and saving those effects which result from labour'; indeed 'the best means of securing the progressive improvement, both of individuals and of nations, is to do justice, and allow labour to possess and enjoy the whole of the produce' (109). The danger of capital export in consequence of successful union activity is totally discounted: 'The most successful and widest-spread possible combination to obtain an augmentation of wages would have no other injurious effect than to reduce the incomes of those who live on profit and interest, and who have no just claim but custom to any share of the national produce' (92).[23]

Now although the general flavour of the argument is quite clearly hostile towards the Ricardians there do exist some Ricardian features in the pamphlet. The notion just alluded to that wages vary inversely with profits is at least consistent with the Ricardian formulation and at the outset of his pamphlet Hodgskin in fact used terminology characteristic of Ricardo: 'I admit that the subject is somewhat abstruse, but there is a necessity for the labourers to comprehend and be able to refute the received notions of the nature and utility of capital. Wages vary inversely as profits; or wages rise when profits fall, and profits rise when wages fall; and it is therefore profits, or the capitalist's share of the national produce, which is opposed to wages, or the share of the labourer' (27-8). In contrast to his position in the early correspondence Hodgskin now made use of the differential rent theory; and he put great weight upon the subsistence wage:

The labourer must, however, live, though the exorbitant claims of capital allow him only a bare subsistence. Mr Ricardo has also been aware of this, and has therefore justly defined the price of labour to be such a quantity of commodities as will enable the labourers, one with another, to subsist, and to perpetuate their race without either *increase* or *diminution*. Such is all which the nature of profit or interest on capital will allow them to receive, and such has ever been their reward. The capitalist must give the labourers this sum, for it is the condition he must fulfil in order to obtain labourers; it is the limit which nature places to his claims, and *he will never give and never has given, more*. The capitalists, according to Mr Ricardo's theory, allow the landlords to have just as much as keeps all the capitalists on a level; the labourers they allow, in the same theory, barely to subsist.

(Hodgskin 1825: 81–2)[24]

It is doubtless the presence of these passages which has created many of the interpretative problems and we need to exercise caution in their evaluation. It is my impression, for the following reasons, that Hodgskin referred favourably to differential rent and the inverse profit–wage relation with tongue in cheek. He himself did not base his case thereupon.

As far as concerns the inverse wage–profit relation it is pertinent that Hodgskin did not enter into the technical details of Ricardo's construction. In brief, *he did not rely on an analysis of exploitation based upon Ricardian value theory*. In the specific context of value theory it is clearly Smith's position that is drawn upon – the adding-up-cost approach – as in the correspondence: 'The *real price* of a coat or a pair of shoes or a loaf of bread, *all* which nature demands from man in order that he may have either of these very useful articles, is a certain quantity of labour. . . . But for the *labourer* to have either of these articles he must give over and above the quantity of labour nature demands from him, a still larger quantity to the capitalist . . . he must pay interest . . . ; and he must, moreover, pay with the produce of his labour the rent of the landlord' (Hodgskin 1825: 75–6).

Rent is thus treated on a par with interest as an extraction from the labourer by way of its effect on cost price, clearly showing that the differential rent theory was not part of the basic argument. Furthermore, Hodgskin has neglected to allow for innovation which, of course, rules out any *necessary* inverse relationship between the rate of profits and *commodity* wages, while, in sharp contrast, very great weight is placed elsewhere upon knowledge and new technology, and the Ricardians are taken to task for their neglect of these considerations. Similarly, in a variety of other contexts Hodgskin *rejected* the principle of diminishing returns as a useful predictive device on grounds of changing technology. The use of aspects of Ricardian theory to taunt the orthodox, as it were, is further suggested by the blatant contradiction implied by the recommendation of union activity as a means of raising wages at the expense of profits, while insisting at the same time that the capitalist employer 'will never give, and never has given' more than a subsistence wage. *To summarize, Hodgskin's case was based on non-Ricardian grounds – the non-productivity of capital and the capitalist (turning upon the notion of synchronized activity) coupled with Smithian value theory – and his positive references to aspects of Ricardian doctrine were not seriously intended.* It may be added that he was quite aware that the Ricardians had not themselves drawn the supposedly obvious conclusions from their own doctrine, although he pretended to be hopeful:

> It is the overwhelming and all-engrossing nature of compound interest, also, which gives to Mr Ricardo's theory and his definitions, as I have already described them, *though this principle is nowhere brought sufficiently into view in his book*, their mathematical accuracy and truth. I refer to them, not as caring much to illustrate the subtleties of that ingenious and profound writer, but because his theory confirms the observations I have just made – *viz.* that the exactions of the capitalist cause the poverty of the labourer.
>
> Political economists, indeed, who have insisted very strongly on the necessity of giving security to property, and have ably demonstrated how much that security promotes general happiness, will not hesitate to agree with me when I say that whatever labour produces ought to belong to it. . . . I take it for granted, therefore, that they will henceforth maintain that the whole produce of labour ought to belong to the labourer.
>
> (Hodgskin 1825: 80–1, emphasis added; 82–3)

Hodgskin's position may be investigated further by reference to *Popular Political Economy* (1827), a work based on lectures delivered in 1825 at the London Mechanics Institution and constituting an appeal for a form of social organization based upon natural law free from all government interference. His roots in this work are evidently firmly in the eighteenth century. No use whatsoever is made of Ricardian conceptions; on the contrary, a profound hostility to the 'Westminster Reviewers' is conspicuous.

Hodgskin's opposition to legislative interference of any kind is expressed in extreme terms and is the theme with which the book opens and closes. His objective is the analysis of the '*code* of natural laws' relating to the production of wealth, and as a matter of principle he eschews all discussion of desirable legislative measures (1827: viii–xxi). The theory of distribution is set aside for a second volume (which never saw the light of day) but a brief passage condemns Smith's successors for their faulty approach which, it is asserted, had generated a general dislike of political economy:

> It was his intention also to have noticed some of the errors of the great Masters of the science, which would have enabled him, as moral

feeling and scientific truth must always be in harmony with each other, to trace to its source the repugnance now felt to some of the doctrines of Political Economy. Men turn away disgusted, not from truth, but from errors dogmatically enforced. . . . [The] writings of Dr Smith's successors are chiefly defective; – they are erroneous chiefly on the subject of distribution. *That great man carefully distinguished the natural distribution of wealth from the distribution which is derived from our artificial right of property. His successors, on the contrary, make no such distinction, and in their writings the consequences of this right are stated to be the laws of Nature.*

(Hodgskin 1827: xxi–xxii; emphasis added)

At the close of the book, similarly, Hodgskin censured economists for their justification of the 'present distribution of wealth' as a 'natural phenomenon', although such a position constituted 'a palpable violation of that natural law which gives wealth to labour and to labour only; and though it is only maintained by an armed force, and by a system of cruel and bloody laws'. And he further condemned the aspirations 'to regulate, not only the present, but the future condition of society' on the part of those 'Political Economists in our time [who] far from imitating the wise conduct of their master, have all participated in this infatuated ambition, and have all aspired to be legislators' (266–7). Hodgskin's profound hostility towards the 'Westminster Philosophers' is crystal clear.[25]

His remarks on contemporary orthodox theory reveal a similarly hostile attitude. As in 1825 his dissension from the orthodox economists (presumably McCulloch and Mill) on the 'utility of accumulated capital' is again elaborated (1827: 238). The general conception of the 'bountiful' consequences of a natural system leads him to reject Malthus's *Essay on Population*. The same negative evaluation is made of the related principle of diminishing returns, and here Hodgskin places the emphasis upon the haziness of the notion of good and bad land, and also upon ill-considered presumptions regarding the limited significance of new technology in agriculture: 'I must confess I am astonished at the hasty and dogmatical manner in which Mr Malthus, Mr Ricardo, and their disciples, have decided, on the single principle of decreasing fertility, this most important, extensive, and complicated question.' In this context Hodgskin makes a plea for the gathering of some evidence before 'adopting a conclusion, which seems at variance with the general system of the universe'. His own belief – and once again Adam Smith is drawn upon for support as well as more recent empirical data – was that there occurs no secular decrease in labour productivity in agriculture except insofar as it is due to what is darkly spoken of as 'social circumstances'; there is no 'natural' or 'necessary' increase in the difficulties of procuring subsistence' (222–3, 232).[26] The book closes on this theme.

Hodgskin's adherence to Smith extends beyond the issue of natural law and the rejection of the supposed 'pessimism' of the current orthodoxy. It is a fundamental principle of the book – as of all Hodgskin's writings – that, in some sense, labour creates all wealth (19–20), the basis for which principle is found in the *Wealth of Nations*. To the extent that labour is responsible for wealth creation it follows that rent and profit must be deductions from labour's contribution (29).[27] It must be emphasized that a strictly defined labour theory of exchange value is not utilized as the basis for the 'exploitation' interpretation of interest. A distinction is drawn between the 'natural price' of a commodity defined in terms of labour embodiment, and the 'social price' reflected by actual money prices. 'No commodity can in the long run be exchanged for less, though it may for more, labour than it cost. Natural price is therefore always the limit in one direction, but in only one, to the money price of all commodities. They cannot be sold for less labour than they cost, but they *may be sold for more*' (219–20; 232–3; emphasis added). We have here an allusion, as in *Labour Defended*, to the difference between labour embodied and labour commanded along Smithian lines.[28]

I have dealt at some length with the pamphlet of 1827 partly because it provides evidence of Hodgskin's hostility towards the Ricardians, but also because it confirms my view that the favourable references to aspects of Ricardian theory in *Labour Defended Against the Claims of Capital* cannot be taken seriously but reflect the intention to embarrass the orthodox Ricardians. For the inverse profit–wage relation, subsistence wages and differential rent make no appearance whatsoever while, on the contrary, great attention is paid to new technology.[29]

There is a rather mysterious reference to contemporary value theory in the pamphlet calling for comment: Smith's approach towards 'the foundations of the science differs very much from that of late adopted in this country. Here it is now generally called after foreign authors the *science of values*; a most limited, and, perhaps, even useless definition; confining the science, were the definition followed, to only a small part of it, and affording no explanation whatever of its most interesting phenomena.' It was unfortunate 'that both the name and the arrangement given to the science by Dr Smith, should have been superseded in his own country, and even among those persons who are proud to call him their master and the founder of the science, by the name and arrangement of his French commentators' (Hodgskin 1827: 43). Presumably it was J. B. Say to whom Hodgskin referred.[30] But precisely what he had in mind may perhaps be clarified in terms of a complaint addressed against Ricardo's value theory, some twenty years later, namely that his procedure *obscured class relationships* – which Smith had with some success brought to the surface – by concentrating on the insignificant issue of the cause of variation in exchange value. The formulation summarizes beautifully the position already adopted in the early correspondence and in both pamphlets:

Mr Ricardo is logically most accurate in ascribing, throughout, according to Smith's own doctrine, 'of labour paying all price', every variation in price ultimately to variation in quantities of labour. We must, however, say, that in one sense, Smith's verbal variation from his own principle serves better to explain some social phenomena than Mr Ricardo's technical adherence to it. Clearly the increase of price which Smith indicated to be caused by rent and profit, meant the increase of labour, which the labourer, who originally possessed the whole commodity produced, had to give, for the same, or an equal commodity, when he, not other men, not certainly the capitalists and the landlords, had to pay profit and rent, or share that commodity with others. Substituting labourer for labour, in Smith's doctrine, it is a truer representation of what actually occurs in society than Mr Ricardo's, which, after all, is of comparatively little importance, because it is limited entirely to the exchangeable *variations in the value of commodities*, and takes no notice of the exchange between the different classes of labourers, capitalists, and landowners, which it was partly Smith's object to explain. Admitting the greater verbal or logical accuracy of Mr Ricardo, it was obtained, we apprehend, by shutting entirely out of his science those important relations of the labourer to other classes, which Smith, by a change in his terms, really discussed.

(Hodgskin, *The Economist*, IV, 28 November 1846: 1557)[31]

II. THE DISSENTERS AND THE LABOUR WRITERS

No serious dependency on the part of Hodgskin upon Ricardian theory is discernible; on the contrary, Ricardian theory was seen to lend itself to social apologetics. I wish now to consider the possibility that the dissenters may have taken for granted that the labour writers were in fact Ricardians – a possibility that must be carefully allowed for given the presence in Hodgskin's work of features which, taken in isolation, do indeed suggest a Ricardian affiliation. If it is found that the dissenters were impressed by such passages, then the hypothesis which we are examining – that the dissenters sought to revise orthodox economic theory because of the 'dangerous use' made thereof by the social critics – would have much in its favour.

I do not intend to examine each and every possible candidate for the designation 'dissenter'. Only four of the better known critics will be considered – Samuel Read, G. Poulett Scrope, Richard Whately and Mountifort Longfield. But this sample includes writers who, it will probably be generally agreed, are amongst the most important. On the basis of this evidence I can see little to suggest a conspicuously held belief on the part of dissenters that the labour writers, such as Hodgskin, drew their inspiration from Ricardian theory.

The general object of Read's work is outlined in the Preface to his *Political Economy*. It is to define the respective rights, and the limits to those rights, of wage and profit recipients. The issue was regarded of immediate import in the light of labour's growing sophistication and power (Read 1829: xxx). During the course of the argument, Smith, Ricardo and Hodgskin were taken to task, in independent critiques, for maintaining the position, explicitly or implicitly, that labour is the source of all wealth: 'Dr Smith himself was not, it must be admitted, wholly free from error in his treatment of the question between the labourers and capitalists. He does not indeed treat that question directly, but he says incidentally, "it is but equity that those who feed, clothe and lodge the whole body of the people should have such a share of the produce of their own labour as to be themselves tolerably well fed, clothed, and lodged"; meaning evidently, from the context that the labourers alone feed, clothe and lodge "the whole body of the people" ' (xxxii).[32] As evidence that the so-called 'Ricardo economists' maintained labour to be the sole source of wealth, Read referred to McCulloch's *Principles*, to Ricardo's pamphlet *On Protection to Agriculture*, and to the first chapter of Ricardo's *Principles*. The latter, he asserted, 'consists of an elaborate, though indirect attempt to prove that labour produces all, as if capital produced nothing, and was not a real source of wealth also!' (xxix n).[33]

Read fully agreed with the position of Hodgskin – 'a very able writer and advocate of the labourers' (xxx) – that the working class would no longer tolerate an 'unjust' social organization. The two shared much in common on fundamentals. As Read phrased the matter, 'the great object of political economy is to point out and demonstrate the natural grounds of right upon which the great laws of property are or ought to be founded, and upon which they must ultimately rest for their justification, and stability'. What is called 'this innovation', he asserted further, 'gives a more important and a more definite object to the science, presents it under a new and totally different aspect from that in which it has hitherto appeared, and causes it to assume an entirely new shape' (xxxi, xxiii–iv, ix). There can be no doubt that the scope of political economy is drawn upon a broader canvas than by either Ricardo or Smith.

I turn now to his critique of Hodgskin. Read objected to Hodgskin's contention that 'all the benefits attributed to capital arise from coexisting and skilled labour', an approach which minimized the significance of (circulating) capital as stored-up goods and emphasized in its stead that of synchronized activity, the labourer requiring nothing but 'a conviction that while he is labouring at his particular occupation, the things which he does not produce himself will be produced for him, and that he will be able to procure them and pay for them by the produce of his own labour' (Read 1829: 125).[34] In his reply, Read insisted upon the empirical fact that pre-existing stocks are necessary for current production to proceed. But Hodgskin had also posed a variety of questions regarding fixed capital goods amounting to the contention that, however productive, they can produce nothing 'independent of the labourer' having 'no utility whatever, possessing no productive power whatever, but as they are guided, directed, and applied by skillful hands' (cited by Read 1829: 127–8). To all this Read objected that Hodgskin's argument disallowed any return to the capitalist, however great the contribution of capital to output, and therefore *proves too much*. The claim to profit by the capitalist in fact rested, Read insisted, 'upon the compact and agreement with the labourer, to whom he pays his wages in virtue of that agreement', and depended 'partly upon the *comparative* degree in which labour can produce *with* and *without* capital, and partly upon the cost and difficulty or privation which the particular contribution of capital requires'. The correct way of determining the respective contributions of the factors from this perspective was to consider the (limited) output of which labour without capital is capable as the 'produce of labour', and all the rest as 'the effects or produce of the machines and instruments or capital' (Read 1829: 128).[35]

The criticism of Hodgskin thus emphasized Hodgskin's special approach to capital and was made quite apart from anything that Read had to say about Ricardo or, for that matter, Smith. There is nothing to suggest that he regarded Hodgskin's position as deriving from Ricardo or the Ricardians.

The error of identifying 'value with labour' and resolving 'cost of production into the quantity of *labour* only' was said by G. Poulett Scrope in his *Principles of Political Economy* (1833) to apply to the 'majority of political economists'. Ultimate responsibility, however, was assigned to Adam Smith. Smith 'and his followers' are criticized for insisting that each commodity has 'a *real* value, which they define to consist of the quantity of *labour* required to produce it' – an error leading them to 'call labour the natural standard or measure of value' (Scrope 1833: 197n, 166n). In his well-known *Quarterly Review* article of January 1831 Scrope took to task 'Ricardo, Malthus, and their several schools' for insisting upon 'a *natural* and *real* measure of value in *labour*, inasmuch as labour enters into, and is the *primary* cause of, the value of everything' (Scrope 1831a: 14). Ricardo doubtless was included amongst the 'majority of political economists' with whom Scrope took issue in 1833.

No formal mention is made of Hodgskin in the context of value theory in the *Principles*, and this is in itself lends additional support for the divorce of Hodgskin's case from any basis in Ricardian value theory; but Scrope had some sharp words for him when he turned to the nature of capital: 'there are persons', he complained, 'who still, – in the present light of civilization, in the nineteenth century, and in the midst of all the evidence which is afforded, wherever we turn our eyes, of the prodigious part which capital is playing in the production of the necessaries, comforts, and luxuries of human life, – declaim against capital as the poison of society, and the taking of interest on capital by its owners, as an abuse, an injustice, a robbery of the class of labourers!' (Scrope 1833: 150). There are also critical references to James Mill and McCulloch but the culprits are in no way linked. In the review article of January 1831 no mention is made of Hodgskin; it is the economists of Mr Ricardo's school, including Ricardo himself, who bear the brunt on the grounds of their supposed denial of the independent productivity of capital goods:

> The economists of Mr Ricardo's school delight in styling capital 'accumulated labour'. It is by no means so exclusively. Ever since the infancy of manhood capital has done its part towards production in conjunction with labour. Indeed it would be fully as correct to call labour 'accumulated capital', since there is no doubt that man himself, and all his several powers, are the result of the expenditure of much capital. But throughout the writings of these authors it is continually repeated that labour does everything, is the only real source of wealth. As if the land, buildings, machinery, live stock, instruments, all raw produce, at any moment existing in a country were utterly useless towards production.
>
> (Scrope 1831a: 12)[36]

More specifically Scrope addressed himself to the errors of James Mill and McCulloch in a sharp criticism of the labour theory of value:

> This . . . brings us to one of the most extraordinary and barefaced fallacies that were ever attempted to be imposed on the understanding of mankind under the mask of science. Messrs Mill and McCulloch, after Mr Ricardo, have entangled themselves so completely in their doctrine as to labour being the only source of wealth, and the prime and sole element of value, as to be driven at length into a confusion of ideas only to be equalled by those of the Catholic arguments on the invisible presence. They uphold that the profits of stock are actually neither more nor less than the wages of labour.
>
> (Scrope 1831a: 16)[37]

Scrope concluded that 'it is needless to waste time in refuting such palpable absurdities' (18).[38] Capital and labour 'co-operate in every useful undertaking, and the one is no more exclusively productive than the other' (12).

Profit, as such, Scrope regarded as 'the inducement of the capitalist to employ his capital in production' and as 'a compensation . . . for *abstaining for a time from the consumption* of that portion of his property on his personal gratification; and the compensation is therefore proportioned to the *time* during which his capital is so engaged instead of being spent on himself, as revenue' (Scrope 1833: 145–6).[39] In this context issue was again taken with McCulloch and Mill for the view that 'time is a mere word', but the notion of profits as compensation for abstinence had 'escaped the penetration . . . even of Mr Malthus' (146–7, 150).

The picture would be incomplete without mention of Scrope's strongly worded rejection, in his review article, of James Mill on the law of markets. An increase in the 'propensity to save' (Scrope's term) might involve a general glut:

> The economists have nowhere committed greater errors than in discussing the relations of the demand to the supply of commodities. They insist, that there can be no falling off in the general demand for goods, because all business being merely an exchange of goods, the general demand is measured by, in fact consists of, the general supply. We have shown, however, that the real demand being for final consumption only, a general increase in the propensity to save, as compared with that to spend, would proportionately diminish the demand as compared with the supply, and occasion a *general glut*.
>
> (Scrope 1831a: 23)[40]

It may be added that Scrope accepted the Smithian approach to the secular behaviour of the profit rate running in terms of 'competition of capitals' which Ricardo, of course, had always rejected as in conflict with the law of markets – formally objecting to the 'economists of Mr Ricardo's school' for their attribution of the downward trend in the return on capital to 'the necessity of resorting to inferior soils for the production of food' (25–6). In this context both Malthus and McCulloch are cited as the guilty parties.

Finally, Scrope objected to Ricardo and 'his followers' (Mill and McCulloch) regarding the inverse profit–wage relationship although it turns out that his major complaint was to the use of the word 'wages' to mean *proportionate* wages. He, in effect, granted the validity of the relationship on Ricardo's use of terms (although as an uninteresting truism) (27f).

Scrope cannot be said to have placed Hodgskin in a central position in his criticism of orthodox theory. And when Hodgskin is mentioned there is not the slightest suggestion that he depended in any way upon Ricardo or Ricardian theory.

Richard Whately condemned those 'demagogues' who attempted to instil in the working class the belief that 'inequality of condition is inexpedient, and ought to be abolished – that the wealth of a man whose income is equal to that of a hundred labouring families, is so much deducted from the common stock, and causes a hundred poor families the less to be maintained; – and that a general spoilation of the rich, and equal division of property, would put an end to poverty for ever' (Whately 1832: 202). Like Scrope he also criticized McCulloch and Mill for their reduction of capital to accumulated labour and their opinion that 'time is a mere word', but also like Scrope, he did not link the 'demagogues' with the Ricardians.

Longfield took issue with Ricardian doctrine on two central matters of theory: first, the supposed indeterminacy of the wage–profit division in a growing economy; and second, the supposed denial of profit-rate decline in the case of capital accumulation with population given (Longfield 1834a: 184f). In his own model, profits are determined by a kind of marginal productivity theory of capital within a demand–supply framework while wages are treated as a form of residual in the product net of rent. Certain very significant implications for social policy were drawn by Longfield from this conception. Thus on the basis of the 'order in which a correct analysis of the sources of revenue can be carried on ... 1st Rent, 2nd Profit, 3d Wages ... it can be proved how impossible it is to *regulate wages generally*, either by combinations of workmen, or by legislative enactments'. What Longfield evidently had in mind was that the treatment of profits as residual – the orthodox doctrine on his reading – implied that, however low the return on capital may fall, there would be no untoward consequences. In fact, he warned, to fix the wage inappropriately high, by legislation or union pressure, would dictate an inappropriately low return on capital with the effects to be expected from any commodity price set below its equilibrium level (vii–viii).[41] Longfield was by no means consistent in his treatment of *wages* as residual, for he did not rule out some dependency of the growth of the labour supply on wages and he made much of the conception of wages as payment for productive services.

There is no doubt that Longfield hoped that his lectures would demonstrate the untenability of radical solutions: 'Political-Economy is merely a defensive science, which attempts to prevent the injudicious interference of speculative legislation.' The labourer should be taught 'that his interest will be best promoted by prudence and industry', and not by the 'violent demolition of the capital destined to his support', 'that the wages of his labour cannot be determined by the wishes of his employer, that they are even as independent of the decrees of the legislature as they are of his own will, and that they are ultimately entirely dependent upon the prudence or improvidence, the industry or idleness, of the labouring classes themselves' (18–19). More strongly he wrote:

> It is frequently complained of as an unjust and an unreasonable thing, that the labourer, who seems to produce every thing by his toil, should not in return receive the entire, or at least a much greater part than he does receive, of what he has assisted to produce. That his wages are so low, is sometimes attributed to the wicked combination of employers, who take advantage of his necessities or his ignorance, to impose unreasonable and unequal terms upon him, in order thereby to secure enormous profits to themselves. Such arguments are, I believe, principally propagated by men who are conscious of their invalidity, and whose object is to create disturbance, by stimulating the passions of the poor and ignorant, and by persuading them that their poverty is caused by oppression or misrule.
>
> (Longfield 1834a: 158)

The tone of Longfield's remarks here and his general emphasis upon the rule of law and the limited potential of union activity suggest that he may have been familiar with Hodgskin's writings. The *Lectures* also contain what is perhaps a more detailed, albeit implicit, reference to Hodgskin. It occurs during the course of a discussion of wages envisaged as the *discounted* product of labour, a discount which the labourer is prepared to pay because he 'does not and cannot wait for his wages until the sale of the commodity which he has assisted to produce'; the capitalist employer for his part 'would have no motive to advance his capital if the additional value of the article were to be only equal to the sums advanced by him to the labourer . . . ; he expects to sell it at a greater price and that difference constitutes his profits' (79). But the payment of profits should not be considered as causing an addition to the prices of commodities. For the function of waiting had in any event to be carried on and the property owner was in a better position to do so – that is, he was able to do so for a lower reward – than the owner of labour. Thus the final price which would have to be paid in the absence of conventional profits would not be lower if the burden of waiting were adopted by the labourer (160f). This argument constitutes an implicit rejection of Hodgskin's case that only by viewing the worker as consumer could the fact of exploitation due to the excess of market price over labour embodied – measured by the difference between labour commanded and labour embodied – best be demonstrated.

In all this – both the explicit condemnation of the radicals and the implicit criticism of Hodgskin – there is no connection made between Hodgskin and Ricardian theory. Longfield's approach to Ricardianism will be further explored in the next section.

III. THE DISSENTERS AND REFORM

The dissenters seem to have understood that Hodgskin's position regarding the non-productivity of capital and against the payment of interest was unrelated to Ricardian theory – at least they were silent about any connection. There remains for us to consider the possibility that the dissenters found Ricardian doctrine inadequate *as a reply* to the labour writers. Now there seems to be something to this view. We have seen in the past section that the Ricardians were indeed sometimes taken to task (as by Scrope) for their approach to value theory and its (supposed) implications for the non-productivity of capital and the capitalist. This aspect of the Ricardian position would have been unsuitable as a reply. But in his account Professor Meek (1967: 70–1) has gone considerably further; he has cited a 'disarmingly frank' admission by Scrope in the 1873 (second) edition of his *Principles* that his dissatisfaction with Ricardian theory originally arose from its failure to yield a convincing defence of current institutions and the current income distribution against the charges of the socialists:

What lessons in this respect were they likely to imbibe from the current doctrines of Political Economy? *Were these lessons fitted to reconcile them to the hardships of a condition of almost ceaseless toil for, in many cases, but a meagre subsistence*; and this in a country overflowing with wealth enjoyed in idleness by some at the expense (as it might at first sight appear to them) of the labour of others? On examination of the works of the most noted economists of that day, Messrs Ricardo, Jas. Mill, McCulloch, Malthus, Chalmers, and Whateley, I could not discover in them any answer likely to satisfy the mind of a half-educated man of plain commonsense and honesty who should seek there some *justification for the immense disparity of fortunes and circumstances that strike the eye on everyside*. On the contrary, these works appeared to me to contain many obvious inconsistencies and errors, to inculcate many false and pernicious principles, and certainly to be little adapted to the purpose which I looked for in them.

(Scrope 1873: vii–viii)[42]

'Approaching political economy in this spirit,' Meek concluded, 'it is hardly surprising that Scrope should have been the first British economist to propound a consistent version of the abstinence theory.' 'Was Marx's "bad conscience and evil intent of apologetic" too strong a characterisation of such as these?' asked Dobb rhetorically (1973: 110).

The foregoing interpretation, I believe, is the precise reverse of Scrope's actual position. *What he intended to convey by the passage is the failure of orthodox theory to provide a convincing rationale for the low standards and gross inequality which the orthodox economists – the Ricardians – themselves, he complained, were attempting to justify.* The mistaken interpretation follows from the presumption that an economist who upholds the abstinence theory of interest is *ipso facto* an apologist for the *status quo*. It suffices to draw attention here to the following passage from the *Principles* where Scrope expressly accepts the necessity for reform but refuses to attribute all the social evils of the day to the existence of capital and the payment of interest:

That those who observe the prevalence of great misery among the inferior classes of workmen in this and other wealthy countries, who witness and deplore the fact, that in spite of all the manifold improvements which are continually adding to the productiveness of labour, the share of the gross production which falls to the common labourer does not increase – perhaps proportionally diminishes; that, on viewing this anomaly, they should conclude *something* to be wrong in the arrangements which at present determine the distribution of the wealth produced in great part by labour is no source of astonishment to me, for I arrive at the same necessary conclusion from the same observation. But that any sane person should attribute the evil to *the existence of capital* – that is, to the employment of wealth in aiding the

148

production of further wealth, instead of being unproductively consumed, almost, if not quite, as fast as it is created, or unproductively hoarded to satisfy the lust of the miser – is indeed wonderful.

(Scrope 1833: 150–1)

To avoid misunderstanding it should be reiterated that Scrope certainly took issue with the Ricardians on the grounds that their position appeared to rule out the independent productivity of capital goods and the notion of interest as a reward for abstinence. *But there is more to Ricardianism than this, and much of it, Hodgskin complained (as we shall see), lent itself as an apologia for the unacceptable conditions of the day.*

There are other statements by Scrope that have been regarded as clear evidence of his concern that Ricardian doctrine did not provide an adequate *apologetic* reply to the labour writers, and this because of its disharmonious implications regarding contemporary institutional arrangements (Blaug 1958: 148–9). The following extract is one such formulation:

In blundering the different subjects that have passed through their hands – rent, profits, wages, population, and morals – they have not merely erred, they have invariably, and with an unhappy pertinacity in error, erred on the wrong, on the most mischievous side.

In their theory of rent, they have insisted that landlords can thrive only at the expense of the public at large, and especially of the capitalists: in their theory of profits, they have declared that capitalists can only improve their circumstances by depressing those of the labouring and most numerous class: in their theory of wages, they have maintained that the condition of the labourers can only be bettered by depriving them of their greatest happiness and their only consolation under trouble, the feelings of the husband and the father: in their theory of population, they have absolved governments from all responsibility for the misery of the people committed to their care: and in their theory of morals, they have impressed on the poor, that the legitimate indulgence of their natural affections is the greatest of all crimes, – on the rich, that the abandonment of the poor to destitution is the most sacred of all duties. In one and all of their arguments they have studiously exhibited the interests of every class in society as necessarily at perpetual variance with those of every other class!

(Scrope 1831b: 116)[43]

That Scrope objected here to the disharmonious implications of Ricardian doctrine – as he read it – is obvious and it could not have served as a convincing defence of contemporary institutions had he wished to formulate one. But if this extract is used as evidence of an apologetic intention on his part – of an insistence upon the mutually beneficial state of contemporary society – it must again be objected that the truth of the matter is quite the reverse. *His complaint was that orthodoxy presented a vision of the economy precluding reform, which he believed to be essential.*

Scrope's bitter criticism of the landlord class and of contemporary institutions as responsible for poverty (1833: 310),[44] his case for insurance schemes,[45] progressive income taxation and property taxation (332-3), his justification of intervention in Ireland in the light of unemployment (1831a: 40),[46] his rejection of the Treasury View on the grounds of a high elasticity in the supply of savings – independently of the interest rate (see discussion below, p. 152) all give the lie to the notion that his economics was imbued with apologetic intent. It was the orthodox school which Scrope believed deserved the charge. Here he had in mind Malthusianism interpreted as a deliberately designed apologetic doctrine which 'directly frees government from all responsibility for the sufferings of the mass of the community, by throwing the blame entirely on nature and the improvidence of the poor themselves, and declaring the evil to admit of no remedy from any possible exertions of the legislature' (1833: 290; also 282-3). Second, he rejected the doctrine of *laissez faire* attributed to the orthodox economists – that individuals are 'certain to pursue that precise line of conduct which is most for the public advantage'; the doctrine, if applied, 'would turn the throne, the pulpit, and the bench into a sinecure' and 'destroys the utility of political economy itself, for what avail rules for the guidance of nations to an increase of either wealth or happiness, if individuals are sure to take the right path of their own accord?' (1831a: 47).[47]

But most important is Scrope's insistence that increased aggregate wealth – the context implies that the caution applies even to increases in *per capita* wealth – cannot be identified with increased social happiness *unless the matter of distribution is also attended to* (1833: 298). In a discussion of the grounds for limitations of the free-trade principle, Scrope charged that 'the fallacy which has misled the writers who have supported free trade, as applicable without limit to all possible cases, has its roots deeply interwoven with the groundwork of political economy' (1831a: 42). What he had in mind was the treatment of the subject by orthodox writers (such as Malthus and McCulloch) solely as a 'science of wealth' and not (what we would now call) one of *welfare* – 'it is utterly false that every increase in wealth is a proportionate increase in the aggregate means of enjoyment' (43-4).[48] As he phrased the issue in detail:

> All we are anxious for is a clear, general, and specific acknowledgment that the theory of wealth is *not* the theory of government; that the laws which regulate the increase or diminution of wealth are not the laws which determine the well or ill being of a nation; that it is of infinitely greater importance *how* the wealth of a community is *distributed*, than what is its absolute amount; that an increase of national wealth may be made at the expense of much national and individual happiness; and

consequently, that the conclusions of the science of wealth, serviceable as we acknowledge they must be, if correctly deduced from true principles, and properly applied, ought, on no account, to be taken by themselves as guides to the knowledge of the real interests of a society, but must be first tested and tried by a reference to other data, upon which the welfare of societies depends, in an equal, if not in a still greater degree, than on their aggregate wealth.

(Scrope 1831c: 52)

The significance of Scrope's complaint against the orthodox doctrine can only be fully appreciated if it is recognized that his position was almost identical to that of William Thompson – one of the so-called 'Ricardian Socialists'. I have in mind Thompson's criticism of the 'political economists', or 'mechanical speculators', as he called them, for their preoccupation with maximum output: 'By them the sublime notions of intelligence, benevolence or mutual co-operation and perfectibility, are held in derision. . . . The problem with them has been, how to raise the greatest produce and to ensure that greatest consumption or efficient demand' (Thompson 1824: v–vi).[49] He spoke sarcastically of the 'noble discoveries' of political economy as useless to social science, 'the application of which becomes the art of social happiness' (viii), and appealed for an approach which made political economy 'subservient to that just *distribution* of wealth which tends most to human happiness' (x). All talk of morals and legislation must be nugatory without attention to distribution: 'the most important portion of our virtues and vices [are] indissolubly connected with the distribution of wealth, that to speak of morals and legislation with an affected contempt of such matters, is to grasp at a shadow and to leave a substance – is to add hypocritical or ignorant insult to the miseries of communities' (xvii–xviii).[50]

The insistence upon the problem of distribution profoundly influenced Scrope's attitude towards political obligation: 'the state has no claim to the allegiance of those citizens upon whom it confers no advantages. An individual to whom the law extends no protection in the extremity of distress is absolved from all duty of obedience to the law. It is the very first duty of a government to secure the means of subsistence to every well-disposed and well-conducted member of the community over whose welfare it presides' (Scrope 1833: 305).[51] It may be added that while Longfield shared with Scrope (and W. F. Lloyd) the view that there exists a 'natural right' to subsistence as the counterpart to any obligation to obey the laws of society, he feared Scrope had gone much too far in implying that 'you must by tyranny understand every government which is not the *best* government to which the rights of man entitle him', a position which he believed, 'would justify resistance to the laws, in every individual who thought any modification of them expedient' (Longfield 1834b: 25–6).[52] Whether this was exactly Scrope's intention is uncertain, but his formulations were certainly read by some to imply dangerous implications for property.

Scrope's abstinence doctrine does not alter this picture of a committed reformer. *Full employment* was specified by Scrope as a deliberate object of social policy, and the fact that capital might not be in excess was not to be used as an excuse against intervention – in effect Scrope rejected the so-called Treasury View: 'It is not true,' he wrote, 'that the opening of any new branch must *necessarily* cause the withdrawal of capital from some other, *in the same country*, in which it is now actively employed' (1831a: 40). He had in mind partly the possibilities open for capital inflows. But more important for us are his comments on (internal) capital supply conditions: 'There is, moreover, a species of elasticity in capital, by which it accommodates itself to the demand for it; and the economists themselves assert, that any new demand for capital is in effect immediately supplied from *new* savings' (40).[53] It is clear that in this fundamental application Scrope assumed what seems to constitute a highly elastic long-run capital supply curve. In any event *no emphasis at all is placed on the problem of assuring capital supplies*. Scrope's theoretical discussion of the abstinence issue is scarcely utilized in an apologetic manner.

Much of what has been said regarding Scrope applies also to the other dissenters. Read, for example, charged the Ricardians with social apologetics; rising real wages, he maintained, 'is a result which Mr Ricardo and his followers deprecate beyond all others' in the interest of profits; and Malthus is charged with opposing Godwin on the basis of 'certain alleged greater difficulties and destitution than would fall upon the poor in consequence of those attempts to relieve them' (Read 1829: 256–7).[54]

Like Scrope, Richard Whately, in his *Lectures* of 1832, emphasized *per capita* national wealth as the object of study ('wealth *in proportion to* the population') (Whately 1832: 188), and insisted upon fair distribution: '[Among] nations equal in wealth, the greatest and most important varieties may exist in respect to its *distribution*. If a large proportion of the wealth of a community consist of the enormous and overgrown fortunes of a few, that community has by no means such promising prospects in respect of the intellectual and moral advancement of the rest of the people, or even of the possessors of those fortunes, with one which enjoys a greater diffusion of wealth' (Whately 1832: 193). Support for this position was drawn from a statement by 'the late Professor [Nassau Senior] in his Introductory Lecture' favouring increased wages as essential to the 'morals and happiness' of the working class.[55] Whately had also based himself upon an earlier article by Senior, citing Senior's position there that great wealth accumulated in the hands of a very few 'may not be favourable to the happiness of the possessor; and, if this be so, Political Economy will best teach us to avoid creating or perpetuating institutions, which promote such inconvenient agglomerations' (Senior 1828: 174). All this must be borne in mind in evaluating Whately's condemnation of demagoguery. To reject strict 'equality' was not to support a distribution entailing 'the enormous and overgrown fortunes of a few'.[56]

Longfield is the most difficult of the dissenters to interpret. We have seen that he was critical of aspects of Ricardian theory, especially its treatment of profits as residual. To this extent it would seem clear that he could not have adopted orthodox doctrine, in his critique of radicalism. But this applies to the *uncorrected* version of the doctrine. It is my contention that Longfield should be envisaged as *making very extensive use* indeed of the Ricardian corpus of theory appropriately corrected or appropriately interpreted.[57] As one conspicuous example, he retained the theory of differential rent, justifying the secular growth of unearned land income on the grounds that landlords are likely to generate a desirable influence on social behaviour, and by the observation that, in consequence of improvements, the secular increase in rents 'takes place without a reduction of wages or profits'. Moreover, the social implications of rising unearned income were said to be diluted by the increase in the *number* of landowners: 'The same quantity of land will be distributed among a greater number of proprietors, and the relative situation of the classes will remain as before, and a greater number of men will be supported by the rent of land, a greater number by the profits of capital, and a greater number by the wages of their labour' (Longfield 1834a: 225).[58] As a second key example, he retained the Ricardian inverse wage–profit relation and used the measure of value in its construction in a manner so convincing as to attract Robert Torrens back to the Ricardian fold. Longfield did not believe that the fundamental theorem on distribution, when correctly interpreted as referring to *proportions* rather than absolute incomes, implied a clash between classes. This was particularly true when the doctrine was supplemented by his new approach to profit-rate determination.

That the (Ricardian) three-fold class approach was *not* necessarily suggestive of class warfare is a case quite explicitly argued by Longfield:

> At first sight it would appear, and many reasonings have proceeded upon the supposition, that the three principal classes have interests directly adverse to each other. That the landlord gets all the produce of the soil, except what is divided between the labourer and the capitalist. The more he gets, the less remains for them; and therefore as rent increases, the portion that is divided between the labourer and the farmer must suffer a corresponding diminution. In the same manner, as the fruits of industry are divided between the capitalist and the labourer, it might hastily be supposed that the gain of one must be the loss of the other.
>
> (Longfield 1834a: 223)

The apparent implication of inter-class hostility is rejected on the grounds of the general principle of competition: 'But the fact is not so. The parties to every contract have just at the time of making it an interest opposed to each other, each being desirous to get as much, and to give as little, as he can. But the competition of others prevent this adverse interest from operating to the detriment of either, and previous to the contract, all parties have a common interest that the articles which are the subject of the exchange should be produced in the best and cheapest manner' (223).

We must now consider the matter of specific policy issues. As we have seen, Longfield opposed direct intervention in the labour market by legislation or union activity, basing his view upon the notion that profits cannot be treated as simple residual, since any fall in the return on capital must have negative effects on the rate of accumulation. His conception of the wage rate as payment for productive services – which I again emphasize does not fit well with the view that wages are to be treated as residual – also had social implications especially for poor law legislation. All of this may appear to suggest an apologetic intent. Yet this would be an unfair conclusion. The fact is that, like Scrope, Longfield pointed squarely to the distribution problem. An emphasis upon the necessity for a 'judicious' distribution is apparent in a contrast drawn between personal wealth and national wealth: 'it is to be observed, that though the wealth of an individual may be expended in procuring vicious luxuries, yet that a rich nation, as distinguished from a poor nation, will be found to consist in the great mass of its inhabitants being comfortably and wholesomely fed, lodged, and clothed, and well rewarded for their industry. If otherwise, that wealth must be wrongly distributed; the cause and cure of which wrong distribution come also within the province of the political-economist to investigate' (1834a: 5).[59] The greatest care was thus taken to warn against international *per capita* comparisons divorced from distribution considerations. *The matter of 'desirable' distribution was placed squarely within the domain of the economist.*[60]

To some extent Longfield's 'solution' amounted simply to an appeal on *standard Ricardian lines* for rapid capital accumulation. But the range of legitimate government intervention extends far beyond anything conceived by Ricardo. In the first place, we must recognize Longfield's assertion of a 'natural right' to subsistence in exchange for the duty to obey the laws of society – the position that 'every individual is entitled to the means of support, from that society which is determined to compel him to obey its laws' (1834b: 19).[61] On these grounds, Longfield rejected the view of J. B. Say – shared with Malthus – that 'if a man does not produce subsistence for himself, or does not possess the means by voluntary gift from some other person, he can have no right to compel any one else to provide subsistence for him' (Longfield 1834b: 16). But this merely provided justification for poor relief according to the 1834 model, whereas Longfield's programme went considerably further. He was prepared to support tax-financed redistributive schemes provided he was satisfied that labour productivity would not be adversely affected thereby (Black 1971: 25). Accordingly, in the

Lectures on Poor Laws he made out a case for 'those whose wants are aggravated by sufferings which put it out of their power to earn their bread; the blind, the insane, the crippled poor', who 'should be liberally assisted by the state'; the establishment of 'hospitals, infirmaries, and asylums' for infectious disorders; 'a very small pension' for cripples and blind poor resident at home; and of particular importance, 'a small pension as a superannuation allowance, to every labourer of sixty years of age' irrespective of whether the claimant could justifiably be defined as 'necessitous' (Longfield 1834b: 31–3). In a lecture of 1872, which formally dealt with 'the limits of state interference with the distribution of wealth', we are told that 'political economy fully proved that as soon as society arrives at a very moderate degree of civilization, the state can give very little assistance to the creation of wealth', and 'that its interference, in general, although with the best intentions, has been absolutely mischievous'; but we also read that certain other issues of policy 'have been utterly neglected, or at least have never been discussed in scientific principles' (1971: 133–4).[62] State interference in distribution is what Longfield largely had in mind, and in the paper we find 'a program of redistribution which anticipates most features of the modern welfare state' (Black 1971: 25).[63]

This progressive approach is unaffected by the analysis of interest in terms of 'abstinence'. The notion of a relationship between interest and savings – although it played a part in Longfield's unwillingness to countenance wage increases *at the expense of profits* – was not used to counter governmental intervention in social affairs. The fact is that the famous analogy between demand–supply analysis relating to final products and to capital was hesitantly made insofar as concerns the supply side:

> You may remember that the effect of demand and supply, in regulating the price of commodities, is frequently slightly influenced by the cost of production, which determines the average prices, and prevents buyers and sellers, especially in the case of the more desirable manufactured commodities, from departing very far from those prices to which they know the value of the article will soon conform itself. But of capital there is not, properly speaking, any cost of production, except that sacrifice of the present to the future which is made by the possessor of wealth, who employs it as capital instead of consuming it for his immediate gratification.
>
> (Longfield 1834a: 195–6)

It would appear, on balance, to have been Longfield's position that although many *individuals* save irrespective of the return on capital, in any *national* capital market a positive relation can be discerned between the profit rate and saving. But the elasticity and the position, so to speak, of the aggregative curve will differ markedly between countries and over time. It is unfortunate that Longfield chose not to go into 'the circumstances which combined with the rate of profit, will have the most influence strengthening the principle of accumulation in any country' (1834a: 196). But there is evidence that, in Longfield's view, such interest-saving nexus as exists will *tend to weaken in the progress of society* while the other 'circumstances' will strengthen. I refer to the final Lecture where the potentially dangerous effects for accumulation of a secular decline of the profit rate are considered, namely 'the reduction in the income of the capitalist' and 'the difficulty it adds to the accumulation of capital'. The first problem is dismissed in the light of a rising *total* profit income; while the second is also minimized in the light of prospective changing attitudes towards saving: 'Those disadvantages are, with the progress of society, counteracted by the abundance of capital which, notwithstanding the low rate of profits, makes their total amount very large, and by the habits of saving, and the prudent regard to the future, which must exist in such a country' (234). Indeed, in his paper dealing with 'the limits of state interference with the distribution of wealth', Longfield apparently *abandoned* the functional dependency of savings on the rate of profits as an empirically significant phenomenon. I have in mind his assertion in 1872 that taxation to finance benefits to the under-privileged is unlikely, on balance, to have any serious consequences for 'the motives to industry, thrift, and self-denial': 'As far as the taxpayer is concerned, I don't think there is need for much caution. The disposition to accumulate depends more upon habit and temperament, than upon any calculations of reason. Its average strength in Great Britain is greater than is necessary, and can bear reduction without loss to the public. Were it not for the outlet afforded by foreign speculations, these islands could not find a profitable employment for the excess of capital that is created for a few years of peace' (Longfield 1971: 135). This is a truly remarkable passage if it is recalled that Ricardo feared that a fall in the return on capital would generate a slackening of accumulation while J. S. Mill emphasized the precariousness of the savings disposition.

IV. SUMMARY AND CONCLUSION

We have seen that the dissenters against Ricardian orthodoxy did not react because of the use supposedly made by the labour writers of the doctrine. Any such position would in any event have been unlikely given the forcibly expressed hostility towards Ricardo on the part of Thomas Hodgskin.

My analysis also casts doubt on the view that the dissenters found Ricardian theory unhelpful as a defence of the institutional and distributional *status quo* against the charges of the labour writers, particularly Hodgskin. I have shown that the argument collapses when faced by the fact that Scrope was as sharp a critic of Ricardianism as an apologia for the *status quo* and of the skewed income distribution, as any labour writer.

In Longfield's case it is more accurate to say that he made much positive use of Ricardian theory in formulating his reply to the radicals, fitting his own theoretical modifications into the existing framework, appropriately interpreted, and thereby avoiding what he envisaged to be negative implications for inter-class relationships.

There remains to add the following fascinating aspects of the record. There does exist one case of an economist who complained bitterly of the ammunition provided by Ricardo (albeit inadvertently) for the socialists. This individual was not, however, one of the 'dissenters' – he was Thomas De Quincey. Writing in the *Logic of Political Economy*, not of value theory or the inverse wage–profit theorem but of Ricardo's minimization of technological progress and the consequent emphasis upon continuously rising rent, De Quincey complained:

> And it happens (though certainly not with any intentional sanction from so upright a man as David Ricardo) that in no instance has the policy of gloomy disorganising Jacobinism, fitfully reviving from age to age, received any essential aid from science, excepting in this one painful corollary from Ricardo's triad of chapters on Rent, Profit and Wages. . . . The class of landlords, they urge, is the merest realisation of a scriptural idea – *unjust men reaping where they have not sown.* They prosper . . . *by* the ruin of the fraternal classes associated with themselves on the land. . . . [The] noblest order of men amongst us, our landed aristocracy, is treated as the essential scourge of all orders beside.
>
> (De Quincey 1970 [1844]: 250–1)[64]

The notion of class hostility – supposedly engendered by Ricardo's distribution theory – providing a handle for the anarchists, is thus a central complaint not of the dissenters but of one of the most faithful of Ricardo's followers.[65] And the supposed connection did not lead De Quincey to seek for an alternative structure.[66]

Second, we should keep in mind James Mill, whose hysterical response to Hodgskin is sharper than that of any of the dissenters. Mill evidently did not believe that the standard Ricardian position failed to provide an adequate response to the radical challenge, and saw nothing therein – even in the labour theory as interpreted by himself – which served the purposes of the socialists. The episode in question commences with Mill's complaint to Francis Place about a working-class deputation to the editor of the *Morning Chronicle*: 'Their notions about property look ugly; they not only desire that it should have nothing to do with representation, which is true, though not a truth for the present time, as they ought to see, but they seem to think that it should not exist, and that the existence of it is an evil to them. Rascals, I have no doubt, are at work among them. . . . The fools, not to see that what they madly desire would be such a calamity to them as no hands but their own could bring upon them' (Mill, letter of 25 October 1831, cited in Wallas 1925: 274n). It was Hodgskin's *Labour Defended*, Place explained to Mill, which the labourers were preaching. In the following year Mill informed Brougham: 'The nonsense to which your Lordship alludes about the rights of the labourer to the whole produce of the country, wages, profits and rent, all included, is the mad nonsense of our friend Hodgskin which he has published as a system, and propagates with the zeal of perfect fanaticism. . . . These opinions, if they were to spread, would be the subversion of civilized society; worse than the revolutionary deluge of Huns and Tartars' (letter of 3 September 1832, in Wallas 1925: 274n).

Clearly there is no self-evident relationship in the post-Ricardian literature between a body of economic theory and the social attitudes of the economist subscribing to it. The positive contributions by some of the labour writers point in precisely the same direction. This is very apparent in Thompson's case. His discussion of value includes the conceptions of differential land use, alternative cost and scarcity value; the principle of diminishing marginal utility is defined and utilized (together with the principle of increasing marginal disutility of effort) in an attempt to define an equilibrium wage rate, and also in a calculation of the effects of income redistribution (Thompson 1824: 71–3). The significance of free exchange is clearly expressed in utility terms: 'All voluntary exchanges of the articles of wealth, implying a preference, on both sides, of the things received to the thing given, tend to increase the happiness from wealth, and thence to increase the motives to its production' (45); whereas labour was said to be the sole measure of value, it was not an accurate measure in the light of changes in preference patterns over time, so that to seek an *accurate* measure of wealth was 'to hunt after a shadow' (15) – as clear-cut a criticism as any by Bailey. In Hodgskin's case, what stands out is his emphasis upon synchronized activity, which in an *Economist* review (XII, 18 November 1854: 1270) was elaborated in terms of the mutual exchange of valuable services. It is precisely conceptions such as these which, when found in the 'dissenting' literature, are said to indicate a developing hostility to Ricardianism and a justification of unregulated capitalism.

NOTES

1 That the roots of British socialism are to be traced to Ricardo's economics was later urged in Anton Menger's *The Right to the Whole Produce of Labour*, and by H. S. Foxwell in his Introduction to that work: 'Whatever qualifications Ricardo may have made . . . in his own mind, ninety-nine readers out of a hundred took him literally, and the main impression left by his book was that while wealth was almost exclusively due to labour, it was mainly absorbed by rent and other payments to the unproductive classes' (Foxwell 1899: xlii).
2 There is an extensive literature adopting this perspective. Elie Halévy emphasizes the opposition of the socialists to the Ricardians, but at the same time insists upon their *dependency* on Ricardo's value theory: 'the democratic opponents of James Mill and McCulloch, the first working-class theorists, instead of

attacking the Ricardian theory of value seized upon its principles to draw from it new conclusions and to refute, by a form of *reductio ad absurdam*, Ricardo's political economy' (Halévy 1956: 180–1). See also Halévy 1955 [1928]: 223–4: William Thompson (and Hodgskin) 'drew inspiration' from Ricardo.

Similarly, G.D.H. Cole refers to Hodgskin's work as the 'working-class answer' to Malthus and Ricardo, and to his 'critique of the orthodox economics of Ricardo and his school'. (Cole 1963: 10–11.) But he also writes, regarding both Hodgskin and Thompson, of their 'deductions from Ricardian assumptions' and their 'inversion of the Ricardian economic system. . . . As Hodgskin argues in his book, if it is admitted – and Ricardo admits it – that labour is the source of all value, then clearly all value belongs to the labourer, who should receive the whole product of his work' (12). See also Cole 1962, I: 106.

Max Beer (1929, I: 154) draws the relationship in these terms: 'But at the same time the socialists appeared and began to make use of the Ricardian theory of value as a weapon against the middle classes and to teach Labour that not the Tory landowner but the Liberal capitalist was their real enemy. Ricardo made labour the corner-stone of his system and yet he permitted the capitalist to appropriate accumulated labour and to decide the fate of the working classes.'

3 See also Marx's rough draft notes of 1857 (Marx 1973: 883).

4 Meek considers Ricardian theory narrowly defined in terms of the labour theory of value and the related conception that profits depend upon 'the proportion of the annual labour of the country . . . devoted to the support of the labourers', or upon the quantity of labour allocated to the wage-goods sector relative to the labour force as a whole; and also other supposed standard doctrines involving future prospects and class relationships. Cf. Meek 1967: 62, 67, 72–3.

5 For much the same general approach see also Meek 1972: 500–1, and Meek 1973: 124–5, where 'the persistent rejection or dilution' of the labour theory by so many economists during the late 1820s and the 1830s is attributed to the 'use (or misuse) of classical value theory by the British radical writers'.

6 In a recent paper, J. E. King argues that 'the 1873 "Afterword" does not do justice to Marx as an historian of economic thought, and cannot be regarded as a definitive exposition of his views on the subject' (1979: 383). My concern is not with Marx as historian of economics but with the hypothesis defined in the text, whether or not it represents his 'true' position. It should, however, be noted that the formulation in the text is not based solely on the Afterword but draws also upon *Theories of Surplus Value*.

7 For an effective demonstration that, on the matter of value, 'Hodgskin was decidedly hostile to Ricardo', see Hunt 1977.

Cf. the evidence presented by Professor P. H. Douglas which demonstrates that the impetus to early nineteenth-century British socialism deriving from the conception of profits and rent as 'deductions from the whole produce of labour' came from the writings of Adam Smith rather than those of Ricardo (Douglas 1928: 95f).

A similar account is given by Mark Blaug (1958: 148). But see 143: 'Unlike Gray and Thompson, who show no signs of having read Ricardo, Hodgskin derived his exploitation theory of profit directly from Ricardo's version of the labor theory of value.'

In her well-known monograph on the subject Esther Lowenthal questioned the legitimacy of the designation 'Ricardian' socialism: 'although . . . the socialist use of the labor theory followed hard on the publication of Ricardo's *Principles*, there is no evidence that the socialists were particularly impressed by his teachings. They all of them quote Adam Smith as their authority for the labor theory of value . . . and only Hodgskin betrays an intimate knowledge of [Ricardo's] work' (Lowenthal 1911: 103). But she also asserted that Hodgskin 'attacks the claims of capital on the basis of the labor theory of value' and 'bases very explicitly on Ricardo's system of economics' his position that 'since labor produces all value, labor should obtain all value' (72, 74–5).

See also J. A. Schumpeter regarding the notion that labour is the only factor of production: 'Though this proposition harks back to Locke and Smith and not to Ricardo, it is likely that the Ricardian theory of value did encourage these socialist writers and also offered suggestions to them' (1954: 479).

8 For a position close to my own see Hutchison 1978: 240f. See also Hutchison 1957: 88–9.

While Professor Hunt has demonstrated Hodgskin's reaction against Ricardian value theory (see previous note), he nonetheless accepts Meek's general position regarding the motive for the bourgeois reaction on the grounds that 'most of Hodgskin's contemporaries . . . were quick to recognize that Ricardo's labor theory of value led quite naturally to Hodgskin's theory of capital. And this undoubtedly contributed to the conservative reaction of the 1820's against Ricardo's value theory' (Hunt 1977: 345).

9 By contrast, 'the practical outcome of Hodgskin's inquiry seems tame, and, as often happens with anarchist essays hardly in keeping with the pretensions of the critical part of the work' (Foxwell 1899: lxiv). On the nature of Hodgskin's own reform programme – more precisely its absence – see also Halévy 1956: 125–6.

10 See also Blaug 1958: 149; Moss 1973: 325; and Dobb 1973: 110.

11 The economists sometimes had to prove their moral and religious *bona fides* and reconcile economics with Christianity to gain entry into the universities. See Moss 1976: 14–15; also Checkland 1951: 52. But it should be noted that the labour writers expressed themselves in much the same language. Rejecting the Malthusian principle, Hodgskin proclaimed that 'moral feelings and scientific truth must always be in harmony with each other' (1827: xxi–xxii). This book ends on the same theme: 'the science of Political Economy . . . will be found when perfectly known . . . to – "Justify the ways of God to man" '(268). And Ravenstone rejected Malthusianism because it cast doubt on the 'veneration of the divine nature' (1821: 17).

12 For an extremely helpful discussion of Hodgskin and his intellectual affiliations, and particularly of his role as reviewer, see Scott Gordon, 1955.

13 Cf. also an unpublished paper by Hodgskin ('On the Moral Influence of an increase in the number of Mankind') cited in Halévy 1956: 61–2, wherein the advantages of a large and growing population are outlined: 'other things being equal, *knowledge* and *ingenuity* and of course the means to produce food must be great in proportion as the numbers of mankind are great, and they must increase as mankind increases in numbers'. Hodgskin refers also to an 'increase in morality owing to an increase of population', for 'collision rubs down and tames passions. The weight of the mass gives force to their opinions which subdues the will of every individual'. The same conception is apparent in Hodgskin 1832: 40: 'As mankind are multiplied, the moral influence of the mass increases over individuals, and each one, feeling the impossibility of resisting a great many, is humbly submissive to the general voice, and therefore prone to respect that right of property, which is acknowledged by all.'

14 Cf. also 1956: 77: Ricardo 'supposes the present rents, except in so far as they are increased by our own restrictions on importation of corn, as the natural and just ones'.

15 Much of this bears a family resemblance to the position adopted by the 'historicist' Richard Jones in his *Essay on the Distribution of Wealth* a decade or so later.

16 Hodgskin also rejected the conception of declining profits in a growing economy, having faith in the potency of technical improvements – improvements which increased the productivity of capital (Hodgskin, cited in Halévy 1956: 75–7).

17 Here there are three facts connected with one another of great importance as to that sum at present paid under the name of Rent. Ist: The soil of Europe was formerly cultivated by slaves, a great portion of whose produce went to their employers or landlords; 2nd: Such classes of men have always been found in European society; and 3rd: The wages of labour are at present and have always been in Europe determined by the reward formerly given to slaves. It is an undoubted fact that land, and with that every means of subsistence, was overrun and monopolised by a few persons in every state of Europe.... That money Rents are merely a commutation for personal services or derived from them I hold to be certain.

(Hodgskin, in Halévy 1956: 70–1)

18 It was an error with widespread consequences: 'There is ... a great difference *between* real natural price and exchangeable value, and by not attending to this Mr R. has been led into – l think – great mistakes relative to the decrease of profit in an improving state of society.'

19 The subtitle of the work is the *Unproductiveness of Capital proved with Reference to the Present Combinations amongst Journeymen*. See Halévy 1956: 89–90, 96, for the view that Hodgskin 'took up Ravenstone's thesis and completed and amended it in his *Labour Defended...*'. Although there is much truth to this, Hodgskin was clearly more familiar with the Ricardian literature and his indebtedness to Smith was also more explicit. Moreover, unlike Ravenstone, Hodgskin accorded no role at all to government. (In his *Popular Political Economy*, 1827: 77, Hodgskin specifically commended Ravenstone for his emphasis upon 'knowledge' in technology.)

20 Hodgskin is somewhat self-contradictory since he himself not infrequently adopts the conception of capital attributed to the Ricardians (e.g. 1825: 95, 107–8).

21 Hodgskin refers to McCulloch's article 'Political Economy', in the Supplement to the *Encyclopaedia Britannica*, presumably that to the fourth to sixth editions, usually dated 1824. With regard to Mill – presumably the *Elements* – Hodgskin remarks on the effects of capital:

Mr Mill's account of these effects, though not so precise, is still more astounding. 'The labourer', he says, 'has neither raw materials nor tools. These are *provided* for him by the capitalist. For *making this provision* the capitalist of course *expects a reward*.' According to this statement, the capitalist provides for the labourer and only, therefore, expects a profit. In other parts of his book it is not the capitalist who provides, but the capital which works. He speaks of capital as an instrument of production co-operating with labour, as an active agent combining with labour to produce commodities, and thus he satisfies himself ... that capital is entitled to all that large share of the produce it actually receives. He also attributes to capital power of accumulation. This power or tendency to accumulate, he adds, is not so great as the tendency of population to augment – and on the difference between these two tendencies he and other authors have erected a theory of society which places poor Mother Nature in no favourable light.

(Hodgskin 1825: 34–5)

22 Barry Gordon (1976: 153) refers to 'a persistent myth that Ricardianism was the creed of a burgeoning urban middle class' which he claims was sponsored mainly by later 'social historians who try to press the realities of the early nineteenth century into some type of Marxian evolutionary mould'. This may be so, but Hodgskin's interpretation of Ricardianism in this manner must not be neglected.

23 But Hodgskin warned not to eat into the return made to employers in their capacity as 'masters' as distinct from that as 'capitalists' (1825: 91–2). He observed too that the accidental circumstance whereby the return to *organization* had been combined with *profits* distorted wage differentials and rendered complex any reform (89).

His position on combination as an efficacious solution was not shared by William Thompson. Thompson (1827: 97–8) took Hodgskin to task for imagining that it would be possible 'under the Competitive System' to assure by way of unions that labour possess 'the whole products of its exertions'. And Hodgskin himself abandoned subsequently his defence of unions; cf. a review for *The Economist*, XII, 29 April 1854, 458–9: 'The principle of observing the natural laws and not interfering with them, is as imperative on governments as on Communists, and combining workmen. In fact, the interference of the former is the parent of the interference of the latter. . . . [The] interferences between capital and labour by Communists, Socialists, and combinations (they are all evil). . . . ' (For attributions of the review here, and also below, see Halévy 1956: 127f.)

24 Cf. also Hodgskin 1825: 31: 'Whatever may be the truth of the theory in other respects, there is no doubt of its correctness in this particular. The labourers do only receive, and ever have only received, as much as will subsist them, the landlords receive the surplus produce of the more fertile soils, and all the rest of the whole produce of labour in this and in every country go to the capitalist under the name of profit for the use of his capital.'

25 Hodgskin's *Labour Defended* was the object of sharp criticism by Charles Knight in his *The Rights of Industry* (1831) – published anonymously on behalf of the Society for the Diffusion of Useful Knowledge. This pamphlet induced Hodgskin, who believed it was by Brougham, to publish in 1832 his *Natural and Artificial Right of Property* based on materials already written (1829). This work constitutes a condemnation of the 'Westminster Philosophers' for their approach to legislation and their desire to replace the existing laws by a new code. In Hodgskin's terms: 'Man, having naturally no rights, may be experimented on, imprisoned, expatriated or even exterminated, as the legislator pleases.' Both Bentham and James Mill are specifically referred to. The latter's statement in his article on 'Jurisprudence' for the *Encyclopaedia Britannica* to the effect that 'all right is factitious, and only exists by the will of the lawmaker' is described as a 'monstrous assertion' (Hodgskin 1832: 21).

On the basis of the distinction between human institutions and the natural order (attributed to Book III of the *Wealth of Nations*) Hodgskin observed 'that the immediate and proximate cause of [labour's] poverty and destitution . . . is the law which appropriates their produce in the shape of revenue, rent, tithes, and profit' (149). The law was intended 'to secure the appropriation of the whole annual produce of labour' (47).

26 A great deal of attention is paid to the influence of observation and knowledge on productivity, and to specialization in its various aspects. The discussion of territorial division of labour does not utilize the Ricardian formulation but cites Smith, Hume and Paley. (See Hodgskin 1827: 127f.) Of Smith, Hodgskin observes that although 'he was aware of the influence of knowledge in adding to productive power', he had not attempted 'to explain the natural laws which regulate the increase of knowledge'. With specific reference to McCulloch, Hodgskin remarks that '[Smith's] successors in this country have humbly imitated his example' (53).

Great emphasis is placed on division of labour, which is not regarded as degrading in its consequences (138–9). Division of labour is said to depend upon the 'extent of the market' (116) and also – here Hodgskin takes issue with Smith – upon 'observation and knowledge' which precede specialization (78f). The development of science itself (as well as the size of the market) is related to the growth of numbers (86f).

27 Hodgskin read a great deal into Smith's famous assertion that ' "all things would gradually have become cheaper" – "with all those improvements of productive power to which the division of labour gives occasion", had it not been *"for the appropriation of land, and the accumulation of stock"* ' (41).

28 While Marx generally took the position that Hodgskin had his roots in Ricardian theory, in commenting on Hodgskin's remarks in the present context (particularly with regard to pages 219–20) he observed that Hodgskin adopts Smith's statement that 'the commodity buys more labour than it contains, or that labour pays a higher value for the commodity than the latter contains'. In this regard, 'Hodgskin reproduces both what is correct and what is confused and confusing in Adam Smith's view' (*Theories of Surplus Value*, Part I, Moscow, n.d., 86–7).

29 Rejection of the inverse profit–wage relation (though with reference to commodity wages) is explicit in a later *Economist* review: '[Ricardo] *puts the wages of the labourer and the profits of the capitalist in opposition, and regards the one as a deduction from the other. These are fatal errors.* We are now fully satisfied by experience that the invention of machinery and the use of canals and railroads raises profits, though they may, after a season, gravitate again to zero, and we know from experience that the same causes raise the rate of wages, and that capitalists and labourers may both get more and become better provided for by means of an improvement in productive power, which Mr Ricardo denies' (*The Economist*, IV, 28 November 1846, 1558). Halévy writes of a change in position since 1825, when in his *Labour Defended*, Hodgskin 'took his stand in his criticisms of capital on the law, enunciated by Ricardo, of the inverse variation of profits and wages' (Halévy 1956: 144). But I can see little evidence of any such change. Consciousness of knowledge and innovation is widespread in Hodgskin's work throughout.

30 An English translation of the fourth French edition of J. B. Say's *Traité d'économie politique* (1819) appeared as *A Treatise on Political Economy* (London, 1821).

31 There is a related complaint in the same review against Ricardo's neglect of the wage structure – his assumption that 'it continues nearly the same from generation to generation': 'We say nothing about the rectitude of any rate of payment, but he must be blind to what is going on in society who is insensible to the facts that *inequalities of reward*, or comparative degrees of estimation in which different kinds of human labour are held, and consequently different

rates of wages, is one of the agitating topics of the day; and the work which, pretending to treat of the greatest of the social sciences, expressly excludes the subject from consideration, casts out a topic, which Adam Smith discussed, of almost overwhelming interest' (1558).

32 But Read played down Smith's slip by allowing that he was 'not led into any further error' thereby, and 'founds none of his future reasonings, or of his doctrines in regard to taxation, on the supposition of labour producing all and capital nothing' (Read 1829: 216).

33 The same proposition is restated subsequently at length in the body of the work (240n); it is clear from Read's formulation in this context that he had before him the first or second editions of Ricardo's *Principles* since in the third edition the chapter 'On Value' is divided into seven sections, not five as Read has it.

34 Cited by Read from Hodgskin's preface to *Labour Defended*.

35 Read's reply to Hodgskin does not contain a genuine empirical means of ascertaining the respective contributions of the factors.

36 Specific attention is paid to Ricardo's chapter 'On Value' in this context.

37 The major objection is to McCulloch's discussion of the increasing value of the cask of wine in the cellar, or the growing oak. Malthus's objections in his *Definitions* are commended (Scrope 1831a: 16–17).

38 The 'logic' of Mill and McCulloch is that the notion that profits are proportional to *time* is meaningless as time is 'a mere word'. Natural agents create fermentation, but such agents are free so that the charge that the capitalist makes for the time he allows nature to work must be a charge for labour.

39 Cf. also Scrope 1833: 197–8n.

40 On this issue see Fetter 1958: 56–7. In the light of Scrope's various qualifications Professor Fetter goes too far in claiming that Scrope 'probably came closer than anything Malthus ever published in anticipating the Keynesian view on the inadequacy of demand as a cause of unemployment'. For the prospect of general glut only reflects excessive savings – 'were every member of society to content himself with the mere necessaries of life' – which he conceded is 'an extreme case which can never happen', thus (inadvertently perhaps) removing all the sting from his condemnation of the orthodox position (Scrope 1831a: 21). Moreover, in the *Principles of Political Economy* (1833: 160–1) we find a somewhat different account. Here Scrope talks of an automatic regulation of savings which precludes any dangerous tendency towards excess: '[If] profits fall through the competition of increased capital, the inducement to save is weakened, while that to spend is increased, by the fall in the cost of all articles consequent on diminished profits. It may, therefore, be safely left to the mutually counteracting influence of the two passions . . . to determine the current average rate of net profit, which is the measure of the degree in which the owners of capital prefer prospective gain to present enjoyment.'

41 See also Longfield 1834a, 159:

[It] is for other reasons important that we should investigate the circumstances which determine the amount of profits and wages, and then we shall incidentally observe that they both are confined within limits which it is beyond the power of the legislature, by any direct exertion of their authority, to extend. Here legislation and combination may do mischief, but cannot do good. They may destroy a source of revenue, but they cannot transfer it to another class. . . . Those propositions will, I trust, be made evident, when we shall have ascertained what profits are, what are the circumstances from which they are derived, and what it is that regulates their amount.

42 *Political Economy for Plain People* (1873) – second edition of the original *Principles of Political Economy* (1833).

43 There is no mention of Hodgskin in this essay.

44 He wrote strongly of the allowance system: 'By this contrivance of paying wages out of poor-rates . . . it is obvious that the whole labouring population is kept up to its full numbers, and maintained *at the lowest possible expense to those who employ and profit by its industry.* And as rent consists of the surplus beyond the expenses of cultivation, the gain resulting from this injurious practise falls to the share of the landowners, who are themselves for the most part the parties who originated and still enforce the abuse' (Scrope 1833: 312). See also his observations regarding agricultural protection: 'the evil suffered by the community from the increase of price far outweighs . . . the benefit derived by the landlord from an increase of rent' (1831a: 35–6).

45 What was involved is a centrally organized system of regular insurance contributions by employers: 'It appears . . . that it is highly desirable, and might be contrived without difficulty, to substitute by degrees for the present mode of raising the poor-rate, a general compulsory contribution by the employers of labour to a fund for assuring their labourers against destitution; a measure which would throw the expense of maintaining the aged, impotent, and destitute poor precisely upon those persons who have profited by their labour, or that of their natural protectors, while capable of work' (Scrope 1833: 316f).

The emphasis in the various versions of the proposal is upon accident, sickness and old-age insurance contributions. And while Scrope had great confidence in the achievement of a high level of employment in the absence of a relief system which artificially encouraged the growth of the labour supply, it would appear that his proposal covered *unemployment* premiums also. This is clarified in a discussion of the effects on a local labour force of the closing of a manufacturing plant, when the pool of labour may even have been created in consequence of the plant in question (321). See also references to the ablebodied poor (306).

46 Scrope described McCulloch's 'doctrine of Absenteeism' as a 'portentous doctrine [which] flows necessarily and immediately from the principle of free trade taken in an unlimited sense' (1831a: 38).

47 See also the following general remark added to the second edition of the *Principles of Political Economy*:

The preceding chapters have dwelt upon a variety of modes of injurious interference by governments with the freedom of industrial operations, in the presumed interests of particular classes or of the community at large. It must not, however, be supposed that every form of interference is objectionable. It is this mistake which has given currency to the charge often brought against Political Economy of requiring a rigid adherence to the principle of allowing to individuals absolute immunity in all commercial transactions from legislative control or supervision. It has been shown, however, that the principle of freedom itself rests only upon the assumption that it is expedient for the general interests. Should these, therefore, clearly require any deviation from that rule, the same expediency will justify its modification.

(Scrope 1873: 336–7)

48 Malthus and McCulloch, runs the complaint, tended to argue as if exchange

value could be identified with utility although in the water case it is realized that a commodity may have 'utility' but no exchange value.

49 He was equally critical of the so-called '*intellectual* speculators', à la Godwin, who 'proclaim man as capable of attaining happiness by his mental powers alone, *almost* independent of material subordinate agency' (Thompson 1824: iii).

50 Cf: 'It is not the mere possession of wealth, but the *right distribution* of it, that is important to a community. . . . 'Tis not the *multitude* but the *use* and the *distribution* of the objects of wealth, with which society is chiefly interested' (1824: ix). Thompson's own objective was to show that via 'Labour by mutual co-operation' there could be achieved a distribution satisfying all *desiderata* – 'the encouragement of production and accumulation, the minimum of administration, political utility and the widest diffusion of moral habits' (xviii).

51 Cf: 'the imperative duty of the government [is] to keep an especial watch over the condition of [the working] class, and lend its aid to prevent their suffering, either from want or oppression, through the peculiarly disadvantageous circumstances in which they are placed' (Scrope 1833: 300).
In 'The Political Economists' (1831a: 48), Scrope quotes Samuel Read (1829: 367) for support of his position.

52 Cf. Longfield 1834b: 29, where he asserts that it is a 'false and dangerous doctrine . . . to lay down that extreme want justifies a disregard of the rights of property'. He himself (19, 30) maintained that the only right was to an income no higher than in 'the savage state'.

53 Nevertheless, the taxation of net profit under given conditions relating to the savings propensity 'must check the rate of increase of national capital, and moreover, occasion its transference to other countries, in which taxation is less onerous, and the rate of profits consequently higher in proportion to the political and legal securities of property' (Scrope 1831a: 23).

54 There are kind words (Read 1829: 350n) for William Godwin's *Of Population* (London, 1820).

55 The reference is to *An Introductory Lecture on Political Economy* (London, 1827), 13.

56 Whately also reacted favourably to Smith's warnings against narrow specialization (Whately 1832: 195f), and to Senior's case for the maintenance of steady employment opportunities (205f); and he supported educational programmes for labour including schools attached to factories (201f).

57 For the details of my argument regarding the Ricardian features of Longfield's economics see my 'The Reception of Ricardian Economics', 1977: 234f. To a lesser extent what is said of Longfield and his relationship with Ricardo applies also to Scrope.

58 Cf. Longfield 1834a: 227, where it is claimed that but for legal restriction on the division of land many more would become landowners. (In Longfield 1834b: 18–19, the justification of landed property is made contingent upon the obligation to accept the rule that '*every individual is entitled to the means of support, from that society which is determined to compel him to obey its laws*'.)
Longfield took issue only with some formal data in Ricardo's *Principles* which imply a continually increasing *proportion* of rent in total produce (1834a: 153f).

59 The object of Political Economy in the *Four Lectures on the Poor Laws* (1834b: 2) is said to be to render the condition of labour 'more comfortable, and more respectable than it has ever been before, by procuring for the labourer a steady market for his industry, and an adequate remuneration for his toil'.

The notion of 'the difference between the wealth of an individual and that of the community' is said to be treated more fully 'by the professor who originally discovered its importance and drew attention to it' (1834a: 6) – probably a reference to Senior to whom Whately also gave due credit as we have seen.

60 In a defence of political economy – which has much in common with that of Richard Whately – against the 'charge that wealth is not a worthy subject for investigation', Longfield observed that 'Political-Economy must be studied, to teach nations the method of avoiding wealth, if it be an evil, or of creating it and distributing it judiciously, if it be a good' (1834a: 3).

61 See also Longfield 1834a: 237, where it is maintained that in conditions of extreme poverty there can be no claim on the individual to obey the laws. But, as we have seen above, Longfield took Scrope to task for going too far. What he himself had in mind was a standard no lower than would have been enjoyed 'had society not existed' (Longfield 1834b: 19). See also note 52.

62 'On the Limits of State Interference with the Distribution of Wealth', *Journal of the Statistical and Social Inquiry Society of Ireland*, Part XLII, Nov. 1872. The issue is formulated with admirable moderation insofar as it is recognized that 'there may be a valid but not sufficient objection to what may be on the whole the wisest policy'.

63 See also Moss 1976, especially chapter 9. Moss argues (179) convincingly that 'his later writings do not represent a repudiation of his early political position but rather an attempt to restore balance'.

64 J. S. Mill, in his review, complained of De Quincey's 'ultra-Tory prejudices' which deformed his work, and which were particularly regrettable since he was so sound on economic theory. Mill had in mind largely De Quincey's support for the corn laws (Mill 1967, VI: 430–4).

65 The American protectionist writer Henry C. Carey also complained of the 'discord' – creating 'hostility among classes' – generated by Ricardo's system; and he described the *Principles* as 'the true manual of the demagogue, who seeks power by means of agrarianism, war, and plunder' (Carey 1848: 74–5). A comment by Marx in this regard is of some interest: 'Closely bound up with Ricardo's scientific merit is the fact that Ricardo exposes and describes the economic contradiction between the classes . . . and that consequently political economy perceives, discovers the root of the historical struggle and development. *Carey* . . . therefore denounces him as the father of communism' (Marx 1968, II: 166).

66 But for an allusion to the view that ideological considerations may have played a part in De Quincey's theoretical contributions see Groenewegen 1974: 193. Groenewegen had in mind De Quincey's insistence upon the mutual determination of exchange value by 'intrinsic utility' and 'difficulty of attainment'. I have demonstrated (Hollander 1977, esp. 242–4) the impressive extent of De Quincey's adherence to Ricardian theory, particularly the inverse profit–wage relationship.

REFERENCES

Beer, Max (1929) *A History of British Socialism*, London: G. Bell and Sons.

Black, R.D.C. (1971) 'Introduction', *The Economic Writings of Mountifort Longfield*, New York: Augustus M. Kelley.

Blaug, Mark (1958) *Ricardian Economics*, New Haven: Yale University Press.

Carey, Henry C. (1848) *The Past, the Present and the Future*, London: Longmans.

Checkland, S. G. (1951) 'The Advent of Academic Economics in England', *The Manchester School of Economic and Social Studies*, 19 (January): 43–70.

Cole, G.D.H. (1962) *A History of Socialist Thought*, London: Macmillan.

—— (1963) [1922] 'Introduction' in Thomas Hodgskin, *Labour Defended Against the Claims of Capital*, 1922, London; 1963, New York: Augustus M. Kelley.

De Quincey, Thomas (1970) [1844] *The Logic of Political Economy*, in David Masson (ed.), *Political Economy and Politics*, Vol. X, [1897] London; 1970, New York: Augustus M. Kelley.

Dobb, M. (1973) *Theories of Value and Distribution Since Adam Smith*, Cambridge: Cambridge University Press.

Douglas, P. H. (1928) 'Smith's Theory of Value and Distribution' in J. M. Clark *et al.*, *Adam Smith, 1776–1926*, Chicago: University of Chicago Press.

Fetter, F. W. (1958) 'The Economic Articles in the *Quarterly Review* and Their Authors, I', *Journal of Political Economy*, 66, 1: 47–64.

Foxwell, H. S. (1899) 'Introduction' in Anton Menger, *The Right to the Whole Produce of Labour*, London: Macmillan.

Gordon, Barry (1976) *Political Economy in Parliament, 1819–1823*, London: Macmillan.

Gordon, Scott (1955) 'The London *Economist* and the High Tide of Laissez Faire', *Journal of Political Economy*, 63 (December): 461–88.

Groenewegen, P. D. (1974) Review, *Economic Journal*, 84 (March): 192–3.

Halévy, Elie (1955) [1928] *The Growth of Philosophic Radicalism*, 1928, London; 1955, Boston: Beacon Press.

—— (1956) *Thomas Hodgskin*, A. J. Taylor (ed.), London: E. Benn.

Hodgskin, Thomas (1825) *Labour Defended Against the Claims of Capital*, 1825, London; 1922, London; 1963, New York: Augustus M. Kelley.

—— (1827) *Popular Political Economy*, London: C. and W. Tait.

—— (1832) *The Natural and Artificial Right of Property Contrasted*, London: B. Steil.

Hollander, Samuel (1977) 'The Reception of Ricardian Economics', *Oxford Economic Papers*, 29 (July): 221–57.

Hunt, E. K. (1977) 'Value Theory in the Writings of the Classical Economists, Thomas Hodgskin, and Karl Marx', *History of Political Economy*, 9 (Fall): 322–45.

Hutchison, T. W. (1957) Review of Halévy's *Thomas Hodgskin*, in *Economica*, XXIV (February): 88–9.

—— (1978) *On Revolution and Progress in Economic Knowledge*, Cambridge: Cambridge University Press.

King, J. E. (1979) 'Marx as an Historian of Economic Thought', *History of Political Economy*, 11 (Fall): 382–94.

Longfield, Mountifort (1834a) *Lectures on Political Economy*, Dublin: Milliken.

—— (1834b) *Four Lectures on Poor Laws*, Dublin: Milliken.

—— (1971) *The Economic Writings of Mountifort Longfield*, R. D. C. Black (ed.), New York: Augustus M. Kelley.

Lowenthal, Esther (1911) *The Ricardian Socialists*, in *Columbia University Studies in History, Economics and Public Law*, Vol. XLVI, New York: Columbia University Press.

Marx, Karl (1965) [1873] *Capital*, Vol. I, Moscow: Progress Publishers.

—— (1968) *Theories of Surplus Value*, [1862–3], Vol. II, Moscow: Progress Publishers.

—— (1971) *Theories of Surplus Value*, Vol. III, Moscow: Progress Publishers.

—— (1973) [1857] *Grundrisse: Foundations of the Critique of Political Economy*, London: Pelican Marx Library.

Meek, Ronald L. (1967) *Economics and Ideology, and Other Essays*, London: Chapman and Hall.

—— (1972) 'Marginalism and Marxism', *History of Political Economy*, 4 (Fall): 500–1.

—— (1973) *Studies in the Labour Theory of Value*, 2nd edn, London: Lawrence and Wishart.

Menger, Anton (1899) *The Right to the Whole Produce of Labour*, London: Macmillan.

Mill, J. S. (1967) *Collected Works of J. S. Mill*, Vol. IV, Toronto: University of Toronto Press.

Moss, L. S. (1973) 'Isaac Butt and the Early Development of the Marginal Utility Theory of Imputation', *History of Political Economy*, 5 (Fall): 317–38.

—— (1976) *Mountifort Longfield: Ireland's First Professor of Political Economy*, Ottawa, Illinois: Green Hill Publishers.

Ravenstone, Piercy [pseudonym of Richard Puller] (1821) *A Few Doubts on the Subject of Population and Political Economy*, London: John Andrews.

Read, Samuel (1829) *Political Economy: An Inquiry into the natural Grounds of Right to Vendible Property or Wealth*, Edinburgh: Oliver and Boyd.

Schumpeter, J. A. (1954) *History of Economic Analysis*, New York: Oxford University Press.

Scrope, G. Poulett (1831a) 'The Political Economists', *Quarterly Review*, 44, 87 (January): 1–52.

—— (1831b) '[Richard] Jones on the Doctrine of Rent', *Quarterly Review*, 46, 91 (November): 81–117.

—— (1831c) 'The Archbishop of Dublin on Political Economy', *Quarterly Review*, 46, 91 (November): 46–54.

—— (1833) *Principles of Political Economy deduced from the Natural Laws of Social Welfare*, London: Longman, Rees, Orme, Brown, Green and Longmans.

—— (1873) *Political Economy for Plain People*, 2nd edn of *Principles of Political Economy*, London: Longmans, Green and Co.

Senior, N. W. (1828) 'Oxford Lectures on Political Economy', *Edinburgh Review*, 48, 95 (September): 170–84.

Thompson, William (1824) *An Inquiry into the Principles of the Distribution of Wealth*, London: Longman, Hurst, Rees, Orme, Brown and Green.

—— (1827), *Labor Rewarded. The Claims of Labor and Capital Conciliated*, London: Hunt and Clarke.

Wallas, Graham (1925) *The Life of Francis Place*, London: Allen and Unwin.

Whately, Richard (1832) *Introductory Lectures on Political Economy*, 2nd edn, London: B. Fellowes.

10

ON P. MIROWSKI'S 'PHYSICS AND THE "MARGINALIST REVOLUTION" '*

I. INTRODUCTION

The central theme of a recent article on the 'marginal revolution' by Philip Mirowski is that 'there was a readily identifiable discontinuity in economic thought in the 1870s and 1880s which was the genesis of neoclassical theory; and both its timing and intellectual content can be explained by developments in physics in the mid-nineteenth century' (Mirowski 1984: 363). Alternatively expressed:

> The adoption of the 'energetics' metaphor and framework of mid-nineteenth century physics is the birthmark of neoclassical economics. . . . [365]
>
> . . . the rise of energetics in physical theory induced the invention of neoclassical economic theory by providing the metaphor, the mathematical techniques, and the new attitudes towards theory construction. Neoclassical economic theory was appropriated wholesale from mid-nineteenth century physics; utility was redefined so as to be identical with energy. . . . [366]
>
> . . . neoclassical economics is bowdlerised nineteenth century physics . . . neoclassicism was not 'simultaneously discovered' because it was 'true', as Jevons and others would have it; instead the timing of its genesis is explained by the timing of the energetics revolution in physics. . . . [377]

(Mirowski 1984: 365, 366, 377)

These are strong assertions. I do not believe that Mirowski has made his case. He has adopted an illegitimately narrow version of 'neoclassicism' from the perspective of those he himself classifies as neoclassical; and even on his own terms he fails to demonstrate the significance of the energy metaphor.

To set the stage for our discussion we should have in mind the meaning attached to 'energy physics' by Mirowski:

---

* Without ascribing any responsibility, I should like to thank Jed Buchwald, Tony Endres, Trevor Levere, Martin O'Connor, Margaret Schabas and Don Walker for helpful comments.

Energetics as a unifying principle was created by Helmholtz's famous 1847 paper 'On the conservation of Force'.... This innovation induced substantial revision of many previous physical doctrines, and created the discipline of physics as the unified study of phenomena linked by energetic principles.... This watershed in physics ... was accompanied by changes in the acceptable standards of theory formation: these included an increasing refusal to specify the underlying nature of phenomena described mathematically ...

Crucial in this revolution in thought concerning physical processes was the transformation of vague 'forces' into a Protean, unique, and yet ontologically undefined 'energy', which could only be discussed cogently through the intermediary of its mathematical eidolon [an image without real existence]. It shifted the description of motion itself away from vectors such as momentum and towards scalars encompassing the new 'energy'. Its divergence from Newtonian concepts became apparent when the conservation law was enunciated, because the conservation law provided the only means by which to identify an energetic system in some sense the 'same' as it underwent various changes and transformations.

(Mirowski 1984: 366)

Mirowski proceeds to describe the displacement of a particle, on the new view, such that the total energy of the particle (unobservable potential energy) is conserved throughout its movement. The path of the particle between A and B – the 'least action path' – is calculated by finding the constrained extrema. The postulate that total energy is conserved allowed a rigorous specification of the principle of least action: 'by the 1860s, the mathematics of unobservable potentials and constrained extrema were extended to all physical phenomena'. In transferring from physics to economics, Mirowski draws an 'exact parallel' in utility to the concept of potential energy. For he refers to a 'scalar function of the goods x and y of the form $U = f(x,y)$, which can ... be interpreted as the "utilities" of those goods. In exact parallel to the original concept of potential energy, utilities are unobservable, and can only be inferred from theoretical linkage to other observable variables. Relative prices are equal to the ratios of marginal utilities by construction: the "potential field" of utility is defined as the locus of the set of constrained extrema' (367–8).

In the foregoing parallel and various amplifications thereof we can discern one aspect of 'neoclassicism' intended by Mirowski. It is essentially 'the calculus of constrained maximization' on the part of the individual (375–6) turning on the principle of diminishing marginal utility. However, 'the mere postulation of diminishing marginal utility is not sufficient to generate a neoclassical theory of price', for which reason Carl Menger must be excluded from the club:

Menger cannot be considered a neoclassical economist because he rejected two basic pillars of that theory: the law of one price, which states that all generic goods in a market (however defined) must trade at the same price in equilibrium . . . and the concept that traded goods in some sense are related as equivalents in equilibrium. . . . Absence of the first subverts any deterministic notion of equilibrium. Absence of the second explains Menger's hostility towards quantification. Absence of both effectively prevented the introduction of the physics analogy into economic theory. In this respect Menger is no different from Dupuit . . . who also recognized diminishing marginal utility, but also repudiated a single equilibrium price.

(Mirowski 1984: 371–2)

There is here insufficient detailed elaboration of the *precise* nature of neoclassicism in its 'energy' garb – and this in itself mars the paper. But if I understand Mirowski correctly his requirements for the designation 'neoclassical' include the mathematical procedures of constrained maximization, assuming diminishing marginal utility; and the principles of 'one price' and of 'equivalence' in exchange. With this in mind I shall consider Mirowski's case that the 'genesis' of marginalism – my concern is largely with Jevons and Walras – can only be appreciated in terms of the energetics revolution.

II. THE EVIDENCE: WALRAS

In his *Elements* (Walras 1954: 71) Walras claimed that 'the pure theory of economics is a science which resembles the physico-mathematical sciences in every respect' (cited in Mirowski 1984: 363). By this declaration, however, Walras did *not* have energy physics in mind; indeed he was in no way concerned with utility at that juncture. Mirowski himself, in fact, points out that Walras was referring to the 'subset of economic phenomena which could be the objects of a pure scientific inquiry: they are the configurations of prices in a regime of "perfect competition" ', for a 'pure science is only concerned with the relationships – the "play of the blind and ineluctable forces of nature" which are independent of human will' (364). 'Such "pure" relationships justify, and indeed for Walras, demand,' Mirowski proceeds, 'the application of the same mathematical techniques as those deployed in mid-nineteenth century physics.'

This latter statement is mere assertion. The analysis of prices in a regime of pure competition amounts to Walrasian general-equilibrium analysis: 'If the pure theory of economics, or the theory of exchange and value in exchange, that is, the theory of social wealth considered by itself, is a physico-mathematical science like mechanics or hydrodynamics, then economists should not be afraid to use the methods and language of mathematics' (Walras 1954: 71). In fact his statement extends beyond exchange:

'the pure theory of economics ought to take over from experience certain type concepts, like those of exchange, supply, demand, market, capital, income, productive services and products'. There is nothing to suggest that he had energy physics in mind by his statements in this context.

In dealing with price formation eighteenth-century writers such as Turgot and Adam Smith frequently adopted a Newtonian metaphor.[1] Walras's vision of general market equilibrium, Jaffé has shown (1983: 313), had been inspired by Turgot, Quesnay, Smith, Ricardo and Say; while for the translation of the vision into mathematical equations Walras owed a debt to A. N. Isnard (1781), Cournot (1838) and Louis Poinsot (1842), the latter 'a textbook on the theory of mechanics bristling with systems of simultaneous equations to represent among other things, the mechanical equilibrium of the solar system [in which] Walras found a pattern for representing the catallactic equilibrium of the market system' (Jaffé 1983: 314).[2] It is a general 'Newtonian' perspective on physics that governed the essentials of Walras's mathematics.

Mirowski makes much of Walras's reading in 1872 of a memorandum by A. P. Piccard which led him to adopt the principle of constrained maximization of utility – the optimization 'of an "unobserved" quantité de besoin'.[3] Certainly Walras learned from Paul Piccard in 1872 'how to construe utility and its derivative with respect to quantity mathematically and how to apply the equi-marginal rule to the theory of value in exchange' (Jaffé 1983: 314–15).[4] But as Jaffé has demonstrated, Walras 'climbed down' from his already formulated general-equilibrium system to absorb the principle of marginal utility. Walras 'did not come into possession of his concept of marginal utility and his method of using it to derive a theoretical demand curve until after he had clearly outlined his mathematical theory of a network of interrelated markets' (313). Piccard provided 'a maximization motor to his all-comprehensive market machine'; for '[it] cannot be emphasized enough that what Walras was after was the completion of his competitive market model, and not the elaboration of a theory of subjective valuation in consumption'.[5]

It is conceivable – though it remains to be demonstrated – that Piccard was trained in the new energy physics, but even so he at most transferred to Walras knowledge of a technique and it is unreasonable to saddle Walras with all the implications of which Piccard might have been aware. (Walras had trouble enough understanding the technique.) And, more important, this technique was absorbed into an already prepared framework. Mirowski, who insists that 'neoclassical economics was not prompted by a Newtonian analogy' (Mirowski 1984: 366; cf. 365), has neglected the general-equilibrium dimension to Walrasian economics.

The only specific piece of textual evidence brought by Mirowski in support of his case is a reference to Walras's late paper 'Economique et mécanique' (1960 [1909]) in which force and *rareté* are considered as vectors and energy and utility as scalars (Mirowski 1984: 364). Mirowski should have indicated that these parallels occur in a specific reference to Fisher (1925 [1892]: 85), and that in correspondence Walras explained that he had altered his article *in proof* to allow for Fisher's definition of energy as a scalar (Walras 1965, III: 417–20).[6] But at least Mirowski does recognize that Walras was 'not prompt[ed] to revise his *Elements* significantly' (Mirowski 1984: 369). Even a restatement in terms of energetics would apply only to utility theory, not the broader general-equilibrium framework and certainly not to that framework as extended to production, capital and money; Walras in fact devotes a separate section in his 1909 paper to the analogy between *l'économique* et *la mécanique céleste* – in contrast to *la mécanique rationnelle* of utility theory.

Walras's admiration for Gossen (1983 [1854]) is pertinent to the Mirowski theme: 'De tous ces écrivains qui nous ont précédés,' he wrote to Jevons in 1880, 'un seul selon moi, a eu vraiment un sentiment sûr et profond quoique imparfait du mouvement et de l'équilibre des forces économiques: c'est Gossen' (Jevons 1977, V: 95–6).[7] I shall take up the implications of this evaluation in the next section.

III. THE EVIDENCE: JEVONS

Mirowski cites Jevons's statement that his equation of exchange does 'not differ in general character from those which are really treated in many branches of physical science', and his subsequent analogy involving the Theory of the Lever (Mirowski 1984: 364). That this 'invocation of the physical realm' is 'always present in Jevons's writings·on price theory', is doubtless true but the question is whether Jevons had in mind the new energy physics based on Helmholtz's 'On the Conservation of Force' (1847), which is Mirowski's main theme.

I certainly do not claim that Jevons makes no references to energy. One such occurs in the Preface to the first edition regarding the lever analogy: 'The Theory of Economy [treated mathematically] presents a close analogy to the science of Statical Mechanics, and the Laws of Exchange are found to resemble the Laws of Equilibrium of a lever as determined by the principle of virtual velocities. The nature of Wealth and value is explained by the consideration of indefinitely small amounts of pleasure and pain, just as the Theory of Statics is made to rest upon the equality of indefinitely small amounts of energy' (Jevons 1924: vii). But in his elaboration of the lever analogy in the second edition of 1879 Jevons relies on Louis Poisson's work of 1833, for he there observes: 'there is no statical problem which is not subject to the principle of virtual velocities', and Poisson, in his *Traité de Mécanique*, which commences with statical theorems, asserts explicitly, 'Dans cet ouvrage, j'emploierai exclusivement la méthode des infiniment petits' (Poisson 1924: 106). More broadly, 'the general principle of virtual velocities' (104) relates back to Lagrange's *Mécanique Analytique* (1788). Surprisingly enough, Mirowski concedes everything: 'Note that at this stage of Jevons's exposition he does not adequately support his statements in the text: since he does not derive the equilibrium of the lever from considerations of potential and kinetic energy, he fails to justify the parallel between the expression for physical equilibrium and his use of differential equations in his own equations of exchange' (Mirowski 1984: 363; the 'stage' at which Jevons did 'support his statements' is nowhere clarified). Similarly, 'Jevons did not explicitly derive the equilibrium of the lever from energetics principles' (373).

Jevons's training and interests – his attendance at lectures by Faraday and his familiarity with Thomson and Joule – are taken by Mirowski (1984: 369) as partial proof of Jevons's adoption of the new energy-physics metaphor.[8] This kind of loose circumstantial evidence will not suffice; the content of the training must be clarified with precision and then shown to have left an impact on the economics. (A recent investigation suggests, in fact, that Jevons never studied energetics at University College, either before or after his Australian odyssey – his training was in an older tradition; Schabas 1983: 250f.) Nor will general references by Jevons to a physical metaphor suffice, such as that to 'the mechanics of self-interest and utility' to which his essay was devoted (Jevons 1924, Preface to 2nd edition, viii), or that in a paper to the Manchester Statistical Society in 1874 involving 'the gravitating force of a material body' (Mirowski 1984: 363). The metaphor must be, specifically, the energy-conservation metaphor applied to economic analysis for Mirowski's case to hold water.

Mirowski (362) also asserts that a 'fundamental break' in theory was achieved by Jevons; and again, in arguing against the notion of 'continuity' in economics, he maintains that 'One cannot read the letters and published works of Stanley Jevons, Léon Walras, Francis Edgeworth, Irving Fisher, Vilfred Pareto and others without repeatedly encountering assertions that their work represented a fundamental break with the economics of their time' (362). But there is good reason to doubt that Jevons's work involves a 'fundamental break'; Jevons himself spelled out his obligations and recognized his precursors generously – albeit largely in his second edition – and to a lesser extent so did Walras.

Thus Jevons traced his intellectual debt at the most basic level to British utilitarianism, paying tribute to Bentham (1823) whose ideas he 'adopted as the starting point of the theory of this work' (Jevons 1924: xxvi), and also to Senior and Jennings and various others 'from which my system was more or less consciously developed' (xxxvii); and to Hutcheson (1728), the earliest to treat pleasure and pain 'in a definitely quantitative manner' (Jevons 1924: 28n) – in short to those who by lending 'precision in their treatment of quantitative ideas . . . have . . . been led to a more or less complete comprehension of the true theory of utility and wealth' (xxv). More importantly for us, Jevons was quite clear regarding common ground with near contemporaries – in the following passage with Gossen and Dupuit: 'I cannot claim to be totally indifferent to the rights of priority; and from the year 1862, when my theory was first published in brief outline, I have often pleased myself with the thought that it was at once novel and an important theory. From what I have now stated in this preface it is evident that novelty can no longer be attributed to the leading features of the theory. Much is clearly due to Dupuit, and of the rest a great share must be assigned to Gossen' (Jevons 1924: xxxviii).[9]

The tribute to Gossen (1983 [1854]) covers *inter alia* the celebrated 'second law', namely that a utility-maximizing individual distributes his income (his 'resources') so as to equalize the marginal utilities of all commodities:

> [Gossen] insists that mathematical treatment, being the only sound one, must be applied throughout; but, out of consideration for the reader, the higher analysis will be explicitly introduced only when it is requisite to determine maxima and minima. The treatise then opens with the consideration of Economics as the theory of pleasure and pain, that is as the theory of the procedure by which the individual and the aggregate of individuals constituting society, may realise the maximum of pleasure with the minimum of painful effort. The natural law of pleasure is then clearly stated, somewhat as follows: *Increase of the same kind of consumption yields pleasure continuously diminishing up to the point of satiety.* This law he illustrates geometrically, and then proceeds to investigate the conditions under which the total pleasure from one or more objects may be raised to a maximum. . . . He then proceeds to give the derivative laws of utility somewhat in the following manner: – That separate portions of the same pleasure-giving object have very different degrees of utility, and that in general for each person only a limited number of such portions has utility; any addition beyond this limit is useless, but the point of uselessness is only reached after the utility has gone through all the stages or degrees of intensity. Hence he draws the practical conclusion that each person should so distribute his resources as to render the final increments of each pleasure-giving commodity of equal utility for him.
>
> (Jevons 1924: xxxiii–xxxiv)

All of this, and also Gossen's geometrical investigation of the marginal disutility of labour and the equilibrium conditions of labour supply, led Jevons to concede (though with some qualifications) that 'Gossen has completely anticipated me as regards the general principles and method of the theory of Economics' (Jevons 1924: xxxv), indeed that 'his treatment of the fundamental theory is even more general and thorough than what I was able to

176

scheme out' – so much so that he was obliged to insist that he had never heard of Gossen's book before August 1878.

This evaluation is an eminently fair one. It is true that Gossen has become famous for his differential coefficient dW/dE' which relates the marginal variation in the sum total of satisfaction with the time during which the sense of satisfaction is being consumed at a uniform rate (Gossen 1983 [1854]: 21). But he extends his analysis to marginal utility proper – his 'Werth der letzten atom' – and to the general problem of maximization subject to a constraint (not necessarily a time constraint). Thus:

> The simple atoms of one and of the same means of enjoyment have very different values, and, in general, for each individual only a definite number of atoms, that is, a definite quantity, has value. An increase in this quantity beyond this point is without any value for that individual, but this point of no value is reached only after the value has little by little moved through many gradations of magnitude. . . .
>
> If the individual's powers are insufficient for providing himself fully with all possible means of enjoyment, he must then provide himself with each means of enjoyment up to the point where the last atom of every means shall represent an equal value to him.
>
> (Gossen 1983 [1854]: 35, 38)

Gossen is fully in the Jevonian line.[10]

As for the physics analogy there is very little to go on. There is no appreciation of the conservation principle. There is no evidence that Gossen was familiar with the Helmholtz paper of 1847; in fact by 1854 he had been at work on his *Laws* for some twenty years. He does have in common with Helmholtz the notion that physical processes constitute matter in motion: 'our action consists merely of the motions by which we bring the various materials available in nature into such an initial combination that the inherent forces of nature produce by themselves determined effects. . . . Even when something is brought about by a chemical process, however, our intervention is limited simply to movement' (Gossen 1983 [1854]: 40). But this same idea is expressed by J. S. Mill (and earlier by James Mill): 'Labour . . . in the physical world, is always and solely employed in putting objects in motion; the properties of matter, the laws of nature, do the rest' (Mill 1965, II: 28).

I turn next to Jevons's tribute to Dupuit in his account of 'coincident' contributions to utility analysis:

> In the . . . most important class of mathematico-economic writers must be placed those who have consciously and avowedly attempted to frame a mathematical theory of the subject, and have, if my judgment is correct, succeeded in reaching a true view of the science. . . . It is the

French engineer Dupuit who must probably be credited with the earliest perfect comprehension of the theory of utility. . . . He establishes, in fact, a theory of the gradation of utility, beautifully and perfectly grounded by means of geometrical diagrams, and this theory is undoubtedly coincident in essence with that contained in this book. He does not, however, follow his ideas out in an algebraic form. Dupuit's theory was the subject of some controversy, in the pages of the *Annalles des Ponts et Chaussées*, and I am not aware that any English economist ever knew anything about these remarkable memoirs.

(Jevons 1924: xxviii–xxix)

Now this tribute has implications for the Mirowski theme. For Mirowski denies Carl Menger the neoclassical label on the grounds that, while like Dupuit he recognized diminishing marginal utility, he also repudiated a single equilibrium price and 'the mere postulation of diminishing marginal utility is not sufficient to generate a neoclassical theory of price', a 'basic pillar' of the energy-physics analogy (cf. above, p. 171–2). Perhaps so, but Jevons's belief that Dupuit's geometrical utility theory 'is undoubtedly coincident in essence with that contained in this book' undermines the broader case regarding the energy dimension. For Jevons (who of course did subscribe to the single price rule) the theory of diminishing marginal utility was important in its own right.

Mirowski's neglect of the general-equilibrium model discussed earlier regarding Walras is relevant also for us at this point. Of course, there are important differences in object and achievement between the two. As Jaffé has pointed out: 'In Walras, the theorem of proportionality of raretés to parametric market prices was used to derive individual demand and offer curves, which, when aggregated over all individuals, served to determine equilibrium prices in a prespecified perfectly competitive market system' (1983: 317). By contrast (as Walras observed) Jevons's ratio of exchange is merely a posited ruling price; he failed to derive 'the equation of *effective demand* as a function of *price* which could have been so easily deduced [from the 'final degree of utility function'] and which is so indispensable for the solution of the problem of the determination of equilibrium price'; and he had not produced 'the theorem of general equilibrium and its corollary, viz. the laws of the emergence and variation of equilibrium prices' (cited from Walras's correspondence, in Jaffé 1983: 318).[11] In Jaffé's words, Jevons focused on utility 'to reduce utilitarian speculations to an exact science which would be useful as a foundation for the theory of value in exchange; while Walras peremptorily and nonchalantly . . . postulated a measurable marginal utility theory without more ado, for the sole purpose of rounding out his previously formulated catallactic theory of price determination'.

Nonetheless, Jevons also begged his readers 'to bear in mind that [his] book was never put forward as containing a systematic view of economics'

(Jevons 1924: xliii–xliv). And it is certain that, while his own immediate project was the mathematical formulation of the utility calculus, he saw the future of the subject as a whole to be in general equilibrium. Walras paid tribute to the 'ten remarkable pages' of Jevons's Preface for the second edition which formulated the correct perspective as he saw it of the relation between distribution and pricing (Walras 1954: 45). There is also Jevons's chapter V containing analysis of the relation between a version of marginal productivity and marginal utility. But most revealing is a tribute to Cournot regarding pricing, and this despite its lack of underpinning in any theory of utility:

> [By] far the most important part of the book commences with the fourth chapter upon the 'Loi du débit'. The remainder of the book, in fact, contains a wonderful analysis of the laws of supply and demand, and of the relations of prices, production, consumption, expenses and profits. Cournot starts from the assumption that the débit or demand for a commodity is a function of the price, or $D = F(p)$; and then after laying down empirically a few conditions of this function, he proceeds to work out with surprising power the consequences which follow from those conditions. Even apart from its economic importance, this investigation, so far as I can venture to judge it, presents a beautiful example of mathematical reasoning, in which knowledge is apparently evolved out of ignorance. In reality the method consists in assuming certain simple conditions of the functions as comfortable to experience, and then disclosing by symbolic inference the implicit results of these conditions. But I am quite convinced that the investigation is of high economic importance, and that, when the parts of political economy to which the theory relates come to be adequately treated, as they never have yet been, the treatment must be based upon the analysis of Cournot, or at least must follow his general method.
>
> (Jevons 1924: xxx–xxxi)

That Jevons's own preoccupation was with the sub-phenomenal level of analysis, does not preclude his recognition that a full-fledged economics is of the general-equilibrium kind.[12]

IV. THE EVIDENCE: MARSHALL

It is Mirowski's position that 'with the single exception of Marshall, all the early neoclassicals used the energetics metaphor; no other economists understood enough physics to discuss its implications and flaws' (Mirowski 1984: 373). Marshall 'certainly discussed some aspects of the physical metaphors . . . ; and he clearly had his reservations' (Mirowski 1984: 374). Marshall in fact was initially unconcerned with utility analysis as such and with constrained maximization by the individual; his concern was supply–demand analysis based on a 'phenomenological' demand curve, turning 'implicitly' upon changes in the number of buyers.

One might think the obvious conclusion of all this – on Mirowski's own terms – is to disqualify Marshall from the 'neoclassical' group, since membership therein hinges critically on constrained utility maximization. But to exclude Marshall (as Menger is excluded) would be inconceivable, and Mirowski chooses a different route.[13] Marshall, according to Mirowski, chose in his *Principles* rather to 'popularize' Jevons *et al.* Specifically: 'The saga of the journey between Marshall's early *Essay* and his *Principles* is the story of a decision to incorporate the innovations of the marginalist revolutionaries in order to shore up the foundations of the demand blade of the "scissors" while preserving his original concerns with the underlying theories of the supply schedule' (Mirowski 1984: 375). The point is that Marshall's ultimate incorporation of utility analysis suffices to allow him formal entry into the club, but is not to be taken seriously, for he was not a committed member: 'Marshall sensed that his concerns could be overwhelmed by the zeal of his marginalist allies, and this partly explains why he does not conform in style to the characteristics of the marginalist cadre identified above'; in brief, he engaged in 'attempts to incorporate energetics into economics while controlling or perhaps altering some of its more objectionable aspects'. (Mirowski alludes to Marshall's defence of Ricardo against Jevons, his soft-pedalling of mathematics, his insistence on continuity of doctrine.) But despite this strategy, and 'however much he might protest, the fact remains that Marshall did render the energetics metaphor palatable for an English audience which would probably have resisted the brash revolution of a Jevons'.

Mirowski is attributing to Marshall (a) a private denial of the importance of utility and (b) a show of support designed to capture and tame Jevonian doctrine for public consumption. To accept that Marshall was thus intellectually twisted requires rather more evidence than we are given. It will also be recalled that Walras too introduced marginal utility analysis belatedly (above, p. 173). His basic preoccupation was the establishment of the general conditions of equilibrium, with the proportionality of marginal utility and prices manifesting itself throughout the system – production, capital formation, money as well as simple exchange. And, as Jaffé puts it, 'surely it is for that reason and for the role he assigned in his grand system to marginal utility, rather than for the now outmoded theory of marginal utility itself, that he is still honored or berated (as in Cambridge, England) by the foremost theorists of our day' (Jaffé 1983: 316–17). Mirowski's position should lead him to say the same of Walras as of Marshall – narrowing early club membership only to Jevons. This is the logical consequence of Mirowski's hyper-narrow perspective on neoclassicism which plays down general-equilibrium analysis to the point of almost total neglect.

It may be added that in his account Mirowski fails to demonstrate any concern on Marshall's part to deal with the energetics metaphor. Citations from the *Principles* (Marshall 1920: xiv, xvi–xvii, given in Mirowski 1984: 375–6) say nothing specifically of that metaphor. As is so usual throughout this paper, Mirowski gratuitously reads energetics into any general reference to mechanics and physics. The case of Marshall is rendered murky rather than 'illuminated by an understanding of energetics' (Mirowski 1984: 374).

V. THE CONCESSIONS

As we have seen, Mirowski asserts that neoclassical economics was 'appropriated wholesale' from mid-nineteenth-century physics and writes of the 'explicit appropriation' of the energy metaphor by every major marginalist innovator except Menger. Energetics 'induced the invention of neoclassical economic theory'; it explains 'the timing of its genesis' and its intellectual content. These themes have not been substantiated for the reasons outlined above. Interestingly enough, Mirowski himself provides a list of potent objections and it is beyond me how he did not draw the obvious conclusion.

We have already encountered Mirowski's allowances regarding the lever analogy used by Jevons (above, p. 175). More generally: 'the early neoclassicals themselves did not adequately understand the physical metaphor and the constraints which it imposed upon social theory' (Mirowski 1984: 373); 'the "inventors" did not understand energetics or the social metaphor with any degree of subtlety' (374).

Second, in his discussion of utility as the counterpart – the unobservable counterpart – of energy which is inferred 'from theoretical linkage to other observable variables' (above, p. 171), Mirowski concedes that 'the early marginalists reversed this logic in their exposition of the principle. Instead of treating utility as a derived phenomenon, they postulated the utility field as the fundamental exogenous data [sic] to which market transactions adjusted' (368). Quite so – as Walras put the matter: 'the utility curves and the quantities possessed contribute the necessary and sufficient data for the establishment of current and equilibrium prices. From these data we proceed . . . to the mathematical derivation of individual and aggregate demand curves. . . . And then, from the individual and aggregate demand curves, we derive mathematically the current equilibrium prices, since there can be only one price in the market' (Walras 1954: 143). Mirowski proceeds to the broad admission that 'although Walras trained originally as an engineer . . . he did not possess a deep understanding of the new energetics' (Mirowski 1984: 369), and that he 'did not comprehend the real thrust' of C. E. Picard's letters which – according to Mirowski, although I am doubtful (see note 6) – prompted him to write his 1909 essay.

We have, too, a peculiar contrast between Jevons and Walras:

If there was a difference between Jevons and Walras it was this: Walras did not evince any deep understanding of mid-nineteenth century physics, and applied the mathematical techniques and the metaphor in a mechanical and unimaginative manner, leaving it for others to draw out the logical and connotative implications of the physical metaphor. Jevons on the other hand, was even less of a mathematician than Walras, but did dedicate his life's work to drawing out the meaning of the metaphor of energetics for the sphere of the economy. This point is not readily apparent.

(Mirowski 1984: 369–70; cf. 363)

This formulation manages to give the impression that at least Jevons had a profound appreciation of 'the meaning of the metaphor of energetics for the sphere of the economy' (and this despite his clumsiness as mathematician) – a position which is never established by Mirowski. Even in this context he concedes: 'this point is not readily apparent'. Indeed not – neither to the reader, nor to Jevons himself.

The conclusion that on Mirowski's own admissions – quite apart from the evidence we have introduced – Jevons in 1871 and Walras in 1874 did *not* base themselves on the new energy physics in any meaningful way, is reinforced by yet a further concession:

There *is* one major difference, however, between the mathematics of energetics and its transplanted version in neoclassical economics. The conservation principle in energetics does not translate directly into neoclassical theory: the sum of income and utility is not conserved, and is meaningless in the context of economic theory. Does this mean that neoclassical economics has managed to dispense with the artifice of a conservation principle? This may appear to be the case, because neither the progenitors of neoclassicism nor any of its modern adherents have ever seriously discussed this aspect of the physical metaphor. . . . Yet to cast any problem in a constrained maximization framework, the analysis must assume some sort of conservation principle. In physics, it is widely understood that the conservation principle is the means by which the system being considered retains its analytical identity.

In other words, the adoption of the energetics metaphor has imposed an analytical regimen, the rigours of which have hitherto gone unnoticed. Neoclassical theorists, from the 1870s onwards have surreptitiously assumed some form of conservation principle in their economic models.

(Mirowski 1984: 368)[14]

We are now so far from the strong assertions which this paper purports to support, that scarcely anything remains. The theme now is merely that 'to cast any problem in a constrained maximization framework, the analysis must assume some sort of conservation principle' – though the originators (indeed neoclassicists to this day) have not realized it. The conservation principle that was initially stated to be at the core of the energetics metaphor turns out to be only a logical 'implication' of constrained maximization.

VI. CONCLUSION

Mirowski's perspective is an extraordinarily narrow one. The mere reference by writers to a physics metaphor (without even being certain that energetics is involved) suggests to him that mid-nineteenth-century physics is the sole significant source of neoclassicism. And this despite his ample concessions that the originators of the 1870s had no idea of what the physics metaphor implied. All other considerations relating to the link between economics and science, including those relevant for the general-equilibrium model, are set at naught. Mirowski himself has written of the 'successful penetration' of mathematics as the key feature of late nineteenth-century economics. In his enthusiasm he has missed a key instance of the extension of mathematics and closed his eyes to the continued use of the Newtonian and possibly other natural science metaphors.

Mirowski asserts that 'classical economists made reference to the Newtonian analogy in non-essential contexts', adding: 'but they could not reconcile the inverse square law, the calculus of fluxions and other Newtonian techniques with their overall conception of social processes' (Mirowski 1984: 366). He is, in all honesty obliged to admit that, on his own showing, just this kind of conclusion should apply to the neoclassicals. For they could not 'reconcile' the various energetic perspectives which require for example, that utility be treated as a derived phenomenon and that conservation be defined meaningfully; worse still, they proceeded to extend the maximization principle to labour, to production, to capital and to money holdings, contexts in which the whole notion of conservation is irrelevant.[15]

There are other problems that Mirowski must face, but which I shall not elaborate here. What will he make of the fact that J. S. Mill accepted the budget constraint, the ranking of alternatives in stable preference ordering and the maximization of satisfaction? The 'law of one price' and the concept that traded goods are related as 'equivalents in equilibrium' (which Mirowski refers to as essential for neoclassicism and the physics analogy) are also conspicuous features in Mill's *Principles*. What happens to the 'discontinuity' of which so much is made in this paper?

NOTES

1 Adam Smith drew explicitly on a Newtonian analogy. His *Wealth of Nations* treats human society as a mechanical system, functioning through internal processes conforming to discoverable natural laws of mechanics, and turning in

a small number of unifying principles (cf. Hollander 1987, ch. 12). His work was, in Jaffé's terms (1983: 101), 'inspired by Newtonian celestial mechanics'.

2 Cf. also Jaffé 1983, 101: 'Walras, having also [like Smith] been guided by the precedent of Newtonian celestial mechanics, used his "rareté" as the connecting common principle in the construction of his general equilibrium model. One of Léon Walras's last publications, *Economique et mécanique* (1909) . . . was a reaffirmation of his reliance on Newtonian mechanics to inform his conception of catallactic mechanics. From the age of nineteen on, when Walras first read Louis Poinsot's *Eléments de statique* [1842], he had sought to create a theory of economics with the same formal properties that characterized celestial mechanics.' Cf. also 275: 'Léon, at the age of 19, was fired by the example of Louis Poinsot's *Eléments de Statique*, a text-book in pure mechanics, including celestial mechanics, which was presented in the form of simultaneous equation systems. It was Poinsot's model that Léon later imitated and adapted to his portrayal of good economic equilibrium.' For some details regarding Poinsot see Walras 1965, III: 149n7.

3 We note first that Picard says nothing about an *unobserved* quantité de besoin (see Walras 1965, I: 308–11).

4 For an elaboration of Walras's debt to his colleague Arnstein, see Jaffé 1983: 77, 90, 206–7, 275, 314–15.

5 Jaffé remarks here on Walras's conspicuous 'inattention to consumption', his marginal utility curves relating to possession.

6 Walras also relied in his paper on advice from Boninsegni. Mirowski's claim (1984: 369) that C. E. Picard exerted some influence does not appear to be valid.

7 See also Walras's Preface to the fourth edition (1900) of the *Elements*: 'I readily acknowledge Gossen's priority with respect to the equation of maximum utility in exchange . . . I am indebted to my father, Auguste Walras, for the fundamental principles of my economic doctrine; and to Augustin Cournot for the idea of using the calculus of functions in the elaboration of this doctrine' (1954: 37).

8 A specific reference given to Jevons 1973: 66 as indicating familiarity with Thomson and Joule is careless. The letter referred to is not *by* Jevons but *to* Jevons (from H. E. Roscoe); and there is no mention in this letter of 'the theory of the conservation of energy'.

9 Cf. letter to Foxwell dated November 1879, conceding that 'all is shelved on the matter of priority', considering the work of Gossen, Cournot and Dupuit (Jevons 1977: 80).

10 For a brilliant account of Gossen's work specifying the specific parallels with that of Jevons, see Georgescu-Roegen (1983).

11 See also Walras's insistence upon his claim to priority regarding 'the general theory of price determination . . . the proper subject matter of pure economics' – in contrast with utility-maximization theorems which he conceded already to be in Gossen and Jevons (Walras 1952 [1885]: 482).

12 Even in 1860, when he was writing with red-hot enthusiasm of his mathematical utility theory, Jevons allowed that 'this law of utility has in fact always been assumed by Pol. Econ. under the more complex form and name of the Law of Supply & Demand' (Jevons 1973: 410); it was the 'definition of capital' and the law of interest that were 'quite new'. And again, when introducing Walras to the English-speaking world in 1874, he repeated this theme: 'the principle inferences from the theory were the laws of supply and demand, and

the doctrine of the relation of value to cost of production already so well known in political economy' (Jevons 1981: 84).

13 A number of commentators, prior to Mirowski, have distinguished Menger from both Jevons and Walras in various respects; cf. Jaffé (1983), Shackle (1972), Streissler (1972).

14 Mirowski proceeds: 'In the period of our present concern, the principle took two forms: (a) the income or endowments to be traded is assumed to be fully spent or traded; thus, for practical purposes, T [total expenditure on goods] is conserved; and/or (b) the transactors' estimation of the utility of the various goods is a datum not altered by the sequence of purchase, nor any other aspects of the trading or consuming process ... so, in effect, the utility field is conserved.' But subsequently it is further allowed that while 'something must be conserved in order to apply the techniques of constrained extrema, the "maximum principle" ... when the physical metaphor is imported into the social sphere, neoclassicists were not at all precise about what the conserved entity was, and they have not yet been able to settle this issue. ... If utility is conserved, then surprise and regret as psychological phenomena have analytically been ruled out of court. If income or endowments are conserved, then Say's Law is implicitly invoked' (1984: 374).

15 Cf. Mirowski 1984, 374: 'In energetics, all physical phenomena are fully and reversibly transformable into any other phenomena. When this idea is transported into the context of the economy, then all goods become fully and reversibly transformable into all other goods through trades. There is no requirement for a specific money commodity or set of financial institutions, because they would be redundant. The analogies of energetics is a barter economy.'

REFERENCES

Fisher, I. (1925) [1892] *Mathematical Investigations into the Theory of Value and Prices*, New Haven: Yale University Press.

Georgescu-Roegen, N. (1983) 'H. H. Gossen: His Life and Work in Historical Perspective', introductory essay to Gossen (1983) [1854], xi–cxiv.

Gossen, H. H. (1983) [1854] *The Laws of Human Relations*, translated by R. C. Blitz, Cambridge, Mass.: The MIT Press.

Hollander, Samuel (1987) *Classical Economics*, Oxford: Basil Blackwell.

Jaffé, W. (1983) *William Jaffé's Essays on Walras*, D. A. Walker (ed.), Cambridge: Cambridge University Press.

Jevons, W. S. (1924) *Theory of Political Economy*, London: Macmillan.

—— (1973) *Papers and Correspondence*, II, *Correspondence, 1850–1862*, R.D. Collison Black (ed.), London: Macmillan.

—— (1977) *Papers and Correspondence*, V, *Correspondence, 1879–1882*, London: Macmillan.

—— (1981) *Papers and Correspondence*, VII, *Papers on Political Economy*, London: Macmillan.

Marshall, A. (1920) *Principles of Economics*, 8th edn, London: Macmillan.

Mill, J. S. (1965) *Principles of Political Economy, Collected Works*, II, III, Toronto: University of Toronto Press.

Mirowski, P. (1984) 'Physics and the "Marginalist Revolution" ', *Cambridge Journal of Economics*, 8, 4: 361–79.

Schabas, M. L. (1983) *William Stanley Jevons and the Emergence of Mathematical Economics in Britain*, unpublished PhD dissertation, University of Toronto. (Revised version published in 1990 as *A World Ruled by Number: W. S. Jevons and the Rise of Mathematical Economics*, Princeton: Princeton University Press.)

Shackle, G. L. S. (1972) 'Marginalism: The Harvest', *History of Political Economy*, 4: 587–602.

Streissler, E. (1972) 'To What Extent Was the Austrian School Marginalist?', *History of Political Economy*, 4: 426–41.

Walras, L. (1952) [1885] 'H. H. Gossen', in H. W. Spiegel (ed.) *The Development of Economic Thought*, New York: John Wiley and Sons.

—— (1954) *Elements of Pure Economics*, translated and edited by W. Jaffé, London: George Allen and Unwin.

—— (1960) [1909] 'Economique et Mécanique', *Metroeconomica* 12: 3–13.

—— (1965) *Collected Papers and Correspondence*, Amsterdam: North Holland.

11

ON A. ARNON'S *THOMAS TOOKE: PIONEER OF MONETARY THEORY*

This book incorporates the substance of several of Arie Arnon's published articles (1984, 1987, 1989). Part I sets the theoretical and factual stage, relying heavily on Feavearyear (1963) for the latter, and includes a chapter on Ricardian monetary thought. Part II on 'Tooke the Follower' – of mainstream monetary theory, largely Ricardo (excluding the posthumous paper *Plan of a National Bank*) – takes the preparatory material further by outlining Tooke's pre-Banking School views in what is called the 'stable conceptual framework' of his first published work, *Thoughts and Details on the High and Low Prices of the Last Thirty Years* (1823) through the first two volumes of *A History of Prices and of the State of the Circulation . . .* (1838). But the core of the book is to be found in parts III and IV. Part III ('Tooke, the Innovator') contains three chapters – one on Tookean Banking School principles as they appear in *An Inquiry into the Currency Principle* (1844), a second on the transition to those principles which Arnon dates largely from 1838 (though in part II reference is made to some early dissensions from Ricardian orthodoxy even in the 1820s), and a third on the post-1844 years. Part IV ('An Attempt at Perspective') comprises two chapters: one on Tooke's knowledge of price trends considering his neglect or ignorance of index numbers; and the second, which contains the substance of the *OEP* paper, on the applicability of the competitive solution to money and credit.

It is a central theme of the book, reflected in the choice of title, that Tooke was a major contributor to monetary theory, a view contrasting with that of Schumpeter but in line with that of T. E. Gregory (and of course J. S. Mill). The early Tooke defended convertibility on the 'Bullionist' lines characteristic of the Currency School that prices are determined by the quantity of the medium in circulation (coins plus banknotes), which quantity should behave as would a pure gold circulation. This position is abandoned in the 1844 *Inquiry* which (a) rejects the distinction between notes and other means of payment; (b) denies the quantity theory, reversing the causal relation between quantity of means of payment and prices – the 'money supply' becoming an *endogenous* variable – with prices themselves determined by consumer income (Arnon 1991: 3, 97). The primary question exercising

Arnon is *when* and *how* this transformation occurred. Gregory, the target throughout, had maintained in his 1928 Introduction to the *History of Prices* that the break was *sudden*, occurring in 1840 immediately after publication of the third volume, and reflected an altered perception of the role of deposits, more specifically the abandonment of the view that deposits are 'unemployed and inert' money distinct from the note issue (Arnon 1991: 3). For Arnon, the transformation was *gradual*, and reflected in its fundamentals the more basic issue of the applicability of free trade to banking, Tooke abandoning his original opposition to free trade in note issue in favour of competition. The chapter devoted to 'The Transition Period' elaborates the thesis that the key years are those following the 1838 volumes and preceding the 1844 pamphlet, during which period 'Tooke was gradually rejecting certain of his earlier premises but had not yet consolidated a complete alternative theory' (Arnon 1991: 120).

Gregory's position that it was only *after* Volume III of *A History of Prices* but *before* the evidence given to the Committee on Banks of Issue later in 1840 that the transition occurred (Gregory 1928: 71, cited Arnon 1991: 120) is said to be misleading, Tooke having already *rejected* the strong distinction between deposits and banknotes in favour of a more balanced position. When this particular change occurred is an open question; it might, one supposes, have been at any time between 1838 and 1840, even in 1840 itself. Potentially significant is the further thesis that the transformation was a gradual one lasting until 1844, turning on various additional reasons for the altered position apparently neglected by Gregory. But Arnon somewhat undermines this potentiality by insisting also that these reasons are already to be found *in Volume III itself* – (a) the argument that banks cannot increase the amount of notes in circulation, the basis for 'the famous law of reflux'; (b) the denial that excess issue of bank notes is responsible for speculation; and (c) an income theory of prices in place of the quantity theory – in which case his difference with Gregory regarding timing may reduce to a few months in 1840. As for the abandonment of the sharp contrast between notes and deposits, that 'did not change after Volume III' and reappears as such in 1844 (Arnon 1991: 122). And though Tooke 'still appears indecisive' about the above-mentioned novelties, one can already distinguish the emergence of those new principles which were to make him an opponent of the Currency School (Arnon 1991: 124). In fact, we are told, the testimony given later in 1840 to the Bank Issue Committee 'add[ed] almost nothing new to Tooke's arguments in Volume III of *A History of Prices*'.

The 'indecision' just alluded to is said to have dissipated by the 1844 *Inquiry* (129), the process of clarification reflecting the resolution of a tension between Tooke's 'meta-theory' relating to free trade and his specifi- cally banking principles (126f). Although his new monetary theory minimizing the Bank's influence on prices should have suggested to him an extension of free trade to banking, Tooke did not take this line immediately and continued to maintain the original exclusion in 1840 – 'free-trade in banking is synonymous with free trade in swindling'; 'the issue of paper substitutes for coin is no branch of productive industry. It is a matter of regulation by the state' (cited Arnon 1991: 129). In 1844 this tension is resolved when Tooke accepted 'that free trade in banking is not dangerous to the production of wealth, its influence on prices is negligible, and so there is no reason not to leave this business outside the "province of police" '. Arnon has some interesting observations here and elsewhere in the book on technical or analytical innovation relative to alterations in broader ideological perspective (e.g. 126, 130, 166, 180).

Here we might profitably consider a broad question raised by this study – the quality of Tooke's theorizing. The innovations alluded to thus far in the context of application of free trade to banking as a reflection of the new monetary theory relates to *note issue*. Arnon allows that his admiration for Tooke as theorist does not extend to the status of free trade with regard to *credit*. That is referred to as 'a critical lacuna', 'a strange omission', and 'the weakest point in his analysis' (Arnon 1991: 115, 131, 173). The mature theory 'seems to avoid and bypass . . . the status of free trade with regard to credit', Tooke failing to build a 'complete system' and engaging rather 'in attempts to discredit his rivals' arguments', so that despite his recognition that (unlike notes) credit does not adjust automatically to the needs of the economy through the law of reflux, he failed to draw the formal conclusion that free-trade principles are *inappropriate* in the case of credit (131).

This 'failure to develop a theory of how credit should be controlled, leaving it totally to the Bank Director's discretion', is one exception to the representation of Tooke as a major theorist: 'If Tooke deserves criticism for being atheoretical, it is in this context'(Arnon 1991: 4, cf. 175). And though there was some progress after 1844, even in the last volumes of *A History of Prices* (1857) there remains 'a gap between Tooke's theories of money and credit and his proposed banking regimes' (Arnon 1991: 142). But what is one to make of the relation between meta-theory and analytical innovation considering so great an exception as the control of credit? And surely Arnon exaggerates when he insists against Gregory on 'a complete reversal in Tooke's attitude to free trade in banking' (Arnon 1991: 132).

The foregoing is by no means the only major reservation allowed by Arnon. There is also the fact that Tooke's original theory of interest (recognizing only a transitory impact of monetary phenomena on the interest rate and emphasizing an effect of the level of the interest rate on the level of prices) remains unchanged despite all the subsequent major revisions: 'In view of the radical changes in his other positions this is somewhat odd' (Arnon 1991: 86, 116). And there is the puzzling question of how Tooke managed to arrive at his accurate conclusion regarding price trends despite the absence of formal indexation 'even when these [data] were not compatible with his general [theoretical] position on the determinants of prices'

(Arnon 1991: 160). Considering Arnon's high opinion of Tooke as theorist, these anomalies require further attention.

The significance of Tooke's theoretical contribution emerges also in the context of filiation of ideas. Tooke's notion that banks cannot increase the amount of their notes in circulation is said to reflect partial acceptance of 'Gurney's argument that any additional supply of notes by the Bank would find its way back to the Bank, which "would lock them up in their tills" ' (Arnon 1991: 123). This idea, it is pointed out, was later developed into the 'famous law of reflux'. (Arnon 1991: 99, 179, contrasts Tooke's restriction of the doctrine to *notes* only with Adam Smith's version.) But that law was *not* due to Tooke, but to Fullarton (Arnon 1991: 135), despite which fact it is Tooke who is represented as 'the innovator of the Banking School' (Arnon 1991: 179).

Much more then should have been said of the relation between Fullarton and Tooke. Only brief mention is made of another major Banking School exponent, James Wilson. Above all, I miss any concerted effort to elaborate on the relationship both from a theoretical and policy perspective between Tooke and J. S. Mill. Mill does not even appear in a brief paragraph in the Introduction on influence or in an Epilogue touching on influence (Arnon 1991: 4, 184).

A word is in order on the representation of the great classics, especially Smith and Ricardo. As for Smith, I am not sure of the edition of the *Wealth of Nations* Arnon has used, since his discussion of Smith's case for free trade in banking opens with the assertion that 'Adam Smith discussed money before discussing the division of labour in the fourth chapter of Book I entitled *The Origins and Use of Money*' (Arnon 1991: 21). More seriously, the exposition of Smith is too neat and tidy. Arnon asserts that 'Smith's theory assumes that a mixed convertible circulation, one based on commodity money, needs no regulation or control. The quantity of the circulating commodity – money – will always be the right one' (Arnon 1991: 24). But the truth is far more complex, since Smith actually maintained that banks *do not necessarily understand their own interest*, and might therefore be responsible for an excessive money supply over an extended period by way of an on-going process of inappropriate discounting, illustrating the case of a circulation 'overstocked with paper money' by Bank of England notes, issued in 'too great a quantity' and this 'for many years together' (Smith 1937 [1776]: 286). Here is a nice instance of a potential clash between technical monetary theory and the free-trade 'meta-theory'.

Arnon has much of interest to say on Ricardo's posthumous paper *A Plan for a National Bank* (1824), particularly its distinction between paper issue as substitute for gold, a function to be carried on by a Commission; and the business of loans which was to be left to competition. This rejection of free trade in note issue, Arnon maintains, has generally been understood as involving *passivity* of the issue authority which was to *respond* to gold movements (Arnon 1991: 31, 38, 98–9, 177). Readers of this pamphlet, including both the main Currency School authorities and Tooke, failed to recognize that it actually constituted a major break with Ricardo's earlier thinking, one which reflected 'growing mistrust in . . . "natural" forces', leading Ricardo to recommend discretionary open-market operations by the Bank to alter the note supply (Arnon 1991: 99, 177, based on Ricardo 1951, IV: 296–7). Arnon insists then on differentiating the Currency School from the late Ricardo, considering the latter's rejection of the meta-theory of free trade in the monetary sphere and 'adoption of a basically central banking theory'.

All this is very difficult and doubtless the last word has not been said on the interpretation of Ricardo's banking principles. Years ago I myself wrote that Ricardo in 1824 'allowed some discretion to the authority by way of the issue of notes against government securities in the event of an improvement of the exchanges and a fall in the market price of gold and the sale of government securities under the opposite conditions' (Hollander 1979: 492–3n). It was not clear to me then, and it is not clear now, precisely what to make of this allowance, but I have the impression that Arnon makes too much of it since the 'discretion' in question is in fact to be strictly a *passive reaction* to movements in the bullion price and exchange rate. It is a major theme of this book that insofar as the mature Tooke (by 1857 at least) and Ricardo (1824) were both pointing towards active Central Bank interventionism – Ricardo for notes and Tooke for credit (Arnon 1991: 180) – there is more in common between them than anyone, Tooke himself and his contemporaries as well as later and modern commentators, ever realized. Because of the various reservations noted above regarding both Ricardo and Tooke, I would say that this position should be viewed as a hypothesis still requiring confirmation.

The reader is not helped by an inadequate index – for example, there is no listing for Gregory, though so much of Arnon's case is directed against him, or for many other characters mentioned in the text including Gurney (we are never told which Gurney), Grenfell, King and Wheatley, and the entry under *Plan for the Establishment of a National Bank* omits the main page references. Throughout one encounters a veritable menagerie of strange creatures such as Lord Grenfeld, Pascue Grenfel, Weatly, Honer, Malet, Sir George Schuckbury Evelyn. The bibliography extends far beyond works actually cited, which practice breaks a useful convention. And some attention might profitably have been paid to Pivetti's contribution on Tooke for the New Palgrave (1987) which also represents Volume III of the *History* as a new stage in Tooke's thought.

REFERENCES

Arnon, A. (1984) 'The Transformation in Thomas Tooke's Monetary Theory Reconsidered', *History of Political Economy*, 16, 311–26.

—— (1987) 'Banking Between the Invisible and Visible Hands: A Reinterpretation of Ricardo's Place Within the Classical School', *Oxford Economic Papers*, 39, 268–81.

—— (1989) 'The Early Tooke and Ricardo: A Political Alliance and First Signs of Theoretical Disagreement', *History of Political Economy*, 21, 1–14.

—— (1991) *Thomas Tooke: Pioneer of Monetary Theory*, Ann Arbor, Mich.: The University of Michigan Press.

Feavearyear, A. (1963) *The Pound Sterling: A History of English Money*, 2nd edn, Oxford: Clarendon Press.

Gregory, T. E. (1928) Introduction to Thomas Tooke and William Newmarch, *A History of Prices and of the State of the Circulation From 1792 to 1856*, London: King and Son.

Hollander, Samuel (1979) *The Economics of David Ricardo*, Toronto: University of Toronto Press.

'On A. Arnon's *Thomas Tooke: Pioneer of Monetary Theory*, *Research in the History of Economic Thought and Methodology*', 13, 1995, 271–6.

Pivetti, M. (1987) 'Thomas Tooke', *The New Palgrave: A Dictionary of Economics*, Vol. 4, 657–9, London: Macmillan.

Ricardo, D. (1951) *Works and Correspondence of David Ricardo*, P. Sraffa (ed.), Cambridge: Cambridge University Press.

Smith, Adam (1937) [1776] *An Inquiry into the nature and causes of the Wealth of Nations*, New York: Modern Library.

12

THE CORN-LAW PAMPHLET LITERATURE OF 1815

Malthus, West, Ricardo and Torrens[*]

I. INTRODUCTION

My concern in this chapter is with the so-called 'canonical' classical growth model as it emerged in the 1815 pamphlet literature on the Corn Laws, with particular but not exclusive reference to the downward trend path of the returns to capital and to labour.[1] I shall preface the discussion by reference to the common belief that the expositions in February 1815 of the diminishing-returns principle were all intimately related to recent wartime circumstances. I also take account of the positions of the protagonists *before* the appearance of their pamphlets. This exercise proves essential in Ricardo's case since his *Essay* proceeds on the assumption of a *constant* (above-subsistence) real wage, though before (and after) he is clear about the shared incidence of increasing land scarcity. Both Malthus and West incorporate this feature in their versions of the model – the former probably influenced by Ricardo's earlier correspondence. Torrens, by contrast, assumes throughout a given *subsistence* real wage, and in that respect comes closest to the 'textbook' view of classical growth theory.

West took for granted both the falling profit rate and the falling agricultural productivity purportedly underlying it as established *empirical* phenomena rather than as analytical propositions in the manner of Ricardo or Torrens.[2] Malthus is somewhat ambiguous on this matter, but approaches the West position. Missing in most accounts of the pamphlet literature is an estimate of the 'seriousness' of the land-scarcity problem; I shall take up this issue by reference to Schumpeter's famous charge of undue pessimism against the contributors of 1815. It proves to be a legitimate complaint in the cases of West and Torrens, but cannot be justified in those of Malthus and Ricardo. And of all the writers Malthus is most intriguing considering his protectionism.[3]

*   This paper is an expanded version of my Introduction (in German) to the pamphlets of 1815 reproduced in the series *Klassiker der Nationalökonomie* (Hollander 1996a).

II. THE DIMINISHING-RETURNS PRINCIPLE AND THE EMPIRICAL DIMENSION

It is common doctrine that the expositions in February 1815 of the diminishing-returns principle were intimately related to recent wartime circumstances. Cannan, for example, has written that 'the early nineteenth-century English economists deduced their doctrines . . . from the actual experience of England during the war', for 'about the year 1813 there were two features in the economic condition of the country which could not fail to strike the most superficial observer – the high prices of corn and the improvement and extension of cultivation' (Cannan 1917: 117). Jacob Hollander asked regarding Malthus's *Inquiry*: 'to what earlier influences [than the Corn Law controversy of 1814], if any, is the genesis of the law of diminishing returns, as stated therein, referable? The general answer is, of course, to that extraordinary condition of British agriculture in the preceding decade, the conspicuous features of which – extension of cultivation and application of capital to land – were familiar to Malthus long before parliamentary blue-books gave them wide publicity' (J. Hollander 1903: 4).

Evaluation of this generalization requires a word on the 1813 Select Committee on the Corn Trade.[4] The report of that Committee made a case against free trade turning upon the asserted facts of low and steady corn prices under effective protection, and high and unstable prices during periods of effectively free importation including the war years (*Parliamentary Papers*, 1812–13 (184), III: 479). Despite the emphasis on heavy importation, the report recognized that 'there had been a great increase of tillage during the last ten years', but also maintained 'that the land now in tillage is capable of being made much more productive by the extension of the improved system of cultivation, and that much land now in grass is fit to be converted into tillage' (3). These themes were elaborated by Sir Henry Parnell in his presentation of the report to the House of Commons on 15 June 1813. Recent corn price increases he blamed on *corn imports* (*Parliamentary Debates*, XXVI, 645);[5] by contrast, the prospect under a *protected* regime was one of low corn prices in consequence of increasing returns. There was, therefore, no uniform reading of the wartime evidence, somewhat undermining the standard generalization alluded to above.

Malthus discussed the report of 1813 with Horner (16 June 1813, in Tucker 1954: 331–2). He read the evidence differently from the 1813 report and Parnell – and also from Horner[6] – perceiving Britain as effectively protected during the war; and in contrast to Horner, who maintained the Smithian position that a rise in the price of corn entails a general price increase leaving the relative price and thus the output of corn unaffected, Malthus insisted that import restriction encourages the expansion of agricultural output (Tucker 1954: 332). He nonetheless *opposed* the protectionist proposals on efficiency grounds in a dynamic context entailing the principle of diminishing returns (Hollander 1997, *ETRM*, 15: II). Diminishing returns, *as a matter of contemporary British relevance*, emerges with Malthus to my knowledge for the first time in this letter to Horner where we also have the precise reverse of the position in the early editions of the *Essay* regarding the level (and stability) of corn prices in a protected economy.[7]

Now the altered perspective *preceded* the evidence of recent extensions to higher cost marginal land given at Parliamentary Committees in 1814–15, while formal and informal discussions of 1813 seem at most to have provided Malthus with evidence *illustrating* the applicability of the increasing-cost principle to the British case. For he explained that his *Inquiry* contained 'the substance of some notes on Rent . . . collected in the course of my professional duties at the East India College' – namely as far back as 1807 – 'and the very near connection of the subject of the present inquiry, with the topics immediately under discussion, has induced me to hasten its appearance at the present moment' (Malthus 1815a: 1).[8] Now the diminishing-returns principle is in fact already to be found in the first and second editions of the *Essay on Population*, though admittedly not its application to the British case. Recent experience, I conclude, could at most have *illustrated* the principle for Malthus.[9]

In his *Observations on the Corn Laws* (first edition, 1814) Malthus elaborated on the themes of the June 1813 letter. Though by this time the evidence given to the Select Committee on the Corn Laws set up in 1814 was available, that he did not formally base himself on that evidence is clear from a retrospective comment in *Grounds of an Opinion* that his position in the *Observations* had been a matter of 'general principle' *confirmed* by the parliamentary evidence (Malthus 1815b: 3–4). And he had indeed in 1814 allowed a high probability of an inflow of imports into Britain in consequence of international cost differentials (Malthus 1986 [1814], 7: 95). Differentials of agricultural technology were admitted, but not to the extent of entirely overcoming productivity relativities of a more basic order, suggesting that – at least in this context – Malthusian diminishing returns (like West's) allowed for improved technology (100).

In this context we also find Malthus referring to the differential-rent property, in his denial 'that the effects of a fall in the price of corn on cultivation may be fully compensated by a diminution of rents', since in the case of 'poor' land, 'the fund of rent will often be found quite insufficient for this purpose' (96). Various empirical references given here to differential rent apparently served an illustrative role considering the clear intimations of that corollary in the second edition of the *Essay on Population* (*ETRM*, 15: II).

West too explained in his essay that the diminishing-returns principle – in his case taking account of technical change – had 'occurred to [him] some years ago', and been 'confirmed by many of the witnesses' cited in the reports of the committees of 1814 and 1815 (West 1815: 1).[10] It thus remains an open question *when* and *how* the diminishing-returns principle had 'occurred' to him.

It is similarly uncertain whence Ricardo obtained the principle, with which he was familiar from, at the least, late December 1810 or January 1811 (Ricardo 1951, III: 287). Now Ricardo actually *applied it* as early as summer 1813 in profit-rate analysis, when he accounted for an observed *upward* movement 1793–1813 in terms of 'decided improvements of agriculture' which rendered the facts 'perfectly reconcilable to my theory. . . . My conclusion is that there has been a rapid increase of Capital which has been prevented from showing itself in a low rate of interest by new facilities in the production of food' (17 August 1813; Ricardo 1951, VI: 94–5). This formulation informs us that for Ricardo secularly diminishing returns *excluded* the impact of new technology (diverging we shall see from West and possibly Malthus); and suggests that he could not have derived his land-based model generating a *falling* profit rate from wartime observations because the profit trend was envisaged as rising, and explicable in terms of *increasing productivity*. Furthermore, the parliamentary materials do not deal with the effect on the general rate of profits of variations in agricultural productivity so that any stimulus provided by the Corn Law debate in 1813 for Ricardo's new theory of profits is not self-evident.

As for Torrens, it is equally unclear whence he obtained the principle of diminishing returns and the differential-rent corollary.[11] But he does imply, in an apologetic remark in his Preface, that he had arrived at his 'first principles' – with some claim to originality – well before actual publication (Torrens 1815: xiv–xv).[12] Torrens' qualified claims to priority are touched on in a further remark in the Preface: '[In the chapter which] treats of the influence of the price of corn on the value of currency, and on the productive powers of industry [Part I, chapter III] . . . many of the discussions are, at least with respect to the author, original. The principles of the natural and market price of labour, he does not remember to have seen previously developed, and, he conceives, they throw a new and important light on the manner, in which the price of subsistence influences wages and production' (xiii–xiv). Here he alluded to the notion of 'natural wages' as a 'subsistence' wage – in the technical sense of a wage assuring constant population – dependent on habits and custom (see 57–8, 62–6, 74, 92). No formal claim to originality is made with respect to diminishing returns or differential rent.[13]

III. ON THE 'ORIGINS' OF THE CANONICAL MODEL

Samuelson finds the full-fledged 'canonical' model in the *Wealth of Nations* (Samuelson 1978, 1980, 1991, 1992). There is some merit to the view that Smith recognized the impact of worsening land scarcity on the profit rate (Hollander 1980; also Brewer 1995). As for the real wage rate, a downward trend path is implicit in the notion of a minimum wage at which population growth ceases (Smith 1937 [1776]: 92f); moreover, Smith explicated the allocative consequences of the fall in wages: whereas contemporary British restrictions on heavy industry in the colonies were of little practical consequence since the high land–labour ratio rendered advanced manufacturing unprofitable, the same restrictions would prove dislocative in 'a more advanced state' where, because of population growth, land has become scarcer and labour more plentiful (549). Yet the 1815 contributors believed that Smith had been wholly unaware of the diminishing-returns principle and *a fortiori* of its use in a land-based growth model. Malthus in his *Inquiry* complained that Smith had neglected 'the explanation of the natural causes which tend to determine the price of corn' (Malthus 1815a: 39–40), and objected to Smith's denial that high corn prices indicated high comparative national wealth (Malthus 1815a: 45–6). West found it 'singular that [the] rise of the real price of corn in the progress of improvement has escaped the attention of the author of the Wealth of Nations' (West 1815: 39–40); and pointed to Smith's discussion of constraints on specialization in agriculture, which neglected *positively* diminishing productivity with secular expansion (West 1815: 5–6).[14] In his *Essay*, Ricardo maintained that the principle whereby 'profits are regulated by the difficulty or facility of procuring food . . . has been almost overlooked in the writings of Political Economists. They appear to think that profits of stock can be raised by commercial causes, independently of the supply of food' (1951 [1815], IV: 13n). And it may also be that Torrens was unaware of the presence of diminishing returns in the *Wealth of Nations*; at least, he later used that principle to contest Smith's notion of an invariable value of corn (see Torrens 1820, Book IV, Chapter I).

Brewer (1988) maintains that since Turgot 'had anticipated the main points of the [classical growth] theory half a century earlier – there is little point in debating which of them (Ricardo, Malthus, Torrens or West) has priority' (512). In my opinion, even were Brewer's interpretation of Turgot correct,[15] there is merit to the exercise since none of the protagonists seem to have based themselves on Turgot, anymore than on Smith.

In any discussion of 'origins,' Malthus's *Essay on Population* is crucial. The principle of diminishing returns such that average (marginal) product falls with increased population density emerges in the context of North American development, and here is found the earliest statement of Malthus's formal growth model involving a declining path of real wages in consequence of a decelerating growth rate of labour demand. *But lacking is any explicit analysis of the profit rate and its secular course.* Moreover, it is not application to land of labour-and-capital in the simple sense that is involved but application entailing land 'improvement' (*ETRM*, 1: V–VI).

Waterman claims that Thomas Chalmers (1808) provides a 'missing link' between Malthus's *Essay* and Ricardo's *Principles*; and that this circumstance 'affords some qualified support for Samuelson's position' (Waterman 1991a: 221).[16] Specifically, 'Chalmers saw, or at least felt ... that the implications of Malthus's analysis of population growth with scarce land must appreciably modify the political economy supposed to have been presented in *Wealth of Nations*' (222). If this is indeed so, it undermines rather than supports Samuelson's position since it implies that the implications of scarce land were unfamiliar to Smith. However, the main issue is whether Chalmers in 1808 developed a land-scarcity based growth model with a downward trend path for both the corn wage and profit rates, and on Waterman's own account the 'canonical' model was at most 'latent' or 'embryonic' or 'implicit' in the 1808 version (Waterman 1991a: 228–9, 231–2, 234). For it is only when 'viewed from 1825' that we can make any such claims. (Actually, Chalmers gets the model wrong even in the 1825 version as cited by Waterman 1991a: 229–30.)

Despite his recognition in the letter of June 1813 (above, pp. 194–5) to Horner of diminishing agricultural productivity as a matter of practical import, in debate with Ricardo during the summer of that year Malthus denied that agricultural productivity conditions had dictated movements in the *profit rate* during the war years. He, like Ricardo (above, p. 196), sought to account for an *upward* trend in the profit rate 1793–1813, but found the explanation (in Ricardo's paraphrase) in 'the opening of new markets or extending the old' (10 August 1813; Ricardo 1951: VI, 93) – a Smithian orientation. And in his correspondence of 1814 with Ricardo, Malthus ascribed to land scarcity an impact *on the real wage rather than the profit rate* – implying, as in the *Essay on Population*, that profits are *insulated* from decline: 'The effects of a great difficulty in procuring corn would ... be ... a diminution in the real wages of labour, or their price in corn; but not a diminution of profits' (6 July 1814; Ricardo 1951, VI: 111). In fact, agricultural protection and domestic expansion of farming might actually *stimulate* the profit rate, the linkage working by way of a negative effect on manufacturing capital and output, which reverses the downward pressure on prices and profits characterizing regular secular expansion or Smithian 'competition of capital' (110).

Under pressure from Ricardo, Malthus came later in the year to accept an impact on the profit rate of agricultural productivity. But the concession applied only in the *limit*; and it worked its way very differently than for Ricardo – a high level of productivity assuring a high agricultural profit rate and generating a high rate of capital accumulation, population and final demand for manufactures, and conversely in the 'ultimate' or stationary state (9 October 1814; Ricardo 1951: 139–40).[17] We have then the manufacturing profit rate kept in line with the agricultural rate via an *indirect* impact of land-scarcity conditions on population and therefore on the demand for final goods. As for intermediate periods, the war decades 1793–1813 illustrated high (agricultural) profits due to pressure of *demand for corn* emanating from a prosperous manufacturing sector (140–1).

Under further pressure from Ricardo, Malthus was obliged to concede an impact on the profit rate of increasing land scarcity over the full secular path – at least as a 'tendency' (23 November; Ricardo 1951, VI: 152). But the downward 'tendency' of the real wage is still represented as a 'more *directly* necessary consequence' of increasing land scarcity (155; emphasis added). I also suspect that Malthus was not quite aware that the secular wage reduction *cannot* insulate the profit rate from decline; for he represents 'the constant tendency' to a fall in real wages (not merely a temporary fall) as acting *positively* on the profit rate, along with the 'prosperous or adverse states of commerce and manufactures' (Ricardo 1951, VI: 152). He had fallen into a common error, failing to ask *why* the wage declines with increasing land scarcity unless it is under pressure from a decelerating labour demand, itself due to a falling profit rate.

Characteristic throughout is Malthus's insistence against Ricardo on Smith's increasing competition of capitals as a supplementary force depressing the profit rate. A letter of 29 December 1814 clarifies that such pressure pertained specifically to manufacturing, not to agriculture; in effect, Malthus applied the Law of Markets to 'necessaries', whereby an increase in corn supply is assumed to be accompanied by an increase in demand (Ricardo 1951, VI: 168). The same letter reiterates that population growth – governed by land-scarcity conditions – impinges on the profit rate via its effect on the demand for manufactures. From these principles it followed that the discovery of new land areas permits renewed or increased population growth and consequently increased demand for manufactures: 'I quite agree with you that a piece of fertile land added to the country upon every increase of capital would prevent the fall of profits, but more in my opinion from its increasing the demand for manufactures by increasing the number of people than by its preventing the rise of wages' (168–9).

It is Ricardo who, in the correspondence with Malthus, first provided a clear formulation of the shared incidence of diminishing returns between labour and capital. This assertion requires justification since the entire issue is a sensitive one and central to the appropriate perspective from which to view the 1815 literature.

On 2 March 1814 Hutches Trower thanked David Ricardo for the loan of his 'very interesting papers on the profits of Capital', which he was returning so that they could be sent on to James Mill (Ricardo 1951, VI: 102). Piero Sraffa noted editorially that the papers were 'Probably an early draft of the *Essay on Profits*, published in 1815' (in Ricardo 1951, I: xxxi–xxxii); and further maintained that although the 'rational foundation' for the determining role of agricultural profits which he attributed to the early Ricardo –

'it is the profits of the farmer which regulate the profits of all other trades' (Ricardo to Trower, 8 March 1814; Ricardo 1951, VI: 104) –

> is never stated by Ricardo in any of his extant letters and papers, he must have formulated it either in his lost 'papers on the profits of Capital' of March 1814 or in conversation, since Malthus [5 August 1814; Ricardo 1951, VI: 117–18] opposes him in the following terms which are no doubt an echo of Ricardo's own formulations: 'In no case of production is the produce exactly of the same nature as the capital advanced, consequently we can never properly refer to a material rate of produce. . . . It is not the particular profits or rate of produce upon the land which determines the general profits of stock and the interest of money'.
>
> (Sraffa in Ricardo 1951, I: xxxi–xxxii)[18]

The closest to an explicit statement is said to be his position in a letter of 26 June 1814: 'The rate of profit must depend on the proportion of production to the consumption necessary to such production' (Ricardo 1951, VI: 108).

Now a corn ratio was, I believe, far from Ricardo's mind in this correspondence of 1814. For in responding to Malthus's objection of 5 August, he maintained that societies *do* 'estimate their profits by the material production' in contrast to individuals *who are subject to money illusion*. Ricardo did not defend the homogeneity of input and output, but rather defended 'materiality' in the specific sense of an avoidance of money illusion: 'Individuals do not estimate their profits by the material production, but nations invariably do. If we had precisely the same amount of commodities of all descriptions in the year 1815 that we now have in 1814 as a nation we should be no richer, but if money had sunk in value they would be represented by a greater quantity of money, and individuals would be apt to *think* themselves richer' (11 August; Ricardo 1951, VI: 121).

As for Ricardo's positive position on secular trends, we are provided with a convenient summary in a letter of 23 October which refers to the strategic role played by *the money wage rate* in the event of a rise in the corn price reflecting secular expansion: 'A rise in the price of raw produce may be occasioned by a gradual accumulation of capital which by creating new demands for labour may give a stimulus to population and consequently promote the cultivation or improvement of inferior lands, – but this will not cause profits to rise but to fall, because not only will the rate of [money] wages rise, but more labourers will be employed without affording a proportional return of raw produce. The whole value of the wages paid will be greater compared with the whole value of the raw produce obtained' (146). This constitutes the main growth model – all in price terms – with one difference: that at this stage Ricardo alludes to two depressing forces at play, whereas he later came to realize that the fall in productivity is in fact reflected in the money wage. A contention by

Malthus (9 October; Ricardo 1951, VI: 141) that the land-based growth
model could not account for the relatively low profit rate 'often' observed in
low-density economies, and conversely in the case of high-density
economies, Ricardo rejected on the grounds that in the first category it
would be found that real wages were 'enormously' high (and constituted a
major source of saving), and should in part be treated as profits, and in the
second that they were 'too low', apparently *artificially* or at least *unnaturally*
depressed (147). The passage in question implies that in the event of less
extreme magnitudes of the real wage – and with appropriate classification of
'profits' – the declining profit trend would be apparent, notwithstanding the
downward trend of wages. On 18 December he insisted that 'permanent'
variation in the profit rate turns *solely* on inverse variation in the real cost of
producing wage goods; in the absence of land scarcity there would be no
downward pressure on profits: 'If with every accumulation of capital we
could tack on a price of fresh fertile land to our Island, profits would never
fall' (162). He further allowed that reduced costs of *manufactured* wage-goods
would also raise the profit rate in a formulation that confirms the strategic
roles accorded the *money* wage rate in profit-rate determination: 'I admit . . .
that commerce, or machinery, may produce an abundance and cheapness of
commodities, and if they affect the prices of those commodities on which the
wages of labour are expended they will so far raise profits . . .' (162). Finally,
the letter contains all the main elements comprising the mature growth
model of the *Principles*, by explicitly indicating that the burden of diminishing returns is shared between capitalists and labourers: 'A diminution of
the proportion of produce, in consequence of the accumulation of capital,
does not fall wholly on the owner of stock, but is shared with him by the
labourers. *The whole amount of wages paid will be greater, but the portion paid to
each man, will in all probability, be somewhat diminished*' (162–3; emphasis
added).

IV. DIFFERENTIAL RENT

These early analyses of land-based theories of profit proceeded without
formal reference to differential rent. Throughout their exchanges of 1813
and 1814 neither Ricardo nor Malthus made explicit mention of the
phenomenon, though Malthus alluded to it in his *Observations* of 1814
(above, p. 195). Ricardo apparently learned the principle from Malthus's
Inquiry, absorbing it rapidly into a well-prepared structure (Patten 1893;
Sraffa, in Ricardo 1951, IV: 4–7; Hollander 1979: 117–18, 134–5). We
must keep in mind a contention by J. S. Mill in 1828 – presumably based
on James Mill – that though Ricardo 'was posterior to the authors named
[West, Malthus], in promulgating the differential-rent doctrine [in 1815],
and less happy in his mode of explaining it than Sir Edward West, it is well
known to many of his friends that he was in possession of the principle, and

was accustomed to communicate it in conversation several years prior to the publication of the earliest of these works' (Mill 1967 [1828], IV: 180). Whether this comment is to be taken at face value is debatable (see Sraffa, in Ricardo 1951, IV: 6). A letter from Ricardo to Malthus dated 6 February 1815 does refer to some earlier discussions of rent, but the details of this letter suggest that Ricardo had then been unclear of the differential property (Ricardo 1951, VI: 173).[19]

As for West's pamphlet, the differential-rent principle emerges not at the outset of the analysis but only in a subsequent application to policy (below, p. 217). Torrens's formulations *are* central to the statement of general principles (e.g. Torrens 1815: 177, 219–20); but still there is not – in Lord Robbins' words – 'the same edge to Torrens' first tentatives in this direction as there is to the statements of West or Malthus or Ricardo' (Robbins 1958: 42). Torrens himself indicates his own dissatisfaction in the preface to the second edition (Torrens 1820: xvii).

V. MALTHUS'S 'INQUIRY INTO RENT'

Before turning to the theory of growth as it emerges in Malthus's *Inquiry*, we note the clarification that by 'rent' or the 'surplus produce from the land', he intended 'the whole fund for the support of those who are not directly employed upon the land' *including farmers' profits*, since '[p]rofits are, in reality, a surplus . . . in no respect proportioned (as intimated by the Economists) to the wants and necessities of the owners of capital' (Malthus 1815a: 16).[20] The all-inclusive notion of surplus is represented as a Providential gift. All this is consistent with the notion of surplus given in the *Essay on Population* as an excess of corn output over 'internal' corn consumption, Malthus differing from the Physiocrats only by his insistence that (agricultural) profit earners share in that excess. But though the agricultural surplus includes profits in excess of some necessary minimum, the primary concern of the pamphlet was rent proper. Profits had to be separated out from rent because they 'take a different course in the progress of society'.[21] What follows provides us with elements of a Malthusian growth model.

A growth model

The essential proposition is that rent proper emerges with manifestations of diminishing returns assuming ongoing growth of capital and labour, the fall in agricultural productivity depressing the profit rate which, together with reductions in the corn-wage rate, assures a payment for land services as such:

> In the early periods of society, or more remarkably perhaps, when the knowledge and capital of an old society are employed upon fresh and

fertile land, this surplus produce, this bountiful gift of Providence, shows itself chiefly in extraordinary high profits, and extraordinary high wages, and appears but little in the shape of rent. While fertile land is in abundance, and may be had by whoever asks for it, nobody of course will pay a rent to a landlord. But it is not consistent with the laws of nature and the limits and quality of the earth, that this stage of things should continue. Diversities of soil and situation must necessarily exist in all countries. All land cannot be the most fertile: all situations cannot be the nearest to navigable rivers and markets. But the accumulation of capital beyond the means of employing it on land of the greatest natural fertility, and the greatest advantage of situation, must necessarily lower profits; while the tendency of population to increase beyond the means of subsistence must, after a certain time, lower the wages of labour.

(Malthus 1815a: 17)

The foregoing account can be read as ascribing the reduction in the profit and corn-wage rates to the reduced productivity of 'inferior' land, the incidence of diminishing returns at the extensive margin falling on both capital and labour. (The intensive margin is also recognized; e.g. Malthus 1815a: 34, 35–6). In this case Malthus would at last have adopted the Ricardian position stated in correspondence of 1814 that the falling wage cannot insulate the profit rate, a matter left in some doubt in the earlier exchange. But there are complexities. There is an apparent reference at the close of the formulation to *excessive* population growth, contrasting with the later full-fledged statement of the growth model in which the corn-wage rate falls despite reduction in the population growth rate as well as the capital (food) growth rate, and in which the profit-rate decline is attributable to a rise in *proportional* wages which itself reflects diminishing returns. A summary of position is more in line with the mature account, attributing *both* the wage- and profit-rate reductions to land scarcity: 'Rent then has been traced to the same common nature with that general surplus from the land, which is the result of certain qualities of the soil and its products; and it has been found to commence its separation from profits, as soon as profits and wages fall, owing to the comparative scarcity of fertile land in the natural progress of a country towards wealth and population' (20–1).

A further complexity in the passage is its reference to 'accumulation of capital beyond the means of employing it on land of the greatest natural fertility' which might suggest downward pressure on the profit rate prior to extension of cultivation onto inferior land (a form of diminishing returns at the intensive margin), which pressure – together with similar downward pressure on the wage – *motivates* the extension. Such motivation is in fact stated explicitly thus: 'When capital has accumulated, and labour fallen on the most eligible lands of a country, other lands less favourably circumstanced with respect to fertility or situation, may be occupied with advantage. The expenses of cultivation, including profits having fallen, poorer land, or land more distant from markets, though yielding at first no rent, may fully repay these expenses, and fully answer to the cultivator. And again, when either the profits of stock or the wages of labour, or both have still further fallen, land still poorer, or still less favourably situated, may be taken into cultivation' (21). Even so, it remains true that the lower marginal product on inferior land suffices only to accommodate a lower profit rate and lower corn wage.

We have, therefore, at the outset of 1815 the essentials of the classical land-scarcity based (single-sector) growth model with its secular downward trend of the profit and wage rates. This simple fact raises the matter of precedence. In laying out the model Malthus says nothing about its origins. But considering the Malthus–Ricardo relation in 1813 and 1814, it is my impression that Ricardo has precedence, leaving his mark on Malthus, who then absorbed the notion into the rent pamphlet. And, in fact, subsequently in his *Principles* Malthus himself claimed precedence only for the declining wage in consequence of land scarcity – allowing Ricardo priority for the declining profit rate (Malthus 1820: 370–1). But there is evidence from later correspondence with Ricardo that Malthus was still not sure of himself (*ETRM*, 4).

Thus far the case has been stated in corn terms. But this is not the full picture, since Malthus also refers to reduced 'expenses' – a lower corn wage and profit rate – *relative to the 'value' of corn*: 'The expense of production will thus be diminished, but the value of the produce, that is, the quantity of labour, and of the other products of labour besides corn which it can command, instead of diminishing, will be increased. There will be an increasing number of people demanding subsistence, and ready to offer their services in any way in which they can be useful. The exchangeable value of food will, therefore, be in excess above the cost of production, including in this cost the full profits of the stock employed upon the land, according to the actual rate of profits, at the time being. And this excess is rent' (1815a: 17–18).[22] But what precisely did Malthus believe happens to the absolute corn price with extensions to increasingly inferior land and the corresponding fall in the corn wage and profit rate envisaged as reduced 'expenses'? Formally, the corn price is said to rise *relative to labour* (and manufactures) – the corn wage falls in effect, though this is difficult to appreciate since the reduction in expenses includes the fall in the corn wage, i.e. the increase in corn command over labour is already taken into account. *But this does not amount to the claim that the absolute corn price will tend to rise.* In fact, in elaborating the process of expansion to increasingly unproductive land with falling labour and capital 'expenses' all that is insisted upon is an assurance against an (absolute) reduction of the corn price, and this is provided by the increasing demand for corn emanating from the non-agricultural sector (the sector supported by the agricultural surplus): 'And, at every step it is clear, that if the price of produce does not fall, the rents of land will rise. And the price of produce will not fall, as long as the industry and ingenuity of the labouring classes, assisted by the capitals of those not employed upon the land, can find something to give in exchange to the cultivators and landlords, which will stimulate them to continue undiminished their agricultural exertions, and maintain their increasing excess of produce' (21–2; emphasis added).

To assert that 'expenses' fall in the sense of falling profits per cent and wages per capita is meaningful at the aggregate level of analysis but unhelpful within an industry framework; it is scarcely surprising that the notion of a corn price should have proven difficult to incorporate. On the other hand, the application of the Law of Markets to food – implicit in the notion that expanded corn supplies assures expanded demand for corn[23] – is inappropriate at the industry level which requires independence of supply and demand. More formally, Malthus justified in his *Inquiry* a value counter-part to the physical agricultural surplus, thereby reinforcing the physiocratic element, in a technical contrast between the demand for 'strict necessaries' and the demand for other goods. Only in the general category is there meaning to *demand independent of or external to supply; and here only does the 'monopoly', or scarcity, property apply.*[24] In agriculture, 'The cause of the higher price of the necessaries of life above the cost of production, is to be found in their abundance, rather than their scarcity' (Malthus 1815a: 13). The analysis is further confirmed in a reiteration that the concept of a negatively sloped demand curve applies only where 'demand is exterior to, or independent of, the production itself' (14). This contrast between speciality products and corn concludes with the generalization that an increased supply of corn is the 'cause' of the excess of price over costs: 'The fertility of soil, and consequent abundance of produce from a certain quantity of land, which, in the former case, diminished the excess of price above the cost of production, is, in the present case, the specific cause of such excess; and the diminished fertility, which in the former case might increase the price to almost any excess above the cost of production, may be safely asserted to be the sole cause which could permanently maintain the necessaries of life at a price not exceeding the cost of production' (15). Malthus is living in the world of Physiocracy. Indeed, we are witness to a *reinforcement* of this bias, since the principle involved had been rejected in the *Essay on Population*: 'On account of the tendency of population to increase in proportion to the means of subsistence, it has been supposed by some, that there will always be a sufficient demand at home for any quantity of corn which could be grown. But this is an error' (1806, II: 264n).[25]

We return to Malthus's opening statement in the *Inquiry* of the separating out of rents narrowly defined (above, p. 202). This appears to attribute the declining profit rate directly to diminishing agricultural returns, accounting for the decline within the confines of the agricultural sector.[26] Yet immediately thereafter there is also a reference to 'such an accumulation . . . as decidedly to lower the *general* profits of stock, and, consequently, the expenses of cultivation, so as make it answer to cultivate poorer land' (Malthus 1815a: 18; emphasis added). Here the fall in the profit rate appears to be determined *outside agriculture* stimulating agricultural expansion at the extensive margin with a *resultant* depression of the agricultural profit rate. The reference to 'the actual rate of profits, at the time being' in the analysis of rent (above, p. 204) points in the same direction. And in an elaboration of the 'main causes' that affect rent by reducing expenses, we apparently have (as the first cause) *capital accumulation as such* depressing the profit rate, which suggests Smithian 'competition of capitals':

> In tracing more particularly the laws which govern the rise and fall of rents, the main causes which diminish the expenses of cultivation, or reduce the costs of the instruments of production, compared with the price of produce, require to be more specifically enumerated. The principal of these seem to be four: *1ˢᵗ, Such an accumulation of capital as will lower the profits of stock*; 2ⁿᵈ, such an increase of population as will lower the wages of labour; 3ʳᵈ, such agricultural improvements, or such increase of exertions as will diminish the numbers of labourers necessary to produce a given effect; and 4ᵗʰ, such an increase in the price of agricultural produce from increased demand, as, without nominally lowering the expense of production, will increase the difference between this expense and the price of produce.
>
> (Malthus 1815a: 22; emphasis added)[27]

What happens to the *direct* depressing effects of land scarcity on the profit rate is left unstated. But since profit-rate equality is the rule, a downward trend in the profit rate in *manufactures* would allow marginal agricultural investments, keeping the agricultural rate in line.

We have thus isolated two perspectives in the *Inquiry*, one agricultural with the falling profit rate and corn-wage rate explained internally, the other entailing manufacturing as lead sector with the manufacturing rate falling under pressure of accumulation, carrying the agricultural rate with it by making possible expansion onto poorer land (or more intensive cultivation) at a depressed profit rate. Malthus might have intended a single model, the initial formulation constituting an incomplete statement designed as convenient summary of the global trends but of this I am not sure. The idea, emerging in the early correspondence, of agriculture as lead sector indirectly governing the manufacturing profit rate via population growth and demand for manufactures is absent from the *Inquiry*.[28]

One other major theme requires mention at this point. It is a presumption that the rental share necessarily *declines* with expansion: 'But though cultivation cannot be extended, and the produce of the country cannot be increased, but in such a state of things as would allow of a rise of rents, yet . . . this rise of rents will be by no means in proportion to the extension of cultivation, or the increase of produce' (29–30); again, 'rent, though greater in positive amount, bears a less, and lesser proportion to the quantity of produce derived from it' (34). This invalid generalization is supported by reference to returns made to the Board of Agriculture, and by the putative logical argument that the rent share *necessarily* declines since the absolute increase of rent on marginal extensions may be 'trifling.' (This we shall see was also West's position.)

On the rising real costs of marginal extensions

The original analysis of growth in the *Inquiry*, outlined above, does not use the diminishing-returns principle in the Ricardian manner to generate a secular upward trend in the corn price reflecting rising *real* costs. On the contrary, the (absolute) corn price might remain *constant* in the face of falling 'expenses', thus generating rent on intramarginal units of output (above, pp. 204–5). However, in a fuller account of diminishing returns later in the essay the order of events does involve expansion of food supply at higher real cost: 'we should consider the soil as a present to man of a great number of machines, all susceptible of continued improvement by the application of capital to them, but yet of very different original qualities and powers. This great inequality in the powers of the machinery employed in procuring raw produce, forms one of the most remarkable features which distinguishes the machinery of the land from the machinery employed in manufactures' (1815a: 37).[29] Here manufacturing is comprised of constant-cost industries, subject to periodic improvement and downward shifts of long-run supply price, that price reflecting productivity conditions of the most efficient firm; by contrast: 'The most fertile lands of a country, those which, like the best machinery in manufactures, yield the greatest products with the least labour and capital, are never found sufficient to supply the effective demand of an increasing population. The price of raw produce, therefore, naturally rises till it becomes sufficiently high to pay the cost of raising it with inferior machines, and by a more expensive process; and, as there cannot be two prices for corn of the same quality, all the other machines, the working of which requires less capital compared with the produce, must yield rents in proportion to their goodness' (38). Subsequently, diminishing returns is explicitly stated as an *empirical* proposition much as West was to do: 'with regard to improvements in agriculture . . . although they are sometimes very powerful, they are rarely found sufficient to balance the necessity of applying to poorer land, or inferior machines. In this respect, raw produce is essentially different from manufactures' (38). In an extension involving differential growth rates between economies, the source of pressure on agriculture is traced to expansion of manufacturing capital, implying population growth *prior to, and responsible for*, expansion of food (42–3).

These formulations suggest a response of food supply to the prior expansion of population and demand. Unfortunately, this conflicts with the formal application of the Law of Markets to agricultural produce – namely '[t]hat quality peculiar to the necessaries of life of being able, when properly distributed, to create their own demand, or to raise up a number of demanders in proportion to the quantity of necessaries produced' (8) – for such interdependence of demand and supply undermines any analysis purporting to trace out the implications of an upward-sloping supply curve in the face of outward shifts of demand. It is difficult to avoid an impression of two unintegrated perspectives, a duality conceivably reflecting the disparate composition of the pamphlet (see above, p. 195).

VI. 'GROUNDS OF AN OPINION': MALTHUS AND AGRICULTURAL PROTECTION

The diminishing-returns principle and the differential-rent corollary were applied in the 1803 *Essay on Population* during the course of a warning against easier agricultural imports (Malthus 1986 [1803], 3: 677; 1806, II: 226). But in his remarkable letter to Horner of 16 June 1813 (above, pp. 194–5), Malthus stated the efficiency advantages of free trade specifically taking account of diminishing returns.[30] The *Observations* of 1814 as a whole also does not convey a protectionist message; its recommendations justifying intervention are designed rather to correct either for distorting internal taxation or for distorting tariffs (see *ETRM*, 17: III). When the letter to Horner of June 1813 is read in the light of the pamphlet, Malthus emerges as an *opponent* of the Corn Laws, at least in the event that all sectors are treated equally, although he desisted in 1814 from committing himself to a formal recommendation.

Malthus's protectionism in his *Grounds of an Opinion* can be traced in part to objective concerns for 'security' in the light of new French export regulations, and for the impact of a reduced price level on *overall activity* directly and also via alterations in distribution, especially in the light of the national debt; in part to new monetary circumstances permitting a better-informed specification of the appropriate limit price below which duties were to be imposed; and in part to the current agricultural depression, and the unrealistically large expansion of manufacturing that would be necessary to absorb even the current unemployed.[31]

Much of this was a matter of expediency rather than principle; and none of it can be said to indicate agricultural bias as such. Yet this was Ricardo's complaint. On reading the *Grounds*, he complained to Malthus not of its protectionism as such, but of its faulty deductions from economic theory: 'you . . . make it appear as if even economically you thought we ought [not] to import corn – such is the approbation with which you quote from Adam Smith of the benefits of agriculture over commerce in increasing production, which I cannot help thinking is at variance with all your general doctrines' (13 February 1815; Ricardo 1951, VI: 178). In the *Essay on Profits* he pointed out that the notion of agricultural superiority clashed with the *diminishing returns* perspective whereby in early stages of development land is free (Ricardo 1951, IV: 37–8); Malthus in his *Inquiry* had correctly taken issue with Adam Smith's agricultural bias when he observed that 'I cannot . . . agree with him in thinking that all land which yields food must necessarily yield rent. The land which is successively taken into cultivation in improving countries, may only pay profits and labour' (1815a: 3n).[32] This was for Ricardo the correct view to take, and it should have led Malthus to reply that 'The same motives will also induce some to manufacture goods, and the profits of both in the same stages of society will be nearly the same.'

Ricardo's charge is justified. The loss of agricultural capital and output is said in the *Grounds* to be pound for pound, more damaging than a loss in other sectors, a reflection of the 'additional value' peculiar to the agricultural sector that would be erased by a free corn trade – Malthus here recommends his *Inquiry* – to the *national* detriment from the perspective both of consumption power and tax revenue: 'And this additional value is not a mere benefit to a particular individual, or set of individuals, but affords the most steady home demand for the manufactures of the country, the most effective fund for its financial support, and the largest disposable force for its army and navy' (1815b: 35). True enough, Malthus conceded – and here he diverges from the main 'physiocratic' line – that 'the last additions to the agricultural produce in an improving country are not attended with a large proportion of rent'; indeed, 'it is precisely this circumstance that may make it answer to a rich country to import some of its corn, if it can be secure of obtaining an equable supply'. Nonetheless, he closed by insisting that 'in all cases the importation of foreign corn must fail to answer nationally, if it is not so much cheaper than the corn that can be grown at home, as to equal both the profits and the rent of the grain which it displaces' (35–6). In order to justify free trade in corn, the savings in resources must be sufficient to compensate for the loss of rent. The logic behind Malthus's argument – the notion of rent as an 'additional value' itself, but particularly when differential rent turning on diminishing returns is allowed – is questionable.[33]

The letter to Horner in June 1813 and the *Observations* of 1814 – in fact large parts of the *Grounds* itself – can perhaps be read as championing free agricultural trade in principle, but not necessarily in practice given the general obstructions to domestic and foreign trade in place. But the powerful element of 'agricultural bias' in the *Grounds* and the *Inquiry* alters the picture, since an optimal allocation for Malthus entailed a larger

agricultural sector than for Ricardo, implying the need for a degree of intervention to assure it, and this certainly played some part in his support of the
1815 legislation – Ricardo's complaint in substance.[34]

VII. EDWARD WEST, 'THE APPLICATION OF CAPITAL TO LAND'

Edward West's pamphlet constitutes almost in its entirety an attempt to
prove, so to speak, the validity of the principle of diminishing agricultural
returns. Of great interest is the presumption that the downward secular
return on capital – itself taken as an accepted *empirical* phenomenon – is
explicable solely by reference to the principle. The main argument proceeds
without reference to differential rent. That differential rent only emerges
towards the close, in an application to contemporary trade policy, confirms
that it was a relatively late supplement to the diminishing-returns principle
itself, which West tells us he had discovered at an earlier period (above,
p. 195).

West's principle, which is contrasted with a version ascribed to Adam
Smith, is stated both in marginal and average terms – rather, a declining
marginal product is presumed necessarily to imply a declining average
product:

> Dr Smith's principle is, that the quantity of work which can be done
> by the same number of hands, increases in the progress of improve-
> ment comparatively less rapidly in agriculture than in manufactures.
> The additional principle to which I allude is, that each equal addi-
> tional quantity of work bestowed on agriculture, yields an actually
> diminished return, and of course if each equal additional quantity of
> work yields an actually diminished return, the whole of the work
> bestowed on agriculture in the progress of improvement, yields an
> actually diminished proportionate return. Whereas it is obvious that
> an equal quantity of work will always fabricate the same quantity of
> manufactures.
>
> (West 1815: 6–7)[35]

The principle is also stated in terms of a diminishing ratio of *net* to *gross*
produce: 'The principle is simply this, that in the progress of the improvement of cultivation the raising of rude produce becomes progressively more
expensive, or, in other words, the ratio of the *net* produce of land to its *gross*
produce is continually diminishing' (2).[36]

As mentioned, at this stage no mention is made of rent; thus the net
produce is identified with profit, generating the outcome that the principle
dictates (or perhaps more accurately is identifiable with) a falling profit rate:
'In the progress of cultivation both the gross produce and the net produce
must be constantly increasing; for additional expense or capital would not be

laid out on land, unless it would reproduce not only sufficient to replace the capital laid out, but also some increase or profit on that capital, which increase or profit is the net produce. But the proposition is, that every additional quantity of capital laid out produces a less proportionate return, and consequently, the larger the capital expended, the less the ratio of the profit to that capital.'[37] The proposition is illustrated in *value* terms: 'Thus suppose any quantity of land such that £100 capital laid out on it would reproduce £120 that is 20 per cent profit, I say that a double capital viz. £200 would not reproduce £240 or 20 per cent. profit, but probably £230 or some less sum than £240. The amount of the profit would no doubt be increased but the ratio of it to the capital would be diminished' (2–3).

We come now to the so-called 'proof' of the 'principle'. West proceeds initially on the assumption of unchanged technology and constant returns in manufacturing. He sets out assertively: 'But would [constant returns] be the case in agriculture? Consider the case of a new colony; the first occupiers have their choice of the land, and of course cultivate the richest spots in the country: the next comers must take the second in quality, which will return less to their labour, and so each successive additional set of cultivators must necessarily produce less than their predecessors' (7–8); similarly, in 'the pastoral state': 'As each cultivator is driven into a narrower compass by the pressure of population, he is obliged to till soils which are comparatively ungrateful and exhausted; the cattle are fed on artificial grasses; and expensive manures are brought from a distance to enable the land to yield successive crops, instead of being left, when exhausted, as in the earlier stages of improvement, to renovate itself' (8–9). But this 'mode of proof' is not carried further, and West proceeds to a 'briefer demonstration of the principle' involving what later came to be called the 'flower-pot argument' – the very fact that extensions are made to increasingly poor land indicated diminishing returns to the intensive cultivation of given land areas (9–11).

The 'proofs', which assume constant technology, are rendered superfluous by the introduction of technical change and increasing returns – 'But the quantity of work which can be done by a number of hands is increased in the progress of improvement, by means of the subdivision of labour and machinery even in agriculture' (12); and a rather clumsy attempt is made to demonstrate that technical progress in agriculture *cannot* fully compensate the negative impact of increasing land scarcity. Were it to do so, the outcome would be a secularly increasing profit rate: 'as we know that labour becomes actually more productive in manufactures, the wealth and stock of the community in the progress of improvement and population would go on, not only increasing, but increasing in a rapidly accelerated ratio. The reproduction of the country would not only each year be larger in amount than in the preceding year, but the ratio of that reproduction to the capital would each year be greater' (13). And a rising profit rate is ruled out, since it implied that 'Population would double with more ease in such a country in twenty-five years than it does in America in the same period; and an acre of land would, in a subsequent stage of improvement, more easily maintain a thousand, or any number of labourers, however great, than it could one in a former stage.'

West was still not satisfied and sought to reinforce his case by reference to the implications for the profit rate of alternative assumptions regarding the relative impact in agriculture of technical change (and/or increasing returns) and land scarcity. Throughout, a falling profit rate is taken for granted; and throughout it is also taken for granted that manufacturing productivity increases.[38] Thus, assuming an across-the-board doubling of productivity (and allowing for a real wage increase proportionate to the productivity change), '[it] is obvious that the profits of stock would, in this case, be doubled; even allowing the wages of labour to be doubled at the same time; for by the productive powers of labour being doubled the net produce of labour would be doubled as well as the gross produce. There would be just twice as much of every article both of rude produce and manufactures as before' (14). (This is scarcely convincing, since West was concerned with the *profit rate on capital* rather than total profits.) Even in the event of constant agricultural productivity – but again allowing a doubling of manufacturing productivity – the outcome would be higher profits (15–16). Assuming agricultural productivity to decline in inverse ratio to the productivity increase in manufacturing, profits would be unchanged (16–17). Only if agricultural productivity declines, indeed declines more rapidly than manufacturing productivity rises, can one be assured of a falling profit rate: 'it is evident that if the decrease of the powers in agriculture should be greater than the increase of those powers in manufactures, the profits of stock must diminish' (17). As for the profit-rate decline itself, West appeals to Adam Smith: 'It is an acknowledged fact that the profits of stock are always lower in a rich than in a poor country; and that they gradually fall as a nation becomes more wealthy. . . . – See Wealth of Nations, Book I. c.9' (18).[39] Thus West works back from a *supposed* factual secular decline in the profit rate, taken to be a well-recognized phenomenon, to falling agricultural productivity. The procedure contrasts with Ricardo's which, we shall see, perceives the 'principle of diminishing returns' as an analytical proposition holding good with technology given.[40]

West rejected various alternative explanations of the falling profit rate. He set out 'to show that it is impossible *wholly* to account for the progressive diminution of the profits of stock by any increase of the wages of labour' (West 1815: 19; emphasis added);[41] were it so, 'the real wages of labour would be constantly and greatly increasing in the progress of wealth and improvement; and population would consequently increase more and more rapidly in the progress of improvement, the contrary of which we know to be the fact.' Unfortunately, the secular course of the real wage is left unclear.

Thus it is not certain that rising secular wages are precluded or only rising wages of a magnitude inconsistent with the purported behaviour of population. The ambiguity is present in the word 'wholly' in the initial statement, and emerges again in the conclusion: 'As therefore the diminution of the net reproduction *is not wholly, at least*, caused by the increasing wages of labour, that is, the expense of maintaining the productive powers; it must be caused partly, at least, by a diminution of those powers. But the productive powers in manufactures, as has been shown, are constantly increasing, and the diminution of the net reproduction or the profits of stock must therefore necessarily be caused by a diminution of the productive powers in agriculture' (19–20; emphasis added).

The course of wages is addressed a little later in the pamphlet. And again there is some ambiguity, implicit in the word 'only' in the following passage: 'We return then to the old question, whether the diminution of the profits of stock in the progress of improvement can be caused by the increase of the wages of labour. Now, 1st, if such were the fact, how comes it that both the wages of labour and profits of stock are high at the same moment in America. The wages of labour being higher in America than in this country, if the rise of the wages of labour were the *only* reason of the diminution of the profits of stock, the profits of stock in America should be lower than they are here. But we know that they are much higher' (22; emphasis added). What follows, however, is somewhat clearer that the secular course involves *both* falling profit and real wage rates.

The argument runs as follows. First, citing Adam Smith on the source of labour demand,[42] West establishes that movements of the real wage are governed by the *relative* growth rates of population and capital such that if 'the stock increases faster than the population, the demand increases faster than the supply, and wages must rise; if the stock and population increase equally, wages will remain stationary; and if population increase more rapidly than the stock, wages must fall' (23).[43] He then – implicitly assuming a constant growth rate of population – emphasizes that the magnitude of any increase in real wage turns on the capital growth rate: 'Nor is it the greatness of the increase alone of stock which causes high wages, but it is the greatness of the ratio of the increase.'[44] And the rate of increase in capital is in turn governed (*ceteris paribus*) by the profit rate: 'supposing a country to be always equally parsimonious, it is upon the rate of profit that the rate of the increase of its stock depends: for the profits of stock are, as I have before mentioned, the net reproduction of stock, and the greater therefore, the profits of stock, if the country be equally parsimonious, the greater the rate of the increase of stock' (24). (Here West silently diverges from Smith for whom, at least in a closed economy, saving is interest inelastic.) West concludes – forgetting that his concern had hitherto been with the *change* in the wage not its *level* – that 'in such a country the greater the profits of stock the higher will be the wages of labour, and vice versa'.

The foregoing implies that the profit and wage rates vary in the *same* direction such that the secular fall in the profit rate (assumed throughout) will be accompanied by a fall in the real wage. That the fall in the real wage cannot compensate for the secular fall in agricultural productivity is, unfortunately, taken for granted rather than proved, i.e. this is the necessary conclusion or else a falling profit rate would not be observed: 'The powers of labour . . . in agriculture, becoming less productive, and the diminished expense of maintaining those powers not compensating such decreased productiveness, which appears from the progressive fall of the profits of stock, the whole produce of land, and consequently the net produce, must diminish in proportion to the expense of production, and the ratio of the net produce to the gross must diminish in the progress of improvement' (26). And the entire formulation, it will be recalled, starts out with the assertion that the real-wage movements turn on the relative growth rates of the factors, which is technically erroneous – the so-called 'dynamic equilibrium' wage path entails a falling trend notwithstanding a common decline.

West thus spells out the main lines of what is known now as the New View, independently of either Ricardo or Malthus.[45] And (at least consciously) his contribution was independent of Smith. For West maintained that he diverged from Adam Smith, whom he charges in effect with serious inconsistency:

> That the demand for labour would be greatest when most could be made of it, that is, when the profits of stock were high, and least when those profits were low, appears too plain to have required proving, and I should not have dwelt on this subject had not Dr Smith, in spite of his clear statement of the subject of wages in the 8th chapter [see West 1815: 22n], seemed to maintain an opposite opinion. 'The rise and fall in the profits of stock,' says Dr Smith, 'depend on the same causes with the rise and fall in the wages of labour, the increasing or declining state of the wealth of the society, but those causes effect the one and the other very differently. The increase of stock which raises wages tends to lower profit.' – [Smith 1937 [1776]: 87]. Dr Smith seems therefore, here to think that the profits of stock and wages of labour vary inversely as each other, the contrary of which I think I have proved to be the fact.
>
> (West 1815: 24–5)

The criticism is somewhat unfair. Though Smith did assert that a rise in the wage reduces the profit rate, the common secular reduction in both the wage and profit rates is implicit in certain contexts, as West himself intimates. And these propositions are perfectly consistent since they entail the cases of constant and declining productivity respectively. Lacking in Smith is a recognition (as in Ricardo's *Principles*) that the inverse wage-profit relation holds good if understood as an expression of *proportionate shares*.

West also took issue with Smithian 'competition of capitals', or the alleged negative effect of aggregate expansion on profits via the effect on prices: 'When the stocks of many rich merchants are turned into the same trade, their *mutual competition* naturally tends to lower its profit; and when there is a like increase of stock in all the different trades carried on in the same society, the same competition must produce the same effect in them all' (Smith 1937 [1776]: 87). West focused on the fallacy of composition implicit in Smith's position in an important statement distinguishing between relative and absolute prices (West 1815: 20–1). It is conceded that there would be a temporary decline in *general* money prices in the case at hand which would, however, be corrected by a monetary inflow: 'The money price of all articles would no doubt be diminished, and therefore the money-profits of stock; but this would not lower the real price of those articles, nor the real profits; even the money price would soon be raised to a level with the real price, by a favourable balance of trade and the consequent introduction of bullion' (21). In all this West's argument bears a close resemblance to that of Ricardo, who insisted that a disturbance affecting all commodities can have no real consequence, and that any change in the general level of prices will be temporary in the light of money flows.[46]

Subsequent general observations by West, on the other hand, appear to accept Smith's proposition whereby a rise in the price of corn will, by way of the effect upon wages, generate a general rise in all prices: 'That this rise too in the price of rude produce is followed by a rise in the wages of labour, and communicates itself, more or less to all manufactures, chiefly of course to those in which rude produce predominates most, and in a less degree to those manufactures of a finer kind in which rude produce bears but a small proportion to the skill of the artist, is also evident' (38).[47] West seems to question only an '*immediate*' and *proportionate* impact of the corn price on general prices, not the fact of some impact (42–3). Conceivably, he intended only a short-run impact prior to a monetary outflow, but the matter is left ambiguous. Had he carried through his earlier observations implying the impossibility of a general (permanent) change in the price level (without additional means of circulation) he would have been led immediately to question the relationship between corn prices and general prices, and to the formulation of the fundamental 'Ricardian' case against Smith.

The relation between diminishing agricultural productivity and corn prices emerges late in the pamphlet where commercial policy is formally debated: 'to make provision for an increasing population, it will be necessary to increase the produce, and this increased produce will, as I have shown, be raised at a greater proportionate expense; or in, other words, the growing price will progressively increase' (34). Unfortunately, West proceeds to relate the rising corn price as cause both to rising general prices and to a falling profit rate – leaving the false impression that he had worked explicitly in price terms in earlier parts of the pamphlet, and failing to clarify how precisely the decline in the general profit rate occurs despite the rise in general prices: 'The price of everything increases rapidly, and the profits of stock fall so low, as I have shown they must do, from the enhanced price of rude produce, that at last even the capital of the merchant, and next of the manufacturer, seeks a more grateful soil' – a reference to capital export (39).

It is an important part of West's argument to demonstrate that free trade would not entail the total abandonment of an agricultural sector, considering the assumption of rising corn costs with (foreign) expansion and reduced corn costs with (domestic) contraction: 'But there are limits to this dependence of any country on foreigners for an article of the first necessity; and these limits are to be found in the principle which I have stated. That principle will show that in such case, as the growth of the foreigner increased, the proportionate expense of his growth would increase, and as the home growth was diminished, the proportionate expense of the home growth would also be diminished, since a larger growth is raised in any given country, at a larger proportionate expense than a smaller growth' (46). Equilibrium would be achieved at some intermediate price, when 'Both the home grower and the foreigner are ... just paid the natural price of their produce, and there is no longer any motive to the one to increase his cultivation, nor to the other to diminish his. ... All I mean to assert is, that the growing price of the former would fall, and the growing price of the latter rise, till they met at some point between the original prices of each' (47–8).[48]

In the main body of his text devoted to proving the fact of diminishing agriculture productivity – account taken of technical change – West had neglected the rent phenomenon, identifying the *net* product with profits (above, p. 210). But he provided a more inclusive definition (following Adam Smith) that 'the natural rent of land is always that part of the net produce of land which remains after payment of the common profits of stock on the tenant's capital' (West 1815: 26–7). That rent relative to 'gross produce' *declines* is taken for granted by West (as by Malthus in his *Inquiry*) as an empirical fact attested to in the Reports of both the Commons and Lords Corn Committees, where it is attributed by witnesses – correctly, one is given to understand – to 'the more expensive mode of cultivation now adopted in order to increase the produce' (West 1815: 28, also 25). Adam Smith, West complained (28–30), had seemed to appreciate the phenomenon of a declining rent share of the gross produce when he wrote that 'In the progress of improvement, rent, though it increases in proportion to the extent, diminishes in proportion to the produce of the land' (Smith 1937 [1776]: 318); but elsewhere Smith took the opposite position that 'the landlord's share of the produce necessarily increases with the increase of the produce' (247).[49]

A *declining* rent share, is thus assumed to be explicable by diminishing agricultural productivity.[50] But surprisingly, it is not *formally* linked to differential rent. Not a word is said about that phenomenon until near the close of the main body of the pamphlet, where it emerges in an analysis designed to show that a free corn trade would not entail the total destruction of the rental income, as would be the case were constant returns to rule: 'our principle [diminishing agricultural productivity] will show that by a diminution of the capital laid out by the farmer, he will be enabled both to reproduce his capital with the common profits of stock on that capital, and also a rent not very much, perhaps, below that which he paid before' (49). There follows an excellent statement of the differential-rent concept and its relation to diminishing returns (50–1), which J. S. Mill estimated as preferable to that in Ricardo's *Essay* (above, p. 201).

Notwithstanding West's technical contribution to the 'canonical' model, a free corn trade is formally recommended on *welfare* grounds rather than to assure against decelerating growth. A closed economy subject to falling agricultural productivity would entail a larger proportion of the (growing) population in the agricultural sector, and reduced general welfare: 'if . . . by any increase of expense in obtaining rude produce the whole wealth and comfort of the community is diminished, the command of each individual over all the necessaries and luxuries, both domestic and foreign, [is] lessened. That such must be the consequence of the increasing expense of raising rude produce is obvious to the slightest consideration. The larger the capital required to raise the rude produce of a country, the less in proportion can, of course, be spared for its manufactures' (43). Assuming a trading partner 'which had not carried its skill in manufactures so far, but grew its corn much cheaper', the domestic economy, 'by turning a part of her hands from agriculture to manufactures, could make as many manufactures as would purchase twice as much corn from the new country as those hands had before raised. The consequence would, of course be, that the former country could draw another portion of her hands from agriculture to manufacture for herself, and the real wealth of the whole community would be increased' (45).[51]

The main body of the pamphlet closes with a caution that the principle of diminishing agricultural productivity provided general policy guidance only; there were other considerations not taken into account, 'such as taxes, poor rates, and the distress of individuals, arising from a rapid shifting of capital from one employment to another . . . and therefore I have not pretended to strike the balance of the arguments for and against some restriction of importation' (55). A provisional conclusion suggested that it would be 'highly impolitic to fix the price below which importation is to be checked at a high point', which, for West, entailed 'for the present, such protection as would keep up the price of corn to 70s., or at the most 75s. the quarter'.[52] (The actual legislation of 1815 fixed an importation price of 80 shillings per quarter.)

VIII. RICARDO'S 'ESSAY ON PROFITS'[53]

Ricardo in his *Essay* paid tribute to Malthus for the theory of differential rent as stated in the *Inquiry*: 'The principles which regulate rent . . . differ in a very slight degree from those which have been so fully and so ably developed by Mr Malthus in his late excellent publication, to which I am very much indebted' (Ricardo 1951, IV: 9). But he also complained that Malthus had failed to utilize logically and consistently the property of rent as a *transfer* payment (Ricardo 1951, IV: 18), or to make proper use of the conception of rent-free marginal land (34).[54] However, the main variable under investigation in the *Essay* was the general rate of profit, and its fundamental determinant was as it had been in the correspondence of 1813 and 1814 when the theory of differential rent was not yet at hand, namely the cost of production of food (26; cf. 13n).[55]

Two crucial assumptions are stated at the outset — that real wages per man are constant (though at an above-subsistence level) and that agricultural technology is unchanged: 'We will, however, suppose that no improvements take place in agriculture, and that capital and population advance in the proper proportion, so that the real wages of labour, continue uniformly the same; — that we may know what peculiar effects are to be ascribed to the growth of capital, the increase of population, and the extension of cultivation, to the more remote, and less fertile land' (12; with regard to the constancy of real wages per head, see also 13, 18n, 23). On this basis Ricardo constructed a model relating to the agricultural sector, which yields a declining profit rate as capital and population expand and are applied to increasingly disadvantageous plots of land (10, 13).[56] It is noteworthy that capital is 'estimated in quarters of wheat',[57] but does not necessarily *consist* entirely of wheat, as we shall see.

The following results yielded by the model are emphasized: that with capital accumulation, net agricultural output (rent and profits) rises absolutely, though in decreasing increments, and also relative to total capital; that aggregate profits rise initially, but subsequently fall — an 'exceedingly curious' property; that the profit rate ('relative profits') declines from the outset; and that the proportion of rent to agricultural capital (the 'share of the landlord') rises (16f). That Ricardo chose to examine the ratio of rent and profits to capital, both fixed and circulating, rather than the rental and profit shares in net or gross produce, suggests that his primary concern was not with the aggregative shares. He was careful to observe that the data 'are assumed, and are probably very far from the truth'. In particular, 'in proportion as the capital employed on the land, consisted more of fixed capital, and less of circulating capital, would rent advance, and [profits] fall less rapidly' (15–16n). Doubtless he had in mind that a *given* increase in aggregate capital, if the fixed-capital constituent is relatively high, would entail a relatively smaller circulating-capital (wages) increment, and support accordingly a lesser increase in population, at the given wage, than if the fixed-capital constituent were lower. Ricardo here touched, for the first time, upon the thorny question of the relationships between different categories of capital, and between capital and labour, providing an inkling of what was to be the centre-piece of Chapter 31 in the third edition of the *Principles*.

It seems to have been Ricardo's intention to apply the model specifically to the agricultural sector,[58] but the fundamental result – the decline in the rate of profit with capital accumulation – was irrelevant unless some explanation for the behaviour of the rate of profit *outside the agricultural sector* could be provided. A preparatory statement at the opening of the essay, where the concern is essentially with the agricultural sector, asserts that 'when the profits on agricultural stock, by the supposition, are fifty per cent. the profits on all other capital, employed either in the rude manufactures . . . or in foreign commerce . . . will be also, fifty per cent. If the profits on capital employed in trade were more than fifty per cent. capital would be withdrawn from the land to be employed in trade. If they were less, capital would be taken from trade to agriculture' (12). The agricultural rate seems to be the 'determining' rate, though this is scarcely surprising given the location of the formulation. All Ricardo sought at this point was to establish provisionally the principle of uniform profit rates: 'I am only desirous of proving that the profits on agricultural capital cannot materially vary, without occasioning a similar variation in the profits on capital, employed on manufactures and commerce' (12n).[59] The statement would be quite inadequate if intended as a formal proposition that the general rate is *governed* by the agricultural rate.

Subsequently, the relationship between the agricultural and general rates of profit is treated in a more sophisticated manner, reminiscent of the letter to Malthus of 23 October 1814 (above, p. 200). Here Ricardo distinguishes two (separable) causal influences on profits – the decline in agricultural productivity in the agricultural sector itself, and the rise in money wages (reflecting the higher corn price) in manufacturing, whereas according to the mature view of the *Principles*, it is the latter force which is responsible for a decline in profits throughout all sectors of the economy, the rise in the corn price merely assuring that farmers are 'compensated' for reduced labour productivity in their sector:

> If the money price of corn, and the [money] wages of labour, did not vary in price in the least degree, during the progress of the country in wealth [capital] and population, still profits would fall and rents would rise; because *more* labourers would be employed on the more distant or less fertile land, in order to obtain the same supply of raw produce; and therefore the cost of production would have increased, whilst the value of the produce continued the same. . . .
>
> [But] the exchangeable value of all commodities, rises as the

difficulties of their production increase. If then new difficulties occur in the production of corn, from more labour being necessary, whilst no more labour is required to produce gold, silver, cloth, linen, &c. the exchangeable value of corn will necessarily rise, as compared with those things.... Wherever competition can have its full effect ... the difficulty or facility of their production will ultimately regulate their exchangeable value. *The sole effect then of the progress of wealth on prices ... appears to raise the price of raw produce and of labour leaving all other commodities at their original prices, and to lower general profits in consequence of the general rise of wages.*

(Ricardo 1951, IV: 18–20; emphasis added)

The second paragraph is evidently the more important of the two since it asserts that (on the given assumption) the corn price and money wage both *do* rise secularly – the first is purely hypothetical – and that the manufacturing rate falls as a result of rising money wages (in turn due to the rising corn price) in the face of constant commodity prices; it is also taken for granted that the exchange value of a commodity reflects the 'difficulty of production', which accounts for the rising price of corn, and the stable price of manufactured goods. To this extent we have already the position of the *Principles*. Ricardo left vague the precise function of the corn price in its 'compensation' capacity in agriculture and the fact that the inverse wage–profit relation in agriculture is precisely the same as in manufactures. A further statement, however, does relate the reduction of profits in agriculture solely to the (inverse) movement in money wages: 'If by foreign commerce, or the discovery of machinery, the commodities consumed by the labourer should become much cheaper, wages would fall; and this, as we have before observed, would raise the profits of the farmer, and therefore, all other profits' (26n).[60]

It is clear then that – as in the letter of 18 December 1814 (above, p. 201) – any force generating a change in money wages would affect the profit rate whether or not it has its origin in the agricultural sector. But in one respect the argument has progressed. For Ricardo now presumes the manufacturing price level to be unchanged during the process of capital accumulation.[61] The increase in the money-wage rate itself in no way disturbs either the price structure, in particular the relative prices of agricultural and manufactured products, or the price level. It remained to be shown precisely why, or under which conditions, this will be the case.

A preliminary attempt was made to deal with the issue in a brief criticism of Adam Smith's proposition that an increase in the price of corn, regarded as the ultimate regulator of wages, will lead to a general price increase. Ricardo objected, distinguishing between causal influences: 'It has been thought that the price of corn regulates the price of all other things. This appears to me to be a mistake. If the price of corn is affected by the rise or fall of the value of the precious metals themselves, then indeed will the price of commodities be also affected, but they vary, because the value of money varies, not because the value of corn is altered' (21n).[62]

Two applications of the general argument illustrate its significance for Ricardo. The analysis is applied to the general theory of foreign trade in the manner of the *Principles*. A relaxation of restrictions upon the importation of corn would not alter the aggregate amount of trade, but profits on capital throughout the economy would be increased since a low price of corn allows reductions in manufacturing costs while selling prices remain unchanged: 'A fall in the price of corn, in consequence of improvements in agriculture or of importation, will lower the exchangeable value of corn only, – the price of no other commodity will be affected. If, then, the price of labour falls, which it must do when the price of corn is lowered, the real profits of all descriptions must rise; and no person will be so materially benefited as the manufacturing and commercial part of society' (35–6). A second application is made to Malthus's argument, based on David Hume, that a low price of corn would have depressing effects on the economy. Ricardo objected on the grounds that there will be *no general decline in prices*, but rather a general increase in profits: 'I must again observe, that a rise in the value of money lowers all things; whereas a fall in the price of corn, only lowers the wages of labour, and therefore raises profits' (37).[63]

One further issue relating to the general rate of profit requires comment. Ricardo had insisted during 1814 that the general profit rate could not rise 'unless capital be withdrawn from the land' (e.g. 18 December; Ricardo 1951, VI: 162), but in the *Essay* he formulated this condition more rigorously. On the assumption that (domestic) demand for corn is a function of population size only, and therefore completely inelastic with respect to price, the margin of cultivation is inexorably determined given population, and so, accordingly, is the agricultural profit rate.[64] Since in the long run there can be only one profit rate, the general rate must come into line following a disturbance in commerce or manufacturing (Ricardo 1951, IV: 23–4). According to this argument, which *takes for granted* that once the margin of cultivation is given the agricultural profit rate is immediately determined, the commercial rate must come into line, following an initial increase thereof, perhaps by new capital investment in commerce (presumably financed by higher retained earnings) rather than by transfers from agriculture: 'there will be such a fall in the price of the foreign commodity in the importing country, in consequence of its increased abundance, and the greater facility with which it is procured, that its sale will afford only the common rate of profits – that so far from the high profits obtained by the few who first engaged in the new trade elevating the general rate of profits – those profits will themselves sink to the ordinary level' (24–5). But it may be asked why equality between the two rates cannot be achieved simply as a consequence of an *attempt* to transfer capital from agriculture to trade, in the face of zero demand elasticity; such an attempt would force up the price of corn relative to that of other goods and tend to bring the rates into equality. If the gap is to be closed, the presumption that the agricultural rate is given once the margin is determined must be justified.

According to Sraffa's hypothesis Ricardo had in mind a model wherein both agricultural inputs and outputs consist of the same physical commodity (corn) so that total profits and the rate of profit on capital (a corn wages-fund) can be determined in physical terms without reference to valuation. Since all other sectors utilize corn as input only, it is the exchangeable value of their products relative to their (corn) capitals which must be adjusted to yield the same profit rate as in agriculture. If this is a justified attribution, then even though an *attempt* is made to transfer capital from agriculture and the price of corn consequently rises, the agricultural profit rate cannot alter. But both the pertinent letters of 1814 (above, 'The diminishing-returns principle and the empirical dimension') and the *Essay* itself, suggest that it is unjustified to regard the argument as implying an analysis in terms of the corn model.[65] The basis for Ricardo's position seems rather to consist of the assumption that the exchangeable value of corn (as of any commodity) depends upon real costs – the 'difficulty of production'. If the agricultural margin is fixed, the productivity of labour (and capital) on land is unchanged and so accordingly is the price of corn. *If, then, the money-wage rate is dependent upon the corn price alone*, it too is constant, so that the agricultural profit rate remains unchanged. In this case the only way equality across the board can be achieved is if the profit rate *elsewhere* comes into line as a result of expansion of commerce and manufacturing.

Ricardo's case for the principle that the general profit rate varies with the money wage (governed in turn by the price of wage goods) has been established; it is much reinforced by his applications as we have seen. But in one passage a fall in the real or corn wage – or an agricultural 'improvement' – is said to act on the profit rate through the intermediary of the corn price rather than directly via the money wage:

> If then, the principles here stated as governing rent and profit be correct, general profits on capital can only be raised by a fall in the exchangeable value of food, and which fall can only arise from three causes: 1st The fall of the real wages of labour, which shall enable the farmer to bring a greater excess of produce to market. 2nd Improvements in agriculture, or in the implements of husbandry, which shall also increase the excess of produce. 3rd The discovery of new markets, from whence corn may be imported at a cheaper price than it can be grown for at home.
>
> (Ricardo 1951, IV: 22)[66]

This formulation is out of step with the rest of the *Essay*; and also, of course, with the *Principles* where a fall in the real wage of either a cyclical or a casual kind acts on profits via the money wage not via the corn price, a real-wage reduction leaving unchanged the price of corn and raising the profit rate by depressing the money wage.

In one essential respect Ricardo's *Essay* is a step backward from the preceding correspondence and the subsequent *Principles*. I allude to the treatment of the *secular path of wages*.[67] As Ricardo was to explain so clearly in the *Principles*, such a decline in the real wage – since it is an outcome of the growth process and incorporates the impact of land scarcity – is not accompanied by a *falling* but by a *rising* money wage, and coincides with the decline in the profit rate. The question now is: what is the course of the secular real-wage path according to the *Essay*? The passage just cited continues as follows regarding the forces acting on (raising) the profit rate: 'The first of these causes [the fall in the real wage] is more or less permanent, according as the price from which wages fall, is more or less near the remuneration for labour, which is necessary to the actual subsistence of the labourer' (22). Taking the word 'permanent' literally, we should read Ricardo as stating that the further the initial real wage is from subsistence, the greater the likelihood a real-wage reduction will be subsequently reversed. This would seem to imply a downward trend in the real wage – at least a *statistical* trend reflecting the circumstance that wage reductions are compensated for to an increasingly small degree by reverse movements. At the same time, what follows *denies* a declining wage trend, though certainly without implying a subsistence-wage path: 'The rise or fall of wages is common to all states of society, whether it be the stationary, the advancing, or the retrograde state. . . . As experience demonstrates that capital and population alternately take the lead, and wages in consequence are liberal or scanty, nothing can be positively laid down, respecting profits, as far as wages are concerned. But . . . in every society advancing in wealth and population, independently of the effect produced by liberal or scanty wages, general profits must fall, unless there be improvements in agriculture, or corn can be imported at a cheaper price' (22–3). Having *implied* a downward trend of the real wage – a statistical if not an analytical trend – Ricardo now seems to abandon any attempt to define a secular pattern. And his justification, earlier in his *Essay*, of the assumption of constant secular wages (12; above, p. 218) followed an allowance that profits might increase either 'because the population increasing, at a more rapid rate than capital, wages might fall' or because of new technology. Ricardo thus failed to take account of the fact – upon which he himself insisted both in the 1814 and later correspondence[68] and in the *Principles* – that the secular process involving diminishing returns necessarily entails falling real wages. To remove wage fluctuations would not, on his own terms before and after the *Essay*, leave a constant secular wage path.

A characteristic of the *Essay* is thus its partial treatment of the secular problem. Ricardo describes the stationary and advancing states; presumably wages are at or above the subsistence level respectively, and so must necessarily fall in the approach to a stationary state. Yet this latter implication, rationalized at length in the *Principles*, is neglected. The argument in the *Essay* constitutes an incompletely formulated analysis, and, from this perspective at least, falls short of the contributions by Malthus and West in their essays.[69]

IX. TORRENS' 'ESSAY ON THE EXTERNAL CORN TRADE'

Though our main concern will be with Chapter III of Part III of the first edition of Torrens's *Essay*, it is important to take note of conspicuous features elsewhere, in particular the extent of adherence to Smithian propositions which emerges early on in the book. For there remains a very fundamental Smithian residue on the main issues that interest us, which distinguishes the work from Ricardo's *Essay on Profits*.

In the first place, Torrens retains the notion that with secular expansion the profit rate declines in consequence of increased 'competition of capitals' in the manufacturing sector. This principle is now combined with that of diminishing returns, but the manufacturing rate takes the lead:

> For the increase of wealth, the accumulation of capital, and the competition amongst capitalists, lower the interest of money, and reduce the rate of manufacturing and commercial profit, until it no longer exceeds, what can be obtained by reclaiming inferior lands. Capitalists, therefore, cease to be induced, by the prospect of greater gains, to leave such lands neglected; nay, if the customary rate of manufacturing and commercial profit should be reduced to nine per cent. the lands lately left untilled, because they could bring a return of only ten per cent. would be eagerly sought after, and capital would flow from manufactures and commerce, and vest itself in agriculture. In the progress of wealth, the profits of stock, and the interest of money, are gradually lowered, while land acquires a higher relative value, and tracts, which can afford a return of nine, of eight, or even of seven per cent. are brought into tillage.
>
> (Torrens 1815: 51)

There are indeed suggestions that pressures will be exerted by diminishing returns upon the general profit rate itself (71, 73–4), but these are not considered in conjunction with the principle of competition of capitals, and their mutual consistency is not investigated.

It will be recalled that Torrens assumed a subsistence wage (above, p. 196). When he turned from 'real' to 'monetary' matters he retained the linkage between the price of corn and general prices working via the *money* wage so characteristic of Smithian theory:

And now we are to consider the manner, in which a rise in the money price of labour raises the money price of all commodities. When, in consequence of a rise in corn, an advance has been effected in the wages of labour, the capitalist who gives it employment, and who pays the advance upon it, must either suffer a diminution in the rate of his profits, or else indemnify himself by charging an advanced price upon his goods. Now when corn has risen, he will be enabled to advance his goods; for the farmer and landowner, receiving a greater sum for the produce of their ground, will have a greater sum to give for other articles. The money demand for commodities being thus increased, the capitalist will be indemnified, by increased money prices, for the increased rate of wages which the rise in corn obliged him to advance.

(Torrens 1815: 81–2)[70]

This passage implies that there will occur no fall in the profit rate in consequence of the rise in money wages, an implication which may be found elsewhere too (e.g. 87). This is a conclusion which does not sit easily beside the contrary implications of the earlier discussion alluding to the *depressing* effects flowing from reduced agricultural productivity; and subsequently too it is expressly stated that 'as a greater quantity of his labour, or (what is the same thing) of the produce of his labour, becomes necessary to the subsistence of the labouring manufacturer, and is consumed by him while at work, a smaller quantity of the productions of labour will remain with the employer' (235).

Torrens himself appears uncomfortable with his own position in the light of questions raised regarding the value of money: 'One other important consideration belongs to this branch of our subject. A rise in the price of corn raises the price of labour, and the rise in labour is communicated to all commodities, both those which it immediately produces, and those to which these are employed as the equivalents. But bullion is a commodity. It is immediately produced from the mines by domestic labour; or, if not, purchased by equivalents, which are. Does it then rise and fall in price with the labour that procures it, when it is a native commodity, and with the produce of labour which purchases it, when it is a foreign one?' (88–9). But he unfortunately declined to enter further into the issue.[71] Conceivably it was this line of thought that led him, the following year, to abandon the Smithian argument.[72]

It is also significant that, despite his formal adherence in 1815 to the Smithian relationship between corn prices and general prices, Torrens did not follow Smith all the way and reject the corn bounty as totally ineffective as a stimulant to agriculture activity (although he was opposed to such intervention on other grounds): 'Bounties upon export, and restrictions upon import, might, indeed, give an increased relative value to land, and raise the price of its produce, until the cultivation of very inferior lands afforded, for a time, at least, a profit sufficiently high to draw labour and capital from other occupations. But this forced and artificial encouragement, afforded to agriculture, would be dearly, much too dearly purchased' (52). Once again it is unfortunate that Torrens did not spell out the argument, for he might then have been led to question the logic of the dependency of general prices upon the price of corn.

Despite the use made of the principle of diminishing returns, Torrens is not always crystal clear about the make-up of the 'natural price of goods', 'since rent is sometimes included within natural price' (57, 62).[73] Yet elsewhere the notion of differential rent is clearly recognized (177, 219–20) and the consequence of trade policy for rent, thus conceived, is developed in the chapter reproduced below, where natural price excluding rent (at the exclusive margin) is unmistakable (324).[74]

We should also have in mind the substance of Torrens's penultimate chapter (Part III, Chapter II) before turning to the final chapter which is the one reproduced. In this chapter Torrens supposes a free external corn trade, and maintains that 'in the present circumstances of these countries, an unrestrained corn trade would lower the price of corn, and bring down the monopoly rents occasioned by the war'; that 'a reduction in the value of corn reduces [money] wages', and 'heightens the productive powers of industry' which in turn 'accelerate[s] the accumulation of stock' and thus 'lowers the rate of profit' (298). He thus concludes: 'a free external trade in corn . . . would effect a reduction in rents, [money] wages, and profits'.[75] We again recall that throughout he takes for granted a subsistence wage in the technical sense of that term, namely that real wage which assures constant population.

We take up now the reproduced chapter which summarizes the alternative effects of a restricted and a free external corn trade.

A characteristic feature of Torrens's case is that corn import restrictions which 'in their first and direct operation . . . extend tillage, and raise the value of land . . . in their second and indirect operation, would, in whatever degree they might prove prejudicial to commerce and wealth, again contract cultivation, and involve the landed interest in the general decline' (315–16). Conversely, in the case of free trade the agricultural interest will benefit in the long run. (There is also the immorality of legislative action to transfer income to landowners: 317.) The elaboration entails sectoral interdependence from both a demand-oriented *and* cost perspective, with the profit rate determined *outside* the agricultural sector and appearing as a cost item in agriculture. Specifically, the distorted resource allocation created by corn import restriction, and aggravated by diminishing agricultural returns entails 'a diminution in the productive powers of industry' (316); for 'a rise in the natural price of corn is not only the same thing as a reduction in the productive powers of the labour and capital employed in cultivation; – but is the same thing as a reduction in the productive powers of industry, in every branch of business carried on by the consumers of corn' (324). And this impediment 'retard[s] the period when the general prosperity of the country, by increasing the demand for corn, and reducing the expense of its production, should allow tillage to be extended over inferior soils' (318). If, however, industry were 'permitted to take its most beneficial direction, the number and wealth of consumers would gradually increase; while the interest of money, and the profits of stock, becoming lower with each advance in opulence, the expense of cultivation would diminish' (319).

The reduction in capital costs with the *general* capital accumulation that is likely to accompany free trade and the desirable stimulus which such a reduction affords agriculture is subsequently elaborated, in a graphic passage which emphasizes that the real increase in costs of such expansion is effectively counteracted so that the 'natural price of corn' remains steady:

To the possible increase of her resources [alluding to a country 'whose position and whose policy permitted her to participate freely in foreign trade'] no limit could be assigned; and her prosperity, instead of becoming every day more tardy, would advance with an accelerated pace. The divisions of employment established with other countries, would enable her to avail herself to the utmost of every natural advantage; and the rapid increase of opulent consumers would speedily bring into cultivation, all her lands of first-rate, and of middling quality. When she had arrived at this point, she would not, at a great waste of labour and capital, force cold and sterile tracts into tillage; but, adopting a more enlightened policy, would receive a part of her subsistence from the foreign grower. Hence, there would be no increase in the natural price of corn, and hence no diminution in the productive powers of industry. The number of opulent consumers would go on increasing, and capital would continue to accumulate as rapidly as before.

As capital accumulated, the rate of interest and of profit would fall; as commerce extended, more accurate divisions of employment would multiply and cheapen all wrought goods. Hence, while the increasing number of wealthy consumers increased the demand for corn, the expenses of cultivation would diminish. Agriculture would flourish beneath the reaction of an enlightened commercial system; the soil would acquire a higher relative value, from the abundance of commodities ready to be exchanged for its produce; and, while tracts of third, fourth, and fifth-rate quality could be profitably tilled, rents would experience a progressive rise.

(Torrens 1815: 326–8)

By the reduced expenses of production attributed to a free corn trade, Torrens intended *labour* as well as *capital* costs. That seems to be the import of the allusion in the above passage to the effect of manufacturing expansion in 'cheapen[ing] all wrought goods' and thus diminishing the 'expenses of cultivation'; and this appears also to be confirmed in what follows:

> In the agricultural country, the rise in rents, and the extension of tillage over inferior soils, would, as has been shewn above, [p. 324] have the effect of raising the natural price of corn; but, in the commercial country, this effect would be counteracted, because the more perfect divisions of employment would require less wages, and the fall in the interest of money, less profits, to be paid for producing any quantity of grain. These causes, co-operating with the competition of an open trade, would necessarily keep subsistence cheap. The natural price of corn would receive no increase, and, consequently, the productive powers of industry sustain no diminution. Prosperity would encounter no check.
>
> (Torrens 1815: 328–9)

The allowance for manufactured wage goods (on which see also 70, 89–93, 292) is particularly important, since some commentators attribute a corn profit model to Torrens.[76] (See on this Hollander 1995b.)

The general social message conveyed by the emphasis on sectoral interdependence is the identity of interests between the 'landed' and the manufacturing classes:

> It cannot be too often repeated, that the interests of the landed, and of the trading, classes of the community, are identical. The rent of proprietors, and the profits of cultivators, must ever be determined by the quantity of other commodities which the manufacturer and merchant are able and willing to give in exchange for agricultural produce. Though it were possible (and, I firmly believe, it is not) that the landowners and cultivators should be uninfluenced by a regard for the good of the public, and for their country's prosperity and power, yet a sensibility to their own true interests should render them solicitous for the adoption of an economical system, which would give increase to the productive powers of industry, and extension to manufactures and commerce. With the flourishing or declining state of these, the value of their produce must ultimately rise or fall. The superiority of a free external trade in corn, with respect to its influence in promoting agricultural improvement, must, in the last analysis, be estimated by its superiority in promoting wealth and commerce.
>
> (Torrens 1815: 319–20)

In expressing this general position Torrens sought to counter 'an inclination occasionally discovered, to revive the exploded paradoxes of the economists' (321); and he might well have had Malthus in mind.[77]

Torrens also rejected the argument for agricultural protection turning on the claim 'that security and independence are of still higher importance than great wealth and population' (Torrens 1815: 330) – again, Malthus's claim, though Torrens makes no explicit mention of Malthus (Torrens 1815: 332–3). This is expanded into a case for the importance of commerce to assure British naval supremacy (334–5).

Torrens insisted on a gradual approach to free trade, for 'sudden change is evil' (341, see also 196–200); and offered a criterion of the desirable rate of change turning on the yield of taxation (347–8). Initial temporary protection of about 70 shillings per quarter is allowed (which is the same order of magnitude as West's; above, p. 217). In estimating the 'remunerating price', Torrens – who complained that 'our economists seem, in a great measure to have overlooked the important influence which the price of corn has upon the expenses of its own production' – drew on 'the extent to which the value of [agricultural] produce regulates most of the items of the cultivator's expenditure' as shown by data provided to the Lord's Committee (342). For: 'When the price of produce falls, the value of tithes, and of seed, will immediately, and in the same proportion, be reduced; and, though neither immediately, nor in the same degree, labour, and all the instruments of production, will come down also' (342–3). None of this necessarily gainsays the earlier allowance for manufactured wage goods.

In closing Torrens reverts back to his insistence on sectoral interdependence, which points against too high a protective duty – a temporary duty of course:

> we never should forget, that every artificial elevation of price secured to the farmer, is not only a direct tax imposed upon the community at large, but a positive discouragement to manufactures and commerce. Now the interests of agriculture, as has repeatedly appeared, throughout this work, are inseparably connected with the flourishing state of trade. If the duty upon the introduction of foreign grain should be laid on so high as to cause our commodities to be excluded from the foreign market, our unemployed manufacturers would no longer have an effectual demand for corn, and prices would ultimately sustain a ruinous fall from the unwise attempt to sustain them at an artificial and unnatural elevation. Of all classes of the community, proprietors and cultivators, would, ultimately, receive the deepest injury from the duty upon importation being laid on too high.
>
> (Torrens 1815: 344)

X. THE CHARGE OF PESSIMISM

Schumpeter charged the contributors of 1815 with an unduly 'pessimistic' conception of economic development. These writers, he contended, 'lived at the threshold of the most spectacular economic development ever witnessed ... [yet] were convinced that technological improvement and increase of capital would in the end fail to counteract the fateful law of decreasing returns. ... They all expected, for the future, the advent of the stationary state, which here no longer means an analytical tool but a future reality' (1954: 571). What justification, restricting ourselves to the 1815 literature, is there for this view?

Malthus, alluding to rising real costs of corn in *Grounds of an Opinion*, recalls his *Observations* of the previous year 'where [he] had endeavoured to shew that ... a considerable fall in the price of corn could not take place, without throwing much poor land out of cultivation, and effectually preventing, for a considerable time, all farther improvements in agriculture, which have for their object an increase of produce' (1815b: 3–4; see above, p. 195). This position is then elaborated by reference to experience since approximately 1795 and especially since 1808, brought out in evidence before parliament,[78] indicating expansion of agriculture by way of the 'high farming' encouraged by rising corn prices during a period of restricted importation (1815b: 4). At the same time, he also emphasized that 'the evidence brought before the two houses of Parliament' indicated *high agricultural potential* to meet further population expansion: 'it is impossible not to be convinced ... that the land was still deficient in capital, and would admit of the employment of such an addition to its present amount, as would be competent to the full supply of a greatly increased population'. And in a further discussion of potentialities based both on parliamentary evidence and Sinclair's formal studies of agricultural productivity of 1812 and 1814, he provided a strikingly optimistic account of British and Irish productivity subject only to the adoption of best *existing* technological and organizational practice (Malthus 1815b: 20–1). He continued by allowing in fact for 'a chance (but on this I will not insist) of a diminution in the real price of corn owing to the extension of those great improvements, and that great economy and good management of labour, of which we have such intelligent accounts from Scotland'.

A note defining the 'real growing price of corn' alludes to a 'tendency' to diminishing marginal returns, but qualifies such a tendency by reference to 'improvements': 'By the real growing price of corn I mean the real quantity of labour and capital which has been employed to procure the last additions which have been made to the national produce. In every rich and improving country there is a natural and strong tendency to a constantly increasing price of raw produce, owing to the necessity of employing, progressively, land of an inferior quality. But this tendency may be partially counteracted by great improvements in cultivation, and economy of labour. See this subject treated in *An inquiry into the nature and progress of rent*, just published' (21n).

Nonetheless, considering the text in the *Grounds* as well as the note, it seems that Malthus, basing himself partly on recent experience, *at most* conceived of a shallow prospective rise of real costs. This is no casual matter, for he proceeded to an explicit assurance that the British economy, if protected, would not be subject to any *serious* constraints as far as concerns growth: 'the united empire [Great Britain and Ireland] has ample means of increasing in wealth, population, and power, for a very long course of years, without being habitually dependent upon foreign supplies for the means of supporting its inhabitants' (Malthus 1815b: 23). Even under protection 'we may certainly look forwards to a progressive increase of population and power'. To his credit, Malthus did not unfairly reinforce his protectionist proposals by emphasizing a prospective absolute *decline* in agricultural costs with domestic expansion; in a final summing-up of the pros and cons of alternative trade policies he pointed to a prospect of secular *rising* corn prices and possible damage to the manufacturing sector in the event of restriction (45). But to focus solely on this caution is misleading; Malthus saw any *major* deterioration in agricultural productivity as unlikely.[79]

Diminishing returns, we have seen, is represented in the *Inquiry* as a relationship incorporating 'improvement' (above, p. 207). And, though various 'modifying' circumstances are allowed, including 'improvements in the modes of cultivation [and] the saving of labour on the land' and foreign trade, implying that diminishing returns is strictly applicable *given technology*, 'improvement' is not treated quite like foreign trade, a contrast which suggests that productivity decline predominates over time *notwithstanding new technology*. For only importation of foreign corn, is said to 'do away, in a considerable degree, [with] the usual effects of great wealth on the price of corn' (1815a: 42).[80] Innovation is thus treated as a 'modifying' force that does not normally reverse the basic *agricultural* cost trend.[81] On the other hand, new technology does assure a reduction in *manufacturing* prices – and this despite the disadvantage of rising corn prices and money wages (45).

As for the specific relevance of all this to British experience, a summary statement at the close of the *Inquiry* ascribes 'part . . . and perhaps no inconsiderable part' of the high British corn price to land scarcity under pressure of 'wealth and population', which 'can only be essentially mitigated by the habitual importation of foreign, and a diminished cultivation of it at home' (54). But there are interpretive problems. An analysis of recent British experience given earlier in the pamphlet has it that expanded agricultural investment since approximately 1794 was financed out of 'temporary' agricultural profits in consequence of 'improved modes of agriculture' supplemented by the rising corn price *unrelated to land scarcity* and accompanied by a lag in other cost items (26).[82] On this reading of wartime developments, major agricultural extension was consistent with an *upward* trend in the agricultural profit rate because of expanding foreign and domestic demand for farm produce acting on the corn price, accompanied by the adoption of cost-reducing technology. *Diminishing returns does not enter the picture.* But what then of the ascription in the same essay of higher corn prices to increasing land scarcity? Conceivably the more optimistic account of productivity trends was formulated earlier, and not adequately reconciled with the change in perspective elsewhere in the pamphlet reflecting the 1814–15 evidence.[83] But of this we cannot be sure. In any event, the great weight placed on demand pressure and new technology is not necessarily inconsistent with some small increase in marginal costs during the war, and *a fortiori* with a prospective secular upward trend. And an allowance for but minimization of the prospect of major productivity decline is confirmed by Malthus's correspondence with Ricardo, where the emphasis is on improved manufacturing not deteriorating agricultural productivity during the 1794–1814 period, though some small deterioration is recognized (see *ETRM*, 15: IV).

Schumpeter's evaluation of Ricardian 'pessimism' is also an exaggeration taking a full overview of Ricardo's writings (see Hollander 1979, chapter 11). We have already seen that in his letter to Malthus of 17 August 1813 Ricardo had accounted for an *upward* trend in the profit rate during much of the period 1793–1813 in terms of technical progress in agriculture (above, p. 196). On 17 March 1815, he similarly wrote to Malthus: 'If it be true that capital has become more and more productive on the land, it can I think only be accounted for on the supposition that great improvements have taken place in agriculture, and that wages have been kept moderate by the improvements in those manufactures which supply the poor with the necessaries on which a part of their wages are expended' (1951, VI: 194). In the *Essay on Profits* itself Ricardo did provide a caution apparently with an eye to the future: 'That great improvements have been made in agriculture, and that much capital has been expended on the land, it is not attempted to deny; but, with all those improvements, we have not overcome the natural impediments resulting from our increasing wealth and prosperity, which obliges us to cultivate at a disadvantage our poor lands, if the importation of corn is restricted or prohibited' (1951, IV: 32). He was unwilling to assume that past patterns could simply be taken for granted. But this is scarcely surprising considering the policy objective of the essay. Even so, he represents technical change in agriculture as an alternative to free trade, his theoretical case showing that 'in every society advancing in wealth and population, independently of the effect produced by liberal or scanty wages, general profits must fall *unless there be improvements in agriculture*, or corn can be imported at a cheaper price' (23; emphasis added). (Even this does not go far enough on Ricardo's own terms since it neglects manufactured goods.)

There is thus a distinct contrast between Ricardo's *analytic* statement of the diminishing-returns principle as holding good *given technology* and West's *empirical* statement as holding good allowance made for changing technology, and it is West who thus seems to approximate Schumpeter's representation. Torrens too treated technical change somewhat as an 'exception' (representing the war years as such) and attacked the protectionists –

Sir Henry Parnell is his *bête noire* – for 'with arrogant ignorance, mistaking casual results for the operation of established laws, [and] erecting exceptions into principles' (Torrens 1815: 245). On the whole, however, Book III, chapter I ('The Effects which a System of Restraints upon the Importation of foreign Corn would produce; I. on the Supply of Subsistence; II on Agriculture; III on Commerce; and IV on Revenue') does paint a depressing picture of the expected outcome of the proposed legislation, though as usual some allowance must be made for the political purpose of the *Essay*.

XI. THE CANONICAL MODEL: SOME CONCLUSIONS ON PRIORITY

I have made the case that Ricardo in correspondence of 1814 had priority over Malthus for the shared incidence of diminishing agricultural returns – the central characteristic of the canonical model – though he neglected to state that feature in his 1815 paper (above, p. 223). As for West's position, I call attention to his charge in 1826 that Ricardo's *Principles* amounted to plagiarism: 'Most of the propositions enunciated in [West's 1815] essay were adopted by Mr Ricardo in his Principles of Political Economy'; Ricardo had only given credit to Malthus and himself for 'the true doctrine of rent',[84] whereas 'other principles of very considerable importance were first enunciated in that essay' (West 1826: v). These include 'the diminution of the net reproduction or the profits of stock, which is observed to take place in the progress of wealth and improvement, [and which] must necessarily be caused by a diminution of the productive powers of labour in agriculture' (v–vi); 'the proposition, which is, however, qualified in the present tract, that in the same state of the productive powers of labour, in providing the necessaries for the maintenance of labour, the real wages of labour and profits of stock are a given quantity; and that, if either of them be increased, that increase of the one must be at the expense of the other' (vi);[85] and 'the principle of the labour which any commodity requires, or costs to produce it, being the measure of its exchangeable value' (vii). 'The author,' he proceeds, 'thinks it not unfair to assert his claim to the discovery of these and other important principles; his essay is before the public, and the public will decide how far this claim is well founded.' In all this there is no *explicit* mention made of the simultaneous *secular* decline in profit and real wage rates. But insofar as West states this proposition in his Conclusion (135, see note 45) and explicitly claims there that Ricardo was totally unaware of it, he is certainly laying claim to priority, and unjustifiably so considering the earlier contributions of both Ricardo (though in correspondence of which he could not have been aware) and Malthus in his *Inquiry*.

Neither in the reproduced extract nor indeed anywhere else in his *Essay* did Torrens recognize the simultaneous decline in the real wage and profit rates.[86] The argument proceeds throughout on the strict assumption of a 'subsistence' wage. In that respect, Torrens is closest to the standard 'text-book' representation of classicism. By contrast, the constant wage of Ricardo's *Essay* exceeds 'subsistence' and thus accommodates logically on-going population growth, though the formulation as a whole is wanting.

NOTES

1 The reproduced materials include: T. R. Malthus, *An Inquiry into the Nature and Progress of Rent and the principles by which it is regulated*, London: John Murray, 3 February (1815a), *The Grounds of an Opinion on the Policy of Restricting the Importation of Foreign Corn*, London: John Murray, 10 February (1815b); [Edward West], *Essay on the Application of Capital to Land with observations showing the impolicy of any great restriction of the importation of corn*, London: T. Underwood, 13 February; David Ricardo, *An Essay on the Influence of a low Price of Corn on the Profits of Stock; showing the inexpediency of restrictions on importation*, London: John Murray, 24 February; and chapter III of Part III of Robert Torrens's full-length book *An Essay on the External Corn Trade*, London: J. Hatchard, also published on 24 February.

2 This raises terminological problems, since the 'principle of diminishing (agricultural) returns' is usually understood as an analytic proposition assuming technology unchanged. The reader must throughout keep in mind that, depending on context, the expression may be used without this presupposition.

3 I shall frequently refer to my *Economics of Thomas Robert Malthus* (ETRM) (1997), indicating as appropriate both chapter and section numbers.

4 I base my account on Hollander 1979, 119–22.

5 The argument involved the machinations of corn-import merchants, price variability in an open system, and the dangers of foreign dependence, suggesting that Parnell may have had before him Anderson's *Calm Investigation* (1801) in preparing the speech.

6 In his parliamentary intervention during the debate of 15 June 1813 on the report (*Parliamentary Debates*, XXVI: 668), Horner maintained that the evidence of the report demonstrated that freedom of trade – which existed in effect in recent years (reference is made to large imports into Great Britain despite the Continental System and the *formal* existence on the books of corn laws) – had resulted in steady prices and a great extension of tillage.

7 Although in the *Essay* Malthus may not have based his case for a lower average corn price with agricultural expansion on any notion of *increasing* returns, there is also no hint of *diminishing* returns in the empirical accounts of 1803 or 1806. Similarly, when it comes to policy, the 1806 edition recommended intervention to encourage Britain's re-emergence as a net corn exporter – to be accomplished in two stages, first corn-import restrictions and subsequently an export bounty (see *ETRM*, 16: II); and there is nothing in this programme to suggest prospective real-cost increases.

8 On the possibility that the pamphlet may have formed the nucleus of lectures on Adam Smith, see J. H. Hollander 1903: 3.

9 J. H. Hollander (1903: 4) suggests also that the appearance of Buchanan's edition of Smith late in 1814, perceiving rent as due to the monopoly character of land ownership, played a part in Malthus's timing.

10 West cited *inter alia* evidence for a falling rent share (see Section VII).

11 The work was completed in 1814.

12 See also the preface to the second edition (1820: xvii), which informs readers that the 1815 version was finished hastily to assure some effect on policy.

13 In the estimate of Lord Robbins, Torrens's initial statement of the principle and the corollary do not live up to those of the other contributors (1958: 39–43). For one thing there is lacking a statement of diminishing returns at the intensive margin.

In his fourth edition (1827: vii) Torrens claimed precedence for the comparative-cost principle (1815: 264–5). On this claim, see Viner 1937: 441–4.

14 West's perspective on Smith is complex. He made his case entailing a downward trend in both factor returns in consequence of diminishing returns, *against Adam Smith's position that the fall in the profit rate is accompanied by a rise in the wage* – that 'the increase of stock, which raises wages, tends to lower profit' (1815: 24). Yet he was aware of and indeed commended those statements in the *Wealth of Nations* (I. 8) entailing contemporaneity of high profit and wage rates, and low profit and wage rates. He found Smith to be self-contradictory.

15 Turgot, it is true, appreciated the diminishing-returns principle and the concept of rent eliminating excess profit on intramarginal land (Brewer 1987). But these concepts appeared in later papers, not in his main work. There the interest rate is determined by 'the abundance or scarcity of capital' (1963 [1770]: 78–9, 85). Brewer's claim that a fall in the interest rate with accumulation allows intensive or extensive marginal expansions is based on a citation from the *Reflections* which cannot support it; the text merely constitutes a fanciful analogy applied to all sectors not just agriculture (86).

For a discussion of James Anderson's early appreciation of the diminishing-returns and differential-rent phenomena, see Hollander 1979: 706–10. On Malthus's intellectual relationship with Anderson, see *ETRM*: 52–3.

16 See also Waterman 1991b: 224: Chalmers' *Inquiry* 'shows an almost complete understanding of the "sophisticated" model of population equilibrium latent in the *Essay {on Population}*, and is the first substantial attempt to consider the impact of Malthusian theory upon the economic analysis of the *Wealth of Nations*'.

17 Though Malthus at this point attributed the position to his *Essay on Population*, the editions of 1798, 1803, 1806, and 1807 contain no such account. He later gave a more accurate evaluation (see above, p. 204).

18 Cf. also Sraffa, in Ricardo 1951, IV: 3: 'In February 1814 Ricardo had written some 'papers on the profits of capital' which he had shown to Malthus, Trower and Mill. These papers have not survived, but a summary of their contents, contained in a letter to Trower of 8th March 1814 shows that the theory of profits, which was to appear in the pamphlet of the following year, was already fully developed.'

19 A newly discovered manuscript raises the possibility that Bentham had many of the ingredients of a land-based growth model at an early date, probably before the evidence of 1813–14 had been accumulated (Hollander 1996b).

20 Cf. 55n: 'I have hinted before, in a note, that profits may, without impropriety, be called a surplus. But, whether surplus or not, they are the most important source of wealth, as they are, beyond all question, the main source of accumulation.'

21 Inclusion of profits (in excess of the minimum) in the surplus defined in 1815 as excess of *corn* output over internal *corn* consumption is to treat profits as a *corn surplus*; and this invites the concept of a rate of profit as a ratio of the corn surplus net of rent to the corn input, Sraffa's rational reconstruction of *Ricardo*. That Malthus later developed this approach is argued in Hollander 1995a.

22 The 'excess' must refer to a *total* or *average* dimension, if we presume that Malthus adopts the notion of a rent-free margin.

23 This concept is also encountered in the earlier correspondence (above, p. 199).

24 Malthus uses the term 'monopoly' to indicate an upward slope to competitive supply curves – in the limit zero elasticity.

25 Malthus objected in the *Inquiry* to Adam Smith and 'more modern writers' – Say, Sismondi and Buchanan – for considering rent (the concern is with *rent proper*) 'as too nearly resembling in its nature, and the law by which it is governed, the excess of price above the cost of production, which is the characteristic of a monopoly'. Later in his *Principles* (1820: 149n) he reacted against Ricardo's adherence (1951 [1817], I: 400) to the scarcity perspective of Sismondi and Buchanan.

26 This applies whether we interpret the contention that 'the accumulation of capital beyond the means of employing it on land of the greatest natural fertility, and the greatest advantage of situation, must necessarily lower profits' (1) as a reference to downward pressure on the profit rate of activity on good land which fall *stimulates* expansion onto poorer land; or (2) as the decline in the profit rate *resulting from* the extensions of poorer land (see above, pp. 203–4).

27 In summarizing, 'the accumulation of capital' is again referred to as if independent of agriculture: 'We see then that a progressive rise of rents seems to be necessarily connected with the progressive cultivation of new land, and the progressive improvement of the old; and that this rise is the natural and necessary consequence of the operation of four causes, which are the most certain indications of increasing prosperity and wealth – namely, the accumulation of capital, the increase of population, improvements in agriculture, and the high price of raw produce, occasioned by the extension of our manufactures and commerce' (32).

28 The correspondence of 1815 and 1816 does, however, elaborate further on this matter (see *ETRM*, chapter 4).

29 This analogy much attracted Ricardo (1951 [1815], IV: 24n).

30 Strange to relate, two years later, after Malthus had stated his support for the Corn Bill of 1815, it was Horner who objected on precisely the efficiency grounds specified by Malthus in June 1813. He evidently had not absorbed Malthus's diminishing-returns lesson of 1813, for he represents the principle as a *novelty* appearing in Malthus's two pamphlets of 1815, with the policy application due to himself (12 June 1815; Horner 1853, II: 222–3).

31 For a full account see *ETRM*, chapter 17.

32 It is only late in the 1815 pamphlet (35–6) that we encounter a *formal* statement of the no-rent principle on marginal units of output and the related principle that the corn price exceeds costs on intramarginal units. The statement on 3n may be an insertion into an earlier text.

33 That the *Inquiry* also contains much physiocratic bias has already been shown (above, p. 202).

34 See Hollander 1992 on Malthus's ultimate abandonment of agricultural protectionism in the 1820s (chapter 16 in this collection).

35 Blaug therefore errs when he attributes to West a notion of diminishing returns 'in terms of diminishing average rather than marginal products of composite doses of capital-and-labour' (1987, IV: 898). As for the matter of 'composite doses', West in fact in our passage refers to 'additional quantit[ies] of work'; elsewhere it is 'additional expense or capital'.

36 'By the gross produce I mean, of course, the whole produce without any refer-

ence to the expense of production; by the net produce, that which remains of the gross produce after replacing the expense of production.'

37 Subsequently, the identification is repeated: 'the profits of stock are the net reproduction of stock' (19; cf. 10–11, 24) – rent is not mentioned.

38 The weights of the two sectors are assumed to be equal (16).

39 For a recapitulation, see above p. 210.

40 Cf. Stigler: West's analysis was 'very similar to Ricardo's ... except that the fall of profits is a historical generalization rather than (as with Ricardo) an analytical theorem' (1965: 177–8). But Grampp makes no such distinction: 'West and the Ricardians believed agriculture was subject to diminishing returns, not only while technology is constant but also when it improves. They did not expect that technological progress would be great enough to offset diminishing returns' (1970: 323).

41 This is preceded by a reminder that 'In the above argument I have supposed the wages of labour to vary with the productive powers of that labour; that is, that the more labour produces the better it will be paid' (18). He promises that he would 'prove presently' that 'this is nearly the case' but, as far as I can see, nowhere fulfils his promise.

42 West cites Smith's position (Smith 1937 [1776], I: ch.viii) that labour demand 'increases with the increase of the revenue and stock', but himself refers specifically to *stock*.

43 West also paraphrases (not very accurately) Smith on the stationary state wage: 'It is not the amount then of the stock of a country which causes high wages; for if the stock of a country be stationary, whatever be its amount, population will soon increase up to the most scanty subsistence which such stock can afford' (cf. 1937 [1776]: 71).

44 An example that follows indicates that he is concerned with the magnitude of the *change* in wages: 'Thus suppose a country with 100 millions increasing its stock annually to the amount of a million, the increase would be as 1 to 100; and the increase of the wages of labour would be but 1/100. But suppose a country with stock amounting to 10 millions, and an annual increase of half a million, though the actual increase of stock would be smaller than in the last case, the increase in the wages of labour would be a half-tenth or one-twentieth' (23–4).

45 For an excellent account of West's analysis of the contemporaneous decline of the real wage and profit rates, see Brewer 1988. Stigler's evaluation is vitiated by insistence that 'Malthusian' population theory – to which West appealed – 'assumes constant real wages' (Stigler 1965: 177n).

In his pamphlet of 1826, West repeated the main lines of the canonical argument, and erroneously claimed that Ricardo in his *Principles* had no inkling of it: 'The diminution of the rate of reproduction will not fall upon profits alone, as Mr Ricardo supposes, but it must inevitably fall in part upon the price or reward of labour' (West 1826: 135). This assertion is preceded by the proposition – West is quite unaware of Ricardo's formulation (see Ricardo 1951, I: 101–2) – that 'The money price of labour would rise, but it could not rise in proportion to the enhanced price of food.' It is followed by the proposition that in the course of secular expansion 'a larger proportion of [the] production goes to the landlord' (see note 49 below).

46 Ricardo touches on this matter in certain *Notes* on Bentham of 1810–11, in correspondence with Malthus of August 1813 and in the *Principles*. The case is alluded to but not elaborated in the *Essay* (above, pp. 220–1).

47 But West also maintained that Smith had *denied* the phenomenon of rising corn

prices in the course of secular growth (above p. 197). The proposition now at hand is of a general analytical nature.

48 West adds that 'This point would, of course, be much nearer the present growing price of the foreign than of the domestic growth, as the effect of the importation divided among many foreign markets would be less to each than the effect of the importation operating on our single market.'

Ricardo in his *Essay* (1951, IV: 32) refers to the withdrawal of capital from 'our poor lands' in the event of free trade and its transfer to the export sector thus implying, though without an elaboration such as West's, the continued maintenance of an agricultural sector. But in his technical chapter on Foreign Trade appearing in the *Principles* he gives but scant attention to the possibility of partial specialization (see Hollander 1979: 464–5).

49 Grampp surmises that West's position in 1815 on the course of the rent share explains why the landlord class 'did not take offense at [his] pamphlet as it did of Ricardo's' (Grampp 1970: 323). West was later to reverse himself on the rent share (see West 1826: 135); he did so without signalling to his readers a change of position.

50 Blaug (1987, IV: 898) mistakenly asserts that West alluded to a fall of *rents per acre*.

51 Cf. p. 42: By free trade 'we might, to a very great degree, unite the advantages of a fresh country, and of one highly improved. By these means we might purchase our rude produce cheap, and manufacture it cheap'.

52 Jacob (1815) wrote a response to West's contribution. He accepted the principle of diminishing returns, but used it to support a *protectionist* case by maintaining that free trade would imply a severe reduction in domestic output since 'poorer lands' constituted by far the greater proportion of the total, and that the transfer of resources from the agricultural sector to the manufacturing sector would entail an excess supply of manufactured goods (Jacob 1815: 4–6, 7–8, 34–5). But in an appendix on the *Essay on Profits* – with reference to Ricardo's observation that free trade would simply entail the transfer of resources between sectors – Jacob maintained that capital could not in practice be withdrawn from agriculture but must be permanently lost. The appendix on Ricardo is unflattering: 'I should deem it trifling with practical men if I were to enter with [Ricardo] into the truisms, mixed with vagaries, which, cloathed in the technical cant of political economy, are to be found in the first twenty-four pages of this work' (34).

53 Sraffa has suggested that the first half of Ricardo's *Essay* is a revised version of a text prepared before the appearance of Malthus's two contributions, while the second half constitutes a direct reply to them (4n).

54 See also above, pp. 208–9.

In his letter of 6 February, Ricardo noted that Malthus had neglected to consider 'the relations of rent with the profits of Stock and the wages of labour'; 'by treating of the joint effect of the two latter on rent' he had 'not made the subject so clear as it might have been' (Ricardo 1951, VI: 174). In reply, Malthus explained that had he proceeded by distinguishing profits and wages in their separate relationships with rent, he 'should have been too much detained by the question of profits about which we differ, and which certainly deserves a separate discussion' (12 February; 176). *The growth model, insofar as concerns the profit rate, was not yet clear to him*; and we must reread the earlier correspondence with this in mind.

55 In what follows, I draw as appropriate on Hollander 1979, chapter 4.

56 Ricardo referred also to an intensive margin (14–15).

57 Cf. the 'Table showing the Progress of Rent and Profit' (17) where reference is also made to 'capital estimated in quarters of wheat'.

58 For example, at the outset Ricardo referred to 'the usual and ordinary rate of the profits of agricultural stock' (10) and also the precise formulation of the results by the model would suggest this.

59 Cf. the assertion that as the profit rate in agriculture declines from 50 to 43 per cent, so 'the profits on all capital employed in trade would fall to forty-three per cent' (14).

60 It is not clear whether the closing phrase should be understood in a *causal* sense. The reference ('as we have before observed') is doubtless to the *Essay*, 12, 14, discussed above.

61 In correspondence of 11 August 1814 prices of manufactured goods were said to *rise* with the money wage, although not in proportion (Ricardo 1951, VI: 119–20). Ricardo subsequently allowed for some change in manufacturing prices but only to the extent that the prices of raw materials increased; this did not alter the main proposition that rising wages left prices unaffected (letter 9 March 1815; 179).

62 Cf. also Ricardo's criticisms of Smith, and Malthus, with regard to the effects of the taxation of necessaries: 'They do not,' he insisted, 'subject us to any of the disadvantages of which Adam Smith speaks in foreign trade' (33–4n).

63 See also 19n, where Ricardo distinguished a variation in the real cost of producing corn from 'an alteration in the value of the precious metals, proceeding from their abundance or scarcity'.

64 In the correspondence of 1814, the notion of zero demand elasticity was not given a formal role in Ricardo's argument. In fact, when the demand curve for corn was considered Ricardo presumed it to be relatively, but not completely, inelastic (1951 VI: 129, 146).

65 This is true also of the subsequent correspondence (see note 68). For criticism of Sraffa's position on the *Essay*, see also Facarello 1982.

66 Also troublesome is the neglect of *costs* in corn pricing in favour of 'the excess of produce [brought] to market'.

67 In what follows I draw on Hollander 1990, 1994.

68 Cf. letter to Malthus of 10 January 1816: 'I cannot think it inconsistent to suppose that the money price of labour may rise when it is necessary to cultivate poorer land, whilst the real price may at the same time fall. Two opposite causes are influencing the price of labour[:] one the enhanced price of some of the things on which wages are expended, – the other the fewer enjoyments which the labourer will have the power to command, – you think they may balance each then, or rather that the latter will prevail. I on the contrary think the former the more powerful in its effects. I must write a book to convince you' (1951, VII: 10). And the *Principles*: the labourer 'will receive more money wages but his corn wage will be reduced; and not only his command of corn, but his general condition will be deteriorated, by his finding it more difficult to maintain the market rate of wages above their natural rate' (1951, I: 102).

69 It is unlikely that Ricardo was deliberately describing a 'dynamic equilibrium' path with wages above subsistence at a constant level. This would require deceleration of population growth, without the inducement of a wage decline, along with (at the same rate as) that of capital (Caravale 1985).

70 Torrens explained further that the price spiral set in motion by the increased corn price will be a damped one, tending to an equilibrium, his argument making allowance for the proportion corn constitutes in the workers' basket and the proportion wage costs constitutes in total costs (83–4).

Regarding the main proposition, Ricardo objected: 'Mr. Torrens' theory . . . appears to be defective, as I think that the price of commodities will be very slightly affected either by a rise or fall in the price of corn. If so every rise in the price of corn must affect profits on manufactures, and it is impossible that agricultural profits can materially deviate from them' (Ricardo to Malthus, 17 April 1815; in Ricardo 1951, VI: 213).

71 'These questions would lead us far. They involve considerations on the value of bullion and of currency, upon which, though they are highly important in themselves, and intimately connected with the external trade in corn, I must, in this place, refrain from enlarging' (89). Cf. also: 'A rise in wages, other things remaining as before, is, as we have seen, communicated to all the articles of life. But a rise in all the articles of life is the same thing as a fall in the value of money. Here, then, every question respecting the price of corn, ultimately resolves itself into a question of currency. Into the discussion of this very important branch of the subject, however, I shall not, at present, enter' (93).

72 On this see Ricardo to Malthus, 23 February 1816, in Ricardo 1951, VII: 24. I discuss some of the implications of Ricardo's comment in Hollander 1995b.

73 Even in this context, rent has something of a residual character (60).

74 Torrens has no concept in 1815 of an *intensive* margin.

75 His argument may imply an *initial* increase in the profit rate – a sort of inverse (money) wage-profit relation – followed by a longer-run decline.

76 But see above, p. 229, regarding a subsequent remark on the role of the corn price in determining agricultural costs.

77 Actually Malthus himself, though subject to physiocratic bias, recognized that manufactures provide a stimulus to or motive for the expansion of the agricultural surplus (see ETRM, 8: III), which is scarcely surprising considering his own demand orientation.

78 The Report . . . on Petitions relating to the Corn Laws, House of Commons, 1814; the Report of the Lords Committees . . . on the Growth, the Commerce and the Consumption of Grain, 1815. Smart provides an excellent summary of the Report of the more important 1814 Committee (Smart 1910, I: 415–16).

79 That any compensating money-wage increases with rising corn prices would discourage manufacturing exports was a somewhat academic concern is also confirmed in the *Inquiry into Rent* (1815a: 50).

80 In fact, it is subsequently conceded that even with a free corn trade the corn price would tend upward, presumably because *all* countries are expanding, albeit some faster than others: 'Even upon the system of importation, in the actual state and situation of the countries of Europe, higher prices must accompany superior and increasing wealth' (47n).

81 See also above, p. 195, regarding the same position in 1814.

82 The higher demand for corn emanated partly from an expanding manufacturing sector – much insisted upon in the correspondence of 1813 with Ricardo.

83 Here we recall that parts of the pamphlet had been in preparation since 1807 (see p. 195).

84 As for the extent of Ricardo's 'credit' there remains some doubt in my mind. The Preface to the *Principles* places West and Malthus together, as jointly responsible for 'present[ing] to the world, nearly at the same moment, the true doctrine of rent'. But this may amount to no more than a factual statement regarding publication priority. And that intellectual debt was not intended is confirmed by Ricardo's notation to his copy of West's 1815 pamphlet: 'This

THE CORN-LAW PAMPHLET LITERATURE OF 1815

was published before my Essay on the Profits of Stock, but it never came into my hands till after I had published my Essay' (see Sraffa, in Ricardo 1951, IV: 6).

85 The 'qualification' alludes to an allowance for a simultaneous increase in profit and wage rates in the event of increased effort or exertion by labour (West 1826: 88).

86 Only in later versions do we find such a conception (Torrens 1826: 125–6, 127–8; 1829: 468–9).

REFERENCES

Anderson, J. (1801) *A Calm Investigation of the Circumstances that have led to the Present Scarcity of Grain in Britain*, London: J. Cumming.

Blaug, M. (1987) 'Edward West (1782–1828)', in J. Eatwell, M. Milgate and P. Newman (eds) *The New Palgrave: A Dictionary of Economics*, London: Macmillan, 4: 898.

Brewer, A. A. (1987) 'Turgot: Founder of Classical Economics', *Economica*, 54 (November): 417–28.

—— (1988) 'Edward West and the Classical Theory of Distribution and Growth', *Economica*, 55 (November): 505–15.

—— (1995) 'Profit and Rent in the *Wealth of Nations*', *Scottish Journal of Political Economy*, 42, 2 (May): 183–200.

Cannan, E. (1917) *A History of Theories of Production and Distribution in English Classical Political Economy from 1776 to 1848*, 3rd edn, London: P. S. King.

Caravale, G. A. (1985) 'Diminishing Returns and Accumulation in Ricardo', in G. A. Caravale (ed.), *The Legacy of Ricardo*, Oxford: Blackwell, 127–88.

Chalmers, T. (1808) *An Enquiry into the Extent and Stability of National Resources*, Edinburgh: Moir.

Facarello, G. (1982) 'Sraffa versus Ricardo: The Historical Irrelevance of the "Corn-profit" Model', *Economy and Society*, 11, 2 (May): 122–37.

Grampp, W. D. (1970) 'Edward West Reconsidered', *History of Political Economy*, 2, 2 (Fall): 316–43.

Hollander, J. H. (1903) 'Introduction' to Sir Edward West, *The Application of Capital to Land* [1815], Baltimore: The Johns Hopkins Press.

Hollander, S. (1979) *The Economics of David Ricardo*, Toronto: University of Toronto Press.

—— (1980) 'On Professor Samuelson's Canonical Classical Model of Political Economy', *Journal of Economic Literature*, 18, 2 (June): 559–74.

—— (1990) 'Ricardian Growth Theory: A Resolution of Some Problems in Textual Interpretation', *Oxford Economic Papers*, 42, 2: 730–50.

—— (1992) 'Malthus's Abandonment of Agricultural Protectionism', *American Economic Review*, 82, 3: 650–9.

—— (1994) 'On the Textual Interpretation of Ricardian Growth Theory: The 'New View' Confirmed (Again)', *History of Political Economy*, 26, 3: 487–99.

—— (1995a) 'Malthus and the Corn Profit Model', in H. Kurz (ed.) *Critical Essays on Piero Sraffa's legacy in Economics*, Cambridge: Cambridge University Press (forthcoming).

—— (1995b) 'Sraffa's Rational Reconstruction of Ricardo: On Three Contributions to the *Cambridge Journal of Economics*', *Cambridge Journal of Economics*, 19, 3: 483–9.

—— (1996a) 'Die "Corn-Law-Pamphlete" von 1815: Malthus, West, Ricardo und Torrens', *Über die 'Corn-Law-Pamphlete' von 1815*, (in the series *Klassiker der Nationalökonomie*), Düsseldorf: Verlag Wirtschaft und Finanzen GMBH, 85–131.

—— (1996b) 'Notes on a Possible Bentham Manuscript', *Cambridge Journal of Economics*, 20, 4: 623–35.

—— (1997) *The Economics of Thomas Robert Malthus*, Toronto: University of Toronto Press.

Horner, Francis (1853) *Memoirs and Correspondence*, Leonard Horner (ed.), London: John Murray.

Jacob, W. (1815) *A Letter to Samuel Whitbread, being a Sequel to Considerations on the Protection required by British Agriculture*, London: J. Johnson.

Malthus, T. R. (1806) *An Essay on the Principle of Population*, 3rd edn, London: J. Johnson.

—— (1815a) *An Inquiry into the Nature and Progress of Rent and the principles by which it is regulated*, London: John Murray.

—— (1815b) *The Grounds of an Opinion on the Policy of Restricting the Importation of Foreign Corn*, London: John Murray.

—— (1820) *Principles of Political Economy*, 1st edn, London: John Murray.

—— (1986) *The Works of Thomas Robert Malthus*, E. A. Wrigley and D. Souden (eds), 8 vols, London: William Pickering.

Mill, J. S. (1967) [1828] 'The Nature, Opinion and Progress of Rent', *Collected Works of J. S. Mill*, Vol. IV, Toronto: University of Toronto Press.

Patten, S. N. (1893) 'The Interpretation of Ricardo', *Quarterly Journal of Economics*, 7 (April): 322–52.

Ricardo, D. (1815) *An Essay on the Influence of a low Price of Corn on the Profits of Stock; showing the inexpediency of restrictions on importation*, London: John Murray.

—— (1951) *The Works and Correspondence of David Ricardo*, P. Sraffa (ed.), (11 vols), Cambridge: Cambridge University Press.

Robbins, L. C. (1958) *Robert Torrens and the Evolution of Classical Economics*, London: Macmillan.

Samuelson, P. A. (1978) 'The Canonical Classical Model of Political Economy', *Journal of Economic Literature*, 16, 4 (December): 1415–34.

—— (1980) 'Noise and Signal in Debates Among Classical Economists: A Reply', *Journal of Economic Literature*, 18, 2 (June): 575–8.

—— (1991) 'Conversations with my History-of-Economics Critics', in *Economics, Culture and Education: Essays in Honour of Mark Blaug*, G. K. Shaw (ed.), Aldershot: Edward Elgar, 3–13.

—— (1992) 'The Overdue Recovery of Adam Smith's Reputation as an Economic Theorist', in Michael Fry (ed.), *Adam Smith's Legacy: His Place in the Development of Modern Economics*, London: Routledge, 1–14.

Schumpeter, J. A. (1954) *History of Economic Analysis*, New York: Oxford University Press.

Smart, E. (1910) *Economic Annals of the Nineteenth Century*, London: Macmillan.

Smith, A. (1937) [1776] *The Wealth of Nations*, New York: Modern Library.

Stigler, G. J. (1965) *Essays on the History of Economics*, Chicago: University of Chicago Press.

Torrens, R. (1815) *An Essay on the External Corn Trade*, London: J. Hatchard.

—— (1820) *An Essay on the External Corn Trade*, 2nd edn, London: J. Hatchard.

—— (1826) *An Essay on the External Corn Trade*, 3rd edn, London: Longman, Rees, Orme, Brown and Green.

—— (1827) *An Essay on the External Corn Trade*, 4th edn, London: Longman, Rees, Orme, Brown and Green.

—— (1829) *An Essay on the External Corn Trade*, A New Edition, London: Longman, Rees, Orme, Brown and Green.

Tucker, G. S. L. (1954) 'The Origin of Ricardo's Theory of Profits', *Economica*, 21 (November): 320–33.

Turgot, A .R. J. (1963) [1770] *Reflections on the Formation and Distribution of Riches*, New York: Augustus M. Kelley.

Viner, J. (1937) *Studies in the Theory of International Trade*, New York: Harper.

Waterman, A. M. C. (1991a) 'The "Canonical Classical Model of Political Economy" in 1808, as Viewed from 1825: Thomas Chalmers on the "National Resources" ', *History of Political Economy*, 23, 2 (Summer): 221–42.

—— (1991b) *Revolution, Economics and Religion: Christian Political Economy, 1798–1833*, Cambridge: Cambridge University Press.

West, E. (1815) *Essay on the Application of Capital to Land with observations showing the impolicy of any great restriction on the importation of corn*, London: T. Underwood.

—— (1826) *Price of Corn and Wages of Labour*, London: J. Hatchard.

Part V

MALTHUS

13

ON *THE WORKS OF THOMAS ROBERT MALTHUS**

Historians of classical economic thought have awaited variorum editions of
T. R. Malthus's major works – the *Essay on the Principle of Population* and the
Principles of Political Economy – with increasing impatience; Adam Smith,
David Ricardo, and J. S. Mill have been splendidly served, but not Malthus.
Anyone who has worked with the essay knows the frustration of having to
isolate variations across six editions published during the author's lifetime:
1798, 1803, 1806, 1807, 1817 and 1826. The eight-volume *Works of
Thomas Robert Malthus* – the published works excluding correspondence and
travel diaries – provides only a half-way house for the researcher as far as the
essay is concerned.

The first volume contains *inter alia* the *First Essay*. (Malthus's works have
been reset, but the original pagination is listed consecutively, so there is no
problem for readers who are used to Bonar's 1926 reprint of the 1798
edition.) The second and third volumes reprint the sixth edition with
variant readings from the second. David Souden, in his introduction to
Volumes 2 and 3, points out that 'essentially, Malthus wrote a new book' in
the five years between 1798 and 1803 (2: 7). E. A. Wrigley, in a general
introduction to the whole set, also maintains that 'the first and second
editions of the *Essay* are so very dissimilar that they may be regarded as separate works, even though the latter is an expansion and elaboration of the
former and there are some passages common to both editions' (1: 8). By
contrast, despite new material, modifications, and reordering of chapters
between 1803 and 1826, 'the work as a whole remained recognizably the
same between the second and sixth editions'.

This contrast is offered as partial justification for the editorial policy, on
the one hand, not to undertake a textual comparison of the first two
editions, and on the other, to compare the 'final' version of 1826 with that of
1803 alone. Evidently the editors were working under severe constraints and
are frank that a full critical edition of Malthus was out of the question.

* *The Works of Thomas Robert Malthus*, edited by E. A. Wrigley and David
Souden, London: William Pickering, 1986 (8 volumes).

Quite apart from this matter, one must ask for whom the edition is intended. Specialists concerned with the progression of Malthus's thought on population over time will be only partly satisfied; the general reader, on the other hand, gets rather too much. To be fair, I must emphasize that this is a personal judgement. Some scholars dislike variorum editions of repeatedly revised works.

Even within the set limits of the edition rather more could have been done to assist readers. The editors state their purpose to be the presentation of a text which is 'as little impeded as possible by obstacles of punctuation, nomenclature and spelling' – obstacles reflecting changing literary conventions (1: 12). In this they have succeeded. But beyond that they provide very little substantive assistance for the reader as he proceeds through the texts. An example or two must suffice. In a 'shorter variant passage' of 1803 (3: 689), Malthus gives two pages (234, 262) obviously relating to his second edition; but we are not provided with the specific places in the present edition to allow a check. Repeatedly we encounter chapters (not to mention paragraphs and sentences) added some time after 1803; internal evidence suggests 1817 but the editors, even in their useful concordance of chapter titles, are miserly with information. Conversely, when was the chapter 'Observations on the Reply of Mr Godwin' (3: chapter 3) removed? Again, no help is forthcoming. An identification of names is simply not attempted. There is, then, much that could have been done, short of a full variorum edition, to render the work more useful.

On the other hand, the apparatus devised to capture the 1826 and 1803 contrasts – the same system applies for most of the other pieces including the *Principles of Political Economy* – is ingenious and works. The reader will find printed the preface to the fifth edition of 1817, and the very important appendix introduced in 1806 and expanded in 1807 and 1817. He will benefit from Wrigley's brief discussion of Malthus's life and thought although it cannot be taken as, nor is it intended as, an authoritative introduction. I myself would be inclined to weigh somewhat more heavily Malthus's appreciation of industrialization than is suggested here (1: 15, 30, 34, 39). And I am not yet convinced that 'Malthus proved to be a poor guide to the future . . . [since] events were to prove that the limitations which he regarded as ineluctable could be overcome' (1: 17). The limitations were, I believe, rather more theoretical than practical. Wrigley appreciates, however, that Malthus recognized the 'solid and extensive evidence to sustain a considerably less bleak view of the future prospects for mankind' (1: 24), and I applaud his attention to Malthus's concern to raise the living standards of the masses.

The first volume contains a useful chronological history of all of Malthus's publications, distinguishing between editions and indicating their location, where appropriate, in the present edition; a selective listing of publications about Malthus and his work; a splendid table, based on the work of J. R.

Harrison, of Malthus's sources in successive editions of the *Essay on Population*; and an equally helpful consolidated bibliography of works cited by Malthus throughout all his writings. Separate bibliographies of works cited by Malthus in the first and the later essays are provided at the end of first and third volumes. (Their comparative lengths provides an index of the change in character of the works.) Similarly, each of the remaining volumes has its respective bibliography.

Volume 4, titled 'Essays on Population', also contains the 1813 'letter' and the 1817 'statements' regarding the East India College. Volumes 5 and 6 print the second or 1836 (posthumous) edition of the *Principles of Political Economy*, and indicate variations between the 1836 edition and the first edition of 1820. Volume 7 includes Malthus's essays on political economy; and Volume 8 has the essay on *Definitions in Political Economy*, and contains the index to all the volumes.

The volumes devoted to the *Principles*, which use the same textual procedures as the essay, are introduced very briefly by D. Souden, who places much weight on the different working methods of Ricardo and Malthus. It is misleading to refer to Malthus's 'professional (if not personal) antagonism towards Ricardo . . . ' (5: 8); this should surely read 'his professional (though certainly not personal) antagonism . . . '. As with the essay, a concordance of chapter (and here also of section) titles between editions is provided to indicate the reorganizations involved. The original editorial notes by John Cazenove are indicated, but again, as with the essay, no substantive set is provided by the present editors.

The volumes, which are beautifully printed and bound, cover *all* Malthus's published works, which will, of course, help determine the ultimate commercial destiny of this edition. I suspect that serious Malthus students will end up with it on their shelves.

14

NEW EDITIONS OF MALTHUS

In 1986 there appeared the eight-volume Pickering edition of *The Works of Thomas Robert Malthus*, edited by E. A. Wrigley and David Souden. Now we have the long-awaited Cambridge variorum editions of the *Essay on Population*[1] and the *Principles of Political Economy*[2], edited by the late Patricia James and John Pullen respectively. A starvation diet, as far as concerns Malthus scholars, suddenly transformed into an embarrassment of riches. It may be helpful to consider the features of the Cambridge editions which distinguish them from the Pickering versions.

The *Principles* printed by Pickering is the posthumous second (1836) edition, with variant readings from the first (1820) using a system of running footnotes for minor variants with extensive variations set apart at the end. The original notes by the editor – now usually identified as John Cazenove – are indicated but there is no substantive set provided by Wrigley and Souden. By contrast, a distinguishing feature of Pullen's edition is its reprinting (Volume 1) of the 1820 *Principles* as in the original, with no modifications except for marginal letters. These have various functions, as we shall see, one of which is to indicate where alterations appear in the second edition and also in a set of Manuscript Revisions made by Malthus and now held in the Cambridge University Library. Volume 2 contains those alterations. Thus while Wrigley and Souden treat the 1836 edition as the primary text, Pullen does the reverse. This major editorial decision turns *inter alia* on the fact that we cannot be sure of the extent to which the second edition of the *Principles* is an authoritative version of Malthus's last thoughts considering the omissions and additions made by Cazenove, coupled with the further circumstance that Malthus made his Manuscript Revisions to the first edition and it was considered desirable to include those Revisions in the new edition (Pullen 1989, 1: xiii). Such easy access for the first time to the Manuscript Revisions will be an important bonus to researchers.

The elements comprising the 1836 edition appear in the Alterations (including the addition of entire sections such as chapter II, Sections vi and vii, covering some twenty-three pages). But I still find it reassuring to have by me the original 1836 volume (reprinted by Kelley in 1964) or the

Pickering version, not because I doubt the accuracy of the new edition but because it is difficult to envisage the second edition as a single unit from the Alterations. It may also be noted that while Pullen provides an excellent analytical index to his edition (and Volume 1 contains the original 1820 index) he does not indicate alterations although there are differences between 1836 and 1820.

Pullen's extensive Editorial Commentary given in his Volume 2 constitutes the second distinguishing feature of his edition. Here he provides supplementary bibliographical materials relating to Malthus's sources, as well as interpretations and assessments of the alterations.

Third, the Cambridge edition differs from Pickering by the provision of a considerable introductory essay. This precedes the 1820 text in Volume 1 and deals with Malthus's works before 1820; the writing of the first edition of the *Principles*; Malthus's works after 1820; and his preparations for the second edition; the identity and role of the editor of the second edition; and a general description of the alterations in the Manuscript Revisions and the 1836 draft.

Pullen has undertaken a Herculean task that has daunted less courageous scholars for over a century and a half. His edition constitutes a research tool which promises to raise significantly the standard of Malthus scholarship. Above all, he forces us to recognize that Malthus's ideas are *in flux* after 1820, and he provides considerable insight into the processes at play. We have been misled long enough by Empson's soporific remark in the *Edinburgh Review* of 1837 that 'In substance and in doctrine, [the 1836 edition] contains the principles of Political Economy taught by Mr Malthus' (Semmel 1963: 234). Similarly, the remark in the advertisement to the second edition – probably by Cazenove – that the major variations relate largely to value theory has not helped (see on this Pullen, 1: lxviii). It is true that Empson also reports Malthus's response shortly before his death to reproaches regarding his failure to publish the revised edition: 'My views are before the public. If I am to alter anything, I can do little more than alter the language.' But this report is belied – or, if a valid attribution, cannot be taken seriously – considering the enormity of the revisions, now so vividly brought to our attention by Pullen. Pullen (lxiv) provides a quantitative index of the revision – 2,399 are recorded, many of them of high doctoral significance.

Pullen also documents the severe problems in the way of achieving valid interpretations of Malthus – worse than in any other classical case. For the 1836 edition was never fully revised by the author himself. That he died suddenly before he had completed the whole of the alterations which he intended is well known. But Pullen points out the revealing fact that the alterations are less extensive in later than in earlier parts of the text; and he raises the possibility that in making his alterations Malthus intended to proceed systematically from beginning to end of the *Principles*, but did not have time to complete his alterations before his death (lxv). It is also conceivable that some of the alterations were by Cazenove. In fact Pullen cautions us that 'Unless further evidence becomes available, the question of the extent of the editor's role in the second edition must remain largely unanswered, and thus there must be some element of doubt in deciding which of the alterations can be attributed to Malthus, and which to the editor' (lxiv). To arrive at any firm conclusion regarding modifications to Malthus's position over time on particular issues requires independent evidence which supplements that obtained from a comparison between the 1820 and 1836 editions. The problem is lessened but not entirely resolved by the availability of the Manuscript Revisions, for the 1836 edition omits a 'large number' of the manuscript revisions and, conversely, only a 'small proportion' of the changes in 1836 are in the Revisions (xxxviii). Pullen concludes that though 'the final manuscript that went to the publisher of the second edition was a very different document from the Manuscript Revisions as they exist now', these latter do 'provide an indication of the development of some of Malthus's ideas after 1820, and the fact that they contain ideas that do not appear in edition 2 of the *Principles* makes them, as it were, an intermediate "edition" of the *Principles*'. Scholars have their work cut out for them, but at least they will know the pitfalls – and opportunities.

In the course of his Introductory essay Pullen discusses personal and professional reasons for Malthus's procrastination and ultimate failure to publish a revised edition (lix–lx, lxviii–lxix). I fully agree that Malthus 'came to regard the second edition as much more than a mere refinement and re-ordering of the first' (lxix). As an example, my recent researches have revealed that over the years 1824–6 Malthus came to abandon his celebrated agricultural protectionism in favour of Ricardo's scheme for countervailing tariffs on efficiency grounds, a transformation reflecting rejection of his long-standing case for balanced growth and, more generally, a severe weakening of his physiocratic biases. It seems to me that this radical transformation – indicated *inter alia* by extensive deletions of protectionist and physiocratic passages from the text of the *Principles* – carries us quite a way in explaining his procrastination. Had his revised position become public knowledge, he would have become the subject of vicious charges of 'treason' from the *Quarterly Review*.

Turning to the editorial apparatus devised for this new edition. As indicated above, alterations between editions are given in a comparison of the two texts and, where relevant, between the texts and the Manuscript Revision. The scheme adopted involves a series of Roman letters in the margin of the 1820 edition indicating the Revisions as such and also the Editorial Comments. This means that there are two locations to consult in the second volume for each marginal letter in Volume 1. This is a little clumsy, but it is the cost of keeping the 1820 edition with its original pagination. In my opinion, it is a cost worth paying since that edition is now so rare. And the layout of the Alterations in Volume 2 is eminently clear. The editor and CUP are to be congratulated on solving a severe technical problem of exposition.

The margins of Volume 1 also have Greek letters. These allude to Editorial Comments which pertain specifically to passages that are not altered, unlike the Roman set which involve alterations. The appropriate extent of editorial commentary is, of course, a matter of taste. Robson in Mill's case and Sraffa in Ricardo's rigorously minimized such interventions. Pullen, who writes that his comments are 'offered as contributions to an understanding of the development of Malthus's thought, but do not pretend to be either comprehensive or definitive' (xiii) has chosen a different route. I understand the minimalist policy of Sraffa and Robson, or conversely a fully fledged analysis of the changes in a separate treatment, but the present policy leaves it unclear how far the analysis of the transition between 1820 and 1836 has been taken. This may sound ungracious; and that is certainly not my intention. On the contrary, Pullen is precisely the person to provide a 'comprehensive', even a 'definitive' treatment of the development of Malthus's thought. And perhaps my concern is after all unjustified. We should be happy to have for now at least, even a non-comprehensive and non-definitive treatment of the development of Malthus's thought from Pullen's pen.

There will inevitably be differences of opinion regarding specific evaluations made in the Commentary. And I suspect we can expect an explosion of debate regarding the development of Malthus's thought. For example, in the test case I have been using, I would add to Pullen's analysis of the removal in 1836 of the notion of an excess of social over private returns to agricultural investment (1: 217–25; 2: 191–2, 392–4) indications of a profound transformation in policy. For this amendment, I believe it can be shown, reflects that *volte face* mentioned above – the abandonment of agricultural protectionism.

Finally, a further characteristic of the Cambridge edition reflects the decision *not* to exclude alterations that are 'doctrinally insignificant' (1: xi). Although some will question this policy – as Stigler questioned Robson's similar decision (1982, 164–5) – I welcome it. Pullen argues convincingly (1: lxiv–lxv) that even apparently inconsequential changes to punctuation and style can be revealing when considered cumulatively. And we need not worry about matters of judgement as to what is and what is not 'insignificant'.

Patricia James's variorum edition of the *Essay on Population* is very different from Pullen's *Principles*. Readers should be aware that no common policy governs the two works.

There is, first, only a minimal editorial introduction. This briefly rehearses Malthus's life, provides information on publication data and makes a couple of comments on doctrine. One of these asserts that because Malthus in 1806 removed a passage of 1803 maintaining that 'A revenue is trans-ferred but not created' by manufacturing activity, he cannot be 'labelled a doctrinaire physiocrat' (James 1989, 1: xiii–xiv). But this sort of haphazard remark scarcely helps since there is pervasive evidence of the retention of a physiocratic perspective in 1806 and long after. The point is that no attempt is made to analyse doctrinal changes and this rule, once set up, should have been strictly followed.

A second major difference is the decision by James not to document apparently inconsequential variations: 'It was not considered necessary to record changes in paraphrasing, the use of capital letters, and small verbal alterations made merely for the sake of euphony or correct grammar: they indicate the care with which Malthus revised his work, but would be distracting to readers who are rightly more concerned with his subject-matter' (xiv). It is precisely the implications flowing from the accumulative impact of 'verbal alterations' that led Pullen to follow the reverse policy.

James's decision is all the more peculiar in the light of a comment in her Editor's Introduction justifying variorum editions, i.e. the 'bringing before the public passages which Malthus himself had cancelled' (xiii) – as if justi-fication were needed! The 'editorial defence', explains James, 'must rest on Malthus's continuing fame and influence, especially outside his own country, which makes everything he wrote, and all his changes of mind, of permanent significance'. Yet readers are not made privy to 'all his changes of mind'.

This characteristic of the James edition is pertinent for the Index. The new analytical index (compiled by John Pullen) certainly proves a very useful tool. But none of Malthus's own indexes are provided although there is an interesting commentary on them with illustrations. Now James there fully recognizes the implications of Malthus's own modifications: 'It is easy to laugh, but the modifications and qualifications which appear in the text of successive editions of the *Essay* are also reflected in the indexes' (James 1989, 2: 358). Or again, after illustrating index entries in the 1806 version, James writes: 'These are the sort of entries which enable anyone, browsing through Malthus's index, to obtain an insight into the views of the author as well as the subjects he discussed, something not usually revealed in the indexes of today' (360). It is scarcely credible that the decision was made not to provide readers with the opportunity to gain such insight. And it is annoying to read at the very close of her 'Note on the Original Indexes' that 'Malthus's indexes, like the *Essay on Population* itself, are a rich field for anybody who enjoys the study of mutation' (361).

That we are in a sense dealing with a *partial* variorium edition is also clear from the treatment of the first edition. Pickering printed the essay of 1798 in the first volume of its eight-volume series and we have Bonar's 1926 photographic reprint, reissued in 1966.[3] The student of Malthus will have to have one or other of these versions at hand if changes between 1798 and 1803 are to be systematically isolated, for the Cambridge edition – which turns on 1803 with variations of 1806, 1807, 1817 and 1826 – provides no systematic comparison with 1798. Thus while it is made clear where passages are incorporated verbatim into the second edition, we frequently find the editorial note that certain passages are 'based on' the 1798 edition which the reader will have to follow up by recourse to the original, the reprint, or Pickering, *Works*, Volume 1. (The relevant pages in 1798 are fortunately given.) As for 1798 passages removed in 1803, little help is provided.

The crucial contribution of the edition is, of course, its primary function – filling in variations *between* 1803 and 1826 – a function not provided by Pickering which compares 1803 and 1826 (taking 1826 as base) with intermediate variations not systematically specified. Here the edition is a boon and we owe a great debt to James. It is unfortunate that the original pagination is not indicated – unlike the Pickering version – so it is difficult to check references in the literature to the 1803 edition. This problem does not arise in the variations of 1806, 1807 and 1826 where full references are provided. Many of the variations appear in footnotes as a sort of commentary rather than in neutral fashion and this is pleasant (but see below for *major* variations). There are helpful cross references, corrections of Malthus's errors, identifications of people and places, and other explanatory comments of contemporary terms and events.

All in all the apparatus works well although it is never made clear why James chose 1803 as the base rather than 1826. Obviously the sort of justification for 'working forward' given by Pullen is irrelevant here. And although the variations emerge clearly enough, there is a certain complexity about the edition. Consider the summary chapter of Book III (Volume 1, 433f). Brief variations to the 1803 text are given in notes as is the normal practice. Major textual insertions made in 1817 are printed in smaller size print. In fact a major note added in 1817 is treated in like manner (445–6). By contrast, where (as in other chapters) quantitatively significant passages have been replaced or altered by Malthus – rather than simply added – note numbers and a large black dot are used at the beginning and end of the relevant segment to forewarn the reader of an extensive change. (Sometimes warning black dots appear without footnotes, as on 1: 430.) Now the change itself is usually given in the footnote indicated, even in very lengthy notes extending over several pages. (One variation of 1806 is printed as a note running for six pages (1: 420–6) with appropriate editorial explanations and further variations of 1807 attached.) But not always. Sometimes major replacements and alterations are given within the text in the same smaller print as permanent additions (see 1: 410–11: on page 410 we have a footnote *number* accompanying the black dots but no corresponding footnote); and elsewhere a major note added in 1826 (2: 74–6) appears as a note rather than in smaller print unlike the case mentioned above. The changes in print size, the great black dots, the sometimes very lengthy notes to incorporate extensive variations with their additional editorial notes and variations, are all a little unpleasing. Fortunately, the apparent inconsistencies of treatment are not pervasive and might have been easily corrected.

Conceivably the complexity I have alluded to would have been reduced by taking the final edition (1826) as base. I cannot be sure. But a Textual Introduction explaining the decision not to work with the last edition – whether on grounds of minimizing inevitable complexity or on other grounds – would have been in order.

This edition has, to my mind, a disconcerting feature which might have been avoided by taking the 1826 version as main text (though doubtless other problems would have been created). The summary chapter of Book III, which in 1803 has the title 'Of the principal Sources of the prevailing Errors on the Subject of Population', constitutes Malthus's chapter xi. James, allowing for the addition in 1817 of a new chapter (vii), labels the summary chapter as xii although in fact it remains 'xi' for Malthus until 1817 (when it actually becomes xiv since four of his chapters in Book III are replaced by six in 1817). In brief, in none of Malthus's own editions is there a Summary chapter numbered xii. And it is disconcerting and potentially confusing that we nowhere find, as such, Malthus's 1817/1826 chapter numbers viii through xiii. (I find myself obliged to consult my own copies of the original editions to avoid confusion.)

Against this must be set a compensating bonus. The four chapters in Book III numbered vii through x in 1803, 1806 and 1807 are printed by James in her Volume 1, and the six chapters numbered by Malthus viii through xiii are printed in Volume 2 as chapters A through F. It is possible by this device to make side-by-side comparisons between 1817 and earlier editions and this is very helpful indeed in dealing with rewritten chapters (although the reader will have to do his own specification of differences). A similar treatment is accorded two rewritten chapters of 1806 in Book II.

The 'Alphabetical List of Authorities quoted or cited by Malthus', which runs to over a hundred pages, raises to a considerable degree the usefulness of the edition. However, on two specific occasions when I followed up this listing – with respect to Malthus's references to Dupont de Nemours and de Mirabeau – I found the contributions to be only partly accurate. In the first case James entertained an unjustified hypothesis regarding the specific edition of *Physiocratie* Malthus was using (2: 281–2); in the second she failed to trace the specific version of *L'Ami des Hommes* that Malthus had at hand (2: 309).[4] I suspect she used the British Library holdings which in these instances proved inadequate. There are substantive consequences flowing from these apparently minor deficiencies for anyone concerned to isolate the precise extent of Malthus's awareness of original physiocratic writings.

James's variorum edition is what we shall have to work with from here to eternity. What seem to me to be weaknesses of the volumes are certainly not ruinous. Serious Malthus scholars will want to own this edition. It is, therefore, appropriate to close by paying tribute to James for her achievement, remembering always that she was not able to bring her work to full fruition. No one else could single-handedly have done a better job.

NOTES

1 T. R. Malthus, *An Essay on the Principle of Population*, Patricia James (ed.), 2 vols, Cambridge: Cambridge University Press for the Royal Economic Society, 1989, pp. 566.
2 T. R. Malthus, *Principles of Political Economy*, John Pullen (ed.), 2 vols, Cambridge: Cambridge University Press for the Royal Economic Society, 1989, pp. liv + 460.
3 The Bonar reprint is not, in fact, a true 'photographic reproduction' since the original long s's are not reproduced.
4 See chapter 15 in this collection.

REFERENCES

Malthus, T. R. (1986) *The Works of Thomas Robert Malthus*, E. A. Wrigley and David Souden (eds), 8 vols, London: William Pickering.
—— (1989) *An Essay on the Principle of Population*, Patricia James (ed.), 2 vols, Cambridge: Cambridge University Press for the Royal Economic Society.
—— (1989) *Principles of Political Economy*, John Pullen (ed.), 2 vols, Cambridge: Cambridge University Press for the Royal Economic Society.
'Semmel, B. (ed.) (1963) *Occasional Papers of T. R. Malthus*, New York: Burt Franklin.
Stigler, G. J. (1982), *The Economist as Preacher and Other Essays*, Chicago: University of Chicago Press.

15

ON MALTHUS'S PHYSIOCRATIC REFERENCES*

The question of Malthus's relation to the Physiocrats has been raised in various recent contributions. Walter Eltis takes the position that Malthus apparently never read the Physiocrats.[1] Now as Thweatt (1987: 30) observes, there are in fact two citations in *Essay on Population* where Malthus 'comes as close as he ever did to citing any of the Physiocrats', one to Dupont de Nemours (Malthus 1803: 458n and the second to 'the author of L'Ami des Hommes' (477).[2] I have investigated more closely the substance and possible implications of these references and this note constitutes some findings. It emerges that, at the least, Malthus had access to a wide range of Quesnay's works and, possibly, a wide range of other physiocratic writings.

THE REFERENCE TO DUPONT (1803: 458n)

The footnote reference to Dupont appears in Book 3, chapter 10: 'Of Bounties on the Export of Corn' in support of the criticism in the text of Adam Smith's position against the corn laws, paraphrased thus by Malthus: 'as the money price of corn regulates that of all other home-made commodities, the advantage to the proprietor from the increased money price is merely apparent, and not real; since what he gains in his sales, he must lose in his purchases'. 'This position, however', Malthus proceeds, 'is not true, without many limitations', to which he attaches the note in question:

> In the Physiocratie, by Dupont de Nemours, it is proposed as a problem in political economy, to determine, whether an advance in the money price of corn is a real or only nominal advantage: and the question is resolved, I think justly, on the side of the reality of the advantage. Tom. ii.

* I much appreciate the help afforded to me by Walter Eltis, Arnold Heertje, Donald Winch, Leanne Pander and Dianne Gutscher (Bowdoin College Library), Jill Richardson (War Memorial Library, Jesus College, Cambridge), and Angela Whitelegge (Goldsmiths' Library, London). Antonella Vergati provided efficient research assistance. Two anonymous referees offered generous comments. Funds for my research are from a Social Science Research Council of Canada fellowship.

We turn now to the treatment of this note in two recent editions of Malthus's *Essay* – the Pickering (Wrigley and Souden, eds, 1986) and Cambridge (James, ed., 1989) editions. As for the first, we find the following modified version:

> In P. S. Dupont de Nemours, *Physiocratie, ou constitution naturelle du gouvernement le plus avantageux au genre humain* (Leiden, 1768), bk ii, it is proposed as a problem in political economy, to determine, whether an advance in the money price of corn is a real or only nominal advantage: and the question is resolved, I think justly, on the side of the reality of the advantage.
>
> (Malthus 1986, 3: 683)[3]

The original note in fact gives neither the full title nor the place and date of publication and refers to *Tom.* ii not to *book* ii. These details, innocuous as they seem at first sight, may prove significant, as we shall see.[4]

In her 'Alphabetical List of Authorities quoted or cited by Malthus', the late Patricia James asserts (like Wrigley and Souden) that Malthus refers to the 1768 Leyden edition, and further – to explain the reference to 'Tom. ii' – that the version Malthus had at hand 'could have been split into two'. Taking this for granted, she isolates Malthus's allusions as referring to Maximes 18, 19 and 20 and their respective Notes:

> The work quoted by Malthus in Bk III, ch. xi, n. 15,[5] is *Physiocratie ou Constitution Naturelle du Gouvernement le plus avantageux au genre humain*: 'Recueil publié par Du Pont, des Sociétés Royales d'Agriculture de Soissons & d'Orléans, et Correspondant de la Société d'Émulation de Londres'. It was published in Leyden in 1768, and the British Library copy is bound in one octavo volume; it could, however, easily have been split into two, the first dealing with Quesnay's *Tableau Économique*, the second (to which Malthus refers) being *Maximes Générales du Gouvernement Économique d'un Royaume Agricole*.

Malthus must have had in mind Maxims XVIII, XIX and XX (pp. 116–17, pp. 162–4 for the Notes thereon) in which Dupont maintains that abundance without commercial value does not constitute wealth: higher prices and scarcity lead to misery, but high prices and plenty lead to opulence. The higher the price of corn, the higher the wages of the common people – whose pay 's'établit assez naturellement' according to the price of grain – so that they had more money for other commodities. Dupont stressed the importance of the masses, as consumers, and as producers of the revenue of the state: poor peasants, poor kingdom.

Malthus's text here, in 1806, is the same as in 1803, and there is no obvious reason why this footnote should have been omitted from the

1806 edition, unless he wished completely to dissociate himself from the physiocrats.

(Malthus 1989, 2: 281–2)

Now the British Library Leyden copy of *Physiocratie* is in fact the *first* volume of a *two*-volume set, a set possessed by the University of Cambridge Library (Pryme. c. 12, 13); there is not the slightest reason to entertain the possibility, as James does, that the *first* volume *was itself divided into two*.[6] The second volume bears the title *Discussions et développemens sur quelques-unes des notions de l'économie politique. Pour servir de seconde Partie au Recueil intitulé: PHYSIOCRATIE*. The publication data read: 'A Leyde, Et se trouve à Paris, Chez Merlin, Libraire, rue de la Harpe. M.DCC.LXVII.'[7] It is evidently to material in this latter part that Malthus refers.[8] For in it there is posed, precisely as Malthus says, the following 'problème économique': 'Le profit qu'une Nation retire de l'accroissement du prix de ses productions surpasse-t-il le désavantage qu'elle éprouve, alors par le rencherissement de ses dépenses' (Table Sommaire, 489, referring to Quesnay's main text, 183–4).[9] Following an elaboration of this issue in terms of alternative assumptions, including those relating to foreign trade, we find as the Dernière Question à Résoudre: 'Quel est dans le cas donné la bénéfice réel que l'on trouve dans l'accroissement qui double le revenu' (Table Sommaire, 491–2, referring to main text, 197–8).[10] The 'real' advantages of a high corn price are then traced out:

> Elle est avantageuse pour tout le monde. Les Fermiers des terres en profitent pendant le cours de leurs baux, & c'est pour une Nation pauvre le bénéfice le plus précieux. L'augmentation de richesses des Fermiers les met a portée de donner de la même terre un plus grand produit net aux Propriétaires & au Souverain, & la concurrence les y oblige.
>
> On voit par le Tableau, pag. 195, que l'effet de l'augmentation, *d'un sixieme* sur le prix des productions augmente la recette de la classe stérile de *sept vingt-deuxiemes* en livres, ce qui lui assure environ *un septieme* de plus de jouissances, de consommations, par conséquent de population: Résultat bien opposé à l'opinion de ceux qui ont cru devoir faire baisser le prix des denrées pour l'avantage de la classe salariée.
>
> En résumé par l'augmentation d'un sixieme du prix des productions dans le cas donné les Propriétaires gagnent *onze douziemes*; la classe stérile environ *un septieme*; la classe productive la jouissance de l'accroît pendant le cours des baux; & la population générale de la Nation accroît d'environ *un dixieme*
>
> (Table Sommaire, 494–5, referring to main text, 212–20)[11]

Before turning to the substantive implications of Malthus's reference to the foregoing text, we must step back to review the evidence that it is the two-volume edition, i.e. the set of two *separate* volumes which Malthus had at hand. The fact is that we *cannot be sure*, though the actual textual matter – in whatever of the possible versions – is certainly that discussed above.

One problem is that the Leyden edition also appeared with its two parts bound together, with pages numbered consecutively (Cambridge, VI.8.25; also Goldsmiths' Library, University of London, [GL] 1768).[12] The point is important. For possibly Malthus had at hand *only* the second part of the work and not the first part; alternatively, he might have had *both* parts at hand.[13] However, I am prepared to hazard the guess that, even if Malthus used the edition of volume 2 issued in separate binding he also had volume 1 at hand. Apart from the lesser likelihood that one would have access only to the second part of a two-part work, there is the further circumstance that only volume 1 makes specific mention of Dupont on the title page.[14]

But we cannot be certain that Malthus read the Leyden edition – whether the first (Pékin) or the second. The fact is that he refers to *Tom. ii* whereas the Leyden version refers to the *seconde partie*; it seems unlikely that an English reader would render 'seconde partie' as 'Tom. ii'. This circumstance is scarcely decisive – only suggestive – but it is reinforced by the existence of a version of *Physiocratie* actually divided into *Tomes* rather than *Parties*. That version was a new edition published at Yverdon 1768–9.[15] The particular set of this edition in the Goldsmiths' Library is made up of six *tomes* bound in three pairs – the first (dated 1768) being the two parts of the Leyden edition (but with pages numbered differently); and the additional material (works by Dupont, Baudeau, Le Trosne and Abeille) in *tomes* III and IV dated 1768, and in *tomes* V and VI dated 1769.[16] It is possible therefore that Malthus had the whole Yverdon set; or only part of it – and if the latter, possibly only the bound set of the first two *tomes*;[17] or, if the Yverdon version was also published in six *separate tomes*, only the second.[18]

The last question can be answered in the earlier manner: In all likelihood Malthus had at hand *at least* the first two *tomes* even if bound separately, for again *tome* I of the Yverdon version (like that of the Leyden version) refers explicitly on the title page to Dupont whereas *tome* II does not – apart from the lesser probability that he would have had access only to the second.

In the event that Malthus was familiar with the Yverdon edition in its entirety he would have covered the full range of physiocratic writing.[19] But we cannot be sure about this. What we can say for certain is that Malthus had access to the second part or volume of the Leyden or Yverdon editions of *Physiocratie*; and probably, for the reasons given above, also to the first part of one or other of the editions either bound with part ii or bound separately. Let us turn now to some substantive implications of this conclusion.

As we have seen, the footnote reference itself (1803: 458, above) draws support from Dupont for the textual criticism of Adam Smith. But this support is of the most general kind. It is the conclusion that a rise in the corn price has 'real' effects that is used, not the precise reasoning on which it is based, and certainly not that part of the argument utilizing the Tableau Economique. Having said this, we note also that part of the case in *Physiocratie* involves the advantage to labour of a high corn price (see above). Now this is a theme developed by Quesnay at length in tom. i (or part i), his formulation, anonymous of course, appearing in a *note* on Maxime 19 of the *Maximes Générales*.[20] It is also one of Malthus's most celebrated theorems that since the money wage is governed by the price of corn, the higher the corn price the greater is the amount available for expenditure on non-agricultural goods and the higher labour's welfare:

> I stated in the *Observations* [1986, 7: 102–3], and more at large in the *Inquiry into rents* [7: 127], that under the same demand for labour, and the same consequent power of purchasing the means of subsistence, a high *money price* of corn would give the labourer a very great advantage in the purchase of the conveniences and luxuries of life. The effect of this high money price would not, of course, be so marked among the very poorest of the society, and those who had the largest families; because so very great a part of their earnings must be employed in absolute necessaries. But to all those above the very poorest, the advantage of wages resulting from a price of eighty shillings a quarter for wheat, compared with fifty or sixty, would in the purchase of tea, sugar, cotton, linens, soap, candles, and many other articles, be such as to make their condition decidedly superior.
>
> (Malthus, *Grounds of an Opinion* [1815] 1986, 7: 162)

James (above) also refers to Maxime 19 and the note but assumes that it is to them that Malthus *specifically* refers in his footnote reference. This is not the case. All we can say is that he probably had access to the part or volume containing the Maximes and notes and, if so, *may* have derived his theorem from Quesnay, though whether or not in that case it was a conscious borrowing, it is impossible to say.[21] But certain it is that Quesnay must be given priority over Malthus for the theorem.[22]

There is much else in both volume 1 and volume 2 that might be relevant for an appreciation of Malthusian Physiocracy. But for present purposes, I am limiting the discussion to the explicit reference made by Malthus in 1803 (458n) and to the theorem on wages touched on in the relevant material and spelled out by Quesnay in part 1 of *Physiocratie*.

THE REFERENCE TO *L'AMI DES HOMMES* (1803, 477)

The reference to de Mirabeau's work is found in the text to Book 3, Chapter 11, 'Of the principal Sources of the prevailing Errors on the Subject of Population':

The author of L'Ami des Hommes, in a chapter on the effects of a decay of agriculture upon population, acknowledges that he had fallen into a fundamental error in considering population as the source of revenue; and that he was afterwards fully convinced that revenue was the source of population.[b] [Note 'b' gives as reference: 'Tom. viii. p. 84. 12 mo. 9 vols. 1762'.][23]

The edition I have consulted in the British Library (shelf-mark 231.e20–26) is a seven-volume Avignon edition.[24] Mirabeau's statement in this edition appears in 'Suite de la VI Partie', p. 84:

TABLEAU OECONOMIQUE. *Considéré dans le dépérissement de la Culture, & dans ses effects relativement a la Population.*

C'est ici le Chapitre qui m'a d'abord fait connoître, & dans lequel j'avois néanmoins fondamentalement erré. J'avois considéré la population comme la source des revenus; un plus habile [Quesnay] m'a heurté de front. J'ai été assez heureux pour écouter, & il m'a appris que ce sont au contraire les revenus qui sont la source de la population.[25]

Malthus, therefore, paraphrased Mirabeau's formulation pretty closely. And something more substantive than a mere 'citation' is involved in the Mirabeau case, as we also concluded in that of Dupont. For there is no doubt that Malthus was familiar with the Tableau Economique – though, from his silence on the matter, he was evidently unwilling to adopt that structure as his own.

NOTES

1 'Strangely there is no evidence that Malthus ever read Quesnay or even Mirabeau.... [T]here is astonishingly no evidence that the two leading English political economists of the early nineteenth century, Malthus and Ricardo, felt any temptation or obligation to read their recent French predecessors' (Eltis 1984: 321).

2 The reference to Dupont is specific to 1803 and disappears from *all* later editions of the *Essay*.

3 As a matter of policy, the editors modify all references to conform to modern practice (1986, 1: 10).

4 There is no bibliography attached to the 1803 edition; Dupont does not even appear in the index. *Physiocratie* is not on the shelves of the Jesus College, Cambridge collection of the Malthus Library and is not listed in the *Pergamon Malthus Library Catalogue*, Pergamon (1983), or in the Supplementary List of Books Published Before 1835 registered in the Dalton Hill Catalogue (attached to the Pergamon main lists) but not forming part of the Jesus College Collection, or in the unpublished Supplement to the Dalton Hill Catalogue prepared by the late John Harrison of the Jesus College Library. For a discussion of the deficiencies of the Pergamon catalogue, particularly its presumption that the books in the present collection comprised Malthus's personal library – a presumption not attributable to the contributors themselves – see Grampp 1984. The *Oeuvres* of Turgot in nine volumes and the anonymous, two-volume *L'ordre naturel* (by Mercier de la Rivière) have the

label: 'EX LIBRIS HENRICI MALTHUS, OLIM PATRIS SUI T. R. MALTHUS. COLLEGIO JESU CANTAB.' There are no other 'physiocratic' items.

5 These references are to the chapter and footnote numbers in James's variorum edition, not to the original.

6 Apart from this, the maxims and notes are not by Dupont as James implies but by Quesnay.

7 There exists a version of the Leyden edition with a title-page reference to publication 'A Pékin, et se trouve à Paris'. It has the same pagination as the Leyden–Paris version. (See National Union Catalog, 477: 189.) The 'Tableau Chronologique des Oeuvres de François Quesnay' (INED, I: 312–13) lists the Pékin–Paris version (in two separate volumes) dated (November) 1767 as the first edition, and the Leyden–Paris edition (also in separate volumes) as the second. Professor Heertje confirms that the Pékin–Paris version is the 'real' first edition, both parts published in 1767. See also Einaudi 1958: 6–7. He mentions the common practice before the French Revolution of giving false locations. On this practice, designed to circumvent censorship, see Murphy 1986: 299–306. There are various complexities regarding the work. For one, Higgs (1935: 423) lists an edition published 'à Leyde, 1768 [for 1767]. Bastard title . . . ' without reference to Paris. (Pagination is identical to the Leyden–Paris version.) A copy owned by Professor Heertje, on the other hand, has only 'à Paris, 1767' on the title page to the second part; and the title itself makes no reference to *Physiocratie*, being reduced to 'Discussions et développemens sur quelques-unes des notions de l'économie politique. Seconde Partie de ce Recueil.'

8 All items, from both volumes (except for the 'First Dialogue'), are in Meek's English translation (1962). Meek's translations are from the text of *Physiocratie* as reproduced in *François Quesnay et la Physiocratie*, published by the Institut National d'Etudes Demographiques, Paris, 1958, volume 2.

The first volume of the Leyden edition entitled *Physiocratie* contains the following sections. I append the INED, vol. 2 references:

1 Discours de l'éditeur, pp. i–ci.
2 Table Sommaire de la Première Partie, [pp. cii–cxx].
3 [Quesnay] *Le Droit Naturel*, pp. 1–38. [INED, 2: 729–42]
  Avis de l'Editeur, pp. 39–42.
4 [Quesnay] *Analyse du Tableau Economique*, pp. 43–98. [INED, 2: 793–812] (including *Observations Importantes*, pp. 67–98).
5 [Quesnay] *Maximes Générales du Gouvernement économique d'un royaume agricole*, pp. 99–172. [INED, 2: 949–76]. Avis de l'Editeur, pp. 101–4. [Quesnay] *Notes sur les Maximes*, pp. 123–72. [INED, 2: 957–76]. The second volume contains:

1 Avis de l'Editeur, pp. 175–180.
2 [Quesnay] *Problème economique*, [pp. 181–234.] [INED, 2: 859–77].
3 [Quesnay] *Dialogues sur le Commerce et sur les travaux des Artisans*
  Avis de l'Editeur, pp. 237–50
  Premier Dialogue, pp. 251–370
  Second Dialogue, pp. 371–442 [INED, 2: 885–912].
4 [Quesnay] *Second Problème Economique*, pp. 443–88 [INED, 2: 977–92].
5 Table Sommaire, pp. 489–520.

9 The original *Question* in the main text as formulated by Quesnay reads thus: 'On demande, si le profit qu'une Nation retire de l'augmentation du prix des

productions de son territoire surpasse le désavantage de l'augmentation des dépenses causées par le renchérissement des productions? car il semble qu'une augmentation de prix qui nous procureroit dans nos ventes un gain que nous perdrions dans nos achats, ne nous laisseroit acun bénéfice' (183).

10 The main text refers to the 'SOLUTION PRECISE ou calcul des effets réels du renchérissement dans le cas donné' (198).

11 Variations in the initial data supposed would alter the precise outcome: 'Un autre accroissement de prix dans d'autres circonstances présenterait des données & par conséquent des résultats différens.'

12 The two-separate-volume edition is also numbered consecutively; it is only a matter of different binding. Similarly, the Pékin–Paris edition exists as two separate physical volumes, each described as *Partie* on the title page with pages numbered consecutively (see Einaudi 1958: 5–6, on the copy from the Menger library in Tokyo); and also bound together in one physical volume (copy held at Bowdoin College Library).

13 There is a minor mystery in that the second part to which Malthus refers is dated 1767, while the first is dated 1768. (This is so in both versions.) In the Goldsmith copy there is a penned solution in Foxwell's hand: 'According to *Schelle* – p. 402 the date 1768 is a printer's error for 1767: as the first part was printed in Nov.ʳ of that year.' For others who take this view, see Einaudi 1958: 5. Einaudi himself (6–8) argues that while it is certain that the Pékin–Paris version was published in 1767, it is not *necessarily* the case that the date given on the first part of the 'normal' edition (Leyden–Paris) is an error. He bases his case on the suppression in the Leyden–Paris version of a reference in the Pékin–Paris edition to the presence of Louis XV in December 1758 at the first printing at Versailles of the Maximes together with the Tableau Economique. Einaudi suggests that the frontispiece of the relevant volume only – the first – was modified from the original 1767 to 1768 when the suppression of the reference was made.

14 This is true both of the first (Pékin) edition and the second edition (see note 7).

15 The French 'Yverdon' equals the German 'Ifferten' in Switzerland. See Chisholm 1902: 1765.

16 Each of the six *tomes* except the first has the title page: 'Discussions et développemens sur quelques-unes des notions de l'économie politique, Pour servir de suite au Receuil intitulé: PHYSIOCRATIE.' The pagination starts afresh with each of the six (unlike the Leyden version).

17 In fact, Higgs (1935) 4266 lists an Yverdon edition which contains only *tomes* i and ii.

18 The Bibliothèque Nationale catalogue lists an Yverdon six-volume edition, 1768–9. The Goldsmiths' card catalogue lists *Physiocratie*, six volumes in three, Yverdon, 1768–9, and 'another edition of vols. 1–2 . . . Leyden, 1768, 1767'. This is reversed in the printed Catalogue of the *Goldsmiths' Library of Economic Literature*, vol. 1: *Printed Books to 1800*, p. 512. The N.U. Catalogue vol. 477, p. 189, clarifies that the Yverdon version is a 'Second edition, containing new material, with works by Du Pont de Nemours, Baudeau, Letrosne, Turgot and Abeille'. On the other hand, INED, 1: 313 represents the Yverdon edition more correctly as the third edition.

19 Higgs's summary of contents (1935: 424) is useful here:

4268 [DU PONT DE NEMOURS] Physiocratie, ou Constitution naturelle du Gouvernement le plus avantageux au Genre Humain. Recueil publié par Dupont. *à Yverdon, 1768. 3 vols. 8°.*

Vol. I. Contents. Tome I.
1 Discours de l'éditeur, and table, *xcii pp.*
2 Le Droit Naturel, *1–30 pp.*
3 Avis, and Analyse du Tableau Economique, *31–54 pp.*
4 Observations importantes, *54–78 pp.* [Quesnay]
5 Maximes générales du gouvernement économique d'un royaume agricole, 79–139 pp.

Tome II. Title 'Discussions et développemens' etc.
1 Avis de l'Editeur, and Problème economique, *to p. 45.*
2 Dialogues sur le Commerce, etc., and Avis, *to p. 254.* Table, *to end p. 288.*

Vol. II. Title repeated. Tome III.
1 De l'origine et des Progrès d'une Science Nouvelle, *1–66 pp.* [Dupont]
2 Lettres d'un Citoyen . . . sur les Vingtièmes et les autres Impôts, *to p. 222.* [Baudeau]
3 De l'administration des Chemins, par Du Pont, and Table, *to p. 288.*

Tome IV. Titles as before.
1 De l'utilité des Discussions Economiques, *1–70 pp.* [Le Trosne]
2 Lettre à Monsr. B. [sur la concurrence des étrangers], *to p. 175.*
3 Discussions sur l'argent et sur le commerce, *to p. 213.*
4 Avis au Peuple sur son premier besoin, Table and Approbation, *to end pp. 266–7.* [Baudeau]

Vol. III. Titles as before. Tome V. Date of this volume, 1769.
1 Avis au peuple (continued), and Table, *1–272 pp.*

Tome VI. Titles as before.
1 Réflexions sur la police des grains en France et en Angleterre, to *1–56 pp.*
2 Faits qui ont influé sur la cherté des grains en France et en Angleterre, *to p. 106.* [Abeille]
3 Lettres sur les émeutes populaires que cause la cherté des bleds, *to p. 152.* [Baudeau]
4 Effets d'un privilège exclusif en matière de commerce sur les droits de la Propriété &c., and Table, *to end p. 231.*

20 Maxime XIX asserts: '*Qu'on ne croie pas que le bon marché des denrées est profitable au menu peuple*; car le bas prix des denrées fait baisser le salaire des gens du Peuple, diminue leur aisance, leur procure moins de travail & d'occupations lucratives, & anéantit le revenu de la Nation' (Leyden, I: 116–17; Yverdon, I: 93–5).
The *Note* reads thus:

La cherté du blé, par exemple, pourvu qu'elle soit constante dans un Royaume agricole, est plus avantageuse au menu peuple, que le bas prix. Le salaire de la journée du Manouvrier s'établit assez naturellement sur le prix du bled, & est ordinairement le vingtieme du prix d'un septier. Sur ce pied si le prix du blé étoit constamment à vingt livres, le Manouvrier gagneroit dans le cours de l'année environ 260 liv., il en dépenseroit en blé pour lui et sa famille 200 liv., & il lui resteroit 60 liv. pour les autres besoins: si au contraire le septier de blé valoit que 10 liv. il ne gagneroit que 130 liv., il en dépenseroit 100 liv. en bled, & il ne lui resteroit pour les autres besoins que 30 liv. Aussi voit-on que les Provinces où le blé est cher sont beaucoup plus peuplées que celle où il est à bas prix.

> Le même avantage se trouve pour toutes les autres classes d'hommes, pour le gain des Cultivateurs, pour le revenu des Propriétaires, pour l'impôt, pour la prospérité de l'Etat; car alors le produit des terres dédommage largemens du surcroît des frais de salaire & de nourriture. Il est aisé de s'en convaincre par le calcul des dépenses & des accroissemens des produits.
> (Leyden, I: 162–3; Yverdon, I: 130–1; for translation see Meek 1962: 257–8)

21 The fact that the theorem is first mentioned only in the *Observations on the Effects of the Corn Laws* (1814), rather than in the *Essay* itself, raises the possibility that Malthus arrived at the idea independently or, if he had derived it from Quesnay, that he may have forgotten its origin.

22 For an apparent attribution to Malthus as originator, see Grampp 1954.

23 The Pickering edition (1986, 3: 455n) renders the note: 'V. R. Mirabeau, *L'ami des hommes, ou traité de la population*, 5th ed., 9 vols. (Paris, 1762–4), viii, p. 84.' This edition is included in the files of the late John Harrison relating to 'Works cited in Eds 1–6 of the "Essay . . . " ' But there is no indication here of where this specific edition is housed; and the standard collections do not refer to it. See: Catalogue of the Goldsmiths' Library of Economic Literature, 1, Printed Books to 1800; The Goldsmiths'-Kress Library of Economic Literature, 2; National Union Catalog Pre-1956 Imprints; Higgs' Bibliography of Economics, 1751–1775; catalogue of the Bibliothèque Nationale.

24 The first and second volumes (actually referred to as *parties*) are dated 1762; the third and fourth, 1758 and 1759 respectively; and the remaining three, 1761. The first volume is entitled *L'Ami des Hommes ou Traité de la Population. Nouvelle édition Corrigée*, Première Partie. Similarly, the second and third volumes, with appropriate adjustment. The remaining four volumes have only the reduced form *L'Ami des Hommes*, but with an additional title page devoted to the particular subject matter. Thus volume 5 has as its special title 'Tableau Economique, avec ses explications' (without attribution to Quesnay).

Professor Heertje informs me that in an Avignon seven-volume (tome) edition (1759–1760) the VI Partie and the 'Suite de la VI Partie' constitute volume 7. (The quote is on p. 131.) Apparently this is the edition used by Meek in his translation of extracts from 'The tableau économique and its explanation'; see Meek 1973: 115, 118. The Explanation, written in co-operation with Quesnay, was first published in 1760. In this edition the 'Questions intéressantes sur la population l'agriculture et le commerce' appears in Suite de la IV Partie (which comprises tome V) without reference to Quesnay, though an informed reader could follow hints regarding authorship.

The reimpression of *L'Ami des hommes ou Traité de la population* by Scientia Verlag Aalen (1970) is of an Avignon edition comprising six *parties* in two volumes. The first three parts (volume 1) are dated 1756; the last three parts (volume 2), 1758, 1760, [n.d.], respectively. The statement by Mirabeau in this edition appears in volume 2, sixième partie, p. 215; it is part of a 'second part' comprising comments by Mirabeau on the 'Tableau Oeconomique avec ses explications par François Quesnay' which precedes it. The fourth part in this edition includes the 'Questions intéressantes . . . par François Quesnay'.

25 James, who may have used this edition, has the following:

MIRABEAU, VICTOR RIQUETTI, MARQUIS DE (1715–1789), of a Provençal family, originally from Naples: this *économiste* should not be confused with his two more dramatic sons, who were conspicuous during the French Revolution. The first three parts of *L'Ami des Hommes, ou Traité de la Population* were published anonymously in 1756; this is presumably why Malthus refers to 'the author of *L'Ami des Hommes*' in Bk. III, ch. xii, n. 17 although it is possible that it was prudent not to mention the name of Mirabeau in an English book in 1803.

Malthus's reference may be found on p. 84 of Vol. VI of the 1761 Avignon edition of *L'Ami des Hommes*. The catalogues of major libraries contain many versions of Mirabeau's works, which changed in character as he came more and more under the influence of Quesnay and the Physiocrats, and this set is described as *nouvelle edition corrigée*. Malthus's quotation is from a section of separately numbered pages – *L'Ami des Hommes, suite de la VI Partie* – and is devoted to the 'Tableau Economique avec ses explications'. Malthus translates Mirabeau fairly literally – 'j'avois . . . fondamentalement erré' – but omits Mirabeau's tribute to Quesnay as one more able than himself, who had confronted him with his mistake, and to whom he had been happy to listen.

(James 1989, 2: 309)

The references to a chapter xii of Book III in the 1803 edition and to note 17 are to James's variorum edition, not the original.

REFERENCES

Chisholm, G. G. (ed.) (1902) *Longman's Gazetteer of the World*, London: Longmans, Green and Co.

Einaudi, L. (1958) 'A propos de la date de publication de la "Physiocratie" ', in INED, 1: 1–9.

Eltis, W. (1984) *The Classical Theory of Economic Growth*, London: Macmillan.

Grampp, W. D. (1954) 'Malthus on Money Wages and Welfare', *American Economic Review*, 46 (December): 924–36.

—— (1984) 'Review: *The Malthus Library Catalogue*, Pergamon Press, 1983', *History of Political Economy*, 16, 4 (Winter): 640–2.

Higgs, H. (1935) *Bibliography of Economics 1751–1775*, Cambridge: Cambridge University Press.

INED [Institut National d'Etudes Démographiques] (1958) *François Quesnay et la Physiocratie*, 2 vols, Paris.

Malthus, T. R. (1986) *The Works of Thomas Robert Malthus*, 8 vols (year of each work given in the text), E. A. Wrigley and D. Souden (eds), London: Pickering and Chatto.

—— (1989) *An Essay on the Principle of Population*, 2 vols, Patricia James (ed.), Cambridge: Cambridge University Press.

'Meek, R. L. (1962) *The Economics of Physiocracy*, London: George Allen and Unwin.

—— (1973) *Precursors of Adam Smith, 1750–1775*, London: Dent.

Murphy, A. E. (1986) *Richard Cantillon: Entrepreneur and Economist*, Oxford: Clarendon Press.

Thweatt, W. P. (1987) 'The Classicals' Citations to the Physiocrats and Turgot', *History of Economic Thought Newsletter*, 38 (Spring): 29–32.

16

MALTHUS'S ABANDONMENT OF AGRICULTURAL PROTECTIONISM
A discovery in the history of economic thought*

Thomas Robert Malthus, it is universally known, opted for agricultural protection in the great Corn Law debates at the close of the Napoleonic Wars. He was the only major economist to do so and has been regarded ever since as something of an anomaly. This essay reports a finding that seems to remove the anomaly – the apparent fact that Malthus as early as 1824 withdrew his support for the prohibitory Corn Laws. The episode lends credence to his persistent claim that his original protectionism was not designed to defend the Class Interests of landowners but reflected rather his perception of the National Interest – a perception which required modification with the beginning of the end of the old Commercial System and in the light of the actual experience of industrial buoyancy. The *volte face* entailed a profound reorientation of analytical perspective, amounting to renunciation of support for balanced growth and self-sufficiency in food in favour of industry-based growth – the Ricardian position. An Historiographical Addendum addresses Malthus's failure to correct the oversight of his contemporaries who were unaware of the change. This discussion also throws light on the puzzling neglect by scholars of the numerous statements by Malthus indicating an abandonment of agricultural protectionism.[1]

I. THE EVIDENCE

I start by taking account of extensive alterations between the first (1820) and second (1836) editions of the *Principles of Political Economy*. In considering this evidence caution is in order since Malthus died suddenly 'before he had completed the whole of the alterations which he had in contemplation, and while he was yet occupied in correcting and improving the latter parts of the work' (Otter 1836: xi). It proves pertinent that alterations

* My sincere thanks for their comments on the numerous drafts of this paper to Bob Black, Giovanni Caravale, Robert Dorfman, Stanley Engerman, Barry Gordon, Noah Meltz, Salim Rashid, Sergio Nistico, Sandra Peart, John Pullen, Bette Polkinghorn, Paul Samuelson, George Stigler, Tony Waterman and Donald Winch.

269

towards the close of the *Principles* are less extensive than those in the early parts, suggesting that the views expressed there 'are not necessarily Malthus's final views' (Pullen 1989: lxv).

The most striking alteration is the removal of material in the chapter on rent involving a supposed excess of social over private return to agricultural investment and a case for protection based upon it. Included in the deletion is a reference to the argument in the chapter 'Of Corn Laws: Restrictions Upon Importation' in the 1817 *Essay on Population* (5th edn) whereby the loss sustained by the landlord from free trade would not usually be 'counterbalanced' by a proportionate gain to the state (Malthus 1820: 218). Also deleted are various specific warnings in 1820 regarding free trade. These include the dire consequences likely to follow significant reliance upon the cotton industry as a means of obtaining food: 'and woe will, I fear, befal us, greater than ever we have yet experienced, if the prosperity of our cotton trade should become necessary to purchase the food of any considerable body of our people!' (236n). Removed too is a note of 1820 justifying agricultural protection on the dual grounds that (a) investment in permanent agricultural improvements constitutes a means of effectively adding to the land supply; and (b) that there had occurred an 'alarming' increase in 'the *proportion* of our manufacturing population' (223n). A further excision is a note warning of the glutted markets likely to result if British capital were devoted largely to manufacturing (331n). And absent too is the relevant text asserting that 'A country, which accumulates faster than its neighbours, might for hundreds of years still keep up its rate of profits, if it were successful in making permanent improvements in the land' (332); the policy conclusion flowing from this perspective – that a growth programme turning on manufacturing and involving corn imports was bound to be stifled prematurely; and the application of these principles to contemporary Britain.

The second edition of the *Principles* leaves unchanged a statement, at the very end of the book, on agricultural protection as the exception to the general free-trade rule: 'I have already stated, in more places than one, why, under all the circumstances of the case, I think it desirable that we should permanently grow nearly our own consumption of corn' (Malthus 1820: 508; 1836: 427). What weight should be given to this formal retention of the protectionist exception? I would say little when placed in the balance against the extensive deletions made in the *Principles* itself – here one must remember that the new edition was never fully revised by Malthus, and that alterations between editions are less extensive in later parts of the book – and against evidence of the rejection of agricultural protection in a famous *Quarterly Review* article of 1824, in a note in the 1826 *Essay on Population* (6th edn) and in three letters of 1832–3.

When exactly the changes to the *Principles* were made is unclear. But

Malthus's article of 1824 on Ricardian political economy intimates a change of attitude by its insistence that no 'forced encouragement should be given to agriculture', and by its reference to the 'improved views of our government in commercial legislation' – the Huskisson reforms (Malthus 1986, 7: 267, 287).[2] Confirmation that these remarks must be taken seriously is provided by a note to the chapter 'Of Corn Laws: Restrictions on Importation' in the 1826 edition of the *Essay on Population*, a work ready for the press by late 1825. This note refers to articles by J. R. McCulloch (1824a) and J. S. Mill (1825) maintaining that a free corn trade assured against major price fluctuations. This Malthus denied, but he conceded that, considering the interests of the commercial world as a whole, a free corn trade was nevertheless desirable. Now Malthus had rejected this universalist concern in the 1817 *Essay* on the grounds that it was 'visionary' considering the potency of nationalist sentiment (1817, 2: 506; 1986, 3: 436). This earlier statement is repeated in the 1826 text, but the added note takes a wholly internationalist perspective implying that the experiment was after all worth trying. The appropriate policy was one that did not 'impeach the principles of free trade':

> I am very far however from meaning to say that the circumstances of different countries having often an abundance or deficiency of corn at the same time, though it must prevent the possibility of steady prices, is a decisive reason against the abolition or alteration of the corn laws. The most powerful of all the arguments against restrictions is their unsocial tendency, and the acknowledged injury which they must do to the interests of the commercial world in general. The weight of this argument is increased rather than diminished by the numbers which may suffer from scarcity at the same time. And at a period when our ministers are most laudably setting an example of a more liberal system of commercial policy, it would be greatly desirable that foreign nations should not have so marked an exception as our present corn laws to cast in our teeth. A duty on importation not too high, and a bounty nearly such as was recommended by Mr Ricardo, would probably be best suited to our present situation, and best secure steady prices. A duty on foreign corn would resemble the duties laid by other countries on our manufactures as objects of taxation, and would not in the same manner impeach the principles of free trade.
>
> (Malthus 1826, 2: 209n; 1986, 3: 436n)[3]

The essential point of the 1826 note is its recommendation to replace the 1815 prohibitory system by a system designed 'not to . . . impeach the principles of free trade'. Much more is involved than a simple recommendation to lower an existing tariff. The plan for a 'substantially free trade in corn' as David Ricardo himself phrased it in 1822 (Ricardo 1951, IV: 266) – a plan overwhelmingly rejected by the House of Commons – entailed a duty on corn imports as countervail for differential taxation imposed on British farmers *relative to British manufacturers*, with an appropriate drawback on exports (243). Ricardo was careful to distinguish his proposed drawback from a regular export subsidy. The purpose of the recommendation was to assure not to distort competitive resource allocation.[4]

Malthus's transformation is further confirmed in three letters, one to Nassau Senior dated 31 March 1829, the second to Thomas Chalmers dated 6 March 1832 and the third to Jane Marcet dated 22 January 1833. The first maintains that even a temporary increase in real wages due to the relaxation of corn import restrictions would be desirable:

> It does not by any means follow from these principles, that we should not use our utmost endeavour to make two ears of wheat grow where one grew before, or to improve our commercial code by freeing it from restraints. An increase of population is in itself a very decided advantage, if it be not accompanied by an increased *proportion* of vice and misery. And the period during which the pressure of population is lightened, though it may not be of long duration, is a period of comparative ease, and ought by no means to be thrown out of our consideration.
>
> (Malthus in Senior 1829: 85)

The letter to Chalmers reads simply: 'I quite agree with you in regard to the moral advantage of repealing the corn laws' (Chalmers papers, CHA4.185.32).[5] James cites this remark, noting that it 'might have surprised Malthus's contemporaries' (James 1979: 433). Indeed so – unless they had read and remembered the 1824 article, the alterations to the *Principles*, and the note in the 1826 edition of the *Essay*.

The third letter of the early 1830s, to Marcet, relates to her *John Hopkins's Notions on Political Economy* and contains the following passage:

> If I were obliged to find any fault, I should say that you have presented in rather too brilliant and unshaded colours the advantages which would accrue from the abolition of the Corn Laws, so as to excite expectations which cannot be realized. *In the actual state of the redundancy of labour in this country, it appears to me scarcely possible to conceive that the money wages of labour will not fall nearly in proportion to the price of corn, and the labourers be greatly disappointed.* It will no doubt give a stimulus to foreign trade; but it must for a considerable time aggravate the redundancy of labour in country parishes; and during the process of the change, there will probably be more thrown out of work than in any other case of the restrictions of the freedom of trade, on account of the largeness of the concerns. It will also tend to raise the value of money and increase the pressure of the national debt. *Still I am for the removal of the restrictions*, though not without fear of the consequences.

(Malthus in Polkinghorn 1986: 845, italics in the original)

The dangers of a free corn trade alluded to here are partly of a transitional nature. What the apparently longer-term 'consequences' to be feared were it is difficult to say, but Malthus might have had in mind the implications of a reduced price level mentioned in the penultimate sentence. But in any event, he closes by calling for 'the removal of the restrictions'.

II. THE RATIONALE

I now consider *why* Malthus called for the transition to free trade. The primary question is whether the new perspective implied the abandonment of various original arguments favouring protection or only their reduced weighting against the often-recognized *disadvantages* of protection – domestic efficiency losses, check to population growth and discouragement of manufactures (e.g. 1817, 2: 475; 1986, 3: 423) – in the light of new theoretical and empirical considerations. I shall focus first on the note in the *Essay on Population* of 1826 and then look further afield.

As will be recalled, that note refers to the contemporary period as one 'when our ministers are most laudably setting an example [to the world] of a more liberal system of commercial policy'; foreign nations should not be allowed 'so marked an exception as our present corn laws to cast in our teeth'. Malthus evidently approved of the first breaches in the old 'Commercial System' and saw the Corn Laws as an impediment to bringing foreign countries into line.[6] The note is not simply a reaffirmation that from a cosmopolitan viewpoint free trade in corn was desirable, but implies an estimate that, given the new British policy, global free trade involving the full range of products was no longer a pipe dream – indeed, liberalization of corn imports would provide a potent weapon for its achievement.[7]

What of the net cost to Britain of the abandonment of agricultural protection? There are a number of considerations here. The original case for protection turned partly on grounds of increased instability of output in a free-trade régime, considering the potential for disruption during wartime (Malthus 1817, 2: 500–1; 1986, 3: 432–3). Conceivably, the newly recognized possibility of global free trade – to which end it was hoped the abandonment of the Corn Laws by Britain would contribute – was envisaged as decreasing the probability of such disturbances. Similarly, the prospect of reductions of French corn-export restrictions in response to the new British policy would be enhanced, reducing the 'security' problem so much emphasized in 1815 (1986, 7: 156). The matter of improved international morality is admittedly speculative, but the enthusiasm with which the prospect was greeted by Malthus suggests that it cannot be dismissed. J. S. Mill, of course, was to take the matter *very* seriously.

There can be little doubt about the destiny of that part of the original

273

case for the Corn Laws turning on the need to counter 'mercantilist' regulations favouring manufactures (1817, 2: 445; 1986, 3: 431). This particular dimension would without question have been rendered increasingly obsolete by the new governmental programme. Even so, it would not account for the transition in its entirety since the full protectionist case related to the prevention of an otherwise 'natural' tendency towards a preponderance of manufacturing.

An important dimension to Malthus's positive response to the new government policy emerges in his 1824 *Quarterly Review* article. There he allowed that expansion of foreign markets for British manufactures had mitigated the worst effects of the post-war depression by drawing labour from the agricultural sector:

> In the period which has elapsed since the return of peace, the difficulty of finding employment, particularly on the land, has been too notorious to require proof; and if, owing to the extraordinary stimulus given to the population by the previous demand for it, it still continues to increase with rapidity, yet there is reason to think that the present demand would not nearly have kept pace with the rate of increase, and that great distress would have been the consequence, if the happy opening of new and large channels of foreign commerce, combined with the improved views of our government in commercial legislation, had not prepared the way for a renewed demand for labour.
>
> (Malthus 1824; 1986, 7: 287)

It is particularly relevant, in the light of the 1826 note, that the expansion of foreign markets is here partly ascribed to the 'improved views of our government in commercial legislation'. The empirical significance of manufactures from the perspective of aggregate activity reinforced the case for free trade since expanded markets could scarcely be relied upon with agriculture 'so marked an exception' to a general free-trade programme. The protectionist case of 1815 had turned partly on the unrealistically large expansion of manufacturing required to absorb even the agricultural workers who were unemployed in 1815 (Malthus 1986, 7: 163, 167). By the mid-1820s, the manufacturing sector was proving itself adequate in that respect. Actually, even when making his case for agricultural protection in 1815 and in the 1817 essay, Malthus had included the discouragement of manufactures amongst the costs of such a policy (1815; 1986, 7: 105–6; 1817, 2: 475; 1986, 3: 423). This concern becomes decisive in 1824.

To appreciate better what is entailed by the free-trade proposal, it is necessary to revert to the original position in *Grounds of an Opinion* (1815). There it is affirmed that the loss of agricultural capital and output is more damaging than a similar loss in other sectors: 'no loss, in proportion to its amount, affects the interest of the nation so deeply, and vitally, and is so difficult to recover, as the loss of agricultural capital and produce' (Malthus

1986, 7: 165). In what consists 'the interest of the nation' which is peculiarly reflected by the health of the agricultural sector? The same question
emerges again in a discussion of the landowning class. Though landowners
'do not so actively contribute to the production of wealth, as either of the
classes just noticed, there is no class in society whose interests are more
nearly and intimately connected with the prosperity of the state' (1986, 7:
167). In this context Malthus adopts Adam Smith's (physiocratic) proposition that 'no equal quantity of productive labour employed in manufactures
can ever occasion so great a reproduction as in agriculture'. Again: 'If we
suppose the rents of land taken throughout the kingdom to be one fourth of
the gross produce, it is evident, that to purchase the same value of raw
produce by means of manufactures [exports], would require one third more
capital. Every five thousand pounds laid out on the land, not only repays the
usual profits of stock, but generates an additional value, which goes to the
landlord.' This 'additional value' would be erased by a free corn trade –
Malthus here recommends his *Rent* pamphlet – to the *national* detriment
from the perspective both of consumption power and tax revenue: 'And this
additional value is not a mere benefit to a particular individual, or set of
individuals, but affords the most steady home demand for the manufactures
of the country, the most effective fund for its financial support, and the
largest disposable force for its army and navy' (Malthus 1986, 7: 167–8).
Ricardo had strongly objected to this physiocratic dimension to the original
protectionist case on 13 February 1815 (Ricardo 1951, VI: 177–8).

The emphasis in 1824 on expenditure derived from export sales and the
rejection of pro-agricultural intervention implies *the abandonment of the case
for unproductive consumption by landlords*. In this regard, the Malthus–Chalmers
correspondence is highly revealing. For in the same letter to Chalmers of
March 1832 in which he wrote of his support for Corn Law repeal (cited
above), Malthus also defended *industrial exports* as essential to national wealth
and power and questioned the quantitative significance of aggregate demand
exerted by the 'dependents upon the landlords' compared with that exerted
by capitalists and traders:

> Have you not pushed too far the doctrine of the non-importance of
> foreign commerce? . . . Without [Britain's manufacturing exports] she
> would be less powerful, and I should certainly add less wealthy, though
> she might still be as strong in defensive war. *It is owing to the abundance
> of her exports, derived from her skill machinery and capital, that money rents
> and the money prices of corn and labour are high, and that with a small quan-
> tity of English labour a large quantity of the products of foreign labour is
> purchased.* The demand for useful and beneficial personal services is
> limited; and after all these have been fully paid, would it not be an
> impoverishing and very disadvantageous exchange to substitute for the

275

rich capitalists and comfortable and independent traders living upon the profits of stock, a body of dependents upon the landlords?

(Malthus, Chalmers papers; emphasis added)

Similarly in a letter of 16 February 1833 to Chalmers, Malthus wrote:

Do not manufactures and commerce increase the *Revenue* of a country, and *enlarge* the *returning power*? I own I cannot but think that if the taste for luxuries and superior conveniences were at an end, the cultivation of the land would be essentially deteriorated, – at least under the present division of landed property. How could the actual number of labourers have an adequate demand for the produce of the soil, if commerce and manufactures were greatly to be diminished? What numbers would be out of work! What constant calls for an extension of Poor Laws, and of all public and private charities.

(Malthus, Chalmers papers)

This is much the same point that Malthus had already made in 1824.[8]

There were indeed earlier allusions by Malthus to the significance of manufacturing (even in 1815), including the export sector, for the maintenance of activity to the advantage of agriculture itself. But now this theme is reiterated forcefully with an eye to the growing empirical significance of the export sector; and it is no longer part of a protectionist case to assure sectoral balance in an economy 'naturally' becoming predominantly industrial, but rather *part of a free-trade case justifying such imbalance.*

In his evidence to the Commons Select Committee on Emigration on 5 May 1827, Malthus commented thus on the view that low wages are favourable to trade and commerce: 'In one respect it is, and in one respect not; it may enable the capitalist to work up his commodities cheaper, and to extend his foreign trade, but it certainly will have a tendency to diminish the home trade, and I think the home trade much more important than the foreign' (House of Commons Parliamentary Papers 1827, V: question 3285). This might seem to suggest no change whatsoever in Malthus's original physiocratic stance. But Malthus was concerned here to emphasize that 'the extent of the effectual demand for manufactures and commodities consumed at home, depends essentially upon the good condition of the labouring classes' (question 3282). His comment compares the positive impact on demand of expanded exports due to wage reductions with the fall in domestic demand entailed by wage reductions, a theme foreign to earlier formulations with their emphasis on the advantage of high expenditure out of *rent*.

More generally, from the viewpoint of labour's welfare, evidence has been provided by Gilbert (1980) of a new emphasis discernible in the 1817 *Essay* upon industry-biased growth as typically characteristic of the later stages of economic development because of growing land and scarcity, and an increasing taste for industrial products, and along with it, the retraction of much of an earlier concern with such growth from *labour's* perspective. The evidence given in this paper points to the implications for trade policy of this orientation.

Can Malthus's new policy position be understood, at least in part, in terms of increasing pessimism regarding British agricultural prospects? In 1814 diminishing returns had been specified as one objection to the proposed Corn Bill (1986, 7: 107–8). When in 1815 he opted for protectionism, he took account of other overriding arguments (arguments which by the mid-1820s were in the course of becoming obsolete). And in the 1817 *Essay* (repeated in 1826) he affirmed that agricultural protectionism was partly justified by buoyant prospects for ongoing accumulation and population growth at steady, even rising, wages and with no downward pressure on the profit rate (1817, 2: 491–4; 1986, 3: 429–30). My question, therefore, is whether Malthus reinstated diminishing returns as a major part of the new case for free trade.

Several of the revisions to the *Principles* discussed above point to this conclusion, including the removal (a) of the justification for protection on the grounds that permanent agricultural improvements effectively add to the land supply, and related statements (applied to Britain) regarding prospective agricultural-based growth proceeding for 'hundreds of years' without decline in the profit rate; and (b) of the proposition that 'a great demand for corn of home growth must tend greatly to encourage improvements in agriculture' (1820: 332, 324). It seems that some allowance is required for a reevaluation of agricultural prospects in approaching the new attitude towards industry-based growth. This too would imply a further undermining of physiocratic bias.

As for other possible considerations, the 'moral' perspective adopted by Chalmers might be relevant. Malthus, it will be recalled, approved in 1832. That it was a consideration in the early 1820s is an open possibility. For the question of 'morality' is implicitly raised in 1823 when Malthus showed marked impatience with the pretensions of the landlords – their proposal to adjust contracts to their own benefit at the expense of fundholders – which is unlike anything he wrote earlier and as sharp as anything written by Ricardo (Malthus 1823: 80–1; 1986, 7: 220–1).

There remains some doubt whether or not Malthus still maintained that balanced growth was essential in *the very long run* since foreign sales of home manufactures could not *ultimately* be relied upon – a central argument against 'Commercial Systems' in the *Essay on Population*.[9] One cannot be certain, but the 1824 article suggests that a matter of principle rather than of temporary expediency was involved: The circumstance that agricultural capital 'adds a *much greater value* . . . than any equal capital employed in manufactures' (1986, 7: 267), did *not* justify 'any forced encouragement . . . to agriculture' since this 'would probably defeat the very end in view'. And a caution retained in the 1826 *Essay*, regarding distant prospects for US diversification threatening British sales of manufactures, is deliberately qualified: 'I am very far from meaning to insinuate that an advantage, while it lasts, should not be used, merely because it will not continue for ever. But if the advantage be in its nature temporary, it is surely prudent to have this in view, and to use it in such a way that when it ceases it may not have been productive, on the whole, of more evil than good' (Malthus 1826, 2: 152; 1986, 3: 404).

III. SUMMARY AND CONCLUSIONS

I have argued that Malthus's transition to free agricultural trade constitutes his positive response to the government's new liberal trade programme with its promise of major expansion of British manufacturing exports – assuming the removal of barriers to corn imports – and his recognition of a contemporary absorption into the industrial sector of surplus agricultural capital and labour. The new liberal policy also undermined that part of his original concern with industry structure reflecting artificial stimuli accorded manufactures.

More is in question than a change of perception regarding the state of the contemporary economy, although growing concern with land scarcity may have played a role in addition to the alteration in government policy. For much of Malthus's original protectionism reflected 'agricultural bias', including a concern to prevent the disproportionate expansion of industry even in a freely operating system. A reorientation of analytical perspective seems to be involved which contributed to the abandonment of agricultural protectionism – renunciation of the case for balanced growth in favour of industry-based growth, and growing dissatisfaction with physiocratic conceptions including the dependency of expenditure levels on the magnitude of rental incomes.[10]

That Malthus championed free trade solely on the cosmopolitan grounds of international morality may also be dismissed. Although the note of 1826 argues for free trade in terms of net *universal* advantage, my analysis of the specifics of the case suggests that Malthus also envisaged prospective net advantages for Britain. He may not have abandoned entirely a secular concern with the reliability of foreign sources of food supply, but this was now given a sufficiently low weight to be outweighed by the advantages of new openings in the more immediate future for British manufacturing exports, in conjunction with the long-recognized efficiency advantages of free trade.

APPENDIX: HISTORIOGRAPHICAL ADDENDUM

Since no one apparently referred to his adoption of the free-trade position why did not Malthus, between 1824 and his death, correct the oversight of his contemporaries? Was it perhaps so trifling a change that it could be left quiescent? Worse still, could Torrens have been mistaken in saying of Malthus that he 'possesse[d], in a very eminent degree, a spirit of candour and a love of truth' (Torrens 1815: xi); or Ricardo when he wrote of Malthus in a letter of 13 October 1819 that 'a more candid or better man nowhere exists' whose 'erroneous opinions respecting the expediency of a free trade in corn . . . are honest conscientious opinions' (Ricardo 1951, IX: 101)? After all, several parliamentary figures (including of course Huskisson) did convert regarding the merits of the 1815 Act and made no bones about it.

There is perhaps a hint of a lessening of concern with the policy question,[11] but the problem can better be resolved in terms of Malthus's failure to complete the second edition of the *Principles of Political Economy*, for had he himself published the revised version – and explicitly pointed out the deletions of protectionist passages – his new view could not possibly have remained a public secret. In the event, the second edition evinced little interest, and the nature and import of the revisions have been camouflaged ever since by the lack of a variorum edition. The only major notice was that by William Empson for the *Edinburgh Review* (1837) and he missed entirely the import of the changes documented in this paper: 'In substance and in doctrine, it contains the principles of Political Economy taught by Mr Malthus' (in Malthus 1963: 234). This is simply misleading. If my case is well made out, Malthus's procrastination in completing the new edition may reflect his need to absorb the implications of the theoretical and policy reorientation, a problem not faced by the politicians. Certainly more than the usual courage would have been required to undertake a concerted campaign to spread the word, for after 1815 Malthus was all but blacklisted by the *Edinburgh Review* because of his prohibitionism, and he was obliged to turn to the ultra-Tory *Quarterly Review*. Had his new position become public knowledge, he would without question have been subjected to virulent charges of treachery.[12] His unwillingness to go further than he did to broadcast his new position is not difficult to appreciate in these terms.

Finally, what of the 1826 note? Several colleagues have shamefacedly admitted to skipping footnotes. Were this common practice, it would partly explain the puzzle that Malthus's new position has been under wraps for nearly 170 years. However, the note is only one of several indications of the change of policy – so one is obliged to revert to the unfinished nature of the revisions to the *Principles of Political Economy* to explain the puzzle. The importance of the 1826 note lies rather in its adoption of Ricardo's specific free-trade scheme as the appropriate policy.

NOTES

1 Patricia James (1979) and Bette Polkinghorn (1986) have brought to our attention Malthus's letters of 1832–33 which suggest an altered position at

that late date on 'moral grounds'. But these taken by themselves raise more questions than they answer. Geoffrey Gilbert has discerned in Malthus an increasingly balanced view of industrial and agricultural growth as potential contributors to working-class welfare (Gilbert 1980: 93). But he denies that this indicates an evolution towards Ricardo's 'pro-industrial' bias, and in any event does not discuss implications for trade policy.

2 The first formal amendments to the Navigation Acts were introduced in Parliament in 1822 followed by more extensive reforms in 1823 (especially the Reciprocity of Duties Bill). A free-trade budget in 1824 reduced protective duties on a wide variety of goods, and removed the linen export bounty, restrictions on the export of British wool and also various prohibitions on the use of foreign silk goods (Smart 1910, II: 192f). A second free-trade budget of 1825 reduced protective duties on *inter alia* cottons, woollens, linens, paper and books, and iron.

3 The last sentence is ambiguous. But I understand 'and would not in the same manner . . .' to refer to foreign *revenue* tariffs – tariffs imposed 'as objects of taxation' – which do not 'impeach' free-trade principles. What Malthus had in mind, however, is unclear, since European countries were increasingly adopting protective legislation.

The penultimate sentence might be said to imply that only the drawback was to be à la Ricardo. But this is unlikely since Ricardo's drawback is part of a package designed to assure competitive resource allocation as we shall see.

4 Robert Torrens claimed priority for the scheme and justified it on free trade grounds (Torrens 1826: vi–vii). J. S. Mill accepted Ricardo's countervailing duty in principle (1825; 1967: 68). J. R. McCulloch (1824b), too, championed the Ricardo scheme and Mill draws on his account in elaborating the case. Malthus may have been reminded of the Ricardo scheme by Mill's 1825 article to which he refers in the note.

5 The moral dimension – which outweighed for Chalmers the danger inherent in dependence on foreign food supplies – entailed avoidance of 'the certain and urgent evil of a dissatisfied population; who feel, and perhaps with justice too, as if defrauded of their rights, by the compulsory restraints of the legislature on the importation of food' (Chalmers 1832: 533–4; see also 539).

6 At precisely this time, Mill was making the same case, that 'the mutual support which every monopoly lends to every other, is one of the strongest reasons why they should all be destroyed' (1825; 1967: 66). Both William Huskisson and the Chancellor of the Exchequer (F. J. Robinson) made the point that to allow exceptions was to impede the whole trend towards free trade.

7 In 1824, Malthus reacted similarly to the freeing of machinery exportation from controls in evidence given to the Commons Select Committee on Artizans and Machinery, 10 May 1824 (House of Commons Parliamentary Papers, V: 600).

8 The Inverarity manuscript – a student's notes of Malthus's lectures delivered c. 1830 – also contains heavy emphasis on the 'advantages of manufactures and commerce' in the course of a critique of Physiocracy (Pullen 1981: 809).

9 The context involves proposals for Europe to devote itself entirely to manufactures in exchange for American corn. The presumption is that each 'landed' country will (with internal population growth) divert increasing fractions of its agricultural output to internal requirements, reducing correspondingly its corn exports. The trade in corn is thus said to be a distinctly *non-permanent* trade; it should be viewed as no more than a means of balancing temporary require-

ments, not as a trade upon which could be based the international division of labour (Malthus 1817, 2: 482–3; 1986, 3: 425–6).

10 The causal sequence may, however, have been the reverse – the undermining of agricultural protectionism on the various grounds documented in this paper obliging a continuous questioning of physiocratic perceptions. In all likelihood, the sequences were mutually reinforcing.

11 The desirability of an artificial maintenance of 'a balance between the agricultural and commercial classes of society' is portrayed in 1817 as 'the most important practical question in the whole compass of political economy'; but in 1826 as 'a most important practical question' (Malthus 1817, 2: 477; 1986, 3: 424). This, however, does not carry one too far since the change in policy itself reflects, or at least parallels, a profound analytical reorientation.

12 Frank Fetter (1965: 431) provides the context.

REFERENCES

Chalmers, Thomas (1832) *On Political Economy*, Glasgow: William Collins.

Empson, William (1837) 'Life, Writings and Character of Mr Malthus', *Edinburgh Review*, 64 (January): 469–506.

Fetter, Frank W. (1965) 'Economic Controversy in the British Reviews, 1802–1850', *Economica* 32 (November): 424–37.

Gilbert, Geoffrey (1980) 'Economic Growth and the Poor in Malthus's *Essay on Population*', *History of Political Economy*, 12 (Spring): 83–96.

House of Commons Parliamentary Papers (1824) *Sixth Report from the Select Committee on Artizans and Machinery*, 10 May 1824, V: 598–601.

—— (1827) *Third Report from the Select Committee on Emigration*, 5 May 1827, V: 311–27.

James, Patricia (1979) *Population Malthus*, London: Routledge and Kegan Paul.

McCulloch, J. R. (1824a) 'Corn Laws and Corn Trade', *Supplement to Encyclopaedia Britannica*, 6th edn, III: 342–73.

—— (1824b) 'Price of Foreign Corn – Abolition of the Corn-Laws', *Edinburgh Review*, 41 (October), 55–78.

Malthus, Thomas R., Correspondence. Chalmers papers, New College, Edinburgh.

—— (1803) *Essay on the Principle of Population*, 2nd edn, London: J. Johnson.

—— (1806) *Essay on the Principle of Population*, 3rd edn, London: J. Johnson.

—— (1814) *Observations on the Effects of the Corn Laws*, London: J. Johnson.

—— (1815) *Grounds of an Opinion on the Policy of Restricting the Importation of Foreign Corn*, London: John Murray.

—— (1817) *Essay on the Principle of Population*, 5th edn, London: John Murray.

—— (1820) *Principles of Political Economy*, London: John Murray.

—— (1823) *Measure of Value*, London: John Murray.

—— (1824) 'Political Economy', *Quarterly Review*, 30 (January): 297–334.

—— (1826)*Essay on the Principle of Population*, 6th edn, London: John Murray.

—— (1836) *Principles of Political Economy*, 2nd edn, London: William Pickering.

—— (1963) *Occasional Papers of T. R. Malthus*, Bernard Semmel (ed.), New York: Burt Franklin.

—— (1986) *Works of Thomas Robert Malthus*, E. A. Wrigley and D. Souden (eds), London: Pickering.

—— (1989) *Principles of Political Economy*, Cambridge: Cambridge University Press.

Mill, J. S. (1825) (1967), 'The Corn Laws', *Westminster Review*, April 1825, 3: 394–420, in *Collected Works of John Stuart Mill*, 1967, Toronto: University of Toronto Press, 4: 45–70.

Otter, William (1836) 'Memoir of Robert Malthus' in T. R. Malthus, *Principles of Political Economy*, London: William Pickering, xiii–liv.

Polkinghorn, B. A. (1986) 'An Unpublished Letter from Malthus to Jane Marcet, 22 January 1833', *American Economic Review*, 76 (September): 845–7.

Pullen, John (1981) 'Notes from Malthus: the Inverarity manuscript', *History of Political Economy*, 13 (Spring): 794–811.

—— (1989) 'Introduction to Malthus', in T. R. Malthus, *Principles of Political Economy*, Vol. I, Cambridge: Cambridge University Press, xv–xix.

Ricardo, David (1951) *Works and Correspondence of David Ricardo*, P. Sraffa (ed.); IV, *Pamphlets, 1815–1823*; VI, *Letters, 1810–1815*; IX, *Letters, 1821–1823*; Cambridge: Cambridge University Press.

Senior, Nassau (1829) (1966), *Two Lectures on Population . . . to which is added, a Correspondence Between the Author and the Rev. T. R. Malthus*, 1829, London: Saunders and Otley; 1966, New York: Augustus M. Kelley.

Smart, William (1910) *Economic Annals of the Nineteenth Century*, London: Macmillan.

Torrens, Robert (1815) (1826), *Essay on the External Corn Trade*, 1815, London: J. Hatchard; 1826, 3rd edn, London: Longman, Rees, Orme, Brown and Green.

17

MORE ON MALTHUS AND AGRICULTURAL PROTECTION

John Pullen summarizes his case against my interpretation thus: 'There is no clear, unambiguous statement of recantation [by Malthus] on the Corn Law. Although Malthus in 1826 recommended a *reduction* in the level of the duty on imported corn, the textual evidence so far produced [in Hollander 1992; essay 16 in this collection] is, on balance, not sufficiently strong to justify the claim that in his later years he *abandoned* this agricultural exception to the "great general rule" of free trade' (Pullen 1995). I am not sure about the 'on balance', since Pullen takes exception to *every* single item of evidence I have brought in support of my case, leaving my pan on the scales quite empty. I shall explain why I am unconvinced by the objections.

A major item of evidence for my case is the 1826 note to the *Essay on Population*. One sentence from the note, Dr Pullen argues, 'clearly indicates that what was intended by Malthus was merely a reduction in the level of the existing tariff on corn imports, not an abolition of the tariff' (section 1.1). I beg to differ. Let me return the sentence to its context:

> The most powerful of all the arguments against restriction is their unsocial tendency, and the acknowledged injury that they must do to the interests of the commercial world in general. The weight of the argument is increased rather than diminished by the numbers which may suffer from scarcity at the same time. And at a period when our ministers are most laudably setting an example of a more liberal system of commercial policy, it would be greatly desirable that foreign nations should not have so marked an exception as our present corn-laws to cast in our teeth. *A duty on importation not too high, and a bounty nearly such as was recommended by Mr Ricardo, would probably be best suited to our present situation and best secure steady prices.* A duty on foreign corn would resemble the duties laid by other countries on our manufactures

as objects of taxation, and would not in the same manner impeach the principles of free trade.

(Malthus 1826, II: 209n; cited Hollander 1992: 652; emphasis added)

Notice that the full passage makes a case 'against restriction' and proceeds to refer to the need to get rid of 'our present corn-laws' in the interests of 'a more liberal system of commercial policy'. The going system would be replaced by a duty on foreign corn resembling foreign duties on British manufactures *as objects of taxation* – suggesting a revenue tariff – 'not impeach[ing] the principles of free trade'.[1] The mere fact that Malthus allows a tariff in no way indicates continued support for *protectionism*; both Ricardo and Smith, after all, also made out cases for a (non-protective) tariff. It is true, as I myself indicated in my paper, that Malthus's reference to Ricardo is ambiguous since it is not absolutely clear that he proposed Ricardo's specific duty designed as countervail against differential domestic burdens imposed on agriculture (Hollander 1992: 652n). But whatever his position on this particular, he was now rejecting *protective* tariffs, or tariffs that do 'impeach' free-trade principles. Consider also the fact that the 'present corn laws' involved the principle of import *prohibition* – in 1815 free imports at corn prices above 80 shillings per quarter and exclusion below 80 shillings; in 1822 a sliding-scale system of duties above 70 shillings and prohibition below 70 shillings. Malthus is calling for the replacement of *this system* by a non-distorting tariff, not reduction in the level of an existing tariff.

I cannot fathom Pullen's paragraph 1.3. As I specify in my article, the section cited from the note is indeed preceded by a denial that a free corn trade would assure greater stability of the corn price. But the fact is that *notwithstanding* this denial, Malthus proceeds very distinctly: 'I am very far however from meaning to say that the circumstance of different countries having often an abundance or deficiency of corn at the same time, though it must prevent the possibility of steady prices, is a decisive reason against the abolition or alteration of the corn laws' (1826, II: 209n).

Pullen argues that since the chapter of the *Essay* in which the note appears ('Restrictions upon Importation') is substantially unaltered in the case it makes out for agricultural protection, 'it is difficult to see how the new 1826 footnote to chapter 12 can be taken as evidence of rejection of agricultural protection'. This is unhelpful. Of course the choice by Malthus of the device of a footnote to a substantially unchanged chapter to state his new position is problematic; my historical addendum was addressed precisely to this problem. Whether my explanation convinces or does not convince – Pullen neglects it entirely – does not alter the *fact* of the insertion and its message.

In my explanation of Malthus's procedure, I sought to avoid the charge of disingenuousness. My suggestion ran in terms of fear of the likely Tory response in the event of a highly publicized declaration, which to my mind is not necessarily to be identified with lack of candour. It has, however, come to my attention that in another context such a charge has been made. Thus Waterman in the theological context has recently maintained that though Malthus 'in attack was an admirable, indeed exemplary controversialist, courteous, magnanimous and fair-minded; in retreat he was less gracious, correcting logical slips by minimal, unadvertised amendments, and camouflaging retraction by a verbal smokescreen' (Waterman 1991: 147). I would prefer to avoid this sort of conclusion, though if, at the end of the day, it proves impossible to do so, then so be it.

There is, however, a further consideration. The fact is that the note closes with a paragraph representing the chapter not as a case *for* protection but as a balanced evaluation of pros and cons, and positively insists that its retention in the new edition of the *Essay* was 'not . . . a kind of protest against the abolition or change of the corn laws': 'But whatever system we may adopt, it is essential to a sound determination, and highly useful in preventing disappointments, that all the arguments both for and against corn-laws should be thoroughly and impartially considered; and it is because on a calm, and, as far as I can judge, an impartial review of the arguments of this chapter, they still appear to me of weight sufficient to deserve such consideration, *and not as a kind of protest against the abolition or change of the corn-laws*, that I republish them in another edition' (Malthus 1826, II: 209n; emphasis added). And it is true enough that in the body of the chapter Malthus had himself stated that the balanced growth policy 'may be purchased too dear', and could not be recommended as a hard-and-fast rule (1817, II: 477–8; 1826, II: 186–7). The stage had been set for a renunciation of the case for balanced growth in the new circumstances that Britain encountered.

III.

Pullen remarks that Malthus supported the Corn Laws in 1815 'not to protect or encourage agriculture as an end in itself . . . [but] to maintain "an independent supply" of corn' (section 2.3; see also section 3). This is far too narrow a perspective since so much more was involved than the so-called 'security' issue. The case extended to *balanced growth* as a matter of developmental principle. But if circumstances are such – as indeed they were given the relative British cost structure – that in an open trading system Britain would import (some of) her corn in exchange for manufactures, then the maintenance of balanced growth assuring self-sufficiency in corn obviously entails the 'forced encouragement' of agriculture. In his 1824 article, Malthus rejected such forced encouragement (Hollander 1992: 657), and thereby intimated rejection of protectionism; continued support of the Corn Laws would be inconsistent with the new opposition to forced encouragement. And the new position can be partly accounted for, I have argued, by awareness of the growing role played by the manufacturing sector (manufacturing exports in particular) in the maintenance of general activity.[2] The observed change in the vision of the economy *undermined* the case for balanced growth and with it agricultural protection.

I might add that the Malthus–Ricardo correspondence is highly pertinent to the original case of protection. In a (non-extant) letter of 1818 reported by Ricardo (24 June; 1951–73, VII: 270–1), Malthus raised 'the question of the comparative advantage of employing capital in agriculture or on manufactures' and implied a physiocratic-Smithian conception of rent as a *net* contribution to wealth generated only in agriculture. To this, Ricardo objected that the increase of real national income in the war years 1793–1813 (a period of effective protection), reflected in an increase of rent, would have been yet larger in the event of free trade, though it would have taken the form of profits. Malthus then attempted to turn the wartime circumstances against Ricardo. The empirical experience of rising profits (without reduction in wages) simultaneously with expansion of national income in the form of rent, indicated for him that rent was a 'creation' not a 'transfer' from profits (16 August; 279). Now this expansion, he maintained, *would not have occurred in the event of reliance on foreign corn*: 'if [rents] have risen chiefly from improvements in agriculture occasioned by the direction of so much capital to the land in consequence of a high price [of] corn, is it not an increase of wealth which would not otherwise have been obtained?' Evidently the original case for agricultural protection turned, *pace* Pullen, on profound matters of analytical principle extending far beyond the issue of 'an independent supply'. By 1824 this was no longer the line taken, at least in the policy context.

IV.

Let me briefly turn to the *Principles* and the references I gave to various omissions from the second edition taken up by Pullen (sections 4.1–4.3). Pullen recognizes the deletion of a series of protectionist passages, but he reverts back to the protectionism of the 1826 *Essay*. This will not do at all, for he deliberately neglects the new footnote. Combined with the insertion of that footnote, the changes to the *Principles* point unmistakably to a major change in perspective on protectionism. Pullen then refers to that 'important non-omitted statement in the *Principles*' (section 5) which I take up in my article (Hollander 1992: 651). Since it is Pullen himself who in his splendid Introduction to the *Principles* points out that 'the alterations in the second edition of the *Principles* are more frequent and more extensive in the earlier chapters than in the later ones', implying perhaps that 'the views expressed in the later, less-corrected parts are not necessarily Malthus's final views' (1989, I: lxv), his hesitancy now is surprising. Moreover, while Cazenove and Empson believed that Malthus had completed all he considered essential

(Pullen 1995, sections 5.2 and 5.3), William Otter pointed to Malthus's sudden death 'before he had completed the whole of the alterations which he had in contemplation, and while he was yet occupied in correcting and improving the latter parts of the work' (cited in Hollander 1992: 650).

V.

Extraordinary it is that Malthus's protectionism did not become common knowledge. This fact reflects the problem which I have openly stated: 'Why did not Malthus between 1824 and his death, correct the oversight of his contemporaries?' (Hollander 1992: 658). For the moment I can offer no fresh insights beyond those given in my addendum; but the textual evidence of the change of position stands unaffected by the problem.[3] At the same time, we should not exaggerate the problem. We must not forget that Malthus *did* speak out to several of his friends. I have referred to them in my paper, and Pullen's negative reaction does not impress me. Malthus's agreement in 1832 with Chalmers on 'the moral advantage of repealing the corn laws', he says, tells us nothing because it does not indicate the significance of this dimension relative to the arguments *for* protection (section 6).[4] This reaction reflects a general weakness of Pullen's paper – that he takes each of my pieces of evidence in isolation from the others, purports to dispose of each, and then proceeds to the next *table rase*. To me, the letter to Chalmers reinforces the validity of my interpretation of the 1824 article, the 1826 note and the omissions from the *Principles*. Pullen's reaction (section 7.2) to Malthus's unambiguous statement that he was, *for the removal of the restrictions*, in the letter to Jane Marcet of 22 January 1833 (Hollander 1992: 652), I also find to be baseless. Why not read the letter in a natural and easy fashion rather than as asserting the opposite of what it explicitly says?[5]

We end up then with Malthus personally informing Chalmers and Marcet (and I have also argued Nassau Senior) of his change of mind, while Cazenove and Empson remained in the dark. A complex picture indeed; and a nice problem to sink one's teeth into. But this problem does not dispose of the evidence for the abandonment of protectionism. It means only that there is more to learn about Malthus's personal contacts – and personality.

NOTES

1 Malthus's general case for revenue tariffs was long-standing (cf. 1820: 508–9; 1836: 427–8).

2 My reference to Malthus's 1824 statement regarding 'the improved views of our government in commercial legislation' is made in context (Hollander 1992: 654) and Pullen should have done the same. The sentence occurs in a passage referring to the maintenance of aggregate demand for labour by a buoyant manufacturing export sector which is itself partly ascribed to the new free-trade policy *of the early 1820s*. There is (as Pullen says) no explicit reference here to agricultural

trade; but my point is that the retention of agricultural protectionism threatened to thwart these newly observed trends.

3 Pullen writes that 'It would have been quite extraordinary . . . if Empson had not been aware of any change in Malthus's views on the Corn Laws; or if being aware of such a change, he deliberately chose to conceal it' (section 5.5). But Pullen himself admits there is evidence that Malthus recommended 'a reduction in the level of the existing tariff' (section 1.1), that is, that there had occurred some sort of change!

4 In a further letter to Chalmers of 6 February 1833 (Chalmers Papers, CHA 4.210.5), Malthus commented that he found Chalmers's 'valuable present' – he alludes to *The Supreme Importance of a Right Moral to a Right Economical State of the Community* (1832) reviewed by Cazenove in the *British Critic* – 'most important, and completely victorious'. In this work, Chalmers advocated repeal of the Corn Laws on 'moral' grounds (cf. Chalmers 1852, 2: 216–17).

5 Strangely, Pullen also allows that it is 'the most persuasive piece of evidence' for my case. Pullen fails to represent me fairly in one respect. I refer to his assertion that '[Malthus's] statement to Mrs Marcet *"Still I am for the removal of restrictions"* is used as a principal piece of evidence of his change of mind, and on the basis of this argument, it is argued that he deliberately intended to conceal his change of mind!' (section 9.4). This is scarcely cricket since my evidence of a change of mind – as is clear from Pullen's paper itself – includes a very wide range of texts among which the letter in question is certainly not a *principal* item and since I did not argue that Malthus disingenuously concealed his new position. On the contrary, I sought to avoid such a conclusion.

REFERENCES

Chalmers Papers, Thomas, New College, Edinburgh.

Chalmers, T. (1852) *Political Economy*, Vol. 2 of *Works of Thomas Chalmers*, Edinburgh: Thomas Constable.

Hollander, S. (1992) 'Malthus's Abandonment of Agricultural Protectionism: A Discovery in the History of Economic Thought', *American Economic Review*, 82, 3: 650–9.

Malthus, T. R. (1817) *An Essay on the Principle of Population*, 5th edn, London: John Murray.

—— (1820) *Principles of Political Economy*, London: John Murray.

—— (1826) *An Essay on the Principle of Population*, 6th edn, London: John Murray.

—— (1836) *Principles of Political Economy*, 2nd edn, London: William Pickering.

—— (1989) *Principles of Political Economy*, edited by John Pullen, Cambridge: Cambridge University Press.

Pullen, J. (1989), 'Introduction to Malthus', in T. R. Malthus (1989).

—— (1995) 'Malthus on Agricultural Protection: An Alternative View', *History of Political Economy* 27 (Fall): 517–30.

Ricardo, D. (1951–73) *Works and Correspondence*, 11 vols, P. Sraffa (ed.), Cambridge: Cambridge University Press.

Waterman, A. M. C. (1991) *Revolution, Economics and Religion*, Cambridge: Cambridge University Press.

18

MALTHUS AS PHYSIOCRAT
Surplus versus scarcity*

This paper investigates the agricultural bias pervading T. R. Malthus's economics. The question arises whether and to what extent the bias reflects a debt to the Physiocrats. That Malthus was aware in 1798 of the French literature, though possibly only at second hand, is clear; that by 1803 he had become acquainted *at first hand* with that literature is also certain. I shall show that though Malthus was sometimes critical – a prime example is his objection to the Single Tax proposal – it was because he regarded the French economists as failing to work out the full logic of their position. He in fact took the doctrine of a surplus peculiar to the agricultural sector further than they did themselves, attempting to strengthen it as its weak points (as in value theory) and seeking to minimize doctrinal differences. The significance of the question of literal 'debt' is reduced considering the *active* contribution made to what may be termed 'doctrinaire' Physiocracy.

I. ON 'SURPLUS': THE ESSAY ON POPULATION (1798, 1803)[1]

Agricultural bias emerges distinctly in the first *Essay on Population*. Malthus was, in fact, critical of the 'Economists' for not going far enough, insisting that even were manufacturing to yield 'a clear rent' that sector should be classified as 'unproductive' at least relative to agriculture: 'supposing the value of the wrought lace to be such, as that besides paying in the most complete manner the workman and his employer, it could afford a clear rent to a third person; it appears to me, that in comparison with the labour employed upon land, it would be still as unproductive as ever' (1798: 330). For though manufacturing activity admittedly added 'to the exchangeable value of [the] annual produce', a transfer to agriculture of labour hitherto engaged on luxury production would involve an increase in 'productive' activity, in terms of 'real utility' or 'the mass of happiness in the society' (329), an index which relates ultimately to population increase. This

* My warm thanks to Lila Costabile, Walter Eltis, Chidem Kurdas, Heinz Kurz, Pier-Luigi Porta, Annalisa Rosselli and Anthony Waterman for incisive criticism.

position held good even when labour after the transfer produces *less* food than it consumes, since the gross output of food rises compared with the original allocation (333–6). In brief: 'A capital employed upon land, may be unproductive to the individual that employs it, and yet be highly productive to the society. A capital employed in trade on the contrary, may be highly productive to the individual, and yet be almost totally unproductive to the society: and this is the reason why I should call manufacturing labour unproductive, in comparison of that which is employed in agriculture, and not for the reason given by the French Oeconomists' (333).

That Malthus offered his own justification of the productive–unproductive contrast in terms of the impact on food, and consequently on population, does not necessarily imply that he was unaware in 1798 that this latter relation was also recognized by the Physiocrats. His complaint was that the Physiocrats were inconsistent on their *own* terms involving 'wealth' defined as the 'gross produce of the land': 'Though according to the reasoning used by the French Oeconomists, the man employed in the manufacture of lace would, in this case [assuming a net revenue], seem to be a productive labourer; yet according to their definition of the wealth of a state, he ought not to be considered in that light. . . . The clear rent, therefore, that a certain produce can afford, after paying the expenses of procuring it, does not appear to be the sole criterion, by which to judge of the productiveness or unproductiveness to a state, of any particular species of labour' (330–1). All this alludes to the peculiar 'productivity' of agricultural activity with reference to its impact on population. We shall see that Dupont de Nemours envisaged the *Essay* as paradigmatically Physiocratic from just this perspective.

Malthus in 1798 thus considered agricultural activity as 'productive' (or relatively so) even in the absence of a net surplus or 'clear rent'; and manufacturing as 'unproductive' (or relatively so) even allowing for a net surplus, represented formally as excess of income over expenses relating to labour and capital, i.e. an income afforded 'to a third person'. This conception is modified or supplemented when it is allowed that in actuality profits on manufacturing or trading capital were frequently high enough to constitute a source of accumulation – a concept involving the character of *disposability*:

> It is, indeed, almost impossible, to see the great fortunes that are made in trade, and the liberality with which so many merchants live, and yet agree in the statement of the Oeconomists, that manufacturers can only grow rich by depriving themselves of the funds destined for their support. In many branches of trade the profits are so great, as would allow of a clear rent to a third person: but as there is no third person in the case, and as all the profits centre in the master manufacturer, or merchant, he seems to have a fair chance of growing rich, without

much privation; and we consequently see large fortunes acquired in trade by persons who have not been remarked for their parsimony.

(Malthus 1798: 333–4)

The two classifications are not inconsistent provided the first – surplus payment to a third party in excess of wage and profit expenses – is interpreted as an excess over 'expenses' incorporating *minimum* factor returns, thus containing no disposable element; with profits and wages assumed to be at their minima the surplus or residual income will take the form of rent payment to the landlord (the 'third person'), which (by implication) is alone disposable for accumulation. The second classification makes explicit the disposability criterion, and specifies that *profit* too might constitute in part a surplus in the sense of an income *disposable* for saving even if no third party exists, as in manufacturing where the land factor is supposedly inapplicable. Should the agricultural profit rate exceed the minimum return and thus contain a disposable element, the identification of surplus with rent fails. (For an elaboration, see below pp. 293–4.)

Malthus's objection to the physiocratic perspective on accumulation by manufacturers as a matter of abnormal deprivation does not suggest that for him net returns in manufacturing are merely apparent, constituting transfer payments out of agricultural income. That national income includes manufacturing (as with Adam Smith) is certain: 'The consumable commodities of silks, laces, trinkets, and expensive furniture, are undoubtedly a part of the revenue of the society' (335). This is no longer the case in the second edition (1803). There we discern the following physiocratic propositions: (1) that a surplus is generated *solely* by agriculture, and (2) and yet more strongly, that manufacturing income (in its entirety) entails a transfer payment. This can without question be described as 'fundamentalist' Physiocracy. Indeed (1) alone would justify such a designation since (2) was by no means universally maintained by the French economists (cf. Hollander 1973: 83).

As in 1798 Malthus points out in 1803 that the physiocratic criterion of productiveness turning on the ability to generate a surplus would oblige one to categorize manufacturing as 'productive' in the event that it generates a surplus, whereas the French economists seemed to want to avoid this conclusion (Malthus 1989, I: 389–90). Again, manufactures were in fact 'essentially different' from agricultural produce, so that even were a surplus generated thereby they should still be designated *unproductive*: 'the question respecting their productiveness or unproductiveness by no means depends entirely upon the largeness of the profits upon them, or upon their yielding or not yielding a clear rent' (391). But Malthus now adds, here turning away from Smith, that in any event manufacturing incomes constitute *transfer* earnings not original incomes: 'But manufactures, strictly speaking, are no new production, no new creation, but merely a modification of an old one, and when sold must be paid for out of a revenue already in existence, and consequently the gain of the seller is the loss of the buyer. A revenue is transferred, but not created.'

This perspective is elaborated in the following representation of the agricultural surplus as 'supporting' the service and manufacturing sectors, a strictly one-way dependency:

> If, in asserting the productiveness of the labour employed upon the land, we look only at the clear monied rent yielded to a certain number of proprietors, we undoubtedly consider the subject in a very contracted point of view. The quantity of the surplus produce of the cultivators is, indeed, measured by this clear rent; but its real value consists in its capability of supporting a certain number of people, or millions of people, according to its extent, all exempted from the labour of procuring their own food, and who may, therefore, either live without manual exertions, or employ themselves in modifying the raw produce of nature into the forms best suited to the gratification of man.
>
> (Malthus 1989, I: 391)[2]

In sharp contrast, 'A net monied revenue, arising from manufactures, of the same extent, and to the same number of individuals, would throw the country in which it existed into an absolute dependence upon the surplus produce of others; and if this foreign revenue could not be obtained, the clear monied rent, which we have supposed, would be absolutely of no value to the nation' (391–2). Yet more strongly, the enrichment of non-agricultural nations, like those of individuals, occurs by way of a transfer process: 'Land, in an enlarged view of the subject, is incontrovertibly the sole source of all riches; but when we take individuals or particular nations into our view, the state of the question is altered, as both nations and individuals may be enriched by a transfer of revenue without the creation of a new one' (392).

A particularly important passage spells out the peculiar role of the agricultural surplus. It makes the 'dependency' case quite generally, i.e. 'whether the exchangeable value of the annual produce of the land and labour is the proper definition of the wealth of a country' – Adam Smith's approach which treats manufacturing income as an original income – or 'whether merely the produce of the land, according to the French Economists, may not be a more correct definition' (389).[3] 'Whichever of these two definitions is adopted . . . the great position [1806: the position] of the Economists will always remain true, that the surplus produce of the cultivators is the great fund which ultimately pays all those who are not employed upon the land. Throughout the whole world, the number of manufacturers, of proprietors, and of persons engaged in the various civil and military professions, must be exactly proportioned to this surplus produce, and cannot in the nature of things increase beyond it' (393; 1806, II: 208).[4]

Malthus cautioned in 1803 against drawing any parallel between monopoly profits and agricultural rent. Monopoly profits reflected only the 'mere monied revenue to an *individual*':

> The ultimate value of everything, according to the general reasoning of the Economists, consists in being *propre à la jouissance*. In this view, some manufactures are of very high value; and in general they may be said to be worth to the purchaser what the purchaser will consent to give. In the actual state of things, from monopolies, from superior machinery, or other causes, they are generally sold at a price above what the Economists consider as their real worth; and with regard to a mere monied revenue to an individual, there is no apparent difference between a manufacture which yields very large profits and a piece of land which is farmed by the proprietor.
>
> (Malthus 1989, I: 392)

The Physiocrats, who in fact understood the fundamental contrast between agriculture and manufactures, had unfortunately concentrated too much on the national surplus taking the specific form of *land rent*: 'I do not mean to say that the Economists do not fully comprehend the true distinction between the labour employed upon land, and the labour employed in manufactures, and really understand the value of the surplus produce of the cultivators, as totally distinct from the net monied revenue which it yields; but it appears to me that they have exposed themselves to be misunderstood, in their reasonings respecting the productiveness of land, and the unproductiveness of manufactures, by dwelling too much on the circumstance of a net rent to individuals' (392n). While '[in] an enlarged sense' – doubtless from an economy-wide perspective – 'it is certainly true, that land is the only source of net rent', that national surplus, albeit generated solely in agriculture, could not be entirely represented by *rent*.

This objection is elaborated in a criticism of the Single Tax proposal. Interest recipients also shared in the net income: 'One of the principal errors of the French economists appears to be on the subject of taxation. *Admitting, as I shall be disposed to do, that the surplus produce of the land is the fund which pays everything besides the food of the cultivators*; yet it seems to be a mistake to suppose that the owners of the land are the sole proprietors of this surplus produce. It appears to me that every man who has realized a capital in money, on which he can live without labour, has virtually a mortgage on the land for a certain portion of the surplus produce' (398n; emphasis added). Malthus maintained the physiocratic notion that *taxation incidence falls solely on the agricultural surplus* thereby supplementing the notion of surplus as net income *disposable for capital accumulation* (above, pp. 290–1), but insisted on the empirical fact that that surplus cannot be identified with land rent. And interest recipients might be taxed with no withdrawal of services resulting: 'those who live upon the interest of money, certainly pay a general tax in the same manner as the landholders, and cannot throw it off from their shoulders, like those who live upon the profits of stock, or the wages of labour'. (Indeed, the incidence falls to some extent even on profits and wages, particularly 'professional' earnings 'for a very considerable time'.) Precisely because landholders do not in practice receive all the surplus, it would be unjust to limit taxation to land rent: 'The real surplus produce of this country, or all the produce not actually consumed by the cultivators, is a very different thing, and should carefully be distinguished from the sum of the net rents of the landlords . . . ; a kind of mortgage is ultimately established on the land, by taxes and the progress of commercial wealth, and in this sense, all taxes certainly fall upon the land. . . . [But] though these taxes may still fall wholly on the land, they will not fall wholly on the landholders. It seems a little hard, therefore, in taxing surplus produce to make the landlords pay for what they do not receive.'

Surplus as disposable income from the perspective of *accumulation* need not coincide with surplus as disposable income from the perspective of *taxation*. They only coincide if we assume capitalists and labourers earn their minimum returns. As we have seen, both perspectives emerge in the texts. Conceivably, Malthus was implicitly utilizing this assumption at least in the long run – in the short run (albeit 'for a very considerable time') even profits may be taxed with no impact on capital supply; and Malthus's earlier allusions to savings by manufacturing capitalists out of profits might well refer to short-run earnings.

We return to the sharp contrast between industrial sectors. Both in 1803 and 1806 Malthus draws the extraordinary physiocratic contrast between the effects on national profitability of corn and industrial exports: 'In the ordinary course of things, the exportation of raw produce is sufficiently profitable to the individuals concerned in it. But with regard to national profit, it possesses . . . peculiar and eminent advantages above any other kind of export' (Malthus 1989, I: 406).[5] For 'raw produce, and more particularly corn, pays [1806: corn pays] from its own funds the expenses of procuring it, and the whole of what is sold is a clear national profit', whereas only that part of the value of manufactured exports exceeding the 'value of subsistence' may be so included (406–7; 1806, II: 231–2). Though Adam Smith (1937 [1776]: 642) had appreciated that the value of agricultural output 'bears a much greater proportion to the expense incurred in procuring it, than that of any other commodity whatever, and the national profit on its sale is in consequence greater', he forgot the rule when it came to foreign sales, failing to allow for the subsistence absorbed in preparing manufactures for export.

II. ON SECTORAL INTERDEPENDENCE

We must keep in mind several allowances for sectoral interdependence. From Malthus's physiocratic perspective focusing on the magnitude of surplus agricultural product, England appeared to be the 'richest' country in Europe relative to its land and population (Malthus 1989, I: 395–6; 1806, II: 213–14). More specifically, an 'agricultural system' – as championed by the Physiocrats – was the only system that assured in the long run a healthy manufacturing sector by encouraging low materials costs, and thus raising international competitiveness. Physiocratic terminology did less than justice to their own *valid* conceptions: 'According to the system of the Economists, manufactures are an object on which revenue is spent, and not any part of the revenue itself. But though from this description of manufactures, and the epithet sterile sometimes applied to them, they seem rather to be degraded by the terms of the Economists, it is a very great error to suppose that their system is really unfavourable to them. On the contrary, I am disposed to believe that it is the only system by which commerce and manufactures can prevail to a very great extent, without bringing with them, at the same time, the seeds of their own ruin' (394–5; 1806, II: 211–12). Here too the idea that at the *national* level, revenue is generated only by agriculture emerges: 'It is in the nature of things, that a state which subsists upon a revenue furnished by other countries must be infinitely more exposed to all the accidents of time and chance than one which produces its own.'

There are also interdependencies involving an impact of manufacturing on agriculture. The first, strictly speaking of a non-physiocratic or even anti-physiocratic nature, is that manufactures provide a stimulus or motive for the expansion of the agricultural surplus (Malthus 1989, I: 393, 396), though with a warning against 'forcing manufactures' since agriculture is the leading sector in that 'the funds for the subsistence of the manufacturer must be advanced to him, before he can complete his work' (393). The second, that improved manufacturing technology raises the real purchasing power of the surplus thereby adding 'virtually' to the real national income, is represented as consistent with the physiocratic system: 'Even upon this system, there is one point of view in which manufactures appear greatly to add to the riches of a state. The use of a revenue, according to the Economists, is to be spent; and a great part of it will of course be spent in manufactures. But if, by the judicious employment of manufacturing capital, these commodities grow considerably cheaper, the surplus produce becomes proportionably of so much greater value, and the real revenue of the nation is virtually increased' (394n; 1806, II: 211n).[6] Despite these allowances, Malthus hesitated in 1803 – this is apparently not so in 1806 – to accept Smith's designation of manufacturing as 'productive' activity: 'There is no light, perhaps, in which we can view manufactures, where they appear to be so productive as in this; and if it do not completely justify Dr Smith in calling manufacturing labour *productive* in the strict sense of that term; it fully warrants [1806: . . . increased. If this view of the subject do not, in the eyes of the Economists, completely justify Dr Smith in calling manufacturing labour *productive*, it must fully warrant] all the pains he has taken in explaining the nature and effects of commercial capital, and of the division of manufacturing labour.'

Malthus thus readily admitted (again both in 1803 and 1806) that 'No great surplus produce of agriculture could exist' without commerce and manufactures, 'and if it did exist, it would be comparatively of little value' (430n). Nonetheless, commerce and manufactures were 'the ornaments and embellishments of the political structure rather than its foundations'. But this is wholly unconvincing since, as we shall see (Section IV), Malthus relied on an increase in the demand for corn emanating from the *manufacturing sector* to absorb all secular increases in corn supply. To accord 'priority' to agriculture is a mere formality.

III. AGRICULTURE AS SOLE SOURCE OF SURPLUS CONFIRMED: THE ESSAY ON POPULATION (1806, 1807, 1817)

We come now to various modifications made in the third and fourth editions of the *Essay* (1806 and 1807). The passages in 1803 treating manufacturing earnings as a transfer payment rather than an original income are eliminated (note 4). And in the edition of 1807 Malthus *formally* dissociated himself from the notion that manufacturing does not generate original income: 'This account of manufactures and revenue is not in my opinion correct; because, if we measure the revenue of the whole state by its whole consumption, or even by the consumption of those who live upon surplus produce, manufactures evidently form a considerable part of it; and the raw produce alone would not be an adequate representation either of its quantity or of its value' (1989, I: 394n; 1807, II: 135n).[7]

In the context also of the Single Tax doctrine (above, p. 293) Malthus in 1806, by deleting the phrase 'Admitting, *as I shall be disposed to do*', withdrew his *own* acceptance of the position that 'the surplus produce of the land is the fund which pays everything besides the food of the cultivators' which implies that non-agricultural incomes are received by way of transfer (Malthus 1989, I: 399n; 1806, II: 217n). In 1807 the note in question is further altered to reinforce objections to the concept of 'wealth' (read *income*) as excluding manufactures: 'The great practical error of the Economists appears to be on the subject of taxation; and this error does not necessarily flow from their confined and inadequate definition of wealth, but is a false inference from their own premises. Admitting that the surplus produce of the land is the fund which pays everything besides the food of the cultivators; yet it seems to be a mistake to suppose that the owners of land are the sole proprietors of this surplus produce' (1989, I: 399n; 1807, II: 142n).

Malthus, however, reiterated in 1807 that 'all taxes certainly fall upon the land', though 'not wholly upon the landholders' (above, p. 294), *confirming continued adherence to the sole source of surplus in agriculture*, albeit that the surplus in actuality takes the form partly of non-rent incomes even in the manufacturing sector. The text of 1806 involving the modern notion of economic rent and *surplus as taxation capacity* (above, pp. 293–4) is elaborated: 'As consumers indeed it cannot be doubted, that even those who live upon the profits of stock and the wages of labour, particularly of professional labour, pay some taxes on necessaries for a very considerable time, and many on luxuries permanently; because the consumption of individuals, who possess large shares of the wealth which is paid in profits and wages, may be curtailed and turned into another channel, without impeding, in any degree, the continuance of the same quantity of stock or the production of the same quantity of labour' (1989, I: 399n; 1806, II: 218n). Also retained are the *defence* of the Physiocrats for essentially comprehending that 'the value of the surplus produce' on land is not identifiable with land rent although they exposed themselves to a misunderstanding on that score (above, p. 293); and the acceptance that 'In an enlarged sense . . . land is the only source of net rent'. Finally, England continues to be represented as the 'richest' country in Europe given the magnitude of its surplus agricultural produce; the notion of net national revenue generated solely in agriculture remains implicit in the caution given regarding a manufacturing-based economy dependent on food imports; and we again find the distinction between the value of corn exports which constitutes in its entirety a net addition to national income and the value of manufacturing exports from which must be deduced subsistence costs to obtain the 'clear national profit'. In sum: *while the 'fundamentalist' notion of manufacturing income as a transfer payment was abandoned in 1806/1807, it remained Malthus's position that agriculture is the only source of surplus.*

In 1817 we again encounter the predominance of agriculture whereby although 'Commerce and manufactures are necessary to agriculture . . . agriculture is still more necessary to commerce and manufactures' (Malthus 1817, II: 396; 1989, II: 29). Agriculture as sole source of surplus again provides the key: 'It must ever be true that the surplus produce of the cultivators, taken in its most enlarged sense, *measures and limits* the growth of that part of the society which is not employed upon the land. . . . [T]hat quality of the earth by which it may be made to yield a much greater quantity of food, and of the materials of clothing and lodging, than is necessary to feed, clothe and lodge the persons employed in the cultivation of the soil . . . is *the foundation of that surplus produce which peculiarly distinguishes the industry employed upon the land*' (397–8; 1989, II: 29–30; emphasis added).[8] An elaboration confirms the national surplus to be the excess of corn output over corn consumption in agriculture itself, which surplus might in part take the form of profits and wages[9]:

> If in asserting the *peculiar productiveness of the labour employed upon the land*, we look only to the clear monied rent yielded to a certain number of proprietors, we undoubtedly consider the subject in a very contracted point of view. In the advanced stages of society, this rent forms indeed the most prominent portion of the surplus produce here meant; but it may exist equally in the shape of high wages and profits during the earlier periods of cultivation, when there is little or no rent. The labourer who earns a value equal to *fifteen quarters of corn* in the year may have only a family of three or four children, and not consume *in kind above five or six quarters*; and the owner of the farming stock, which yields high profits, may consume but a very moderate proportion of them in food and raw materials. All the rest, whether in the shape of wages and profits, or of rents, *may be considered as a surplus produce of the soil*.
>
> (Malthus 1817, II: 399–400; 1989, II: 30; emphasis added)[10]

I conclude that there was no further significant dilution of physiocratic perspective in 1817 such as has sometimes been discerned (cf. Winch 1987: 61).

IV. SURPLUS VS SCARCITY: THE PAMPHLETS (1815) AND 'THE PRINCIPLES'

We consider next the rationalization of the surplus unique to agriculture to be found in Malthus's contribution to the pamphlet literature of 1815 and in his *Principles of Political Economy*. We should note first the clarification in his *An Inquiry into the Nature and Progress of Rent* (1815), after establishing the course of 'rent' or the 'surplus produce from the land', that by that designation he had intended 'the whole fund for the support of those who are not directly employed upon the land' *including farmers' profits*, since 'Profits are, in reality, a surplus . . . in no respect proportioned (as intimated by the Economists) to the wants and necessities of the owners of capital' (Malthus 1815: 16n). All this is consistent with the notion of surplus given in the *Essay on Population* as an excess of corn output over 'internal' corn consumption, Malthus differing from the Physiocrats only by his insistence that (agricultural) profit earners share in that excess. The *all-inclusive* notion of surplus is represented as a Providential gift: 'Is it not . . . a clear indication of a most inestimable quality in the soil, which God has bestowed on man – the quality of being able to maintain more persons than are necessary to work it . . . ' (Cf. a similar formulation, Malthus 1820: 149–50; 1836: 147–8.) But though the agricultural surplus includes profits in excess of some necessary minimum, the primary concern of the pamphlet was rent proper. Profits had to be separated out from rent because they 'take a different course in the progress of society'.[11]

The protectionist *Grounds of an Opinion* (1815) affirms that, pound for pound, the loss of agricultural capital and output is more damaging than a similar loss in other sectors: 'no loss, in proportion to its amount, affects the interest of the nation so deeply, and vitally, and is so difficult to recover, as the loss of agricultural capital and produce' (Malthus 1986, 7: 165). This is an assertion. In what consists 'the interest of the nation' which is peculiarly reflected by the health of the agricultural sector? The same question emerges again in a discussion of the landowning class. Though landowners 'do not so actively contribute to the production of wealth, as either of the classes just noticed, there is no class in society whose interests are more nearly and intimately connected with the prosperity of the state' (167). Here Malthus adopts Adam Smith's (physiocratic) proposition that 'no equal quantity of productive labour employed in manufactures can ever occasion so great a reproduction as in agriculture'. Again: 'If we suppose the rents of land taken throughout the kingdom to be one fourth of the gross produce, it is evident, that to purchase the same value of raw produce by means of manufactures [exports], would require one third more capital. Every five thousand pounds laid out on the land, not only repays the usual profits of stock, but generates an additional value, which goes to the landlord.' This *additional value* would be erased by a free corn trade – Malthus here recommends his *Rent* pamphlet – to the *national* detriment from the perspective both of consumption power and tax revenue: 'And this additional value is not a mere benefit to a particular individual, or set of individuals, but affords the most steady home demand for the manufactures of the country, the most effective fund for its financial support, and the largest disposable force for its army and navy' (167–8). A typically physiocratic formulation focusing on the productivity contribution of land (presumably reflected in rent) appears in a query addressed at this period to Ricardo: 'Supposing two nations with the same population and wealth, and the same rate of profits; and one of them to be merely manufacturing and commercial, and the other mainly agricultural, would you not say, that the agricultural country would produce the given quantity of wealth and population with less labour, and would therefore have a greater mass of disposeable wealth, and could maintain larger fleets and armies?' (11 June 1815, in Ricardo 1951, VI: 229–30).

Yet the allowance that agriculture is subject to diminishing returns distinguishes Malthus from the Physiocrats, and introduces a complexity. For Malthus concedes, even while he sings the praises of the 'additional value' constituting rent, that 'the last additions to the agricultural produce in an improving country are not attended with a large proportion of rent' (Malthus 1986, 7: 168). It is 'precisely this circumstance that may make it answer to a rich country to import some of its corn, if it can be secure of obtaining an equable supply'. Nevertheless, he closes by insisting that *in order to justify free trade in corn, the savings in resources must be sufficient to compensate for the loss of rent*: 'in all cases the importation of foreign corn must fail to answer nationally, if it is not so much cheaper than the corn that can be grown at home, as to equal both the profits and the rent of the grain which it displaces'. The logic of Malthus's argument is questionable – the notion of rent as an 'additional value' itself, but particularly when differential rent turning on diminishing returns is allowed.

In the *Inquiry* of 1815 and the *Principles* – the latter containing an elaboration, sometimes a duplication of the former – Malthus objected to Adam Smith, the Physiocrats,[12] and 'more modern writers' (Say, Sismondi and Buchanan), who are all charged with considering rent (the concern is now with *rent proper*) 'as too nearly resembling in its nature, and the law by which it is governed, the excess of price above the cost of production, which is the characteristic of a monopoly [1820: common monopoly]' (Malthus 1815: 2; 1820: 135; 1836: 136).[13] As for the Physiocrats, while accurate in 'some of their views' on the nature of rent, they had 'mixed them with so much error, and have drawn such preposterous and contradictory conclusions [1820, 1836: such unwarranted inferences] from them, that what is true of their doctrines has been obscured and lost in the mass of superincumbent error, and has in consequence produced little effect [1820, 1836: that what is true of their doctrines has produced little effect]' (1815: 3–4; 1820: 136; 1836: 137). The substantive complaint is the 'monopoly' implication of the Single Tax recommendation: 'the propriety of taxing exclusively the neat rents of the landlords, evidently depends upon their considering these rents as completely disposable, like that excess of price above the cost of production which distinguishes a common monopoly'. The posthumously published version is slightly more elaborate: 'Their great practical conclusion, namely, the propriety of taxing exclusively the neat rents of the landlords, evidently depends upon their considering these rents not only as completely disposable, like that excess of price above the cost of production, which distinguishes a common monopoly, but also that every indirect tax operates as a deduction from neat rents in proportion to its amount' (1836: 137).

The objection here is much the same as that to be found earlier in the *Observations on the Effects of the Corn Laws* of 1814, namely that to reduce rent by taxation endangered the rate of accumulation in land improvement. There Malthus had expressed special concern with the dynamic consequences for 'the future improvement of land' of a reduced 'real' (relative) corn price, and he charged the Physiocrats with an essentially static orientation detrimental to growth of the food supply and population: 'It was a fatal mistake in the system of the Economists to consider merely production and reproduction, and *not the provision for an increasing population*, to which their territorial tax would have raised the most formidable obstacles' (1986, 7: 97; emphasis added).[14] For though the 'motive' to expand was governed by 'the expected returns' on new capital investments, landlords must also be assured 'rent at least equal to the rent of the land in its former [uncultivated] state'; and while there typically existed a 'disposable surplus' on 'the greater part of the [already] improved lands', any reduction in the corn price would necessarily impede expansion (96–7).

Here in effect Malthus rejects the concept of no-rent land, though elsewhere he had allowed it. The notion of no-rent land introduces a serious technical challenge to physiocratic principle.[15] The allowance for rent at the margin, although it undermined physiocratic taxation policy, paradoxically strengthened the basic doctrine itself.[16]

We return to Malthus's reaction to 'modern writers'. In his discussion of Sismondi, he objected to a note in *De la richesse commerciale* (1814, I: 49) which takes the Physiocrats to task for *failing* to envisage rent as a transfer payment made possible by dint of landowners' 'privilège' and pressure of demand for food (Malthus 1815: 5; 1820: 136–7; 1836: 138). The same was true of Adam Smith's editor, Buchanan, who took issue with the physiocratic perspective on the grounds that a relaxation of the scarcity constraint would allow a transfer of real income from landowners to the rest of the community. Buchanan in fact had gone further than any of the others in spelling out that, from the 'monopoly' perspective, rent was *not* 'a clear addition to the national wealth' but an imposition on the rest of society.

We are faced by an apparent difficulty. Malthus himself objected to the Physiocrats for adopting a monopoly or scarcity perspective on rent, but now objects to Sismondi and Buchanan for their monopoly perspective on rent as opposed to the 'neat surplus' position they attributed to the Physiocrats. It is unclear how precisely Malthus read the Physiocrats, unless we envisage him (as we must) as rejecting only the supposed monopoly implication of the Single Tax proposal, rather than the position that rent represents a net creation of wealth as opposed to a transfer due to land scarcity (or 'monopoly').

We come now to a reinforcement of the surplus as opposed to the 'monopoly' perspective on rent. We recall the emphasis thus far on a *physical* corn surplus. This is now supplemented by the assurance that *value* surplus can look after itself. Thus in the *Principles* Malthus ascribed to the Physiocrats what he perceived as the valid proposition that 'the power of yielding rent' turns on the physical surplus – 'the fertility of the land . . . yielding a surplus quantity of necessaries beyond the wants of the cultivators', fully confirming the definition of 1817 – coupled with 'the peculiar quality belonging to the necessaries of life, when properly distributed, [which] tends strongly and constantly to give a value to this surplus by raising up a population to demand it' (Malthus 1820: 143; 1836: 144). Adam Smith too had maintained this position, at least 'in those passages of the *Wealth of Nations*, in which he approaches the nearest to the doctrines of the Economists [1836: to their doctrines]. But modern writers have in

301

general been disposed to overlook them, and to consider rent as regulated upon the principles of a common monopoly, although the distinction is of great importance, and appears obvious and striking in almost any instance that we can assume [1836: take].' The insertion of the above passage in the *Principles implies formal adherence by Malthus to physiocratic doctrine, and confirms that his earlier criticism related only to the Single Tax because of its (possibly unintended) implication that rent could be accounted for in terms of 'monopoly'*.

The *Inquiry into Rent* also elaborates on the technical contrast between the demand for 'strict necessaries' and the demand for other goods. Only in the general category is there meaning to *demand independent of or external to supply; and here only does the monopoly (or the scarcity) property apply*. In agriculture 'The cause of the higher price of the necessaries of life above the cost of production, is to be found in their abundance, rather than their scarcity' (Malthus 1815: 13). Here in effect Malthus applies Say's Law to food in a strong form – *supply creates its own demand without lag*. Although this particular formulation in question is absent from Malthus's *Principles*, its substance is retained in a contrast between the effects of a reduction by 50 per cent in the fertility of the mines producing precious metals and that of the land;[17] and also in the analysis of the impact of a cheaper diet on rent, which involves the presumption that expansion of food supply generates its own demand via population growth, assuring the maintenance of food prices and rents (Malthus 1820: 231; 1836: 211).

The analysis is fully confirmed in a reiteration, common to both the texts of 1815 and 1820, of the allowance that land which yields speciality products rather than basic necessaries is to be treated in scarcity rather than surplus terms. For the concept of a negatively sloped demand curve is only applicable where 'demand is exterior to, or independent of, the production itself' (Malthus 1815: 14; 1820: 147; 1836: 145). Then only does *contraction* of supply raise price above costs – as in the case of the produce of particular vineyards; the more complex case involving an *increase* in demand concomitantly with a reduction in supply could also be treated in that manner. But *this was ruled out in the case of corn*. Here an increase in demand was inconsistent with a decrease in supply. More generally, an increase in supply does not generate a fall in price – rather, such increase is the 'cause' of an excess price over costs; and a decrease does not raise price but depresses it.

It is, in brief, to a surplus physical produce that the excess value return is ascribed, in that the former assures an increase in population external to agriculture and a demand for food in addition to that generated within agriculture. All this is summed up in the *Principles* in a contrast between the *scarcity* approach applicable to all goods other than necessaries, and the *surplus* approach applicable to necessaries: 'in the one case, the *power* of the produce to exceed in price the cost of production depends [1836: depends mainly] upon the degree of the monopoly [1836: and of the external demand]; in the other, it depends entirely upon the degree of fertility [1836: fertility natural or acquired]. This is surely a broad and striking distinction' (1820: 148–9; 1836: 147; italics in 1836 only). We are evidently still in the world of Physiocracy. Indeed, we are witness to its *reinforcement* since the basic principle involved had apparently been rejected in 1806: 'On account of the tendency of population to increase in proportion to the means of subsistence, it has been supposed by some, that there will always be a sufficient demand at home for any quantity of corn which could be grown. But this is an error' (1806, II: 264n; 1989, I: 425n).

V. MALTHUS AND LAND SCARCITY

Malthus reacted strongly to Ricardo's adherence to the scarcity perspective of Sismondi and Buchanan: 'It is extraordinary that Mr Ricardo [1951, I: 400] should have sanctioned these statements of M. Sismondi and Mr Buchanan. Strictly, according to his own theory, the price of corn is always a natural or necessary price [1836: and, independent of agricultural improvements, the natural and necessary condition of an increased supply of product]. In what sense then can he agree with these writers in saying, that it is like that of a common monopoly, or advantageous only to the landlords, and proportionably *injurious* to the consumers?' (1820: 149n; 1836: 147n). Ricardo's position that agricultural rent reflects land scarcity, not 'the advantages which the land possesses over every other source of useful produce', he rejected in terms of surplus as a gift of Providence: 'It seems rather extraordinary that the very great benefit which society derives from that surplus produce of the land which, in the progress of society, falls mainly to the landlord in the shape of rent, should not yet be fully understood and acknowledged. I have called this surplus a bountiful gift of Providence, and am most decidedly of opinion, that it fully deserves the appellation' (1820: 226; 1836: 207).

Yet despite everything, a scarcity requirement *is* specified by Malthus. Thus he spelled out that the 'causes' of rent are, in fact, *three fold*:

> The causes of the high price of raw produce [1820: the causes of the [1836: ordinary] excess of the price of raw produce above the costs of production] may be stated to be three. First, and mainly, that quality of the earth [1836: soil], by which it can be made to yield a greater portion [1836: quantity] of the necessaries of life than is required for the maintenance of the persons employed on the land. 2^{ndly}, that quality peculiar to the necessaries of life, of being able [1820: when properly distributed] to create their own demand, or to raise up a number of demanders in proportion to the quantity of necessaries produced. And, 3^{rdly}, the comparative scarcity of the most fertile land [1820: The comparative scarcity of fertile land, either natural or artificial].
>
> (Malthus 1815: 8; 1820: 139–40; 1836: 140)

This latter condition is elaborated thus:

> That there are some circumstances connected with rent, which have an affinity to a natural monopoly, will be readily allowed. The extent of the earth itself is limited, and cannot be enlarged by human demand. And the inequality of soils occasions, even at an early period of society, a comparative scarcity of the best lands; and so far [1820: this scarcity] is undoubtedly one of the causes of rent properly so called. On this account, perhaps, the term *partial monopoly* might be fairly applicable [1820: to it]. But the scarcity of land, thus implied, is by no means sufficient to produce the effects observed. And a more accurate investigation of the subject will show us how different the high price of raw produce is, both in its nature and origin, and the laws by which it is governed, from the high price of common monopoly.
>
> (Malthus 1815: 8; 1820: 139; 1836: 140)

It was the first characteristic that generated a physical surplus – the concern extends beyond rent proper – without which, however scarce land might be, 'neither rent, nor any essential surplus produce of the land in the form of high profits [1820: and high wages] could have existed' (1815: 9; 1820: 140; 1836: 141). In the *Principles* the emphasis is, in fact, formally placed on the *maximum rent potential* allowing that this surplus might take the form of high wages and profits: 'On the other hand, it will be allowed, that in whatever way the produce of a given portion of land is divided, whether the whole is distributed to the labourers and capitalists, or a part is awarded to a landlord, the *power* of such land to yield rent is exactly proportioned to its [1836: natural or acquired] fertility, or to the general surplus which it can be made to produce beyond what is strictly necessary to support the labour and keep up the capital employed upon it.' This physical potential, the 'foundation or main cause of all rent', had to be supplemented since (in 1815) 'if the necessaries of life . . . had not the property of creating an increase of demand proportioned to their increased quantity, such increased quantity would occasion a fall in their exchangeable value'. Or again (in the *Principles*): 'this surplus, necessary and important as it is, would not be sure of possessing a value which would enable it to command a proportionate quantity of labour and other commodities, if it had not a power of raising up a population to consume it, and, by the articles produced in return, of creating an effective demand for it'.

A passage appearing in the *Principles* alone also allows the scarcity dimension: 'It is so obviously true, as to be hardly worth stating, that if [1836: the] land of the greatest fertility were in such excessive plenty compared with the population, that every man might help himself to as much as he wanted, there would be no rents or landlords properly so called' (1820: 206; 1836: 195). Moreover, '[it] will also be readily allowed, that if in this or any other country you could suppose the soil suddenly to be made so fertile, that a tenth part of the surface, and a tenth part of the labour now employed upon it, could more than support the present population, you would for some time considerably lower rent'.

There is one further significant allowance for the scarcity requirement; though it appears only in 1815 it is in line with the argument thus far. Malthus remarks in the pamphlet that should cotton machinery have those qualities of land which permit it to yield 'food, clothing and lodging, in such proportions as to create an increase of population equal to the increased supply of these necessaries', there would result a *rent* to such machinery – since 'the demand for the products of such improved machinery would continue in excess above the cost of production' (1815: 11). And here is attached a most revealing note: 'I have supposed some check to the supply of the cotton machinery in this case. If there was no check whatever, the effects would show themselves in excessive profits and excessive wages, without an excess above the cost of production'. This note – as well as the imaginary case to which it is attached – is removed in 1820, but in all versions the supposed contrast between land and cotton machinery is elaborated, namely that in the latter case alone increase of output eradicates the value product (1815: 11; 1820: 143–4; 1836: 143).

Where then do Malthus and Ricardo differ, since Malthus too specifies a scarcity requirement? The answer would seem to lie in Malthus's primary concern with the *total surplus* or excess of corn output over internal (agricultural) consumption, and its *value* counterpart – the first accounted for by a Providential quality in land, the second by the population reaction to food which assures appropriate demand. The third or land-scarcity condition accounts only for the surplus taking the specific form of rent narrowly defined. Were land free – recall the cotton machinery example – 'the effects would show themselves in excessive profits and excessive wages'. *But those excessive returns too were to be explained (a) by the Providential surplus of corn output over minimum internal consumption and (b) by a corresponding value excess assured by population growth in almost automatic response to any increase in the food supply.* Malthus's concessions regarding land scarcity actually undermined his objections to those 'moderns' who insisted on rent as a transfer; but they did not affect the peculiar qualities attributed to agriculture.

Ricardo, by contrast, refused to countenance any *analytical* distinction between sectors. Malthus's first condition said only that land 'yields a greater value in return than the value of the labour expended on it', which was true of 'every occupation in which man engages. If produce of all kinds did not fulfil those conditions it would not be produced' (Ricardo 1951, II: 106). Moreover, land ('natural agents') contributed to manufacturing activity as well as to agriculture; the notion of some 'third' productive factor in agriculture *alone* was an optical illusion reflecting the circumstance that land had a zero price in manufacturing (1951, I: 75). The second quality was 'quite fallacious' since population increase did not *follow* increase in food but the reverse, the supply of food, like that of all other products, responding to prior increase of demand (1951, II: 107, 110–111, 114–115).

VI. THE DIMINISHING-RETURNS COMPLEXITY ELABORATED

Ricardo correctly objected in 1815 that Malthus's elaboration of the diminishing-returns conception in his *Inquiry* according to which 'land which is successively taken into cultivation in improving countries may only pay profits and labour' conflicted with the so-called *preeminence* of agriculture (Ricardo 1951, IV: 37–8). This same issue arises in the *Principles* (1820) where in discussing definitions of 'productive labour' Malthus proposed tentatively that all labour – even service labour – be categorized as 'productive' but to different degrees, upon which principle 'the labours of agriculture would, *generally speaking*' – not universally – 'be the most productive; because the produce of nearly all the land actually in use is not only of sufficient exchangeable value to pay the labourers employed upon it, but the profits of the stock advanced by the farmers, and the rents of the land let by the proprietors' (1820: 38; emphasis added).[18] This definitional approach 'would determine . . . the natural pre-eminence of agriculture, which Adam Smith is obliged to explain afterwards, and, at the same time, shew the numerous cases where *an increase of manufacturing and mercantile labour would be more productive, both to the state and to individuals, than an increase of agriculture*; as in all cases where, from a greater demand for manufactured and mercantile products, compared with the produce of land, *the profits of manufacturing and mercantile capital were greater than both the rent and profits combined of labour employed upon new and less fertile land*' (39; emphasis added). This important qualification reflects the small rent (if any) generated on marginal land. The principle of diminishing returns was undermining the notion of a preeminent agriculture.

We now revert to common ground between the 1815 *Rent* pamphlet and the *Principles* with respect to diminishing returns. In all versions Malthus used the increasing-cost principle to argue that were landlords to *relinquish* rent, the corn price would be unchanged – since price is determined at the no-rent margin (Malthus 1815: 57–8; 1820: 201–2; 1836: 191–2). Ricardo approved Malthus's statement (1951, I: 74–5). But Malthus read much more into it than did Ricardo, representing it as confuting the objectionable 'monopoly' (scarcity) approach to corn pricing and rent maintained by the 'more modern' authors Say, Sismondi and Buchanan. If the corn price is a 'necessary' price reflecting marginal costs under pressure of demand, and rent the outcome, any notion of the price of corn (and the return to land) arising from 'monopoly' – with the implication that rent constituted a transfer and was injurious to consumers – was unacceptable.

Malthus was on shaky ground. The increasing-cost characteristic of agriculture, whereby the corn price (however high it may rise) is a *necessary* price to assure the requisite output, and rent the necessary result, entails standard competitive demand–supply analysis, the equilibrium price determined at the intersection of an upward-sloping supply curve and the *independent* demand curve. Now Malthus had to all intents and purposes admitted that rent *was* a scarcity payment, clinging however to his *general* notion of agricultural value surplus (above, p. 305). Unfortunately, that notion turned on the *dependence* of the demand for corn on supply, which assured that an increase in supply did not depress the corn price. He had fallen into a logical trap – insisting upon the physiocratic view of rent as surplus while allowing the differential principle of rent. Eltis has observed that Malthus 'set out a Physiocratic analysis with the modification that there were diminishing not constant returns in agriculture' (Eltis 1984: 321). But the fact is that to adopt diminishing returns is inconsistent with the physiocratic position. Malthus's theoretical position was, as Ricardo insisted, untenable.

VII. MALTHUS'S 'DEBT' TO THE PHYSIOCRATS

We have been concerned with characteristically 'physiocratic' concepts in Malthus's economics. There is no evidence that in 1798 he had read any physiocratic literature in the original; his general references to the French economists may reflect second-hand familiarity, derived in part from Adam Smith.[19] This may be so but the fact remains that in 1798 he sought to spell out the full implications of the *physiocratic* definition of 'national wealth' involving the gross output of land, envisaging it to be in conflict with their own approach to productivity involving the *net* produce. For agriculture was the preeminent sector because of its impact on population growth; and its superiority held good independently of the question of net product, even indeed if labourers transferred from manufacturing to agriculture were to consume more food than they produced.

For Semmel (1965: 534), the notion that the means of subsistence limit population was reached independently, since Malthus in 1798 was unaware of that particular notion in the French literature. He cited the Preface to the 1803 edition as evidence. But actually that Preface refers to *excessive* population growth relative to the growth of food as a notion to be found in a wide range of literature – including 'some of the French economists' – of which Malthus had originally been unaware (Malthus 1989, I: 1–2). It remains possible that the more general proposition relating population growth to food supply *was* derived originally in part from physiocratic sources indirectly if not directly. In any event, a powerful index of this 'physiocratic' dimension is provided by the reaction to the 1806 version of the doctrine by Dupont de Nemours (1817), the only Physiocrat to live long enough to comment on Malthus: 'Dans ce qu'il y a d'évidemment incontestable, l'ouvrage de M. *Malthus* est un long, mais savant et curieux commentaire de cette maxime des economistes Français: *La mesure de la subsistance est celle de la population*' (Dupont de Nemours 1817: 2).

Two specific and favourable references to the Physiocrats – to Dupont and de Mirabeau – are given in the second edition. The first occurs in a note to a text controverting Smith's position against the Corn Laws on the grounds that any increase in the price of corn will be purely nominal (Malthus 1803: 458; 1989, I: 416). Dupont's case in *Physiocratie* (which involves an application of the *tableau économique*) purports to demonstrate the real advantage to all classes including labour of a high corn price. The advantage to labour is elaborated by Quesnay in that work in terms of the approximately proportionate rise in the money wage upon a corn-price increase but lag in the prices of non-corn wage goods. And there is a considerable likelihood that Malthus had access to that case. The second reference is to *L'ami des hommes*, specifically to an admission of an earlier error in representing 'population as the source of revenue' rather than the reverse (Malthus 1803: 477; 1989, I: 440).[20] Clearly by 1803 he had encountered *at first hand* important samples of the French literature including the food and population nexus.[21]

There is, we have also seen, a *strengthening* of the 'physiocratic' orientation in the 1803 version, manifested (a) in the representation of agricultural income alone as 'original' and (b) in the insistence on surplus as generated in agriculture alone – even when as in subsequent editions of the *Essay* (a) is abandoned, (b) is retained – and the discussion of these features suggests first-hand familiarity (above, p. 291f). His reference to the physiocratic concept of 'the ultimate value of everything' as '*propre à la jouissance*' (above, p. 293) points to the same conclusion; as does also his reference to profits 'intimated by the Economists' to be 'proportioned . . . to the wants and necessities of the owners of capital' (above, p. 298).

In reviewing the evidence of first-hand familiarity, I am not attempting to represent Malthus as slavish follower. On the contrary, we know he was frequently critical, especially regarding the Single Tax doctrine which implied an identification of surplus with land rent narrowly defined. Nonetheless, the essential fact remains that he accepted and sought to reinforce their agricultural bias, supplementing the notion of a *physical* surplus pertinent to agriculture by arguing for a corresponding *value* surplus. In fact, his support for agricultural protection to avoid loss or contraction of that surplus, effectively transplanted into the going circumstances involving Britain as net corn importer the same policy conclusions as the Physiocrats had earlier drawn when France was a net corn exporter and free trade assured the world price as floor.

That Malthusian doctrine was *perceived* to be physiocratic by some contemporaries is evident from the reaction by Dupont in 1817 to the food–population linkage. In fact, he went much further, for he disliked Smith's chapter 'Of the Agricultural Systems' and described Malthus as 'encore plus profond et plus tenace que *Smith*, sur les bons principes relatifs à l'administration de l'agriculture, des manufactures et du commerce . . . et qui sait relever les erreurs de *Smith* même, lorsque celui-ci se trompe ou exagère' (Dupont de Nemours 1817: 30). Relevant too is the reaction of William Spence who cited Malthus's statement in the *Essay* of 1803 that 'A revenue is transferred [by manufacturing], but not created', in defence of his own *Britain Independent of Commerce* (1807, 1808) (see his *Agriculture, The Source of the Wealth of Britain*, 1822 [1808]: 152). But Spence – who recognized 'that nearly all the main tenets of the Economists, have been embraced and defended by Mr Malthus' – added that 'the sentiment of this gentleman will be deemed of greater weight, when it is recollected, as I have before observed [129–30], that he is no blind admirer of the Economists; but admits that in some senses, manufactures may be said to create national wealth'. Malthus's assertion that 'the great position of the Economists will always be true, that the surplus produce of the cultivators is the great fund which ultimately pays all those who are not employed upon the land' (above, p. 292) is similarly cited in his defence (Spence 1822: 130).[22]

VIII. THE DISINTEGRATION OF MALTHUSIAN PHYSIOCRACY

In a letter to Macvey Napier of 8 October 1821, Malthus compared the Ricardians who had 'adopted a theory which will not stand the test of experience', with the Physiocrats. Their system 'takes a partial view of the subject, like the system of the French Economists; and like that system, after having drawn into its vortex a great number of very clever men, it will be unable to support itself against the testimony of obvious facts, and the weight of those theories, which though less simple and captivating, are more just, on account of embracing more of the causes which are in actual operation in all economical results' (letter to Napier, 8 October 1821, B.L. Add. MSS 34,612. f. 453). A similar identification appears in a *Quarterly Review* article of 1824 (Malthus 1986, 7: 297). Here he gives as 'the specific error of the French economists . . . the having taken so confined a view of wealth and its sources as not to include the results of manufacturing and mercantile industry'.

Much the same complaint, again in a comparison with the Ricardians, appears in the *Principles* itself. The first chapter sets out by defining national income in Smith's fashion to include 'material objects which are necessary, useful or agreeable to mankind' (Malthus 1820: 28; 1836: 32); and the final chapter objects to any definition limited to *net revenue* in the sense of 'disposable' income. Although his own (Smithian) definition '[did] not include the question of what may be called the amount of disposable produce, or the fund for taxation', the Economists had 'destroyed the practical utility of their works by referring exclusively to the net produce of the land';[23] while those who limited wealth to 'rents and profits, to the exclusion of wages – a position attributed to Ricardo – committed an error exactly of the same kind though less in degree' (Malthus 1820: 423; 1836: 368).[24] Wages in fact – he here includes even service labour – accounted for most of national income and constituted a significant source of expenditure and also of taxation: 'Those who live upon the wages of labour, unproductive as well as productive [1836: including of course those engaged in personal services], receive and expend much the greater part of the annual produce, pay a very considerable sum in taxes for the maintenance of the government, and form by far the largest portion of its physical force. Under the prevalence of habits of prudence, the whole of this vast mass might be nearly as happy as the individuals of the other two classes, and probably a greater number of them, though not a greater proportion of them, happier.'

It is not clear whether all this should be represented as a truly *novel* attack on Physiocracy. After all, the refusal to limit national income to the farm sector was an old story, and Malthus had long before insisted that others apart from landowners – interest recipients, and even capitalists and labourers – if only in the short run, bore in part the burden of taxes and engaged in accumulation. This insistence underlay his objection to the Single Tax proposal – that the national surplus albeit generated in agriculture, must not be identified with land rent. Nonetheless, the reference to 'the prevalence of habits of prudence' in our present context is striking. For it implies that with appropriate social attitudes and policy the subsistence minimum could not be envisaged as the long-run norm; a *major* part of the national surplus – wherever its ultimate source – might permanently take the form of wages (even of service labour). If this is so, it would be the case that Malthus's primary policy concern – to encourage population control – was proving incompatible with physiocratic bias.[25] Certainly the prospect of prudential control undermines the perspective taken in 1798 on an aggregate volume of 'happiness' defined in terms of population magnitude, a perspective that had justified the original preoccupation with the agricultural sector.

Here we should note a new emphasis in the 1817 version of the *Essay on Population* on industry-biased growth as typically characteristic of the later stages of economic development, reflecting growing land scarcity and an 'increasing taste for conveniences and luxuries' which tends to 'direct the greatest part of new capital to commerce and manufactures' (Malthus 1817, III: 6; 1989, II: 79), and along with it retraction of much of an earlier concern with such development from labour's perspective. To allow a natural tendency to *industry-biased* growth – and concede the possibility of improved living standards notwithstanding[26] – and yet to champion agricultural protection to assure balanced growth implies a *reinforcement* of the physiocratic dimension, not its weakening. But as I have demonstrated elsewhere (Hollander 1992b [essay 16]), Malthus over the period 1824–6 in fact came to *abandon* his protectionist position. The modifications in question reflect in large part Malthus's recognition that expanded *manufacturing* exports had mitigated the worst effects of the postwar depression, i.e. that the manufac-turing sector was proving itself, leading to an abandonment of an earlier case for unproductive consumption by landlords (see above, p. 299). Although there are earlier allusions to the significance of manufacturing in main-taining activity to the advantage of agriculture itself (above, Section II), the theme is now underscored with particular reference to the growing empirical significance of the *export* sector; and it is no longer part of a protectionist case to assure sectoral balance despite a 'natural' trend to industrial supremacy, but rather part of a free-trade case justifying the imbalance. Possibly pertinent – though this is not definitive – is a suggestion of growing concern for British agricultural prospects, which also would imply an undermining of physiocratic bias.

Much of what is retained in the text of the *Principles*, to appear in the posthumous 1836 edition, reflects the surplus-oriented physiocratic theory outlined in the account above. My tentative conclusion is that Malthus could never shelve a powerful theoretical bias that governed his economics from the beginning. The fact that deletions of *protectionist* passages are more systematic suggests that dissatisfaction emanated initially from policy considerations, and that Malthus was unwilling or unable to return and reconstruct the theoretical framework. But of his discomfort there can be no doubt.

In documenting and rationalizing the apparent disintegration of Malthusian Physiocracy allowance should also be made for the charge against the French Economists of downplaying, indeed of denying, the impact of *trade* in raising Aggregate Demand, a matter of increasing concern to him: 'The [1836: French] Economists, in their endeavours to prove the unproduc-tive nature of trade, always insisted that the effect of it was merely to equalize prices, which were in some places too high and in others too low, but in their amount the same as they would be after the exchange had taken place. This position must be considered as unfounded. . . . [It] is impossible to doubt for a moment the direct tendency of all internal trade to increase the value [1836: both the quantity and value] of the national produce' (1820: 441; 1836: 383).

The informal Inverarity report of lectures given in 1830 goes further. It is so hostile as to suggest that by that date Malthus had abandoned the entire system though he failed to record such a thoroughgoing renunciation in the revisions to the *Principles*. The 'fundamental error of the Economists' was '[t]heir confined definition of wealth as well as their confined definition of the term *productive* which does not even include all the rude produce of the land. This definition has led them to overlook the accumulation of capital and the better distribution and division of labour in the hands of what they call the sterile class' (Pullen 1981: 809). Other 'important errors and omis-sions . . . which render[ed] their works of comparatively little use' are then listed: 'They overlook the advantages of manufactures and commerce; the accumulation of capital in the sterile class; the value super-added to the raw produce by the manufacturers; the benefit the raw produce derives from the extension of its market through its more transferable form; the benefits of machinery and the better division of labour; the cheapness of commodities from the last two causes.'

IX. SUMMARY AND CONCLUSION

It has emerged that there was a physiocratic dimension to Malthus's economics, more positive, specific and lasting than usually suggested in the literature (cf. Meek 1962; Semmel 1965; Eltis 1984; Winch 1987). Was Malthus *indebted* to the Physiocrats for the agricultural bias discussed in this essay, or was it a matter of parallelism? His knowledge of the French literature in 1798 was probably second hand. But that he had become acquainted at first hand with the literature by 1803 is certain and this reading seems to have left its mark. Moreover, he was envisaged as 'physiocratic' by William Spence and by Dupont. Most important of all, he reinforced the French doctrine, supplementing the notion of a physical (agricultural) surplus by the assurance of a corresponding value surplus. The question of literal *debt* is secondary considering the active contribution he made to doctrinaire Physiocracy.

NOTES

1 Where appropriate I shall insert into my extracts from 1803 minor variations of 1806. Substantive modifications will be taken up in the section 'Agriculture as sole source of surplus confirmed . . . '.
2 The statement implicitly assumes wage and profit rates to be at their *minima*; otherwise, the surplus is *not* measured by the rent paid land proprietors.
3 Cf. the equivalent statement in 1798 specifying 'the gross produce of the land, according to the French Economists' (327). But in 1803 (392), the definition of 'most of the Economists' is said to be 'the clear surplus produce of the land' rather than the *gross* produce.
4 This is troublesome. On the Smithian definition of national income it cannot strictly be said that the agricultural surplus 'ultimately pays' the non-agricultural sector; this formulation only applies if we treat manufacturing income as a transfer. The retention of the passage in 1806 after Malthus had himself reverted to the Smithian definition is presumably an oversight. A modification in 1807 excises the expression 'ultimately pays': 'it must always be true that *the surplus produce of the cultivators measures and limits* the growth of that portion of the society which is not employed upon the land' (1989, I: 393n; 1807, II: 132; emphasis added). See also the 1817 version (above, p. 297).
5 In 1806, Malthus adds various reasons explaining the 'national advantage' of agricultural exports, but the first remains as in 1803 (1806, II: 231).
6 This is consistent with Adam Smith's representation of Physiocracy (1937 [1776]: 633–4).
7 He still recognized that *even for the Physiocrats* manufactures 'appear greatly to add to the riches of the state' because of the impact of manufacturing tech-

nology in raising the purchasing power of the agricultural surplus (395n; 1807, II: 135n).

8 While the *motive* for the production of the surplus turns on non-agricultural activity, the same priority is accorded the surplus produce as in earlier versions: 'the funds for the subsistence of the manufacturer must be advanced to him before he can complete his work; and no step can be taken in any other sort of industry unless the cultivators obtain from the soil more than they themselves consume' (1989, I: 398; 1989, II: 30).

9 Earlier definitions of surplus as excess of national income over 'expenses' can be accommodated provided the wage and profit rates are at their minima.

10 By the same token, in a growing system approaching stationariness subject to falling returns to labour and capital the agricultural economy had the particular advantage that its 'disposable income' was maintained: 'It should also be observed that in a state, the revenue of which consists solely in profits and wages, the diminution of profits and wages may greatly impair its disposable income. The increase in the amount of capital and in the number of labourers may in many cases not be sufficient to make up for the diminished rate of profits and wages. But where the revenue of the country consists of rents as well as profits and wages, a great part of what is lost in profits and wages is gained in rents, and the disposable income remains comparatively unimpaired' (425; 1989, II: 47).

11 Inclusion of profits (in excess of the minimum) in the surplus defined in 1815, as in 1817, as excess of *corn* output over internal *corn* consumption is to treat profits as a *corn surplus*; and this invites the concept of a rate of profit as a ratio of the corn surplus net of rent to the corn input, the so-called Sraffa rational reconstruction of *Ricardo*. That Malthus later developed this approach is argued in Hollander 1997, chapter 10.

12 'The Economists' (1815, 1820); 'the *Economists* of the school of M. Quesnay' (1836). Doubtless the alteration in 1836 is to indicate the wish to draw a line between more recent French economists, especially Say and Sismondi, from the earlier eighteenth-century Quesnay group.
As for Smith, Malthus allowed that 'in some parts of the eleventh chapter of his first book he contemplates rent quite in its true light', but was less clear elsewhere and 'leaves the reader without a definite impression of the real difference between the cause of the high price of the necessaries of life, and of monopolized {scarce} commodities'.

13 Malthus was using the term 'monopoly' to indicate an upward slope to competitive supply curves – in the limit zero elasticity; cf. Viner 1958: 360, on this usage.

14 A further charge was made against Adam Smith for illegitimately excluding corn from treatment in terms of the standard scarcity, or demand-supply, model (90–1). This criticism creates a severe anomaly since much of Malthus's own treatment of rent – above all the argument in the 1815 *Rent* pamphlet and in the *Principles* that a *physical* surplus ensures a corresponding *value* surplus – turns on just such an exclusion as we shall see.

15 Interestingly, the tendency to diminishing returns at the extensive agricultural margin is even to be found in the French literature; see Spengler regarding Dupont (1942: 198n). Turgot has remarkable statements of the principle (Brewer 1987; Hollander 1987: 55).

16 The 1814 allowance for rent in marginal cost should not be read as a denial of diminishing returns and differential rent. These concepts are clearly intimated in a discussion of war-time experience and trade policy (96, 107–8). The differential

rent principle and the no-rent margin make a (casual) appearance as early as 1806.

17 In the former case, as population may be supposed unaffected, it was conceivable that rents, profits and wages at the mines would be unaffected and even rise; in the latter case the impact would be disastrous (1820: 145–6; 1836: 144–5).

18 Although the classification was not finally adopted, the substantive difference between sectors stands.

19 A. M. C. Waterman denies any reliance by Malthus on the Physiocrats suggesting Richard Paley as a likely source of anything apparently 'physiocratic' in Malthus (letter dated 1 February 1994).

20 For a detailed discussion of the two references see Hollander 1992a [essay 15].
Since the context involves the Tableau Economique, we may conclude that Malthus had access to this device although he never adopted it as such. His familiarity with the tableau is further confirmed by a letter to Horner, 14 March 1815, pointing to the Economists' calculation that 'one third of the raw produce obtained by the farmer is advanced to the steril [sic] classes' (in Ricardo 1951, VI: 187).

21 See Landry on Quesnay's ideas on population (Landry 1958, I: 11–74). Landry maintains that despite certain ambiguous formulations made before 1757 Quesnay was never a 'populationist' in the sense of encouraging population increase by direct means independently of prior food expansion. In any event, he objected successfully to Mirabeau's formulations in *L'Ami des hommes* (1757) which could be read in a populationist sense. (Landry maintains that in fact Mirabeau too held that population growth, though desirable, should turn on prior land improvement.)
   The specific references to Dupont's *Physiocratie* and to *L'Ami des hommes* treating, respectively, the advantage to labour of a high corn price and the dependency of population on 'revenue' (food) rather than the reverse are removed in 1806. But since the relevant texts remained unaltered, there is no obvious analytical reason for the deletions, and presumably Malthus sought to dissociate himself from the physiocrats for political reasons (James in Malthus 1989, II: 282).

22 In addition, Spence commended Malthus's criticisms of one aspect of Physiocracy – 'the confined and erroneous conceptions of those, who, in contemplating the importance of the revenue derived from the land, restrict their view to the net money revenue received by the class of land-proprietors' (132).

23 Malthus at times represented the French definition in terms of *gross rather than net agricultural output*. And in fact, a chapter in *Definitions in Political Economy* (1827) commences with the insistence that the term 'wealth' not be restricted 'either to gross raw produce', or the net raw produce, and is entirely devoted to the objection that the Physiocrats excluded 'the results of manufacturing and mercantile industry' (1986, 8: 9, 38).

24 In this context, Ricardo pointed to an ambiguity running through Malthus's *Principles*: 'When we meet we must agree upon the meaning to be attached to "a neat surplus from the land" – it may mean the whole material produce after deducting from it what is absolutely necessary to feed the men who obtained it, or it may mean the value of the produce which falls to the share of the capitalist, or to the share of the capitalist and landlord together. . . . This term neat produce is used ambiguously in your book' (24 November 1820; Ricardo 1951, VIII: 301).

25 I owe to Anthony Waterman the observation that 'the seemingly "fundamentalist physiocratic" theorem that "the number of manufacturers, of proprietors, and of persons engaged in the various civil and military professions, must be exactly proportioned to [the] surplus produce" (cited above, p. 292; see also p. 297) contradicts Malthus's population theory. In particular, it destroys the possibility of treating the "subsistence" wage as a policy parameter' (letter dated 1 February 1994).

26 The novelty of the 1817 version is its recognition of the possibility of decelerating population growth relative to that of food so as to assure a rising corn wage (and thereby also higher command over non-food components of the basket), irrespective of the actual growth rate of food. Conceivably the corn wage may rise with prudential control despite decelerating growth of food.

REFERENCES

Brewer, A. (1987) 'Turgot: Founder of Classical Economics', *Economica*, 54: 417–28.

Dupont de Nemours, P. S. (1817) *Examen du livre de M. Malthus sur le Principe de Population*, Philadelphia: Lafourcade.

Eltis, W. (1984) *The Classical Theory of Economic Growth*, London: Macmillan.

Hollander, S. (1973) *The Economics of Adam Smith*, Toronto: University of Toronto Press.

—— (1987) *Classical Economics*, Oxford: Basil Blackwell; 1992, Toronto: University of Toronto Press.

—— (1992a) 'On Malthus's Physiocratic References', *History of Political Economy*, 24, 2: 369–80.

—— (1992b) 'Malthus's Abandonment of Agricultural Protectionism', *American Economic Review*, 82, 3: 650–59.

—— (1997) *The Economics of Thomas Robert Malthus*, Toronto: University of Toronto Press.

Landry, A. (1958) 'Les idées de Quesnay sur la Population', *François Quesnay et la Physiocratie*, I: 11–49, Paris: INED.

Malthus, T. R. (1798) *An Essay on the Principle of Population*, London: Macmillan, facsimile, 1926.

—— (1803) *An Essay on the Principle of Population*, 2nd edn; in Malthus (1989).

—— (1806) *An Essay on the Principle of Population*, 3rd edn, in 2 vols, London: J. Johnson.

—— (1807) *An Essay on the Principle of Population*, 4th edn, in 2 vols, London: J. Johnson.

—— (1814) *Observations on the Effects of the Corn Laws*, London: J. Johnson.

—— (1815) *An Inquiry into the Nature and Progress of Rent*, London: John Murray.

—— (1817) *An Essay on the Principle of Population*, 5th edn, in 3 vols, London: John Murray.

—— (1820) *Principles of Political Economy*, 1st edn, London: John Murray.

—— (1824) 'Political Economy', *Quarterly Review*, 30, 60, in *Occasional Papers of T.R. Malthus*, B. Semmel (ed.), New York, 1963, 171–208.

—— (1827) *Definitions in Political Economy*, London: John Murray.

—— (1836) *Principles of Political Economy*, 2nd edn, London: William Pickering.

—— (1986) *The Works of Thomas Robert Malthus*, edited by E. A. Wrigley and D. Souden, London: William Pickering.

—— (1989) *An Essay on the Principle of Population*, 2 vols, Patricia James (ed.), Cambridge: Cambridge University Press.

Meek, R. L. (1962) *The Economics of Physiocracy*, London: George Allen and Unwin.

Pullen, J. M. (1981) 'Notes from Malthus: the Inverarity Manuscript', *History of Political Economy*, 13: 794–811.

Ricardo, D., (1951) *Works and Correspondence of David Ricardo*, 11 vols, P. Sraffa (ed.), Cambridge: Cambridge University Press.

Semmel, B. (1965) 'Malthus: Physiocracy and the Commercial System', *Economic History Review*, 17: 522–35.

Smith, A. (1937) [1776] *The Wealth of Nations*, New York: Modern Library.

Spence, W. (1822) [1807, 1808] *Tracts on Political Economy*, London: Longman, Hurst, Rees, Orme and Brown; reprinted and privately published New York, 1933, 1–92.

Spengler, J. J. (1942) *French Predecessors of Malthus*, Durham, North Carolina: Duke University Press.

Viner, J. (1958) *The Long View and the Short*, Glencoe, Ill.: Free Press.

Winch, D. (1987) *Malthus*, Oxford: Oxford University Press.

19

INTRODUCTION TO FACSIMILE REPRINTS OF MALTHUS'S *ESSAY ON POPULATION**

The primary purpose of this Introduction is to illustrate the value of working through the various editions of Thomas Robert Malthus's *Essay on Population*. My illustrations will be drawn from the following broad topics in Malthusian economics: the theory of economic growth and various applications; the case for 'prudential' population control; the intellectual 'debt' to the French Physiocrats; empirical estimates of both agricultural productivity and contemporary population growth; the perception of the 'population problem' and implications for social reform; and the theological dimension. I close with a discussion of Malthus's agricultural protectionism and its ultimate abandonment. This limited selection reflects a personal evaluation of what is interesting and important, but there is enough to indicate how close attention to the variora confirms Malthus's powerful reformist orientation and his optimistic evaluation of actual and prospective productivity and population trends.

I. ON EXISTING VARIORUM EDITIONS

Before proceeding to substance, I shall briefly indicate why a full reprint is required notwithstanding the recent publication of two variorum editions.[1] Anyone who has worked with the *Essay* knows the pains and pleasures of having to isolate variations across the six editions published during the author's lifetime: 1798, 1803, 1806, 1807, 1817 and 1826. The eight-volume *Works* (1986) edited by Wrigley and Souden provides only a half-way house. Malthus's works have been reset, but the original pagination is listed consecutively. The first volume contains the 1798 version; the second and third volumes reprint the 1826 edition with variant readings from 1803. Wrigley maintains that the first and second editions 'are so very dissimilar that they may be regarded as separate works, even though the latter is an expansion and elaboration of the former and there are some

* I gratefully acknowledge financial aid from the Social Science Research Council of Canada.

317

passages common to both editions', whereas, despite new material, modifications, and reordering of chapters between 1803 and 1826, 'the work as a whole remained recognizably the same between the second and sixth editions' (1986, 1: 8). This contrast is offered as partial justification for the editorial policies (1) not to undertake a textual comparison of the first two editions, and (2) to compare the final version of 1826 with that of 1803 alone. A full critical edition of Malthus was thus not attempted; and, accordingly, specialists concerned with the progression of Malthus's thoughts over time will be only partly satisfied.

The editors state their purpose to be the presentation of a text which is 'as little impeded as possible by obstacles of punctuation, nomenclature and spelling' – obstacles reflecting changing literary conventions (1: 12). This will not be regarded as a desirable feature by those whose interest resides precisely in the *original* 'conventions'. Moreover, little substantive assistance is provided as the reader proceeds through the texts. An example or two must suffice. In a 'shorter variant passage' of 1803 (1986, 3: 689); Malthus himself gives two pages (1803: 234, 262) obviously relating to his own second edition; but we are not provided with the specific places in the present edition to allow a check. Repeatedly we encounter paragraphs, sentences, and entire chapters added some time after 1803 but without guidance as to dating. Conversely, when was the chapter 'Observation on the Reply of Mr Godwin' (vol. 3, chap. 3) removed? Again, no help is forthcoming. On the other hand, the apparatus devised to capture the 1826 and 1803 contrasts is ingenious and works. The reader will find printed the preface to the fifth edition of 1817, and the very important appendix introduced in 1806 and expanded in 1807 and 1817.

Patricia James's variorum edition of the *Essay* omits apparently inconsequential variations: 'It was not considered necessary to record changes in paraphrasing, the use of capital letters, and small verbal alterations made merely for the sake of euphony or correct grammar: they indicate the care with which Malthus revised his work, but would be distracting to readers who are rightly more concerned with his subject-matter' (1989, I: xiv).[2] But the cumulative impact of 'verbal alterations' is surely essential to attain a full appreciation; even apparently inconsequential changes to punctuation and style can be revealing when considered cumulatively. James's decision is, in fact, at odds with her own justification of a variorum edition: the 'editorial defence must rest on Malthus's continuing fame and influence, especially outside his own country, which makes everything he wrote, and all his changes of mind, of permanent significance' (I: xiii). Similarly, none of Malthus's own indexes are provided, though James fully recognizes the implications of Malthus's own modifications: 'It is easy to laugh, but the modifications and qualifications which appear in the text of successive editions of the *Essay* are also reflected in the indexes' (II: 358). Or again, after illustrating index entries in the 1806 version, James writes: 'These are the sort of entries which enable anyone, browsing through Malthus's index, to obtain an insight into the views of the author as well as the subjects he discussed, something not usually revealed in the indexes of today' (II: 360). Yet the decision was made not to provide readers with the opportunity to gain such insight.

That we are in a sense dealing with a *partial* variorum edition is also clear from the treatment of the first edition. As mentioned above, Pickering printed the essay of 1798 in the first volume of its eight-volume series (and we also have Bonar's 1926 reprint, reissued in 1966, and a more recent photographic reprint by Klassiker der Nationalökonomie). The student of Malthus will have to have one or other of these versions at hand if changes between 1798 and 1803 are to be systematically isolated, since the Cambridge edition provides no systematic comparison with 1798. It is made clear where passages are incorporated verbatim into the second edition, but we frequently find the editorial note that certain passages are 'based on' the 1798 edition which the reader will have to follow up by recourse to the original, the reprint, or Pickering. As for 1798 passages removed in 1803, little help is provided.

The Cambridge edition provides the variations *between* 1803 and 1826 taking 1803 as base. Here we owe a very great debt to James. Unfortunately, the original pagination of 1803 is not indicated so that it is impossible to check references in the literature to that crucial edition. Although this problem does not arise in the variations of 1806, 1807, 1817 and 1826, where full references are provided, there is a complexity to the edition reflecting changes in print size to indicate major insertions, extensive replacements or alterations of text, these sometimes taking the form of very lengthy notes with additional editorial notes and variations attached. And there is a disconcerting feature which might have been avoided by taking the 1826 version as main text. The important summary chapter of Book III, which in 1803 has the title 'Of the principal Sources of the prevailing Errors on the Subject of Population', constitutes Malthus's chapter xi. James, allowing for the addition in 1817 of a new chapter (vii), labels the summary chapter as xii although in fact it remains 'xi' for Malthus until 1817 (when it actually becomes xiv since four of his chapters in Book III are replaced by six in 1817). In brief, in none of Malthus's own editions is there a Summary chapter numbered xii. And nowhere do we find, as such, Malthus's 1817/1826 chapter numbers viii through xiii. One is obliged to consult the original editions to avoid confusion.

II. GROWTH THEORY AND APPLICATIONS

We turn now to our series of 'illustrations'.[3] It is a matter of debate whether Malthus had in mind the principle of diminishing returns by his celebrated 'arithmetic ratio' of food increase and 'geometric ratio' of population increase, in the sense that if population were smaller average product would be higher. A close reading of the *First Essay*, particularly Chapter X which applies the contrasting ratios to William Godwin's idealistic schemes, indicates that quadrupled labour *might* yield quadrupled product if appropriate preparatory investments are made in land improvement or other forms of real capital accumulation before the higher rate of application of labour is undertaken (see Hollander 1997: *ETRM*, 1, II). That average product would not necessarily fall with increased population density is immaterial to the polemical purpose of the essay which is satisfied by demonstrating the necessity for a reduction of the population growth rate below its maximum potential. This conclusion is also supported by the discussion of the Poor Law institution (Malthus 1798: 91). That the *ratios* do not turn on the principle of diminishing returns does not, however, imply the absence of that principle in the first *Essay*. It manifests itself elsewhere in contexts constituting the origin of Malthus's formal growth model, namely a model involving a declining path of real wages in consequence of a decelerating rate of growth of labour demand. Still lacking is an explicit analysis of the profit rate and its secular course. Moreover, it is not application to land of labour-and-capital in the simple sense that is involved, but application entailing land 'improvement'.

Conspicuous in all this is a criticism of David Hume's *Essay on the populousness of ancient and modern nations* for neglecting to distinguish between growth rates and absolute size of population. Specifically, Malthus rejects Hume's theme that the record of early marriage and low celibacy in ancient times indicates a large absolute population, and that of high celibacy and late marriage in modern nations, a smaller population:

> If I find that at a certain period in ancient history, the encouragements to have a family were great, that early marriages were consequently very prevalent, and that few persons remained single, I should infer with certainty that population was rapidly increasing, but by no means that it was then actually very great; rather, indeed, the contrary, that it was then thin, and that there was room and food for a much greater number. On the other hand, if I find that at this period the difficulties attending a family were very great; that, consequently, few early marriages took place, and that a great number of both sexes remained single, I infer with certainty that population was at a stand; and, probably, because the actual population was very great in proportion to the fertility of the land, and that there was scarcely room and food for more.

> (Malthus 1798: 58)

We have here the two-fold notion that population growth depends on the magnitude of *per capita* income which in turn is governed by the population/land ratio.

The related notions of reduced per capita output at higher absolute population sizes (with a minimum to earnings and a corresponding maximum to population size) and of a *decelaration* of population growth with increase in population density are applied in Malthus's chapter VI in an analysis of North American development. There, because of high per capita income in consequence of low population density the growth rate of population was extremely high, which is to say that the 'checks' are removed (1798: 101–2). There follows an important statement describing the effect initially on per capita output and secondarily on the population growth rate, of a reduction in absolute population size (109–10).

In his chapter VII Malthus goes further in formulating a model of growth along the lines thus far outlined. It is highly suggestive of what later on he came to state with impressive precision – namely the land-scarcity based growth model. The argument appears in the context of a comparison of British demographic data for two periods (Elizabeth I to the mid-seventeenth century compared with late-seventeenth to mid-eighteenth century): 'there are many reasons for expecting to find a greater excess of births above the burials in the former period than in the latter. In the natural progress of the population of any country, more good land will, *caeteris paribus*, be taken into cultivation in the earlier stages of it than in the later. And a greater proportional yearly increase of produce, will invariably be followed by a greater proportional increase of population' (123–4). The passage thus alludes to an increasing scarcity of 'good' land, and to a more rapid increase in food production in early than in later stages of development, a differential related to the increasing land scarcity. The more rapid rate of food production at early stages will 'invariably be followed' by a similarly rapid rate of population growth; and by implication (the context makes clear this was Malthus's intention) the subsequently decelerating growth rate of food production will be followed by a deceleration of population growth.

Now if the population growth rate decelerates in line with that of food, then with food growth at zero, population growth too will cease. Such is the stationary state. Malthus also alludes to the 'forcing' of population as in China (1798: 130). But the major European states (England and France) were not subject to this problem of excessive population growth. The data regarding birth and death rates indicated that 'population has accomodated itself very nearly to the average produce of each country', so that periodic plagues 'to repress what is redundant' were not a feature of the recent record (125–6). It is the impact of low real wages which discourages population growth and assures that it stays in line with the growth of food supplies in the course of regular secular expansion. Similarly, an acceleration of food production, by raising real wages, will encourage an appropriate population increase (133).

What now of the course of real wages in the normal course of secular development? Evidently they are at their lowest in the stationary state –

setting aside the possibility of 'forced' reductions – and by implication they must tend downwards over time. But we can be more explicit than that, for Malthus brings in the North American case – characterized by plentiful land resources – where 'the reward of labour is at present so liberal' (131), adding that 'it might be expected, that in the progress of the population of America, the labourers will in time be much less liberally rewarded'.

As for Malthus's analysis in 1798 of the contemporary British situation, the 'model' there applied is *not* the land-scarcity version. That related specifically to new colonies. The picture rather is one of very slow growth of population and food proceeding for centuries at roughly constant real wages and motored by periodic bursts of new technology (see below, Section V; *ETRM*, 1, VII). The analysis of the British case is undertaken with an eye to explaining what Malthus considered to be the surprisingly *slow* growth of population, i.e. there is no question of excessive population growth such as one so often finds attributed to him.

We find in 1803 the same perspective as in 1798 regarding North America involving the dual linkages: (1) of per capita output to population density and (2) of population growth to per capita output, the latter mediated via the labour market and turning on capital accumulation in agriculture or the growth rate of food supplies (Malthus 1798: 101f; 1803: 336f). The notion of diminishing returns – in the guise of a decline in per capita output with increases in the population/land ratio – is central to the analysis. There is a repetition of the reference to the 'expectation' (indeed a trend actually under way) that 'in the progress of the population of America, the labourers will in time be much less liberally rewarded', i.e. a falling real wage path (1798: 131; 1803: 348). And in both, there is lacking any formal discussion of the profit rate and its trend.

We call attention now to a reformulation in 1803 of the original criticism of David Hume's proof that absolute population size had declined over the ages: 'the more productive and populous a country is in its actual state, the less probably will be its power of obtaining a further increase of produce, and consequently the more checks must necessarily be called into action to keep the population down to the level of this stationary, or slowly-increasing produce. . . . [The] difficulty of rearing a family may arise from the very circumstance of a great absolute population, and the consequent fullness of all the channels to a livelihood; though the same difficulty may undoubtedly exist in a thinly peopled country, which is yet stationary in its population' (1803: 178–9). This reformulation adds precision to the notion of reduced per capita output and accordingly of population growth at higher absolute population size.

But whereas this restatement reinforces the discussion of 1798, the case is reversed in another context. One brief statement in the first *Essay* of the land-scarcity based growth model, including deceleration of food production due to diminishing returns at the extensive margin accompanied by (or rather 'followed' by) a corresponding decline of population growth (above, p. 321), is *removed* in 1803 (316–17). The context suggests why. The issue in 1798 is the accuracy of the village and market town 'registers', particularly the accuracy of the registers for the earlier period which indicated a higher excess of births over deaths than subsequently. Richard Price in 1792 had questioned the early data but Malthus argued tentatively in their favour and provided a possible rationale, namely the encouragement given population growth by relatively good land resources, and, by implication, the deceleration of population growth with increasing land scarcity manifested in diminishing returns at the extensive margin. Now by 1803 Malthus was newly aware of the fact of *accelerating* population growth attributing it to 'the more rapid progress of commerce and agriculture' (303). He had come to question the accuracy of the registers (his main concern in 1803 is actually a comparison of the early and later years of the eighteenth century), so that the theoretical rationale originally offered in support of a *decelerating* growth rate was no longer relevant. That fact does not, however, necessarily touch on the validity of the model itself.

An Appendix of 1806 was devised to correct specific misinterpretations of the *Essay* and to summarize its central message. The 'chief object' of the essay, it is clarified, was, in fact, not to provide a 'proof' of the arithmetic and geometric differential ratios. These are represented as self-evidently true: 'the first of these propositions I considered as proved the moment that the American increase was related, and the second proposition as soon as it was enunciated' (Malthus 1806, II: 520n). Malthus's concern was rather 'what effects these laws, which I considered as established in the first six pages had produced, and were likely to produce on society'. The wholly rhetorical purpose of the arithmetic–geometric contrast is hereby confirmed. And he complained of readers who, while accepting 'the different ratios of increase on which all [his] principal conclusions are founded', yet claimed 'that no difficulty or distress could arise from population, till the productions of the earth could not be further increased' (517). There emerges here by implication a notion of *deceleration* of the food growth rate as the 'limit', albeit 'indefinite', is approached. But that was evidently not Malthus's concern, which remained the simple fact of an excess of 'unrestricted' growth of population over the maximum conceivable growth rate of food.

The 1817 edition of the *Essay* contains a considerably sharpened analysis of the land-based growth model, with particular reference to the falling trend paths of the corn wage and the profit rates until their respective minima when capital and population growth cease (Malthus 1817, II: 433–5). This contrasts with earlier versions of the *Essay* where only the declining wage is allowed. In this new formulation Malthus also spelled out the conditions – including that of unchanged technology – that have to be satisfied for a 'regular' deceleration of population growth and of the wage and the profit rates, for in practice a steady pattern was not to be expected.

And he further emphasized that the approach to stationariness of capital and population, setting aside disturbing causes, is a very slow one (440–1).

These themes are elaborated in the chapter – it appears with variations in all editions except the first – 'Of Increasing Wealth, as it affects the Condition of the Poor' (1817, Book III, ch. 13). The context is a long-standing objection to Adam Smith's notion that the demand for labour varies with 'wealth' (i.e. national income or 'annual produce'). Expanding national income might take the form of manufactured luxuries alone and thus fail entirely to stimulate population growth. This, however, is a limiting case; the normal case entails only a lag of population growth behind the increase of 'wealth': 'in the usual progress of improvement the increase of wealth and capital is rarely accompanied with a proportionately increased power of supporting an additional number of labourers' (Malthus 1817, III: 4). This lag parallels that of agriculture behind general activity – a lag noted by Smith – which is attributed primarily to land scarcity. The position that the (agricultural) wage fund does not necessarily increase with the increase of wealth and rarely in proportion to it, was – as we have seen – already developed in the earlier editions, including the diminishing returns rationale. But in 1817 Malthus put greater weight on the land-scarcity phenomenon, taking Smith to task for an undue emphasis upon *faulty institutions* in his analysis of stationariness of population, 'wealth', and agriculture (9–10). In arguing thus, Malthus was revising his position, since in 1803 (438–9) and in 1806 (II: 214–15) he too had offered an institutional rationalization for observed lags in agricultural activity.

III. ON PRUDENTIAL POPULATION CONTROL

A further proposition in 1817 weakens the dependency of working-class welfare on growth in the food supply – thus relaxing the criticism of Smith – by recognizing 'that the condition of the lower classes of society does not depend exclusively upon the *increase* of the funds for the maintenance of labour, or the power of supporting a *greater* number of labourers' (Malthus 1817, III: 2–3; emphasis added). That the wage basket is mixed had long been recognized, but the full argument of 1817 provides the basis for one of the most important statements of the growth process in the classical literature (10–11). Here Malthus identifies demand for labour (or employment capacity) with food advances – at least food advances constitute the 'main ingredient' – yet envisages the real wage basket as including 'conveniences and even luxuries'. He alludes also to a highly elastic labour-growth supply such that as the growth rate of food increases the response of population prevents any 'great [positive] effect' on the (corn) wage. This version, which turns on 'the tendency in population *fully to keep pace with* the means of subsistence', differs from a notion of tendency given at the outset of the essay, namely 'to increase beyond the means of subsistence' (1817, I: 5). But a qualification sets the 'tendency' (in either sense) aside, *by recognizing the possibility of deceleration of population growth relative to that of food so as to assure rising corn wages, irrespective of the actual growth rate of food*: 'the cause which has the most lasting effect in improving the situation of the lower classes of society depends chiefly upon the conduct and prudence of the individuals themselves, and is therefore not immediately and necessarily connected with an increase in the means of subsistence' (1817, III: 11). Conceivably the wage may even rise due to such self-imposed prudential control despite decelerating growth of food.

The textual amplification spells out further the elements of a growth model based on diminishing returns as population density rises, with an ultimate limit to food (and thus to population size). Increasing land scarcity accounts for the necessary deceleration of food supply in a growing economy and the consequentially necessary deceleration of population growth. But whether the corn wage declines or not turns on labour-supply conditions. In the absence of increasing prudential control, the corn wage necessarily declines, for it is this decline that acts to impede population growth. With increasing prudential control, however, any decline in corn wages can be avoided:

> A diminished power of supporting children is an absolutely unavoidable consequence of the progress of a country towards the utmost limits of its population. . . . This state of things is generally accompanied by a fall in the *corn* price of labour; but should this effect be prevented by the prevalence of prudential habits among the lower classes of society, still the result just described must take place; and though, from the powerful operation of the preventive check to increase, the wages of labour estimated even in corn might not be low, yet it is obvious that in this case the power of supporting children would rather be nominal than real; and the moment this power began to be exercised to its apparent extent, it would cease to exist.
>
> (Malthus 1817, III: 12–13)[4]

A new Appendix of 1817 explains precisely what is entailed in practice and what stimulated the elaboration. The context is a proposal by Arthur Young in 1812 'so to adjust the wages of day-labour as to make them at all times equivalent to the purchase of a peck of wheat' (419). Malthus objected to the plan that 'in its general operation, and supposing no change of habits among the labouring classes, it would be tantamount to saying that, under all circumstances, whether the affairs of the country were prosperous or adverse; whether its resources in land were still great, or nearly exhausted; the population ought to increase exactly at the same rate, – a conclusion which involves an impossibility' (420). (For a similar formulation, in the context of 'the poor-laws as a general system', cf. 1817, II: 350. In earlier editions the message is the same but expressed in much less formal terms; cf. 1806, II:

188.) Here we have an appeal to the standard model; the corn-wage path *must* fall to assure the appropriate deceleration in the population growth rate. But allow for prudential control and the picture is transformed; constancy of the corn wage might be achieved despite increasing land scarcity:

> If however this adjustment, instead of being enforced by law, were produced by the increasing operation of the prudential check to marriage, the effect would be totally different, and in the highest degree beneficial to society. A gradual change in the habits of the labouring classes would then effect the necessary retardation in the rate of increase, and would proportion the supply of labour to the effective demand, as society continued to advance, not only without the pressure of a diminishing quantity of food, but under the enjoyment of an increased quantity of conveniences and comforts; and in the progress of cultivation and wealth the condition of the lower classes of society would be in a state of constant improvement.
>
> (Malthus 1817, 420–1)

We now come to a potent relationship that entirely negates any notion of Malthus as 'dismal scientist'. Malthus does not treat increasing prudential control solely as a matter of exogenous change in habits (stimulated perhaps by education or propaganda programmes). Rather it is *endogenous to the growth process*. Already in 1803 there is brief reference to the possibility that rising wages stimulate improved prudential control by way of more sophisticated tastes: 'Supposing the people to have been before in a very depressed state, and much of the mortality to have arisen from the want of foresight which usually accompanies such a state, it is possible, that the sudden improvement of their condition might give them more of a decent and proper pride' (1803: 245–6). The improved degree of prudence in turn would reduce the mortality rate: 'the proportional number of marriages might remain nearly the same, but they would all rear more of their children, and the additional population that was wanted, would be supplied by a diminished mortality, instead of an increased number of births' (246). The 1817 formulation goes a major step further, finding a role for a rising ratio of corn to manufacturing prices in the process of changing taste patterns. From 'experience' Malthus drew a relationship linking a taste for manufactured wage goods to diminishing returns on land, the upward pressure on the corn price itself encouraging inward shifts of the labour growth curve which check and possibly prevent reductions in the corn wage: 'it seems to be proved by experience, that the lower classes of society seldom acquire a decided taste for conveniences and comforts till they become plentiful compared with food, which they never do till food has become in some degree scarce. . . . It is under these circumstances, particularly when combined with a good government, that the lower classes of society are most likely to acquire a decided taste for the conveniences and comforts of life; and this taste may be such as even to prevent, after a certain period, a further fall in the corn price of labour' (1817, III: 23–4). A general summary allows for the maintenance of good conditions even in a slowly growing economy, and conversely possibly poor conditions with rapid growth. All depends on the population-growth function (25–6). Here we have a rejection of the Smithian view that with capital growing only slowly, real wages *must* be low.

IV. MALTHUS'S 'DEBT' TO THE PHYSIOCRATS

There is nothing to indicate that at the time of the first *Essay* Malthus had read any physiocratic literature in the original; his general references to the French economists may reflect second-hand familiarity, derived in part from Adam Smith. Nevertheless, in 1798 he sought to spell out the full implications of the physiocratic definition of 'national wealth' involving the gross output of land, which he envisaged to conflict with the Physiocrats' own approach to 'productivity' involving the *net* produce; agriculture, he insisted, was the preeminent sector because of its impact on population growth, and its superiority held good independently of the question of net product, even indeed if labourers transferred from manufacturing to agriculture consumed more food than they produced (Malthus 1798: 330–2).

The Preface to the 1803 edition of the *Essay* refers to *excessive* population growth relative to the growth of food as a notion to be found in a wide range of literature – including 'some of the French economists' – of which Malthus had originally been unaware. Yet it remains possible that the more general proposition of 1798 relating population growth to food supply was derived originally, at least in part, from physiocratic sources, indirectly if not directly. In any event, a powerful index of this 'physiocratic' dimension is provided by the reaction to the 1806 version of the doctrine by Dupont de Nemours, the only Physiocrat to live long enough to comment on Malthus: 'Dans ce qu'il y a d'évidemment incontestable, l'ouvrage de M. *Malthus* est un long, mais savant et curieux commentaire de cette maxime des economistes Français: *La mesure de la subsistance est celle de la population*' (Dupont de Nemours 1817: 2).[5]

Two specific and favourable references to the Physiocrats – to Dupont's *Physiocratie* and to *L'ami des hommes* (de Mirabeau) – are given in the second edition. The first occurs in a note to a text controverting Smith's position against the Corn Laws on the grounds that any increase in the price of corn will be purely nominal (Malthus 1803: 458). Dupont's case purports to demonstrate the real advantage to all classes including labour of a high corn price. The advantage to labour is elaborated by Quesnay in Dupont's work in terms of the approximately proportionate rise in the money wage upon a corn-price increase but lag in the prices of non-corn wage goods. And there is a considerable likelihood that Malthus had access to that case.[6] The reference to *L'ami des hommes* relates to de Mirabeau's admission of an earlier error in representing 'population as the source of revenue' rather than the reverse (Malthus 1803: 477). Malthus does not mention de Mirabeau by name (either because he was unaware of the identity of the anonymous author or because of political discretion) and omits de Mirabeau's reference to 'un plus habile' (Quesnay) who corrected the error. But evidently by 1803 he had encountered at first hand important samples of the French literature including the food–population nexus. The specific references to Dupont's *Physiocratie* and to *L'Ami des hommes* are removed in 1806. But since the relevant texts remained unaltered, there is no obvious analytical reason for the deletions, and presumably Malthus sought for political reasons to dissociate himself from the Physiocrats.

Passages in 1803 treating manufacturing earnings as a transfer payment rather than an original income (1803: 430–4) are eliminated from the 1806 edition. And in 1807 Malthus *formally* dissociated himself from the notion that manufacturing does not generate original income (1807, II: 135n). Also omitted in the 1806 revisions is a *defence* of the Physiocrats for essentially comprehending that 'the value of the surplus produce of the cultivators' is not identifiable with land rent although they exposed themselves to a misunderstanding on that score (1803: 434n). Malthus, in the context of the Single Tax doctrine, by deleting in 1806 the italicized phrase 'Admitting, *as I shall be disposed to do*', withdrew his own acceptance of the position that non-agricultural incomes are received by way of transfer: 'One of the principle errors of the French Economists appears [1806: The principle errour of the French economists appears] to be on the subject of taxation. Admitting, *as I shall be disposed to do* [1806: omitted], that the surplus produce of the land is the fund which pays every thing besides the food of the cultivators; yet it seems to be a mistake to suppose that the owners of land are the sole proprietors of this surplus produce' (1803: 440n; 1806, II: 217–18n; emphasis added). In 1807 the note in question is further altered to reinforce his objections to the concept of 'wealth' (read *income*) as excluding manufactures: 'The great practical error of the Economists appears to be on the subject of taxation; and this error does not necessarily flow from their confined and inadequate definition of wealth, but is a false inference from their own premises. Admitting that the surplus produce of the land is the fund, which pays every thing besides the food of the cultivators; yet it seems to be a mistake to suppose, that the owners of land are the sole proprietors of this surplus produce' (1807, II: 142n).

Malthus, however, reiterated that 'all taxes certainly fall upon the land' though 'not . . . wholly on the landholders' (143n), confirming continued adherence to the sole source of surplus in agriculture, albeit that the surplus in actuality takes the form partly of non-rent incomes even in the manufacturing sector. The formulation of 1803 involving the notions of economic rent and surplus as taxation capacity (1803: 440n) is elaborated (1806, II:

218n; 1807, II: 142n). And England continues to be represented as the 'richest' country in Europe given the magnitude of its surplus agricultural produce; the notion of *net* national revenue generated solely in agriculture remains implicit in the caution given regarding a manufacturing-based economy dependent on food imports; and we again find the distinction between the value of corn exports which constitutes in its entirety a net addition to national income and the value of manufacturing exports from which must be deduced subsistence costs to obtain the 'clear national profit' (see *ETRM*, 8, II, III). In sum: while the 'fundamentalist' notion of manufacturing income as a transfer payment was abandoned in 1806/1807, it remained Malthus's position that agriculture is the only source of surplus.

In the 1817 version of the *Essay* we again encounter the predominance of agriculture – reminiscent of the 1806 or 1807 weighting[7] – whereby although 'Commerce and manufactures are necessary to agriculture . . . agriculture is still more necessary to commerce and manufactures' (1817, II: 396). Agriculture as sole source of surplus again provides the key: 'that quality of the earth by which it may be made to yield a much greater quantity of food, and of the materials of clothing and lodging, than is necessary to feed, clothe and lodge the persons employed in the cultivation of the soil . . . is the foundation of that surplus produce which peculiarly distinguishes the industry employed upon the land' (397–8). An elaboration confirms the national surplus to be the excess of corn output over corn consumption in agriculture itself, which surplus might in part take the form of profits and wages (399–400). Although, as in earlier editions (1803: 433, 436; 1806, II: 209, 214), the *motive* for the production of the surplus turns on non-agricultural activity – scarcely a physiocratic notion – the same priority is accorded the surplus produce: 'the funds for the subsistence of the manufacturer must be advanced to him before he can complete his work; and no step can be taken in any other sort of industry unless the cultivators obtain from the soil more than they themselves consume' (1817, II: 398).

I conclude from all this that there occurred no further significant dilution of physiocratic content in 1817 such as has sometimes been discerned. We should certainly note a specifically new emphasis in the 1817 version on industry-biased growth as typically characteristic of the later stages of economic development, reflecting growing land scarcity and an 'increasing taste for conveniences and luxuries' which 'would naturally and necessarily direct the greatest part of this new capital to commerce and manufactures' (1817, III: 6), and along with it retraction of much of an earlier concern with such development from labour's perspective. But to allow a natural tendency to *industry-biased* growth – and concede the possibility of improved living standards notwithstanding – and yet to champion agricultural protection to assure balanced growth as Malthus did in this period (see Section IX) implies rather a *reinforcement* of the physiocratic dimension than a weakening.

V. EMPIRICAL ESTIMATES OF AGRICULTURAL PRODUCTIVITY

As shown in Section II, the principle of diminishing returns (though not its differential-rent implication) is apparent already in the 1798 *Essay*; but it was applied to the North American case, not to contemporary Britain. As for Britain, Malthus alludes to a slow growth of population supported by a moderate expansion of agriculture, the latter reflecting 'the inclosure of waste lands, and the general improvements in husbandry', 'improvements in agricultural instruments' and a 'generally increased fertility of the soil' rather than a growing agricultural work force (Malthus 1798: 316–19). Malthus actually asserted that the agricultural work force had fallen absolutely as a result of reorganization and labour-displacing technology. Land scarcity as such, reflected in diminishing returns, thus plays no part in the 1798 account of actual British circumstances.[8]

The 1803 edition of the *Essay* provides further references to the high productivity of British agriculture, the recent census data indicating that 'the number of persons employed in agriculture is very unusually small in proportion to the actual produce' (Malthus 1803: 438). If agricultural development was constrained it was because of 'undue encouragement' afforded manufactures – the Navigation Acts and the colonial trade monopoly – which had 'robbed [land] of much of the capital which would naturally have fallen to its share'. As for future domestic agricultural development Malthus was optimistic in 1803, at least in the event of an 'enlightened system of agriculture' which would 'undoubtedly be able to produce food beyond the demands of the actual population' (467–8). He objected only to the 'prejudice' that any conceivable system 'can ever be made to keep pace with an unchecked population'. He even denied practical limits to growth in an 'enlightened' system (443).

The 1803 formulation goes further and actually predicts *reduced* corn prices in consequence of the stimulus afforded output by a corn-export bounty, Malthus insisting, against Smith, that a bounty provided an incentive to expansion and thus generated lower prices (463). Despite the first impression, it is by no means certain that Malthus intended to assert *increasing* agricultural returns by his prediction of a *reduced* corn price with expansion. What he may have intended is a contrast, clarified in the 1806 edition, between the 'direct' effects a corn-export subsidy, which were to raise the domestic corn price, and its indirect effects, which were 'both to lower the average price, and to prevent the variations above and below that price' (1806, II: 259), the latter turning on a distinction between the 'growing' price of corn in normal years and an 'average' price over all years (261–2). But even so, there is no hint of *diminishing* returns in the empirical accounts of 1803 or 1806. Similarly, when it comes to policy, the 1806 edition recommended intervention to encourage Britain's re-emergence as a net corn exporter – to be accomplished in two stages: first corn-import restrictions and subsequently an export bounty (see *ETRM*, 16, II); and nothing in this programme suggests prospective real-cost increases.

The account of productivity trends emerging in the 1817 *Essay* is strikingly optimistic, emphasizing the disturbing causes at play which accounted for an increase in the profit rate over the preceding two decades or so, despite 'prodigious' accumulation and agricultural extensions. Since mid-century 'it cannot be doubted that the capital of the country has been prodigiously enlarged, and its cultivation very greatly extended; yet, during the last twenty years, we have seen the interest of money at above 5 per cent., with profits in proportion [nearly twice the level 1720–50]; and, from 1800 to 1811, an increase of population equal to 1,200,000 on 9,287,000, a rate of increase about two and a half times as great as at the former period' (1817, II: 440). When precisely this striking passage was formulated is unclear. The reference to 'the last twenty years' during which the interest rate exceeded 5 per cent was conceivably inserted at the time of writing rather than publication; 1814 or thereabouts is a likely date for the passage considering the fact that the profit rate declined during the postwar downturn. In any event, that the twenty-year period ending in 1814 was intended is confirmed in a similar passage in the chapter 'Of Corn Laws' (Book III, chapter 12) regarding the impact of new technology and other disturbing causes in reversing the downward pressure on the profit and wage rates. Here it emerges that Malthus's celebrated agricultural protectionism was partly dictated by his vision of buoyant prospects for ongoing accumulation and population growth at steady, even rising, wages and with no downward pressure on profits. He conceded a case for a free corn-import trade where an economy approached stationariness (491). This was far from the case in contemporary England; considering the impact of new technology and the various other disturbing causes 'the British isles shew at present no symptoms whatever of this species of exhaustion' (491–2).[9]

It seems that this optimistic view of 1817 coloured even the evaluation of the war years. Yet at the same time, there are references in 1817 – appearing also in 1826 – to an *ultimate* deceleration of population growth, attributable to land scarcity although with no suggestion of any immediate manifestation (see Section VI). And Malthus specified a variety of 'limits' all based on diminishing returns, including an ultimate limit to population at which the subsistence wage equals the marginal product (430). Even so, in all this there is still no suggestion that such limits had any *immediate* relevance.[10]

VI. CONTEMPORARY POPULATION GROWTH

It is common for commentators to understand the first essay as conveying the message that population was *actually and invariably* increasing faster than subsistence. This is an untenable reading. It is not *actual* but maximum or *potential* population growth that exceeds the growth of subsistence. The 'principle states of modern Europe' were in fact experiencing slow population growth, Malthus maintained in 1798: 'instead of doubling their numbers every twenty-five years, they require three or four hundred years, or more, for that purpose' (1798: 62). (See also 314–15 regarding 'very slow' English population growth.) The reason for the short fall of actual behind potential growth turns, of course, on the operation of the preventive and positive checks, the wage acting in an *equilibrating* fashion to assure that population growth keeps in line with (in the present case) a slowly growing food supply by acting appropriately on birth and death rates. Conversely, an acceleration of food production, by raising real wages, would encourage an appropriate population increase (133). The slow growth of the British food supply is not, be it noted, explained in terms of proximity to the stationary state; that the food supply had been growing only slowly, despite an increased agricultural potential created by reorganization and new technology, is explained rather by undue manufacturing expansion and diversions of capital to satisfy rising upper-class demands (318–19). The problem, as Malthus saw it, was to raise the growth rate of agricultural output and rely on population growth to respond to higher real wages. Direct encouragement of the birth rate (extensions of the poor laws and the various idealistic proposals of the day) promised disaster by giving free reign to the ever-existing potential of population to expand faster than food supplies (132–3). Population growth could look after itself. And though there were limits to what could be achieved by this programme deriving from the constrained possibilities for agricultural growth in an 'old settled' country, this was scarcely a practical concern and there is certainly no suggestion that the higher real wages that were attainable by agricultural growth would be effaced by *excessive* increases in labour supply. Without the institutional encouragement of population, labour supply would rise, at most, at a rate corresponding to that of labour demand. This theme is carried over to all later editions of the essay.

The 1803 version places greater emphasis upon the preventive (as distinct from the positive) check in the accounts of modern history.[11] At various points will be found references to that check where none existed in 1798 (1803: 347, 350). Most striking is an entirely new passage representing delayed marriage as 'the most powerful of the checks, which in modern Europe keep down the population to the level of the means of subsistence' (351). Malthus was ill-advised to retain in 1803 the original frame of reference (the first two chapters of 1798) with its general presumption that population growth must be constrained within the limits imposed by a *slowly* growing food supply. Evidence of the higher effectiveness of the prudential check would contribute to explain a slowly growing population. But the same evidence has a totally different implication at a time of *rapid* population growth; reduced nuptuality (and a reduced birth rate) obviously do not serve to explain that phenomenon.

The revised picture of population growth was brought to light by the census data made available between editions as Malthus himself stresses. In 1798 he had estimated British population ('this island') at about 7 million (1798: 23) when it was in fact closer to the 10.9 million reported by the 1801 census – some 56 per cent higher.[12] The census data also revealed that the English population had been increasing steadily since the 1740s and at an accelerating rate. (In fact, in the early 1820s it reached the highest level it was ever to attain.) Such a rate of growth, given evidence of increasing prudence, could only be rationalized in terms of reduced mortality: 'It would appear, by the present proportion of marriages, that the more rapid increase of population, supposed to have taken place since the year 1780, has arisen more from the diminution of deaths, than from the increase of the births' (1803: 311n). This is removed in 1806. In its place there is inserted a reference to 'the absolutely stationary number of deaths during the last twenty years, notwithstanding a considerable increase of births . . . ' (1806, I: 466–7). But this statement still implies a falling *rate* of mortality. And indeed almost immediately Malthus implicitly reaffirms the primary role of reduced mortality in accounting for the population explosion: 'as the increase of population since 1780 is incontrovertible, *and the present mortality extraordinarily small*, I should still be disposed to believe that the greater part of the effect [a reference to the "most striking" increase in life span experienced since 1780] is to be attributed to increased healthiness' (469; emphasis added; see 1803: 312 for the almost identical version).[13] In 1817, the altered reference of 1806 is deleted entirely; but the passage regarding the 'incontrovertible' population increase and the 'extraordinarily small' mortality is retained (1817, II: 65), and in fact the word 'much' (removed temporarily in 1806) is reinserted in the conclusion: 'I should still be disposed to believe, that much the greater part of the effect [expanded life span] is to be attributed to increased healthiness'. The position of 1803 regarding the source of the contemporary population increase in reduced mortality – all the more striking considering the 'crowd[ing] together in close and unwholesome rooms' which characterized manufactures in the 1798 account (1798: 313) – is thus confirmed and indeed reinforced in 1817.

In 1803 Malthus inserted the proposition that nuptuality need not rise with an acceleration of economic activity. For *rapid economic growth might itself generate improved prudential habits*, a most important contribution to demographic theory (above, p. 326; see *ETRM*, 5, IV); and the higher degree of prudence in turn would reduce the mortality rate. Now 'improving cultivation and trade', improved 'habits with respect to prudence and cleanliness', and the fact that population growth reflected 'diminished mortality, instead of an increased number of births', characterized contemporary Britain on Malthus's own estimate. Higher British earnings did not in that case generate a higher marriage rate; and indirectly contributed to the reduced mortality rate.

Consider now Malthus's reaction in 1817 to the 1811 census results indicating rapid population growth with no downward pressure on real wages: 'The returns of the Population Act in 1811 undoubtedly presented extraordinary results. They shewed a greatly accelerated rate of progress, and a greatly improved healthiness of the people, notwithstanding the increase of the towns and the increased proportion of the population engaged in manufacturing employments. They thus furnished another striking instance of the readiness with which population starts forwards, under almost any weight, when the resources of a country are rapidly increasing' (1817, II: 80). The experience of accelerating population growth is thus again taken as evidence of the essay's major theme, namely that population growth is constrained below its maximum physiological level by the *relatively* sluggish expansion of 'resources' (read food supply); a relaxation of this constraint allows population growth to rise towards its full potential. The validation of this theme was all the more impressive given the expansion of urban centres and a rising proportion of the work force engaged in manufactures.

The new data presented a challenge, for they indicated an *acceleration* of population growth in an old-settled country where a *deceleration* was to be expected. Specifically, evidence available at the beginning of the century indicated a population growth rate amounting to a doubling in eighty-three and a half years; the 1811 census figures raised the estimate to a doubling in fifty-five years: 'This is a rate of progress which in a rich and well-peopled country might reasonably be expected to diminish rather than to increase. But instead of any such diminution, it appears that as far as 1810 it had been considerably accelerated' (81).[14] Or again, even the lowest of alternative birth/death rate ratios then under debate was 'quite extraordinary for a rich and well-peopled territory . . . [which] were it to continue, would . . . double the number of inhabitants in less than fifty-five years' (103). This rate of increase, however, and by implication its prerequisite – a rapidly increasing food supply – could not be 'permanent'; Malthus apparently contemplated ultimate deceleration of food supplies and consequently of population. But not seriously; its onset would not occur for some three or four decades (66).[15]

The postwar depression years left their impression, but long-term optimism shines through. Malthus in 1817 blamed the 'distresses' partially on the high population growth rate in the face of a *temporary* downturn in accumulation. The problem was envisaged as a temporary one first, because some deceleration of population growth might be expected considering the going circumstances of agricultural scarcity similar to 1800–1, but more significantly because of the expected reestablishment of the high trend path of capital accumulation: 'The great object to be kept in view, is to support the people through their present distresses, in the hope (and I trust a just one) of better times', which would 'restore the labouring classes to full employment and good wages' (359). Apparently, 'full employment and good wages' are envisaged as the secular norm.

When we come to the sixth edition, the accelerating population trend is again much emphasized. With the results of the census of 1821 in hand – 1801–11, a 13.3 per cent increase, or a doubling in fifty-five years; 1800–21, a 15.6 per cent increase, or a doubling in forty-eight years – Malthus declaimed regarding 'a most extraordinary rate of increase, considering the actual population compared with its territory, and the number of its great towns and manufactories' (1826, I: 444). The expectation in 1817 of renewed 'full employment and good wages' is now said to have been 'in a considerable degree' confirmed (II: 102n). This outcome reflected not a relative constraint on population growth by way of reduced marriage and birth rates – labour-supply constraints – but the rapid expansion of labour demand. In fact Malthus alludes to *too rapid* a population expansion impeding a total recovery:

> This has, in a considerable degree, taken place; but it has been owing rather to the latter causes noticed than to the former. It appeared, by the returns of 1821, that the scarce years of 1817 and 1818 had but a slight effect in diminishing the number of marriages and births, compared with the effect of the great proportion of plentiful years in increasing them; so that the population proceeded with great rapidity during the ten years ending with 1820. But this great increase of the population has prevented the labouring classes from being so fully employed as might have been expected from the prosperity of commerce and agriculture during the last two or three years.
>
> (Malthus 1826, II: 102n)

Considered in isolation this latter paragraph might seem to imply a substantive change in position, since so much had been made in earlier editions of a *secular reduction* in the marriage and birth rates, the rapid population growth turning on reduced mortality. But we should not make too much of the passage, for in all other contexts the original weighting is retained; and moreover, a new note is added to the original 1806 Appendix which reinforces that weighting: 'It appears from the three returns of the Population Act, in 1801, 1811, and 1821, that the proportion of marriages has been diminishing with the increasing health of the country, notwithstanding the augmented rate of increase in the population' (462n). There was then no reversal in the last edition of the earlier estimates. They were indeed in one respect reinforced. For the loose prediction given in 1806 and 1817 of decelerating growth of food supplies and therefore of population within some three or four decades *is extended to a full century* (1826, I: 414), and this despite *acceleration* of the population growth rate revealed by the third census.

VII. THE POPULATION PROBLEM SUMMARIZED AND SOCIAL POLICY OBJECTIVES

Our exegesis has demonstrated that land scarcity and rising real costs of food make no appearance in the accounts of contemporary and prospective agricultural development given in the *Essay*. We should also have in mind the striking observation that '[f]rom a review of the state of society in former periods, compared with the present, I should certainly say, that the evils resulting from the principle of population have rather diminished than increased' – which suggests reduced misery, i.e. higher real wages – and could be expected to diminish further with increasing prudential control (1803: 603). All this implies the absence of a population problem in the sense of *excess* population growth relative to food.[16] The denial of a population problem in this sense is the same in 1803 as in 1798, with one difference: In 1798 Malthus was seeking to explain the *slow* growth of population and found it in the slow growth of food supplies, whereas in 1803 (with the census results of 1801 at hand) his attention was on the newly discovered fact of *accelerating* population growth which he accounted for by *reduced mortality* due partly to exogenous improvements in health and partly to accelerating domestic food supplies and, to a limited degree, imports.

But if in normal circumstances, and from a secular perspective, excess population growth was not the issue, what is the sense of the *immediacy* of the problem upon which Malthus repeatedly focused? The answer turns on the maximum *capacity* of population to grow at a rate exceeding the maximum capacity of food. This is nicely put in 1803 in a statement wherein Malthus disclaims concern with ultimate stationariness. The issue is whether corn could be increased at a rate equal to the 'natural' (maximum conceivable) growth rate of population. Since it could not, there is continuous need for the operation of checks (positive and/or preventive). In this sense the 'principle of population' poses a *permanent* problem, not one for some future period: 'with regard to the principle of population, it is never the question, whether a country will produce *any more* but whether it may be made to produce a sufficiency to keep pace with an unchecked increase of people. . . . [It] is not the question whether, by cultivating all our commons, we could raise considerably more corn than at present; but whether we could raise sufficient for a population of twenty millions in the next twenty-five years, and forty millions in the next fifty years' (1803: 481–2).

This, of course, is not a statement of *actual* population doubling every twenty-five years that must necessarily be restricted, but of its *potential*. The problem of population therefore existed even under conditions of accelerating food production since population growth still had to be restrained below its maximum. And, in fact, somewhat paradoxically, the newly recognized acceleration of population growth served to vindicate the initial position of 1798: 'That the checks which have been mentioned, are the true

[1826: immediate] causes of the slow increase of population, and that these checks result principally from an insufficiency of subsistence, will be evident from the comparatively rapid increase, which has invariably taken place, whenever, by some sudden enlargement in the means of subsistence, these checks have been in any considerable degree removed' (1803: 336; 1826, I: 514).

Marx's famous charge that 'the parson Malthus . . . reduces the worker to a beast of burden for the sake of production and even condemns him to death from starvation, and to celibacy' (Marx 1968, II: 119) is, it will now be clear, a parody. Malthus himself gave the reply to this sort of charge in 1803 and all later editions:

This prudential restraint, if it were generally adopted, by narrowing the supply of labour in the market, would, in the natural course of things, soon raise its price. This period of delayed gratification would be passed in saving the earnings which were above the wants of a single man, and in acquiring habits of sobriety, industry and economy, which would enable him, in a few years, to enter into the matrimonial contract without fear of its consequences. The operation of the preventive check in this way, by constantly keeping the population within the limits of the food, though constantly following its increase, would give a real value to the rise of wages . . . .

(Malthus 1803: 495)

Reduction of the birth rate was the key to increased wages, and one of the desirable consequences of the improved conditions would be reduced mortality. Exogenous improvements in health, including vaccination, which cut the mortality rate were championed, subject to a compensatory reduction in the birth rate, to prevent an excessive growth rate of population.

In his 1806 Appendix Malthus forcefully protested against blatant misinterpretations of his position on this matter:

In many parts of the Essay I have dwelt much on the advantage of rearing the requisite population of any country from the smallest number of births. I have stated expressly, that a decrease of mortality of all ages is what we ought chiefly to aim at; and as the best criterion of happiness and good government, instead of the largeness of the proportion of births, which was the usual mode of judging, I have proposed the smallness of the proportion dying under the age of puberty. Conscious that I have never intentionally deviated from these principles, I might well be rather surprised to hear that I had been considered by some as an enemy to the introduction of the vaccine inoculation, which is calculated to attain the very end which I have uniformly considered as so desirable.

(Malthus 1806, II: 513–14)

Malthus did not favour a stationary state (even at high wages) as the ideal. He wanted 'a market rather understocked with labour', but not 'in such a degree as to affect the wealth and prosperity of the country' (1803: 511), an illusion to aggregative indexes. It was 'of the very utmost importance to the happiness of mankind, that they should not increase too fast' (492) – not that population should be stationary. For as he explained in 1806, he favoured growth of population at 'high' wages: 'It is an utter misconception of my argument to infer that I am an enemy to population. I am only an enemy to vice and misery, and consequently to that unfavourable proportion between population and food which produces these evils. But this unfavourable proportion has no necessary connection with the quantity of absolute population which a country may contain. On the contrary, it is more frequently found in countries which are very thinly peopled, than in those which are populous' (1806, II: 507–8). His critics had failed to appreciate that the proposed programme of checks to the birth rate, designed to avoid 'poverty and premature mortality', was consistent with population expansion, and had erroneously supposed 'that the *ultimate* object of my work is to check population, as if any thing could be more desirable than the most rapid increase of population unaccompanied by vice and misery' (515).

What of the internal consistency of the *desiderata* alluded to in the foregoing passage? The key to higher standards is a reduction in the birth rate by way of postponed marriage, and such a programme would be consistent with achieving population increase assuming a reduced *mortality* rate: 'Two or three years in the average age of marriage, by lengthening each generation, and tending, in a small degree, both to diminish the prolifickness of marriages, and the number of born living to be married, may make a considerable difference in the rate of increase, and be adequate to allow for a considerably diminished mortality' (536–7). Moreover, the potential for productivity increase (due *inter alia* to land improvement) is greater in the case of a population comprising a high proportion of healthy adults; the programme, by altering the age distribution, would result ultimately in the creation of 'fresh resources' for the support of population growth under relatively favourable circumstances: 'without a diminished proportion of births, we cannot attain any *permanent* improvement in the health and happiness of the mass of the people, and secure that description of population, which, by containing a larger share of adults, is best calculated to create fresh resources, and consequently to encourage a continued increase of efficient population' (550). The immediate policy implications are unambiguous. An increase in population size that is otherwise achievable only at low wages might with patience be attained with no deterioration: 'there is no man who has the slightest feeling for the happiness of the most numerous class of society, or has even just views of policy on the subject, who would not rather choose that the requisite population should be obtained by such a price of labour, combined with such habits, as would occasion a very small mortality, than from a great proportion of births, of which comparatively few would reach manhood' (551–2n). It is clear that population increase was an objective; that the means to that end were either a high birth rate accompanied by low wages and high mortality, or a low birth rate accompanied by high wages and low mortality; and that Malthus unambiguously championed the latter alternative.

Some statements are so 'optimistic' as to suggest that population increase can be *indefinitely* maintained at constant wages provided its *rate of increase* is suitably restrained. In that case stationary states will at most constitute temporary breathing stops. But in all likelihood this does not constitute Malthus's considered opinion. At the outset he had clarified that an *unlimited* potential to the expansion of food supplies was an unrealisable supposition; and this clarification is emphasized in the 1806 edition: 'I have allowed the produce of the earth to be unlimited, which is certainly going too far' (516–17). In brief, the potential for land preparation tends to weaken. Malthus certainly favoured population expansion, but he believed there to be absolute limits. It was his objective to assure that in the stationary state wages should be high. But 'ultimate' stationariness was a far distant prospect; in the meantime population might grow without a fall in wages provided its rate of increase was appropriately limited.

Malthus's 'pessimism' is considerably constrained on our reading. It amounts to the proposition that in the absence of checks to the growth rate of population, average living standards must fall. In this limited sense both the effect of land scarcity and the need for time-consuming land improvements are continuously making themselves felt. These notions of population pressure are, however, not to be equated with actual population pressure in a literal sense of the term. Malthus in 1803 unfortunately retained the remark that 'there are few states in which there is not a constant effort in the population to increase beyond the means of subsistence. This constant effort as constantly tends to subject the lower classes of society to distress, and to prevent any great permanent amelioration of their condition' (1803: 12).[17] But a 'tendency' is not to be understood as a 'prediction'. Similarly, he was asking for trouble by introducing a reference in 1817 to a *'natural tendency* of population to increase beyond the powers of the earth to produce food for it' (1817, III: 413) when he himself was pointing out the solution.

VIII. UTILITARIANISM AND THEODICY

'Prudential' restraint refers to delayed marriage probably accompanied by vice: 'The effects, indeed, of these [preventive] restraints upon marriage are but too conspicuous in the consequent vices that are produced in almost every part of the world; vices, that are continually involving both sexes in inextricable unhappiness' (1798: 69–70). Similarly, prudential considerations 'are calculated to prevent, and certainly do prevent, a very great number in all civilized nations from pursuing the dictate of nature in an early attachment to one woman. And this restraint almost necessarily, though not absolutely so, produces vice' (28–9). Yet notwithstanding, in the course of his case against the outdoor poor-relief system, Malthus intimated a preference for prudence as a necessary evil for the sake of avoiding misery: 'Every obstacle in the way of marriage must undoubtedly be considered as a species of unhappiness. But as from the laws of our nature some check to population must exist, it is better that it should be checked from a foresight of the difficulties attending a family, and the fear of dependent poverty, than that it should be encouraged, only to be repressed afterwards by want and sickness' (89–90).

By 'moral restraint' – the check to population growth formally introduced in the second edition of 1803 – was intended the restraint from marriage 'which is not followed by irregular gratifications' (1803: 11).[18] Malthus himself pointed to the new check and its practical implications in a famous Preface to the second edition:

> Throughout the whole of the present work, I have so far differed in principle from the former, as to suppose another check to population possible, which does not strictly come under the head either of vice or misery; and, in the latter part, I have endeavoured to soften some of the harshest conclusions of the first essay. In doing this, I hope that I have not violated the principles of just reasoning; nor expressed any opinion respecting the probable improvement of society, in which I am not borne out by the experience of the past. To those who shall still think that any check to population whatever, would be worse than the evils which it would relieve, the conclusions of the former essay will remain in full force; and if we adopt this opinion, we shall be compelled to acknowledge that the poverty and misery that prevail among the lower classes of society are absolutely irremediable.
>
> (Malthus 1803: vii)

This statement, which has done much to stamp the first *Essay* as a thoroughly depressing document, is misleading. Malthus had *not* shown in 1798 that 'the poverty and misery that prevail among the lower classes of society are absolutely irremediable' – only that they are so in the absence of prudence. And he had from the outset recommended delay of marriage despite the 'vicious' consequences. Equally important, the implications of 'moral restraint' must not be exaggerated, since Malthus did not believe that the period before marriage would by-and-large be spent chastely (cf. 1806, I: 20n).

To have allowed much weight in practice to 'moral restraint' would have been to concede too much to Godwin, and this Malthus did not do despite the Preface of 1803. Indeed, the embarrassing implications of Malthus's championship in the first *Essay* of delayed marriage – despite the high probability of accompanying vice – are brought out yet more strongly in a rejection introduced in 1806 of Arthur Young's criticism of 1804 that Malthus had assumed 'perfect chastity in the single state': 'Whatever I may have said in drawing a picture *professedly* visionary, for the sake of illustration, in the practical application of my principles I have taken man as he is, with all his imperfections on his head. And thus viewing him, and knowing that some checks to population must exist, I have not the slightest hesitation in saying, that the prudential check to marriage is better than premature mortality. And in this decision I feel myself completely justified by experience' (1806, II: 538). Even in the absence of moral restraint, prudential delay of marriage was to be welcomed, and this because misery also entails vice. On a balance of costs and benefits, prudence with 'irregular gratification' was preferable; Malthus was prepared to tolerate *immoral* restraint as the lesser of two evils. (For the full evidence, see *ETRM*, 18, V.)

The final two chapters of the first edition treat the compatibility of the 'disheartening' outcome of the population principle with a beneficent deity (see *ETRM*, 19). These chapters establish a 'moral' dimension to Malthus's utilitarianism, and illustrate his attempt to combine the viewpoint of moralist and objective scientist (though the same may be said, of course, of Bentham and J. S. Mill). But the fact remains that Malthus's explanation of 'disharmonies' by reference to Divine Wisdom is irrelevant for the analysis and without influence on the theory of policy. More strongly, the last two chapters in the 1798 essay turn out to be an embarrassment, as is apparent from the famous Senior–Malthus correspondence of 1829. For Malthus rejected Senior's original attribution to him of the view that reform was to no purpose; he had intended only to convey that the solution to low wages, or the permanent maintenance of improved wages, lay in population control since 'population was always ready, and inclined, to increase faster than food, if the checks which repressed it were removed' (see *ETRM*, 18, IX). To write two chapters expressly designed to 'Vindicate the ways of God to man', having in mind the 'constant pressure of distress' (1798: 348–9) could only have misled readers in just the manner Senior complained of. In sum: the theological chapters worked on a presumption of *actual* population pressure, whereas Malthus had in mind elsewhere in his first edition and throughout the later editions *potential* population pressure.

There is a further matter of high relevance – the fact that comparison of the 1798 and later editions reveals a completely changed 'vision' of the population problem (above, Section VI). The empirical issue originally, as far as concerns contemporary Britain, was a supposedly low population growth rate accounted for proximately by low wages, in turn due to sluggish agricultural progress. In 1803 and thereafter the picture was transformed in the light of information revealed by the censuses of 1801, 1811 and 1821. The new problem was to explain accelerating population growth at steady (even rising) real wages. The explanation offered turned on reductions in mortality rates – not increases in marriage and birth rates – in conditions of, and partly due to, rapid growth of national income and capital accumulation. The 'vision' was a *bright* not a *dismal* one, for 'the evils resulting from the principle of population have rather diminished than increased, even under the disadvantage of an almost total ignorance of their real cause' (1803: 603).[19] The original theological problem had thus been entirely superannuated by events; and the revised theological problem of the need for the 'painful' check of chastity before marriage (487) was merely *theoretical*, considering the ongoing acceleration of national product, or at the worst, a problem for some distant future.

The empirical dimension alone would account for the removal of the theological chapters. But there may be other reasons including the abandonment of the theodicy there outlined, reflected in the contrast between God's grand spiritual end or purpose of 1798 extending *beyond* this world and thus assuring an overwhelming net balance of good, and the *mundane* ends of material existence, namely the replenishment of the earth and the cultivation of the soil. As far as concerns actual demographic policy in the *Essay on Population*, Malthus effectively eschewed theological considerations. His utilitarianism in these contexts is almost entirely earthbound.

There is, however, a 'theological' issue which emerges in the body of the first essay but is conspicuously absent from the theological chapters – namely the fact that any reduction in misery entails, in practice, vice. Such a choice would cast doubt on the benevolence of the Deity, and is a problem brought to Malthus's attention by critics of the first essay. This led him to introduce the matter of 'moral restraint' in 1803 (Book IV). A theological dimension thus certainly remains in 1803 and thereafter – the mere fact that the two concluding chapters of 1798 disappear as such is of no consequence. Indeed, it is fair to say that the defence of the Deity is reinforced – though only if limited to an ideal rather than the real world considering the practical insignificance of restraint. Even so, its substance differs from that of 1798. First, there is no longer any emphasis on the training of mind for a *future* existence, the most characteristic feature of the 1798 theodicy.[20] Second, the case for a reduction of poverty is now formally conspicuously represented as a 'moral' issue, so that the theological problem is no longer to explain 'distress' but to explain the need for 'painful' checks to *avoid* distress.

IX. AGRICULTURAL PROTECTIONISM AND ITS ABANDONMENT

A case for agricultural protection appears in earlier editions of the *Essay* (those of 1803, 1806 and 1807) with particular reference to Malthus's opposition to 'Commercial Systems'. The static efficiency gains of free trade were not at issue. Rather the object of agricultural protectionism – in 1803 by way of a corn-export bounty and in 1806 with greater attention to import restriction – was to assure 'security, independence, and permanent prosperity' even at the cost of a slight deceleration of growth (see *ETRM*, 17, II). It is the presumption here that a faster expansion of manufacturing relative to domestic agriculture exacerbates the problem of seasonal instability; and puts upward pressure on the level of money costs to the ultimate disadvantage of manufacturing itself. There was also a danger to national negotiating power of reliance on imported food. Moreover, to rely on imports was foolhardy because of the prospective transition of agriculturally based economies to mixed systems and the drying up of foreign surpluses for export. A more formal case for corn-import restriction is spelled out in 1817 in the chapter 'Of Corn Laws: Restrictions on Importation'. To this chapter an extraordinary note retracting protectionism is added in the sixth edition.

Malthus commences his case by repeating the central argument against 'commercial systems' in 1803, 1806 and 1817 itself, in the context of proposals for Europe to devote itself entirely to manufactures in exchange for American corn. Even were such a trade pattern the natural outcome in the absence of controls, the manufacturing economies would ultimately suffer when the United States itself took up manufactures (as it inevitably would), and restricted its corn exports (1817, II: 483). The trade in corn was a distinctly *non-permanent* trade, to be viewed as no more than a means of balancing temporary requirements, not as a trade upon which could be based the international division of labour (482). Corn is contrasted with 'the peculiar products of each soil and climate' which are *permanent* objects of trade: 'The peculiar products of each soil and climate are objects of foreign trade, which can never, under any circumstances, fail. But food is not a peculiar product; and the country which produces it in the greatest abundance may, according to the laws which govern the progress of population, have nothing to spare for others' (481–2).

It is allowed that with a free corn trade the absolute size and rate of growth of population would be greater than with reliance on domestic agriculture, but the cost was too high, namely – here is a nice summary of the main objections to a 'commercial system' – 'a greater degree of uncertainty in its supplies of corn, greater fluctuations in the wages of labour, greater unhealthiness and immorality owing to a larger proportion of the population being employed in manufactories, and a greater chance of long and depressing retrograde movements occasioned by the natural progress of those countries from which corn had been imported' (495–6). Malthus downplayed the price instability frequently attributed to a '*protected* economy – the magnitude of the corn-price decline required to expand exports abroad in the event of a glut: "a nation with an ample capital"' would find little difficulty carrying over any surpluses to future years (504). A worse source of instability was that occasioned by a flood of imports. And in any event those nations 'which habitually grow their own supplies' would lessen the magnitude of price increases in years of general scarcity, thus diminishing the potential range of variability (505). On balance, 'the range of variation will be the least under such a system of restriction as, without preventing importation when prices are high, will secure in ordinary years a growth equal to the consumption' (505–6).[21]

It is precisely at this point that Malthus inserts into the 1826 edition his note which maintains that notwithstanding the greater stability of prices under protection, he did *not* favour protection (1826, II: 209n). The appropriate policy was one that did not 'impeach the principles of free trade': 'I am very far however from meaning to say that the circumstance of different countries having often an abundance or deficiency of corn at the same time, though it must prevent the possibility of steady prices, is a decisive reason against the abolition or alteration of the corn-laws. The most powerful of all the arguments against restrictions is their unsocial tendency, and the acknowledged injury which they must do to the interests of the commercial world in general. The weight of this argument is increased rather than diminished by the numbers which may suffer from scarcity at the same time.' Moreover, 'at a period when our ministers are most laudably setting an example of a more liberal system of commercial policy' – a reference to Huskisson's free trade reforms – 'it would be greatly desirable that foreign nations should not have so marked an exception as our present corn-laws to cast in our teeth. A duty on importation not too high, and a bounty nearly such as was recommended by Mr Ricardo, would probably be best suited to our present situation, and best secure steady prices. A duty on foreign corn would resemble the duties laid by other countries on our manufactures as objects of taxation, and would not in the same manner impeach the principles of free trade.' A final statement at the close of the note makes explicit that the specification of the pros and cons of the Corn Laws in the body of the chapter was not designed as a 'protest' *against* their abolition or change: 'But whatever system we may adopt, it is essential to a sound determination, and highly useful in preventing disappointments, that all the arguments both for and against corn-laws should be thoroughly and impartially considered; and it is because on a calm, and, as far as I can judge, an impartial review of the arguments of this chapter, they still appear to me of weight sufficient to deserve such consideration, and *not as a kind of protest against the abolition or change of the corn-laws*, that I republish them in another edition' (emphasis added). And it is indeed true that in the body of the chapter Malthus had stated that the balanced-growth policy 'may be purchased too dear' (1817, II: 477; 1826, II: 186), and could not be recommended as a hard-and-fast rule. The stage had already been set for a renunciation of the case for balanced growth – with the requisite agricultural protection – in the new circumstances that Britain encountered.

It is particularly relevant, considering the 1826 note, that the contemporary expansion of foreign markets is partly ascribed by Malthus in the *Quarterly Review* for 1824 to the 'improved views of our government in commercial legislation' (1986, 7: 287). The empirical significance of *manu-factures* from the perspective of aggregate activity reinforced the case for free trade, since expanded export markets could scarcely be relied upon with agriculture 'so marked an exception' to a general free-trade programme. Thus by the mid-1820s the manufacturing sector was proving itself adequate in that respect. Actually, even when making his case for agricul-tural protection in the 1817 essay (1817, II: 475–6), Malthus had included the discouragement of manufacturing exports amongst the *costs* of such a policy. This concern becomes decisive in the 1820s.

There is a related matter – the classical proposition that the relatively high manufacturing (export) productivity of a particular trading nation allows and assures that nation a higher price level in international monetary equilibrium. This proposition would put paid to the original concern – that of 1803, 1806 (it does not appear in 1817) – with the undermining of competitiveness in consequence of a higher price level generated by a disparate expansion of manufactures. The causal sequence is reversed; general prices are high because of high export efficiency. Malthus's subscription to that position appears in a further note added in 1826 to the very chapter 'Restrictions upon Importation' which has preoccupied us (1826, II: 198n).

More generally, from the viewpoint of labour's welfare, there is evidence of a new emphasis discernible in the 1817 *Essay* on industry-biased growth as typically characteristic of the later stages of economic development, and along with it, the retraction of much of an earlier concern with such growth from *labour's* perspective (see *ETRM*, 5, IV). The evidence given above from the 1826 version points to the implications for trade policy of this orienta-tion, and suggests that Malthus had in fact thrown in his lot with the Ricardians. There is, however, a possible lessening of concern with the policy question in one respect. For the problem 'whether a balance between the agricultural and commercial classes of society, which would not take place naturally, ought, under certain circumstances, to be maintained artificially' was described in 1817 as 'the most important practical question in the whole compass of political economy', whereas this is modified in 1826 to read simply 'a most important practical question' (1817, II: 477; 1826, II: 187).

NOTES

1 I draw here on two reviews of these editions (Hollander 1988 [essay 13], 1991 [essay 14]).
2 A selection from the two James volumes has been prepared by Winch (Malthus 1992).
3 I shall provide references where appropriate to my *Economics of Thomas Robert Malthus* (forthcoming 1997). This will be cited as *ETRM* with an indication of chapter and section.
4 The alternative outcomes are in fact already apparent, though less formally expressed, as early as 1803: 'if the lower classes of people had acquired the

habit of proportioning the supplies of labour to a stationary, or even decreasing demand, without an increase of misery and mortality, as at present; we might even venture to indulge a hope, that at some future period, the processes for abridging human labour, the progress of which has of late years been so rapid, might ultimately supply all the wants of the most wealthy society with less personal labour than at present; and if they did not diminish the severity of individual exertion, might, at least, diminish the number of those employed in severe toil' (594). See also below, pp. 333, 337.

5 Dupont's *Examen du livre de M. Malthus sur le Principe de Population* (1817) includes a translation of four chapters in the 1806 edition of the *Essay* absent in P. and G. Prévost's translation of 1809. These chapters are Book III, chapter VII, 'Of increasing Wealth as it affects the Condition of the Poor'; chapter VIII, 'Of the Definitions of Wealth. Agricultural and Commercial Systems'; chapter IX, 'Different Effects of the Agricultural and Commercial Systems'; chapter X, 'Of Bounties on the Exportation of Corn'.

6 But the Quesnay case is never alluded to formally in the *Essay*, and first appears (without attribution) in Malthus's pamphlets of 1814 and 1815.

7 Thus a statment in 1803 (442) that 'upon the whole . . . our commerce has not done much for our agriculture; but . . . our agriculture has done a great deal for our commerce', is altered in 1806 (II: 220) to read: 'that our commerce has not done so much for our agriculture as our agriculture has for our commerce' – a nice instance of Malthus's fiddling with his texts. In 1807, he fiddled a bit more: 'It must be allowed therefore, upon the whole, that our commerce has not done more for our agriculture, than our agriculture has for our commerce' (1807, II: 144).

8 There is a qualification to this generalization. Increasing land scarcity is alluded to in an application to the analysis of a supposedly higher British population growth rate c. 1600–50 compared with c. 1680–1750 (above, Section II). But despite this statement, Malthus did not perceive Britain in his own day as densely populated; it is expressly described as 'thinly inhabited' or at least 'not . . . extremely crowded and populous' (1798: 116). He had in any event applied the land-scarcity analysis to seventeenth-century data circumspectly (123 and note). This particular analysis of the demographic data, though of theoretical importance, does not have much relevance for the appreciation of Malthus's considered view of English development.

9 This formulation raises problems. The land-scarcity based growth model so brilliantly formulated in the same 1817 edition (above, Section II) was apparently *not* a reflection of contemporary events. Yet in the pamphlets of 1814 and 1815 the principle of diminishing returns is said to have been confirmed by wartime experience as revealed by the parliamentary evidence, albeit not to any great degree. What transpired between 1815 and 1817 to lead Malthus to a reorientation is discussed in *ETRM*, 15, V.

10 The 1820 and the 1836 (posthumous) versions of the *Principles* both emphasize an increasing rate of return on capital over the war years attributable *inter alia* to higher productivity and effort supply. Taking the *Principles* as a whole, we can discern no revision of the optimism expressed in the 1817 (and 1826) *Essay* regarding prospective productivity increase. Only in the second version of the chapter on Rent are there possibly new doubts, but these are not sustained or carried through. For these reasons Malthus's new recognition in the 1820s that Britain's future prosperity turned on industry-led growth (Section IX) cannot be attributed with any confidence to a growing concern with prospective agricultural productivity.

11 Even in 1798, however, Malthus had expounded on the widespread practice of the preventive check 'through all the ranks of society in England' (1798: 63).

12 In 1803 the base population figure used in illustrating the geometric and arithmetic progressions is 11 million in place of the original 7 million (1803: 8). For details of the inaccurate estimates brought to light by the census see 1803: 300f.

13 In 1806 too Malthus observed that 'the increased healthiness observed of late years could not possibly have taken place without this accompanying circumstance' of delayed marriage (1806, II: 536), a reference to the special necessity for a reduced birth rate during a period of falling mortality.

14 In the 1806 edition after a reference to a doubling in eighty-three and a half years Malthus added: 'and as we cannot suppose that the country could admit of more than a quadrupled population in the next hundred and sixty-six years, we may safely say that its resources will not allow of a permanent rate of increase greater than that which is taking place at present' (1806, II: 535). This is unchanged in 1817 (III: 361), but altered in 1826 to read 'a permanent rate of increase greater than that which was then taking place' (II: 461).

15 Malthus repeats the passage from 1803 (313) to this effect. As early as 1806 (I: 470), he removed a note regarding the 'late scarcities' of 1800–1 and their impact on birth and death rates, indicating that he came to consider those years to be aberrations.

16 At least in a system avoiding dependence upon foreign corn supplies with the danger that posed of providing an unreliable stimulus to population growth.

17 In the first *Essay*, the formulation was stronger: 'Yet in all societies, even those that are most vicious, the tendency to a virtuous attachment is so strong, that there is a constant effort towards an increase of population. This constant effort . . . ' (1798: 29).

18 Cf. the explanatory note added in 1806: 'It will be observed, that I here use the term *moral* in its most confined sense. By moral restraint I would be understood to mean a restraint from marriage, from prudential motives, with a conduct strictly moral during the period of this restraint; and I have never intentionally deviated from this sense. When I have wished to consider the restraint from marriage unconnected with its consequences, I have either called it prudential restraint, or a part of the preventive check, of which indeed it forms the principal branch' (1806, I: 19–20n).

19 Since the empirical problem in Britain is *not* represented even in 1798 as one of excess population growth – rather, low real wages reflected remediable impediments to agricultural growth – the theological chapters were strictly speaking unnecessary.

20 A sentence in the 1803 Preface referring to continued adherence to the original theology is deleted in 1806.

21 Nowhere in the chapter is falling agricultural productivity – diminishing returns – taken into account.

REFERENCES

Dupont de Nemours, P. S. (1817) *Examen du livre de M. Malthus sur le Principe de Population*, Philadelphia:Lafourcade.

Hollander, S. (1988), 'Review of *The Works of Thomas Robert Malthus*' 1986, *Journal of Economic History*, 48 (December): 987–9.

—— (1991) 'New Editions of Malthus', *Utilitas*, 3, 2 (November): 303–10.

—— (1997) *The Economics of Thomas Robert Malthus*, Toronto: University of Toronto Press.

Malthus, T. M. (1798) *An Essay on the Principle of Population*, 1st edn, London: J. Johnson.

—— (1803) *An Essay on the Principle of Population*, 2nd edn, London: J. Johnson.

—— (1806) *An Essay on the Principle of Population*, 3rd edn, London: J. Johnson.

—— (1807) *An Essay on the Principle of Population*, 4th edn, London: J. Johnson.

—— (1817) *An Essay on the Principle of Population*, 5th edn, London: John Murray.

—— (1826) *An Essay on the Principle of Population*, 6th edn, London: John Murray.

—— (1986) *The Works of Thomas Robert Malthus*, 8 vols, E. A. Wrigley and D. Souden (eds), London: Pickering.

—— (1989) *An Essay on the Principle of Population*, 2 vols, Patricia James (ed.), Cambridge: Cambridge University Press.

—— (1992) *An Essay on the Principle of Population*, selected and prepared by D. Winch, Cambridge: Cambridge University Press.

Marx, K. (1968) *Theories of Surplus Value* (1862–3), II, Moscow: Progress Publishers.

20

ON THE AUTHORSHIP OF 'SPENCE ON COMMERCE' IN *THE EDINBURGH REVIEW*, JANUARY 1808*

I. INTRODUCTION

This essay concerns the disputed authorship of the article 'Spence on Commerce' – William Spence's *Britain Independent of Commerce* (third edition, 1807) – in the *Edinburgh Review* (No. XXII, January 1808, 429–48). Fetter (1953: 246) maintained that the article was 'probably' by Malthus; subsequently, he attributed it to Malthus without qualification (Fetter 1957: 10). Henderson's analysis of 'Malthus and the *Edinburgh Review*' takes for granted that Malthus was the reviewer (Henderson 1984: 118–23); so does Fontana (1985: 128); and the item appears under Malthus in Waterman's bibliography (1991: 279).

Semmel questioned Malthus's authorship: 'it seems to be more probable that Malthus did not write the January article' (Semmel 1963: 15; 1970: 56n). His suspicions are based on two considerations: (1) that many of Spence's views were 'too congenial to Malthus to have received such a full-scale drubbing from him', and (2) that Spence subsequently quoted Malthus in defending himself against the review. Internal and external evidence suggested to Semmel that Henry Brougham was 'probably' the author, though he did not spell out the full case. Pullen (1989: xix–xx) does not explicitly commit himself on the matter of authorship. The doubts expressed by Semmel (1963) that it was by Malthus are supported, he suggests, by the absence of any references to it by Malthus; yet he finds it difficult to accommodate a statement by Francis Horner to Francis Jeffrey (editor of the *Edinburgh Review*) of 17 February 1808 that 'Malthus has begun to contribute', and he discerns 'a number of themes that were to appear in Malthus's later thoughts'.

It is my argument that we may *definitely* exclude Malthus and accept Brougham as author of the 1808 review.[1] Horner's statement to Jeffrey presents no difficulty. The only cloud on the horizon for our thesis is a belief

* I gratefully acknowledge financial aid from the Social Science Research Council of Canada.

that *Brougham himself* some half a century later (1855) attributed the review to Malthus.[2] This matter will be taken up in Section V.

Why does authorship of the review matter? It is doubtful whether the Malthus canon will be much affected, since the item has never attracted so much attention as to affect the general perspective on Malthus. (We are not dealing with the *Essay on Population*!) And there is certainly no 'received' interpretation, for one encounters diametrically opposed perspectives on its central message amongst those who attribute it to Malthus. Waterman, for example, focuses on its championship of industrialization and trade: 'William Spence (1807) had argued that the Continental System would benefit rather than harm the British economy by stimulating more balanced development. He was decisively answered in the *Edinburgh* (1808, pp. 429–48) by Malthus, who showed that foreign trade and industrialization increased domestic employment and raised living standards for all' (Waterman 1991: 227). Henderson asserts the very opposite – that the article 'showed that Malthus would not likely be sympathetic to unlimited manufacture', a circumstance putting him 'on the wrong side of Whig and *Edinburgh Review* policies' (Henderson 1984: 111); Pullen, similarly, finds a resemblance between the statement that 'the internal commerce of a country is of infinitely greater consequence than its external', and Malthus's statement in 1827 to the Select Committee on Emigration that 'I think the home trade much more important than the foreign' (Pullen 1989, I: xix–xx).

Our attribution is important rather for what is added to our knowledge of Brougham, for there are several themes which confirm his position as it had emerged in his *Colonial Policy* (1803a). It is certainly more 'natural' to relate the review to what is known to have been already stated, than to what was 'to appear in Malthus's later thoughts'. Indirectly, however, our finding does throw light on Malthus. I refer to the reviewer's frequent reliance on the *Essay on Population*, a reliance partly accounting for the faulty attribution. Since Spence himself also drew on the *Essay*, the episode speaks volumes for the complexity of Malthus's contemporary impact. And it is of course essential simply to set the record straight. After all, if I am correct *The Wellesley Index* requires adjustment (see note 2).

II. THE EVIDENCE: MATTERS OF FORM

The article was written by an established contributor to the *Edinburgh Review*. This fact emerges in the course of an apologetic justification for bothering to treat what the author estimated to be a poor production: 'we perhaps owe some apology to our readers for making it the subject of serious discussion; but it will be recollected, that one of our professed objects, has always been to use our feeble endeavours in assisting the public judgement on those topics to which its attention was actually directed; and consequently, that the mere popularity of any work gives it a claim upon our attention, independently of its definitively intrinsic merits' ('Spence on Commerce': 430). It is surprising that more has not been made of this statement which to my mind positively excludes Malthus who at that time had published *nothing* in the *Edinburgh Review*. The only regular contributors to economics at that early stage were Francis Horner and Henry Brougham, together responsible for twenty-one of the first twenty-eight economic articles appearing between 1802 and 1806 (Fetter 1953: 243–5). Of these, Horner wrote eight and then ceased to contribute economic articles; and Brougham thirteen. Brougham seems the only candidate.[3]

The statement of Horner to Francis Jeffrey dated 17 February 1808 requires attention at this point: 'Since Malthus has begun to contribute, I hope it will not be for want of solicitation on your part, if he does not continue to supply you with articles. Of all subjects, political economy is at present the most productive of all useful publications, and though his general views are sometimes imperfect, he is always candid, and an advocate for what he believes to be most liberal and generous' (Horner 1853, I: 446). Fetter (1957: 10) presumed that this remark refers to the January review of Spence, thus establishing Malthus's authorship. And so does Pullen: Horner's statement 'implies that an article by Malthus had recently been submitted and published. It is unlikely that Horner's statement referred to Malthus's article on Newenham in the *Edinburgh Review* of July 1808, because that article was not read by Jeffrey, the editor of the *Review*, until just before 21 April 1808', on which date he wrote to Malthus: 'I have just read your review of Newenham' (Pullen 1989, I: xix n).[4] To my mind this objection is not to be taken seriously. That 'Malthus has begun to contribute' may very well refer to Malthus's acceptance of the commission to contribute on Newenham; it by no means necessarily implies reference to an article 'recently . . . submitted and published'. (Even Fetter – 1953: 246 – allowed that the remark might refer to Malthus's review of Newenham of July 1808. James – 1979: 149 – takes for granted that it does refer to this review.)

There is a further indication of Brougham's authorship, even limiting ourselves to matters of form. Compare the 'apology' to readers in the foregoing citation with precisely the same sort of justification given in a review appearing in April 1803 known to be by Brougham: 'Nothing but the subject of this tract [*Guineas an Unnecessary and Expensive Incumbrance on Commerce*], and the attention which we are astonished to hear it has received from the public, could have induced us to trouble our readers with any account of it' (1803b: 101). Similarly, in Brougham's review of Lauderdale's *Inquiry into the Nature and Origin of Public Wealth*: 'There are errors indeed, as it appears to us, in the present publication, of a tendency so dangerous as to counteract much of the benefit which the noble author's patronage is calculated to confer upon the science: and this consideration, together with the unquestionable importance of the subject, must plead our excuse for lending the work a greater portion of our attention than its actual merits may seem to justify' (1804a: 343–4); and at the close: 'We have now only to apologize for drawing this article to so great a length. We conceived that talents, and a station like Lord Lauderdale's, might have the effect of misleading the public' (376). And if more of the same is needed, there is Brougham's review of Arthur O'Connor's *The Present State of Great Britain*: 'The origin and the object of this pamphlet may appear to some of our readers to render an apology necessary for the notice we propose to bestow upon it' (1804b: 104); and later: 'Such are the elements of which Mr O'Connor's political reasonings are compounded. We have only to refer our readers to the introductory remarks, as an apology for detaining them as long on this work – if, indeed, the importance of the general speculations that have grown out of our examination of it have not already pleaded our excuse' (124). Brougham's authorship of the Spence review seems certain on the formal indications till this point.[5]

An objection might be raised that Brougham may have edited a *Malthus* document to bring it in line with the *Edinburgh's* 'corporate persona'. This possibility is highly unlikely. First, the apology contained in the review would then be directly misleading readers into a belief that the author was the same individual who had written several of the other economics articles, since the reference to 'one of our professed objects' (above, p. 350) is clearly not to *every* article appearing in the *Review*. Moreover, the fact that it does not relate to every article itself points away from general policy. And most important, the substance of the review suggests Brougham rather than Malthus, as we now show.

III. THE EVIDENCE: MATTERS OF SUBSTANCE

We turn now to the content of the review. It is characterized by unstinted acceptance of Smith's inclusion of manufacturing within national income, in contrast with Spence's physiocratic position: 'we are of opinion, that [Smith's arguments] really do prove, that manufactures are productive of national wealth, independently of the circumstance of whether they do or do not produce a net rent' ('Spence on Commerce': 431); in fact the reviewer denied that 'the production of a net rent is essential to the increase of wealth'. Now on this matter Malthus would not perhaps have objected, at least in 1808. For by then he had withdrawn the position that manufacturing income is paid as a transfer payment – that 'manufactures, strictly speaking, are no new production, no new creation, but merely a modification of an old one, and when sold must be paid for out of a revenue already in existence, and consequently the gain of the seller is the loss of the buyer. A revenue is transferred, but not created' (Malthus 1803: 433).[6] But his strong agricultural bias remains conspicuous and sets him apart from the reviewer.[7] Particularly relevant, considering that the debate turned on the nature and role of commerce, is his rejection of Smith's preference for the export of manufactures over food: 'In the ordinary course of things, the exportation of corn is sufficiently profitable to the individuals concerned in it. But with regard to national advantage, there are . . . very strong reasons why it is to be preferred to any other kind of export'. These reasons include the fundamental contrast that 'corn pays from its own funds the expenses of procuring it, and the whole of what is sold is a clear national profit', unlike manufactures from the value of which must be deducted subsistence costs 'before we can estimate the clear national profit' (1806, II: 231–2; 1807, II: 155–6). The review is more critical of physiocratic categories, as indeed is Brougham's *Colonial Policy* which contains a strong attack on the essential French contrast between agriculture and industry, referring to an 'apparent fallacy in their fundamental principles' (Brougham 1803a, Note I, 572; also 142–3).

We also recall Malthus's cautions regarding a manufacturing economy dependent on food imports (1806, II: 273–6n; 1807, II: 197–201n), and his opposition to Commercial Systems on grounds of 'security, independence, and permanent prosperity' (1806, II: 258–9; 1807, II: 182–3). Now admittedly the reviewer qualified his defence of foreign commerce. Though he opposed Spence's position that 'no national wealth is derived from the commerce of import', he yet excluded himself from 'the blind admirers of this species of commerce' ('Spence on Commerce': 443). 'Every rational political economist considers it greatly inferior, both in magnitude and importance, to the internal trade of a country; and always places it below its two elder sisters, agriculture and manufactures' (446).[8] This position is attributed to 'the Economists, Dr Smith, and almost all modern writers' with no explicit mention of Malthus. But Malthus had maintained in 1798 and 1803 that 'the home trade of consumption is by far the most important trade of every nation' (1798: 335; 1803: 432);[9] were he the author, he would surely have mentioned his own *Essay* at this point.

Moreover, the rationale offered by the reviewer is not characteristic of the *Essay on Population*.[10] It involves a *monetary* argument (attributed to Hume), namely that a prosperous commerce will be accompanied by an inflow of precious metals and a higher price level so that 'foreign commerce cannot be expected permanently to bring into any country such a rapid accession of wealth as of late years has flowed into Great Britain' ('Spence on Commerce': 447; also 449 regarding the 'bad consequences' of a 'great expansion' of foreign commerce 'similar to the excessive accumulation of the precious metals'). The language used in this context – 'more peculiarly than . . . agriculture and manufactures [commerce] contains within itself the seeds of its own decay' – is, admittedly, similar to that used by Malthus in 1803, 1806 and 1807 when he defended Physiocracy on the grounds that 'it is the only system by which commerce and manufactures can prevail to a very great extent, without bringing with them, at the same time, the seeds of their own ruin' (1803: 437; 1806, II: 212; 1807, II: 136), or again in applying the 'doctrine of proportions' to the problem of the increasing riches of the commercial part of any nation – 'there seems to be a point, beyond which [luxury] must necessarily become prejudicial to a state and bring with it the seeds of weakness and decay' (1806, II: 274n; 1807, II: 199n). But, as mentioned, Malthus did not base himself on Hume's case that commerce implied a monetary inflow; while it is perfectly conceivable that the author of the review borrowed some of Malthus's forms of expression.

The problem of attribution is aggravated by the fact that the reviewer was no fanatical opponent of the Physiocrats. Were he one, it could be counted as definitive evidence that he could not be identified with Malthus. He insisted in fact that Spence had distorted the physiocratic position in key respects – including his reintroduction of mercantilist prejudice 'which those ingenious writers had long since most successfully exposed' ('Spence on Commerce': 429; on this matter see below, pp. 355–6). This rather balanced position emerges also in comments on Spence's case for the purchase of durable goods: 'One of Mr Spence's most constant themes is his strong preference for manufactures of an imperishable nature, compared with those which are speedily consumed, and "leave not a wreck behind". This is another of his doctrines, which he did not learn from the Economists. Their system is dreadfully mangled in his hands. He has retained their errors, and rejected their excellences' (444n). More specifically, the reviewer himself warns against 'dependency' and the threat of trade disruption, with intimations of a case for some protection:

> And if a nation has habitually conducted itself upon the true principles of acquiring wealth, and has purchased all its commodities where they may be had the cheapest, it may have become dependent upon other countries for some of the most necessary and important articles of its consumption. Under these circumstances, a sudden check to foreign commerce from violent causes, can hardly fail of being attended with the most distressing consequences; and its liability to checks of this kind, forms with us a sufficient reason against pushing to an excessive extent, and habitually importing articles of the first necessity which might be raised at home.
>
> ('Spence on Commerce': 447)[11]

Subsequently he alludes to 'security and independence, with moderate wealth' as 'preferable to greater riches subject to frequent reverses' (448). Now Malthus too of course favoured a degree of agricultural protection, and expressly sought 'security, independence and permanent prosperity' even at the 'sacrifice [of] a small portion of present riches' (Malthus 1806, II: 258–9; 1807, II: 182–3). The argument and language of the review is very similar. It is probable that the reviewer was writing with the *Essay on Population* at hand.[12]

The reviewer attacks Spence's idea 'that expenditure is the duty of the landholders', himself maintaining that their savings 'would operate in the same manner on the general prosperity of the country as the accumulation of the profits of trade. . . . There cannot, in our conception, be a more gross error, than to consider, as Mr Spence does, the land proprietors as almost the sole, or, at least, the principal consumers in the country' ('Spence on Commerce': 433–4). Thus he rejects Spence's assertion that British manufacturers would be devastated by landlords cutting consumption, but unconcerned were foreign commerce (and demand for British goods) to cease. Now we know Malthus's view on that issue – at least in 1815: '[rent] affords the most steady home demand for the manufactures of this country, the most effective fund for its financial support and the largest disposable power for its army and navy' (Malthus 1986 [1815], 7: 167–8). (I do not, however, know of so explicit a formulation in 1806/1807.)

There is also the argument in the review that accumulation (by landlords) as effectively generates 'prosperity' as does their consumption. This is somewhat generalized:

> We are perfectly ready to admit, that consumption must exist somewhere, or there could be no production; and that there are limits to the accumulation of capital, though we do not know where to place them: but we are strongly disposed to believe, that production generates consumption, as well as consumption production; and that an increasing capital naturally produces an increased use of consumable commodities, from the greater cheapness of manufactures, the comparatively higher price of labour, the improved cultivation of the soil, the more rapid increase of population, and the constant growth of an important class of consumers living upon the profits of stock, and the interest of money.
>
> ('Spence on Commerce': 434)

Now Pullen sees this as presaging later Malthusian themes: 'its statements on the importance of consumption, on the dangers of an excessive accumulation of capital, and on the reciprocity of the causes of growth, foreshadow similar ideas in the *Principles*' (Pullen 1989, I: xix–xx). It may be argued to the contrary that the *primary* message conveyed is that capital accumulation *does* assure demand: 'We are strongly disposed to believe . . . that an increasing capital naturally produces an increased use of consumable commodities.'[13] The allusion to 'limits to the accumulation of capital' is by way of qualification ('we are ready to admit that'). But even an emphasis on the dangers of excessive capital accumulation would not undermine attribution to Brougham, since Brougham had long before elaborated the theme of 'superabundant' capital for which the colonies would provide a partial solution (e.g. Brougham 1803a, I: 159–63, 214–22; and 1804a: 373–4).

A further 'internal' indication of authorship deserves mention. The reviewer reverts on several occasions to what he sees as an error on Spence's part in retaining mercantilist prejudice in his defence of the doctrine of the 'exchange of equivalents' attributed to the Physiocrats – the notion that trade, envisaged as a swapping of commodities of equal value, has no positive effect on national wealth ('Spence on Commerce': 435–6).[14] The doctrine is said to underlie 'Mr Spence's main argument against foreign commerce, which we suppose must be considered as the one by which he means to stand or fall, as it is only by the establishment of this argument to the satisfaction of the public, that he can justify his title-page, to which he has called so much attention'; Spence was 'totally unconscious . . . of the true nature of foreign commerce'. This argument is fully in accord with Brougham's earlier denial that trade constituted an 'exchange of equivalents', on the grounds that it generates a gain to both parties: 'Trade enriches a nation, by enabling it to exchange what it has no use for, against what it stands principally in need of' (Brougham 1803c: 240–3).

IV. FURTHER CONSIDERATIONS

There remains some evidence of a different order pointing away from Malthus's authorship. Malthus in 1806 excluded his two formal references of 1803 to physiocratic literature – to Dupont's *Physiocratie* and to (de Mirabeau's) *L'ami des hommes* (see Hollander 1992 [essay 15]). But on three occasions the reviewer refers specifically to *Physiocratie* in making his case.[15] This does not suggest common authorship, though the anonymity of the review disallows any strong conclusion on this particular.

The reviewer cites *Colonial Policy* (Brougham 1803a) in insisting, against Spence, on colonies as 'provinces of the mother country' ('Spence on Commerce': 440–1). Semmel (1963: 15) reads this reference as partial evidence for Bougham's authorship. This is convincing. It is noteworthy that nowhere in his *Essay on Population* does Malthus refer to Brougham on colonies, a circumstance pointing away from Malthus as author of the review.

Semmel found that Spence's subsequent appeal to Malthus in his *Agriculture, The Source of the Wealth of Britain* (1808) – a defence of his *Britain Independent of Commerce* against the review – points away from Malthus as reviewer (above, p. 349). Spence in his defence maintained that while most of the main tenets of the Physiocrats had been adopted by Malthus, 'the sentiments of this gentleman will be deemed of greater weight', when it is recollected, as I have before observed [129–30] that he is no blind admirer of the Economists; but admits that 'in some senses manufactures may be said to create national wealth' (1822 [1808]: 151–2).[16] Now Spence drew here on the 1803 edition of the *Essay*,[17] specifically Malthus's strong formulation of manufacturing income as 'a revenue . . . transferred, but not created' (above, p. 352) citing Malthus 1803: 433 (a passage that does not appear in the 1806/1807 editions). In this same work (Spence 1822 [1808]: 130), he also cited Malthus's argument that 'the great position [1806: the position] of the Economists will always remain true, that the surplus produce of the cultivators is the great fund which ultimately pays all those who are not employed upon the land' (Malthus 1803: 435–6; 1806, II: 208). But Malthus had modified this formulation in 1807 (note 7).[18] Since Malthusian 'Physiocracy' is rather weaker in 1807 than in 1806, and in 1806 than in 1803, it would not be inconceivable that our review of 1808 was written by Malthus, critical of Spence for leaning too far towards Physiocracy by drawing on features of his second edition that he no longer maintained. In and of itself, therefore, the appeal to Malthus by Spence provides inconclusive evidence against Malthus's authorship of the original review.

V. SUMMARY AND CONCLUSIONS

For the reasons given above, I conclude that Brougham was the author of the review of Spence. To summarize: The reviewer in 1808 refers to himself as a frequent contributor to the *Edinburgh Review*, and Brougham is the sole candidate; his characteristic 'excuses' to readers in earlier contributions introduce the review; and detailed internal arguments are more consistent with Brougham's position elsewhere, including his opus *Colonial Policy*, than with Malthus's *Essay on Population*. Yet some attribute the article to Malthus on *Brougham's own authority* (above, pp. 349–50).

This attribution originates with entries made in the hand of Anthony Trollope in a set of *Edinburgh Review* once owned by Trollope, entries which apparently derive from a list prepared by Brougham (together with Murray and William Brougham) in 1855 (Griggs *et al.* 1945, 1946). Now even Fetter, who accepted the attribution to Malthus by these authors – the Temple University group – as 'probable', implies some doubt: 'no list prepared by Brougham so long after the appearance of the articles could be accepted without reservation', though he estimated that 'most of the assignments of authorship are plausible and check with evidence from other sources' (Fetter 1953: 244). 'Most' doubtless – but in the specific case of the review of Spence, Fetter cited (apart from Trollope) only the circumstantial support afforded by Horner's remark of 17 February 1808 ('Since Malthus has begun to contribute . . . '; see above, p. 349). Since the latter is an exceedingly weak reed (see above, p. 351), we are left solely with the Trollope entry.[19] To rely on it we must suppose that Trollope accurately recorded Brougham's attribution in our specific case. Now since the work of Fetter and the Temple group various Brougham lists have come to light, including one neat version by a copyist from which Trollope apparently obtained most of his entries (New 1961: 419f). These Trollope entries therefore now 'have no independent value' (Houghton 1966: 426), and the case for Malthus as author turns on the putative attribution by Brougham on the copyist's list.[20]

Against this must be set the evidence given in this essay that Brougham himself was the author. If that evidence stands, we must presume either that an error crept in at some stage in the preparation of the lists – even Houghton, who accepts the attribution, admits that 'the lists must be used with great caution'; or that Brougham's memory had totally failed him. (That he had some ulterior reason to attribute his own work to Malthus can surely be dismissed.) The former alternative seems more likely though the latter cannot be excluded, since as Fontana points out, '[Brougham's] writings, in the ninety years of his life ... attained an utterly unmanageable amount. The contributions to the *Edinburgh Review* alone were so numerous that in their later life even Francis Jeffrey and Brougham himself were unable to provide an entirely reliable reconstruction of their authorship' (1985: 126).

NOTES

1 A recent study of Brougham's economics makes no mention of the 1808 review; and it is not included in a list of 'possible' economic works by Brougham (Sockwell 1994: 207).

2 Houghton (1966, I: 442) attributes the article to Malthus on these grounds, supplemented by Horner's letter to Jeffrey.

3 Semmel mentions Jeffrey but finds him an unlikely candidate. He was not an economic 'sophisticate' and 'although he tried his hand at economic articles, was rather a novice in such matters' (Semmel 1970: 56n). Other early contributors (some 'possible' or 'probable') were Macvey Napier, John Allen, Alexander Hamilton, David Buchanan and George Ellis.

4 The letter is actually dated 21 April 1809 in Cockburn 1852, II: 125, but presumably 1808 is correct, at least if one supposes that an editor does not wait to read his contributor's work until several months after it appears in print.

5 Brougham was responsible for several other articles in the January 1808 issue including one other on economics, 'Orders in Council' (Houghton 1966: 442–3). This latter (the last in the issue) commences: 'We have received this interesting and very able publication, just as we were preparing to close our labours for the present quarter' (*The Edinburgh Review*, January 1808: 484).

6 For a detailed account of Malthus's chopping and changing with respect to Physiocracy, see Hollander 1997, chapter 8.

7 The reviewer's denial that incorporation of manufacturing into national income depended on the question of surplus may perhaps be read as an implicit concession that only agriculture generates a true surplus, notwithstanding which fact manufactures had to be included. But with Malthus the matter was spelled out with considerable care. Thus he retained the position that 'all taxes may be said to fall wholly upon the land, though not wholly on the landholders' (Malthus 1806, II: 219n; 1807, II: 143n). In 1806, he also repeated the declaration of 1803 that whichever of the Smithian or physiocratic definitions of 'wealth' (read 'income') was valid, 'the great position [1806: the position] of the Economists will always remain true, that the surplus produce of the cultivators is the great fund which ultimately pays all those who are not employed upon the land' (1803: 435–6, cited above, p. 357; 1806, II: 208). Although this is watered down in 1807 to read: 'it must always be true that the surplus produce

of the cultivators measures and limits the growth of that portion of the society which is not employed upon the land' (1807, II: 132). Malthus's agricultural bias in the *Essay* remains more conspicuous than the reviewer's.

8 Similarly, the reviewer concedes that 'nations may be great and powerful without much foreign trade and that the internal commerce of a country is of infinitely greater consequence than its external' ('Spence on Commerce': 447). Pullen (above, p. 350) finds this statement similar to a Malthus formulation of 1827, and implies that this might suggest Malthus as author of the review. But the reviewer is explicit that he is drawing on Hume and Smith.

In this context the reviewer is critical of those who see imports and exports as a 'barometer of our public prosperity' and who oppose higher wages as damaging to British competitiveness: 'We certainly are most ready to acknowledge, that the sale of these articles abroad [cottons, woollens, etc.] tends to enrich Great Britain; but we think at the same time, that there are other objects worthy of the attention of Great Britain besides mere riches'; and he opposed 'great extensions' to foreign commerce because 'the happiness of the lower classes of people ought not to be put in competition with the sale of a few more woollens and cottons' (447–8). These positions had been long before expressed by Smith and Hume (Hume figures large in the review).

The reviewer himself hoped that he would not be judged inconsistent in attacking Spence's bias against foreign commerce while conceding that he too objected to the 'great extension of this species of trade'. For his agreement with Spence did not turn on Spence's view that foreign commerce is 'not productive of wealth' but on other broad reasons – inflationary pressure, security and workers' welfare.

9 This is withdrawn in 1806 as part of a major deletion of paragraphs at the outset of Book III, chapter ix ('Of the definition of Wealth') representing manufacturing income as a *transfer*. But the proposition itself was not abandoned; cf. 'The quantity of a country's exports is a very uncertain criterion of its wealth. The quantity of produce permanently consumed at home is, perhaps, the most certain criterion of wealth to which we may refer' (Malthus 1986 [1815], 7: 166).

10 Malthus's secular concern was that increase in demand for corn relative to supply, reflecting manufacturing expansion at a faster rate than agriculture, implied upward pressure on the corn price and thus on money wages with potentially serious implications for the international competitiveness of manufacturing itself. The impact of a rising corn price on the money wage is further reinforced by 'scarce years' – unavoidable in the 'present system' – bearing in mind downward wage rigidity. Rising wages in turn play back on corn costs again reinforcing the upward trend of food and materials prices. The ultimate threat is to the competitiveness of the export industries, on the (Smithian) grounds that manufacturing cost prices are governed by money wage costs (Malthus 1803: 443–4; 1806, II: 222).

11 Here he attaches a reference to Berkeley's *Quirist*: 'There can be no doubt of the truth of Bishop Berkeley's opinion, that a nation with a large and fertile territory might grow richer every year, although surrounded with a wall of brass a thousand cubits high; but it would neither grow rich so fast, nor to such a degree, as if it had the advantage of foreign commerce.' Interestingly, Spence also cited Berkeley to the same effect (Spence 1822 [1808]: 38) as did Malthus in his fifth edition (1817, II: 427).

12 However, the reviewer does not specify *agricultural* protection; his 'articles of the first necessity' or 'some of the most necessary and important articles of . . .

consumption' may have a wider connotation, as is the case in Brougham's review of Lauderdale (Brougham 1804a: 361–2).

13 Cf. also 'Spence on Commerce': 445: 'We have the greatest possible respect, as our readers already know, for the accumulation of capital, considering it as the great mean [sic] of future production, and of future consumption.'

14 The reviewer maintains that Spence distorted the French view – and in fact was inconsistent – because they had rejected the idea of wealth comprising *bullion* and yet Spence ended up with the result that national wealth increases only if foreign trade results in a net import of the precious metals: 'Mr Spence retains some of the prejudices which they have so easily refuted' (438; also 429, 430). 'We are astonished that the manner in which Mr Spence states the instance of the exporting merchant, did not lead him to the true source of the national profit derived from the commerce of import; for, as to the commerce of export, we can only consider it as profitable, because it is the necessary condition of getting imports' (438–9).

15 The first is the basic proposition that 'a balance of trade paid in the precious metals, is the *pis-aller* of foreign commerce' ('Spence on Commerce': 438), where reference is made to 'Physiocratie, Seconde partie, p. 344'. The second (440) is to the physiocratic position on colonies (which did not coincide with Spence's), namely that *Des colonies sont des provinces de la metropole*, in 'Physiocratie, Seconde partie, Sommaire, p. 506'. The third occurs in the course of a brief remark on price theory: 'We intended to have noticed a few other subjects in Mr Spence's production, such as his deviation from the economists into a wrong path on the subject of price; and his inconsistency in allowing home made laces to stimulate agriculture, and not foreign wines and teas; his hopeful recommendation to wear more coats than we want; his strong project for a standing navy, &c&c' (445–6). A note is attached to 'price' referring to the superiority of the physiocratic conception over Smith's: 'On the subject of price, the economists may boast a superiority over Adam Smith; but we cannot reconcile their just views, in general, on this important point, with the very false doctrine which they apply to commerce, that, *Les prix précédent toujours les achats et les ventes*. Physiocratie, Vol. II, p. 259.'

16 He probably intended here two specific allowances by Malthus for sectoral interdependence – the stimulus provided by manufactures for the expansion of agriculture from the point of view of motive (Malthus 1803: 436, 438); and the higher real purchasing power of agricultural incomes due to 'the judicious employment of manufacturing capital' (436–7n).

17 Even in his later *Objections Against the Corn Bill Refuted* (1815) he did not refer to the 1806 and 1807 versions.

18 A nice example is the following sequence of alterations: 'our commerce has not done much for our agriculture; but . . . our agriculture has done a great deal for our commerce' (Malthus 1803: 442); 'our commerce has not done so much for our agriculture as our agriculture has for our commerce' (1806, II: 220); 'our commerce has not done more for our agriculture than our agriculture for our commerce' (1807, II: 144).

19 Similarly, Griggs *et al.*: 'It is likely that we have here a hitherto undiscovered article by Malthus' (Griggs *et al.* 1946: 204). Apart from Horner's letter to Jeffrey they offer no substantial support, merely the assertion that 'The subject and treatment of this review, together with the absence of any other ascription to [Malthus] before the following July, make the identification highly probable.'

20 New does not provide the full list; he only records Brougham's contributions

excluding, of course, the Spence review. The full list is in C. K. Ogden's papers, University College Library. I am most grateful to Professor F. Rosen and Dr J. Harris for their efforts, albeit unsuccessful thus far, to trace the current whereabouts of the list.

REFERENCES

Brougham, Henry (1803a) *An Inquiry into the Colonial Policy of the European Powers*, 2 vols, Edinburgh: E. Balfour, Manners and Miller, and Archibald Constable.

—— (1803b) 'Guineas an Unnecessary and Expensive Incumbrance on Trade', *Edinburgh Review*, III (April), 101–16.

—— (1803c) 'Wheatley's remarks on Currency and Commerce', *Edinburgh Review*, V (October), 231–52.

—— (1804a) 'Lord Lauderdale on Public Wealth', *Edinburgh Review*, VIII (July), 343–77.

—— (1804b) 'O'Connor's Present State of Great Britain', *Edinburgh Review*, IX (October), 104–24.

—— (1808) 'Examination of the Late Orders in Council: *Edinburgh Review*, XXII (January), 484–98.

Cockburn, Lord Henry (1852) *Life of Lord Jeffrey*, Edinburgh: A. and C. Black.

Fetter, Frank W. (1953) 'The Authorship of Economic Articles in the *Edinburgh Review*, 1802–47', *Journal of Political Economy*, LXI (June), 232–59.

—— (1957) 'Francis Horner and the *Edinburgh Review*', in *The Economic Writings of Francis Horner in the Edinburgh Review 1802–6*, New York: Kelley and Millman.

Fontana, Biancamaria (1985) *Rethinking the Politics of Commercial Society: The 'Edinburgh Review' 1802–1832*, Cambridge: Cambridge University Press.

Griggs, I., Kern, J. D. and Schneider, E. (1945, 1946) 'Brougham's Early Contributions to the Edinburgh Review: A New List', *Modern Philology*, XLII (February 1945), 152–73; XLIII (February 1946), 192–210.

Henderson, John P. (1984) 'Malthus and the *Edinburgh Review*', in Warren J. Samuels (ed.), *Research in the History of Economic Thought and Methodology*, 2, 107–24.

Hollander, Samuel (1992) 'On Malthus's Physiocratic References', *History of Political Economy*, 24, 2 (Summer): 369–80.

—— (1997) *The Economics of Thomas Robert Malthus*, Toronto: University of Toronto Press.

Horner, Francis (1853) *Memoirs and Correspondence of Francis Horner, MP*, Leonard Horner (ed.), London: John Murray.

Houghton, Walter E. (1966) 'The Edinburgh Review, 1802–1900', in *The Wellesley Index to Victorian Periodicals 1824–1900*, Toronto: University of Toronto Press, I, 416–29 .

James, Patricia (1979) *Population Malthus: His Life and Times*, London: Routledge and Kegan Paul.

Malthus, T. R. (1798) *An Essay on the Principle of Population*, facsimile edn, 1926, London: Macmillan.

—— (1803) *An Essay on the Principle of Population*, 2nd edn, London: J. Johnson.

—— (1806) *An Essay on the Principle of Population*, 3rd edn, London: J. Johnson.

—— (1807) *An Essay on the Principle of Population*, 4th edn, London: J. Johnson.

—— (1808) 'Newenham and Others on the State of Ireland', *Edinburgh Review*, XXIV (July), 336–55.

—— (1817) *An Essay on the Principle of Population*, 5th edn, London: John Murray.

—— (1986) [1815] 'Grounds of an Opinion on the Policy of Restricting the Importation of Foreign Corn', in *The Works of Thomas Robert Malthus*, E. A. Wrigley and David Souden (eds), vol. 7, 151–74, London: William Pickering.

New, Chester W. (1961) *The Life of Henry Brougham to 1830*, Oxford: Clarendon Press.

Pullen, John (1989) Introduction to the Variorum Edition of T. R. Malthus, *Principles of Political Economy*, Cambridge: Cambridge University Press, I: xv–lxix.

Semmel, Bernard (1963) 'Introductory Essay: Malthus and the Reviews', in *Occasional Papers of T. R. Malthus*, 3–29, New York: Burt Franklin.

—— (1970) *The Rise of Free Trade Imperialism*, Cambridge: Cambridge University Press.

Sockwell, William D. (1994) *Popularizing Classical Economics: Henry Brougham and William Ellis*, London: St. Martin's Press.

Spence, William (1822) [1807; 7th edn 1808] *Britain independent of Commerce; or, Proofs deduced from an Investigation into the True Causes of the Wealth of Nations, that our Riches, Prosperity, and Power are derived from Resources inherent in ourselves, and would not be affected, even though our Commerce were annihilated*, London: Cadell and Davies; in *Tracts on Political Economy*, London: Longman, Hurst, Rees, Orme and Brown, reprinted and privately published, New York, 1933, 1–92.

—— (1822) [1808] *Agriculture, The Source of the Wealth of Great Britain*, ibid., 95–192.

—— (1822) [1815] *The Objections Against the Corn Bill Refuted*, ibid., 193–235.

Waterman, A. M. C. (1991) *Revolution, Economics & Religion: Christian Political Economy, 1793–1833*, Cambridge: Cambridge University Press.

Part VI

SHORT REVIEWS

21

SHORT REVIEWS

21.1 *James Mill: Selected Economic Writings*, edited by Donald Winch, Edinburgh and London: Oliver and Boyd for the Scottish Economic Society, Toronto: Clarke, Irwin, 1966, pp. vii, 452
(*The John Stuart Mill News Letter*, 2, Spring 1967, 16–17)

This book is one of a series of volumes containing the main economic works of Scottish economists of the eighteenth and early nineteenth centuries. The edited works of Sir James Steuart have recently appeared; those of Lauderdale, James Anderson and J. R. McCulloch are in preparation, and further issues are planned. If these volumes maintain the standard established by Dr Winch, the series is likely to be a great success.

In this volume five major pieces are reproduced in full or, from the economist's viewpoint, with minor deletions: *An Essay of the Impolicy of a Bounty on the Exportation of Grain*, 1804 (in full); *Commerce Defended*, 1808 (in full except for the omission of materials relating specifically to the probable outcome of the Napoleonic conflict); extracts from 'Thomas Smith on Money and Exchange', *Edinburgh Review*, 1808; *Elements of Political Economy*, third edition, 1826 (in full); and extracts from the essay 'Whether Political Economy is Useful', *London Review*, 1836. Extracts are also reproduced from Book II ('Of the Hindus') of the *History of British India*, third edition, 1826, and from submissions by Mill to the Select Committee on the Affairs of the East India Company, 1831 and 1832.

These materials are organized into four sections: 'Early Economic Writings, 1804–1808'; 'James Mill and David Ricardo' (*The Elements*); 'James Mill on Scope and Method'; and 'James Mill and India'. For each section Dr Winch has prepared an introduction. There is also a Biographical Sketch and a *partial* bibliography. The texts are annotated.

Each of the major works is summarized clearly and placed in a meaningful context. The choice of extracts and the introductions provide an excellent account of Mill's contribution to economics, his relationship with the classical school of political economy, and his intellectual sources.

It is difficult to take Mill's direct contribution to theoretical economics seriously. He presented the most extreme and least justifiable version of almost every one of the principal elements constituting classical, or perhaps more specifically, Ricardian economic theory. One suspects that he did not understand Ricardo, although the *Elements* was designed to provide a simplified account of the Ricardian structure. This view appears to be quite commonly accepted in histories of thought, and the reader of this volume is not given cause to reject it. But here is a further element to be considered. Dr Winch traces briefly the influences upon Mill emanating from his Scottish education, emphasizing particularly the historical approach to the study of social institutions, the idea of progress developed by the eighteenth-century Scottish philosophers, and the Smith–Millar analysis of political changes in terms of economic and property relations. From these sources there ultimately developed Mill's bitter hostility towards the landowning classes, and his deep suspicion of those who were in control of parliament. It becomes very clear that the Ricardian system was a blessing in disguise, in that it accorded perfectly with Mill's initial outlook. His preoccupation was not with the analytics but with the propaganda value of the system, and any admission of error and any qualification would, he apparently feared, prejudice its effectiveness.

An issue which remains a little hazy – probably as a result of the conciseness with which an editor must write – is the relation between Mill and his fellow classical economists. For example, in the 1808 review of Thomas Smith, Mill recommended a return to gold, although at the same time he denied the possibility of bank-induced price increases. 'It required Ricardo's intervention later to end Mill's indecision' (36). But it is never made unambiguously clear that it was in fact Ricardo's influence which did the trick. The problem relates in part to the uncertain authorship of a review of Ricardo's *High Price of Bullion* (180n).

Similarly, in a discussion of Mill's attack in *Commerce Defended* upon Spence's under-consumptionist fear of capital accumulation, Dr Winch refers to the creation of 'an important link in the continuity of "orthodox" macroeconomic views between Smith and Ricardo' (32). But in what sense was it an important link? Was Mill's argument in any way influential? This may be asked as well of Mill's move away from the 'vent-for-surplus' doctrine of Smith (35), and, at the most general level, of the Law of Markets. In his section devoted to 'Mill and Ricardo', Dr Winch, following Sraffa, expresses the view that 'on questions of theory Mill had little to offer Ricardo' (186).

Dr Winch traces not only the Smith–Mill, Mill–Ricardo relation but also that between Mill and Bentham. We get a glimpse of the antagonism which developed between Mill and McCulloch, who had so much in common that they are usually bracketed together in histories of thought as the weak links in classical political economy. It is noteworthy that the members of the Political Economy Club did not take Mill's economics very seriously. But it is the relation between Mill and his son which will be of particular interest to the readers of this newsletter. Dr Winch takes a more balanced view than most in his discussion of Mill's educational methods (20). In pure theory John's ideal stationary state is traced back to James (195). But it is largely in methodology that a really significant influence on John by his father is emphasized (369–70). Yet it should not be forgotten that John was only too well aware of his father's 'impatience of detail' and of his exaggerated trust in 'the intelligence of the abstract, when not embodied in the concrete' (quoted 189). There seems to be a qualitative difference between father and son.

Mill comes into his own when he turns away from pure economics. In this regard, the extracts from the *History of British India* are welcome. Here are combined Mill's scientific methodology, his utilitarianism, his debts to the Scottish philosophers, and the application of his economics to practical issues. The economist will be able to obtain from this volume a more complete and accurate picture of the man than is usually at hand.

21.2 *The Years of High Theory: Invention and Tradition in Economic Thought, 1926–1939*, by G. L. S. Shackle, Cambridge: Cambridge University Press, 1967, pp. 328
(*Canadian Journal of Economics*, 1, November 1968, 846–8)*

This book is intended not only as an account of the developments which occurred in economic theory during the extraordinarily fruitful years 1926–39 but also as a 'case study' which might cast some light on the broader issue of the processes whereby changes in economic analysis are generated. We agree with the author's basic methodological position that no alternative approach exists at present in our quest for a 'theory of theories', although at the same time we must note the regrettable paucity of results attributable to the 'empirical' method in the case of another (increasingly distant) revolutionary period, namely the 1870s. The difficulty is that an empirical investigation requires ideally a clearly defined initial set of hypotheses and it will not be easy to develop hypotheses without prior extensive interdisciplinary study. Thus, for example, one might ask, upon noting Professor Shackle's amazement at the 'slowness' with which the seeds of economic theory tend to germinate, how slow is slow? We ought, in principle, to have criteria for such evaluations. At the same time, it would certainly be unsatisfactory to halt further investigation until a suitable set of hypotheses had been developed: indeed, the present work hopefully may itself contribute to the generation of hypotheses for scholars working in this or other periods. Professor Shackle's extension of the frontier in the history of economics is therefore welcome, although the degree of objectivity that can be maintained in a study of recent events must remain a matter of personal judgement.

* This review was erroneously attributed by the Journal to Karl F. Helleiner.

This book will require of its readers familiarity with the theoretical techniques dealt with and is not designed to serve as a textbook. The first two and the final chapters are methodological in content; chapters 3–8 deal with developments in price theory in Britain and the United States, and chapters 9–15 largely with British and Swedish macroeconomics; there is one chapter (16) on cycles and growth, and another (17) on input–output analysis.

The principal microeconomic topics that are investigated are the full exploitation of indifference-curve analysis and the abandonment of the assumptions of perfect competition. This section contains a fascinating discussion of the historical development of the marginal revenue concept and throughout the emphasis is on the 'slow' fruition of earlier contributions. The principal moral the reader is encouraged to draw seems to be the recognition of the stultifying effects of received doctrine – in this instance the model of perfect competition – and the great difficulty of posing any other questions than those for whose answer there are readily available tools at hand (e.g. 41–2). At the same time the ultimate success of those struggling to escape from the grip of a set of well-learned preconceptions is likely to be more lasting and meaningful than the brilliant contributions made by those on the outside (31). It is this moral which must have contributed to Professor Shackle's choice of title. One may wonder, however, to what extent the 'greater insight' and 'the more extensive view' resulting from the laborious task of dismantling and replacing the original model is not a reflection of the conservatism of the audience rather than the method of the actors. But if Professor Shackle is correct, an analogy might profitably be made between his period and the 1870s, where may be found the debilitating effects of classical orthodoxy on the one hand and (perhaps) the beneficial results of the patient and lengthy attempts to introduce changes from within on the other.

A single theme governs the macroeconomic chapters, namely the crucial role played by *uncertainty* both in the Swedish (Myrdalian) and the British (Keynesian) formulations. A detailed and most useful critical analysis of Myrdal's *Monetary Equilibrium* (1931) is given in chapter 10. Shackle here argues for the view that in the absence of the *General Theory* the same results would have been 'eventually supplied' by Myrdal's work (124ff), any delay apparently being attributable to Myrdal's lack of showmanship. Two key chapters ('Keynes' Ultimate Meaning' and 'The Anatomy of the *General Theory*') present the essence of Keynesian thought; what Shackle calls the 'engine room' of the system is seen to lie in chapter 12 ('The State of Long-term Expectation') of the *General Theory*, and considerable attention is paid also to Keynes' clarificatory paper in the *Quarterly Journal of Economics* for February 1937. Several more detailed chapters on particular Keynesian concepts follow and, throughout, the relationship between the *General Theory* and the *Treatise* is borne in mind. A discussion of the multiplier is developed around Hegelund's *The Multiplier Theory* (1954); Professor Shackle correctly insists on the differential effects of changes in consumption expenditure and in investment expenditure regarded as initial stimuli, and warns against identifying the true multiplier with historical concepts which bear a family resemblance. One of the most important chapters in the book concerns liquidity preference; here Shackle traces the celebrated debates on interest-rate theory published in the *Economic Journal* for 1937. The basic lesson is that we should recognize the ultimate 'nihilism' implied in Keynes' logic, a step taken by Keynes himself more explicitly in the *QJE* paper than in the *General Theory*.

There can be little doubt that Professor Shackle has served a most beneficial service by his emphasis on the role of uncertainty and his objections to the ever-present tendency to interpret Keynes in mechanistic fashion, as though he contributed no more than an alternative *technical apparatus* for classical macroeconomic theory. In this book, however, we get only a glimpse of the overwhelming implications of Shackle's interpretation followed through to its logical conclusion. We would indeed be in a state of nihilism: The interest-rate depends on expectations of its own future. It is expectational, subjective, psychic, indeterminate. And so is the rest of the economic system' (247). As one implication one might mention Shackle's scorn at the statistical investigations of the interest rate (157–8). And one senses Shackle's own disappointment in his observations that Keynes himself was not at ease with such implications. This is clear, for example, in Shackle's rejection of a 'precautionary motive' for holding money (158); and we read with specific reference to Keynes:

> Theories give knowledge, and so (it is unconsciously felt) knowledge must be ascribed to the people who play a part in our theories. It is almost as though the writers said to themselves: We cannot theorize rationally about conduct which is not completely rational. The dominance of the equilibrium idea, in one or other of its many forms, goes very deep in economics. Is it beneath the dignity of humans to recognize the human predicament of uncertain expectation? The *General Theory*, of course, is wholly concerned with uncertain expectation, but still allows itself (except in chapter 22, on the Trade Cycle) no liberty to connect sequential states of mind with each other (270).

The more general implications of Professor Shackle's study for the evolution of economic theory are not easy to pin down. One may argue with some of the details of the following statement but in general it is presumably true: 'Theoretical advance can spring only from theoretical crisis: either internal crisis, as when for example, the analytically indispensable assumption of perfect competition is recognized to conflict with the notion of economies of large scale, or when the notion of a unit of utility is found to be incapable of operational definition; or external crisis, as when the established theory of value seems to declare general heavy unemployment impossible, in self-destructive contradiction of the facts, or as when political alarms at the doctrines of Marx called for a replacement of the labour theory of value' (288). As an explanation for the simultaneous crop of inventions during the years 1926–39 Professor Shackle emphasizes, I think, 'external crisis'. Of the simultaneous investigations of Myrdal and Keynes (and Kalecki) we read: 'The depression of the 1920s and its drastic worsening in the early 1930s was not only a disaster in the real lives of millions but a profound intellectual shock. It exposed the established theoretical picture of the economic system as fallacious and helpless' (127–8); or similarly: 'When, in 1914–18, the settled assumptions of life for ordinary people dissolved, the economics of tranquillity became inadequate and partly inappropriate. Its obsolescence, becoming abruptly evident as soon as there was time again to think, after years of war and of absurd, gigantic inflations, is the greatest single explanation of the theoretical ferment of the 1930s' (291). The pressure of events thus forced a new concern with reality. The war also acted, it is argued, as a 'psychic release' from traditional patterns of thought (291). But the developments in theory were the product of human minds and did not spring directly from the events ready made, and it is precisely this simple fact that renders attempts to understand the development of economics so difficult: 'A handful of audacious and imaginative minds, who happened for this reason or that to be crouched upon the mark when the starting-gun was fired, outdistanced all pursuit' (128). If only we understood some of those reasons.

21.3 *The Church and Economic Activity in the Middle Ages*, by J. Gilchrist, London, Melbourne, Toronto: Macmillan; New York: St Martin's Press, 1969, pp. xi, 328
(*Canadian Journal of Economics*, 3, August 1970, 522–4)

The primary objective of this book is to evaluate the influence of the Church on the medieval economy. The task is one of great complexity, because the influence of the Church on behaviour operated not only through legal sanctions imposed by ecclesiastical courts, but also by way of men's consciences. A closely related issue which is considered is whether there is evidence of a conflict between the economic behaviour of Christians and Church doctrines.

The author concludes that the Church's doctrines in the period of economic recovery and expansion of the eleventh, twelfth and thirteenth centuries were sufficiently flexible to prevent a clash with the emerging economic forces. The subsequent period of stagnation, however, according to the author, was characterized by a 'tightening up of previously relaxed teachings' (126), and a failure by the Church to offer solutions to pressing social problems. By this time, however, the Church was being successfully challenged by secular institutions, and its stature and influence with economic processes had passed. The implication of the author's argument is that Church doctrine did not restrain the transition from a 'natural' to a 'money' economy and the development of the latter, although in some respects it may have altered certain details of the process. Moreover, the Church by its own activities in the economy contributed on balance positively to the economic and social achievements of the early Middle Ages. The emphasis upon the accommodation achieved by the Church with the secular world during the period of economic expansion brings the author into direct conflict with the general positions of Weber and Tawney, which denied the possibility of compromise between the medieval Catholic Church and the 'capitalist' mentality.

A novel feature of the investigation is the detailed attention paid to the canons and constitutions of the General Councils of the Church. The book contains a valuable appendix consisting of a translation of selected texts from the first eighteen General Councils, with particular emphasis on the Latin councils commencing with Lateran I (1123). The author seems at times to forget his own warnings (16, 29–30) that the import of the Conciliar evidence must be evaluated with the greatest caution. Thus he points out (63) that while Lateran II (1139) *extended* the prohibition against usury, it would be misleading to see this as the whole picture. Yet as evidence of a change in position during the period of economic contraction we are told that after Lateran IV (1215) 'the Church leaders became increasingly concerned with narrow issues' (20), the Conciliar decrees of the fifteenth century, for example, dealing with the 'by then arid questions of the previous century' seemingly 'unaware of the changing nature of society' (84). Whether or not this reflects an increasingly rigid attitude on the part of the papacy to the secular world, the fact is that in the later Middle Ages there occurred a continuous relaxation in the approach of canonists and theologians: *damnum emergens* became a commonly accepted title to interest in the fifteenth century, and an increasing number of authorities came to the defence of *lucrum cessans* as a title. The 'triple contract' was first legitimized in 1485. And the 'liberal' view of canonists and theologians on the Just Price did not undergo a reversal after 1300: as Professor Gilchrist remarks, the position of Langenstein represented only a 'minority tradition' (58).

That the theologians and canonists of the later Middle ages were – along with the papacy – 'removed from real problems' (85) is therefore doubtful. As J. T. Noonan in his *Scholastic Analysis of Usury* has suggested, a chief cause leading to the growing acceptance of the titles to interest noted above was the need to justify the financial practices in the Italian city states, particularly the charging of interest by the *montes pietatis*. Furthermore, Lateran V (1515) actually *sanctioned* the *montes* (115), a fact which seems to conflict with the proposition that the papacy 'in the later Middle Ages, became increasingly rigorous in its condemnation of usury' and 'failed to accommodate itself any longer to the economic policies of the city states' (96); or, even more explicitly, that Lateran V – in contrast to Lateran IV – 'instead of attempting a similar compromise on matters affecting Church and State, pursued the extremist line of clerical independence' (101).

More attention should perhaps have been paid to hypotheses which might account for the greater rigidity attributed to the Church during the period of economic stagnation. The author explains, in part, the ability of the Church to come to terms with the economic forces of the earlier (expansionary) period by reference to the social origins of clergy, bishops, and popes which reflected the general social order, *including the merchant class* (136–7). But there was no reversal of this pattern in the later period of stagnation. If anything, it seems that the trend was reinforced: 'By the time of the Avignonese papacy [1309–78] the Curia was staffed largely by men who were themselves sons of merchants' (37); and during the later Middle Ages the English bishops were recruited less and less from the 'saints and scholars', and increasingly from the great baronial families. As Professor Gilchrist himself points out, such bishops 'were hardly likely to adopt a high-minded attitude towards the secular world. . . . Opposition was almost certain to come to any measure that proposed a return to basic Christian teachings' (136–7). This scarcely explains or even accords with the view that in the fourteenth and fifteenth centuries the Church tightened up its previously relaxed teachings.

21.4 *The New Political Economy of J. S. Mill*, by Pedro Schwartz, Durham, North Carolina: Duke University Press, [1968] 1972, pp. viii, 341
(*Journal of Economic Literature*, 11, December 1973, 1374–6)

Professor Pedro Schwartz at the outset of this impressive book discusses the common charges that J. S. Mill lacked originality, insofar as he followed the abstract Ricardian doctrine, and that he was inconsistent, both in his profound preoccupation with historicist and institutionalist themes while at the same time remaining loyal to Ricardo, and in matters of internal logic. The first accusation is categorically rejected, and justly so, largely on the basis of Stigler's evidence (*Economica*, 1955). Nevertheless, the piecemeal nature of Mill's technical innovations, it is argued, implies merely an attempt to add improvements to the Ricardian system rather than to rebuild anew. It is the object of this book to describe and evaluate Mill's attempt to construct a new 'progressive' and 'more hopeful' political economy *on a Ricardian foundation*. The matter of Mill's consistency in undertaking this sort of project is dismissed rather casually but perhaps justifiably as 'unrewarding', 'irrelevant' and 'unimportant'. Other issues preoccupy the author: Mill's relationship to his teachers; his objective in devising a new political economy; the degree of his success; and the value of his work for modern economists and social philosophers. The book raises these matters within the context of Mill's approach towards trade unions, government intervention, socialism and the future of society.

Professor Schwartz talks of a rapid decline of the Ricardian 'school' very shortly after Ricardo's death – with only James Mill and J. S. Mill remaining – which he attributes to empirical evidence countering its pessimistic predictions and also to growing optimism regarding the ultimate achievement of political reform. The *Principles* of 1848 thus constitute the beginning of a 'tardy Ricardian renascence' after an eclipse during the 1830s and 1840s, induced, it is argued, by the 'profound modifications' made by Mill to the doctrine – although not to the original analytical pattern. Mill's contribution, according to this view, involves 'conservation in the analytical field, and modification in the practical'.

These are fundamental and fascinating issues, and Professor Schwartz's treatment constitutes an outstanding and challenging contribution to the literature on the classical school, which deserves the serious attention of historians of economic thought. Particularly important is the critical yet constructive analysis of the famous methodological distinction between the 'laws of production' and the 'laws of distribution', which provided Mill with a framework for an improved appreciation of institutional assumptions in economics. This work successfully portrays Mill's aim of restoring the Smithian conception of a political economy 'which instead of confining itself within the limits of a narrow professionalism, would use economic knowledge to interpret and change society'.

I shall restrict my comments to three central issues raised in the study, namely the nature of Ricardianism; Mill's relationship with Ricardo; and the wages-fund 'recantation' in 1869. These matters, it must be emphasized, involve notoriously difficult problems of interpretation.

Professor Schwartz's various accounts of 'Ricardianism' are, to my mind, insufficiently precise. What requires particular emphasis is the assumption of an absolute standard of value and the doctrine, formally dependent on it, regarding *proportionate* wages and *proportionate* profits. It can be shown that, despite their formal criticisms, Bailey and Torrens were obliged to concede – and Torrens did so with amazing candour – the logical validity of the Ricardian position. Furthermore, the analysis of deviations of price from labour value, which served as a preliminary step in the complete derivation of the inverse profit–wage relationship, is reproduced clearly by McCulloch. As I read the literature, there was no early decline of Ricardianism – evidence to the contrary drawn from the meetings of the Political Economy Club recorded by J. L. Mallet is inconclusive – and Mill was scarcely engaged in mounting a counter-revolution in 1848.

While Mill also maintained the essentials of Ricardianism outlined above, it seems illegitimate to regard his admittedly remarkable innovations in theory as simply a matter of adding improvements. It seems rather – and the point is made not only by Marx but also by Jevons in the second edition of his *Theory of Political Economy* – that we have here elements which fit into a very different general theory. Mill's conception of scientific development as proceeding cumulatively rather than by way of revolutionary changes may help account for his fidelity to Ricardo, as the author suggests, but it is putting the matter in a false perspective to play down the incompatibilities which are apparent in the *Principles*.

Finally, a word on the wages-fund issue. Professor Schwartz suggests that Mill took advantage in 1869 of the appearance of W. T. Thornton's work to express independently acquired ideas of his own regarding the illegitimacy of the wages-fund conception. This assessment seems to be confirmed by a letter to Cairnes dated 9 April 1869 (Mill 1972, XVII: 1587). Much of the remainder of the argument is, however, less convincing. It is based on the belief that Mill rejected the one-year production period since income did not accrue at yearly intervals but the employer made advances continually, and replaced them continually, from his returns. Now, on my reading, Mill did not abandon the one-year production period. His innovation lies in the recognition that consumption outlays by capitalists can be reduced during the period in favour of wages, and conversely, although the sum available for distribution remains constant. But there is more to the matter. Mill's new position is an appendage to a basic contention that the demand for labour is of zero elasticity, at least in the short run and within limits. This interpretation (advanced elsewhere by the reviewer) is rejected by Professor Schwartz on the grounds that Mill had no clear idea of the elasticity of the demand for labour in the short run, a position which I believe is unacceptable in light of explicit statements that the demands for an input (in the short run) and for a final commodity have distinct characteristics, the latter only being price responsive.

All of these complex questions lie in a domain of scholarship which is still not clearly mapped out; differences of opinion are to be expected and welcomed. The contribution of the work as a whole to our understanding of nineteenth-century economic thought is unquestionably of the highest order.

21.5 *The Structure of Classical Economic Theory*, by Robert V. Eagly, Oxford: Oxford University Press, 1974, pp. 142
(*The Times Literary Supplement*, 1 August 1975, 870)

Mathematical 'restatements' of Smithian, Ricardian and Marxian economics are now quite common. *The Structure of Classical Economic Theory*, however, has as its object the restatement of 'classical economics' in its entirety; it is designed to provide a synthesis of over a century of theorizing from the French Physiocrats to Walras, including the major British luminaries as well as Marx. The scope of this book is thus unique. (Earlier mathematical renditions of 'classical' economics turned largely on the specific question of the differences between Keynes and his predecessors with regard to the monetary mechanism.)

The book offers what is called a *gestalt* approach, and Robert V. Eagly is not basically concerned with individual economists who are named 'only with respect to their most significant contributions to the analytical structure'. This structure is seen as turning upon a single concept, that of capital: 'The centrality of capital cannot be overemphasized. . . . In all, the capital concept provided the analytical scheme around which the component parts of classical economics are built'. Labour was envisaged as a produced rather than an original productive factor in the light of the conception of advances of wage goods; and the focus of attention was upon the manner whereby the total capital stock is divided between its constituent elements (fixed and variable) – called by Dr Eagly 'the allocation problem' – and upon activity envisaged as occurring in the form of discrete time intervals, each involving a 'production period'. In this structure the product and factor markets are treated as independent, and the money supply is deprived of any important role. The book is composed of a variety of sophisticated mathematical formulations of themes relating to the main topic, including 'The Quesnaysian Revolution', 'The Analytical Role of Money', 'Malthusian Aggregative Analysis', and 'Business Fluctuations' (with reference to Karl Marx).

To render the analytical structure of classical theory concisely but accurately, from both a technical and a historical perspective, would be a truly extraordinary feat. And, considered as a set of analytical exercises centring upon the capital concept, this book is indeed most impressive. But a number of questions may be raised regarding its historical dimension.

No one will want to question any account which emphasizes the preoccupation of the eighteenth- and nineteenth-century literature with the problem of capital, manifested in the distinction between productive and unproductive labour, the advances conception, the analysis of the sub-categories into which the stock is divided and the determinants of accumulation. At the same time the total subordination to this problem of all the issues with which the economists were concerned might be thought exaggerated. One might question, for example, the severe constraint imposed upon the role allotted to exchange – 'important certainly, but only in regard to the contribution it made as clearing mechanism for capitalists in a multi-industry system, facilitating and enabling the reconstitution of capital stock' – on the grounds that an accurate perspective calls for a broader conception of its allocative function. (Certainly little attention is devoted to the price mechanism in all its manifestations as it is analysed in *The Wealth of Nations*.) This is not to say that Dr Eagly's view of the balance to be ascribed to the various parts of classical theory is necessarily wrong – it is simply that justice must not only be done but also seen to be done.

The *gestalt* approach which is adopted here also tends to play down certain fundamental differences of outlook and analysis between economists, which it is surely one of the functions of the historian of economics to distinguish. In particular, the sharp objections raised by Ricardo against Smith's treatment of the effects of wage-rate changes upon profits and prices are nowhere discussed, although it was in matters relating to value and distribution that many contemporaries observed in 1817 a major – indeed a 'revolutionary' – break in economic theory.

Let us turn to the treatment of the 'basic classical model' itself. The fundamental assumption here ascribed to the classicals is an exogenously fixed labour–machinery ratio. With this assumption, Dr Eagly constructs an ingenious model deriving the demand curve for labour on the basis of a given total capital stock and equilibrium in the market for machine goods. But how much of all this is 'classical economics', and in what sense, it is not always easy to discern: 'It is the purpose of this section to illustrate how the classical demand for labour *can be derived* as a joint-demand function and to show how supply-demand equilibrium is established in the factor markets'; it is nowhere stated that any classical writer actually derived the function in this way, so that it remains an open question how the labour demand function has been envisaged. Similarly, Dr Eagly devotes a section to the question of the 'full utilization of capital stock' and 'infers' the answer '*from the logic* of the classical system' (italics added). And, while it might be expected that the ascription of the basic assumption itself would be carefully justified, all we have to rely on is the cryptic assertion that 'classical economists, J. S. Mill in particular, implicitly assumed an exogenously fixed ratio of labour to machinery'.

Given the author's prefatory assurance that individual economists would be named 'with respect to their most important contributions to the analytical structure', the neglect of Ricardo's chapter 'On Machinery' is incomprehensible. (There is probably no more significant single discussion in the entire literature dealing with the conversion of circulating into fixed capital, and it is central for a full appreciation of Marx's subsequent treatment of technical change.) Furthermore, the relation which is envisaged between the 'basic model' and the 'Ricardian model of relative income shares' is not adequately explained.

21.6 *Classical Economics Reconsidered*, by Thomas Sowell, Princeton, New Jersey: Princeton University Press, 1974, pp. 152
(*Journal of Political Economy*, 84, August 1976, 899–902)

This book is one of three that have appeared within the last year or so on the same topic. The other works are in the nature of a technical monograph (R. V. Eagly, *The Structure of Classical Economic Theory*, 1974) and a general textbook (D. P. O'Brien, *The Classical Economists*, 1975). There are no indications in the present work regarding intended readership.

We consider first the scope of the book. The Keynesian and Marxian definitions of 'classical' economics are rejected as 'tendentious', 'egocentric', and 'idiosyncratic'. In their place we read at the outset (4–8) of a tradition established in the *Wealth of Nations* and lasting until the marginalist revolution of the 1870s. The major contributors are Ricardo and the younger Mill as well as Smith and, in the second rank, McCulloch and James Mill. There were also those who 'contributed key concepts to classical economics without sharing all its methods and conclusions' (such as J. B. Say, Malthus, West) and those who were 'classical in some respects but not in others' (Torrens, Senior, Marx). It would appear therefore to be the author's view that there existed a 'small solid core' sharing a common set of philosophical presuppositions, and common methods and conclusions relating to matters of substantive economic analysis. The major propositions listed include the labour theory of value, Say's Law, the Malthusian population theory, and the quantity theory of money, while throughout (33, 74) it is emphasized that the orientation of the classicals in their theoretical and policy writings was toward the issue of economic growth. Professor Sowell describes most effectively some of the features common to the group in his discussions of the breakaway by Smith from mercantilist conceptions relating to the nature of wealth, international commercial relations, and the scope of the 'nation' (8ff, 54).

Yet for all that the general impression left by the work as a whole is one of much less coherence than implied above. This is true of many of the basic theoretical positions. To define a clear-cut 'classical' view of Say's Law turns out to be all but impossible. Most striking of all is the contrast between Smithian and Ricardian method which emerges in the final chapter on methodology. Smith's approach is represented as 'eclectic', entailing an intermingling of 'the empirical, the theoretical, the institutional, the philosophical, the static and the dynamic'. With Ricardo, we are told, 'economics took a major step toward abstract models, rigid and artificial definitions, syllogistic reasoning – and the direct application of the results to policy. The historical, the institutional, and the empirical faded into the background, and explicit social philosophy shrank to a few passing remarks. Comparative statics became the dominant – though usually implicit – approach' (113–14). Reference is made (121) to classical economics in its 'contemporary Ricardian form', and in fact, the final chapter is almost entirely devoted to contemporary and subsequent criticisms of Ricardo and 'the Ricardians', with very great weight placed on Schumpeter's charge relating to the so-called Ricardian Vice (122, 135–6, 146–7). On the author's own reading of the record, therefore, there were profound modifications introduced into political economy in 1817. We are obliged to raise the question whether any good purpose is served by thinking in terms of a common tradition commencing in 1776 and lasting for approximately 100 years delineated by the term 'classical' economics.

We turn now to the substance of the argument. In the first chapter ('Social Philosophy'), a number of interpretations of the 'classics' are turned down in rather spirited terms. Attention is paid in particular to the contention that they were apologetic defenders of the status quo, that they believed in a harmony of class interests, and even that they were motivated by personal interest (8ff, 17, 26ff). I am totally in sympathy with Professor Sowell's position as far as concerns Smith, Ricardo, Mill, and others to whose defence he comes. Nonetheless, it seems unnecessary to fight the battle with such energy. One still meets occasionally the distorted picture of a group of hard-hearted grinders of the faces of the poor, but surely the air has been sufficiently cleared – for example, by Lord Robbins's *Theory of Economic Policy*. This impression may reflect wishful thinking, but the author gives not a single reference to the secondary literature to demonstrate the need for a new refutation.

The core of the work as far as concerns analytical matters is contained in two chapters entitled 'Macroeconomics' and 'Microeconomics', respectively. It is not certain whether much is gained by this particular division of the materials which reflects our modern tastes. To some extent there is a net loss in comprehension. It is, for example, difficult to appreciate fully the discussion of limits to growth treated in the first of the two chapters without taking into account the effect of accumulation upon the profit rate in consequence of diminishing agricultural returns, a matter considered only in the second chapter. The discussion of the Malthusian population theory in a chapter on microeconomics also seems poorly placed.

There is much that is valuable in the analytical sections. Their merit lies in an attempt to spell out the ambiguities of various key theoretical conceptions, to fit the argumentation into a suitable frame of reference reflecting contemporary preoccupations, and to demonstrate how confusion was sown by terminological and methodological differences between disputants – and above all by Ricardo's ascriptions to his opponents of his own, largely comparative-statics approach.

Sowell's discussion of Say's Law, which constitutes the essence of the first two theoretical chapters, is particularly worthwhile. As in his well-known *Say's Law: An Historical Analysis* (1972), the author takes issue with those who believe that the great controversy turned upon the question of secular stagnation. Both the general-glut and the orthodox economists, he insists, accepted that there were no permanent or secular growth constraints, and the debate turned entirely upon the possibility of short-run excess supply. Thus while Malthus, for example, maintained that increments of saving (investment) might fail to yield an adequate return and would be followed by subsequent disinvestment, the Ricardians insisted that there was no such thing as an equilibrium level of aggregate output (42ff).

Sowell's position is a little difficult to grasp in the light of a summary statement to the effect that 'Say's Law answered those who feared that economic growth had reached, or was approaching, some ultimate limit to what the economy could profitably absorb' (72). Since he does not here have in mind the dissenters from Say's Law it would have been most desirable to give the reader some idea of the identity of those contemporaries who did fear secular stagnation. Second, Malthus *et al.*, on Sowell's own showing (50–1, 72), recognized that further advance beyond the short-run limit to sustainable investment hinged upon technological innovations, but little is said about the prospects for such improvement in their writings. We are told also that J. S. Mill developed a position on oversaving similar to that of Malthus, Lauderdale, and Chalmers (50, 70), but full justice is not done to Mill, since the question of the effects of accumulation on the profit rate by way of the rising cost of wage goods, which played a large part in his work, is not discussed in the present context but, as already noted, in the chapter on micro-theory.

A most important feature of the discussion is the emphasis upon Say's conversion in the fifth edition of the *Traité* (1826) regarding the possibility of short-run limits to production and his acceptance of Sismondi's particular version of aggregate output equilibrium. The recantation, Sowell observes, 'made no impression on the British classical school' (48) and has been neglected by modern commentators.

Sowell insists that none of the major general-glut economists based his position on leakages from the income flow (45). But although this is a common view, it probably requires some modification. Say himself on at least one occasion recognized deficient money demand as a cause of contemporary depression. (A famous footnote to this effect in Say's *Letters to Mr Malthus*, 1821, is mentioned no less than four times in Sowell's book: 50, 56, 61, 65.) Now while Ricardo objected that Say 'concedes too much', Malthus himself was delighted observing that 'he fully concedes all that I contend for' (Sraffa 1951–73, VIII: 260, 267). There is at least an element in Malthus's position in his debate with Ricardo turning upon the possibility of leakages.

As mentioned earlier, the labour theory is listed among the major propositions of classical economics at the outset of the book. But we read, in the chapter on microeconomics, that 'the substantive theories of [the classical] system can be presented without the so-called labor theory of value' (75), and, in the final chapter, that 'for all the controversy generated by the "labor theory of value" it was tangential to classical value theory' (110). There is no doubt that Ricardo, for one, recognized numerous qualifications to the labour theory of exchange value, but it is also true that he used the theory consistently (indeed more so in the third than the first edition of his *Principles*) in the derivation of his major results. It is possible to restate his conclusions in other terms, but the flavour of the argument is diluted in consequence. Sowell seems here to have neglected one of his own rules of desirable procedure.

The chapter on microeconomics gives what is now the standard view of Ricardian profit theory, namely that version which runs in terms of the subsistence wage, based upon the Malthusian population principle, combined with the law of diminishing agricultural returns. The notion of profit-rate decline is presented not merely as an analytical but also as an historical proposition (83–5).

This is a work which can be warmly recommended to the serious student. But it would have been even more useful as a text had the author allowed himself considerably more space to expand his position and relate it to the voluminous secondary literature which now exists.

21.7 *Economic Analysis Before Adam Smith: Hesiod to Lessius*, by Barry Gordon, London: Macmillan, 1975, pp. xiii, 282
(*Canadian Journal of Economics*, 10, February 1977, 170–3)

In the preface to his work the author cites Samuelson's concern that there exist too few basic disagreements on fundamentals between Western economists. A book which considers a variety of alternative approaches towards economics, Professor Gordon suggests, might serve as an effective antidote. The coverage of the book, both temporally and conceptually, is vast indeed. Chapters are devoted to Greek literature prior to Plato, the Socratic tradition, the Old and New Testaments, the legal traditions of the Rabbis and Canonists and the Roman Law, St Thomas Aquinas, and subsequent Scholastic thought relating both to money and value. A separate chapter is devoted to Lessius, especially his *De Justitia et Jure* (1605). Nonetheless, the general impression is that the author has been led to portray a process of progress – albeit not in straight-line fashion – from erroneous conceptions towards the true gospel which, in the event, amounts largely to that body of theory presented in modern (orthodox) texts. The perspective, in brief, turns out to be much the same as that of Schumpeter, according to which the function of the historian is the description of the successive increments of 'truth' and the explanation of the impediments which inhibited their more rapid accumulation. One or two instances of the methodology to which we refer must suffice. With respect to Aristotle's *Politics* we read: 'It is noteworthy, however, that nowhere is there any clear perception that accumulated capital yields a meaningful service to its possessor by satisfying, through its very possession, the owner's need for liquidity. This failure on Aristotle's part is most inhibiting for his theory of money. It has serious consequences also for the subsequent development of monetary theory. However, the lack of perception at this point is consistent with his adherence to a conception of human personality which stressed public role-playing rather than the existence of a private, internal calculus of loss and gain' (38–9; cf. also the references to Aristotle's 'failure' in the *Ethics* to perceive a basis for interest in foregone opportunities, 50–1). Similarly, reference is made to Aquinas's 'failure' to develop 'a general theory of price determination', which, it is suggested, may be explained by a predominant concern with commutative, as distinct from distributive, justice (176–7). Most striking of all is the excellent press accorded Lessius when considered in the light of a continual emphasis upon his 'anticipation' of Léon Walras in a wide variety of contexts including the nature of markets and money (65f, 254f). We do not suggest that Professor Gordon is in error in his various hypotheses and interpretations; on the contrary, his judgement is usually well substantiated. It is the method of approach we wish to emphasize, given the initial statement of objective. It is unlikely that the desired 'corrective' function can be accomplished by the 'absolutist' procedure adopted in effect if not by intention.

The book is in fact best envisaged as an analytical study of the Greek philosophers and the Scholastics; the sections on the Bible and the Rabbinic literature, although in themselves of great interest, appear – in consequence of the teleological flavour of the study as a whole – as digressions. A central theme of the discussion of the Pentateuch and the Wisdom literature is that of man's 'stewardship' over worldly resources, a conception which discounts 'the significance of use-values and the end of rational economic activity' we are told (79), and one which contrasts sharply with the 'Hesiod–Robbins' definition of the economic problem in terms of scarcity (3, 73, 78). But the discussion is *in vacuo*, as it were, and little is made of it in the remainder of the work. Similarly, the discussion of Talmudic literature appears to lead nowhere. Thus we find the rather innocuous statement that 'given the importance of the Jewish presence in trade and finance, it is reasonable to suppose that Talmudic economic thought cannot be discounted as a force in the gradual emergence of economic analysis in Christian Europe' (122); at the same time we also read of the difficulty in gauging 'with any certainty the degree of influence it [Jewish religious tradition] exerted in the development of the mainstream of Western economic thought' (121) – and there the matter is allowed to rest.

The Gemara (a fifth-century compilation) is mentioned only in passing; the entire section on the Rabbinic tradition is devoted to the Mishnah. But it may be of some interest to note that the text of the Gemara which relates to one of the Mishnayot reproduced by Gordon (117) contains a crystal-clear indication of the appreciation by the Amoraïm of the psychic pleasure derived from the holding of money stocks, having in mind the possibility of meeting expenditure requirements, for which an individual was required, under certain conditions, to make some form of payment (*Babylonian Talmud*, Vilna edition, Baba Mezia: 43a). This is but one casual instance of a veritable host of similar insights. It is essential to reiterate that there exists a vast body of literature which has been scarcely touched by historians of economic thought.

The analysis of Aristotle on money is, to this reviewer's mind, first rate – particularly the demonstration that Aristotle did not, as is so often maintained, hold a 'metallist' position (44–5, 48). Gordon has much of great importance to say on various fundamental aspects of the Scholastic literature, especially the role of external events in generating an ever-widening legitimization of *lucrum cessans* as a justification for interest payments and, in the case of Lessius, a further legitimization in terms of *carentia pecuniae* (a form of liquidity preference). The work of Lessius, it is convincingly maintained, constitutes 'an important stage in the movement towards seeing an economy as composed of a number of related markets [including the labour and money markets] which, despite special features in each, operate according to the same basic set of principles' (262).

On the whole, Gordon appears to emphasize the subjective dimension in Scholastic literature on the theory of value (58f, 215, 218, 235, 238). Yet it is also conceded that 'demarcation between the different schools and streams of scholastic opinion on price and value are difficult to establish with any precision' (220–1), and a cost emphasis is attributed to a number of important later authorities including Molina (241) and Lessius himself (260f). There is some question whether, perhaps, Gordon does not rather exaggerate Lessius's appreciation of the nature of long-run normal supply price (268).

A final word regarding the general perspectives of the study is in order. The influence of Greek literature upon the later Christian analysts is well documented, but by contrast there is an unfortunate lack of concerted discussion of the subsequent filiation of ideas. There are, it is true, numerous *analogies* made between the Scholastic and more recent writing (especially late nineteenth- and early twentieth-century literature) – some convincing and some a little forced – but very little on the lines of influence exerted by the Scholastics. This is particularly unfortunate in the light of Gordon's great emphasis upon the remarkable analytical qualities of Lessius. Who amongst the seventeenth- and eighteenth-century economists read him? Did he exert any effect upon, say, Pufendorf, or for that matter on Smith? In the final paragraphs of his work Gordon addresses himself all too briefly to the matter. It is implied that the later Scholastics had little effect upon Physiocracy, mercantilism, or classical economics. While nothing further is said of the classics, reference is made to the 'regressive aspects' of the former two categories. In particular the mercantilists 'regressed to the ancient form of economic enquiry practised by the Sophists. They were concerned with the economics of nation-state building and aimed at achieving the concrete, practical result. In their hands, economics reverted again to a technology. Most of them cared very little for analysis in the abstract and were frankly derisory concerning the careful distinctions and often tedious legalistic logic of the moralists. In the process some valuable analytical initiatives of the latter were neglected' (271). Now, it seems to me that there *were* significant contributions made by mercantilist writers to economic analysis, and in fact only a few pages earlier Gordon himself makes the same point: 'Not only Petty, but a number of other significant economists of the era of Mercantilism show marked traces in their work of ideas already current in later scholastic debate' (243). Furthermore, in the present context the allusion to the Sophists is unclear in the light of the discussion at the very outset of the work: 'The manner in which economics was taught by the Sophists has a strong affinity with the approach which has come to be dominant in the twentieth century. In fact, their approach is much closer to that of the majority of modern professional economists than are those adopted by Plato, Aristotle, and the scholastics. For the Sophists, economics is a technology. Its techniques can be taught and mastered without reference to the desirability attached to the ends or purposes which the technique can be made to serve' (16).

Professor Gordon's book is likely to prove a most valuable guide through the maze of Greek and Scholastic economic literature. It is also to be warmly welcomed for posing a variety of serious problems regarding the origins of the modern paradigm.

21.8 *Mountifort Longfield: Ireland's First Professor of Political Economy*, by Lawrence S. Moss, Ottawa, Illinois: Green Hill Publishers, 1976, pp. 249
(Canadian Journal of Economics, 11, May 1978, 378–80)

There is growing interest in the immediate post-Ricardian period on the part of historians of economics. In recent years we have had substantial studies of the economics of Torrens, Bailey, Malthus and Lauderdale, McCulloch, and James Mill (by Robbins, Paglin, Rauner, O'Brien, and Winch respectively) to add to the earlier work on Senior by Bowley. The journals also indicate a growing preoccupation with the post-Ricardians. There can thus be no question of the timeliness of a full-length investigation of Longfield, to supplement the Kelley reproduction (1971) of Longfield's economic writings.

The most attractive feature of Professor Moss's work is the manner in which his subject is throughout placed in suitable historical perspective. A central theme relates to the Longfield–Ricardo nexus. It is the firmly held view of the author that the *Lectures on Political Economy* of 1834 'contained an essentially complete theory of value and distribution that departed both in tone and content from the one developed by Ricardo' (16); and furthermore that Longfield was the only one of the dissenters to present an alternative theoretical system to Ricardo (185, 187). These related propositions are presented as conflicting with the 'improper verdict', attributed to the secondary literature, that Longfield was merely a 'modifier' of Ricardo's economic theory (17, 66). It may be remarked that one authority only is cited in this regard (Mark Blaug, *Ricardian Economics*, 1958). It is not at all clear that Blaug's position constitutes the general verdict; Schumpeter after all wrote of Longfield that 'he overhauled the whole of economic theory and produced a system that would have stood up well in 1890'; Professor Bowley awards Longfield the title of 'first of the neoclassics'; and Professor Black observes that Longfield's analysis of pricing and distribution 'is a fundamentally and systematically different analysis from the Ricardian one. . . . Only Longfield, among those who wrote in English at this period, offered his readers a theory of value which was complete – and completely original' (Schumpeter 1954: 465; Bowley 1973: 217; Black 1971: 15–16). Moss's conclusion regarding the status of Longfield as a brilliant and successful precursor of neoclassicism is quite consistent with these evaluations.

What of the details of the central argument? All depends in the first place on the nature of the Ricardian system envisaged. Moss adopts a version running in terms of the agricultural model of distribution in a growth context. Essential to this model is the separation of the landlord's share by the differential theory of rent and the explanation of the profit–wage division by use of the subsistence–wage conception (17–18, 96–7). Longfield's major divergence does not relate to the differential-rent theory – this served the same function as in Ricardo's scheme – but to the determination of the rate of profit. What is entailed is a theory of profit turning upon the 'marginal productivity of machinery employed in manufacturing' (20; cf. 69f, 98f).

Is the picture of 'Ricardian' economics adopted here convincing? The striking feature as this reviewer sees it is the total omission of the role of the measure of value as basis for the inverse profit–wage relation. Professor Moss in fact is explicit that this indeed is a secondary feature of the structure (23–4). Now I believe that to take this position is to ignore a key characteristic of Ricardianism as Ricardo understood it and one which occupied a conspicuous place in the post-Ricardian literature. It is an omission with consequences, for Longfield himself explicitly adopted the Ricardian position in this regard, and moreover was responsible for a celebrated *volte-face* by Torrens in favour of Ricardo. Professor Moss is aware of this latter fact and is nonplussed: 'What a curious turn of events that Longfield, who set out to supplant the English theory of wages and profits with a new one of his own, should be hailed in England as one who defended the central pillar of the Ricardian theory of distribution' (120–1). The decision to define Ricardian economics in terms of the agricultural model has, it seems to me, blocked a potentially fruitful avenue of approach towards the relationship between the Ricardian and non-Ricardian elements in Longfield's work, leaving an impression of a sharper divergence than may be justified.

We proceed to consider the picture of Longfield's theory itself. A mathematical statement is presented in the central analytical chapter of the book which has the formal object of demonstrating that 'the number of postulated relationships between the variables is equal to the number of variables to be determined'. The discussion concludes with the observation that Longfield presented 'something approximating a complete theoretical system' (105). In the mathematical model the wage is equated to the value of the marginal product of labour; and the law of diminishing returns is applied whenever the quantity of one factor is varied holding the quantity of the other factor constant. The general picture is one of 'neoclassical' procedure: 'Each time Longfield analysed one of the three distributive shares he tried to relate his account to the supply-and-demand theory of price that he presented in the early chapters of his *Lectures on Political Economy*'; he proceeded under the assumption of given total factor supplies in the 'Austrian' fashion; and 'his analysis of marginal demand in the commodity market and his marginal productivity account of capital pricing deserve recognition as great anticipations of the neoclassical theory of distribution of the last quarter of the nineteenth century' (107).

If, however, the account of Longfield in the work as a whole is considered, it becomes clear that the foregoing perspective must be qualified. At an early stage the reader is expressly warned to 'avoid imputing to Longfield more than he intended' (51). When solving the problem of distribution, Longfield used the differential rent theory in precisely the same way as Ricardo (as before observed) but reversed the order of procedure in dealing with profits and wages – wages rather than profits were now treated as 'residual'. He was, to quote Moss again, 'unable to generalize the concept of marginal productivity to arrive at a general theory of resource pricing' (50). I conclude that, if Ricardo failed to recognize distribution as a *general* problem in the pricing of productive services in the neoclassical fashion, the same charge must be addressed to Longfield.

Furthermore, it is strictly speaking illegitimate to refer to the marginal product of (fixed) capital in the central analysis of profits itself. This too is emphasized by Moss: 'It is significant that Longfield does not consider the possibility that an increase in the ratio of machines to labor could itself have an effect on the *physical* product of the last machine employed. . . . The idea that the actual proportion in which labor and capital are combined can itself account for alterations in the efficiency of capital is not part of Longfield's discussion' (78). In the light of these qualifications the reader is inevitably led to suspect that the author may on occasion have exaggerated the degree of neoclassicism implicit in Longfield's work.

There is much in this book which will be found of profound interest to historians of economics. In particular there are most fruitful discussions of Longfield's pioneer contributions to the theory of international trade and money, his academic status, the general ideological climate and the consequences flowing therefrom for his work, the relationship between analysis and policy, and (most impressive) the reception of his theory. Students of nineteenth-century economic thought are fortunate to have an addition to the literature of this calibre.

21.9 *Adam Smith's Politics: An Essay in Historiographic Revision*, by
Donald Winch, Cambridge Studies in the History and Theory of Politics,
Cambridge, New York and Melbourne: Cambridge University Press, 1978,
pp. xi, 204

(*Journal of Economic Literature*, 17, June 1979, 542–5)

Donald Winch takes strong issue, in this essay, with a wide variety of
modern interpretations, both Marxist and non-Marxist, which, presupposing
a 'liberal capitalist' or 'liberal individualist' tradition extending back to
Hobbes and Locke, make Smith appear as the first major economic
spokesman for an emerging capitalist order. An implication of this perspective, Winch complains, is that the 'political' dimension of Smith's work is
faded out. He himself reads the evidence in precisely the reverse way: 'I . . .
wish to maintain that Smith has a "politics" which is far from being trivial'
(23). A demonstration of this proposition and the discernment of what
precisely Smith's politics amount to constitute the primary tasks of this
essay.

The early part of the essay is devoted to what is regarded as the relevant
intellectual background. Winch alludes to a body of recent 'revisionist'
history – the work of Peter Laslett, Caroline Robbins, Bernard Bailyn, and
(above all) J.G.A. Pockock – which is said to demonstrate conclusively the
inadequacies of the notion of a continuous genealogy of liberal or bourgeois
individualism flowing from Locke to the nineteenth century and beyond,
and which places great emphasis upon the emergence of a body of 'Anglo-
American oppositional literature' reflecting 'Country' ideology opposed to
the 'Court' or official Whig position. This ideology insisted upon an (idealized) balanced constitution, and was, accordingly, concerned about excessive
executive power and royal influence as a threat to the authority of a landed
parliament, was critical of the 'moneyed interest' supporting the Court
against the landed interest, and was opposed to a standing army because of
its potential independence of parliamentary control. What Pockock *et al.*
have revealed, we learn, is 'evidence of a profound concern with the challenge posed to the existing political order – or rather, an idealized version of
it – by the new moneyed interest and forms of property which appeared to
have none of the citizenly or virtuous qualities possessed by visible or landed
property' (122–3).

What are the specific implications for Smith's politics of this background
material, apart from a clarification – important though it is – of relevant
linguistic usage, which in turn reveals the appropriate agenda of debate?
Where did Smith stand, in brief, on the Country–Court controversy?

The great attention paid by Winch to Smithian methodology is relevant
to this question. The notion of Smith as 'political' or 'social scientist' is
much stressed and reinforced by repeated references to his 'scepticism', his
'irony', his 'cynicism', and his 'complacency'. Duncan Forbes's recent work

on 'Sceptical Whiggism' (1975) with its message that Smith, like Hume, was a 'sceptical' Whig *because* he was a political scientist, is warmly adopted. And Winch alludes to the opinion expressed by Adam Ferguson and Dugald Stewart to much the same effect. All this would seem to imply that Smith did not 'take sides'.

Now it seems to me that Smith's 'objectivity' as social scientist can be overdone. And it is interesting that there is much in the present work to suggest this – indeed much of the value of the essay resides precisely in the evidence pointing to this conclusion. We are shown, for example, how wide-ranging were Smith's educational recommendations, designed to counter some of the consequences of over-specialization. The state had educational responsibilities extending far and wide to include the maintenance of the 'martial spirit' of the common people – and this because of a common concern with the preconditions for effective citizenship; the whole issue of 'defence' should be viewed from the perspective of Smith's concern with the martial virtues as human and moral qualities; the discussion of the relative merits of militias and standing armies falls into this range of considerations as does also the matter of religious sects. Winch's analysis leads him to conclude that Smith presents political arguments for strengthening the mechanisms of social control and that these arguments certainly convey 'something that is central to an understanding of Smith's brand of political analysis' (120). I have no doubt that this is so, but in that case we surely have a picture of a profoundly committed advocate.

A chapter on the public debt points in the same direction. Smith is shown to be tolerant of those expenses of the sovereign related to necessary services, which include the upkeep of public buildings, and Winch observes that 'durable magnificence of the kind that is a credit to the genius and achievements of a collectivity, such as a city or nation, conforms – as Jacob Viner indicated – to a classical-renaissance view of communal enrichment' (134). This too falls within the domain of mechanisms of social control and implies a degree of advocacy. Similarly, Winch elaborates on Smith's tolerant attitude towards those interest groups upon which depend the prestige and stability of government – for a distinction had to be made between mere faction and healthy opposition – in which context Winch himself insists that Smith was neither ironic, nor cynical, but had to be taken at face value.

It is my impression from all of this that the medium is *not* the message in Smith's case. His style is often cynical, but not the substance. This is not, however, to deny one of Winch's main themes – his insistence that along with Hume, following in Montesquieu's footsteps, Smith attempts to develop a 'science' of politics. There is surely no reason why one cannot be both scientist *and* advocate! It is perhaps a weakness of the present work that it sometimes implies otherwise, but by no means a fatal weakness, for we are given the materials which allow a balanced interpretation.

We are now able to return to our original question. Smith *was* an advocate but evidently not of the Country or oppositional position. He was opposed to the agrarian laws recommended by his teacher Hutcheson as a device to prevent immoderate acquisition (50, 66–7, 90–1); he was not particularly worried by the political strains due to a growing national debt (138); he minimized the risks to civil liberty emanating from a standing army (108–9); he justified interest groups relating to the prestige and stability of government (153–3); and he spoke favourably of the contemporary British governmental system (161). Winch makes it clear that 'liberty' to Smith meant primarily personal and civil liberty – the impartial administration of justice and security of property and contracts – and as such was compatible with a wide variety of governmental forms. He did not share the fears of the Country Party regarding a change in the balance in consequence of royal influence. The dangers to moral identity and citizenship posed by the advance of commercial society smacks rather more of the Country way of thinking, but the difference lies in Smith's willingness to endorse modernization, subject always to the corrective steps to be taken by the state. Similarly, Smith recognized some of the potential dangers to civil liberty inherent in standing armies, but was again prepared to accept this consequence of modern society – provided care was taken in the selection of the high officers, that military training was given to the population at large, and that the regular army was kept at a minimum (108–9, 112–13). The picture that emerges from the present work is one that places Smith much closer to the Court than the Country position, but certainly not as complaisant observer. *Smith had very positive proposals for the solution to, or at least mitigation of, the defects attributed to commercial society.* It is worth noting that matters of value and principle are said, in the conclusion, to have played a part in the total picture (171, 183), and Winch writes at one point of Smith's 'pervasive concern with injustice and oppression' (98–9).

Winch makes much of the 'fact that "capitalism" was not available to Smith, and that he did not find it necessary to coin the term' (142). This is an important part of the argument, for it reflects Winch's protestations against anachronistic readings. It seems to me, however, that nothing that can be deduced about Smith's position on the Country–Court controversy precludes the possibility that he may also have been addressing himself to issues peculiar to 'capitalist' society – an advanced form falling within the broader category of 'commercial' society. I can accept many of the valuable things that Winch has to say regarding the significance of 'polity', including his insistence that 'economy' was but *one* branch of the science of legislation, which had not yet swamped the rest, but I cannot conceive of any accurate reading of the *Wealth of Nations* that does not place the capitalistic labour–employer relationship in a very central position indeed. More generally, I suspect that the economic element has been unduly played down in the discussion of long-term historical transitions – one does not have to subscribe to the four-stages interpretation, understood as a theory implying inevitable determinism, to insist upon the very central role given to self-interest in the transition from a service to a money nexus.

This elegant study provides an effective antidote to traditional ahistorical interpretations. History must surely be read forward not backward. But it is my impression that the author may have been following the dictum (cited by a famous moral philosopher in a different context) – 'If the rod be bent too much one way . . . in order to make it straight you must bend it as much the other.'

21.10 *The Economist in Parliament: 1780–1868*, by Frank Whitson Fetter, Durham, North Carolina: Duke University Press, 1980, pp. xii, 306
(Victorian Studies Newsletter, 25, 1982, 505–7)

In this masterly compendium Frank Whitson Fetter has encapsulated the results of a massive body of research relating to the parliamentary roles of British economists during the 'classical' period 1780–1868. It is an impressive achievement indeed.

With broad strokes he paints in the relevant background, describing the nature of the sociological, technological, and intellectual circumstances which after mid-century led increasingly to the treatment of economics as 'an organized and systematic analysis', its practitioners focusing upon the economic problem – the production of wealth and its distribution – and emphasizing 'economic considerations in judging national policy' (5, 200). Fetter finds his chosen period exceptional in the large number of economists who became MPs (6), although he shows that in terms of numbers, the nature of controversy, and the attitudes adopted, the years 1800–50 constitute a more homogeneous period from the perspective of the central argument of his book: that economists sought reforms to pave the way for the solutions envisaged for the economic problem – 'Smithian' solutions largely – reforms depending for passage upon their parliamentary representation and requiring, more profoundly, the creation of a legislature responsible to public opinion and public wants (213, 228).

Most of the book is made up of a series of analyses of the parliamentary roles of economists focusing on international trade, government in economic life (including the regulation of working conditions), monetary and banking policy, public finance, education, and poor relief and emigration. These are the strictly economic issues. Further chapters are devoted to church and state, civil rights and religious disabilities, the humanitarian movement, imperial Britain, and parliamentary reform. There is a brief closing chapter evaluating the economists' influence in parliament.

It is a principal theme of this study that the economists 'were well to the left of centre by the standards of the age. They were liberals in the historic sense of being receptive to, even eager for, orderly changes to be defended in the light of reason' (15). But who were the 'economists'? Without a resolution of this fundamental issue, an investigation of the present kind cannot get off the ground. I doubt whether much exception can be taken to Fetter's general principles of selection (7–8). He effectively catches within his net those who would conform broadly to the types of modern academic and business or financial economists. My only serious reservation applies to the inclusion of 'politicians whom the accidents of history forced to be economists' (13) – preeminently Sir Robert Peel.

I suspect that the inclusion of Peel was a most difficult decision. Fetter repeatedly excludes from his various generalizations the Tory 'politician economists' (13, 228, 233). He also maintains that what influence economists exerted was in their capacity as backbenchers, not government members, and seems to set aside the formal classification when he writes that 'the carrying out of the changes, economic, political and social, for which parliamentary economists argued and battled was largely in the hands of men not ordinarily thought of as economists' (233). The inclusion of Peel is thus hard to understand and perhaps colours Fetter's estimate of a generally positive 'influence' exerted by economists (230).

This matter of influence is extremely tricky. Fetter talks of a 'typical economist's approach' (200). But apart from the Corn Laws, the Navigation Acts, and public finance, there was, he shows, no broad consensus of viewpoint on economic policy, including government interference in the market for commodities and labour (59, 67) and the role of the Bank of England (134). Furthermore the economists are shown to have been 'generally on the losing side of both economic and political issues' (240). The ultimate adoption of their positions, sometimes long after their passing from the scene, Fetter apparently accepts as evidence of influence – 'when [Joseph] Hume fought doggedly for measures that were eventually adopted it is reasonable to believe that he had influence' (235) – but this perspective surely requires defence.

There is, moreover, the paradox that the more significant the name the less may be the influence in parliament. Of Ricardo and J. S. Mill Fetter says that 'their votes and speeches in Parliament may have been but a minor influence on legislation as compared with the influence of their extraparliamentary activities' (33–4). But there are no rules. Of Cobden we are told that his greatest contribution 'may be' as MP rather than as leader of the Anti-Corn Law League, 'relentlessly pressing on a reluctant Peel the case for free trade in corn' (236–7).

I am a little troubled also by the matter of the direction of influence; Fetter sometimes wants to have it both ways. Thus Thomas Attwood 'may have influenced Peel in sponsoring the rigid provisions of the Bank Act of 1844, in the thought that this would strengthen the defenses of the gold standard' (234). But Ricardo is also accorded an 'influence' from the opposite direction: 'How many votes may have been influenced, even after his death, by his ideas is conjecture, but it is plausible that he did much to strengthen parliamentary criticism of the Corn Laws and support of the Gold Standard' (235). There is rather too much conjecture here. I fear that the issue may be quite intractable by its very nature.

It is noteworthy that Adam Smith is given pride of place in the account as most responsible for the thinking of the parliamentary economists (239). The characteristic nineteenth-century analyses of value, machinery, the law of markets, and the wages fund, would seem to have played little part. Most conspicuous for its absence in the summary statement of the story is the Ricardian growth model with its prediction (*ceteris paribus*) of a falling profit rate and ultimate secular stagnation in a closed economy. There are profound implications here for the interpretation of classical economic doctrine.

21.11 *The Classical Theory of Economic Growth*, by Walter Eltis, London: Macmillan, 1984, pp. xv, 372
(*The Economic Journal*, 95, March 1985, 234–5)

Walter Eltis has succeeded brilliantly in capturing the essence of the classical theory of economic growth and income distribution, in an extraordinarily brief span. The great merit of this work lies not so much in its isolation of the central themes of classical growth theory, which will be familiar to many readers (the contrast between surplus-producing activities and surplus-using activities, and the dependence of the rate of economic growth upon surplus), but rather in the pellucid and original exposition of those themes.

The author has no axe to grind. This emerges strikingly in two chapters on Marx, which provide the most objective yet sympathetic coverage of Marxian economics and method known to me. More generally, Eltis is careful to indicate how far the models presented constitute 'restatements' of the master economists themselves, and how far they extend or correct the originals; this he achieves by close attention to the texts to assure accuracy of attribution as far as concerns the axioms, and by effective application of Stigler's principle of 'scientific exegesis' whereby 'we increase our confidence in the interpretation of an author by increasing the number of his main theoretical conclusions that we can deduce from (our interpretation of) his analytical system' (Stigler 1965).

This is an intellectually rich work. Apart from his concern with the filiation of ideas (the concluding summary chapter constitutes in itself a *tour de force* in this regard), Eltis relates the theoretical 'reconstructions' to contemporary circumstances, institutional and quantitative, with an eye to both analytical structure and policy application; he draws parallels and contrasts between the classical and modern theoretical approaches; and he considers the relevance of the classical models for current policy issues. Eltis argues convincingly that classical procedures and even results cannot safely be neglected in today's world.

I am much impressed by the process of model construction with a minimum of fuss and just the right degree of mathematics. Eltis brings out the essentials of the 'magnificent dynamics', and in so doing provides case studies of the method of model building with wide applicability. To follow his examples would be a pretty good way of learning economics.

Of the five economists studied, Quesnay seems to be Eltis's favourite; at least he impresses Eltis most, and understandably so since he had much less to go on than his successors in his model building and applications. Of the five, Ricardo is the only one for whom Eltis does not provide a *formal* restatement, and this doubtless because Ricardo was himself a deliberate and successful formal model builder to a greater degree than any of the others. It is good to see confirmed that Ricardo 'was the classical economist who came closest to complete logical consistency', since readers of recent Samuelson articles referring to Ricardo would gain from them the impression that Ricardo is far from the impeccable logician of the legend.

Of the many impressive specific contributions in this work I am particularly struck by the clarification of the *tableau économique*; the tracing through of the implications of increasing returns in the Smithian and Marxian structures; the marvellously succinct treatment of the applications to policy of their respective models by Quesnay and Ricardo; the clarification of the 'Keynesian' dimension in Malthus's analysis of effective demand; the exposition of the Marxian 'transformation' and 'realization' issues; and the interpretation of the contrast between those who were concerned by impediments to the 'right' structural proportions between subsectors of the economy (Quesnay, Malthus, and Marx) and those who relied on the market process to do the job (Smith and Ricardo).

There will inevitably be differences of judgement regarding detail. The precise logic of various criteria which arise for the output of the productive sector, particularly the relation between surplus generation and 'materiality' and 'marketability', requires perhaps more elaboration. The basic physiocratic axiom regarding agricultural surplus is not always firmly enough grounded, especially the relation between physical and value surplus: similarly, the weight placed upon the increasing 'capital–output ratio' as rationale for Smith's falling profit rate stays too much on the physical plane; and I suspect that, considering the main theme, somewhat more explicit attention should have been accorded changing resource-endowment patterns in an open economy in the account of Smith's position on the role of the agricultural and manufacturing sectors in the growth process. Had Samuelson's canonical classical model (Samuelson 1978) been taken into account, it may have been found necessary to modify several uncompromising statements asserting the absence of diminishing returns in the *Wealth of Nations*. (The Samuelson and Eltis versions of Ricardo, incidentally, are similar in essentials although arrived at by different paths.) The confusion in *Wealth of Nations* between the process of saving and the result of saving, notwithstanding the considerable attention accorded fixed capital, remains troublesome. The notion of Malthus as 'pessimist' regarding the living standards of the masses requires revision (Hollander, *History of Political Economy*, forthcoming [1986]). In the discussion of Marx the falling wage trend and the role of population pressure are given no part (on this issue see Hollander, *American Economic Review*, 1984); and Marx on the source of profits in surplus labour is, I believe, no different from the orthodox writers including McCulloch and J. S. Mill.

But which reviewer can resist any opportunity to take his hobbyhorses out of the paddock? This important book is to be warmly welcomed. It will surely help give the history of economic thought a good name.

21.12 *History and the Economic Past: An Account of the Rise and Decline of Economic History in Britain*, by D. C. Coleman, New York: Clarendon Press, Oxford University Press, 1987, pp. 150

(Albion, 21, Fall 1989, 525–7)

The subtitle accurately defines the theme of this small volume. It is another lament for the parlous state of economic history. Professor Coleman commences with the Scottish historical school (chapter 2), represented as 'the first British signpost to the examination of the economic past as an essential element in the understanding of human society' (5), with special reference to David Hume, Adam Smith and John Millar, and other celebrated contributors to 'speculative' or 'hypothetical' or 'conjectural' history. Following these 'progenitors of what we now call economic history' (17) comes 'The English Reaction' (chapter 3), a reference largely to the Ricardo school – Ricardo, James Mill and J. R. McCulloch are harshly treated for attempting to abort the embryo; and then 'Rebels, Outsiders and Economic Historians' (chapter 4) which treats the English inductivist critics of 'Ricardian abstraction' (42), the German historicists and those responsible directly or indirectly for assuring a toe-hold for economic history in British universities between 1880 and 1910. The heroes include Cliffe Leslie, Cunningham, Ashley and Hewins; Coleman is particularly warmly disposed towards Arnold Toynbee. A feature in this chapter is the Cunningham–Marshall controversy and the victory of the latter, assuring the distancing of the subject as it emerged from economic theory. Chapter 5 ('Reformists and Neutralists') covers the impact of Tawney committed to social reform, and Clapham, not thus committed in his technical work which allowed 'some limited use of the tools of neo-classical economics' (63). These two men are seen to provide the typical modes of approach throughout the following decades. But even in 1926 when the Economic History Society was formed 'the subject still had only a rather slender hold in the formal establishment of British universities' (93). To the reputation of the new *Economic History Review* is attributed the survival of economic history. The extraordinary blossoming of the subject, by various indexes, from 1945 to the mid-1970s is the theme of chapter 6; and so too is its subsequent 'decline'.

Coleman's book is far from a mere parading of names and a classification of periods. Its attraction lies in an attempt to account for the perceived trends. An extraordinary range of considerations are introduced. One of the most interesting themes emerges in an account of the late nineteenth-century enthusiasm for the subject: 'Perhaps the most potent immediate force helping to stimulate the later nineteenth-century concern for the economic past was unease. It had more than one origin: middle-class social guilt at poverty amongst wealth; distaste for aggressive industrialism; nostalgia for a supposed age of pre-industrial bliss; and, especially pervasive, apprehensions at evident setbacks in Britain's economic performance' (56). The theme of social 'guilt' and the use of the subject as a weapon in the struggle for social reform (and for protectionism and nationalism) is pervasive (e.g. 59, 69, 79). The same conceptions emerge in the account of the blossoming after 1945: 'post-war recovery stimulated a new fascination with the historical problems of production, technical change, and, above all, economic growth' (98).

The problem is that this sort of rationalization can explain almost anything or nothing. Both pessimism and optimism regarding economic performance and prospects apparently account for periods of vigour. The rationale offered for the late nineteenth-century upswing scarcely explains the Clapham line emerging soon after, its preference for 'quantification, some limited use of the tools of neo-classical economics, and an attempted stance of ethical neutralism in relation to the course of economic change' (63). Apparently the on-going decline of the subject since the mid-1970s is compatible with precisely the same apprehensions as a century ago regarding the British economy. (Perhaps there is some hope for a renewal of interest in economic history – if things should go badly enough!) But I admit that my criticism is a little unfair to Coleman, for he is clear enough that a multiplicity of forces is always at play.

As for the present decline, there are hints of a certain inevitability: 'The great [postwar] boom could not last. Soon it began to go the way of all such phenomena: retardation appeared in some indicators, absolute decline in others' (98; cf. 101). But Coleman puts most of the onus squarely on the subject's practitioners, especially their self-imposed isolation from both the historians and economists, the latter going back to the celebrated Cunningham–Marshall dispute (45–6, 62, 78–9, 93, 102–7). Coleman writes strongly here – 'sterility' and 'complacency' are the terms employed – of the lack of intellectual stimulus that came with 'success' and the establishment of an 'orthodoxy' isolated from the outside. Interestingly, the British response (or rather lack thereof) to cliometrics is explained in these terms. In the last resort, however, these attitudes have to be accounted for at a deeper level than suggested here. The problem of 'numeracy', and lack of mathematical and statistical training, related back to the British school system, takes us some way. (On these themes see especially 1–2, 108–10, 125–7.)

Clearly Coleman is not opposed to theory as such. This emerges frequently (e.g. 74, 102, 109, 113, 125); indeed, any hope he has for the future seems to reside in a linkage of economic history with theory and, of course, history (127). The problem is: what sort of theory? I cannot escape a sense of ambivalence on Coleman's part towards neo-classical economics and a strong attraction to the so-called 'stages of economic growth' approach that characterized the Scottish historians (e.g. 28, 103, 113). Neo-classical theory – as used by the 'neutralists' – can go so far and is better suited for industry studies than for the magnificent themes of growth and decay (102–4). This is confirmed in the closing chapter ('The Future of the Economic Past'). Marshall himself was aware of the limitations of what Coleman refers to as 'short-period neo-classical analysis', but moderns engaged in the study of secular trends apparently are not (128–30). Coleman's doubts regarding 'bold abstractions' over lengthy periods 'based on the primacy of economic motives' sit uneasily beside his warmth towards Smith's 'philosophic' history based on 'the psychological assumption of continuously operating self-interest' (133, 10).

What of the future? The 'American trail' would lead to economic history being confirmed simply as a branch of economics. This is not Coleman's ideal. He champions concentration by economic historians on 'manageable historical entities' and sees promise in local, urban and business history – the latter especially calling for 'more than economics': 'It is clear that the standard set of theoretical questions and methods available in the new economic history is of very limited value when tackling the history of the firm, the most important single organizational entity of modern economic life' (141). And it is the 'neo-institutionalism' of A. W. Chandler that he commends with its limited use of advanced orthodox economic theory. I do not quite fathom the final paragraph which suggests that the subject is after all intimately bound up with national (or global) and secular issues (146).

These are fascinating issues – especially for a member of a department headed at various times by Sir William Ashley, Harold Innis and W. T. Easterbrook. It is especially revealing to see the decline of the subject at Toronto as part of a world-wide phenomenon (cf. also *The Future of Economic History*, ed. A. J. Field, 1987). One might cavil at some of Coleman's rationalizations of the trend – his preoccupation with Britain inevitably means that a variety of global forces are neglected – but what he has to say of the British case and his proposals for the future are well worth pondering.

My serious reservations relate to his forays into doctrinal history. Least acceptable is the representation of David Ricardo, whose speculations are contrasted with Adam Smith's historical orientation (19–24). I must immediately declare an interest, a matter to which fortunately there is an amusing side. In a recent *Times Literary Supplement* review of my *Classical Economics* (1987), T. W. Hutchison recommends Coleman as a corrective, to demonstrate 'that economic history was originally developed by Smith and the Scottish historical school . . . but was then almost strangled in infancy by the non-historical dogmatism of Ricardo and his associates' (11–17 December 1987). Unfortunately, Coleman's representation of Ricardo and his relation with James Mill derives almost entirely from Hutchison's own *Revolutions and Progress in Economic Knowledge* (1978) – scarcely cricket on Hutchison's part – and is demonstrably faulty. Coleman, moreover, like Hutchison neglects the powerful component of abstract theory in the *Wealth of Nations* and seems unaware of Malthus's severe objections to Smithian abstraction and application; he fails to comment on Cliffe Leslie's debt to J. S. Mill, that champion of Ricardian economics; and there is no recognition of the similarity between Willhelm Roscher's 'historicism' and that of Mill. Interested readers will find in the conclusion to my *Economics of J. S. Mill* (1985) and in a trio of chapters on classical method in my *Classical Economics* the reasons why the old-fashioned dichotomies which characterize Coleman's historiography should be abandoned.

21.13 *Theories of Surplus and Transfer*, by Helen Boss, London: Unwin Hyman Ltd, 1990
(This item appeared as a Preface to the book.)

In *Theories of Surplus and Transfer* Helen Boss subjects to close analysis and with remarkable liveliness the logic and history of the celebrated productive–unproductive dichotomy in its various senses – surplus-generating vs. surplus-absorbing; material vs. immaterial; marketable vs. non-marketable; final vs. intermediate. The coverage is ambitious, extending from the late seventeenth-century national income accountancy of Petty and King to the Physiocrats, Adam Smith, the British and the French classics, the marginalists and early neo-classicists, nearly the whole range of modern orthodox literature, and also Marx, Marxist and Soviet writings. As such it constitutes a veritable *tour de force* dealing with the central issue at the foundation of all economic reasoning: who are the producers and what do they produce?

Sir John Hicks emphasizes a too often neglected contrast between the history of the natural sciences and the history of economics. For the working natural scientist the history of his subject is typically of no practical significance: 'Old ideas are worked out; old controversies are dead and buried.' Not so in economics: 'we cannot escape in the same way from our own past. We may pretend to escape; but the past crowds in on us all the same' (Hicks 1976: 207). The themes of this book provide a case in point. Far from constituting the dusty museum piece of Schumpeterian legend, the controversies relating to the boundaries of the economic domain – within which income-generating activity occurs and upon which 'non-producers' (the author's 'parasites') are dependent – yield a range of perspectives on the nature of output, and therefore on appropriate national income accounting, which are of abiding theoretical and practical significance. Students would do well to become familiar with the struggles of the mind surrounding these issues, both to develop their understanding of the bases of economic logic and as a means of avoiding the arrogant provincialism in space and time which is encouraged by *Principles* texts, which imply that past debates reflect nothing but confusion at last settled to everyone's satisfaction, at least to every right-thinking person's satisfaction.

The source of this narrowness of perspective seems to derive from the exclusion of history from courses and training in economics. I have long held that logic and history should be co-requirements in any self-respecting program for the training of economists. The great economists of the past did not approach their subject solely as a matter of 'pure' theory but had particular visions of the environment in mind as requiring explication. The point was made by J. S. Mill: 'The deductive Science of Society will not lay down a theorem, asserting in an universal manner the effect of any cause, but will teach us to frame the proper theorem for the circumstances of any given case. It will not give the laws of society in general, but the means of determining the phenomena of a given society from the particular elements or data of that society' (*System of Logic*, 1843, in Mill 1973, VIII: 899–900). E. Phelps Brown has urged that a 'clinical commitment' be made to resist 'the temptation to seek the job for the tools instead of the tool for the job' (Phelps Brown 1972: 8). For teachers and students of modern economics who welcome this orientation and are curious to see the effects of extending it broadly to matters of definition and classification as well as to mechanisms and mathematical tools narrowly perceived, the present work will be a boon. It is illuminating to look at changes in fashion regarding such central concepts as 'production', 'capital formation', 'consumption' and 'surplus' with an eye to the relative influences of the theoretical, ideological, computational and historical context.

That the productive–unproductive dichotomy is indeed far from a dust-covered relic is manifestly apparent in that aspects of it continually reemerge with changes in the economic situation and therefore in the focus of our attention. It is disconcerting to see that our own concern with improving the performance of Western mixed economies characterized by high levels of public expenditure raises issues in some respects identical to those debated in the eighteenth century.

The book charts with pleasing impartiality the shifting emphases economists and social thinkers have placed on markets and on 'mode' of production, generally in their quest for an optimal mix of institutions. Dr Boss relates concern over declining proportions of 'material production' and growing service shares in Western and socialist economies to the sovereignties (producer, consumer, dictator) which drive economic outcomes. A study of this book would I suspect prove particularly illuminating to Soviet, Eastern bloc and Chinese reformers.

In its full development of the implications of the productive–unproductive dichotomy, Helen Boss's *Theories of Surplus and Transfer* is a unique contribution so far as I am aware. It provides a fine balance of history of economic thought, economic history, welfare theory and policy, growth economics and economic systems. The quality of the scholarship is impressive; whether or not one accepts all of its provocative interpretations or indeed its agenda for an economics of the future is of secondary importance.

21.14 *Ricardian Politics*, by Murray Milgate and Shannon C. Stimson, Princeton, New Jersey: Princeton University Press, 1991; pp. xiii, 169
(*Journal of the History of Economic Thought*, 16, 1994, 159–61)

The authors of this book make the claim for a 'distinctive' Ricardian politics involving democratic reform and deriving from David Ricardo's economic thought. Specifically, 'in Ricardo's more explicitly political writing, one encounters an attempt to construct an argument for democratic reform that is at once based upon, and consistent with, an account of the operation of the new market mechanism itself' (x). It is part of their case that by 'Ricardian' is intended Ricardo, not James Mill or others often included within the rubric. It is an enterprise, they assure the readers, approached 'almost entirely without any preconceptions as to what we would find' (x–xi).

A chapter on Representative Government attributes to Ricardo a recommendation for immediate parliamentary reform by expanding the franchise 'just short of' universal suffrage (37). A companion chapter ('The Reasonable Part of the Country') points to the exclusion of 'the poor' – those dependent on relief – on grounds of their general incapacity for citizenship at least in going conditions (63); and a further supplementary chapter extends the discussion to arrive at 'The Principle of Exclusion' covering (apart from Ricardo's position on religious toleration, but silent on the matter of gender) the principle that 'the rights of property should be held sacred', justifying depriving those of the franchise 'against whom it could justly be alleged that they considered it their interest to invade them' (cited p. 91). Property ownership as such was not to provide the test. A chapter entitled 'Co-optation and Incorporation' argues that Ricardian politics was not 'a politics of unanimity or harmonization', but rather an arena for 'structuring such conflict [by] putting competing class interests on a more equal footing' (106, 119). A final substantive chapter is devoted to the duration of parliament (the case for triennial parliaments).

I have the impression that what would certainly be a substantial article has been stretched out to book length, exaggerating Ricardo's *bonâ fides* as political thinker. Nevertheless, I welcome the work in any form since I share the authors' belief that Ricardo's differences with James Mill in the political (as well as the economic) sphere require recognition and since I have been objecting for years to the appellation 'the Ricardian Vice' to describe Ricardo's policy applications, themes that are here amply corroborated. (It does not surprise me in the least that this book should have already been vilified by one reviewer as 'hagiography'.)

There are, however, some details which I would question. Milgate and Stimson assert that 'Ricardo's arguments were at once attacked [as by Hodgskin] as being essentially preservative of the existing political order', and 'at the same time incorporated into a new theoretical discourse of working-class radicalism' (9). The authors here fail to note that the Ricardian Socialists to whom they refer were neither Ricardian nor Socialist. The authors are covered by a later qualification: 'Although there has been some debate . . . that their real inspiration' was Adam Smith (146), this is set aside without much ado and we return immediately to Ricardo's 'dangerous doctrines' (149). This issue is particularly important since bourgeois apologists – 'socialist adversaries' – are said to have reacted to the use made of Ricardo's economics 'by the likes of Hodgskin to mandate a thorough-going restructuring of society rather than merely a measure of political reform' (9–10). This perspective has been debated in the literature at considerable length and one might have expected the pros and cons to have been properly dealt with.

That the authors have not fully absorbed the literature seems confirmed by their brief reference to the pseudonymous 'Piercy Ravenstone'. They fail to realize that he has long been identified as Richard Puller. Far more serious, they unnecessarily weaken their own case by failing to discuss – or even to mention – Ricardo's partially laudatory comments on Ravenstone's explanation of working-class distress as reflecting the extractions made by landlords, capitalists and tax-gatherers, a matter raised by Jacob Viner sixty years ago.

As mentioned, it is the major claim of this book that Ricardo's politics derive from his economics. The economics in question is the Cambridge version based on Sraffa's rational reconstruction, but stated here as a demonstrated fact: 'A theory of distribution without recourse to the theory of value at all', based on the assumption that in agriculture the same commodity, corn, appeared as both the means of production (corn wages) and as output, so that the rate of profit of the farmer (determined on land that commanded no rent) regulated the profits of all other trades (147; see also 23). I cannot quite fathom why Ricardo's support for parliamentary reform – broadening of the franchise, limited parliaments, vote by ballot – and his case for restriction of the franchise based on his profound respect for property rights require the Corn Model. The claims to this effect are all the more surprising given the prefatory declaration noted at the outset of this review that Ricardo's case for democratic reform 'is at once based upon, and consistent with, an account of the operation of the new market mechanism itself'. It is a pity that this potentially promising theme was not in fact carried through. Perhaps a significant element of preconception was unconsciously present after all?

21.15 *Capital and Wages: A Lakatosian History of the Wages Fund Doctrine*, by John Vint, Aldershot: Edward Elgar Publishing Company, 1994, pp. x, 278
(The European Journal of the History of Economic Thought, 2, Autumn 1995, 501–3)

This elegant book provides first-rate accounts of Imre Lakatos's methodologies of scientific and historiographical research programmes, of debate surrounding Lakatosian philosophy of science, and of recent applications to various episodes in the history of economics. Dr Vint's own purpose is to apply the structure to the wages fund doctrine. It is one of the merits of this book that the Lakatosian categories (such as hard core, protective belt, heuristic, progressiveness, degeneration, monster-adjustment, recovery of hidden lemmas) reduce to pretty common-sensical notions in the specific applications provided by Vint. Accordingly, even those who might be a little old-fashioned in their approach to doctrinal history need not be put off by the complex inventory of concepts.

What did the 'hard core' of the wages fund doctrine amount to? A Foreword by Professor Mark Blaug summarizes what I imagine the 'representative' reader expects: 'Of all the doctrines of English Classical Political Economy that modern readers find difficult to understand there is none so bizarre as the wages fund doctrine. According to this doctrine, there is at any moment in time a predetermined stock of wage goods in an economy available for payment to workers, setting an upper limit to the wages bill, at least in real terms. . . . How could intelligent men, like Ricardo, Malthus, McCulloch and John Stuart Mill, have believed so absurd a doctrine and not just for a few years but for almost two generations?' But strange to relate, this is positively *not* the picture Vint's reader obtains. (Moral: abolish the imprimatur and let authors speak for themselves.) Thus Vint over and again makes it clear that this version was *not* held by Ricardo: 'There is no simple, clear statement of the wages fund doctrine [the short-run version] . . . to be found in Ricardo's *Principles of Political Economy* (1817), or any of his other published works or correspondence' (50); 'Ricardo's approach to wages runs counter to the simple wages fund doctrine' (51); 'Further evidence for Ricardo's rejection of the wages fund doctrine is seen in his attitude to combinations revealed in correspondence with Malthus' (55). Even Malthus is an uncertain adherent: 'hard core elements are quite clear in the first edition of the *Essay* in 1798, whereas they are not as well developed in the first edition of the *Principles of Political Economy* in 1820. Hard core development then, in Malthus's case, is not a linear process' (65). And in J. S. Mill's *Principles* – not only in his famous recantation – will be found important examples where increased money wages paid fully-employed labour allow increases in their real wage even in the 'short run' (93–5). That I have not got Vint wrong is confirmed by a summary statement regarding the short-run wages fund, reaffirming that 'there was something of a tradition among the major writers in arguing that workers could improve their living standards, albeit temporarily, by consuming luxuries under certain circumstances when their money wages were increased' (86). McCulloch is the major exception, but 'the more limited rigid theorem was never so accepted except by the popularizers'. And in the concluding chapter we read: 'The major Classical economists . . . did not consistently adhere to the rigid doctrine' (252) – unlike Marcet and McCulloch.

Vint refers repeatedly to *the* wages fund doctrine. Yet the hard core for him also includes a long-run version entailing the following propositions: '1. In the long run increases or decreases in capital accumulation will lead to increases or decreases in the wages fund. 2. In the long run the population may change in response to changes in the real wage rate. 3. The trend of the wage rate over time will depend on the relationship between capital accumulation and population growth' (42). A 'hard-core' that contains both a strict *short-run* version à la Blaug and a *dynamic-growth* version is in fact a marshmallow. Since it is perfectly consistent firmly to reject the first and enthusiastically subscribe to the second version, or abandon the second but retain the first, the very notion of *a* or *the* hard core breaks down. It is revealing that the concluding chapter turns entirely on the short-run version. The issue seems to have troubled Vint (e.g. 3, n2); and takes on particular significance given his own recognition that 'An important starting point is . . . the notion of the research programme itself and the associated hard core', namely 'a wages fund research programme with a clearly identifiable hard core' (31–2). Yet there is still much to be learned from this book regarding the nature of classical economics, since one can read Vint without first donning Lakatosian clothing if one prefers less formal dress.

Vint takes for granted – and expects his readers to follow suit – that the 'wages fund doctrine is false if assessed from the perspective of Neoclassical economics' (256). I would remind readers of Jacob Viner's partial defence in 1930 against Cannan's total rejection: 'the common type of attack on it [the wage fund theory] . . . in destroying it also destroys the foundation of a sound interest theory. Assuming continuous production, no stock of provision wholly ready for consumption needs to be accumulated in advance of payment of wages. But current wages are paid out of a flow of finished products to which current labor has contributed only the finishing touches. What current labor produces is in the main future and not current real wages' (Viner 1958: 402). This dimension should not be neglected.

REFERENCES

Black, R. D. C. (1971) Introduction, *The Economic Writings of Mountifort Longfield*, New York: Augustus M. Kelley.

Blaug, Mark (1958) *Ricardian Economics*: New Haven: Yale University Press.

Bowley, M. (1973) *Studies in the History of Economic Theory before 1870*, London: Macmillan.

Field, A. J. (1987) *The Future of Economic History*, Boston: Kluwer-Nijhoff Publishing.

Forbes, Duncan (1975) 'Sceptical Whiggism, Commerce and Liberty', in A. S. Skinner and T. Wilson (eds), *Essays on Adam Smith*, Oxford: Clarendon Press, 179–201.

Hicks, J. R. (1976) 'Revolutions in Economics', in S. Latsis (ed.), *Method and Appraisal in Economics*, Cambridge: Cambridge University Press, 207–18.

Hollander, Samuel (1984) 'Marx and Malthusianism: Marx's Secular Path of Wages', *American Economic Review*, 74 (March): 139–51.

—— (1985) *The Economics of J. S. Mill*, Toronto: University of Toronto Press.

—— (1986) 'Malthus's Population Principle and Social Reform', *History of Political Economy*, 18 (Summer): 187–236.

—— (1987) *Classical Economics*, Oxford: Basil Blackwell.

Jevons, W. S. (1879) *Theory of Political Economy*, 2nd edn, London: Macmillan.

Mill, J. S. (1972) *The Later Letters, 1849 to 1873, Collected Works of J. S. Mill*, XVII, Toronto: University of Toronto Press.

—— (1973) *A System of Logic* (edn 1, 1843), in *Collected Works*, VII—VIII, Toronto: University of Toronto Press.

Phelps Brown, E. H. (1972) 'The Underdevelopment of Economics', *Economic Journal*, 82 (March): 1–10.

Robbins, L. C. (1952) *Theory of Economic Policy in English Classical Political Economy*, London: Macmillan.

Samuelson, P. A. (1978) 'The Canonical Classical Model of Political Economy', *Journal of Economic Literature*, 16, 4 (December): 1415–34.

Schumpeter, J. A. (1954) *History of Economic Analysis*, New York: Oxford University Press.

Sowell, Thomas (1972) *Say's Law: An Historical Analysis*, Princeton: Princeton University Press.

Sraffa, P. (ed.) (1951–73) *Works and Correspondence of David Ricardo*, (11 vols), Vols VI–VIII: *Letters*, Cambridge: Cambridge University Press.

Stigler, G. J. (1955) 'The Nature and Role of Originality in Scientific Progress', *Economica*, 22 (November): 293–302.

—— (1965) 'Textual Exegesis as a Scientific Problem', *Economica*, 32 (November): 447–50.

Thornton, W. T. (1869) *On Labour*, London: Macmillan.

Viner, J. (1958) *The Long View and the Short*, Glencoe, Ill.: Free Press.

INDEX

403